WITHDRAWN

# SHAKESPEARE SURVEY

## 72

## Shakespeare and War

EDITED BY

EMMA SMITH

**CAMBRIDGE**
UNIVERSITY PRESS

# CAMBRIDGE
## UNIVERSITY PRESS

University Printing House, Cambridge CB2 8BS, United Kingdom

One Liberty Plaza, 20th Floor, New York, NY 10006, USA

477 Williamstown Road, Port Melbourne, VIC 3207, Australia

314–321, 3rd Floor, Plot 3, Splendor Forum, Jasola District Centre,
New Delhi – 110025, India

79 Anson Road, #06–04/06, Singapore 079906

Cambridge University Press is part of the University of Cambridge.

It furthers the University's mission by disseminating knowledge in the pursuit of
education, learning and research at the highest international levels of excellence.

www.cambridge.org
Information on this title: www.cambridge.org/9781108499286
DOI: 10.1017/9781108588072

First published 2019

Printed in the United Kingdom by TJ International Ltd, Padstow Cornwall

*A catalogue record for this publication is available from the British Library.*

ISBN 978-1-108-49928-6 Hardback

# EDITOR'S NOTE

It is a great honour to assume the editorship of *Shakespeare Survey* with volume 72. 'Shakespeare and War' draws on the programme of the International Shakespeare Conference held in Stratford-upon-Avon in the summer of 2018.

Cambridge University Press and the *Survey* Advisory Board join me in recording our warmest thanks to Peter Holland for his nineteen-year editorship. Under his direction, *Survey* confirmed and extended its role in presenting lucid, critical scholarship from established and up-and-coming scholars. It continued to reach for contributions and readers beyond the Anglophone world, and to develop its founding commitment to Shakespeare in performance and adaptation. Peter brought to *Survey* his own extraordinary intellectual range and scholarly generosity, and has left it a more inclusive and exciting forum. With his predecessors as editors – Stanley Wells, Kenneth Muir and Allardyce Nicol – Peter has created a Shakespearean institution. Do help me to steward its continued development: I am grateful for your feedback, contributions and recommendations.

The next issue, 73, on 'Shakespeare and the City' will be in press by the time this volume appears. The theme for 74 is 'Shakespeare and Education' (drawing on the ISC in 2020, and with additional submissions by 1 September 2020), and for 75, '*Othello*' (submissions by 1 September 2021). There is limited space in each volume for articles that are not on the theme: these can be submitted for consideration at any point in the year. Please send any correspondence, including submissions as email attachments, to emma.smith@hertford.ox.ac. uk. All submissions are read by me as Editor and at least one member of the Advisory Board. We warmly encourage both early-career and more senior scholars to consider *Survey* as a venue for their work.

Part of *Survey*'s distinctiveness is its reviews. Review copies, including article offprints, should be addressed to the Editor at The Shakespeare Institute, Church Street, Stratford-upon-Avon, Warwickshire CV37 6HP; our reviewers inevitably have to exercise some selection about what they cover.

EMMA SMITH

# CONTRIBUTORS

MELISSA CROTEAU, *California Baptist University*
GABRIEL EGAN, *De Montfort University*
SAMUEL FALLON, *SUNY Geneseo*
MICHAEL GRAHAM, *independent scholar*
MICHAEL HATTAWAY, *New York University in London*
DIANA E. HENDERSON, *MIT*
LISA HOPKINS, *Sheffield Hallam University*
RUSSELL JACKSON, *University of Birmingham*
ROS KING, *University of Southampton*
PETER KIRWAN, *University of Nottingham*
SONYA FREEMAN LOFTIS, *Morehouse College*
IRENA R. MAKARYK, *University of Ottawa*
ZOLTÁN MÁRKUS, *Vassar College*
RANDALL MARTIN, *University of New Brunswick*
ELIZABETH MAZZOLA, *City College of New York*
REIKO OYA, *Keio University, Tokyo*
ELENA PELLONE, *University of Birmingham*
PAUL PRESCOTT, *University of Warwick*
EOIN PRICE, *Swansea University*
STEPHEN PURCELL, *University of Warwick*
JUDITH ROSENHEIM†, *independent scholar*
DAVID SCHALKWYK, *Queen Mary University of London*
CHARLOTTE SCOTT, *Goldsmiths College University of London*
JAMES SHAW, *University of Oxford*
PETER J. SMITH, *Nottingham Trent University*
ELISABETTA TARANTINO, *University of Oxford*
CHRISTINA WALD, *University of Konstanz*
RAMONA WRAY, *Queen's University Belfast*

# CONTENTS

# CONTENTS

# ILLUSTRATIONS

# LIST OF ILLUSTRATIONS

# *HENRY V* AFTER THE WAR ON TERROR

## RAMONA WRAY[1]

In the debate around Shakespeare and 9/11, the question of Shakespeare's political uses tends to be addressed only in the most oblique of ways. As Matthew Biberman, the editor of *Shakespeare Yearbook*'s special issue on the theme, notes, criticism typically retreats into a looser discussion of 'the role that canonical texts can play in the development of ethical, philosophical and civic frameworks'.[2] The one exception is the discussion generated by *Henry V*. Critics have noted the way in which *Henry V* is marshalled to support the language of contemporary militarism, with Diana E. Henderson and others citing the controversial manner in which the play was 'issued to US soldiers ... and repeatedly invoked in speeches ... and on websites supporting military actions'.[3] In complementary work, critics have noted the popular comparisons between Henry V and figures such as George W. Bush, Tony Blair and Tim Collins.[4] But what tends to be dramatized most fully in these encounters is the gulf between academia and popular usages of Shakespeare's text. Critical discussion is directed towards demonstrating the inappropriateness of contemporary parallels, and users are encouraged to engage more subtly with the play (undoubtedly good advice for succeeding British and American administrations, but unlikely to be heeded).[5] Hence, while such commentary implicitly acknowledges that *Henry V* has a special resonance inside the discourses of Afghanistan and Iraq, the precise ways in which *Henry V* signifies in the here-and-now remains to be fully considered.

Part of the difficulty is the scant attention afforded in such work to imaginative/creative productions of

*Henry V*. As Matthew Woodcock notes, 'the twenty-first century stage has gone much further than academic criticism in drawing comparisons between Henry's campaign and the Iraq War'.[6] In fact, the period since 9/11 has seen unprecedented numbers of *Henry V* productions, as well as the first

[1] Many thanks to Pascale Aebischer, Michael Dobson, Ewan Fernie and Martin Wiggins for invitations to lecture on this theme and for insightful and enabling feedback.

[2] Matthew Biberman, 'Introduction: Shakespeare after 9/11', in *Shakespeare After 9/11: How a Social Trauma Reshapes Interpretation*, ed. Matthew Biberman and Julia Reinhard Lupton (Lewiston, NY, 2011), pp 1–18; p. 8.

[3] Diana E. Henderson, 'Meditations in a time of (displaced) war: *Henry V*, money, and the ethics of performing history', in *Shakespeare and War*, ed. Ros King and Paul J. C. M. Franssen (Basingstoke, 2008), pp. 226–42; esp. pp. 226–7.

[4] See Richard Burt, 'Civic ShakesPR: middlebrow multiculturalism, white television, and the color bind', in *Colorblind Shakespeare: New Perspectives on Race and Performance*, ed. Ayanna Thompson (London, 2006), pp. 157–86; esp. pp. 158–9; Ewan Fernie, 'Action! *Henry V*', in *Presentist Shakespeares*, ed. Hugh Grady and Terence Hawkes (London, 2007), pp. 96–120; esp. pp. 99–100; David Coleman, 'Ireland and Islam: Henry V and the "War on Terror"', *Shakespeare* 4 (2008), 169–80; pp. 172–6; Emma Smith, '"Freezing the snowman": (how) can we do performance criticism?' in *How to Do Things with Shakespeare: New Approaches, New Essays*, ed. Laurie Maguire (Oxford, 2008), pp. 280–97; esp. p. 286; Scott Newstok and Harry Berger Jr, 'Harrying after VV', in *Shakespeare After 9/11*, pp. 141–52; p. 141; Hugh Grady, 'Shakespeare and the dialectic of enlightenment: a presentist perspective', in *Shakespeare After 9/11*, pp. 137–40; p. 138.

[5] Newstok and Berger, 'Harrying', p. 150.

[6] Matthew Woodcock, *Shakespeare – Henry V: A Reader's Guide to Essential Criticism* (Basingstoke, 2008), p. 146.

major film in almost thirty years. Thea Sharrock's *Henry V* (2012), starring Tom Hiddleston, was crafted to form the high point of the cultural Olympiad, internationally co-produced (the BBC joined forces with Neal Street Productions, NBC Universal and WNET Thirteen) and distributed to great acclaim.[7] Like most of the theatrical productions of *Henry V* since 2001, the film draws on discursive strategies shaped by the 'War on Terror', the now-defunct term which signifies the international military campaign waged in the aftermath of 9/11, including the Iraq War and the War in Afghanistan.[8] Sharrock's film – the first *Henry V* to be directed by a woman – crystallizes a trend initiated by a number of productions which, in the wake of the successful National Theatre production of *Henry V* directed by Nicholas Hytner in 2003, refract the Iraq and Afghanistan conflicts in the action on stage.[9]

In reconceiving of Shakespeare's history in a way which is inseparable from contemporary understandings of conflict, Sharrock follows in the footsteps of Laurence Olivier and Kenneth Branagh and their now-canonical film adaptations of the play.[10] In common with these directors, Sharrock also offers a reading of *Henry V* in part determined by the contemporary representational landscape. Recent work in film studies has highlighted 'the way in which ... depictions of war have shifted since the mid-1980s', signalling, in particular, a move away from the anti-war Vietnam films.[11] As exemplary of this development, critics highlight a group of late 20th- and early 21st-century World War II films such as *Saving Private Ryan* (dir. Steven Spielberg, 1998), which, revisionist and recuperative in orientation, illuminates the rise of what Andrew J. Bacevich has identified as a 'New American Militarism'.[12] Spotlighting a 'tendency to see military power as the truest measure of national greatness', Bacevich describes a romanticized and nostalgic conception of wars, armies and soldiers that 'pervade[s] the American consciousness' and 'ultimately pervert[s] US [foreign] policy'.[13] Linked to this cultural phenomenon, but distinctive in style and approach, is a more recent and controversial series of films based

on the Iraq War experience. Films such as *Generation Kill* (dir. Susanna White and Simon

[7] Sharrock's *Henry V* forms part of *The Hollow Crown* – four television film versions of the Henriad produced by Sam Mendes. For an article on the production context of the series, see Ruth Morse, 'The hollow crown: Shakespeare, the BBC, and the 2012 Olympics', *Linguaculture* 1 (2014), 7–20. More broadly, for a discussion of Shakespeare's place as 'a ubiquitous presence throughout the Cultural Olympiad', see Paul Prescott, 'Shakespeare and the dream of Olympism', in *Shakespeare and the Global Stage: Performance and Festivity in the Olympic Year*, ed. Paul Prescott and Erin Sullivan (London, 2015), pp. 1–37; p. 4. For a discussion of the production contexts of *The Hollow Crown*, see Ramona Wray, 'The Shakespearean auteur and the televisual medium', *Shakespeare Bulletin* 34 (2016), 469–85.

[8] In 2009, the phrase was quietly dropped by the Obama administration. On the problematics of the term, see Marc Redfield, *The Rhetoric of Terror: Reflections on 9/11 and the War on Terror* (New York, 2009), pp. 51–2.

[9] Subsequent productions of *Henry V* which reference Iraq and/or Afghanistan include those directed by Jonathan Munby at the Royal Exchange Theatre, Manchester (2007); Michael Boyd at the Roundhouse, London (2008); Henry Filloux-Bennett at the Old Red Lion, London (2012); and Michael Grandage at the Noël Coward Theatre, London (2013). For analyses of Hytner's production, see Michael Dobson, 'Shakespeare performance in England, 2003', *Shakespeare Survey 57* (Cambridge, 2004), 258–89; pp. 278–84; Catherine Silverstone, *Shakespeare, Trauma and Contemporary Performance* (London, 2011), pp. 109–35; Mark Steyn, 'Henry goes to Baghdad', *The New Criterion* 22 (2003), 40–4.

[10] As Emma Smith notes, *Henry V*'s 'topicality' has historically revolved around war 'as it reflects, recalls and participates in military conflicts from the Crimea to the Falklands' – see *Shakespeare in Production: King Henry V* (Cambridge, 2002), p. 1. For a historical survey of the reception of the histories, see Andrew Hiscock, '"More warlike than politique": Shakespeare and the theatre of war – a critical survey', *Shakespeare* 7 (2011), 221–47; pp. 236–9; Ton Hoenselaars, 'Introduction: Shakespeare's history plays in Britain and abroad', in *Shakespeare's History Plays: Performance, Translation and Adaptation in Britain and Abroad*, ed. Ton Hoenselaars (Cambridge, 2004), pp. 9–34.

[11] H. Louise Davis and Jeffrey Johnson, 'One nation invisible: unveiling the hidden war body on screen', in *The War Body on Screen*, ed. Karen Randell and Sean Redmond (London, 2008), pp. 134–46; esp. p. 136.

[12] Andrew J. Bacevich, *The New American Militarism: How Americans are Seduced by War* (Oxford, 2013).

[13] Bacevich, *New American Militarism*, pp. xi, 2.

Callas Jones, 2008), *Redacted* (dir. Brian de Palma, 2007) and *In the Valley of Elah* (dir. Paul Haggis, 2007) are often edgy, uncomfortable and interrogative in their attitudes towards the War on Terror.[14] Guy Westwell notes that the Iraq War films generally proved unpopular, failing 'to find an audience', and the few that did, such as the Oscar-winning *The Hurt Locker* (dir. Kathryn Bigelow, 2008) and *American Sniper* (dir. Clint Eastwood, 2014), were notably much less political – less critical – in orientation.[15] Typically, the vision of war in the commercially successful Iraq War films embeds a human experience divorced from larger questions of political accountability. Sharrock's *Henry V* begs comparison with this new wave of war films in that it retains a heroic emphasis while largely avoiding engagement with the politics of war – the 'cause' (4.1.133), as Shakespeare's play has it – and it executes this dual manoeuvre through a narrow focus on the bodily experience of a small group of soldiers.[16]

This focus on a trajectory of suffering allows Sharrock to negotiate in a unique way 'the essential doubleness' that critics from Norman Rabkin to Stephen Greenblatt have identified around Shakespeare's Henry V.[17] In particular, the film invokes the associations around post-traumatic stress disorder (PTSD), which Anthony Oliver Scott 'argues ... is the defining feature' of the Iraq War films, to reconcile and explain antithetically opposed images of Henry while connecting with the anxieties of present-day audiences.[18] Situated inside a new – post 9/11 – Shakespearian aesthetic which prioritizes the solider as spectacle, Sharrock's film, energized by a decade of theatrical innovation, realizes a *Henry V* very different in complexion, scale and significance from that of her predecessors – hence, the unfamiliar effects of a film which cuts scenes and soliloquies traditionally regarded as essential, reintroduces episodes conventionally bypassed, invests in daring interpolations and capitalizes on a performative style that overturns received interpretation. Caught in a net of its Olympic contexts, the film has thus far been seen only inside its commemorative paradigms.[19] In arguing that Sharrock's production manifests

a fresh conceptual template for Shakespeare's history, this article suggests that the contemporary applications of *Henry V* move beyond the simplistic parallels which have so exercised and animated critical discussion. By prioritizing the fields of debate that surround *Henry V*, it identifies, for the first time, the extent to which the War on Terror has transformed the meanings of Shakespeare's greatest history.

## A MODERN OBITUARY

In Sharrock's production, a radical take on the narrative is encapsulated in the scenes of Henry's funeral which open and close the film. Merging the play's prologue and epilogue, the film enables us to *hear* the former (the invocation to the muse) but to *see* the events associated with the latter (the death of the protagonist). The symbolism of the opening

---

[14] For a general overview, see John Markert, *Post 9/11 Cinema: Through a Lens Darkly* (Lanham, MD, 2011), pp. 209–309; Stephen Prince, *Firestorm: American Film in the Age of Terrorism* (New York, 2009), pp. 281–309.

[15] Guy Westwell, 'In country: mapping the Iraq War in recent Hollywood', in *Screens of Terror: Representations of War and Terrorism in Film and Television Since 9/11*, ed. Philip Hammond (Bury St Edmunds, 2011), pp. 19–35; esp. p. 22. *American Sniper* has been described as the highest-grossing war film of all time, the sum of $547 million in global box office earnings being identified – see Johnny Rico, 'Top 10 highest grossing war movies', 30 April 2017, www.thoughtco.com/highest-grossing-war-films-3438701.

[16] Pascale Aebischer writes that Branagh's film adaptation of Henry V 'works to amplify [a] ... concern with the martial male body's precariousness' – see 'Shakespeare, sex, and violence: negotiating masculinities in Branagh's *Henry V* and *Taymor's Titus*', in *A Concise Companion to Shakespeare on Screen*, ed. Diana E. Henderson (Oxford, 2006), pp. 112–32; esp. p. 112.

[17] Woodcock, *Shakespeare – Henry V*, p. 112.

[18] Westwell, 'In country', p. 30, citing A. O. Scott, 'Apolitics and the war film', 6 February 2010, www.nytimes.com/2010/02/07/weekinreview/07aoscott.html.

[19] See David Livingstone, 'Silenced voices: a reactionary streamlined *Henry V* in *The Hollow Crown*', *Multicultural Shakespeare* 12 (2015), 87–100; pp. 87–8; L. Monique Pittman, 'Shakespeare and the cultural Olympiad: contesting gender and the British nation in the BBC's *The Hollow Crown*', *Borrowers and Lenders* 9 (2015).

shot – a dirty-faced child plucking a wild flower (its shape evokes the epilogue's 'star of England' (6)) and running past the Boar's Head (the scene of revelries now eclipsed) – speaks of loss and impermanence. Dark painterly effects, tenebrous lighting and alienating medieval architecture match this mood and confirm the anti-heritage landscape characteristic of many recent Renaissance appropriations. Although the end reveals that he has been in attendance all along (he is finally revealed as Shakespeare's 'Boy' offering a retrospective viewpoint), the Chorus is apprehended at this point only via a gravelly, sombre voiceover. In keeping with the muted emotional contours – and despite the verse's aspiration towards elevation and an upward movement – the slow delivery and downward intonation of the prologue's lines – 'O for a muse of fire, that would ascend / The brightest heaven of invention' (1–2) – strikes a defeatist note, with viewers being invited to imagine great possibilities (not least, ideas of animation and resurrection) in the context of brute mortality (the death/funeral) and communal devastation (the assembled mourners). Bolstering the emotional contours is the score – a doleful Celtic strain characterized by strings and minor chords – that, in contrast to the rousing epic film music of Branagh's and Olivier's adaptations, lends the scene a subdued melancholy and an elegiac air.

For Lindsey Scott, the summoning of different stages in the story of Henry V reminds us of 'how Shakespeare's audiences would have been aware of Henry's short reign from the preceding performances of the *Henry VI* plays'.[20] But the crane-shot of the laid-out corpse covered by a heavy flag invokes 21st-century iconography of soldiers' bodies being brought home from conflict; contrary to the historical record, the effect is to suggest the King as casualty of the war in France.[21] This is confirmed in the voiceover's identification of the corpse as 'warlike Harry' (Prologue, 5), establishing the funeral under way as that of a military combatant. (A choreographed glimpse of the guard of honour stepping forwards reinforces the soldierly associations.) Pointed up in the scene, then, is what Andrew Hill terms 'the hard Real of the body-corpse … the

material presence of combat, which … constitutes the incontrovertible detritus of war'.[22] Like contemporary soldiers William James (*The Hurt Locker*) and Chris Kyle (*American Sniper*), Henry, from the start, is limned in terms of a fatal trajectory. By filtering the narrative through the depressive events described by the Chorus at the close, Sharrock's *Henry V* not only prepares an audience for what is to come but also begins the process of elaborating the hero in terms of victimhood. Long before the English army lands on French soil, mourning infuses the endeavour, with viewers recognizing Henry as a 'dead man walking'. The perspective is one that the ensuing narrative never moves beyond, not least because the continuing voiceover keeps us connected to the idea and import of the funeral in what is – by a large margin – the most extended use of the Chorus on screen.[23]

More broadly, the mutedly retrospective method functions to downplay the triumphant associations of what Crystal Bartolovich describes as 'the most overtly "nationalistic" and Anglophilic text in the Shakespearian canon'.[24] The demythologizing

---

[20] Lindsey Scott, 'Review of *The Hollow Crown*', *Shakespeare* 9 (2013), 108–14; p. 112.

[21] The flag covering Henry's coffin combines the red lion alongside the French *fleur de lis* and illustrates how Sharrock's production deploys signifiers of Welshness to soften the 'Englishness' of Shakespeare's text. All of Henry's 'I am Welsh' asseverations are retained, while the production follows Branagh's lead in amplifying Fluellen's contribution. See Courtney Lehmann, *Shakespeare Remains: Theater to Film, Early Modern to Postmodern* (Ithaca, NY, 2002), p. 206.

In the 2013 live broadcast of the RSC production of *Richard II*, directed by Gregory Doran, the Duchess of Gloucester (Jane Lapotaire) is represented grieving over a draped coffin, a crane-shot emphasizing her hunched posture.

[22] Andrew Hill, 'Hostage videos in the War on Terror', in Randell and Redmond, eds., *War Body*, pp. 251–65; esp. p. 263.

[23] In an adaptation which retains only about one-third (34 per cent) of the lines overall, nearly two-thirds (65 per cent) of the Chorus's statements are included. The only choric speech to be amputated is Act 5 (only six of the forty-six lines are retained), presumably because of its triumphalist tone.

[24] Crystal Bartolovich, 'Shakespeare's Globe?', in *Marxist Shakespeares*, ed. Jean E. Howard and Scott Cutler Shershow (London, 2001), pp. 178–205; esp. p. 179.

tendency is specifically realized in the opening's reference to Agincourt as a traumatic memory. At the Chorus's lines, 'the very casques / That did affright the air at Agincourt' (Prologue, 13–14), overlaid sounds of the clash of swords, men's cries and horses' screams are heard. These combine with a close-up on Exeter, the source of the experience, who blanches, closing his eyes at the inadvertent recollection. This eruption of the past into the film's present looks forward to similar episodes involving psychologically afflicted soldiers. *Henry V*, as Jonathan Baldo notes, is a play deeply engaged in the 'consolidation of the collective memory', but, in Sharrock's adaptation, remembering is, first and foremost, a traumatic endeavour.[25]

The moment prefigures the fantasy of England's remembering celebrated in Henry's St Crispian speech but models instead a contemporary concern with the place of the personal story inside the commemoration of national conflict. Henry's passing is figured simultaneously as a collective loss (the death that makes England and France bleed, as the epilogue has it) and as a private domestic tragedy. The latter is bolstered by the camera's focus on the loving looks bestowed by Katherine on the corpse. Ideas of personal affliction are further emphasized when the corpse is unveiled and a giddy 180° camera pan mimics Katherine's grieving perspective. Via self-conscious camera work, the production constructs the Henry–Katherine relationship as a love match, pre-emptively diffusing the later difficulties of staging Act 5, Scene 1. Re-envisioning a play 'famous for the relative absence of women', the interpolation characteristically amplifies the significance of Katherine (Mélanie Thierry), signalling a felt responsiveness to a world of heroism previously construed – by Olivier, by Branagh and by Shakespeare – almost wholly in masculine terms.[26] The sense that this is a tragedy belonging in the first instance to Henry's nuclear family is strengthened by the appearance here of a character only mentioned in the epilogue – 'Henry the Sixth' – for, behind the spectating widow, a waiting-woman is seen carrying a vulnerable new-born in 'infant bands' (Epilogue, 9). As in Iraq films such as *The Hurt Locker*, Henry here is realized not in terms of the larger political landscape but at the level of the career path characterizing 'the individual soldier'.[27] The method is exemplified as the camera zooms into the exposed corpse and pauses on a close-up of Tom Hiddleston's fine (if fixed and pallid) features. At this moment, the music climaxes and the production title freezes, with title, theme and subject succinctly being brought into union. Made apparent via his lover's gaze, but discovered simultaneously in terms of a soldier's funeral, Henry – and his march towards death – is cemented as subject, object and theme. The effect is to substitute the customary Henrician trajectory of boyhood to manhood with a single focus on manhood cut off in its prime. That generational movement so beloved by adapters of the play is replaced by an arc that begins with the protagonist's death, goes on to his war and circles back to the flag-covered corpse (we return to the same funeral at the end). Bracketing the proceedings thus, Sharrock telescopes the dramatization of warring nations into a modern obituary.

## THE MILITARIZED, VULNERABLE BODY

The business of Act 1 proper is jump-started by a match-cut which shifts the audience from a close-up of the exposed corpse to a close-up of Henry alive. The shot which links the two views of Henry – that of eyes being jolted open – implies a Lazarus-like resurrection, self-consciously recalling both the ways in which film is the medium that reanimates Shakespeare's play and the revivifying powers, as described by the Chorus, of the audience's imagination. Moving from death to life, it is appropriate that the first shots of Henry privilege physicality, and, as the scene plays over the

[25] Jonathan Baldo, *Memory in Shakespeare's Histories: Stages of Forgetting in Early Modern England* (London, 2012), p. 103.
[26] Kate Wilkinson, '"A woman's hide": the presentation of female characters in Michael Boyd's *The Histories*', *Shakespeare* 7 (2011), 56–69; p. 56.
[27] Philip Hammond, 'Introduction: screening the War on Terror', in *Screens of Terror*, pp. 7–18; esp. p. 9.

dialogue between Canterbury and Ely, an extended sequence shows Hiddleston – minus the crown – astride a galloping white horse.[28] As Canterbury and Ely discuss his transformation, Henry is realized leaping from his horse and rushing into the palace, stripping off clothes and, as he runs, snatching up the crown.[29] The stress on action contrasts with the earlier stillness of the corpse, while simultaneously – in the words of Yvonne Tasker – providing 'a narrative justification for ... physical display'.[30] Sharrock's *Henry V* is seductively oriented, with the pleasures of Hiddleston's gym-honed body being played up throughout.[31] Even when Henry is in armour, the viewer's eye is invited to dwell on the eroticized body because the battle attire is so precisely – unfeasibly – tight-fitting. The designer explains that Hiddleston's armour was 'made ... out of rubber, and he was sewn into things ... so he could move and look sexy'.[32] For Sharrock, there was an intimate connection between Hiddleston's physique and the production's 'feel': 'I wanted him to have a look that was ... [a]ttractive', she notes. 'He's an amazing, beautiful man. It seems crazy to [give him] a bowl haircut or put him in a pair of tights.'[33]

If Sharrock here marks her distance from the traditional stage and screen image of Henry V, the distinction is disingenuous. In fact, Sharrock's sense of Henry's appearance is perfectly aligned with a recent trend in theatre and cinema which has been to highlight – to 'sex up' – the militarism of Shakespeare's male roles. Thus, *Coriolanus*, the 2012 film directed by Ralph Fiennes, *Othello*, the 2013 National Theatre production directed by Nicholas Hytner, and *Othello*, directed by Iqbal Khan for the RSC in 2015, prioritized conflict-zone settings, relying, variously, on the military training undertaken by the casts and such identifiers as hard bodies, replica guns, flak jackets and desert fatigues.[34] In these instances, costuming, in particular, intimately equates the sexuality of the Shakespearian hero with his military identity, bringing to mind the romanticized construction of militarism in the contemporary war film. Unlike the French (who are dressed to appear 'shiny and ... mannered'), in Sharrock's film the English mostly wear leather, which costume designer Annie Symons describes as giving the actors 'sexuality and a warrior-likeness'.[35] Caught up in this reification are the intertexts of Hiddleston's earlier parts in Hollywood films such as *Thor* (dir. Kenneth Branagh, 2011) and *Avengers Assemble* (dir. Joss Whedon, 2013).[36] As Loki, brother to Thor, Hiddleston established himself as an ambiguated intergalactic warrior, while his role as Captain Nicholls in *War Horse* (dir. Steven Spielberg, 2011) suggests most strongly the identification of the Shakespearian type as a sexualized military protagonist. In Sharrock's film, the interpolated Agincourt scenes show Henry fighting aggressively and stress how an audience's gaze is directed towards a moving, spectacular property. Minus both horse and crown (the latter shoved dismissively away as battle commences), Henry functions as a summation of innate athleticism

---

28 Emblematic of the 'wildness' (1.1.27, 65) that Canterbury claims Henry has now abandoned, the scene points up the wrongness of the ecclesiastical narrative (our first indication that the words of Henry's bishops are not to be relied upon): they don't know of what they speak.
29 Typical of the cinematography, Henry is placed in centre-shot and allowed to dominate the middle of the frame.
30 Yvonne Tasker, *Spectacular Bodies: Gender, Genre and the Action Cinema* (London, 1993), p. 2.
31 See Ramona Wray, 'Franco Zeffirelli', in Mark Thornton Burnett, Courtney Lehmann, Marguerite H. Rippy and Ramona Wray, *Welles, Kurosawa, Kozintsev, Zeffirelli: Great Shakespeareans: Volume XVII* (London, 2013), pp. 141–84; pp. 183–4.
32 Eliza Kessler, '*Henry IV* and *Henry V*: Q&A with the costume designer', 5 July 2012, www.bbc.co.uk/blogs/tv/2012/07/henry-iv-v-shakespeare.shtml.
33 Phil Harrison and Gabriel Tate, 'Interviews: "The Hollow Crown"', www.timeout.com/london/events/interviews-the-hollow-crown.
34 On comparisons between *Coriolanus*, *The Hurt Locker* and the James Bond film *Skyfall* (dir. Sam Mendes, 2012), see Graham Holderness, *Tales from Shakespeare: Creative Collisions* (Cambridge, 2014), pp. 89–125.
35 Kessler, 'Costume'.
36 On intertextuality and Hiddleston's previous roles, see Anna Blackwell, 'Adapting *Coriolanus*: Tom Hiddleston's body and action cinema', *Adaptation* 7 (2014), 344–52; p. 346.

1  Henry V (Tom Hiddleston) with his nobles before the walls of Harfleur. Courtesy of Photofest.

and soldierly accomplishment that collapses boundaries of rank and class. The notion of the contemporary soldier is most stridently enunciated in scenes where, face muddied and shadowed, Henry's appearance recalls the familiar contours of the War on Terror forces; a medieval setting notwithstanding, the visual complexions suggest camouflage, besmirching, nocturnal encounters and a particular enunciation of 21st-century warfare. The so-called 'charred face' (which supersedes the mud-bespattered *mise-en-scène* of Branagh's adaptation) is the signature of the authenticated battle experience.[37]

This fine adjustment in visual detailing sits well with the filmic motif of the victim-soldier. Echoing Iraq War films which delineate the vulnerability of American troops in Baghdad, Henry's campaign in France is marked by a concentration on the beleaguered situation of the English. Characterized by inhospitable wintry terrain and formidable stronghold walls, France is alien territory and the war effort a depressed undertaking – coughing, exhausted men, some carrying compatriots, are the downcast corollaries for what is conjured as a wholly dispirited enterprise. At Harfleur, fearful and defensive camera work establishes the perspective as that of the 'noble English' (3.1.17) (Figure 1). Because screams, images of affliction and shots of burning oil being poured from the battlements are associated with the English experience, the dynamic of the historical siege is reversed, and Henry's army is limned as the

---

[37] On the 'intertextual and cultural uses' of mud in Branagh's adaptation, see Donald K. Hedrick, 'War is mud: Branagh's *Dirty Harry* and the types of political ambiguity', in *Shakespeare: The Movie II: Popularizing the Plays on Film, TV, Video, and DVD*, ed. Richard Burt and Lynda E. Boose (London, 2003), pp. 213–30; esp. p. 215.

imperilled constituency. Eschewing the Union Jacks which so often accompany theatrical productions, Sharrock's *Henry V* privileges a period-suitable tattered and dirty flag of St George which, fluttering in sorry fashion, emblematizes both the state of Henry's army and its distance from patriotic imperatives. The flag finds a psychic correlative in the ways in which Henry's soldiers, soon after arriving in France, begin to exhibit the 'thousand-yard stare', perhaps the most cinematically recognizable aspect of post-traumatic stress sufferers. Tracing the history of PTSD, Martin Barker notes that discourses around the condition serve as a point of consensus between all sides in American politics, and facilitate a reading of the US military as victims rather than perpetrators.[38] In Sharrock's film, the representation of the pervasiveness of PTSD suggests that the condition is one of soldiering's inexorable effects. The theme is expressed personally at Agincourt via the image of a foetally positioned Pistol who is paralysed and horrified by what he is witnessing – PTSD is triggered by his exposure to atrocity. Discovered in the next scene as crying, shaking and rocking his head, Pistol registers in his behaviour the disorder's pre-eminent symptoms.[39] Interestingly, Pistol's later lines are cut; PTSD, it is suggested, has become his defining story.

Notwithstanding the subtle colour distinction between the armies ('dark congealed bloods for England and beautiful blues, whites and golds for France'), Agincourt is characterized by an overwhelming sense of visceral brutality.[40] Alternately accelerated and slow-motion representations of the battle make prominent the various acts of impaling and skewering in which both forces participate.[41] Thanks to a quasi-documentary style, realist details and hand-held filming techniques, a viewer is quickly immersed in battle scenes which invite comparison with Peter Babakitis's lesser-known 2004 cinematic version of the play, *Henry V*. Sarah Hatchuel notes that, in this adaptation, the 'cinematography ... seems heavily influenced by media footage provided by ... commentators during the 2003 British and American invasion of Iraq'.[42] In the Sharrock adaptation, the interpolated injunction from Henry ('Advance the army

thirty paces – now!') and the scene which sees Essex wait for the perfect moment for the arrows to be loosed ('Steady lads!') simultaneously situate military success while allowing for the suspense so integral to contemporary depictions of warfare.[43] As befits this mode of representation, instead of the heavy classical orchestration of Branagh's and Olivier's scores, the soundtrack is merged with the noise of the combatants' pain, anguish and blows in a critical cacophony of violence. Key military moments are backgrounded by a wall of smoke that rises from behind the combatants, and a sense of chaos dominates. When Henry pronounces, 'I know not if the day be ours or no' (4.7.82), the disorientation is absolutely

---

[38] Martin Barker, '"America hurting": mapping the Iraq War in recent Hollywood', in *Screens of Terror*, pp. 37–50; esp. p. 39.

[39] Ros King similarly accounts for Pistol's 'outbursts of violence ... bragadocchio and ... language' in terms of 'shell shock, post-traumatic stress disorder' – see '"The disciplines of war": Elizabethan war manuals and Shakespeare's tragicomic vision', in *Shakespeare and War*, ed. King and Franssen, pp. 15–29; esp. p. 18.

[40] Kessler, 'Costume'.

[41] Here, Henry's later claim – 'God fought for us' (4.8.120) – is undermined by the film's insistence on accounting for the English victory. If Shakespeare's play 'removed the real, secular reasons for the ... disparity in casualties', the fashion in recent productions has been for recognizing, in the words of one director, 'the decisive role played by [the] archers': Sharrock's film extends the tendency. See Gary Taylor, 'Cry havoc', 5 April 2003, www.theguardian.com/stage/2003/apr/05/theatre.classics; ' The director's cut: interviews with Kenneth Branagh, Edward Hall, Nicholas Hytner and Michael Boyd', in *Henry V*, ed. Jonathan Bate and Eric Rasmussen (Basingstoke, 2010), pp. 176–201; esp. p. 187.

[42] '"Into a thousand parts divide one man": dehumanised metafiction and fragmented documentary in Peter Babakitis' *Henry V*', in *Screening Shakespeare in the Twenty-First Century*, ed. Mark Thornton Burnett and Ramona Wray (Edinburgh, 2006), pp. 146–62; esp. p. 150.

[43] As in *American Sniper*, in which the 'enemy' is held in the rifle's sights in the tense seconds before the trigger is pulled, Sharrock's film deploys shots of taut bowstrings, slow motion and the increasing noise of the horses' hooves to raise the tension of the viewing experience.

convincing, for it is one that is filtered through a distinctly contemporaneous aesthetic.

Inside this contemporary understanding of warfare sits Sharrock's daring re-envisioning of the play's great set-speeches. If, as Linda K. Schubert argues, 'Branagh's choices ... [were] deliberately the opposite of those informing Olivier's movie', then Sharrock, in turn, sets herself against Branagh by avoiding, in her words, 'the huge rhetorical thing'.[44] Playing down excess and working in conversational ways, her *Henry V* utilizes the rhetorical underplay characteristic of the Iraq War film to make its set-speeches the most understatedly delivered in the screen record. 'Once more unto the breach' (3.1.1) is realized instinctively, as evolving spontaneously from the contexts in which the protagonist finds himself, and Henry himself is represented on his knees (debris falling all around). In the 'Feast of Crispian' (4.3.40) address, low-key tones predominate, and most of the speech proceeds without scoring; the suggestion of a private farewell is assisted by emotive sighs and weighty pauses.[45] Recognized in both is an uneasiness with the declamatory mode – what Nicholas Hytner, reflecting on his own stagecraft, has termed a public 'mistrust of ... rhetoric'.[46] Sharrock's *Henry V* is sensitive to the evisceration of rhetoric in the public sphere and, by dampening its force, endeavours to ensure that Henry is never figured in directly political terms.

Crucial to the construction is Henry's participation in a shared experience of vulnerability. Hiddleston, as one reviewer notes, is a 'cerebral actor', and nonverbals – a broken delivery and pained facial expressions – make for a revisionist reading that places emphasis on the King's own fears.[47] Given that the wearisome accoutrements of leadership are already written through Hiddleston's body, the soliloquy on the 'hard condition' (4.1.227–81) of kingship (traditionally regarded as 'central to the complex modern Henry') is cut.[48] Instead of lonely communion, the emphasis is on Henry's connection with a small group of individualized soldiers. Hence, the cropped camerawork of 'Once more unto the breach' underlines the closeness of the encounter,

and Shakespearian plurals are suitably contracted – the general 'yeomen' (3.1.25) become a solitary 'yeoman'. Such decisions make sense given the nature of contemporary warfare – no longer fought by large armies but by small detachments.[49] As in the Iraq films in which, as Martin Barker notes, 'soldiers are shown bonding with each other, giving this as their first loyalty', it is the values of the unit (the group whose interests Henry represents and defends) that are accorded the greatest importance.[50] In the St Crispian speech, this change of emphasis is encapsulated in the climactic delivery of the expression, 'band of brothers' (4.3.60), and in the registration of the hero's sentimental mood in the tears of his listening soldiers. Accordingly, a break with performance tradition accents the inclusive 'us' (4.3.67), in contradistinction to the exclusive 'not' – the situation of 'gentlemen' (4.3.64) who do not participate – so that the

---

[44] Linda K. Schubert, 'Scoring the fields of the dead: musical styles and approaches to postbattle scenes from *Henry V* (1944, 1989)', in *Shakespeare and the Middle Ages: Essays on the Performance and Adaptation of the Plays with Medieval Sources or Settings*, ed. Martha W. Driver and Sid Ray (Jefferson, NC, 2009), pp. 62–80; esp. p 68; Harrison and Tate, 'Interviews: "The Hollow Crown"'. For a comparative discussion of the speeches in the Olivier and Branagh films, see David Margolies, '*Henry V* and ideology', in *Shakespeare on Screen: 'The Henriad'*, ed. Sarah Hatchuel and Nathalie Vienne-Guerrin (Rouen, 2008), pp. 147–55.

[45] Only at the reference to the 'good man' who teaches 'his son' (4.3.56) does non-diegetic music feature.

[46] See 'The director's cut', p. 180. In Hytner's production of *Henry V*, the issue is addressed via the self-conscious screening of the speeches as 'spin'.

[47] Ben Lawrence, '*The Hollow Crown: Henry V*, BBC Two, Review', 22 July 2012, www.telegraph.co.uk/culture/tvandradio/9415849/The-Hollow-Crown-Henry-V-BBC-Two-review.html.

[48] James N. Loehlin, *Shakespeare in Performance: Henry V* (Manchester, 1997), p. 3.

[49] In addition, the English army's camp – wreathed in mist, provisional and populated with green-coloured tents – evokes in its visual language the temporary structures of 'Camp Bastion' and 'Camp Cooke', US military bases in Iraq and Afghanistan respectively.

[50] Martin Barker, *A 'Toxic Genre': The Iraq War Films* (London, 2011), p. 43.

significance of the saint's day becomes about affirming male relations.

More generally, Sharrock's *Henry V* visualizes man-on-man relationships in a way that is unprecedented in the stage and film history of the play. During Henry's night-time meetings, the 'comfort ... pluck[ed]' (4.0.42) is granted physical exposition, as hands are shook, smiles exchanged, backs patted and hugs welcomed from a singularly tactile protagonist. Consonant with the stress on male bonding, the production omits the discovery of the traitors' conspiracy, eschews mention of the Scottish rebellion (1.2.136–220) and cuts that 'furious repudiation of difference', the four captains' scene.[51] The infamous question – 'What ish my nation?' (3.3.66) – becomes untenable in a production where relations between men take precedence over national affiliation. Distinctively, the development is given a racial inflection through the casting of the black actor Paterson Joseph as York. The mode of representation accords with the 'colour-blind' casting of most contemporary *Henry V* productions, but – complicating Jami Rogers's view that, in *The Hollow Crown*, no 'ethnic minority actors' were cast in 'major roles' – York is a notable presence, with extensions deepening and stretching the part.[52] These, and the fact that York is consistently visualized, mean that Henry's soldierly fraternity appears, as L. Monique Pittman has discussed, as a contemporary, multicultural phenomenon.[53] It is also possible to read York as enacting a symbolic role, not least in the light of Martin Barker's observation that, in the Iraq War film, 'special figures ... [often] representatives of minorities ... stand out ... [to] embody a new kind of soldier: the hero-victim'.[54] York's death is staged as the centre point of the Agincourt scenes, with Surrey's death (4.6) extracted out so as not to blur the solitary focus. Caught in an off-guard moment while comforting the Boy, he is violently stabbed in the back, the reprehensibility of the French Constable's actions brutally realized in York's abject condition and lingering death. York's blood-steeped torso contrasts with the draped and cleansed corpse of Henry at the start, stressing the former's status as a symbolic victim of derelictions in military conduct.

The symbolism is carried forward in the film's most important property – the talismanic flag stained with York's blood and retained by the Boy as an arm-band. A *memento mori* not only of the wounded war body but also of the war crime, the flag makes manifest the film's memorializing strategies. As relic, it newly locates the monarch's predictive claims: in the scrap of material, it is the illegitimacy of York's death that is 'freshly remembered' (4.3.55).

## THE IDEOLOGY OF THE SUFFERING SOLDIER

Director Nicholas Hytner has argued that, post-Iraq, any contemporary reworking of Act 1, Scene 2 (in which the justification for war is set out) is 'far more interested in the *ways* our war leaders ... take us to war than it is in the *rights or wrongs* of the cause'.[55] Sharrock's production similarly prioritizes process. The church's plan to go to war to avoid financial ruin (1.1.7–11, 79–81) is captured in close-up, and Henry's cynicism around ecclesiastics is stressed via a delay in Hiddleston's pentameter. Henry's response to Canterbury's unctuous greeting, 'Sure we thank you' (1.2.8), is ruptured to read, 'Sure', with a notable pause before the subsequent expression of thanks. The meaning is akin to the modern 'whatever', a signal that the protagonist recognizes as insincere the archbishop's

---

[51] Philip Edwards, *Threshold of a Nation: A Study in English and Irish Drama* (Cambridge, 1979), p. 76.

[52] Jami Rogers, 'The Shakespearean glass ceiling: the state of colorblind casting in contemporary British theatre', *Shakespeare Bulletin* 31 (2013), 405–30; p. 406. For example, York is lent speeches from other nobles, is the first to penetrate the inner sanctum of Harfleur, and tosses his sovereign a sword on the battlefield.

[53] L. Monique Pittman, 'Colour-conscious casting and multicultural Britain in the BBC *Henry V* (2012): historicizing adaptation in an age of digital placelessness', *Adaptation* 10 (2017), 192–209.

[54] Barker, A 'Toxic Genre', p. 43.

[55] 'The director's cut', p. 189.

rhetorical persiflage.[56] The warning 'take heed' (1.2.21) is delivered formally as a righteous affront, and the question 'May I with right and conscience make this claim?' (1.2.96) is highlighted because transposed to the start of Henry's address. Typically for this production, nonverbals continue as indices of meaning: the expressions that flash across Henry's face and the restless tapping of his fingers suggest hesitation, a monarch unsure whether there really is a persuasive case for war.

At the same time, semi-circular blocking (mimicked by the claustrophobic circling of the camera around Henry) suggests the combined forces – ecclesiastical and political – ranged in opposition to Henry's questioning, and in this regard it is noticeable that the production includes all of the nobles' supportive assurances (1.2.122–31), along with a series of response shots that point up a shared encouragement.[57]

The speech on the Salic law (1.2.37–95) is cut, its content transposed instead onto a scroll. The material surrogate is reminiscent of the National Theatre production (where Canterbury handed out 'copies of an elaborately produced dossier ... explain[ing] England's right ... to take military action'), but, of course, has its raison d'être in the Blair government's 'dodgy dossier' (which fraudulently detailed Iraq's 'Weapons of Mass Destruction').[58] Sharrock's film extends the use of this property, as the scroll passes between king and nobles and is also substituted for the 'paper' later handed to the French King by Essex.[59] In this way, the narrative bypasses any exploration of the rationale for war, shifting attention instead onto texts that visibly circulate but are never revealed or interrogated. The effect is to keep ideas about the 'cause' circulating and to suggest that, throughout the narrative, it remains a matter of irresolution. Uncertainty around the 'cause' is given additional emphasis in Henry's later discussions with Williams: the latter's arguments are retained, while the former's theological justifications are cut. Comments such as 'That's more than we know' (4.1.128) echo moments in the Iraq War films in which discussion about the reasons for military presence are opened up only in order immediately to be closed down.

With the 'cause' displaced, endlessly deferred or never adequately addressed, it is Henry's conduct in war on which an audience is obliged to focus. Here, as in the film adaptations *A Midsummer Night's Dream* (dir. Adrian Noble, 1996) and *Titus* (dir. Julie Taymor, 1999), the interpretive lens of a child affords a vantage point from which Henry's actions are scrutinized. Because the end of the film reveals the Boy to have the Chorus's retrospective viewpoint, he is allowed a cross-narrative authority and an experiential – interpretive – knowledge. Although most of his lines (including the long speech at 3.2.29–54) are cut, the Boy consistently appears in the margins of the *mise-en-scène*: war and its attendant horrors are mediated through his gaze. Following the 2013 Michael Grandage production of *Henry V*, in which Boy and Chorus are similarly doubled, then, Sharrock positions the Boy/Chorus as a type of 'embedded reporter' imbued with authenticity.[60]

The Boy's function is exemplified in the Bardolph scenes. Unlike Branagh, who uses the episode 'to emphasise the personal cost for Henry', Sharrock directs the spotlight onto the

---

[56] More broadly, Henry's attitude towards God registers not the piety of the historical king but, rather, 'doubt' – the situation of a secular monarch motivated more by hope than by faith. See Mathew Lyons, 'Review: *The Hollow Crown*: Henry V', 25 June 2012, www.mathewlyons.wordpress.com/2012/06/25/review-the-hollow-crown-henry-v.

[57] Later, as the Chorus intones 'Whose state so many had the managing / That they lost France and made his England bleed' (Epilogue, 11–12), the camera pans over the bowed heads, implicitly indicting them, the 'many'. The canvassing of responsibility has a 21st-century charge, bringing into the sphere of accountability political leaders as opposed to soldiers and military personnel.

[58] 'The director's cut', p. 179.

[59] The property is implied in the play's language and made explicit in some editions: see the Arden *Henry V*, ed. T. W. Craik (London, 1995), 2.4.95 SD.

[60] As a review notes, 'the effect [of doubling the boy and the Chorus] is ... to minimise the spin-doctoring gloss that the Chorus puts on ... war'. See Michael Billington, '*Henry V* – Review', 3 December 2013, www.theguardian.com/stage/2013/dec/03/henry-v-review-jude-law.

implications of Bardolph's offence.[61] As in Iraq War films, which are distinctive for including moments of culpable, even criminal, soldiering, an uncompromising reading of Bardolph as an example of aberrant soldierly behaviour is prepared for at Harfleur where he is visualized stealing a large gold cross.[62] 'We would have all such offenders so cut off' (3.6.108) is staged without excision as a rhetorical set-piece, a statement about conduct in war delivered for the benefit of the attendant audience of troops. In the context of concerns about the conduct of coalition forces in Iraq and Afghanistan, the only place for rhetoric in this production is when a condemnation of war crimes is required. Crucially, the Boy's assessment concludes the episode. The camera lingers on the Boy as he stops to contemplate the significance of Bardolph's swinging corpse. The tree from which the body hangs is located to the left of the frame, while the troops (which Nym and Pistol move to join) are seen on the right, suggesting a division of paths, a choice to be made. Most obviously, the Boy conveys the 'rightness' of Henry's judgement as he physically turns away from the Boar's Head fraternity to follow the army on its onward march. In Sharrock's film, then, the traditional Henrician rejection of Bardolph is displaced onto the Boy in such a way as to play up the humanitarian significances of the protagonist's stance on military ideals.

The episode's reification of standards looks backwards to the manner of York's death and forwards to the prisoner scenes. Distinctively, and again in contrast to Branagh's film, in which, as the director states, 'I rather flunked and avoided ... the issue', Sharrock's production includes *both* deathly royal directives – 'Then every soldier kill his prisoners!' (4.6.37) *and* 'we'll cut the throats of those we have' (4.7.61).[63] The inclusion is contextualized, of course, against the background of related controversies at the Abu Ghraib prison in Iraq, at Bagram in Afghanistan, and at Guantánamo, but goes further than other contemporary representations. While the Iraq War films never explicitly realize prisoner abuse on screen, Sharrock's period setting permits her to follow all the major theatrical productions of the last decade in featuring the prisoner scenes. (Typical is

the National Theatre production which has the French kill the boys and plunder the luggage, resulting in Henry's bloody order.)[64] In Sharrock's *Henry V*, Fluellen's reference to the 'poys and the luggage' (4.7.1) is removed, and the decision presented in some part as an angry reaction to the news of York's death. But the order is primarily understood in terms of the post-traumatic associations which gather about Henry in the battle scenes – the inhuman injunction over which he presides, it is suggested, can be seen as a catastrophic error emerging from exhaustion and stress.

It is Henry's traumatized condition that is pointed up in the scenes immediately preceding the order. Staggering about a burning field littered with bodies, he picks his way through numerous corpses, the *mise-en-scène* a spectacle of devastation that confirms, in the words of Karen Randell and Sean Redmond, 'the relationship between trauma and witnessing a terrible event'.[65] Chiming almost exactly with cinematic representations of American soldiers *in extremis*, Henry's wild-eyed expression and panicked breathing are the symptoms of a psychic disturbance triggered by exposure to battle. 'I was not angry' (4.7.53) is a screamed pronouncement directed heavenwards, the minor strains of strings and the reeling pans of the camera suggesting the depths of an emotional

---

[61] Pamela Mason, '*Henry V*: "the quick forge and working house of thought"', in *The Cambridge Companion to Shakespeare's History Plays*, ed. Michael Hattaway (Cambridge, 2002), pp. 177–92; esp. p. 185.

[62] See Barker, *A 'Toxic Genre'*, p. 36.

[63] Ramona Wray and Mark Thornton Burnett, 'From the horse's mouth: Branagh on the Bard', in *Shakespeare, Film, Fin de Siècle*, ed. Mark Thornton Burnett and Ramona Wray (Basingstoke, 2000), pp. 165–78; esp. p. 172.

[64] See Robert C. Doyle, *The Enemy in Our Hands: America's Treatment of Enemy Prisoners of War from the Revolution to the War on Terror* (Lexington, 2010), pp. 292–349. Although examples such as *In the Valley of Elah* might hint at the possibility, prisoner abuse is never realized explicitly onscreen. For an extended discussion of this scene, see Silverstone, *Shakespeare, Trauma*, pp. 120–1.

[65] Karen Randell and Sean Redmond, 'Introduction: setting the screen', in Randell and Redmond, eds., *War Body*, pp. 1–13; esp. p. 7.

crisis. The idea of an irreparably disoriented protagonist is reflected in Essex's startled (and interpolated) response to the order – 'My lord?' Simultaneously, the accompanying wide-shot of a seemingly physically reduced Henry, ringed by slaughtered men, reminds us of the overwhelming contexts underpinning his behaviour. Direct engagement with the viewer falls to the Boy whose sorrowful look to camera invites an empathetic response to Henry as a soldier pressurized into violence of action. In this way, the film not only asks us to accept that Henry orders the prisoners to be killed, but also – and uniquely – urges an audience to view that action with a degree of understanding.

The subsequent unwillingness of Henry's men to execute the order reinforces its aberrancy while echoing the National Theatre production. There, the response of Henry's soldiers points up, as Lois Potter notes, 'the commander's callous indifference'.[66] In Sharrock's production, however, the emphasis lies with Henry's felt participation in the fate of the prisoners and on the physical manifestations of his traumatized interiority. In a tightly sequential montage, we see the prisoners assembled for death (they kneel, with their backs to their guards), then move to a close-up of Henry's tight face and, still with the close-up, we watch the King flinch at the prisoners' screams as the arrows are fired. Throughout the close-up, Henry's eyes are closed, suggesting an experience that is uncommunicable. The moment marks a transformation in Henry's physical relationship with the camera. Distinctively, the Iraq War films have inaugurated a different – and more distanced – relation with viewers: the contemporary war hero is shot side on, head bowed, eyes averted. And, from this point in Sharrock's film, Henry, while remaining centre-frame, increasingly looks away from camera, gesture and bodily comportment betokening knowledge, regret and recognition of his own complicity.

The change in camera angle reflects the ways in which the episode operates in a climactic capacity; put simply, the order to kill the prisoners is seen to overshadow all else. When told that 'The day is yours' (4.7.84), Henry struggles to compose himself, finally falling to his knees, a posture that recalls the previous situation of the prisoners and suggests that their fate has become part of the film's psychic memory. Like Exeter's traumatic memory at the start, the French prisoners' fate subsequently haunts the action. 'Praisèd be God' (4.7.86) and 'Then call we this the field of Agincourt' (4.7.88) are commensurately downbeat and understated, played as tokenistic gestures emptied out of any meaningful substance. Similarly, when Henry reads aloud the 'note' (4.8.80) of 'English dead' (4.8.102), simultaneous shots of blinded noblemen and mutilated soldiers, and the general air of demoralization and deadened sensitivities, unhinge any note of affirmation (Figure 2). In this respect, Sharrock's film throws into sharp relief the equivalent sequences in the National Theatre production where spectators were 'invited to read the celebration of the victory at Agincourt as an analogue for British and American action in Iraq'.[67] In 2003, the year of the National Theatre production, it was still possible to imagine 'victory' in the War on Terror, but today, a decade and a half later, 'the actual experience of war after 9/11 [has] demolished all such expectations'.[68] Instead, Sharrock's film mirrors the view widely held in both popular and military realms that the costs of conflict are out of proportion to the outcome and that there never will be any kind of 'victory' – that its very prospect is unrealizable. Traditionally, critics have argued about whether adaptations of *Henry V* are pro- or anti-war. In representing a new kind of warfare, Sharrock's film moves beyond these debates and suggests their contemporary irrelevance. Envisaging conflict as self-defeat, the film speaks to incompleteness, irresolution and regret as the only available realities.

---

[66] Lois Potter, 'Shakespeare performed: English and American Richards, Edwards and Henries', *Shakespeare Quarterly* 55 (2004), 450–61; p. 454.

[67] Silverstone, *Shakespeare, Trauma*, p. 125. This celebration was marked by a 'dance to pumping heavy metal music ... evident communal delight and relief, and the screening of the victory video' (p. 126).

[68] Bacevich, *New American Militarism*, p. 233.

2  Henry V (Tom Hiddleston) in a state of psychic disturbance after Agincourt. Courtesy of Photofest.

## THE HOMECOMING AND
## COMMEMORATION

Even though we remain in France, Act 5's alteration in pace and mood signals the idea of a return, recalling a cycle of war films whose narrative trajectories are often directed towards the homecoming that concludes a 'tour of duty'.[69] Like the returning soldiers of *The Hurt Locker* and *American Sniper*, Henry is awkward in the unfamiliar domestic setting and his civilian velvet. Of course, the film's framing device (we begin and end with Henry's funeral) and construction – through the representation of the weeping widow – of a 'love match' helps make plausible the romancing of Katherine. Yet it is the echo of the homecoming that really makes sense of the scene: Henry's uneasiness is situated as an inevitable accompaniment of the traumatized soldier's difficult reintegration,

thereby imbuing the episode – often stilted in production – with a naturalized logic. As the French King joins the pair's hands, a match-cut from a close-up of a smiling Katherine moves us to a close-up of her grieving at his funeral. The dissolve from left to right underwrites the change in her circumstances (and clarifies the status of the wooing scene as the princess's private commemoration). Reinforcing the course of a journey from

---

[69] According to Phil Klay, '[i]n his roundup of the fiction and poetry coming out of the Iraq and Afghan wars, US journalist George Packer declared the return home to be the "moment of truth" for modern war fiction, in the same way that scenes of mass slaughter in the trenches were for the first world war and patrols through the jungle were for Vietnam'. See 'The top ten books about returning from war', 28 January 2015, www.theguardian.com/books/booksblog/2015/jan/28/top-10-books-about-returning-from-war-phil-klay.

mortality to vitality and back again, the *mise-en-scène* reverses the earlier match-cut from Henry's corpse to the monarch alive and astride his horse, bringing the narrative full circle. Skilful elisions between Act 5 and the film's epilogue inhere in the repetition of the 'Amen' (Burgundy's prayer is echoed in Canterbury's funeral mass) and in the close-up on the baby, who is, of course, both the 'Issue' (5.2.344) anticipated in the French King's speech and the unfortunate offspring, 'in infant bands crowned King' (Epilogue, 9). Act 5, then, returns us to our starting point in a structural move which mimes the ways in which, in the Iraq War films, non-linear narratives register, as Guy Westwell notes, 'the circular, endless, and ultimately impossible task of imposing order'.[70]

Further bringing things full circle is the camera's focus on the Boy, who is pictured gazing at the corpse while cradling the production's most eloquent symbolic property – York's bloodied flag. When exactly, according to the play, the Boy dies Shakespeare does not make clear, but most directors choose to stage his death. Uniquely, Sharrock's adaptation leaves the Boy alive. The film's third and final match-cut takes us, in a downwards–upwards movement, from a Boy to an old man (a veteran), a switch that moves the action on fifty years. Just as veterans figure as voices of experience on commemorative occasions, and their autobiographies are placed on record, Sharrock's film constructs the Boy as the last survivor of the French campaign. The grown-up Boy – now played by the late John Hurt, an actor whose ravaged countenance underscores the costs of cyclical wartime experience – is revealed as having voiced the Chorus. And, as the now fully orchestrated score rises to a crescendo, the Chorus directly addresses the camera for the first time. The epilogue is quoted almost in full, but a single cut significantly adjusts the conventional petition to the audience. In the play, the plea 'for their sake, / In your fair minds let this acceptance take' (13–14) asks for the actors and the staging to be viewed favourably. Thanks to the loss of the meta-theatrical reference – 'oft our stage hath shown' (13) – in Sharrock's film, it is the medieval soldier (rather than the theatrical

performer) who features as subject. The final request, then, is to look on Henry, his army and his actions with compassion, to acknowledge the new realities of war and to accept the playing-out of a flawed humanity.

Via the traumatic experiences we have been pressed to remember, Henry, York and the English troops take on a larger representativeness. Just as the play's epilogue looks forward to the next instalments in the history, so does Sharrock's anticipate the myriad wars to come. Divorced from its theatrical provenance, 'for their sake' echoes the familiar motto of 'Remembrance Day', dedicated to the memory of all military casualties across the Western world. Enfolding the epilogue and 'Remembrance Day' still further is the idea of an appeal (as in the 'Poppy Day Appeal') to conscience and good will. Bridging Agincourt, Afghanistan and Iraq, Sharrock's *Henry V* offers a bleak and inglorious vision of warfare as a continuum, a universal. The film merges the insights of contemporary theatrical and filmic interpretation to suggest the present as a recapitulation of the past, and to affirm war crimes – the misconduct of troops and the mistreatment of prisoners – as realities for which there is sustained historical precedent. Sharrock's *Henry V* realizes the protagonist in elegiac fashion, and vital to this understanding is the construction of Henry's damaged heroism and its inherent capacity for error. It is a vision replicated in the way in which, out of favour for many years, a cyclical presentation of the history plays is increasingly becoming the dominant paradigm.[71] Playing the Henriad in this way accentuates a mourning note, a serial concern with the inevitability of war, the transience of governance, the vulnerability of kings, and the plaintiveness of the historical process. The features of the individual play alter in the long shadow cast by the War on Terror, and the Shakespeare who emerges is darker and more doubtful than ever before.

---

[70] Westwell, 'In country', p. 23.
[71] See, for example, the Druid Shakespeare touring production of *Richard II, Henry IV* and *Henry V* in 2015 and the RSC's 'London Season' 2015–16 production of the same.

# ECONOMIES OF GUNPOWDER AND ECOLOGIES OF PEACE: ACCOUNTING FOR SUSTAINABILITY

## RANDALL MARTIN[1]

In his magisterial account of the early modern scientific revolution, historian David Wootton excludes Shakespeare from the educated minority who recognized that discoveries such as the heliocentric universe, the magnetic compass, the New World, the printing press and gunpowder were changing orders of knowledge passed down from the ancient and medieval worlds. Wootton's claims of Shakespeare's ignorance could be disproved in any of these areas; but in the case of gunpowder the playwright's texts show him to be fully conscious of its world-changing tendencies, as Charles Edelman has documented comprehensively in *Shakespeare's Military Language: A Dictionary*.[2] Moreover, when Shakespeare's plays were performed, they invited London spectators to *feel* the pressures of technological innovation, since the sensational stagecraft of playhouse cannon-fire made gunpowder explosions an embodied imaginative experience, expanding the physical resonances and theatrical memories of squibs and fireworks (about which Jonathan Gil Harris has written suggestively in relation to *Macbeth*).[3] Rather than seeking to layer pre- and post-Reformation associations of gunpowder, my article will explore Shakespeare's representations of its military, civilian and environmental disruptions. These generated new empirical arguments for peace and sustainability which challenged war's traditional myths, while also introducing a modern conceptual horizon of unpredictable futurity.

Shakespeare's cognitive and sensory pathways into awareness of gunpowder called into question two commonplaces about war. One was the classical theory, based on Galenic physiology, that war

[1] Earlier versions of this article were presented in 2018 at a Shakespeare Association of America seminar on 'Peace', a Columbia University Early Modern Graduate Student Conference on 'World-Making', and finally the International Shakespeare Conference at The Shakespeare Institute, Stratford-upon-Avon. I am very grateful for useful responses from participants at these events. I should also like to thank Madeline Bassnett, Gretchen Minton and Adrian Tronson for their helpful discussions and comments.

[2] Charles Edelman, *Shakespeare's Military Language: A Dictionary* (London, 2000); David Wootton, *The Invention of Science: A New History of the Scientific Revolution* (New York, 2015), pp. 5, 10, 451–3, 511–12. For instance, Wootton observes that the word 'modern' in titles of Renaissance books on warfare 'show[ed] that they acknowledged the revolutionary consequences of gunpowder' (p. 36). Shakespeare's deliberately contemporizing representations of gunpowder, discussed below, point to his similar awareness of gunpowder's modernity.

[3] Jonathan Gil Harris, *Untimely Matter in the Time of Shakespeare* (Philadelphia, PA, 2009), pp. 119–39. Shakespeare's first simulations of cannon-fire in *The First Part of the Contention* (later revised as *2 Henry VI*) and *The True Tragedy of Richard Duke of York* (later *3 Henry VI*) followed those of his sometime collaborator George Peele, who introduced the use of chambers in the English theatre in *The Battle of Alcazar* (c. 1587–9) (3.4 and 5.1). Shakespeare then outdid Peele and other contemporaries in calling for cannon sounds twice in the multi-authored *1 Henry VI Part One* (1.6, 2.3) and *Henry V* (Prologue and 3.1), and three times with multiple volleys in Q2 *Hamlet* (1.2, 1.4, 5.2), followed by a possible encore in *Othello* (2.1.93, but without a Q or F SD), and an envoi with Fletcher in *Henry VIII* (which became devastatingly realistic when a piece of burning wadding from one of several chambers (*Henry VIII* 1.4.49 SD) set alight the thatched roof of the Globe and burnt down the theatre). See Sir Henry Wotton's report of 2 July, reproduced in *Henry VIII*, ed. Jay L. Halio (Oxford, 1999), p. 17. Credit for the innovation should also go to Strange's Men, the acting company which originally performed *Alcazar, The Contention* and *True Tragedy*. As Charles Edelman shows, the stage directions calling for cannon-fire in all three texts were likely written by the same playhouse annotator – see 'The Battle of Alcazar, Muly Morocco, and Shakespeare's *2* and *3* Henry VI', *Notes and Queries* 49 (2002), 215–18.

corrected the corrupting effects of masculine inactivity during peacetime.[4] This gendered medical assumption naturalized alternating historical cycles of war and peace as a healthy social pattern.[5] The other commonplace was that war paid for itself because its costs were always recovered or exceeded by conquest and spoils. Yet the unprecedented devastation of gunpowder weapons, in addition to their soaring financial and social costs to emerging European nation-states, undercut these claims.[6] Shakespeare takes notice of these new realities in the opening scene of *Hamlet* – a play which, not incidentally, calls for cannon-fire to be simulated more often than any other early modern play. Marcellus observes that Denmark's polity is being radically altered by Claudius's orders for 'daily cast of brazen cannon'. A nascent military-industrial complex is producing artillery to supply battleships being built by involuntarily enforced shipwrights, working like machines in 'sweaty haste', 24/7, to sell at 'foreign mart[s] for implements of war' (*Hamlet*, 1.1.72–8). This 'post-haste and rummage', as Horatio calls it, reflects more than just precautions against Fortinbras and his sharked-up mercenaries. It implies: new state and private capitalized investment in resource extraction and industrial production; the mechanization of human life and death in war; profit-driven global trade in armaments; and national aspirations to overseas empires.[7] In short, this was a new economic paradigm of maximal growth through innovation, competition and domination, which Shakespeare shadows by relating it to *Hamlet*'s ethos of apocalyptic revenge tragedy.

Like other major discoveries that gradually invented the modern world, gunpowder demanded new words and stories to describe both its unprecedented killing power and its emptying-out of chivalric-heroic traditions – changes Jaques encapsulates in his mordant seven-ages-of-man quip about the soldier '[s]eeking the bubble reputation / Even in the cannon's mouth' (*As You Like It*, 2.7.152–5).[8] And, like the dialogue between Marcellus and Horatio, contemporary printed news about war made gunpowder's staggering losses publicly visible. Their reframing of war as *calculable* material, human and ecological costs,

I shall suggest, was informed by a wider shift that social historian Alexandra Shepard calls a 'culture of appraisal'. Its quantitative and qualitative constructions opened gunpowder's excesses to

---

[4] 'Gunpowder exploded the old cyclical conceptualisation of the art of war, exalting the grimy artilleryman as the personification of "modern warfare"' – see Mark Charles Fissel, *English Warfare 1511–1642* (London, 2001), p. 181. As Fissel also observes, the English were especially reputed for gunpowder-and-siege warfare, partly owing to experience gained in France and the Netherlands.

[5] Exemplified, respectively, by Virgil's *Aeneid* and *Georgics*. See R. Martin, *Shakespeare and Ecology* (Oxford, 2015), pp. 78–111. An example is Arcite's prayer to Mars from *The Two Noble Kinsmen*, cited by my fellow panellist Sharon O'Dair in her International Shakespeare Conference paper, '"To the Edge of All Extremity": On the Eco-Necessity of War and Ruin':

> Oh great corrector of enormous times;
> Shaker of o'er-rank states; thou grand decider
> Of dusty and old titles, that heal'st with blood
> The earth when it is sick and cur'st the world
> O'th'pleurisy of people.
>
> (5.1.61–5)

Significantly, Shakespeare immediately undercuts this commonplace with a striking gunpowder metaphor describing the victorious Arcite being thrown fatally from his horse (5.6.61–5).

[6] For example: 'What conquest [i.e. booty] brings [Caesar] home?'; 'Like to the senators of th'antique Rome, / With the plebeians swarming at their heels, / Go forth and fetch their conqu'ring Caesar in' (*Julius Caesar* 1.1.32; *Henry V* 5.0.26–8). Partly because of gunpowder's escalating costs, the risks on capital invested in globalizing English trade offered potentially greater profits than military ventures (Fissel, *English Warfare*, p. 200).

[7] Represented originally in Peele's *Alcazar*, whose contemporary background was England's sale of firearms and cannons to Morocco in exchange for the latter's plentiful supplies of high-grade saltpetre, the key ingredient in gunpowder. Artillery contributed to the victory of the Moroccan Sultan Ahmad Al-Mansur and the death of Sebastian I of Portugal, which allowed Philip II of Spain to take over the latter's country. See Edelman, *Shakespeare's Military Language*, p. 296; *The Stukeley Plays*, ed. Charles Edelman (Manchester, 2005), note to 5 Prol. 29; Miranda Kaufman, *Black Tudors: The Untold Story* (London, 2017), pp. 138–44.

[8] Wootton brilliantly demonstrates how geophysical and scientific discoveries necessitated finding new vocabulary and metaphors to explain their workings and significance (*Invention of Science*, esp. pp. 22–9, pp. 15–54).

empirical critique and began to transform knowledge of war from a state of human nature and an arena of masculine honour to a discourse of accountability and sustainability.[9]

Following a preliminary discussion of the early seventeenth-century Siege of Ostend and *Troilus and Cressida*, my article will argue that Shakespeare's sceptical attitudes towards spoils as an alleged offset to the costs of war began to represent the sustainability of peace as a positive reason of state. I shall trace this viewpoint to biographical and contextual sources respectively: Shakespeare's personal experience of financial accountancy, recently examined by economic historian David Fallow; and a ground-breaking treatise written by Sir James Cotton in support of King James's pacific foreign policy. Cotton's research not only quantifies the insupportable costs of war but also expands the definition of what counts as a cost to include social and environmental factors. It thus offers an early example of today's Ecological (or Environmental) Full-Cost Accountability. And it reconceives the value of peace-making in ways that anticipate the post-conquer-and-profit ethos of sustainable prosperity, a key principle of economist Tim Jackson's seminal study, *Prosperity Without Growth*. This ethos, I shall also argue, becomes more prominent in Shakespeare's plays during the second half of his career. It counters the emergent paradigm of relentless economic expansion which gunpowder militarization helped to introduce into the West, and which we now belatedly recognize is a root cause of the incipient environmental calamities of the Anthropocene.[10]

## THE GAME EXPLODES

The most prolonged and devastating example of gunpowder's new capacity for destruction, since its introduction into Europe in the late fifteenth century, was the 1601–4 Siege of Ostend – or 'The New Troy', as contemporary pamphlets dubbed this epic battle of the Eighty Years' War.[11] Ostend was a strategically vital, Dutch-controlled town on the North-Sea coast of Spanish-occupied Flanders. It was besieged by Spanish and Catholic-allied forces, and defended by Dutch and English troops commanded by Sir Francis Vere. During three years of what became a brutal war of attrition, both sides suffered more than 100,000 casualties. The final Spanish victory was pyrrhic. Princess Isabella reportedly wept when she entered Ostend and saw (and no doubt smelled) the ruins. There were no spoils. The siege's financial drain contributed to the bankruptcy of the Castilian treasury three years later.

The catastrophic scale of destruction and direct English involvement made reporting events of the siege irresistible to both Continental and English news writers. And, like them, Shakespeare evidently saw parallels between the seemingly never-ending stand-off at Ostend and the archetypal one at Troy. The earliest English news was *The*

---

[9] Douglas Bruster, 'On a certain tendency in economic criticism of Shakespeare', in *Money and the Age of Shakespeare: Essays in New Economic Criticism*, ed. Linda Woodbridge (New York, 2004), pp. 67–95, argues that the various approaches of New Economic Criticism in the 1980s and 1990s produced a critical tendency to binarize economic aspects of literary texts in terms of either a 'reckoned' quantitative perspective, or a 'rash' qualitative one. Within this framework, 'green Shakespeare', as it was then, was situated on the 'rash', anti-economic side of the tendency. My article reflects the evolution of economic critique within the interdisciplinary practices of materialist and scientific ecocriticism, and the Anthropocene's rescaling of human epistemologies within the deep-time forces of planetary systems and changes. See also next note.

[10] Tim Jackson, *Prosperity Without Growth* (London and Washington, DC: 2010; rev. 2017). The Anthropocene is the epoch in which humans collectively have acted as a geological, biological and atmospheric force to alter the natural state of the planet. It follows 11,000 years of relative biospheric stability called the Holocene. A scientific commission, the Anthropocene Working Group, is currently studying possible time-frames for the Anthropocene. See http://quaternary.stratigraphy.org/working-groups /anthropocene.

[11] A. H. Burne, 'The horrible, bloudie, and unheard of Siege of Ostend', *Journal of the Royal Artillery* 65 (1938/9), 238–53; Fissel, *English Warfare*, pp. 185–8; Anna E. C. Simoni, *The Ostend Story: Early Tales of the Great Siege and the Mediating Role of Henrick van Hastens* ('t Goy, 2003). Bones from the siege are still turning up today: see http://en.wikipedia.org /wiki/Siege_of_Ostend.

*Oppugnation* (1601), describing initial assaults on the town.[12] According to the *OED*'s 2004 revised entry, Shakespeare coined the related word 'oppugnancy', meaning antagonism, in *Troilus and Cressida*, presumably after seeing this pamphlet. In a play marked by conspicuous neologisms, Ulysses flaunts the word in his 'specialty of rule' speech to describe the 'discord' that allegedly follows the subversion of hierarchical authority:

> [e]ach thing melts
> In mere oppugnancy. The bounded waters
> Should lift their bosoms higher than the shores,
> And make a sop of all this solid globe.
>
> (1.3.110–13)

Shakespeare's surrounding image of dissolving land and sea aptly recalls contemporary Ostend, since it was a fortified town built on a sandy wetland estuary, served by extensive canals and sluices.[13]

Printed news pamphlets such as *The Oppugnation*, and their related maps and images, were shaped by new modes of visual perception that turned sieges into theatricalized spectacles, and in turn made the entanglements of Ostend's natural resources, military tactics, and human and environmental devastation highly visible to English readers.[14] The prominence of artillery and firearms also invited writers to quantify these relationships in ways that made their losses and costs measurable. In the opening paragraph of *A breefe declaration of that which has happened ... [in] Oastend* (1602), the anonymous writer conveys the lengthy intensity of the siege by reporting that Spanish cannons have fired 136,000 shots since the assault began the previous July, and an additional 1,300 shots from 7 January to the present.[15] In *The Oppugnation*, the writer keeps count of the shifting number of artillery-pieces and rounds fired on both sides. On 26 July, for example, after de Vere's forces had repulsed three Spanish assaults, their commander Archduke Albert increased the number of his cannon on the west side of town to twenty-six, and on the east to nine, and together that day they fired 16,000 shots, with the Dutch–English defenders countercharging with 9,000 shots.[16] By contrast with chronicle narratives of pre-gunpowder battles such as

Holinshed's, the accuracy of this artillery reporting is striking. *A breefe declaration*'s figures indicate that cannonballs at Ostend were being counted and/or retrieved by the master of the ordinance or master gunner for re-use as they were fired, and their numbers recorded in civilian journals and military records.[17] Each one carried a cost that contemporary

---

[12] *The Oppugnation and fierce siege of Ostend by the Arch-duke Albertus his forces* (London, 1601).

[13] Nick de Somogyi's *Shakespeare's Theatre of War* (London, 1998) argues that the events of Ostend relate to *Hamlet*, and Q2 4.4 in particular (pp. 5, 77–8, 238–43). But 'oppugnancy', as well as the cognate 'propugnancy' (2.2.136, Shakespeare's only usage), point to *Troilus and Cressida* as the more apt connection with the 'New Troy' (both words were sixteenth-century coinages to describe modern gunpowder-and-siege warfare, as the *OED*'s citations show); and *Troilus and Cressida*'s dates of composition (c. 1601–3) fit better than those of *Hamlet*, which Shakespeare began writing soon after *Julius Caesar* in 1599. The topical allusion to Ostend through 'oppugnancy' may provide a *terminus ad quem* for the play's much-debated date of composition. I am grateful to Gretchen Minton for this suggestion.

[14] Brian Sandberg, '"To have the pleasure of this siege": envisioning siege warfare during the European wars of religion', in *Beholding Violence in Medieval and Early Modern Europe*, ed. Allie Terry-Fritsch and Ellen Felicia Labbie (Farnham, 2012), pp. 143–62.

[15] *A breefe declaration of that which is happened as well within as without Oastend sithence the vij. of Ianuarie 1602* (London, 1602), A1r.

[16] *Oppugnation*, B2r–v.

[17] Sandberg, '"To have the pleasure"', p. 147. A Master Gunner and his apprentice surprise the English with defensive cannon-fire at the siege of Orléans (1429) in *1 Henry VI* ('Here they shot [sic] [chambers] and Salisbury falls downe'), killing Thomas Gargrave and the Earl of Salisbury, who previously '[i]n thirteen [field] battles ... o'ercame', thereby illustrating the disproportionate killing power of gunpowder weapons. Although the chivalric traditionalist Talbot rails against them as underhanded, Salisbury was 'first trained to the wars' by the gunpowder innovator Henry V (1.5–6, 1.6.47 SD, 1.6.56–7). For visual recreations of this moment and the off-stage firing of chambers, see Walter C. Hodges, *Enter the Whole Army: A Pictorial Study of Shakespearean Staging 1576–1616* (Cambridge, 1999), pp. 22, 54–7. Thomas Digges's *Arithmetical Warlike Treatise Named Stratioticos* (1579, 1590) states that the master of the ordinance, 'one of the principal Officers of the field', must be a man of mathematical knowledge 'to suppitate and forecast what quantitie of shot, powder, etc. shalbe

readers with some knowledge of modern warfare could estimate, as did the barrels of gunpowder consumed in firing the shots. As the siege unfolds, similar figures specify the number of companies, soldiers in combat, and casualties. Such quantification shapes the writer's narrative and certifies its reliability.[18] A comparable numerical calculation inviting physical and ethical evaluation occurs in *1 Henry IV* when Falstaff boasts he has deliberately exposed his 150 men to lethal cannon-fire. Only 3 remain alive, 'and they are for the town's end, to beg during life' (4.2.14, 5.3.35–8). Implicitly admitting his ulterior aim is to pillage his dead soldiers' pay and widows' pensions, Falstaff's callous precision represents his corruption as a different order of knowledge, and a darker jest, than his later 'sacking' of a 'city' with a hidden bottle (5.3.54). I'll consider further Shakespearian examples of quantification and spoils in a later section.

## ACCOUNTABLE KNOWLEDGE

That some readers and spectators might ponder the material costs of Ostend's disaster seems likely because the calculation of wealth had become essential to early modern transactions of property and credit in daily life. In her book *Accounting for Oneself*, Alexandra Shepard shows that the later sixteenth- and early seventeenth-century conditions of rising incomes and social mobility for all but the poorest classes created a 'culture of appraisal', based on mutually reinforcing financial and moral judgements.[19]

The most influential method of calculation was bookkeeping of either the single- or double-entry kind.[20] Its process of reducing material and human transactions to numeric ciphers of monetary value enabled merchants to judge whether their businesses were sustainable, and to make rational decisions about future investments by revealing patterns in their sales and purchases. And it preserved a record of prudence and prosperity which could serve as social confirmation of the nascent Protestant ethic later

requisite for any Battery' (1590 Y3r; 'supputate' = calculate, a word coined by Thomas's father Leonard Digges, whose writing on artillery his son incorporated into *Stratioticos*). Digges's earlier phrase 'the Auncient Romane Discipline for the Warres', and his illustration of classical field tactics with examples from Roman history, are the presumed source of Fluellen's old-school martialism in *Henry V*. But in his updated 1590 edition, Digges shows how mathematical knowledge necessary for ballistics, proper artillery use, fortification-building and gunpowder warfare in general are rendering classical paradigms of warfare obsolete: 'Modern Warres … [are] altered, and the furie of Ordinaunce such, as all those Romane Orders were meere toyes once to be talked of in these our days: As though the Heauens and Elementes had chaunged their Natures, or Men and Weapons so altered, as no humaine reason might attaine to consider the difference' (B2r). This quantifying episteme is visible in Shakespeare at moments such as when Iago complains about the 'great arithmetician' Cassio, whose 'bookish theoric' – or technical knowledge of mechanized warfare – he is studying. This forward-looking knowledge earns him promotion, since Othello himself is imaginatively and materially invested in modern warfare's 'mortal engines', evident also in his inspection of fortifications being rebuilt on Cyprus, implicitly to accommodate more artillery. The traditionalist Iago, on the other hand, still values squares and divisions in hand-to-hand field battles like his Italian mentor Machiavelli, who failed to take account of gunpowder weapons in his instantly obsolescent *The Art of War* (1519–20, translated 1573; *Othello* 1.1.18–25, 3.23–5, 3.3.357, 3.4.13–34).

[18] It also suggests how contemporary warfare was diverging from early modern stage battles in which soldiers fight only with swords or pikes. Pistols were never used in onstage battles (Edelman, *Shakespeare's Military Language*, pp. 261–2; Alan C. Dessen and Leslie Thomson, *A Dictionary of Stage Directions in English Drama, 1580–1642* (Cambridge, 2001), p. 164).

[19] Alexandra Shepard, *Accounting for Oneself: Worth, Status, and the Social Order in Early Modern England* (Oxford, 2015), esp. p. 36. Shepard's analysis of civil-law-court records shows that measuring the value of personal goods and financial worth became a customary way of assessing taxes, seizure for debt, eligibility for the franchise and public offices, and sumptuary laws.

[20] As Wootton, Alfred Crosby and Adam Smyth each explain, double-entry bookkeeping was formally a three-book procedure of incremental quantification aimed at representing reality in mathematical language and monetary values. A first 'waste book' took on-the-spot notes of any goods and services transactions. The 'register' then reduced the waste book's circumstantial details to an itemized list. The final 'account book' recorded monetary debts and credits on facing pages and kept

theorized by Max Weber.[21] Situating bookkeeping in the wider historicity of truthfulness through quantification, Adam Smyth has shown that accounting practices were disseminated by a new generation of sixteenth-century manuals, and that their models were informally absorbed into commonplace books, diaries and other forms of life-writing – or drama, as Falstaff's lop-sided tavern bill illustrates in *1 Henry IV* (2.5.538–43), a play thematically focused in political and material senses on debts and redemption.

Accounting was shunned in grammar schools for class reasons,[22] but it could be learned in new 'reckoning schools' which sprang up in Southwark near The Globe theatre. Although Shakespeare was a grammar-school boy, he was also the son of an alderman-merchant who managed both his own finances and those of Stratford-upon-Avon. David Fallow shows that, as first-born son and heir, Shakespeare would have been his father John's 'apprentice' in financial numeracy and business practices, which must have included bookkeeping.[23] He would also have made an inventory of his father's debts and assets following his death in 1601, and integrated them into his own accounts. *Twelfth Night*, also written in 1601, possibly alludes to this event when Olivia facetiously 'inventories' her facial assets, 'every particle and utensil labelled to my will' (1.5.234–5). This and other non-dramatic evidence of Shakespeare's financial networks, recently explored in *The Shakespeare Circle*, edited by Paul Edmondson and Stanley Wells, indicates that he participated meaningfully in Shepard's 'culture of appraisal'.[24]

Sir Robert Cotton brought such thinking to bear in a substantial defence of King James's foreign policy, *Warrs with Foreign Princes Dangerous to our Common-wealth* (written and circulated in manuscript *c.* 1610; printed 1657).[25] Gathering factual information from his famous library and government records to refute pro-war arguments presented to Prince Henry by militant Protestants, Cotton presents a reign-by-reign comparison of financial gains and losses caused by English foreign and civil wars in terms of debits and credits.

His work begins by briefly rehearsing his opponents' 'Arguments for Warre', and then summarizes commonplace objections by Cicero, Erasmus and other humanists – above all, that war may be morally justified only as a last resort in self-defence: 'War is to that man just and lawfull, who

---

a running tally. See Wootton, *Invention of Science*, pp. 163–210; Alfred Crosby, *The Measure of Reality: Quantification in Western Europe, 1250–1600* (Cambridge, 1997), pp. 199–223; Adam Smyth, *Autobiography in Early Modern England* (Cambridge, 2010), esp. pp. 57–122.

[21] *The Protestant Ethic and the 'Spirit' of Capitalism, and Other Writings*, ed. Peter Baehr and Gordon C. Wells [1905, trans. 1930] (London, 2002).

[22] E.g.:

MOTH. How many is one thrice told?
ARMADO. I am ill at reckoning. It fitteth the spirit of a tapster.
(*Love's Labour's Lost* 1.2.39–41)

See Smyth, *Autobiography*, pp. 40–1; Linda Woodbridge, 'Introduction', in *Money and the Age of Shakespeare: Essays in New Economic Criticism*, ed. Linda Woodbridge (New York, 2003), pp. 1–18. The 'reckoning schools' were accompanied by a surge in printed works about arithmetic, mathematics and bookkeeping, especially after the Armada event made 'studying math … patriotic' (Woodbridge, p. 8). While this cultural moment drew attention to the new epistemological link between waging war and mathematics, the essays in Woodbridge's volume are focused on money, commerce and early capitalism and do not discuss military production. Yet all these sectors were economically enmeshed and mutually enabling.

[23] 'Like father like son: financial practices in the Shakespeare family', *Studies in Theatre and Performance* 28 (2008), 253–63; 'His father John Shakespeare', in *The Shakespeare Circle: An Alternative Biography*, ed. Paul Edmondson and Stanley Wells (Cambridge, 2015), pp. 26–39. At the time of writing, knowledge of John Shakespeare's financial practices is being opened up by soon-to-be published archival discoveries: see www.roehampton.ac.uk/humanities/news/unknown-shakespeare-records-found-in-the-national-archives.

[24] See especially the essays in Part Two, 'Friends and Neighbours', in *The Shakespeare Circle*, pp. 149–233.

[25] The full title is: *Warrs with Foreign Princes Dangerous to our Common-wealth: or, Reasons for Foreign Wars Answered: With a List of all the Confederates from Henry the first's reign to the end of Queen Elizabeth; proving, That the Kings of England always preferred Vnjust Peace before the Justest Warre*. Subsequent citations are given in the text.

hath no hope of help but by war' (B4r).[26] Like Elizabeth and James, Cotton had been educated in the irenic Christian-humanist ethos instilled by English grammar-school curricula, or personal tutors such as Roger Ascham. He recalls Shakespeare's Erasmian portrait of the much-maligned Henry VI, for example, noting that Henry, 'to save the expence of his people and treasure, offered many large and liberall conditions, but received in exchange nothing but scoffes: he was contented to part with the Dutchy of *Mayne*, to make up a peace with his uncle of *France*' (B5v; *2 Henry VI*, 1.1.48–50). Cotton then begins to materialize the ethical arguments of Erasmian pacifism, implicitly to counter the allegedly rational *realpolitik* of its ideological opponent, Machiavelli, by documenting how war-related taxation has repeatedly incited revolts against monarchs such as King John, Edward II and Richard II (B8v–C2v).

The heart of Cotton's treatise demonstrates that the fiscal burdens of war, borne by virtually all classes and occupations, always exceed any gains (C6r–F3v). Because his packed figures appear in narrative rather than ledger form, the effect on the page – at least to modern eyes – can be dizzying. But the persuasive impression is of 'the intolerable miseries of the Nobility and Commons inseparably accompanying the times of war' (D4v). In particular, Cotton critiques the hoary claim that the spoils of war always outweigh its expenditures (E6r–F3v). Focusing on war-related costs between 1585 and the end of Elizabeth's reign, for instance, Cotton argues:

[u]ntill the late *Queen* was drawn into wars, she had in Treasure 700,000. *l.* [=livres, pounds] but after she was once intangled, it cost her before the 30. of her Reign [1588–9] 1,517,351. *l.* at which time she was but entering into the vastness of her future Charge. For the annuall expence of 126,000. *l.* in the *Low-Countries*, from 1587. untill 1593 the yearly disbersment for *Flushing* and the *Brill* 28,482. *l.* the debts of the States [General of the United Provinces of the Netherlands] 800,000. *l.* and the Aides of the *French* King ... above 401,734. *l.* Thus by reason of warre, besides Taxes upon her people to the Summe of two Millions, and 800,000. *l.* by Subsidies, Tenths &

Fifteens, she hath spent of her Lands, Jewells and Revenues an infinite proportion [i.e. disproportion].
(E7r–v, numbers edited with commas)

Carrying forward such evidence to contemporary debates over James's peace-making with Spain, Cotton demolishes the militarist fantasy that the '[s]poils we have brought away in our *French & Spanish* attempts [have exceeded] ever the charge in getting' (B2r).[27]

But Cotton's account is more than a treasury audit. He expands categories relating to the costs of war and the benefits of peace to include social, political and environmental gains or losses. He also lays bare the hidden subsidies and loans that promoters of war pass over. His treatise thereby demonstrates an early example of what is known today as Ecological Full-Cost Accounting. This model identifies both direct and indirect expenditures of private- or public-sector projects according to the so-called 'triple bottom line' of social, economic and environmental costs.[28] Cotton identifies *social costs* such as:

- territorial invasion
- destroyed towns
- shedding of Christian blood
- ship requisitioning
- property expropriations
- suppression of agriculture
- changed land and sea-port uses
- military impressment
- reduced hospitality
- destruction of churches

---

[26] The extended title paraphrases Cicero: an unjust (i.e. imperfect, self-sacrificing) peace is always preferable to the justest war. Nicholas Grimalde, *Marcus Tullius Ciceroes thre bokes of duties* [1556], ed. Gerald O'Gorman (Washington, DC, 1990), p. 65.

[27] Malcolm Smuts, 'The making of *Rex Pacificus*: James VI and I and the problem of peace in an age of religious war', in *Royal Subjects: Essays on the Writings of James VI and I*, ed. Daniel Fischlin and Mark Fortier (Detroit, 2002), pp. 371–87. For Elizabethan debates in printed news that preceded James's peace with Spain, but which advanced mainly political and religious arguments rather than economic ones, see Alexandra Gajda, 'Debating war and peace in late Elizabethan England', *Historical Journal* 52.4 (2009), 851–78.

[28] See http://en.wikipedia.org/wiki/Triple_bottom_line.

Economic costs:

- tenths, fifteenths
- parliamentary subsidies
- poll taxes
- fines
- mortgages
- loans
- rack-renting
- poundage and tonnage
- victuals
- soldiers' pay
- munitions
- clothing and armour
- carts and wagons
- sale of crown assets such as jewels, plate and forests

And environmental and animal costs:

- wood
- hemp
- wool
- canvas
- metal resources
- oats
- wheat
- wine
- horses
- pigs
- oxen and other cattle

There is obviously overlap among these items, and my lists are not exhaustive. But Cotton is not only accounting more pragmatically for war's costs but also showing conclusively that quantification is an ecological discovery tool, and that it has peace-making value which can contribute to the nation's long-term well-being. For one of the goals of ecology is to find relatively stable patterns in the complexly entwined and variable condition of the natural and human worlds, or what (with a posthumanist inflection) Donna Haraway calls 'naturecultures'.[29] Sifting the diverse contingencies of war, Cotton secures irrefutable ecocritical arguments: that the classical theory of 'healthy' cycles of war and peace is unsupported by economic or material evidence; and that the conventional rationale of spoils, typically defined in monetary or commodity terms, is erroneous. These conclusions allow

him to move forward in the last third of his treatise to advance practical benefits of peace, such as trade co-operation and national prosperity. Cotton's justification of King James's pacific turn concludes by reasserting that the 'Utility' of increasing revenues 'by the addition of Forreign *Dominions*' is always a delusion, and that alliances with neighbouring countries is the means to avoid the debilitating expenses of war, especially in the new era of gunpowder (E6r–G8v).

## 'SLUTTISH SPOILS'

Shakespeare's comparable scepticism about conquest and spoils similarly implies the economic and ecological benefits of peace. In the opening scene of *2 Henry IV*, for example, Shakespeare changes Holinshed's report that the battle of Holmedon (or Holmildon Hill) was won by English archers. Westmorland instead reports that the armies 'did spend a sad and bloody hour, / As by the discharge of their artillery / And shape of likelihood the news was told' (1.1.56–8). By attributing the terrible enemy casualty numbers at Holmedon – '[t]en thousand bold Scots, two-and-twenty knights' – mainly to gunpowder weaponry, Shakespeare deepens the contrast with the 'honourable spoil' of two high-ransom noblemen. This effect also seems to explain his change of Holinshed's 23 knights to 22: the repeated cardinal number enables a quick division of 11 knights or 5,000 commoners killed for every nobleman taken captive, driving home the reality of an appalling imbalance. Such disparities epitomize the historical shift from medieval to modern warfare. For, according to military historians Michael Roberts, Geoffrey Parker and Clifford J. Rogers, artillery and firearms transformed the strategic goals of warfare in two key ways: from capturing prisoners for ransom, to killing as

---

[29] Donna Haraway, 'Encounters with companion species: entangling dogs, baboons, philosophers, and biologists', *Configurations* 14 (2006), 97–114; pp. 98, 110, 111.

many soldiers and/or civilians as possible; and from an individualist focus of combat, and the chivalric tradition of knight-service, to 'undiscriminating slaughter at a distance'.[30] This was a shift, in other words, from a recoverable future to a precarious one. The disproportion in lives valued or written off explains Westmorland's laconic response to Henry's myopic enthusiasm: '[i]n faith, it is a conquest for a prince to boast of' (1.1.76).[31] As David Bevington also notes, Shakespeare's change in weaponry looks forward to Hotspur's (sarcastically distorted) recollection of the disgust of the 'neat lord' at the stinking slaughter wrought by 'these vile guns' at Holmedon (1.3.60, 63).

Although, historically, no gunpowder weapons were deployed at Holmedon, Shakespeare's representation of them there is not entirely anachronistic, for in England the gunpowder revolution that began in Henry IV's reign became a world-changing phenomenon in Henry V's. As Dan Spencer explains, the former greatly expanded the royal artillery and spent heavily on the production of larger guns that began to be used regularly in sieges. These included Henry IV's assaults on the Percy strongholds of Warkworth and Berwick Castles in 1405, where contemporary observers reported the artillery damage to be as much psychological as physical.[32] Shakespeare captures the mentally shattering impact of 'basilisks ... cannon, [and] culverin' in the PTSD symptoms Hotspur suffers, and which estrange him from his wife Lady Percy (*1 Henry IV* 2.3.38–62).[33]

Henry V invested even more heavily in ordnance than his father, hoping to recoup the expenditures from territorial conquest. As scholars have long observed, the 'profits' that Pistol shamelessly expects to 'accrue' in France expose the true aims of King Henry's spoiling masculine aggression, culminating in his 'capital demand' for Princess Katherine. Following the opening Chorus's lofty rhetoric, Canterbury mundanely inventories potential losses in a conflict between church and parliament, if the latter is allowed to seize half the church's lands:

... all the temporal lands ...
Would they strip from us – being valued thus:
As much as would maintain, to the King's honour,
Full fifteen earls and fifteen hundred knights,
Six thousand and two hundred good esquires;
And, to relief of lazars and weak age,
Of indigent faint souls past corporal toil,
A hundred almshouses right well supplied;
And to the coffers of the King beside
A thousand pounds by th' year.

(1.1.9–19)[34]

---

[30] On the 'principle of mass-subordination' created by gunpowder warfare, see Michael Roberts, 'The military revolution, 1560-1660', in *The Military Revolution Debate: Readings on the Military Transformation of Early Modern Europe*, ed. Clifford J. Rogers (Boulder, CO, 1995), pp. 13–35; pp. 15, 28–9; also Geoffrey Parker, 'The military revolution – a myth?' (pp. 37–54), and Clifford J. Rogers, 'Military revolutions of the Hundred Years War' (pp. 55–93), in the same volume; Fissel, *English Warfare*, p. 184.

[31] William Shakespeare, *Henry IV Part Two*, ed. David Bevington (Oxford, 1987), note to 1.1.57. The shock of gunpowder devastation and its affects in the retelling may be coded by Westmorland's temporally compressed timeframe (e.g. '[a] sad and bloody hour'), and by his metrically truncated line. His report retrospectively magnifies the carnage of Henry's opening speech when the King deplores 'intestine shock' and 'furious close' of 'civil butchery'.

[32] '"The scourge of the stone": English gunpowder artillery at the Siege of Harfleur', *Journal of Medieval History* 43 (2017), 59–73; pp. 59–62.

[33] Cotton documents Henry IV's onerous taxes, above all 'a Contribution *ita gravis*, so heavy, that it was granted ... upon ... condition, that it should not be made an Example to following times, and that after the Account the Evidences should be burnt' (D7v–8r). Nonetheless, this exceptional levy was effectively reimposed in Henry VI's time by means of a huge array of old and new taxes devised by his counsellors, 'who of purpose plotted to make a consumption of Duty and Affection towards him' (D8v–E1v). Compare the complaints against Duke Humphrey by his enemies: '[t]he commons hast thou rack'd, the clergy's bags / Are lank and lean with thy extortions' (*2 Henry VI* 1.3.128–9); and yet these exactions failed to reverse the chronic debts of 'war and waste' that persisted through Henry VI's reign.

[34] These lines are almost never spoken fully in performance. Like the opening Chorus, this scene is absent in the quarto text of the play, which begins with Henry calling in two Bishops to expound the Salic Law.

The bill was aimed partly at paying down the debts of Henry IV's expansion of artillery production and deployment in his civil wars. To prevent it, Canterbury invents a scheme to claim the French crown supported by a huge clerical subsidy (1.1.80–2). This offer flatters Henry's dynastic ambitions and pays for the massive firepower he unleashed at Harfleur.[35] For, as Spencer also shows, an essential element of Henry's invasion plans was the build-up of a colossal artillery train. Cotton confirms its deepening of long-term debts. He reports that, six years after Agincourt, 'the *Chancellour* bewailed ... in Parliament the Feebleness and Poverty of the People by reason of [the King's] wars and scarcity of money' (D8r). Shakespeare traces the origins of Henry's ultimately bankrupting campaign in its escalating military and gunpowder expenditures:

*from* Henry's vague 'let our proportions [i.e. taxes] for these wars / Be soon collected' (1.2.304–5);

*to* 'expectation' hiding a sword embossed with 'crowns imperial' (2.0.8–10);

*to* the 'well-appointed' (i.e. powerfully armed) 'fleet majestical / Holding due course for Harfleur' (3.0.4, 16–17);

*to* the 'ordnance on their carriages' at the siege, play-house chambers being fired twice, and the 'devilish cannon' smashing 'all before them', thereby fulfilling Henry's earlier vow to 'break' a stubborn France 'all to pieces' (3.0.26, 33–4; 1.2.225).

As Spencer explains, the firepower at Harfleur was so prolonged and intense there were no munitions left for Agincourt, only large breaches in national finances.[36] Shakespeare's *Henry V* creates a theatrical emblem for this blowout victory by calling for chambers to be fired twice at Harfleur (3.0.33, 3.1.34) yet omitting any mention of the famous longbowmen at Agincourt. This modernizing orientation recalls his substitution of artillery for archers in *1 Henry IV*, and implicitly intervenes in the sixteenth-century debate about the superiority of longbows versus cannon among traditional and forward-looking militarists. Burgundy's moving apostrophe to peace (*Henry V* 5.2.17, 29–67)[37] later underlines the terrible environmental damage and social displacement caused by the English army's

'fatal balls of murdering basilisks', which the aggressors, as well as their French victims, had to repair.[38] The play's epilogue continues to red-flag these deficits in its pointed reminder of Henry's early death, his son's untimely succession, and England bleeding.

At the end of *Hamlet*, Fortinbras can at first make sense of Elsinore's corpse-strewn court only by comparing it to annihilation by cannon-fire: 'O proud Death ... so many princes at a shot / So bloodily hast struck?' (5.2.319–20).[39] He swiftly

---

[35] Canterbury again later thirsts for spoils. His lengthy bee metaphor (1.2.187–213) extolling hierarchical obedience to authority (the equivalent of Ulysses' 'specialty of rule' speech in *Troilus*) begins with a king, officers, magistrates and trading merchants working harmoniously in peacetime. But bees, as 'soldiers, armed in their stings', deviates Canterbury's metaphor into violent foreign plunder: '[m]ake boot upon the summer's velvet buds, / Which pillage they with merry march bring home' (193–5). This shift sets up Canterbury's conclusion – '[t]herefore to France, my liege' – and reiterates the 'blood and sword and fire' trope of his Salic Law speech. Topically, it echoes the apocalyptic rhetoric of warmongering clergy, opposed to peace with Spain, which Cotton's treatise aimed partly to refute.

[36] Holinshed's account of Harfleur states that Henry raised bulwarks and 'a bastell' for his artillerie, '[a]nd dailie was the towne assaulted: for the duke of Gloucester, to whom the order of the siege was committed, made three mines under the ground, and approaching to the wals with his engins and ordinance, would not suffer them within to take any rest'. The material and mental barrage forced the Harfleurais to promise to surrender within a fortnight if no relief came. When the Dauphin could not arrive in time, the town capitulated. See Geoffrey Bullough, *Narrative and Dramatic Sources of Shakespeare*, 8 vols. (London, 1957–75), vol. 4, pp. 387–8.

[37] Burgundy's speech alludes to the genre and content of Erasmus's fullest statement of his pacifist arguments, *Querela pacis* (1517, translated by Thomas Paynell in 1559 as *The Complaint of Peace*, possibly known by Shakespeare).

[38] Which is perhaps one reason why Laurence Olivier's 1944 film of *Henry V*, which otherwise cut all lines that might darken the English victory, unexpectedly retained this speech; its environmental and mental devastation connected emotionally to British experiences of the Blitz.

[39] As per the 1604 Q. F reads ambiguously, 'at a shoot', whereas the 1603 Q text makes it clear that arrows are meant: '[h]ow many princes / Hast thou at one draught bloodily shot to death?'. See *Hamlet: The Texts of 1603 and 1623*, ed. Ann Thompson and Neil Taylor (London, 2006), 17.115. The discrepancies between archery and gunpowder shots recall those between Holinshed's

takes charge by rechannelling the erratic fury of gunpowder into ritual peals for Hamlet's 'passage' (5.2.352, 357). Earlier in 4.4, however, there is no mention of cannon when the Captain tells Hamlet about Fortinbras's campaign against Poland. Fortinbras may be emulating the pre-gunpowder chivalry of his father when he fought Old Hamlet in order to prove his 'hot mettle'. Applying cost–benefit thinking, however, the Captain derides the waste of 20,000 ducats and 2,000 men for a 'spoil' worth less than 5 ducats. Hamlet echoes his reasoning by deploring the inordinate death of 20,000 men for an 'egg-shell', 'a fantasy and a trick of fame', and 'a plot / Whereon the numbers cannot try the cause', juxtaposing Fortinbras' zealous but wasteful action with the urgency of his own motives for revenge (4.4.44, 52, 53–4).

To return to *Troilus and Cressida*, its core debate about the war's sustainability and justice in 2.2 centres on Helen's status as a spoil of war and the related theme of appraisal: 'What's ought but as 'tis valued?' (2.2.51). Hector has previously sent a covert personal challenge to Achilles under the guise of a courtly-love combat touching the honour of the Greeks. He does so half expecting the challenge to be redirected; and Ulysses confirms his suspicion by rigging a lottery to choose 'blockish Ajax' as Hector's competitor, thus diverting the provocation into a 'sportful' contest aimed at humbling Achilles (1.3.256–385). But in 2.2, the Greeks issue the Trojans a more serious and substantial challenge. They not only repeat their demand for the return of Helen but also add a far-reaching list of accountables, reminiscent of Cotton's treatise, which reconfigures Helen's release as a cancellation of war-debts and a practical means of buying peace:

all damage else –
As honour, loss of time, travail, expense
Wounds, friends, and what else dear that is consumed
. . .
Shall be struck off.

(2.2.3–7)

Hector sees the logic of this offer:

[l]et Helen go.
. . .

If we have lost so many tenths of ours
To guard a thing not ours – nor worth to us,
Had it our name, the value of one ten –
What's merit in that reason which denies
The yielding of her up?[40]
. . . she is not worth what she doth cost
The holding. . . .
'tis mad idolatry
To make the service greater than the god.

(2.2.16, 20–4, 50–1, 55–6)

Yet, whereas Hector redefines Helen's value as an irrational imbalance of costs and losses, Troilus sees it as beyond arithmetic or computation. He compares it to the biblical 'pearl of great price', even though that supposedly uncalculable 'pearl / Whose price hath launched above a thousand ships / [Has] turned crowned kings to merchants' (2.2.80–2).[41] Troilus rejects Hector's rhetoric of measurement, marshalling snobbish disdain for its marketplace associations:

[w]eigh you the worth and honour of a king
. . . in a scale . . .
Of common ounces? Will you with counters sum
The past-proportion of his infinite,
And buckle in a waist [read also 'waste'] most fathomless
With spans and inches so diminutive
As fears and reasons?[42]

(2.2.25–31)

---

account and Shakespeare's dialogue in *1 Henry IV*. Most modern editors follow Stevens's lead in assuming that the 'warlike noise' and 'warlike volley' which Fortinbras's army gives to the English ambassadors when it arrives in Denmark refer to cannon-fire, and add an SD for '*shots within*' (e.g. 5.2.333, 336). But a corroborating SD is absent in the 1604 Q, while F's SD calls for '*shout within*'. The moment is not represented in the 1603 Q.
40 See also '[e]very tithe-soul, 'mongst many a thousand dimes, / Hath been as dear as Helen' (2.2.18–19).
41 An allusion to Matthew 13.45. Note the deflating effect of the metrical shortfall and trochaic foot in line 82.
42 Ferdinand echoes Paris's disdain for accountancy in *The Duchess of Malfi* by referring to Antonio as '[a] slave, that only smell'd of ink and counters'; see John Webster, *The Duchess of Malfi*, ed. John Russell Brown (London, 1964), 3.3.72.

After's Cassandra's jarring prophecy, Hector and Troilus continue to argue the respective merits of 'discourse of reason' against 'the goodness of a quarrel / Which hath our several honours all engaged' (2.2.115, 122–3), while Paris rationalizes the option of a 'redemptive' rape (2.2.147–8). Suddenly, Hector reverses his opinion to maintain Trojan solidarity (2.2.188–90), raising suspicions about whether his subversive arguments were merely a pose (in a play of continual posturing).

The relation of Helen-as-spoil to the war's epic costs in lives, *matériel* and treasure is subsequently taken up by the aggressively anti-romantic Diomed, who weighs up their imbalances in terms of human biomass:

> He merits well to have her that doth seek [Helen],
> Not making any scruple of her soilure,
> With such as hell of pain and world of charge . . .
> With such a costly loss of wealth and friends . . .
> For every false drop in her bawdy veins
> A Grecian's life hath sunk; for every scruple
> Of her contaminated carrion weight
> A Trojan hath been slain.
>
> (4.1.57–9, 62, 71–4)

This passage recalls the scales, measurement, carrion flesh and scruple metaphors of *The Merchant of Venice*, another play that embroils material value, human worth and aspirational justice (e.g. 'many a purchased slave'). In *Troilus and Cressida*, Hector loses his sense of discrimination and proportion in the appetitive blood-heat of combat, tragically miscalculating in exactly the way Cicero, Erasmus and other humanists argued became unavoidable in war. Unable to distinguish mercenary possession from chivalric propriety, Hector viciously hunts down a nameless Greek opponent for the spoil of his rich armour (5.6.27–31). His frenzy recalls Troilus's anxious apprehension about consummating his passion for Cressida:

> I do fear besides
> That I shall lose distinction in my joys
> As doth a battle when they charge on heaps
> The enemy flying.
>
> (3.2.24–7)

Hector, in turn, is spoiled by Achilles in revenge for Ajax's slaughter of Patroclus. The consequences of ignoring the Greek revaluation of Helen as an instrument of reparation pessimistically represents the rejection of rationally favourable costs of peace.

As in *Troilus and Cressida*, there is no gunpowder in *Coriolanus*, but there is considerable debate about the culture of spoils in relation to Rome's transition to a more equitable polity, and to peacetime as a sustainable alternative to war. Coriolanus bitterly resists this reorientation, but the patricians make partial concessions to it under popular pressure. Yet when Cominius celebrates his victory at Corioles, he propagates the traditional heroic myth that Coriolanus ran 'reeking o'er the lives of men as if / 'Twere a perpetual spoil' (2.2.119–20). This recycles one of the patricians' dearest conceits: that war converts enemy bloodshed into Roman sustenance. Raised on Volumnia's hyper-masculine fantasy that Hector's bleeding forehead was more vitalizing than Hecuba's nursing breasts (1.3.40–5), Coriolanus embodies an ideology of predation and survival but scoffs at measuring conquest in terms of prizes or trophies: '[o]ur spoils he kicked at', Cominius adds, '[a]nd looked upon things precious as they were / The common muck of the world' (2.2.124–6). This recalls his earlier disdain for spoils at Corioles. After one soldier mistakes the value of his booty ('I took this for silver'), Coriolanus ridicules the supposedly mercenary greed of Rome's commoners:

> See here these movers that do prize their honours
> At a cracked drachme! Cushions, leaden spoons,
> Irons of a doit, doublets that hangmen would
> Bury with those that wore them, these base slaves,
> Ere yet the fight be done, pack up.
>
> (1.5.4–8)

Yet *Coriolanus*'s citizens in fact prefer the personal security and prosperity of peacetime to the illusory hopes and unequal profits of war. Their voluntary behaviour converts peace from a beleaguered ideal into a communally regenerative economy:

> the present peace
> And quietness of the people, which before
> Were in wild hurry. Here do we make his friends

Blush that the world goes well ...
Our tradesmen singing in their shops and going
About their functions friendly.

(4.6.2–9)

The play's repeated clashes suggest that the Roman citizens' appraisal of their own political interests matures through their bitter experiences of the patricians' refusal to distribute the spoils of Corioles fairly. This bad faith prolongs the hoarding policies which originally created an artificial famine that fabricated a pretext for capturing Corioles' granaries and mills (1.1.77–9, 1.11.31, 3.3.4–5). Towards the end of the play, the irenic arguments Martius makes to the Volscians to justify abandoning his destruction of Rome is palpably an inauthentic consciousness, imposed on him by Volumnia to save her family and sate her hunger for public fame:

> Our [i.e. Volscian] spoils we have brought home
> Doth more than counterpoise a full third part
> The charges of the action.

(5.6.77–9)

The Volscians understandably see Coriolanus's surprising embrace of military accountancy as both a betrayal of their alliance and a failure to recover their war expenses. The First Volscian Lord complains that Coriolanus has

> give[n] away
> The benefits of our levies, answering us
> With our own charge [i.e. costs], *making a treaty*
> *Where there was a yielding.*

(5.6.65–68; my emphasis)

If we understand 'yielding' in this passage to mean a voluntary and reasoned, rather than forced, capitulation (the way Hector used the word to describe surrendering Helen), the phrase might alternatively identify a wider breakthrough in cultural attitudes.

Analysing such moments in relation to Shakespeare's overall career, Steve Marx argued that the playwright's thinking about pacifism shifted markedly in James's reign from pro- to anti-war. R. S. White nuanced this oversharp distinction by showing that Shakespeare represents peace positively across his entire career (and I would note

that topical connections between late-Elizabethan *Troilus* and Ostend are evidence of this), and Paola Pugliatti further substantiated this reading.[43] Shakespeare never underestimates the challenges of negotiating peace or acting selflessly to achieve it, or the temptation to fall back into war. Yet I would agree with Marx that his Jacobean plays seem to represent such efforts more optimistically. Scotland overthrows Macbeth and purchases a regenerative security (within the husbandry imagery of the play, at least) in part because Malcolm puts aside his country's dislike of 'the English epicures', accepts a degree of co-dependency on King Edward's army, and adopts the foreign title of 'earl' for 'thane'. King Lear's loyalists are aided by a French army co-led by a Marshal la Far and Cordelia, the King of France having conveniently turned back before crossing the Channel and avoided a claim of sovereignty (4.3; Q only). Shakespeare stages this Franco-British collaboration in a short dumb show at the beginning of 5.2: '[e]nter the powers of France over the stage, Cordelia with her father in her hand' (Q SD).[44] Although Cordelia and her allies lose the war, Edmund quietly esteems his opponents by admitting that his own forces 'sweat and bleed'. He also observes that '[t]he friend hath lost his friend, / And the best quarrels in the heat are cursed / By those that feel their sharpness' (*King Lear* 5.2.54–6; Q only). Edmund not only laments his army's casualties but also seems to regret how the wrath of war has exceeded the boundaries of its ethical

---

[43] Steven Marx, 'Shakespeare's pacifism', *Renaissance Quarterly* 45 (1992), 49–98; R. S. White, 'Renaissance pacifism' and 'Pacifist voices in Shakespeare', in *Pacifism and English Literature: Minstrels of Peace* (Basingstoke, 2008), pp. 110–38, 139–77; 'Troilus and Cressida: Shakespeare's anti-war play', in *Vintage Shakespeare: New Perspectives from India and Abroad*, ed. Prahsant K. Sinha and Mohini Khot (Jaipur, 2010), pp. 14–24; Paola Pugliatti, *Shakespeare and the Just War Tradition* (London, 2016), esp. pp. 37–52.

[44] By contrast the F SD does not identify the army as French: '[e]nter with drum and colours Lear, Cordelia, and Soldiers over the stage'. See Gary Taylor, 'The war in *King Lear*', *Shakespeare Survey 33* (Cambridge, 1980), 27–34, which discusses differences between Q and F representations of the war.

arguments, thereby destroying the future potential for a French and British *entente cordiale*. In *All's Well That Ends Well*, the Florentines make an overture of peace even though they have had 'success' against the Sienese (but also after being denied official support from the King of France for pacific 'reasons of state', and losing their own soldiers in 'friendly fire' (3.2.10, 3.6.49–58, 4.3.41–2)). Pericles absents himself from Tyre, risks his political lineage by devolving personal rule onto Helicanus, and exposes himself to shipwreck, all to avoid Antiochus's making war on his guiltless people (1.2.24–8, 90–100, 1.4). In *Cymbeline*, to come to the most obvious example, 'a Roman and a British ensign wave / Friendly together' in its idealized ending: '[n]ever was a war did cease, / Ere bloody hands were washed, with such a peace' (5.6.481–2, 485–6). The King has actively purchased sustainable peace and voluntarily accepted a limitation on his sovereignty by resuming the mutually negotiated payment of tribute to Rome – despite the fact that the British won the war. Contrary to what historical Romans believed, peace cannot be imposed by conquest; it must entail sacrificing a certain amount of freedom and autonomy, just as obligations to the environment and non-human lifeforms necessarily involve limiting human privilege and power.[45] Written in the same year as Cotton's treatise, *Cymbeline* exemplifies its concluding advice: that power-sharing reciprocity curtails expensive stand-alone belligerence, and cosmopolitan multilateralism reduces the soaring expenses of gunpowder militarization (F4r–G8v). As White's and Pugliatti's research reminds us, moreover, we can trace Shakespeare conceptualizing this attitude of co-operative altruism, in both Erasmian and accountability terms, in his earlier plays. In *2 Henry IV*, for example, after the Archbishop of York and his allies believe they have negotiated a peace with Prince John, York invokes the logic of bookkeeping to define their agreement as a double 'conquest': '[f]or then both parties are nobly subdued, / And neither party loser' (4.1.315–17). In other words, when both sides embrace the mutual interests of other and self, it's a win-win. Unfortunately, Prince John

double-crosses York and his allies, sparing physical damage to Gaultres, but denying them the legal clemency that royal forest law afforded.

As a reflection of James's peace-making ideology, *Cymbeline*'s worldview proved to be short-lived, but economically beneficial in one far-reaching way. By keeping the country out of the devastating Thirty Years' War, Britain got a crucial head-start on the development of key industries that set the Industrial Revolution in motion.[46] Regrettably, we recognize, in ecological hindsight, that this opening accelerated the wrong kind of growth. For the next 400 years, Western nation-states concealed the problem of inherent resource limits while simultaneously scaling up their balance of payments deficits through imperial conquest and exploitation of the entire planet.

## SUSTAINABILITY IN THE ANTHROPOCENE

Max Weber famously theorized that modernity's disenchantment of the natural world was attributable partly to emerging principles of mathematical quantification, because '*by means of calculation*', 'we can in principle *control everything*'.[47] Such technocratic power, Weber also argued, served as 'the handmaiden' to the development of Western capitalism and its now global dream of endless

---

[45] See Aldo Leopold, *A Sand County Almanac: And Sketches from Here and There* [1949] (New York, 1987), pp. 201–14.

[46] John Nef, *The Rise of the British Coal Industry*, 2 vols. (London, 1932), vol. 1, pp. 165–89; Sybil M. Jack, *Trade and Industry in Tudor and Stuart England* (London, 1977), pp. 66–121. For iron manufacturing represented through the lens of a neo-classical 'iron age', see Todd A. Borlik, 'Iron Age as Renaissance Anthropocene: periodization and the ecology of war in Shakespearean history', *Early Modern Culture* 13 (2018), article 9.

[47] But, Weber argued, it 'does *not* imply a growing understanding of the conditions under which we live', because we leave technical understanding of their workings to specialists (original italics). See 'Science as a vocation' (1917), in *The Vocation Lectures*, ed. David Owen and Tracey B. Strong, trans. Rodney Livingstone (Indianapolis, IN, 2004), pp. 1–31, pp. 12–13; cited in Wootton, *Invention of Science*, p. 449.

economic growth and consumption. Increasingly although by no means universally, governments and citizens recognize that this ideology is an essential cause of today's global ecological crisis, and is plainly unsustainable as the earth's population approaches 9 billion by mid-century.[48] Moreover as Richard Fortey, Baird Calicott and Timothy Clark all show from a deep-time perspective, it has widened the disjunction between the pace of human technological and cultural domination over the past 20 millennia or so, and the much slower rate of natural evolution over billions of years.[49] But biophysical realities in the (ironically named) Age of Man are now forcing human control to repurpose itself as geocentric preservation.[50] Cotton and Shakespeare, I have suggested, anticipate this epistemic shift by using quantification and reappraisal to frame narratives of ecological accountability and sustainability that critique the nascent gunpowder-and-growth worldview. Historically, their thinking addresses a practical weakness in Erasmian-humanist arguments for peace, which were dominated by philosophical and ethical discourses that had little to say about world-changing scientific discoveries and modern economic developments.[51]

Yet my presentist analogy cannot end there, because at least since the 1984 Brundtland Commission asserted that robust economic growth was compatible with environmental conservation, the idea of sustainability has been a politically contested proposition, and an ecocritically disputed one,[52] although not a *scientifically* questionable principle. Brundtland and its supporters unleashed a flood of corporate greenwashing, and licensed the 'triple bottom line' to skew almost always in favour of profit over people and planet. Re-prioritizing this beguiling trio has been the goal of post-growth economists such as Tim Jackson. He redefines sustainability according to a complex-systems and global-futures paradigm. It resituates the monoculture of private profit and GDP-obsessed metrics within an intersectional economics of distributed ownership and growth. This model places greatest value on public goods and non-monetary assets that build up the earth's interdependent human

and non-human communities.[53] Shakespeare's critique of spoils and Cotton's full-cost accountability work to similar ends by reframing the balance-sheet of war's profits and losses according to the long-term needs of society and its environments.

---

[48]  See http://ourworldindata.org/world-population-growth.

[49]  Richard Fortey, *Life: An Unauthorised Biography. A Natural History of the First Four Billion Years of Life on Earth* (London, 1997); *Survivors: The Animals and Plants that Time has Left Behind* (London, 2011); Baird Callicott, 'Lamark redux: temporal scale as the key to the boundary between the human and the natural worlds', in *Nature's Edge: Boundary Explorations in Ecological Theory and Practice*, ed. Charles S. Brown and Ted Toadvine (Albany, 2007), pp. 16–40; Timothy Clark, *Ecocriticism on the Edge: The Anthropocene as a Threshold Concept* (London, 2015), pp. 139–57.

[50]  As novelist Amitav Ghosh argues, Anthropocene conditions challenge conventional literary and dramatic forms and present significant new difficulties for writers because many of their disorders cannot be immediately seen or comprehended on an everyday level in today's era of global commodity exchanges and economies of scale. Even when $CO_2$-intensified storms and droughts *are* seen and felt, their causal synergies resist explanation by conventional modes of realist fiction. See Amitav Ghosh, *The Great Derangement: Climate Change and the Unthinkable* (Chicago, 2016). To put this in Bakhtinian terms, there is as yet no chronotope, or subjectively defining correlation of time and space, for the Anthropocene's multi-scaled intersecting contingencies. Adaptations of Shakespeare's polygeneric and temporally fluid narratives represent possible paths into discovery of Anthropocene chronotopes. See Steve Mentz, 'Shipwreck and ecology: toward a structural theory of Shakespeare and romance', *Shakespeare International Yearbook* 8 (2008), 165–82; R. Martin and Evelyn O'Malley, eds., 'Eco-Shakespeare in Performance', special issue, *Shakespeare Bulletin* 36.3 (2018).

[51]  As Robert Ginsberg also argues, this kind of pacifist rhetoric is constrained by its constituting ethics of non-violence to remain within the domain of peaceful (if often verbally powerful) discussion, whereas pro-war arguments can go beyond words to coercion, since violence is the aim of pro-war rhetoric. See Robert Ginsberg, 'The rhetorical dilemma of peace', *Peace and Change* 80 (2009), 1–6.

[52]  See Stacey Alaimo, 'Sustainable this, sustainable that: new materialisms, posthumanism, and unknown futures', *PMLA* 127 (2012), 558–64; Steve Mentz, 'After sustainability', *PMLA* 127 (2012), 586–92; Sharon O'Dair, 'Growing pains', *Early Modern Culture* 13 (2018), article 7.

[53]  Tim Jackson, *Prosperity Without Growth: Foundations for the Economy of Tomorrow*, 2nd edn (Abingdon, 2014), esp. pp. 159–84.

To echo Jackson's terms, they propose an alternative vision of growth, prosperity and progress based on nurturing capabilities for flourishing within earth-bound ecosystems.[54] Shakespeare's post-gunpowder pacifism presents a comparable vision of peace-building and multilateralism. Ultimately, this vision insists upon a conception of human nature shaped by co-operation and altruism, not merely selfishness, aggression and survival of the strongest, as the yoked ideologies of social Darwinism and growth-driven capitalism have maintained. Disseminating this hopeful but always vulnerable ethos of sociable flourishing and reimagined relations with non-human lifeforms is the task of culture, as Jackson observes, and represents a fresh opportunity for Shakespeare in the Anthropocene. Because gunpowder helped to transform concepts of historical time from repeated cycles into a *discoverable and re-shapable* futurity, it inspired the playwright, and now obliges his present-day interpreters and performers, to loosen the fixations of human-centred history, to rethink his war-and-battle plays in early modern and postmodern terms, and to shift public consciousness by staging imaginative re-creations of Shakespeare's ecological knowledge.

---

[54] Jackson, *Prosperity*, pp. 61–5. For a nuanced argument about how Shakespeare might model an ecocentric economics based on degrowth principles, see Charles Whitney, 'Green economics and the English Renaissance: from capital to the commons', in *Shakespeare and the Urgency of Now: Criticism and Theory in the 21st Century*, ed. Cary DiPietro and Hugh Grady (Basingstoke, 2014), pp. 103–25.

# SHAKESPEARE AND RELIGIOUS WAR: NEW DEVELOPMENTS ON THE ITALIAN SOURCES OF *TWELFTH NIGHT*

## ELISABETTA TARANTINO

The century in which Shakespeare was born and started his career as a playwright saw two major instances of mass violence linked to religious issues: the Sack of Rome in 1527, and the 1572 Saint Bartholomew's Day massacre in Paris. These events were mirror images of each other in more than just their dates: in the former case, it was the See of Catholicism that was attacked by the Emperor's troops, which included a Lutheran contingent; in the latter, it was the French Protestants, or Huguenots, who were attacked by the Catholic population.[1]

New elements that have come to light concerning the dramatic sources of Shakespeare's *Twelfth Night* suggest that, between them, the long-known and newly adduced sources for this play refer to those two instances of religion-tinted war. We have known for a long time that the main plot of *Twelfth Night* is linked to a series of works derived from *Gli Ingannati* (*The Deceived*), a comedy staged in 1532 by the Sienese Academy of the Intronati.[2] In this play, the 1527 Sack of Rome is what separates the brother and sister. On the other hand, a 2012 article by Hilary Gatti convincingly links the gulling of Malvolio to Giordano Bruno's *Candelaio* (*The Candle-maker*, 1582).[3] This play was printed in Paris on the tenth anniversary of the 1572 Saint Bartholomew's Day massacre, which is also mentioned within the play itself.[4]

The present article shows that the subplot of *Twelfth Night*, like the main plot, draws on a cluster of interconnected works, and that some of its elements can be linked to a comedy entitled

*La Strega* (*The Witch*, pr. 1582), by Antonfrancesco Grazzini, also known as Il Lasca. Grazzini's play has several important features in common with both Bruno's *Candelaio* and *Gli Ingannati*. Not only does it, therefore, function as a lynchpin between the two clusters of Italian sources: as we shall see below, the connecting features include some of the specific elements that, in the other two plays, refer to Saint Bartholomew and the Sack of Rome.

To my knowledge, *La Strega* has not been mentioned before in connection with *Twelfth Night*, though in 1874 Wilhelm König linked it

---

[1] On how this 'mirroring' is reflected in Shakespeare, and especially in *Twelfth Night*, see Elisabetta Tarantino, 'Mountainish inhumanity in Illyria', in *Compassion in Early Modern Literature and Culture: Feeling and Practice*, ed. Katherine Ibbett and Kristine Steenbergh (Cambridge, forthcoming), where I argue that, together with the reference to war-related Italian sources, the numerous mirror-like opposites in *Twelfth Night* represent both a warning and a plea for tolerance: they remind the late Elizabethan audience of how easily they too might fall prey to the violence that led many French and Dutch craftsmen to seek refuge in England. See also Tarantino's Shakespeare Birthplace Trust e-exhibition: http://collections.shakespeare.org.uk/exhibition/exhibition/shakespeare-connected-shakespeare-and-religious-war.

[2] See '*La Strega* and *Gli Ingannati*' below.

[3] See Hilary Gatti, 'Giordano Bruno's *Candelaio* and possible echoes in Shakespeare and Ben Jonson', *Viator* 43 (2012), 357–75.

[4] See Elisabetta Tarantino, 'Bruno's *Candelaio*, Shakespeare and Ben Jonson: building on Hilary Gatti's work', in *Authority, Innovation and Early Modern Epistemology: Essays in Honour of Hilary Gatti*, ed. Martin McLaughlin, Ingrid D. Rowland and Elisabetta Tarantino (London, 2015), pp. 118–36.

to passages in *The Merchant of Venice* and *Hamlet*. By relating *La Strega* to *Twelfth Night*, we gain a precedent for the name Viola, in a way that additionally explains a one-off variant found in the First Folio. We also acquire an antecedent for the character of Sir Andrew Aguecheek, including his flimsy desire to attack Malvolio on religious grounds. In addition, a passage from *La Strega* is relevant to the famous 'mountainish inhumanity' phrase in the Hand D speech in *Sir Thomas More*, and to its analogue in *Twelfth Night*.[5]

Overall, the evidence we can draw from linking *La Strega* and *Candelaio* with *Twelfth Night* significantly adds to our knowledge of the way in which Shakespeare worked with Italian sources. He seems actively interested in Italian lexical items, in a way that does *not* suggest a matter-of-course familiarity with the language. He works with clusters of sources – i.e. sources that are linked to one another. He also displays a knowledge of a wider range of Italian plays than he has been credited with so far, in a way that is compatible with the list of works prefixed to John Florio's dictionaries, and with volumes of Italian plays in early modern English bindings that can still be found in UK libraries today.

In this article, I start by suggesting a possible model of source studies and related taxonomy that will accommodate the type of Shakespearian sources that will be discussed here. I then go on to explore, in 'La Strega and Candelaio', the links between these titles and, in 'La Strega and Gli Ingannati', the links between these, highlighting in the process the historical elements of *Candelaio* and *Gli Ingannati* that are relevant to *Twelfth Night*. 'Clusters of plays' and 'Grazzini and early modern English drama' show how Shakespeare could have been aware of Grazzini's *Strega*. 'The strangers' case: *La Strega* and *Twelfth Night*' examines the relationship between *La Strega* and *Twelfth Night*, and its relevance to *Sir Thomas More*. My aim is not only to point out these new – and relatively new – sources for the subplot in *Twelfth Night*, but also to show how these intertextual clusters function as a denunciation of war and its human costs.

## THE IDEA OF A SOURCE

An article that appeared recently in *Shakespeare Survey* represents a milestone in the reflection on what constitutes a (Shakespearian) source. In the article, Laurie Maguire and Emma Smith review recent uses of the term, and conclude that 'the stand-alone word "source" has outlived its usefulness'.[6] The authors go on to list an array of synonyms that critics have used in order to allay what is obviously an uneasiness towards the use of the plain old-fashioned word 'source', concluding that, nevertheless, 'source studies are still without the rethinking this lexis implies'.[7] Their reading of the influence of Marlowe's *Dido* on Shakespeare exemplifies what shape such rethinking could take by seeking to merge two apparently opposite categories identified by Stuart Gillespie: 'indistinct haunting' and 'clear citation'.[8]

Despite this intellectual unease with the idea of a source, as Maguire and Smith point out at the beginning of their discussion, Shakespeare editions have continued to carry a sources' section, which has continued to 'do the same intellectual work' across the decades.[9] There thus seems to be a perceived pragmatic usefulness in the investigation of Shakespeare's sources, despite the 'methodological shrug' and the calling into question of authorial agency that characterizes our poststructural age – an agency that, as I discuss below, would have included the process whereby an author *intentionally chooses* a specific source for a given purpose.

Also, in terms of literary production, the practice and purpose of literary imitation tends to vary from period to period, often upstaging its theory. *Imitatio* with *variatio*, or the interplay of

---

[5] *Twelfth Night* and *Sir Thomas More* are both given a 'best-guess date' of 1601 in Martin Wiggins and Catherine Richardson, *British Drama, 1533–1642: A Catalogue*, 10 vols. (Oxford, 2012– ), vol. 4.

[6] Laurie Maguire and Emma Smith, 'What is a source? Or, how Shakespeare read his Marlowe', *Shakespeare Survey 68* (Cambridge, 2015), 15–31; p. 16.

[7] Maguire and Smith, 'What is a source?', p. 17.

[8] Maguire and Smith, 'What is a source?', p. 18.

[9] Maguire and Smith, 'What is a source?', p. 16.

similarity and difference, was fruitfully deployed by ancient authors for centuries in order to claim their place within a classical canon. In the great cultural flourishing that would lead to the Italian Renaissance, it was not the authors' derivative theorizing but their truly individual and effective imitative practices that signalled the literary self-consciousness of a new era.[10] And in Elizabethan England, where authors and even their publishers were liable to have their hands cut off for intervening too openly in public affairs, the appeal of a relatively safe semantic strategy would have been quite obvious.

Maybe some taxonomic agreement could, then, be reached to help us describe this varied practice from a pragmatic point of view. We could, for instance, agree to sort the relationship among texts into three progressively narrower sets and subsets. At the most general level, we could talk of 'analogues', which can enlighten our reading of a text even when they are not intentional, or indeed when the authors in question were unaware of each other's work. The only criterion for this broader intertextual relationship would be *relevance*. In a first subset, adding the element of *knowledge*, we might call 'intertexts' those analogues that were known to an author and surface in their work, whether or not the author in question is intentionally alluding to them. *Intention* or *choice* would then be the characterizing element of the third kind of intertextual relationship, which is the one with which I am concerned in this article. And it is for this final group that I reserve the name of 'sources'. From the point of view of the hermeneutic effort, sources function as actual signs within the text. A non-source intertext would be more akin to a symptom, while a non-intertext analogue is simply used by the critic as an interpretive tool.

The 'sources' I discuss here are intertexts that were intentionally chosen by an author to convey some meaning that is relevant to his text. In all utterances, intention is a semantic *sine qua non*, above and beyond difference. Difference is a necessary condition if there is to be choice, but is not a sufficient condition in itself: two sets of traffic lights at either end of a road, one constantly red, the other constantly green, are 'different', but do not convey any meaning.

Accordingly, in what follows, I consider a 'source' to be a practical textual element, one of the farthest links in a chain that begins with phonemes, morphemes, lexemes and so on. While the recognition of a generic analogue or an 'unintentional' intertext can still give rise to enlightening readings of a target text, the discussion of a source is a rather less optional exercise, and indeed, as Maguire and Smith reminded us, it has been the practice of editors since time immemorial. Such a reading is part of the same operation as identifying the correct reading of a letter or word, and, once we accept this, refusing to investigate its relevance would be akin to saying that it is not necessary for us to understand the meaning of the words that form a text in order to engage with that text.

In both cases – i.e. both for the correct reading of sources and for the interpretation of other textual components – context is of paramount importance. The likelihood that an analogue is worth taking into account increases exponentially as more aspects or elements are uncovered that connect that particular element to general aspects and themes of the work under examination. Of course, there will always be a degree of subjectivity in determining what is relevant. But as long as we make intellectual honesty a fundamental requirement in both the proponent and the assessor of this kind of study, there should be no more disagreement than is normally the case as to the overall interpretation of a text.

The idea of a 'cluster of sources' is a powerful tool in the attempt to prove relevance and thus identify an intertext as a source. In the study that follows, this element is especially prominent. It occurs at both a physical and a conceptual level: 'Clusters of plays' shows how the Italian plays under discussion were encountered as, or indeed turned into, a cluster by their early modern English readers, while the remaining sections reveal how our three main intertexts for *Twelfth Night* are interconnected 'at the source', making it all the

---

[10] See Martin McLaughlin, *Literary Imitation in the Italian Renaissance: The Theory and Practice of Literary Imitation in Italy from Dante to Bembo* (Oxford, 1995), pp. 276–7.

more likely that any one of them would call to mind the other two.

## LA STREGA AND CANDELAIO

We should start with the links between *La Strega* and *Candelaio*, since the influence of *Candelaio* on *Twelfth Night* provides an important clue to the political concerns of Shakespeare's play.

Unlike the main plot of *Twelfth Night*, discussed in '*La Strega* and *Gli Ingannati*', until recently the gulling of Malvolio had not been assigned a totally convincing source. Personages from real life were indicated as the original of Malvolio, but none of them had suffered the kind of treatment to which the steward is subjected in *Twelfth Night*.[11] Incidents from sources related to the main plot had been adduced as antecedents for that treatment, but they referred to characters that did not match the general profile of Malvolio.[12] There was thus a 'vacancy' in this respect, should something be found that provided an overall closer fit. This 'something' was identified by Hilary Gatti in *Candelaio*, the only play by philosopher and heretic Giordano Bruno. In this play, a character called Bonifacio – a name that means 'I do good', and is thus a significant parallel to Malvolio's name, which refers to 'ill will' or 'wishing evil' – is made to believe that a lady (in this case, a courtesan) is in love with him. He is then persuaded to dress in a certain way for an assignation with her, only to end up being imprisoned by fake representatives of the law. After the publication of *Candelaio*, Bruno spent two years in London, where he frequented John Florio and other members of the intellectual and political élite. He was burned at the stake in Campo de' Fiori in Rome on 17 February 1600, news of which reached England by the summer of that year.[13]

Gatti's 2012 article also pointed to the influence of *Candelaio* on Ben Jonson's *Bartholomew Fair*. This gives us an important clue as to why Shakespeare would want to use Giordano Bruno's play for the gulling and 'punishment' of a character who is presented as 'a kind of Puritan' (*Twelfth Night*, 2.3.135), anticipating the actual Puritans depicted in Jonson's play.[14] In an article in honour of Hilary

Gatti, I followed up her discovery with the identification of an important political-historical theme in Bruno's play. The play features a character called Bartolomeo and was printed in Paris in 1582, i.e. on the tenth anniversary of the Saint Bartholomew's Day massacre, an event to which it refers explicitly by using the phrase 'la furia francesa' (French fury; *Candelaio*, 4.5). Some of its incidents have similarities with other political events that followed the massacre. Ben Jonson, for one, would recognize this affiliation of *Candelaio* with the Saint Bartholomew's Day events. He takes elements from Bruno's play and explicitly connects them to this particular day in his 1614 comedy *Bartholomew Fair*, which also contains an explicit reference to the massacre.[15]

This connection with the Saint Bartholomew's Day massacre is what gives *Candelaio* its relevance as a source for English plays that, in different ways, acknowledge the presence of a critical attitude towards Calvinists (the religious denomination to which the Paris Huguenots were linked).[16] It may also be worth noting that Bruno and his play have in the past been linked to *Love's Labour's Lost*, whose character names explicitly reference the French wars of religion.[17] More recently, Richard Wilson has

---

[11] See Geoffrey Bullough, *Narrative and Dramatic Sources of Shakespeare*, 8 vols. (London, 1957–75), vol. 2, pp. 371–2. See also J. J. M. Tobin, 'Gabriel Harvey in Illyria', *English Studies* 61 (1980), 318–28.

[12] See Barnaby Rich's tale of 'Two Brethren and their Wives' in *Rich's Farewell to Military Profession* (1581), the collection that contains 'Apolonius and Silla'. This was first adduced by W. A. Neilson in the *Atlantic Monthly*, 1 May 1902.

[13] See Tiziana Provvidera, 'A new English document on Giordano Bruno', *Bulletin of the Society for Renaissance Studies* 19 (2002), 23–9.

[14] In the quotation, I have restored the capital 'P' from the First Folio.

[15] See Tarantino, 'Bruno's *Candelaio*'.

[16] On Bruno's critique of Calvinists in the philosophical dialogues that he published in London in 1584–5, see Tarantino, 'Bruno's *Candelaio*', p. 124. Rather than to any specific doctrinal points, Bruno was opposed to the idea of a religion that placed doctrinal concerns above issues of peace and order.

[17] Lia Buono Hodgart, '*Love's Labour's Lost* di William Shakespeare e il *Candelaio* di Giordano Bruno', *Studi*

demonstrated Shakespeare's engagement with this topic throughout his career.[18]

Grazzini's *Strega* shares several elements with *Candelaio*, including aspects that in Bruno's play point to the Saint Bartholomew's Day massacre: a character called Bartolomea (*Candelaio* features a male character by this name), a character called Bonifazio (Bonifacio in Bruno), and the fact that in both plays these two characters are taken in by fake magicians or alchemists. In fact, a purported magical feat in *La Strega*, to be executed at their behest, involves making a woman fall in love by modelling her figure in gold. This anticipates both 'scams' in *Candelaio*, suffered respectively by the characters who bear the same names as those in *La Strega*, Bonifacio and Bartolomeo, one of which involves using a wax doll to secure a woman's love, the other turning base metal into gold. A formal aspect that these two plays have in common is the presence of multiple, strikingly argumentative presenters of the plays who state that a prologue is unnecessary.

More work needs to be done on the relationship between Bruno and Grazzini. While *La Strega* was printed for the first time in 1582, the same year as *Candelaio*, we know that it was written decades earlier, though never performed.[19] For our present purposes, it is enough to note that anyone who picked up both these plays would be struck by these similarities, regardless of how they came into being and of whether they were deliberate. We already know that, when composing *Twelfth Night*, Shakespeare used several works related to *Gli Ingannati* (and see 'Clusters of plays' below on the role of character names in signalling a play's enrolment in a specific cluster). For these reasons, *Candelaio* could easily have provided the point of entry of *La Strega* into the complex of sources for *Twelfth Night*.

## LA STREGA AND GLI INGANNATI

There are also links between *La Strega* and the main source of Shakespeare's play, and these were definitely deliberate.

As already mentioned, the ultimate source for the main plot of *Twelfth Night* is *Gli Ingannati* (*The Deceived*), a comedy by the Sienese Academy of Gli Intronati, first printed in 1537, but performed in 1532 (o.s. 1531, the date given on the title page). The Prologue tells us that the play was meant to atone for the misogynist entertainment *Il Sacrificio* (*The Sacrifice*), which had taken place on the night of the Epiphany, or Twelfth Night, of the same year. An entry dated 2 February 1602 (o.s. 1601) in the diary of John Manningham, describing *Twelfth Night* as 'most like and neere to that [play] in Italian called Inganni' is cited in most editions of the play, including the *Norton Shakespeare* (p. 3334). The discovery of the diary and of its author is described in detail by Joseph Hunter, who was the first to point out that the Intronati play was much closer to the main plot of *Twelfth Night* than either of the two sixteenth-century comedies actually called *Gli Inganni*, by Niccolò Secco and Curzio Gonzaga.[20]

The Intronati's *Ingannati* was an extremely successful play and from it derived several versions in five different languages and three different genres (plays, *novelle* and romances): a cluster of works that

---

*Secenteschi* 19 (1978), 3–21, additionally surveys the play's connection with John Florio, who is one of the most likely vehicles for Shakespeare's knowledge of *Candelaio* and of Italian culture in general. Other aspects of Bruno's work are referred to in Frances A. Yates, *A Study of Love's Labour's Lost* (Cambridge, 1936), and Gilberto Sacerdoti, *Sacrificio e sovranità: teologia e politica nell'Europa di Shakespeare e Bruno* (Turin, 2002).

[18] Richard Wilson, 'Too long for a play: Shakespeare and the wars of religion', in his *Worldly Shakespeare: The Theatre of Our Good Will* (Edinburgh, 2016), pp. 53–72.

[19] *La Strega* is included in a list of his works drawn up by Grazzini in September 1566 (see 'Grazzini and early modern English drama'). The Argument refers to the play being staged by aristocratic performers, but in the address to the reader prefaced to the 1582 individual edition of *La Strega* in 12° (an inferior collective edition of Grazzini's plays in 8° was issued by the same printers, Giunti of Venice, the same year), Grazzini states that the play was never performed. See *La Strega*, in Antonfrancesco Grazzini, *Teatro*, ed. Giovanni Grazzini (Bari, 1953), pp. 179–242; pp. 181, 185. In this article, I quote from this edition and give my own translation.

[20] See Joseph Hunter, *New Illustrations of the Life, Studies, and Writings of Shakespeare*, 2 vols. (1845), vol. 1, pp. 370–6, 391–7.

I term the 'Ingannati franchise'.[21] The tale of 'Apolonius and Silla' in Barnaby Rich's *Farewell to Military Profession*, first printed in 1581, being the closest work in the 'Ingannati franchise' to have been written in English, is sometimes mentioned as *the* source for *Twelfth Night*. However, we do know that Shakespeare went back specifically to *Gli Ingannati* for more than simply the main plot.[22] He even echoes lexical items from the original Italian, in a way that recalls a language learner's keen ear for striking expressions: see the famous 'accost', used by Sir Toby as an exhortation to Sir Andrew Aguecheek to approach Olivia's waiting woman Maria, and that Sir Andrew mistakes for Maria's surname: 'Good Mistress Mary Accost' (*Twelfth Night*, 1.3.46–56). As already recorded by Geoffrey Bullough in his collection of Shakespeare's sources, this verb is found in *Gli Ingannati*, and is used to comic effect in Act 2, Scene 6, where two servants observe Isabella – the Olivia equivalent – as she invites 'Fabio' (in fact, Lelia) to come closer.[23] (Could the fact that Aguecheek here is wrong or 'deceived' as to the meaning of the word 'accost' be a metalinguistic reference to the Italian source?)

In '*La Strega* and *Candelaio*', we saw how the link between the Saint Bartholomew's Day massacre and *Candelaio* provides a rationale for the presence of Bruno's play in *Twelfth Night*. When we re-read the main source of Shakespeare's play with this in mind, we find that *Gli Ingannati* also refers to an episode of metropolitan warfare with a religious dimension: in this case, the 1527 Sack of Rome. In *Gli Ingannati*, Lelia, the Viola equivalent, is separated from her brother Fabrizio not through a shipwreck, but through its political equivalent: the Sack of Rome by the imperial troops of Charles V. As a result of this event, the girl was held captive by the Spaniards until she was ransomed. Most of the family fortune was lost, and her brother disappeared. Eventually, Lelia and her father fetched up in Modena, where the play is set. All this is mentioned at the start of the play. Then, in Act 1, Scene 3, a flippant – but, in fact, rather emotional – conversation takes place between Lelia and her nurse Clemenzia; and we should bear in mind that this character's name recalls that of the

reigning Pope at the time of the Sack, Clement VII, who was himself held prisoner by the Spaniards. In this scene, Clemenzia has spotted Lelia in men's clothes, a ruse that the girl adopted in order to enter the service of Flaminio, with whom she is in love:

CLEMENZIA. And no shame at all! Oh, Lelia, have you become a woman of the world, as some people call it nowadays?
LELIA. Yes – I'm a woman of the world, all right, if it's this world you're talking about. How many women of the other world have you seen? I've never been there in my life, that I can remember.
CLEMENZIA. Well, then, have you lost your virgin name?
LELIA. Not so far as I know – not in Modena at least. Not the *name* of virgin – but if you want to know about anything else, you'd better ask the Spaniards who held me prisoner at Rome.

(*Deceived*, pp. 203–4)[24]

[CLEMENZIA. Parti forse che si vergogni? Saresti mai diventata femina del mondo?

---

[21] See Rich's '*Apolonius & Silla*', *an Original of Shakespeare's 'Twelfth Night'*, ed. Morton Luce (London, 1912), pp. 7–8; Bullough, *Narrative and Dramatic Sources*, vol. 2, p. 270.

[22] For instance, both Fabrizio in *Gli Ingannati* and Sebastian in *Twelfth Night* decide to go sightseeing, which has been adduced as a common element from Hunter onwards: See Hunter, *New Illustrations*, vol. 1, p. 396. See also Bullough, *Narrative and Dramatic Sources*, vol. 2, pp. 278–85, for a detailed comparison between the two plays; and René Pruvost, 'The *Two Gentlemen of Verona*, *Twelfth Night*, et *Gl'Ingannati*', *Études anglaises* 13 (1960), 1–9.

[23] See Bullough, *Narrative and Dramatic Sources*, vol. 2, pp. 279, 298, 307. On *Twelfth Night* and Italian linguistic elements, see also Elisabetta Tarantino, 'John Florio's *A World of Words* (1598) as link between plot and subplot in *Twelfth Night*', *Notes and Queries* 63 (2016), 422–4. On Shakespeare and Italian, see Naseeb Shaheen, 'Shakespeare's knowledge of Italian', *Shakespeare Survey* 47 (Cambridge, 1994), 161–70; Jason Lawrence, '*Who the devil taught thee so much Italian?*': *Italian Language Learning and Literary Imitation in Early Modern England* (Manchester, 2005).

[24] Quotations are: for the original Italian, from Accademici Intronati di Siena, *Gl'Ingannati*, in *Commedie del Cinquecento*, ed. Nino Borsellino, 2 vols. (Milan, 1962), vol. 1, pp. 195–289; for the English translation, from *The Deceived*, in *Five Italian Renaissance Comedies*, trans. and ed. Bruce Penman (Harmondsworth, 1978), pp. 193–278.

LELIA. Sì, che io son del mondo. Quante femine hai tu vedute fuor del mondo? Io, per me, non ci fu' mai, ch'io mi ricordi.

CLEMENZIA. Adunque, hai tu perduto il nome di vergine?

LELIA. Il nome no, ch'io sappi, e massimamente in questa terra. Del resto, si vuol domandarne gli spagnuoli che mi tenner prigiona a Roma.

(*Ingannati*, 1.3; p. 214)]

A little later in this conversation, Lelia reminds the nurse of the effect of what happened:

LELIA. … in that miserable business of the sack of Rome … And you know that for all that time I had a hard and difficult life, shut off from thoughts of love, and almost shut off from humanity; for I thought everyone would be pointing at me because I'd been in the hands of the soldiers, and however honourably I lived, I didn't see how I could escape calumny.

(*Deceived*, pp. 204–5)

[LELIA. … dopo il miserabil sacco di Roma … Sai anco quanto, in que' tempi, fu aspra e dura la mia vita e, non pur lontana dai pensieri amorosi, ma quasi da ogni pensiero umano: pensando che, per essere io stata in mano di soldati, che ognuno m'aditasse; né credevo poter vivere sì onestamente che bastasse a far che la gente non avesse che dire.

(*Ingannati*, 1.3; p. 215)]

Indeed, the play features several derogatory comments against Spanish soldiers, who were more or less an occupying army in Italy, and takes some small revenge against them through the mistreatment of a Spaniard called Giglio by the servant Pasquella.

In the previous section, we saw how the names of the *dramatis personae* in *La Strega* duplicate one of the features of *Candelaio* that point to the Saint Bartholomew's Day massacre. *La Strega* also echoes those elements in *Gli Ingannati* that refer to the Sack of Rome – and in this case the link is obviously deliberate.

The first instance of this occurs in the conversation between the presenters, where the Argument and the Prologue discuss how historical and social conditions have changed, and how modern comedy differs from ancient comedy. The Argument concludes by pointing out that nowadays:

should these soldiers get their hands on any girls or married women they would rob them of their virginity and their honour (unless they were planning to obtain a good ransom for them).

[se per sorte capitasser loro [ai soldati] nelle mani, o fanciulle grandicelle o donne maritate (se già non pensassero cavarne buona taglia), torrebbero loro la virginità e l'onore

(*La Strega*, 'Interlocutori nel principio', p. 187)]

This is precisely the situation described by Lelia in *Gli Ingannati* to her nurse Clemenzia as one in which she had found herself at the Sack of Rome. The latter character – whose name, as we have seen, is itself a pointer to the Sack – provides an additional parallel with *La Strega*: just as the nurse Clemenzia voices her fear that Lelia may have become 'femina del mondo' ('a woman of the world'), the servant Clemenza in *La Strega* 5.6 (p. 233) declares her belief that her young mistress, Violante, must have become 'femmina di mondo' and that it was 'impossible' that she could have preserved her virginity.

Here we catch a glimpse of a theme that would require a study in its own right: how the ravages of war are represented in terms of sexual assault on female characters (of course, the link is more obvious in Romance languages, since the gender of cities is feminine). There are indications that successive authors saw Lelia's possible rape at the Sack of Rome in these terms, and correctly understood this to be a fundamental, though implicit, issue raised by *Gli Ingannati*. In Curzio Gonzaga's 1592 *Inganni*, the name Lucretia, effectively a synonym for a 'Roman rape', plays a prominent role.[25] In both Grazzini and Shakespeare, the heroines' names directly voice the concept of violation (Violante and Viola).

Terence Cave mentions this in a completely different context, where Viola herself is the 'violator':

---

[25] Another coincidence that is at least worth recording, because it again links Rome and Paris as victims of 'rape', is the assonance between 'Lucretia' and the French capital's ancient name, 'Lutetia'. There is obviously no room here to pursue the implications of this for Shakespeare's *Rape of Lucrece*.

[Viola] represents, indeed, a particularly fruitful violation of the laws of rational discourse no less than of sexual decorum: the fact that her proper name echoes the erotic flowers and music of the opening scene, insidiously rearranges the letters of Olivia's name, and comes close to naming violation itself, appears to be yet another of the verbal accidents to which the play is prone.[26]

These are not, in fact, 'verbal accidents'. It is true that, in Italian grammar, 'viola' is an active rather than passive form of the verb, and the same applies to the name 'Violante' in *La Strega*. However, as we have seen, the strong link with the '*Ingannati* franchise' points us in the other direction. My contention is that this unavoidable contradiction is put to good use by Shakespeare. As the gulling of Malvolio gets underway, in *Twelfth Night* 2.5.84, we are told that Lucrece features in Olivia's seal. The idea of rape, which is unequivocally evoked here, establishes a link between the female ruler and the female refugee, just as the idea of the violating and the violated are merged together in the heroine's name and intertextual derivation. This whole semantic complex then becomes another way in which *Twelfth Night* hints at the levelling effect of war on apparent opposites.[27]

I return to the similarity in name between Shakespeare's and Grazzini's heroines in 'The strangers' case', where I discuss how Shakespeare's attention in *Twelfth Night* focuses specifically on the episode from *La Strega* that has given Clemenza reason to despair of the heroine's virtue. But, first, I will support my argument that Grazzini's play intervenes directly in Shakespeare's cluster of sources by referring to some methodological aspects, and then to other ways in which Grazzini was present in early modern English drama.

## CLUSTERS OF PLAYS

The important methodological point to be made here is twofold: first of all, Shakespeare is working with a cluster of interconnected sources; second, clusters such as this physically existed in Elizabethan England, and were in fact one of the main ways in which the Elizabethan readership consumed these plays. These texts were imported

from Italy in loose sheaves, customers selected and bought the plays that appealed to them most, and then had them bound together. Joseph Hunter describes one such volume that he believes to be particularly significant in relation to *Twelfth Night*. It contained:

a small collection of Italian comedies, all printed at Venice, between the years 1546 and 1592. The plays were the following; and in the following order:

[Gonzaga's] Gl'Inganni, 1592.
Il Capitano, del Dolce, 1547.
Il Viluppo, del Parabosco, 1547.
La Notte, del Parabosco, 1546.
Il Sacrificio, de gli Intronati, 1585 [which included Gl'Ingannati].[28]

This volume is indeed interesting, also because the *dramatis personae* of the third play listed, *Il Viluppo*, include an 'Orsino in love' (*Orsino innamorata* [sic]), which means that at least three of the five plays listed have some connection with *Twelfth Night*.[29]

I believe that this specific volume has not been traced. However, what we now know is that it did not contain the entire cluster of Italian plays relevant to *Twelfth Night*. Also, similar collections, which include one or more of the Italian comedies that are of interest in relation to *Twelfth Night*, are far from unusual. They can be found in several English repositories, including Oxford's university and college libraries.[30]

---

[26] Terence Cave, *Recognitions: A Study in Poetics* (Oxford, 1988), p. 280. Mentioned in Lorna Hutson, 'On not being deceived: rhetoric and the body in *Twelfth Night*', *Texas Studies in Literature and Language* 38 (1996), 141–74; p. 165.

[27] See n. 1.

[28] Hunter, *New Illustrations*, vol. 1, p. 393. See also Lawrence, '*Who the devil?*', pp. 168–9, n. 35.

[29] See Hunter, *New Illustrations*, vol. 1, p. 398.

[30] An example of this is All Souls' mm.17.17, which is a 12° volume in an early modern English binding. This volume contains Grazzini's 1582 *Strega* together with nine more Italian plays, including a 1567 *Viluppo* and a 1585 edition of Secco's *Inganni*. (I am grateful to the Codrington Librarian, Gaye Morgan, for her help.) Bruno's *Candelaio* had an entirely different publishing history and is not part of these *Sammelbände*.

Another kind of physical cluster gathering these plays together in early modern England is the list of works consulted in John Florio's dictionaries, *A World of Words* (1598) and *Queen Anna's New World of Words* (1611). The earlier of these only contains three entries that refer to comedies, but the greatly expanded list in the Queen Anna version includes some thirty plays, the great majority of which are comedies. Virtually all the plays that come within the radar of our discussion feature in this list: 'Il viluppo. Comedia', 'Inganni. Comedia' (we do not know which, but it is probably Gonzaga's, since Florio's list does not include Secco's *L'Interesse*), 'Sacrificio, Comedia' (this would have included *Gli Ingannati*), 'Spiritata. Comedia', 'Strega. Comedia'. Bruno's *Candelaio* does not appear, but his philosophical dialogues do.[31] Unsurprisingly, these titles often correspond to those found in English *Sammelbände*.

Florio's list and the collections of plays bound together provide evidence of the availability of these plays in London in the decades around the end of the sixteenth century. They also show how readers tended to encounter, and arrange, them as clusters.

A final piece of evidence concerning the ways in which these plays were grouped together, this time by their authors, is provided by character names. We saw this at work in the second and third sections of this article, as links between *La Strega* on the one hand and *Candelaio* and *Gli Ingannati* on the other. In 'The strangers' case' below, we shall find another link of this type, between Grazzini's play and *Twelfth Night*. Character names play an important part – alongside plot incidents – in allowing us to identify a cluster of sources derived from *Gli Ingannati*. Niccolò Secco was the author not of one but of two plays belonging to the 'Ingannati franchise': one signals this fact through its title, *Gli Inganni*; the other, *L'Interesse*, by giving its four main characters names that echo those found in the Sienese play – including 'Lelio' as a girl's pseudonym.

As for Shakespeare, he took the name of the slightly enigmatic minor character Fabian from *Gli Ingannati*, while his 'Cesario' comes from Gonzaga's *Inganni*, his 'Orsino' possibly from *Il Viluppo*, his 'Olivia' from Emanuel Ford's *Parismus*, and so, at least in part, does his Viola (but see more on this below). That there was conscious artifice in this seems likely when we look at another device that Shakespeare reproduces from elements of the 'Ingannati franchise': the assonance between the first syllable of the heroine's real or assumed name and her brother's name – a way of reiterating the confusion and assumption of identities. In *Gli Ingannati*, Lelia calls herself 'Fabio', obviously in remembrance of her lost brother 'Fabrizio'; Barnaby Rich's heroine takes on her brother's name, Silvio, without any modification – but the assonance is already in her own name, Silla. What we find in *Twelfth Night* is a variation on this onomastic game: the lost brother is called *Se*bastian, and Viola calls herself *Ce*sario.

## GRAZZINI AND EARLY MODERN ENGLISH DRAMA

Antonfrancesco Grazzini, also known as Il Lasca, was born in 1505 in Florence, where he died in 1584.[32] Most of his comedies were not printed until two years before his death. However, they are mentioned in the prologue to his farce *Il Frate*, first performed in 1541, and again in a list drawn up by the author in 1566. For *La Strega*, we also have a censored manuscript, presumably the result of Grazzini's attempt to obtain the necessary *imprimatur* from the Florentine Inquisition. There are indications that this attempt failed.[33] However, Grazzini's works are found in several early

31 See John Florio, *Queen Anna's New World of Words* (1611), STC 11099, *EEBO* images 6 and 7. On *La Spiritata*, see 'Grazzini and early modern English drama'.
32 See Robert J. Rodini, *Antonfrancesco Grazzini* (Madison, 1970); Roberto Trovato, *Anton Francesco Grazzini: un commediografo fra tradizione e modernità* (Genoa, 1996); Michel Plaisance, *Antonfrancesco Grazzini dit Lasca (1505–1584): écrire dans la Florence des Médicis* (Manziana, 2005).
33 The play was eventually printed in Venice rather than Florence. See Michel Plaisance's critical edition of *La Strega*, based on this manuscript (Abbeville, 1976), esp. pp. 15–18. See also Matteo Durante, 'L'inquieta tradizione della

manuscripts, which denotes a high degree of popularity. In this section, I explore three instances that indicate how these works had an influence on early modern English drama beyond *Twelfth Night*.

The only comedy by Grazzini to be printed before 1582 was *La Spiritata*, first published by Giunti in Florence in 1561.[34] Within a few years of its publication, an English writer (possibly the John Jeffere named on the manuscript) made a version of it entitled *The Bugbears* (exact date unknown). This English version is of interest for our discussion from several points of view, also bearing in mind that 'a bug-beare' is the first translation listed in Florio's dictionary for 'Beffana', the witch-like figure whose name is a corruption of the word 'Epiphany' and who personifies the Twelfth Night holiday.[35] Firstly, this manuscript play testifies that Grazzini's work was read with interest in Elizabethan England. Secondly, the author of *The Bugbears* adds to *La Spiritata* incidents taken from *Gli Ingannati*, thus anticipating the conjunction of sources to be found in *Twelfth Night*. Finally, he adds a sarcastic reference to the difficulty in procreating that had initially beset Henri II of France and had been blamed on his wife, Catherine de' Medici, before they went on to produce ten children (an allusion that is spoken by a character whose name Shakespeare would use in *The Taming of the Shrew*):

BIONDELLO.O sir, you would wonder what miracles I
        did hear
    Of those that did know him [the fake astronomer and
    physician Nostradamus] in Orleans this other year,
    And in Paris what a cure he did on the French King –
    I would have said the queen – how he brought down
    her teeming.

                                    (*Bugbears*, 3.3.23–6)[36]

As Warwick Bond remarks, '[t]he mention of Orleans, apart from its repute for magic ... may be dictated by the importance the town had recently assumed as the centre of the religious struggle in France, a struggle sufficiently interesting to Elizabethan England'.[37] Even if *The Bugbears* was indeed written in the 1560s, as argued by Bond, after the 1572 'massacre at Paris' this passage would

have looked like a double reference to the hot spots of religious trouble in France, a background that, as we have seen, is relevant to the inclusion of *Candelaio* among the sources for *Twelfth Night*.

We turn now to two parallels between *La Strega* and works by Shakespeare other than *Twelfth Night*. These were pointed out by Wilhelm König in 1874, and concern two other plays from the middle period of Shakespeare's career.[38]

In *The Merchant of Venice*, Portia says of her English suitor, young Falconbridge: 'How oddly he is suited! I think he bought his doublet in Italy, his round hose in France, his bonnet in Germany, and his behaviour everywhere' (*Merchant*, 1.2.70–3). This is indeed quite similar to a passage in Grazzini:

TADDEO. Why, are my clothes so very odd?
FARFANICCHIO. Extremely odd. You are – forgive me:
    Your Lordship is – wearing a German bonnet,
    a French cape, a Florentine gown, a Spanish ruff,
    Gascony stockings, Roman shoes, a Fiesole face,
    a Sienese brain, and a Jennet plume. Do you not
    call this odd?

[TADDEO. Oh, è egli però abito sì stravagante questo?
FARFANICCHIO. Stravagantissimo. Voi avete, cioè la signoria vostra ha la berretta alla tedesca, la cappa alla franzese, il saione alla fiorentina, il colletto sòpravi alla spagnuola, le calze alla guascona, le scarpette alla

---

Strega del Lasca', *Studi medievali e umanistici* 7 (2009), 291–353, and tables XX–XXVII.

[34] Grazzini's farce *La Gelosia* had been printed in 1551, with a French version appearing in print in 1579.

[35] See Tarantino, 'Florio's *A World of Words*'.

[36] *The Bugbears*, ed. James D. Clark (New York, 1979).

[37] *Early Plays from the Italian*, ed. R. Warwick Bond (Oxford, 1911), p. 82. The reference to Catherine de' Medici is reinforced at 5.7.89, where Formosus is asked: '[w]ill you take Rosimunda di Medici to your wife ... ?' Bond points out that the addition of a surname to the bride's name is due to the English adapter, who may have had in mind Grazzini's dedication to Raffaello de' Medici (*Early Plays*, p. 301). However, this 'Rosimunda di Medici' would certainly bring to mind the French Queen alluded to in Act 3, Scene 3.

[38] See Wilhelm König, 'Ueber die Entlehnungen Shakespeare's, insbesondere aus Rabelais und einigen italienischen Dramatikern', *Jahrbuch der Deutschen Shakespeare-Gesellschaft* 9 (1874), 195–232; pp. 227–30.

romanesca, il viso alla fiesolana, il cervello alla sanese e lo spennacchio alla giannetta: non vi pare stravaganza questa?

(*La Strega*, 2.1; pp. 205–6)]

English eclecticism in clothing was proverbial at this time, and other analogues are mentioned by modern editors of *The Merchant of Venice* – though the German bonnet is common only to Shakespeare and *La Strega*. One parallel by Robert Greene is especially close: '[i]n truth, quoth Farnese, to digress a little from your matter, I have seen an English gentleman so diffused in his suits, his doublet being for the wear of Castile, his hose for Venice, his hat for France, his cloak for Germany, that he seemed no way to be an Englishman but by the face'.[39] However, there is at least the possibility that Greene too was aware of the *Strega* passage, especially given the concluding remark about 'the face': see 'The strangers' case' below, for the meaning and significance of the reference to a 'Fiesole face' in *La Strega*.

The other parallel adduced by König refers to Hamlet's famous speech to the Players:

HAMLET. . . . [f]or anything so overdone is from the purpose of playing, whose end, both at the first and now, was and is to hold as 'twere the mirror up to nature, to show virtue her own feature, scorn her own image, and the very age and body of the time his form and pressure.
A PLAYER. I hope we have *reformed* that indifferently with us, sir.
HAMLET. O, *reform* it altogether.

(*Hamlet*, 3.2.19–38; emphasis added)

I quote a few lines from *La Strega* for comparison's sake:

PROLOGUE. What can you do? That is the way the world goes nowadays: one must accept today's ways.
ARGUMENT. Today's ways! It used to be that one wrote interludes that went with the comedies: now we are writing comedies to go with the interludes. What do you say to that?
PROLOGUE. I am with you on this, but neither you nor I are going to *reform* people's brains now.
PROLOGUE. . . . don't you know that comedies are images of truth, examples of customs and a mirror of life?

[PROLOGO. Che vuoi tu fare? il mondo va oggidì così: bisogna accomodarsi all'usanza.

ARGOMENTO. Un'usanza da dirle voi! Già si solevon fare gli intermedi che servissero alle commedie, ma ora si fanno le commedie che servono agl'intermedi: che ne di' tu?
PROLOGO. Intendola come te in questa parte, ma né tu né io semo atti a *riformare* i cervelli di oggidì.
PROLOGO. . . . non sai tu che le commedie sono immagini di verità, esempio di costumi e specchio di vita?

(*La Strega*, 'Prologo e Argomento', pp. 185–6; emphasis added)]

Indeed, a reading of the whole of this scene in *Hamlet* alongside the entire dialogue between the Argument and the Prologue in *La Strega* brings out the strong overall similarity in the two dramatists' concern for the 'reformation' of comedies and in their scathing disregard for newer, competing forms of dramatic entertainment.[40]

While individual elements of these parallels surface elsewhere, their cumulative effect, together with the arguments adduced below for a relationship between *La Strega* and *Twelfth Night*, make it extremely unlikely that these could be simply a series of coincidences.

## THE STRANGERS' CASE: LA STREGA AND TWELFTH NIGHT

Having shown how Shakespeare's attention could have been drawn to Grazzini's *Strega* at the time that he was writing *Twelfth Night*, we can now turn

---

[39] Robert Greene, *A Farewell to Folly* (London, 1591), C3v. Another parallel often quoted is with Thomas Nashe, *The Unfortunate Traveller* (London, 1594), I4r: '[a]t my first coming to Rome, I being a youth of the English cut, wore my hair long, went apparelled in light colours, and imitated four or five sundry nations in my attire at once: which no sooner was noted, but I had all the boys of the city in a swarm wandering about me' (I have modernized the spelling in both quotations). A more distant, virtuoso variation on the theme is found in the Induction to Ben Jonson's *Every Man Out of His Humour* (1599; lines 108–12), on which see also the following note.

[40] The description of comedies as 'specchio di vita' ('mirrors of life'), that 'hold the mirror up to nature', etc., common to both passages, was originally ascribed by Donatus to Cicero, and was widely quoted in the Renaissance, including in Ben Jonson's *Every Man Out of His Humour* (3.1.526–7).

to examine the relationship between these two plays. While *La Strega* has obvious points of contact with *Gli Ingannati*, as discussed above, its links with *Twelfth Night* consist more in specific plot elements than in the general plot, which in *La Strega* is as follows. The titular witch, Sabatina, is really no such thing: she is an old widow who has some dealings with a young man called Fabrizio. Fabrizio has information that others do not have and uses it to make other characters believe that the so-called 'witch' can help them achieve certain things they want. In fact, what Fabrizio knows is that those things were going to happen anyway. Luc'Antonio's son, Orazio, believed to have drowned, was already back in Florence. He was hiding at Sabatina's house with Violante, a girl he had rescued after two friends of his had led her away from her home in Genoa, and then killed each other over her. Fabrizio also knows that, as a consequence of Orazio's reappearance, the fatuous Taddeo, on whom his mother's and uncle's livelihoods depend, will be persuaded not to go off to war out of disappointed love. Geva, the woman that Taddeo wishes to marry, is Luc'Antonio's widowed daughter: when Orazio resurfaces, Geva will no longer be an heiress, and will thus be within reach of Taddeo, who will be allowed to marry her.

As with *Candelaio*, the most immediately obvious link between *La Strega* and *Twelfth Night* is in the characters' names. As already mentioned, the name Viola is often said to come from Violetta in Emanuel Ford's *Parismus* (1598), which must have something to do with this complex because it also contains a Queen Olivia. However, in *Parismus*, Violetta's love interest is called Pollipus, while in *La Strega* we have a Violante–Orazio pair, which is a much closer match to the Viola–Orsino pair in *Twelfth Night*. One of the First Folio stage directions announcing Viola's entrance actually reads 'Enter Violenta [*sic*]' (1.5).

Besides this, Taddeo's dependent uncle is in the same position as Sir Toby Belch in *Twelfth Night*. While Bonifazio is far less vivid a character than Olivia's uncle, in a play like *Twelfth Night*, with its underlying theme of the identification of opposites

and opponents, it was indeed a nice touch to derive Sir Toby and Malvolio from characters bearing the same name, i.e. respectively, *La Strega*'s Bonifazio and *Candelaio*'s Bonifacio.[41]

As for Taddeo, he is a source for Sir Andrew Aguecheek. In the scene in which these characters make their first appearance, i.e. *La Strega* 2.1 and *Twelfth Night* 1.3, both threaten to leave because their courtship is unsuccessful, are made fools of by subordinate characters, allude to a missed encounter with academic pursuits, and demonstrate their prowess in fatuous pastimes of a physical nature (children's games in Taddeo's case, galliards and capers in Sir Andrew's). Bonifazio successfully undertakes to make Taddeo delay his departure (*La Strega* 3.3 and 4.3), and so does Sir Toby with Aguecheek in *Twelfth Night* 1.3. Taddeo and Sir Andrew are both rich fools, but Taddeo does get his woman in the end. We do not see his bride's reaction because Geva never actually appears in the play. This is emblematic of the difference between Shakespeare and Italian comedy: whole volumes could be written on why, in Shakespearian comedy, Andrew Aguecheek could never be allowed to marry Olivia.

Although the striking name Aguecheek does not come from *La Strega*, it can be linked to both the other Italian sources of *Twelfth Night*, in a way that confirms two important aspects of the intertextual scenario that is described in this article: that these plays form a macrotext thanks to their intersecting elements; and that Shakespeare seems to be drawn to linguistic peculiarities and to be making connections between near-homophones in the Italian texts that he is handling. Critics have long been aware of the possible relevance to either or both 'Malvolio' or/and 'Aguecheek' of the name of 'Agnolo Malevolti'.[42] This is the only fully named participant in *Il Sacrificio degli Intronati*, the prelude to *Gli Ingannati* that in the sixteenth century was

---

41 On Bonifacio and Malvolio, see '*La Strega* and *Candelaio*' above.

42 See Morton Luce's introductory matter to *Rich's 'Apolonius & Silla'*, pp. ix and 13; Bullough, *Narrative and Dramatic Sources*, vol. 2, pp. 271–2.

invariably printed with the play itself. Semantically, *volto* is an alternative Italian term for 'face', and *male* as a noun can mean 'ague'. Florio does not include this meaning among the twenty-seven alternatives he gives for *male* on its own (starting with 'harm, hurt, evil, ill, mischief, sickness, disease', etc.), but two entries above we find *Mal di febbre* translated as 'an ague or fever'. On the same page, the entry for *Mala* reads 'the ball of the cheek. Also taken for the jaw or cheek bone'.[43] Thus, the name found in the prelude to *Gli Ingannati* phonetically recalls that of Malvolio while it is semantically allied to that of Aguecheek. Similarly, we find a double relevance to both these characters' names in the way in which the name 'Bonifacio' is jokingly modified by other characters in *Candelaio*, as 'Malefacio' ('I do evil', twice in Act 5) and as 'Buon'infaccia' ('Good in the face', an implied accusation of hypocrisy, in *Candelaio*, 4.8).[44] In this instance, Shakespeare seems to be reacting to the homophony between 'faccio' ('I do') and 'faccia' ('face'), which is used to create intriguing resonances between Bruno's Bonifacio and both Malvolio and Aguecheek. Thus, both *Gli Ingannati* and *Candelaio* contributed to Sir Andrew's name, while *La Strega* gave this character his main features.

In fact, there is a point of similarity between Aguecheek and the character of Taddeo in *La Strega* that is especially relevant to our discussion of the theme of war in these plays, and it is the fact that Taddeo and Aguecheek display gratuitously aggressive behaviour towards Lutherans and Puritans, respectively. For Taddeo ('woe betide the first Lutheran that crosses my path' – 'guai al primo Luteriano [sic] che mi si parerà davanti'; *La Strega*, 4.2; p. 213), Lutherans are no more than the most convenient opportunity to fulfil his notion that going off to war was what someone did when thwarted in love. Aguecheek's equally flimsy aggressiveness towards another branch of Protestantism elicits a baffled response even from someone like Sir Toby:

MARIA. Marry, sir, sometimes he [Malvolio] is a kind of Puritan.

SIR ANDREW. O, if I thought that I'd beat him like a dog.

SIR TOBY. What, for being a Puritan? Thy exquisite reason, dear knight.

SIR ANDREW. I have no exquisite reason for't, but I have reason good enough.

(*Twelfth Night*, 2.3.135–40)

A connection that is particularly interesting has to do with this aspect, and provides a three-way link between *La Strega, Twelfth Night* and *Sir Thomas More*. Not only that: this connection also helps to confirm a slightly doubtful reading in the manuscript of the *Thomas More* play.

*Sir Thomas More* contains a justly celebrated speech in which the eponymous character harangues the London populace who wanted to banish or even kill all foreigners in London. While this scene depicts historical riots that took place on the so-called 'Ill May Day' of 1517, it is generally recognized that it had topical relevance, and that it referred to episodes of intolerance against the Huguenot refugees in London at the end of the sixteenth century.[45] The speech in question is found in the Hand D fragment of the play, generally believed to be in Shakespeare's own handwriting. The play only exists in a manuscript that features threatening comments from the censor, Edmund Tilney, and we believe that it was never performed or printed in Shakespeare's time. After conjuring up images of banished foreigners, 'their babies at their backs', Thomas More concludes:

> What would you think
> To be thus used? This is the strangers' case,
> And this your mountainish inhumanity.
>
> (*Sir Thomas More*, 6.154–6)

The adjective 'mountainish' is not recorded in the *OED*. Here I would like to offer, if not an actual

---

43 See John Florio, *A World of Words* (1598), STC 11098, *EEBO* image 117.

44 See Elisabetta Tarantino, 'History and religion in Giordano Bruno's Candelaio', in *Giordano Bruno: Will, Power and Being: Law, Philosophy, and Theology in the Early Modern Era*, ed. Massimiliano Traversino Di Cristo (Paris, forthcoming).

45 See *Sir Thomas More*, ed. John Jowett (London, 2011), pp. 43–7. Quotations are from this edition.

source, at least an enlightening intertext for this concept from an episode in *La Strega* that has additional resonances with *Twelfth Night*. If the phrase has an ultimately foreign origin, it explains why it sounds somewhat strange.

In *La Strega* 4.5, Violante comes face to face with her mother, Madonna Oretta, who has come to Florence from Genoa looking for her. The play's audience would have recognized the mother's name as that of a witty and appealing character in Boccaccio's *Decameron* (4.1), and for this reason Violante's mother would immediately have commanded their sympathy. Violante has been staying willingly in Florence with Orazio. When she sees that her mother has come looking for her, she is afraid that she will be taken back to Genoa, away from Orazio, and therefore asks Sabatina to pretend that she is not Oretta's daughter at all but a different Violante altogether, and Sabatina's own daughter. Obviously Oretta is flabbergasted, as well as hurt. This is part of the argument in *La Strega* between Clemenza and Oretta on one side and Sabatina on the other:

ORETTA. O Lord! Is this possible? And is this how you treat strangers?
SABATINA. And is this how you address a citizen?
CLEMENZA. You a citizen? A citizen of the mountains!

[ORETTA. O Signore! è possibil però questo? e fannosi queste cose ai forestieri?
SABATINA. E diconsi queste parole ai cittadini?
CLEMENZA. Cittadina tu? di quelle di montagna.

(*La Strega*, 4.5; p. 221)]

On the surface, the situation here is quite different from that in *Sir Thomas More*: this is a private quarrel among women, while the Shakespearian fragment describes a popular uprising. And yet there are telling similarities. In both scenes, an accusation of unkindness towards strangers, i.e. foreigners, is coupled with the metaphorical suggestion that this denotes a 'mountainish' origin on the part of the perpetrators. In order to accuse Sabatina of being an uncouth, uncivil person, Clemenza says that the only place of which she is fit to be a 'citizen' is 'la montagna' ('the mountains'). While the *Thomas More* phrase is undeniably odd, the Italian

expression is immediately recognizable as a way of accusing someone of incivility (literally, of not belonging to or in a 'city').[46]

In fact, a reference to the discussion between the Argument and the Prologue at the beginning of *La Strega* helps us identify a prestigious literary affiliation for this trope. When the Prologue utters his evaluation of comedies, which, as we have seen, has been linked to Hamlet's advice to the Players, the Argument accuses him of being old-fashioned, and as uncouth as someone from Fiesole: '[t]u sei all'antica, e tieni del fiesolano sconciamente' (p. 186). The reference to the hillside town near Florence is used here in much the same way as the generic 'di montagna' in the more extended passage from *La Strega* 4.5. It is also behind the servant's jibe, in the passage that we saw in the previous section in connection with *The Merchant of Venice*, about Taddeo having 'il viso alla fiesolana' ('a Fiesole face'). A foreign reader who came across the 'fiesolano' phrase in these two passages from *La Strega* and asked someone well versed in Italian culture to explain its meaning would have been referred to a famous passage from Dante's *Inferno*:

But that ungrateful, malicious people
who came down from Fiesole of old,
and still smack of the mountain and the granite,
will become your enemies because of your just actions.

[Ma quello ingrato popolo maligno
che discese di Fiesole *ab* antico,
e tiene ancor del monte e del macigno,
ti si farà, per tuo ben far, nimico

(*Inferno*, 15.61–4)][47]

It is impossible to know to what extent Shakespeare was aware of the literary origin of this phrase: we

---

[46] For an occurrence of the Italian phrase in the English context, see Giordano Bruno, *The Ash Wednesday Supper* [1584], ed. Hilary Gatti (Toronto, 2018), pp. 82–3. I am grateful to Hilary Gatti for drawing my attention to this passage and offering helpful comments on an earlier draft of this article.

[47] Quoted from the facing-page edition of the *Inferno*, trans. and ed. Robert M. Durling (New York, 1996). I am grateful to Martin McLaughlin for the reference to this passage, and other helpful comments on a draft of this article.

should note, however, that an echo from the Ulysses episode in *Inferno* 26 has been detected in Scene 11 of his collaborative play with which we are dealing here.[48]

In any case, the repeated accusations of what we might call 'mountainishness' in *La Strega* and their application to the treatment of foreigners throw light on the use of this unusual adjective in *Sir Thomas More*. If accepted as a source or intertext, this establishes not simply a link between *La Strega* and *Sir Thomas More*, but a triangulation between these two plays and *Twelfth Night*. At the beginning of the fourth act in *Twelfth Night*, Sir Toby has attacked, as he thinks, 'Cesario', though in fact it was Viola's brother, Sebastian. This means that Toby has been fighting against one of the 'strangers' in the play, at which point he is reproached by Olivia in these terms:

> [w]ill it be ever thus? Ungracious wretch,
> Fit for the mountains and the barbarous caves,
> Where manners ne'er were preached
>
> (*Twelfth Night*, 4.1.46–8)

The parallel between the two Shakespearian works has been pointed out by Catherine Lisak.[49] Now we can see that the argument between Clemenza and Sabatina in *La Strega* 4.5 provides a clear antecedent for the use of this phrase in relation to the treatment of 'forestieri'. The thematic relevance of this passage is even more obvious when we consider that, as pointed out by Lorna Hutson in an article on *Twelfth Night* and *Gli Ingannati*, the theme of 'civility' plays an important part in *Twelfth Night*: immediately after reproaching Toby for his 'mountainous' qualities, Olivia asks Sebastian to excuse his 'uncivil' behaviour (*Twelfth Night*, 4.1.52).[50] As we have seen, this theme is alluded to in the 'cittadina' element of the *Strega* passage.

It is no coincidence, therefore, that the concluding scene in Act 3 of *Twelfth Night* (i.e. the previous scene to the one that we have just discussed) mirrors the emotional encounter between Oretta and Violante in *La Strega*. In Shakespeare's play, Antonio, who has rescued Sebastian from the waves and then entrusted him with all his money, has been arrested. Cesario

(that is, the disguised Viola) arrives on the scene, and Antonio, thinking that he is speaking to Sebastian, asks for his money back, which he needs for bail. Cesario obviously knows nothing about it. Even though Cesario's denial of Antonio is due to a case of mistaken identity, we are made to feel awkward and saddened by Antonio's perceived betrayal on the part of his friend. Therefore, the situation between Oretta and Violante is similar to that between Antonio and Cesario in *Twelfth Night*, but it is in fact its mirror situation: in *Twelfth Night*, there is mistaken identity that is perceived as conscious rejection; in *La Strega*, there is conscious rejection that is passed off as mistaken identity.

## CONCLUSION

An awareness of the role played by Bruno's *Candelaio* and Grazzini's *Strega* in the source cluster for *Twelfth Night* proves illuminating on several counts. In terms of specific intertextual elements, we can now definitely say that we have found the missing source for the subplot of *Twelfth Night*. *Candelaio* and *La Strega* form an interconnected cluster and, between them, account for the gulling of Malvolio (identified by Hilary Gatti in *Candelaio*), the figure of Sir Andrew Aguecheek (including his particular brand of foppishness, his frustrated courtship of an heiress, his flimsy excuse for attacking the religious 'other'), and the social and economic position of Sir Toby Belch. We also have thematic elements that link up with the main plot of *Twelfth Night*, and a pair of protagonists with

---

48 See *Sir Thomas More*, p. 277, where Jowett refers to Vittorio Gabrieli and Giorgio Melchiori's edition of *The Book of Sir Thomas More* (Manchester, 1990), p. 169 (4.2.23–6).

49 See Catherine Lisak, 'Domesticating strangeness in *Twelfth Night*', in *Twelfth Night: New Critical Essays*, ed. James Schiffer (London, 2011), pp. 167–83; p. 181. For other verbal echoes between *Twelfth Night* and this scene in *Sir Thomas More*, see MacDonald P. Jackson, 'The date and authorship of Hand D's contribution to Sir Thomas More: evidence from "Literature Online"', *Shakespeare Survey* 59 (Cambridge, 2006), 69–78; p. 76.

50 See Hutson, 'On not being deceived', p. 173, n. 66.

similar names. Geva's position has elements of both Olivia's and Viola's position as her status depends on her brother being believed to have drowned.

In terms of Shakespeare's compositional technique in *Twelfth Night*, our discussion confirms that we are dealing with a cluster of sources, involving Italian plays that can be found bound together in physical clusters in Elizabethan England, and that Shakespeare is alert to linguistic elements of the original Italian.

Perhaps most importantly, *La Strega* intervenes in the expression of political concerns in *Twelfth Night* – those concerns that, roughly at the same time, Shakespeare and his colleagues had been prevented by censorship from expressing in the play of *Sir Thomas More*. *La Strega* provides an additional, illuminating link between these two Shakespearian plays, and confirms and explains the reading of a word in the manuscript of *Sir Thomas More*. As we saw in 'La Strega and Candelaio', Giordano Bruno's references to the religious strife of his time are relevant to the political implications of both *Twelfth Night* and *Bartholomew Fair*. The figure of Grazzini and his fortune in England would also repay further study. As in Shakespeare's deployment of the two Bonifa(c)ios from *Candelaio* and *La Strega* in his depiction of arch-enemies Malvolio and Sir Toby, it is a nice twist that he used Italian (officially Catholic) sources to highlight the plight of the Huguenots in London in the 1590s. But the kind of sources that he used remind us of how porous the Catholic–Protestant divide appears when faced with the common problem of how to stop senseless violence.

# 'THOU LAIDST NO SIEGES TO THE MUSIC-ROOM': ANATOMIZING WARS, STAGING BATTLES

## MICHAEL HATTAWAY

In this article, I want to review evidence, from the early modern period, for the staging of siege scenes in particular, and battle sequences in general. This reveals that playhouse combats were often ritualized or emblematized, and very often minimalized. It is plausible that they were less prominent than in many contemporary stage productions and in most screen versions. Filmmakers, in order to satisfy contemporary demands for spectacle, can film on location and exhibit the vasty fields of France, but they also tend to magnify the battles, making them both more life-like and more climactic than they originally were. By doing this, screen directors have kept alive the tradition of Victorian and Edwardian directors such as Sir Frank Benson, who deployed spectacle in the interests of theatrical illusion. His stage settings and costumes came out of the pictorial tradition. He glorified war and converted Shakespeare's political texts into historical reconstructions and jingoistic contests between goodies and baddies. These filled the stage with fake castles, heraldic insignia and chunky men in armour.

There is a measure of detailed investigation of stage directions in what follows. A coda follows in which I examine some under-remarked images from Olivier's film of *Henry V*. Before that, I wish to test out my speculation that onstage fighting was often avoided, implicitly disparaged.[1] But, as I found when editing the Henry VI plays for the New Cambridge Shakespeare, there are, as in structuralism, few positive terms and therefore little certainty. My evidence readily slides into contiguous quicksands. In relation to the last fifteen years

of the sixteenth century, textual problems entail dating problems, entail authorship problems, entail company affiliation problems, and now, as we shall see, archaeological problems. It is hard to break into this hermeneutic circle. Some of my evidence from stage directions is problematic and somewhat skimpy.

This skimpiness has led some theatre historians to claim that, in early modern playhouses, spectacular battles were expanded from very brief suggestions. One might conjecture, however, that the small amount of time available for rehearsal meant that elaborate set-piece stage fights in pitched field sequences were often impracticable. Moreover, Elizabethan playing companies were much smaller than those we encounter these days in well-funded theatres – let alone the armies of extras some film directors can afford to deploy. Not surprisingly, therefore, clashes between bands of soldiers were often reduced to single combats between champions.

There is, moreover, no way of determining whether Shakespeare was himself pugnacious or pacifist. It was fashionable around 2003, the year of the Iraq and Bosnian Wars, to claim that a bellicose national poet had saturated the consciousness of the English-speaking empire.[2] At certain times, his texts have indeed done that, and

---

[1] J. MacIntyre, 'Shakespeare and the battlefield: tradition and innovation in battle scenes', *Theatre Survey* 23 (1982), 31–44.
[2] Gary Taylor, 'Cry havoc', www.theguardian.com/stage/2003/apr/05/theatre.classics.

war has been glamorized on stage and screen. However, directors, very properly, can and do argue from either side. Sometimes from both: it was, in fact, in 2003 that Nicholas Hytner directed *Henry V* in modern-dress at the National Theatre, with a black actor, Adrian Lester, as the King. As Michael Billington wrote:

Hytner's intentions are clear from the start: to undercut the rhetorical glamour surrounding war. William Gaunt's pragmatic Archbishop of Canterbury has prepared fat dossiers supporting Henry's dubious claim to the French throne. No sooner has Penny Downie's cardiganed Chorus told us 'Now all the youth of England are on fire' than we cut to the pub where Nym zaps TV channels, preferring the snooker to the king's bellicose warmongering.[3]

Charles Spence, however, saw it differently, perhaps because of the use of a television screen: 'The battle scenes are both deafening and thrilling, and with inventive use of live video, the production also shows how war has become a media event, with Henry's big moments projected on to a screen at the back of the stage.'[4] There is a counter-argument to this: screen depiction onstage turns war into theatre or a kind of media exhibition, and some members of the audience may have been turned off by what could easily be read as an opportunistic public relations stunt on the part of Harry.

Shakespeare, although dramatizing many *wars*, did not always place extended *battles* at the centre of, or as the climax to, his works. In *Henry V*, Agincourt occurs in Act 4 and not Act 5. Moreover, montage techniques often strip away both skirmishes and glory: at Harfleur, in Act 3, Shakespeare cuts quickly from Harry's fustian oration ('Once more into the breach ... ' (3.1.1ff.)), first to a sequence in 3.2 involving Falstaff's sad relics, Pistol and his crew, then to another, in the next scene, giving us a report on the state of the union by showing the giddy minds of an Englishman, a Welshman, an Irishman and a Scotsman. Harry re-appears to deliver a huffing speech (3.3.84ff.), supercharged with threats of weaponized rape against the people of Harfleur, a tirade that seems to reveal a lot about himself. There is little or no actual *fighting*. (Harfleur, of

course, can be spectacular: at the time of the Second Boer War (1899–1902), and regularly thereafter annually on St George's Day, Sir Frank Benson, who played the King, pole-vaulted in full armour on to the city walls.) Shakespeare, however, wanted not just to show war but also to anatomize the politics of war and the make-up of men of war. After his improbable victory at Agincourt, Henry claims the victory was not his but God's: in 1975, in Terry Hands's production in Stratford, Henry's men fell to their knees not in gratitude but, as I read it, in terror. Texts are open to directorial choices, and performances to the readings of individual spectators.

The quotation in my title comes from Jasper Mayne's posthumous tribute to Ben Jonson, which appeared in *Jonsonus Virbius* in 1638. 'Thou laidst no sieges to the music-room': the implication is that music-rooms, in some playhouses at least, were part of the structure aloft, which also accommodated upper stages.

So, let's start with sieges. These presumably entailed scaling-ladders: we find them in the stage directions to the scene depicting the recapture of Orléans in *1 Henry VI* (2.1.7 SD)[5] and, in the Folio text, at the siege of Harfleur in *Henry V* (Folio 3.1.0 SD). However, although Henslowe lists no ladders in his 1598 inventory of properties, it is highly likely that, for these scenes at least, scaling-ladders were used to reach the stage balconies of the Rose and (possibly) the Globe.[6]

There is in fact no mention of a 'music-room' in a stage direction before the publication of a text that appeared some twenty-five years after Shakespeare's early histories. This is *A Chaste Maid in Cheapside* of 1613: '*there is a sad song in the*

---

3  Michael Billington, 'Henry V', *Guardian*, 14 May 2003.
4  Charles Spencer, 'A tale for our time summons the blood', *Telegraph*, 15 May 2003.
5  Quotations from the three parts of *Henry VI* are taken from the Hattaway editions for the New Cambridge Shakespeare, 3 vols. (Cambridge, 1990–3).
6  Oxford conjectures that they would have been required at the beginning of 1.4 of *Cor.*

*music-room'* (4.4.0 SD).[7] (A slight problem: 'room' could just possibly mean any space where music was performed rather than a designated onstage 'box'.) *A Chaste Maid*, according to its title page, was acted by the Lady Elizabeth's Men at the Swan, a public amphitheatre playhouse. De Witt's well-known sketch of the Swan suggests that the music-room could have been on the balcony or, conceivably, in the hut. At the Globe, however, and other amphitheatre playhouses, music, for emblematic scenes and for songs – as well, as we shall see, for sound effects – seems to have been performed 'within'; at the Blackfriars, the balcony was used. Possibly, after the King's Men had acquired that playhouse, music was played 'aloft' at the Globe as well.[8] However, both music-rooms and upper stages may have been equipped with windows, useful for balcony scenes, but presumably obstructive in siege scenes.

Not all London playhouses were amphitheatres: the newly excavated Curtain, in particular, was rectangular. Heather King, lead archaeologist for Museum of London Archaeology's excavation, reports a stage 14 metres wide, with a passage underneath. She has pointed out remarkable similarities between its footprint and that of the Corral de Comedias in Almagro which also has a traverse passage under the stage and which shows boxes in the balcony that could have been music-rooms (Figure 3). Both playhouses have soak-aways in front of the stage and under the end of the roof.[9]

Now I speculate that that wide but shallow stage would have suited the single combats that are salient features of two Curtain plays, *Romeo and Juliet* and *1 Henry IV* (see the Battle of Shrewsbury sequence). Could they (and *Henry V* – if its prologue derives from a Globe revival) have been written with that playhouse in mind?

Sieges, therefore, are and were simply staged – easily accommodated by the basic stage structures of both public and private playhouses, and sometimes requiring fewer players than hand-to-hand conflicts between two armies. Two levels might amplify the effect of a 'skirmish' or 'excursion', or the penetration of a walled city, presumably after an attack on the stage doors. However, in Henslowe's inventory of properties, one entry lists a 'wheel and frame in *The Siege of London*',[10] a lost Admiral's Men play of the 1580s or early 1590s, possibly the basis of *1 & 2 Edward IV*, and probably by Heywood and others.[11] All we can do is speculate: the play's title suggests this could have been a pulley device for use in a siege, a siege catapult (known variously as an 'onager' or 'magonel'), or even a wheeled siege tower, known, in the Middle Ages, as a 'belfry' (*OED*, belfry 1). (They could also have been instruments of torture or execution.)

As for the rest of the *frons scenae*, in *1 Henry VI*, the scene before Orléans for the French Gunner and his Boy, there are references to 'yonder tower' (1.4.11) and, in a stage direction, to 'turrets' (1.4.21 SD):

[GUNNER] . . . The Princes espyals have informed me,
    How the English, in the Suburbs close entrencht,
    Went through a secret Grate of Iron Barres,
    In yonder Tower, to ouer-peere, the Citie . . .
BOY. Father, I warrant you, take you no care,
    Ile neuer trouble you, if I may spye them.
Exit.
        *Enter Salisbury and Talbot on the Turrets,*
                *with others.*
(*1 Henry VI*, 1.4.8–11, 1.4.20–1 SD; TLN 472–88)[12]

---

7 Alan C. Dessen and Leslie Thomson, *A Dictionary of Stage Directions in English Drama, 1580–1642* (Cambridge, 1999), p. 148.

8 Richard Hosley, 'Was there a music-room in Shakespeare's Globe?', *Shakespeare Survey* 13 (1960), 113–23; Michael Dobson and Stanley Wells, eds., *The Oxford Companion to Shakespeare* (Oxford, 2001), p. 312; for music 'above' in other private playhouses, see Dessen and Thomson, *Dictionary*, p. 1.

9 See www.mola.org.uk/blog/curtain-theatre-citizens-playhouse-high-octane-drama.

10 Carol Chillington Rutter, ed., *Documents of the Rose Playhouse* (Manchester, 1999), p. 137.

11 Alfred Harbage, ed., *Annals of English Drama 975–1700*, 3rd edn (London, 1989), p. 78; however, it has been argued that the property referred to a well in *A Larum for London*, possibly the same play: see Laurie E. Maguire, 'A stage property in *A Larum for London*', *Notes and Queries* 231 (1986), 371–3. I owe the reference to Gabriel Egan.

12 All citations from the Folio were transcribed from Charlton Hinman, ed., *The Norton Facsimile: The First Folio of Shakespeare* (New York, 1968).

3 Corral de comedias de Almagro (*c.* 1628).

The words 'yonder Tower' and 'yonder Turret' also occur in 3.2 (lines 23 and 30), when Joan, in disguise, has entered the city gates of Rouen: they implicitly gloss the word '*top*', which occurs in the SD that marks Joan's entrance:

> *Enter Charles, Bastard, Alanson.*
> CHARLES. Saint *Dennis* blesse this happy Stratageme,
>   And once againe wee'le sleep secure in Roan.
> BASTARD. Here entred *Pucell*, and her Practisants:
>   Now she is there, how will she specifie?
>   Here is the best and safest passage in.
> REIG[NIER]. By thrusting out a Torch from yonder Tower,
>   Which once discern'd, shewes that her meaning is,
>   No way to that (for weaknesse) which she entred.
>     *Enter Pucell on the top, thrusting out a*
>        *Torch burning.*
> PUCELL. Behold, this is the happy Wedding Torch,
>   That ioyneth Roan vnto her Countreymen,
>   But burning fatall to the *Talbonites*.

> BASTARD. See Noble *Charles* the Beacon of our friend,
>   The Burning Torch in yonder Turret stands.
> CHARLES. Now shine it like a Commet of Reuenge,
>   A Prophet to the fall of all our Foes.
> REIG[NIER]. Deferre no time, delayes have dangerous ends,
>   Enter and cry, the Dolphin, presently,
>   And then doe execution on the Watch.
>                                          *Alarum.*
>   (*1 Henry VI*, 3.2.17 SD – 35 SD; TLN 1442–62)

A few lines later, Joan and others appear '*on the walls*' (3.2.40 SD) – this time, presumably, the balcony.[13] This encourages me to hypothesize that the 'top' was indeed not the tiring-house balcony but the

---

[13] In Marlowe, the Governor of Babylon appears '*on the walls*' in 5.1.0 of *2 Tamburlaine* (references to plays by Marlowe are taken from Christopher Marlowe, *Doctor Faustus and Other Plays*, ed. David Bevington and Eric Rasmussen (Oxford, 2008).

playhouse hut. It creates a simple special effect, but its theatricality was as important as any kind of lifelikeness.

Immediately after that, and after a second 'alarum', Talbot enters '*in an excursion*':

> *An Alarum. Talbot in an Excursion.*
> TALB. France, thou shalt rue this Treason with thy teares,
> If *Talbot* but suruiue thy Trecherie.
> *Pucell* that Witch, that damned Sorceresse,
> Hath wrought this Hellish Mischiefe vnawares,
> That hardly we escap't the Pride of France.
>
> *Exit.*
>
> *An Alarum: Excursions. Bedford brought*
> *in sicke in a Chayre*
> *Enter Talbot and Burgonie without: within,*
> *Charles, Bastard, and Reignier on the Walls.*
> PUCELL. God morrow Gallants, want ye Corn for Bread?
> I thinke the Duke of Burgonie will fast,
> Before hee'le buy againe at such a rate.
> 'Twas full of Darnell: doe you like the taste?
>
> (*1 Henry VI*, 3.2.36–44; TLN 1463–76)

Presumably he entered by one door, crossed the stage to exit from another, into an imagined town-space, whence he rescues a wounded Bedford. Hand-to-hand fighting does not have to be shown. I shall inspect several more examples of this theatrical trope.

As pitched fields were more difficult and were even disparaged, Shakespeare, like many before him, resorted to choric narration. The most conspicuous example is the depiction of the Battle of Towton, where anything between 2,800 and 28,000 men were killed.[14] After a brief skirmish between Richard of Gloucester and Clifford in *3 Henry VI* 2.4, most of what we see is what King Henry sees and meditates upon, and these moments are emblematic – the entrances of '*a son that hath killed his father, at one door*' and of '*a father [that hath killed his son at another door]*'.[15] After that, Clifford enters mortally wounded in 2.6 and dies onstage. Shakespeare uses the same device in 5.4 of *Troilus* – an off-stage battle with 'excursions' and with narration, in a very different key, from Thersites. However, the death of Hector and the preceding skirmishing is fully enacted. There is another version of choric narrative when we hear

of the defeat of Talbot and the cowardice of Sir John Fastolfe in a 32-line set speech by a messenger in *1 Henry VI* (1.1.108–40)

In the following scene, there is an example of what turns out to be that formulaic technique we have already encountered, an exit to an off-stage battle within followed by a re-entrance. I have some eight examples of this sort of thing. I wish, very tentatively to lay aside any hypothesis of a visible music-room and float the notion of a 'battle-box' – not a word to be found in the period, but possibly more useful in that it conjures an unseen off-stage area. How might that have functioned?

We see how it may have worked in 1.2 of *1 Henry VI*, the siege of Orléans:

> CHARLES. Sound, sound Alarum, we will rush on them.
> Now for the honour of the forlorne French:
> Him I forgiue my death, that killeth me,
> When he sees me goe back one foot, or flye.
>
> *Exeunt.*
>
> *Here Alarum, they are beaten back by the*
> *English, with great losse.*
> *Enter Charles, Alanson, and Reignier.*
> CHARLES. Who euer saw the like? What men haue I?
> Dogges, Cowards, Dastards: I would ne're haue fled,
> But that they left me 'midst my Enemies.
>
> (*1 Henry VI*, 1.2.18–24; TLN 212–21)

After marching proudly onto the stage with a drummer, and challenging the English besieging Orléans from off-stage, a stage direction marks an exeunt for the French leaders – i.e. to leave the stage, sallying forth from the imagined 'city' through a stage door representing a city gate. What follows is a stage direction: '*Here Alarum; they are beaten back* [onto the stage] *by the English, with great losse.*' Dialogue and stage directions indicate that again the fighting is to take place mainly off-stage, suggested by the alarum – probably the

---

[14] See 'The Towton Battlefield Archaeology Project' (http://towtonbattle.free.fr/index.php/re-interpretation).

[15] William Shakespeare, *The Third Part of King Henry VI*, ed. Michael Hattaway (Cambridge, 1993), 2.5.54 SD and 78 SD; see also 2.5.54 SD – 122 SDn., and p. 206 n.10.

sounds of trumpets, drums, clashing swords and battle cries. The *'great losse'* could be signified by walking wounded extras (1.2.21 SD). I see this as one sequence, which is why, unlike the Oxford editors, I did not begin a new scene here.

My next example is a very similar sequence in 2.3–4 of Marlowe's *1 Tamburlaine*, and again I question the decision of the Revels editor to introduce a new scene.

[TAMBURLAINE] *Vusumcasane and* techelles *come,*
　We are enough to scarre the enemy,
　And more than needs to make an Emperour.
　　*To the Battaile, and Mycetes comes out alone with*
　　*his Crowne in his hand, offering to hide it . . .*
MYCE. O Gods, is this Tamburlaine the thiefe,
　I marueile much he stole it not away,
　　*Sound trumpets to the Battell, and he runs in.*
　　　　(Marlowe, *1 Tamburlaine*, 2.3.63–2.4.0 SD
　　　　　　　and 2.4.40–41 SD)

Editors insert an 'Exeunt' for Tamburlaine and his henchmen at 2.3.65. This means that they move 'within', and Mycetes emerges from the off-stage battle with his crown. He is surprised by Tamburlaine, who takes and then gives back his crown. Mycetes does likewise: he *'runs in'* to join the off-stage fight: *'Sound trumpets to the battle, and he runs in'* (2.4.41 SD).

It seems the same 'Gestus' is quoted some 150 lines later: in 2.6–7.

[COSROE] . . . Then strike up Drum, and all the Starres that make
　The loathsome Circle of my dated life,
　Direct my weapon to his barbarous heart,
　That thus opposeth him against the Gods,
　And scornes the Powers that gouerne Persea.
　　*Enter to the Battell, & after the battell, enter Cosroe*
　　*wounded, Theridamas, Tamburlaine, Techelles,*
　　*Usumcasane, with others.*
COS. Barbarous and bloody Tamburlaine,
　Thus to deprive me of my crowne and life . . .
　　　　(Marlowe, *1 Tamburlaine*, 2.6.36–2.7.2)

Again, I would not start a new scene: Cosroe leads his troops to battle, is wounded, and re-enters, having been taken by Tamburlaine. Interestingly the SD reads *'Enter to the battle.'* The battle is off-stage – should editors, for modern readers, emend to *'Exeunt'*?

In 3.3 of *1 Tamburlaine*, a flyting match between Xenocrate and her maid Anippe, on the one hand, and Zabina and her maid Ebea, on the other, is interrupted by noises off, an off-stage battle:

ZEN[OCRATE]. Hearst thou Anippe, how thy drudge doth talk,
　And how my slaue, her mistresse menaceth.
　Both for their sucinesse shall be employed,
　To dresse the common souldiers meat and drink.
　For we will scorne they should come nere our selues.
ANIP[PE]. Yet sometimes let your highnesse send for them
　To do the work my chamber maid disdaines.
　　*They sound the battell within, and stay [cease] . . .*
　　　*To the battell againe.*
ZEN. By this the Turks lie weltring in their blood
　And tamburlaine is Lord of Affrica:
ZAB. Thou are deceiv'd, I heard the trumpets sound,
　As when my Emperor ouerthrew the Greeks:
　And led them Captiue into Affrica.
　Straight will I vse thee as thy pride deseruest:
　Prepare thy selfe to liue and die my slaue.
ZEN. If Mahomet should come from heauen and sweare,
　My royall Lord is slaine or conquered.
　Yet should he not perswade me otherwise.
　But that he that liues and will be Conquerour.
　　*Baiezeth flies, and he pursues him.*
　　*The battell short, and they enter,*
　　　*Baiazeth is ouercome.*
TAM. Now king of Bassoes, who is Conqueror?
BAI. Thou, by the fortune of this damned foile.
　　　　(Marlowe, *1 Tamburlaine*, 3.3.169–223)

Trumpet calls to battle sound intermittently throughout (*'stay'* in the first SD means 'cease'), until Bajazeth, pursued by Tamburlaine, enters from one door, flies across the stage and exits by the other.[16] He is brought back, having been overcome off-stage – although 'Baiazeth is ouercome' and the reference to the foil suggests the two kings might have entered to fight it out onstage.

---

[16] Something similar happens in *Edward II*, 4.5.0 SD; there, however, the direction stipulates 'flying *about* the stage'.

I conjecture, however, that the stage direction has become displaced and should have been printed four lines earlier. Zenocrate's four lines would make more sense if spoken while that fight takes place off-stage.

There is something similar in *Edward II*:

> [EDWARD] ... Soldiers, good hearts, defend your
> souueraignes right,
> For now, euen now, we march to make them stoope,
> Away.
>
>                      *Exeunt.*
>
> *Alarums, excursions, a great fight, and a retreate.*
> *Enter the King, Spencer the father, Spencer the sonne*
> *And the noblemen of the Kinges side.*
>
> EDW. Why doe we sound retreat? vpon them Lordes,
> This day I shall powre vengeance with my sword
> On those proud rebels that are vp in armes,
> And doe confront and countermaund their king.
>
>        (Marlowe, *Edward II*, 3.2.182–3.3.4)

I think the '*great fight*' would have been a '*great noise*', perhaps even '*loud music*', a phrase found in several stage directions.[17] '*A retreat*' is a very frequent direction for trumpet or drum sounds played within to signify a turn in an unseen battle.[18]

One further example from the Henry VI plays – here Edward IV is asleep in his 'tent':

> *Enter three Watchmen to guard the Kings Tent ...*
> *Enter Warwicke, Clarence, Oxford, Somerset,*
> *and French Souldiers, silent all.*
>
> WARW. This is his Tent, and see where stand his Guard:
> Courage my Masters: Honor now, or neuer:
> But follow me, and *Edward* shall be ours.
> I. WATCH. Who goes there?
> 2. WATCH. Stay, or thou dyest.
>
> *Warwicke and the rest cry all, Warwicke,*
> *Warwicke,and set vpon the Guard, who flye, crying, Arme,*
> *Arme,*
> *Warwicke and the rest following them.*
> *The Drumme playing, and Trumpet sounding.*
> *Enter Warwicke, Somerset, and the rest, bringing the King*
> *out in his Gowne, sitting in a Chaire: Richard*
> *and Hastings flyes ouer the stage.*
>
> SOM. What are they that flye there?
>
>        (*3 Henry VI*, 4.3.0 SD, 4.3.22 SD – 28;
>                 TLN 2220, 2246–60)

Warwick and his faction have entered from one stage door and presumably pause before a curtained discovery space or a tiring-house entrance, behind which the scuffle takes place that leads to the capture of Edward offstage. He is brought out downstage, possibly bound to the chair, while, upstage, Richard of Gloucester and Hastings escape by running across the stage to the other stage door. (There do seem to have occasionally been tents on stage: for example, in the sequence before the Battle of Bosworth in *Richard III* and for Achilles and Patroclus in 3.3 of *Troilus and Cressida*. Thomas Platter, from Basel, saw tents (*Zelten*) on stage at the Globe playhouse in 1599.[19])

In *2 Henry VI* 4.3, a stage direction, which probably derives from an authorial manuscript,[20] is ambivalent: it is difficult to decide whether the Staffords are slain on- or off-stage:

> CADE. But then are we in order, when we are most out
> of order. Come, march forward.
> *Alarums to the fight, wherein both the Staffords are slaine.*
> *Enter Cade and the rest.*
> CADE. Where's Dicke, the Butcher of Ashford?
>
>       (*2 Henry VI*, 4.2.164–4.3.1; TLN 2509–13)

However, in the light of the Marlovian examples, I hypothesise that by '*Alarums to the fight*' we should understand '*Sound trumpets. Exeunt to the fight*'. This hypothesis is supported by Cade's re-entrance.

Onstage fighting was again eschewed at the opening of 4.7:

> CADE. Come, then let's go fight with them:
> But first, go and set London Bridge on fire,
> And if you can, burne downe the Tower too.
> Come, let's away.
>
>                    *Exeunt omnes.*
> *Alarums. Mathew Goffe is slain, and all the rest.*
> *Then enter Iacke Cade, with his Company.*
>
> CADE. So, sirs: now go some and pull down the Sauoy:
> Others to'th Innes of Court, downe with them all.
>
>      (*2 Henry VI*, 4.6.11 – 4.7.2 SD; TLN 2629–36)

---

[17] Dessen and Thomson, *Dictionary,* p. 147.
[18] Dessen and Thomson, *Dictionary,* pp. 179–80.
[19] Michael Hattaway, *Elizabethan Popular Theatre: Plays in Performance* (London, 1982), p. 38.
[20] Hattaway, *Popular Theatre,* p. 215.

Matthew Gough was one of the King's commissioners: Lord Scales orders him to take on the rebels in 4.5, but he does not appear in the play. After an offstage skirmish, a body with a livery suggesting an association with Lord Scales may have been brought out, along with sundry severed property heads impaled on pikes. Alternatively, Gough and others may have been flushed out onto the stage and finished off there. In my 1991 edition, I followed Capell and started a new scene here. Now I think I was wrong to do so.

Talbot does fight onstage in *1 Henry VI*. We cannot, of course, recover the impact of staged battles in Shakespeare's time. Nashe wrote about Talbot on stage, not about his *fighting* but about the great lord *dying*: was this admiration, possibly a puff for the play to which he may have contributed himself, or was he mocking the desire of spectators to encounter lifelikeness in the playhouse?

How would it have joyed brave Talbot (the terror of the French) to think that after he had lyne two hundred years in his tomb, he should triumph again on the stage, and have his bones new embalmed with the tears of ten thousand spectators at least (at several times), who, in the tragedian that represents his person, imagine they behold him fresh bleeding.[21]

Shakespeare wrote a very distinctive death scene or 'passion' for the English champion (4.7) – distinctive because it is in couplets. Interestingly, Gary Taylor ascribed that passage to Shakespeare.[22] So might there be a privy note of irony in Nashe's praise?

As well as narration and the alternation of 'within' and 'without' sequences, we find high levels of stylization, or minimalization. Another example comes in 3.3 of *1 Henry VI*:

PUCELL. Your Honors shall perceiue how I will worke,
To bring this matter to the wished end.
*Drumme sounds a farre off.*
Hearke, by the sound of Drumme you may perceiue
Their Powers are marching vnto Paris-ward.
*Here sound an English March*
There goes the *Talbot*, with his Colours spred,
And all the Troupes of English after him.

*French March*

Now in the Rereward comes the Duke and his:
Fortune in fauor makes him lagge behinde.
Summon a Parley, we will talke with him.

*Trumpets sound a Parley*
CHARLES. A Parley with the Duke of Burgonie . . .
(*1 Henry VI*, 3.3.27–36; TLN 1612–25)

The presence of three contesting armies is heard off-stage. It is a kind of musical battle between two tunes: a French march was, according to Dekker, slower than an English one.[23]

There is a significant little *mis en abîme*, 3.5 of *Richard III*, where the Dukes of Gloucester and Buckingham pretend to be protecting an invisible castle from imaginary enemies:

*Enter the Lord Mayor*
RICHARD GLOUCESTER (*aside to Buckingham*)
Here comes the Mayor.
BUCKINGHAM (*aside to Richard*)
Let me alone to entertain him. – Lord Mayor –
RICHARD GLOUCESTER (*calling as to one within*)
Look to the drawbridge there!
BUCKINGHAM Hark, a drum!
RICHARD GLOUCESTER (*calling as to one within*)
Catesby, o'erlook the walls!
BUCKINGHAM Lord Mayor, the reason we have sent –
RICHARD GLOUCESTER Look back, defend thee! Here are enemies.
BUCKINGHAM God and our innocence defend and guard us.
*Enter [Sir William Catesby] with Hastings' head*
RICHARD GLOUCESTER O, O, be quiet! It is Catesby.
CATESBY Here is the head of that ignoble traitor,
The dangerous and unsuspected Hastings.
(*Richard III*, 3.5.11 SD – 22)[24]

---

21 Thomas Nashe, *The Works of Thomas Nashe*, ed. Ronald Brunlees McKerrow and Frank Percy Wilson, 5 vols. (Oxford, 1958), vol. 1, 212.
22 Gary Taylor, 'Shakespeare and others: the authorship of *1 Henry VI*', *Medieval and Renaissance Drama in England* 7 (1995), 145–205.
23 William Shakespeare, *Henry V*, ed. Gary Taylor, The Oxford Shakespeare (Oxford, 1982), 3.3.32 SDn.
24 I reprint a modernized text as F's SDs are very scanty for this play within a play.

4 The Entertainment at Elvetham (1575).

Various things are going on here: perhaps Shakespeare is invoking an iconic tradition, England as a castle, as depicted at the Entertainment at Elvetham (Figure 4).

Perhaps the scene is metatheatrical: Shakespeare, without using the balcony or stage doors, can demonstrate that war, for dissimulating politicians, is a kind of theatrical game. The scene is the obverse of 'Pyramus and Thisbe': there spectators mock amateur players for trying to establish illusion. Here players mock onstage spectators who are frustrated by having no validating images to sustain their credulousness.

However, it is obvious that the playing companies did have the wherewithal for battle sequences. Henslowe's inventory of properties lists a good variety of martial accoutrements: eight lances, eight 'vizards' (which could have been either military visors or masks for courtly entertainments), one long sword, one buckler, one copper and four wooden targets (light and round small shields or bucklers), one 'greve armer' (which I take to be armour for a governor or sheriff), one helmet with a dragon, one shield with three lions, and seventeen foils.[25] Only one military sword, however, but fighting with lances was described in fencing manuals. Moreover, it is notable that 'foils' occur in only three stage directions in Dessen and Thomson. Sword-play sequences, as in *Romeo and Juliet*, obviously allowed those players who, like Richard Tarlton, had been allowed as Masters of Fence to show off their skills.[26] Fencing was both a form of sport and a skill for combat, and Shakespeare creates notable moments of shock, in *Romeo and Juliet* and *Hamlet*, when one turns to the other. What is notable is that the weapons of choice for early modern English soldiers, longbows and their arrows, scarcely appear – except in *Titus Andronicus* when the crazed hero shoots arrows

---

[25] Rutter, *Documents*, pp. 135–7.
[26] Hattaway, *Popular Theatre*, p. 63; Robert Eustis Morsberger, *Swordplay and the Elizabethan and Jacobean Stage* (Salzburg, 1974).

into the heavens. These are not weapons for the stage. Nor is there much armour for men at arms.

To return to swords, Dessen and Thomson have located 375 examples. We have to remember that swords were often worn as costume properties in civilian life to indicate rank, but a large number indicate mood ('with sword drawn') or are 'as froms': 'as from battle', for example. Presumably many players themselves owned swords, or at least daggers or knives.

This list must be supplemented by the table of references to stage blood drawn up by Lucy Munro, most of which refer to bloodied garments or weapons.[27] From this, we may gather that blood, like a riding crop, was often an 'as from property': as from a fight, as from horseback. Textual skimpiness makes certainty impossible. In *Coriolanus*, we read, '*Enter Martius bleeding, assaulted by the enemy*' (1.5.32 SD): does this mean 'being' or 'having been' assaulted? However, there is a note of '3 vials of blood and a sheep's gather [heart, liver, and lungs]' in the 'plot' of *The Battle of Alcazar* (c. 1589), and of '*A little bladder of vinegar pricked*' in *Cambises* (c. 1561).[28] That said, explicit instructions for filled bladders are very rare indeed, and are too easily linked to common stage practice. I feel, moreover, that 'cultural evidence' for stage practice – critical gestures towards the sensationalism of bloody executions and their aftermaths as evidence for *mentalités* that took pleasure in grisliness on stage – are also too readily made.

So, although all these weapons would have been available to Shakespeare, after *H6* and *R3* when he and his company were at the Rose, he does not seem to have used them much in battles, as opposed to single combats. There is a similar kind of theatrical synecdoche in 5.3 of *1 Henry VI*:

PUCELLE ... Now France, thy glory droopeth to the
    dust.                               *Exit.*
   *Excursions. Burgundie and Yorke fight hand to*
            *hand. French flye.*
YORKE. Damsell of France, I thinke I haue you fast ...
            (*1 Henry VI,* 5.3.29–30; TLN 2659–62)

After the scene in which the fiends leave Joan La Pucelle and she exits, proclaiming the fall of France, the battle, between the French and Burgundians on one hand and the English on the other, narrows down to a hand-to-hand fight between Burgundy and York. York pursues Burgundy off-stage where he takes Joan prisoner and drags her back out.

*2 Henry VI* draws to an end at the first Battle of St Albans. Shakespeare shows a series of hand-to-hand combats: between Cade and Iden (4.10), York and Old Clifford (5.2), and Richard of Gloucester and Somerset (5.2) – larger contests are signalled by alarums and excursions.

The whole of the Battle of Bosworth at the end of *Richard III* is virtually violence-free and is conjured by three stage directions: '*Alarum. Excursions. Enter CATESBY*', '*Alarums. Enter RICHARD*', and then this:

*Alarum, Enter Richard and Richmond, they fight, Richard
is slaine.*
*Retreat, and Flourish. Enter Richmond, Derby bearing the
Crowne, with diuers other Lords.*
    (*Richard III,* 5.8.0 SD (Folio); TLN 3841–4)

Richard and Richmond come on, presumably from 'several' doors, and the end of the battle and the end of the Wars of the Roses focuses down on a single combat – in effect, a duel. A duel, of course, is a kind of trial. In both Hall and Holinshed this encounter takes place in the midst of clashes between the armies of the King and 3,000 of Sir William Stanley's men.[29] However, why does Richmond go off only to re-enter? I conjecture that, as to the corpse of Hotspur at the end of the Battle of Shrewsbury in *1 Henry IV*, some kind of beastliness may have been done to Richard's corpse before it was dragged off.

[27] Farah Karim-Cooper and Ryan Nelson, *Shakespeare's Globe Theatre History Seminar. Stage Blood: A Roundtable* (London, 2006), www.shakespearesglobe.com/uploads/files/2015/02/seminar_stage_blood_roundtable_2006.pdf.

[28] See Karim-Cooper and Nelson, *Shakespeare's Globe.*

[29] W. G. Boswell-Stone, ed., *Shakespeare's Holinshed: The Chronicle and the Historical Plays Compared* [1896], (New York, 1966), pp. 419–20.

My main conclusion from all of this is confirmed by Dessen and Thomson's entry for 'battle' in the *Dictionary of Stage Directions*. This reveals that many more battles were reduced, represented iconically or by sound effects. I suggest that these 'battles' were alike in mode to 'discovery' scenes, revealed within the tiring-houses of public playhouses. They were ritualized and constituted a kind of theatrical shorthand, an image rather than a spectacle of battle. The function of battle scenes was diegetic rather than mimetic. In that they were often heard rather than seen, they were like programme music: it was pictorial sound that rendered whatever degree of lifelikeness they exhibited.

*The Famous Victories of Henry V* is typical: there are staccato and skimpy stage directions for the Battle of Agincourt. The text is believed to derive from a memorial reconstruction for the Queen's Men,[30] which was later passed to the Chamberlain's Men.[31] Yet again, the battle takes place off-stage, signified by drumming and shouts, by the soldiers and by Mountjoy, from within what I described as the 'battle box':

HEN.5. Then is it good time no doubt,
For all England praieth for vs:
What my Lords, me thinks you looke cheerfully vpon me?
Why then with one voice and like true English hearts,
With me throw vp your caps, and for England,
Cry S. George, and God and S. George helpe vs.
Strike Drummer.

*Exeunt omnes.*
*The French men crie within, S. Dennis, S. Dennis, Mount Ioy S. Dennis.*
*The Battell.*
*Enters King of England, and his Lords.*
(*The Famous Victories of Henry the Fifth*, 1598, Sig F1r)[32]

So, here, there is a mixture of special effects and action – little more than a brawl ridiculous, it would seem. Sidney was not impressed, but remained tolerant of this kind of thing: 'Two armies fly in, represented by four swords and bucklers, and then what hard heart will not take it for a pitched field.'[33]

Battles were often rendered more by sounds from 'within' than by what was seen. In their 'battle' entry, Dessen and Thomson list some sixteen plays – five by Marlowe or Shakespeare in which 'battles' were sounded 'within'. It was the plethora of sound effects, not endless stage skirmishing, that caused *1 Henry VI* to be disparaged by Maurice Morgann, who dismissed it as 'that Drum-and-trumpet Thing'.[34] We know that 'chambers' were used in *2 Henry VI* in the scene in which Suffolk is captured by pirates (4.1). In the expanded stage direction that heads the scene in the quarto edition we read '*Alarms within, and the chambers be discharged, like as it were a fight at sea . . .*'. 'Chambers' were small cannon used for salutes and in playhouses for sound effects.

In *3 Henry VI*, 5.4, the course and final turn-around of the battle of Tewkesbury, a huge defeat for the Lancastrians, is suffused by sound effects, including those made by chambers: '*Alarmes to the battell, Yorke flies, then the chambers be discharged. Then enter the king, Cla[rence]. & Glo[ucester]. & and the rest, & make a great shout, and crie. for Yorke, for Yorke, and then the Queene is taken, & the prince, & Oxf[ord]. & Sum[merset]. and then sound and enter all againe*' (*3 Henry VI* ['*The True Tragedy . . .* '], octavo, 5.4.82 SD). This is a bit like watching a football match from outside the ground. In *Henry VIII* or '*All is True*', we read '*chambers discharged*' to magnify the drum and trumpet that sounded to signify the entrance of the King and his fellow masquers ('*All is True*', 1.4.49 SD). As Andrew Gurr reminds us, 'It is now a cliché that Elizabethan audiences were hearers before they were spectators.'[35]

[30] Laurie E. Maguire, *The 'Bad' Quartos and their Contexts* (Cambridge, 1996), pp. 324–5.
[31] Andrew Gurr, *The Shakespearian Playing Companies* (Oxford, 1996), pp. 76 and 280.
[32] Transcribed from *The Famous Victories of Henry the Fifth 1598*, ed. Chiaki Hanabusa, *The Malone Society Reprints* (Manchester, 2006).
[33] Sir Philip Sidney, *An Apology for Poetry*, ed. Geoffrey Shepherd (Manchester, 1973), p. 134.
[34] *An Essay on the Dramatic Character of Sir John Falstaff* [1777], in David Nichol Smith, *Eighteenth Century Essays on Shakespeare*, 2nd (revised) edn (Oxford, 1963), p. 226.
[35] Andrew Gurr, *The Shakespeare Company, 1594–1642* (Cambridge, 2004), p. 47.

In a single sequence in *Edward I*, probably staged by the Queen's Men in 1591, Peele deployed just about every trick: '*Alarum, a charge, after long skirmish, assault, flourish. Enter King Edward with his train and Baliol prisoner*' (2207). The skirmish was embedded in conventional musical devices: alarums were generally sounded by drums; charges, assaults and flourishes by cornets or trumpets.[36]

Indeed, the Mayne quotation does suggest that the 'wiser sort', including Christopher Marlowe, were not entirely drawn to scenes in which heroic men fought it out on stage. *1* and *2 Tamburlaine*, which we may remember as epic in scope and subject, actually contain very few examples of stage fighting – although fight scenes might have been included among the 'fond and frivolous gestures', 'purposely omitted and left out' according to the printer.[37] (One may have eluded him: at *1 Tamburlaine*, 5.1.401 SD, we read, '*They sound to* [commence] *the battle, and* TAMBURLAINE *enjoys the victory. After,* ARABIA *enters wounded.*') But this is ambivalent. Tamburlaine may have stood outside the stage door while his army fought within.

All this notwithstanding, not surprisingly in 1616 Ben Jonson loftily disparaged pitched battles (along with descending thrones and sound effects, and short swords rather than long swords):

> . . . with three rusty swords,
> And help of some few foot and half-foot words,
> Fight over York and Lancaster's long jars,
> And in the tiring house bring wounds to scars.
>
> (*Everyman in His Humour*, Prologue, 9–12)

But, if this is partly a gentle gird at Shakespeare, he was pushing at an open door: is there not a touch of self-disparagement in the Chorus to Act 4 of *Henry V*?

> And so our scene must to the battle fly,
> Where O for pity, we shall much disgrace,
> With four or five most vile and ragged [damaged] foils,
> Right ill-disposed in brawl ridiculous,
> The name of Agincourt.
>
> (48–52)

In *Henry V*, Shakespeare artfully segues from narration to action. At the end of the third chorus,

we hear, 'the nimble gunner / With linstock now the devilish cannon touches . . . ', then comes the stage direction '*Alarum, and chambers go off*' (3.0.31–32 SD), sandwiched between those two lines and the end of his sentence – 'And down goes all before them' (3.0.34). (It seems a bit literal to infer that the Chorus is 'clearly identified as present and thus involved in the action described'.[38])

The quoted sound is a nice device, but it frames a staging crux. Did Henry and his men enter through the yard, equipped with the scaling ladders called for in the F version, en route to a siege to the music-room? This was long ago suggested by Nevill Coghill.[39] Andrew Gurr asserts that such entrances, in contrast to recurrent practice at Shakespeare's Globe, were not made.[40] This second '*alarum*' is the first bookend to Henry's 'Once more into the breach, dear friends', the other being '*Alarum, and chambers go off*' (3.1.34 SD). That comes just after the lines: ' . . . upon this charge / Cry, "God for Harry! England and Saint George!"'. I am inclined to take 'charge' as a trumpet sound; Gary Taylor reads it as an action.[41] There seems no point in carrying on scaling ladders without using them, but possibly they were carried out through one of the side entrances.

So, who's right? All we can say is that Harry may have laid siege to a music-room – if there was one at the Globe.

The thrust of my argument is that battles were probably less prominent in the histories than we think. Maybe some of us have our minds stuffed

---

[36] Dessen and Thomson, *Dictionary*, pp. 3–4, 17, and 94; *OED* does not record 'assault' as a musical device.

[37] Christopher Marlowe, *Tamburlaine the Great*, ed. J. S. Cunningham (Manchester, 1981), p. 111.

[38] William Shakespeare, *King Henry V*, ed. Emma Smith, Shakespeare in Production (Cambridge, 2002), p. 138.

[39] William Shakespeare, *King Henry V*, ed. Gary Taylor, The Oxford Shakespeare (Oxford, 1982), p. 157n.

[40] Andrew Gurr, 'Enter through the Yard?', *Around the Globe: The Magazine of Shakespeare's Globe* (1999), 32–3.

[41] William Shakespeare, *Henry V*, The Oxford Shakespeare (Oxford, 1982), 3.1.34.1n.

with the balletic fights seen through clouds of stage mist that were a cliché of RSC productions in the 1960s and 1970s.

When we think of battles on screen we inevitably think of Olivier's *Henry V*. When I first saw it, as a boy, my favourite bit was a couple of seconds of sound from the Agincourt sequence, a wonderful zing and phew as the English shot their arrows into the air in a shot worthy of Eisenstein, one to which Kenneth Branagh paid homage in his screen version of the play.

I have recently revisited the film. The battle is almost as good as I remember, but I was also interested in the production design. Olivier drew upon a range of genres and styles and generated not just illusionistic sequences but also varieties of pastiche. The visual tropes of medieval illuminations inform its portrayal of the countryside; the music, by William Walton, moves from early modern dance (played by a full symphony orchestra) to Elgaresque religiosity.

One detail caught my eye: a procession of the seasons at the end, doubtless set up by the Art Director, Paul Sheriff. First, a glorious summer evening after Agincourt (Figure 5):

The film then abandons battle for a montage of musical merriment and painterly cheer. Cut to a picture-postcard scene of a snow-covered village where Fluellen humiliates Pistol – the wintriness is a fit setting for Pistol's narrative of his Doll's death from the pox 9 (Figure 6).

From this icy interlude, we cut to a shot of a painted castle bathed in glorious spring sunshine; inside, the court are singing merry roundelays (Figure 7).

The scene begins to cloud with Burgundy's lament for the state of France, abandoned by Peace, accompanied by a flashback to panning autumnal shots of the ruined countryside (Figure 8).

Yet this is but a contrasting prelude to a completely unironical treatment of the handfasting of Henry and Katherine. It turns into a kind of apotheosis, with musicians visible aloft (Figure 9).

5 *Henry V* directed by Laurence Olivier (1944), *Summer: After Agincourt* (4.8), at 1:42:44.

6  *Henry V* directed by Laurence Olivier (1944), *Winter: The Fluellen and Pistol sequence* (5.1) at 1:42:53.

7  *Henry V* directed by Laurence Olivier (1944), *Spring: Henry and Charles* (5.2), at 1:48:37.

8  *Henry V* directed by Laurence Olivier (1944), *Autumn: Burgundy's speech* (5.2), at 1:51:43.

9  *Henry V* directed by Laurence Olivier (1944), *Apotheosis: After the Handfasting 1*, at 2:3:12.

10 *Henry V* directed by Laurence Olivier (1944), *Back at the Globe: Laurence Olivier and George Cole.*

Hal and Kate progress in matching robes, perhaps inspired by the gown worn by Spring/Flora in Botticelli's *Primavera*, to chairs of state in the 'castle'.

All these morph into their equivalents back in the Globe. Kate is now played by a 'boy actress' (George Cole) (Figure 10).

If Agincourt is the political climax, the marriage is its moral or mythical one. It is all oddly Spenserian: the play's content resembles what Spenser called 'fierce warres and faithfull loues',[42] and Olivier's film opens into the landscape of *The Faerie Queene*, even offering a demonstration of constancy in mutability.

---

[42] Edmund Spenser, *The Faerie Queene*, ed. A. C. Hamilton (London, 1977), 1 Proem, 1.9.

# SHAKESPEARIAN NARRATIVES OF WAR: TRAUMA, REPETITION AND METAPHOR

## ROS KING

This article concerns the repetition of war motifs in Shakespeare's writing, and the uses and meanings to which the plays are currently being put in therapeutic interventions with veterans suffering from post-traumatic stress disorder (PTSD). It is part of two larger projects: on repetition and on applied arts. The emotional and cognitive work that veterans bring to performing Shakespeare, and the intense enjoyment and camaraderie they derive from the experience, are exceptionally moving to behold. But the juxtaposition of their modern stories with the stories that Shakespeare is telling (and usually re-telling) also completes a circle of writing and interpretation. I argue that, in confronting stories that for many ex-servicemen often remain un-told, the veterans are tapping in to the very structure of the plays, and have something to offer both criticism and professional performance.

The evidence of war in Shakespeare's London was never far away. War manuals, mostly aimed at the armchair soldier, were pouring off the presses. And although Elizabeth was careful to keep England out of broader national involvement, there were Englishmen garrisoning a number of the Channel ports. Mercenaries and private soldiers, returning destitute and probably traumatized, constituted a social problem at home, becoming the subject of successive royal proclamations. They also provided inspiration for a number of memorable, dangerous characters on the stage. The villains Black Will and Shakebag in *Arden of Faversham*, a play in which Shakespeare may well have had a hand, are veterans of the defence of Boulogne,

which had haemorrhaged both men and money throughout the 1540s. Black Will excuses his current lifestyle by recourse to that trauma, explaining that his very survival had depended on 'theft' of food.[1] The play tellingly intermingles his continuing violent criminality with that of other, 'respectable', middle- and upper-class characters, who are making legal – but actually dishonest – fortunes, and need him as an enforcer.

Shakespeare's acknowledged creations, Pistol and Iago, likewise exhibit damaged psyches. Both are designated 'ancient' or ensign, the standard bearer of the regiment. In that very visible position, they would be a prime focus for enemy attack in any operation 'in the field', as Iago puts it (*Othello*, 1.1.21). But, as William Garrard explains in *The Arte of Warre* (1591), the ensign should also be the 'conserver' of the standards or 'general reputation of all the band and companie'.[2] The ensign's is therefore a potentially crippling level of responsibility, and both characters, in their different ways, fail to live up to it, even though the other military characters in their respective plays presume them to be both 'honest' and 'valiant'.[3]

---

[1] *Arden of Faversham*, in *A Woman Killed with Kindness and Other Domestic Plays*, ed. Martin Wiggins (Oxford, 2008), pp. 1–68; 2.18–24.

[2] William Garrard, *The Arte of Warre, . . . Corrected and Finished by Captaine Hitchcock* (London, 1591), p. 62. See Ros King, '"The Disciplines of War": Elizabethan war manuals and Shakespeare's tragicomic vision', in *Shakespeare and War*, ed. Ros King and Paul J. C. M. Franssen (London, 2008), pp. 15–29.

[3] See *Othello*, 2.3.6, 326; *Henry V*, 3.6.12–17.

## PTSD AND COGNITIVE BEHAVIOURAL THERAPIES

Because of improved medical treatment, increasing numbers of people are surviving profound physical injury, but with equally profound, continuing and intransigent mental conditions, for which various types of talking therapy have come to be seen as the best treatment. There is now a large body of literature on the treatment of PTSD through different forms of Cognitive Behavioural Therapy (CBT), including narrative therapy.[4] There are variations on the theme, but the narration by the patient of his or her own life choices and life events before and after the trauma is seen to help that person articulate the things that go on to make them *as a person*. It is designed to let them see that the events that trouble them, the traumatic problem itself, is *not* them. The narrative, it is claimed, externalizes the problem, and enables it to be shared with others:

Telling your story and enacting your story about your fears and your regrets, and so on, makes an internal stage external and it is then witnessed by the group and it is no longer your story – it belongs to the group and they feel relief and they feel they've dropped it and they can let go so that they can use the energy to get on with their lives.[5]

There are numerous accounts in the specialist literature that movingly describe the use of such therapy with traumatized children, veterans and other mental patients. There are now, likewise, a wealth of papers on drama therapy, music therapy, dance therapy and art therapy, many published in the journal *The Arts in Psychotherapy,* and mostly arguing along similar lines. Arts therapies, however, do not have the persuasive big bucks behind them of big pharma, or the influence of established psychiatric services. Assumptions by service providers, and in society more generally, about the frilly nature of the arts, combined with the difficulty of supplying large-scale, statistical, quantitative, randomized controlled trial assessment of arts interventions, mean that practitioners are continually on the back foot, trying to argue again (and again) for the value of what they do, according to the standards used for measuring pharmacological symptom control. By its very nature, participation in an arts event involves one or two professional practitioners and a handful of clients. Writing it up is more 'anecdotal' than 'scientific', and the result tends to be read only by other practitioners in that particular arts area. Hard-pressed institutions on inadequate budgets are inevitably most concerned with management.

It is not, of course, the function of the arts to supply symptom control; we should also remember that neither should symptom control be equated with 'cure'. There is, however, 40,000 years of evidence of the human need to make art, perhaps 60,000 years if the recent re-dating of cave handprints as Neanderthal is accepted.[6] So the real question is not 'To what extent does this or that arts intervention result in a reduction of symptoms?', but 'What is it about participation in this or that arts intervention that the human being, as a person, values?'[7] Qualitative assessments by the participants themselves constitute the only evidence for this.

## SHAKESPEARE'S NARRATIVES: REPETITION WITH DIFFERENCE

Narrative therapy derives partly from the work of various anthropologists working in the 1980s, who were interested in the stories that societies tell about themselves, and the way these are structured

---

4 See Martin Payne, *Narrative Therapy: Making Meaning, Making Lives* (London, 2006).

5 Patient interview with Marvin Westwood, cited in Michael Balfour, Marvin Westwood and Marla J. Buchanan, 'Protecting into emotion: therapeutic enactments with military veterans transitioning back into civilian life', *Research in Drama Education: The Journal of Applied Theatre and Performance* 19 (2014), 165–81.

6 The famous Lion Man statue found in the Ulm cave system is 40,000 years old, and there is research suggesting the artistic use by Neanderthals of pigments and perforated shells, but see Maxime Aubert, Adam Brumm and Jillian Huntley, 'Early dates for "Neanderthal cave art" may be wrong', *Journal of Human Evolution* 125 (2018), 215–17.

7 See Tia DeNora, 'Time after time: a Quali-T method for assessing music's impact on well-being', *International Journal of Qualitative Studies on Health and Well-Being* 8 (2013).

and, most importantly, repeated. In his edited collection of such essays, Edward Bruner argued, 'life experience is richer than discourse. Narrative structures organize and give meaning to experience, but there are always feelings and lived experience not fully encompassed by the dominant story.'[8] In the same volume, Clifford Geertz observed '[t]he wrenching question, sour and disabused, that Lionel Trilling somewhere quotes an eighteenth-century aesthetician as asking – "How Come It that we all start out Originals and end up Copies?" – finds ... an answer that is surprisingly reassuring: it is the copying that originates.'[9]

About 400 years earlier, Shakespeare was using both these principles in structuring his own narratives. Famously, he often borrowed a story but never borrowed a plot, and his play structures regularly interweave multiple similar but different stories, culled from a variety of sources. No doubt this habit of mind derives partly from his grammar school education devoted to the imitation of classical literary models, but it was a habit he manifested in different ways throughout his career. For instance, his re-use of the lock-out scene from Plautus's *Menaechmi* for the furtherance of a simple pretence in *The Taming of the Shrew* (5.1) becomes, in *The Comedy of Errors*, a *tour de force* of farce that derives from his other decision to double Plautus's single pair of twins (3.1). He had realized that the 'dominant story' is better understood when it is compared with other similar stories; and it is this realization that marks his 'originality'. It is this, too, which makes the plays reinterpretable and reusable over time, for spectators faced with multiple variations on a theme are thereby encouraged mentally to contribute their own additional, similar stories.

It is almost as if Shakespeare deliberately set himself an ongoing technical exercise to explore the number of ways in which a story, image or device can be repeated. Thus, Hamlet is only one of five young people in his play who have lost a father. The characteristic reactions to this loss by the other four (impetuous, revenging Laertes, mad Ophelia, war-mongering Fortinbras, and the 'painted tyrant', revenging Pyrrhus) are all aspects

of the characterization of Hamlet himself, who is also shocked that, unlike the player who recounts the story of Hecuba's loss of family, he cannot weep (2.2.550–82). These repetitions create the illusion of the complexity of Hamlet's character and, importantly, also contribute to the sense that there is a debate to be had about the appropriate response to the problem he faces. Hamlet might wish that he had Fortinbras's capacity to go to war, but we are not forced to agree with him; the captain's calculation – 'two thousand souls and twenty thousand ducats' for a patch of ground not worth farming – is a reminder of the futile cost of that action (*Hamlet* Q2, 4.4.11–16).

In *Henry IV*, the repetition with difference is of an entire play. The events of its two parts follow a broadly historical chronology, capitalizing on the repetitions and correspondences that the chroniclers had already used to structure their narratives, but the second part also replicates the dramaturgical shape and action of the first, albeit in a different key. Thus, in rewriting the jolly fat knight, originally named after the Lollard Sir John Oldcastle, as Falstaff, Shakespeare places Part 2's now tired, ageing character in a darker, more politic, more complex and uncertain world. Part 2 marks this transition with an extra scene, an Induction, with the allegorical character Rumour dressed in a gown painted 'full of tongues', stating that he has been spreading stories (his own 'fake news') about the outcome of the battle of Shrewsbury: 'from Rumour's tongues / They bring smooth comforts false, worse than true wrongs' (Induction, 39–40).

Part 1 had begun with King Henry reflecting on an earlier victory, but delaying a planned pilgrimage to give thanks in order to discipline his layabout son, Prince Harry. Part 2 correspondingly starts with Northumberland still shamming sickness so as to avoid going to reinforce the rebel cause,

[8] V. Turner and E. Bruner, eds., *The Anthropology of Experience* (Chicago, 1986). Cited in Michael White and David Epston, *Narrative Means to Therapeutic Ends* (New York, 1990), p. 143.

[9] Clifford Geertz, 'Making experiences, authoring selves', in Turner and Bruner, eds., *Anthropology of Experience,* cited in White and Epston, *Narrative Means*, p. 143.

before he learns that his own son, a hot-headed, warlike Harry (Hotspur), has been killed in the battle. Where Oldcastle had simply described his corrupt recruiting practices in a single speech (*1 Henry IV*, 4.2.10–46), Falstaff is given an entire lengthy scene (*2 Henry IV*, 3.2), not only to demonstrate these, but to expose the mendacity of the country justices by, ironically enough, telling us that they were not in their youth the rakehells they are now pretending they were. And, whereas in Part 1, Prince Henry is described as riding to Shrewsbury 'full of spirit as the month of May, / And gorgeous as the sun at midsummer' (4.2.102–3), now his brother, Prince John, tricks the rebels into disbanding their forces so that he can round up the ringleaders (*2 Henry IV*, 4.1). Across its varying scenes of elegy, pastoral, comedy, history and, yes, tragedy, the war in Part 2 is one of cold calculation.

The difficulty of knowing the truth of what happens in conflict, later described as the 'fog of war', is a recurring theme across Shakespeare's plays. The F text of *Henry V* shows Henry ordering the killing of prisoners in response to a report that the French are regrouping and about to attack. It is, perhaps, mitigated by the urgency of that situation. But, later, F confuses the events it has shown us: Gower and Fluellen are certain that Henry's order is given *after*, not before, he learns of the slaughter of the boys in the baggage train. That this honest and upright pair of English and Welsh soldiers *need* it to be a response to an enemy atrocity turns the whole sequence of events into an ethical issue for us to ponder. The Q version of the play reorders the scenes to remove the contradiction and thereby prevents the question. In F, the common soldier Michael Williams later poses a series of questions about the justness of Henry's entire military campaign. Henry (in disguise) makes a long obfuscatory answer, which Williams clearly feels has merely sidestepped his question. He is unable to identify quite how this happens – although for the rest of us it is a good lesson in the skilled politician's use of rhetoric – and his inchoate frustration has nowhere to go but to erupt in violence. Q again airbrushes the scene. It deprives Williams of his specifying name, elevating him to 'Lord', and, by combining different bits of dialogue, makes it appear that Henry's position is entirely endorsed by his troops (4.1.85–221, and Q equivalent).[10]

In *Macbeth*, Shakespeare's technical problem is to involve his audience in the psychologies of both tyrant and tyrannized. He does this by punctuating the play with a repetition of killings, each presented differently from the next. He manages, glosses and sanitizes them in order to manipulate audience response. After the witches have told us of a battle 'lost and won' (1.1.4), we see a poor, bloody, wounded soldier, but the reality of his wounds is subsumed in the way he relates the victory. He presents Macbeth's slaughter of his opponents as a neat unpicking of the human body, simply 'unseamed' from the 'nave to the chops', not eviscerated, with its guts mingling in the mud (1.2.22). The Macbeths will be unsettled by their killing of Duncan, and will be unable to get the sight of his body out of their minds. But for us, it is unseen offstage, and later beautifully, archetypally, religiously described by MacDuff as an 'anointed temple', its 'silver skin laced with golden blood' (2.3.67, 112). Later, the escape of the child Fleance, even though his father is hacked to death, permits us to feel some relief (3.3). We can even laugh as the murderers make possibly the worst bad joke in the whole of Shakespeare – '[w]hat, you egg! / Young fry of treachery!' – before sticking Macduff's young son in the ribs (4.2.84–5). The child may be a knowing brat, but he didn't deserve that, and neither does his mother, dragged off as she (no doubt) is to both rape and murder. As we may by now have realized, we have been made complicit. It puts us in a better position to appreciate the potential horror of Macduff's willingness to accept Malcolm's own pretended tyrannous habits – although that scene (4.3) is too often heavily pruned in performance. The whole spectrum of modern war and its management is thus present in just this one play. Presumably, war has always been like that, although, until recently, histories have tended to focus on the strategy and the troop movements

---

[10] Laurence Olivier's film makes similar changes in this scene.

rather than the abuse of civilians. Just occasionally, those other stories are so shocking as to make it into the historical record, but usually only if they serve some political purpose. For instance, it has perhaps suited Protestant historians to deplore the 'Spanish Fury' during the Eighty Years' War, in which a succession of towns in the Netherlands were sacked by the armies of their Catholic Spanish Habsburg rulers. It was not, of course, against the law of war to sack a town that had held out under siege; there was biblical precedent for so doing (Deuteronomy 20.10–20), and looting was the accepted method of paying troops. Shakespeare's Henry V threatens the townsfolk of Harfleur with that fate if they do not surrender (3.3), although in the play at least (though not in history) he later orders that they should be well treated. The complaint against the Spanish is that they sacked and looted whether the town had surrendered or not. A letter to Lord Burghley in the Cecil archives (4 August 1572) describes their sacking of Haarlem (one of those towns with an English garrison): '[t]he slaughter of the burghers and common soldiers was so bloody in the streets, that they tied their heads between their legs and threw them into the mere'. Another document in that archive (dated ?1572) weighs up the pros and cons of getting involved: the crown is already seriously in debt; it cannot be seen to defend rebels; and it has to juggle the need to resist alliances between the Pope, Spain, France and the Queen of Scots, and between Spain and Ireland. Not only can it not afford all-out war, it cannot afford to upset the diplomatic balance in Europe.[11]

Art is perhaps the only space where such problems can be aired on a human emotional level, although it is subject to censorship. The Dutch, in the persons of Pieter Bruegel, both elder and younger, allegorized the conflict in their country in paintings of The Massacre of the Innocents, where Herod's troops wear Spanish uniforms, but the Royal Collections example of this series was overpainted, sometime between 1604 and 1621, to make it look like a mere plundering of agricultural goods by generic soldiers, rather than a slaughter of babies by the Spanish.[12] Politics and perceived national interest have always trumped morality.

## TELLING STORIES

There are two issues that may confront those who survive active service. One is the continuing trauma stemming from what they have experienced – the condition that has gone by various names but is currently known as PTSD. The other, less often acknowledged – perhaps because it would implicate more damagingly the structural processes of warfare itself, rather than just the individual's 'incapacity to cope' – is the desensitization that is an essential part of the training process. Whether or not it is true that in World War II only 30 per cent of all soldiers ever fired their weapons directly at the enemy (and Brigadier General Samuel Lyman Atwood Marshall's research has been discredited), the post-war US army believed it to be true, and trained their troops accordingly for action in Korea, Viet Nam and beyond. There are currently no formal programmes of re-sensitization; individuals undergo maybe two or three days of debriefing and are then sent home.

Part of the desensitization process is also, as we have seen in *Macbeth*, a verbal *sanitizing* process. Western military commanders are adept in the use of euphemism to disguise the brutality of military procedures and tactics. From 'ground zero' via 'surgical strike' to 'extraordinary rendition', the horrible actuality of events is rendered palatable and normal, while the 'we'll train you while you holiday in the sun'-type recruiting adverts in both the USA and UK have meant young pilots returning from their first sorties, whether in Iraq or the Falklands, expressing genuine shock to camera that they might actually have killed someone. But military personnel rarely feel they can talk about it; civilians will not understand. Indeed, how could they? My father only once got even remotely close to revealing his feelings about 'bombing his way up the coast of Italy' (but there were plenty of tiny black-and-white photos of him in the family

---

[11] *Calendar of the Salisbury MSS Part II* (London, 1888), pp. 40–2.
[12] www.royalcollection.org.uk/collection/405787/massacre-of-the-innocents.

albums, grinning in uniform while on training, standing next to landmarks like a barrier marking the line of the equator). Life goes on, and I didn't feel I could press him for details, but, looking back, I am conscious of a huge hole. His father, my grandfather, H. R. King (1897–1983), had refused a commission but accepted promotion to company Sergeant Major, and returned a hero from World War I, with an MM, DCM and the Belgian Croix de Guerre. But he had lost an older brother, and was himself severely deafened. He became a very remote figure to his sons and later to us, his grand-daughters. He dedicated his life to education (for which he was again decorated), becoming head-master of the first boys' comprehensive school, a stalwart of the Worker's Educational Association, a tireless worker for better relations with Germany, and a supporter of England's mem-bership of the Common Market. He had the same story as my future father-in-law, one Peter Alexander (the Shakespearian, 1893–1969, whom I never met), of struggling back to his dug-out, unwounded, but with his haversack shot from his back. Peter had been an undergraduate at Glasgow University in 1914, and was one of hundreds who had attended a recruitment lecture on 4 August organized by the university's Principal (i.e. Vice-Chancellor), marching straight down to the recruit-ing office to enlist in the newly formed 6th Cameron Highlanders. He spent the rest of that autumn training in southern England, initially living in a tent, with no uniform, and a broom stick instead of a rifle. Once in France, the following year, he rarely mentions the fighting in his letters home, and then only in the most general terms, stressing the periods of rest behind the lines rather than the stretches in the firing line; he wouldn't want to alarm them, and in any case military details would be censored. But, more tellingly, he excuses himself for not providing a 'hair-raising' account: '[i]n action certain channels of feeling ... are numb and as the fight drags on one's energies are more and more concentrated on merely keeping oneself going'. Instead, he describes the French countryside, and any (rare) comfortable billet at length, and sends precise instructions for purchasing and sending to him both books and essential equipment, such as a portable 'Tommy's Trench Cooker', a 'housewife' or sewing kit, Eiffel Tower Lemonade Crystals and boric acid powder (for use as an insecticide and treating infections such as athlete's foot) – the ban-ality of war, perhaps. He spends many pages writing to his sister about his reading (Anatole France, Wordsworth, 'Pericles to the Athenians', Lamb's essays, as well as Shakespeare), or describes himself in his 'cubby hole' in the trench, reading the TLS his mother has sent him. There is one unsigned Christmas card, a souvenir of the first day of the Battle of Loos, 25 September 1915, showing a printed cartoon of a wild highlander, kilt and moustache flaring and gun at the ready, charging across an empty field – just a small ruined church outlined in the far background. This battle – though Peter, of course, does not say so – was the first time the British had used chlorine gas, and it had blown back in places along the line. Despite this, that first day had been a moderate success, but there was no follow-through, and the result was at least 50,000 British losses to 25,000 Germans. One of Peter's letters equates the 'disaster' of losing all his possessions in that haversack with the 'other disas-ter' (struck out for the censor), which was that battle. In another, the one time he gets close to an emotional confrontation of the way the war is being managed, he refutes published newspaper reports that one division had been cowardly; they were new, he said, just out from England, never having heard live gunfire before, and had been marching for days just to get there. They were exhausted before they started, and had been deci-mated. But it is not until several months later, walking in the town behind the line, that he describes coming across one of many posters advis-ing what to do if, as was likely, gas were to drift in from the line. 'Les chefs de familles', he reads, must show calm and 'sang froid' as an example to children, the sick and the elderly. He comments, 'the most professional of all the military virtues – sang froid'.

As Major Alexander, he served again for most of World War II. In 1943, at the age of 9, his youngest son Nigel (who was also to write a good book on Hamlet), wrote to his dad, still on active service, that he'd seen a school production of *Hamlet*, thought it 'super', and 'now I understand why you like Shakespeare so much'. Peter had returned home by the time his eldest son was killed, shortly after D-day, standing up in his tank while attempting to command its progress across the countryside near Amiens.

If anyone could have reflected on the nature of war in Shakespeare, it could – perhaps should – have been Peter, but there is as little on this topic in his books and articles as there is of actual fighting in his letters home. Instead, he locked himself in his study and edited the complete works, continuing a career devoted to methodical exploration of textual problems, and the forensic unpicking of myth from evidence in Shakespeare's life.[13] The family never spent another Christmas at home together because the loss was unbearable, and Nigel, I think, never recovered. The story he told himself about his brother's death made him feel guilty. Such stories – acknowledged, but more usually unacknowledged – are ubiquitous. They cannot but affect the way families behave to each other, and societies conduct themselves, sometimes for generations.

## 'FEAST OF CRISPIAN': A SHAKESPEARE PROGRAMME FOR US VETERANS

There are several Shakespeare programmes for vets now operating in the USA.[14] I shall describe just one: 'Feast of Crispian', based near the huge military hospital in Milwaukee run by the Department of Veterans Affairs. It is the brainchild of the actor Nancy Smith-Watson, and of Bill Watson and Jim Tasse, both professional theatremakers and teachers in the drama programme at the University of Wisconsin–Milwaukee; Jim is also a veteran of the war in Vietnam.[15] The main technique employed is a development of a well-known rehearsal method (which I have also used with undergraduates studying English literature). That exercise involves a reader who splits a speech into thought-sized chunks, whispering each in turn to an actor who, when ready, repeats the thought accompanied by some suitable gesture. The gesture

is held while the reader reads the next thought, and so on. The idea is to align language with the actor's body, allowing the actor to experience physically the many turns in direction of a typical Shakespeare speech, and to realize that each spoken thought is itself also an action that must influence another person. It is a slow, careful and interesting process, but, although it is embodied, it does not usually result in anything one might class as a performance.

Feast of Crispian's version of this technique, 'feed and drop in', is adapted from one initially developed by Tina Packer and others at Shakespeare & Co. (Lenox, MA). It is much faster and more intense. In this case, a facilitator gives the line or idea (the 'feed') to the person performing, who immediately repeats it. Sometimes the facilitator then asks a question (it is always a question) – the 'drop in'. This is designed to prompt some memory of the performer's military experience – memories that may lie deep, even buried. The facilitator immediately repeats the feed, and the actor repeats the line again. The facilitator generally then moves straight on to the next feed. The result the afternoon I was there was some of the most raw and powerful performances of Shakespeare (scenes from *Julius Caesar* and *Cymbeline*) I have ever seen.

The implications of this work go in a number of directions. The first is the therapeutic effects on the participants, the vets. They themselves report more control over their PTSD than they have hitherto derived from conventional talking therapies. The joy from their involvement in these sessions is palpable, as is the support – and indeed

---

[13] Peter Alexander, *Shakespeare's Life and Art* (New York, 1961); Peter Alexander, ed., *The Complete Works of Shakespeare* (Glasgow, 1951; regularly reprinted); Peter Alexander, *Hamlet: Father and Son* (Oxford, 1955); Nigel Alexander, *Poison Play and Duel: A Study in Hamlet* (London, 1971).

[14] See also the De-Cruit programme described in Alisha Ali and Stephan Wolfert, 'Theatre as a treatment for posttraumatic stress in military veterans: exploring the psychotherapeutic potential of mimetic induction', *The Arts in Psychotherapy* 50 (2016), 58–65.

[15] www.feastofcrispian.org.

love – they show for each other. But the technique raises interesting questions that are of relevance to educators at all levels, therapists in other areas of mental health, and theatre professionals alike.

Playing extensively on US TV networks at the time of my visit was an ad for T-Mobile. A voiceover intones: 'sometimes a day at the ball park is not just a day at the ball park'; the camera pans round a packed stadium and another voice comes over the tannoy asking all military and ex-military to stand up. Dotted round the stadium, a succession of men of all ages, shapes, sizes and colours rise slowly, shyly and proudly to their feet. But there are no obvious injuries – no missing limbs, or burnt faces – and no females, apart from one little girl who looks up adoringly at her good-looking, apparently well-adjusted dad. T-Mobile is offering half-price contracts to all who have served. There is so much so wrong with all this that it is difficult to know where to start, though I need to point out that the Veterans' Affairs organization itself is currently under some pressure to change or at least adapt its motto (a direct quotation from Abraham Lincoln's second inaugural address), since it does not acknowledge that a significant proportion of vets are now women:

[w]ith malice toward none, with charity for all, with firmness in the right as God gives us to see the right, let us strive on to finish the work we are in, to bind up the nation's wounds, *to care for him who shall have borne the battle and for his widow, and his orphan*, to do all which may achieve and cherish a just and lasting peace among ourselves and with all nations. (my emphasis)

But what do you do if the particular action that troubles you is one that you not only do not think was 'right', but which you know to have been an immoral abuse of power? One of the vets recounted just such an event, one that he had buried for twenty-five years, but which had resurfaced during a Feast of Crispian production of *Othello*: 'we were on a search and destroy mission; I came across a soldier raping a 16-year-old; he jumped me; I pulled a gun and he calmed down; but he jumped me again'. I was not quite clear what

the outcome had been, and at that moment did not feel I could ask. But he went on, 'I took it out on the actors'; there were supportive nods of assent from round the room: 'it's a safe place; no one's going to judge'. But perhaps the issue is not what precisely happened in that out-of-the-way place so many years ago; we know, if we care to acknowledge it, that rape is a commonplace in war, and that civilians rather than military make up the bulk of all war casualties. What goes unrecognized is the Cartesian paradox that, in the military, there is 'no place for emotions' and, at the same time, 'no time to think – you react' (I quote the same man). And things don't improve when they leave the service. They cannot (as we have seen) talk to their families, who cannot cope either with hearing what they've gone through or, often, with the way they have changed. In fact, it gets worse, since they have lost the camaraderie of their fellows, and the security of the little card that every soldier carries in his pocket, printed with the rules of engagement which, in the circumstances laid down, absolves him (or indeed her) from guilt. Neither emotion, nor thinking. No wonder theatremaking can be such a powerful tool, since it allows you to have both simultaneously.

## THEATRE V. THERAPY

In a typical therapy session, experienced by these vets, participants will sit around in a circle; they may talk, but if the talk gets too heated, too dangerous, the therapist will pull it back and, as Smith-Watson described, 'manage it down'. Yet, since memory is not laid down as on some computer hard drive, but remade every time one 'remembers', there is considerable evidence that simply retelling an event can cause it to be relived; as she puts it, one of the effects of PTSD is that it 'stops time': sufferers get stuck in the story, and express themselves as sick of retelling it. There are also ethical issues in official therapeutic settings. If a participant discloses a crime, whether historical infringement of the rules of war, or something more recent – marital abuse, maybe, or theft to fuel a drugs habit – doesn't the therapist have a duty to report it? Is that a safe space?

Feast of Crispian participants do not sit round and talk about their stories. They get on their feet and act a part. It is the character's story and the character who has the emotion; the actor, as these vets were fully aware, has to feel for what the character may be feeling, but also has a responsibility to his fellow actors. He cannot just lash out. 'Charlie', who is built seemingly of steel, has a history of doing just that. He reports having tremendously violent incidents where he blanks out and cannot remember what he has done. After such incidents, he can understand that he 'did not need to go there', but he has hitherto been unable to stop himself. That afternoon, he played Cassius in a feed and drop-in version of the row with Brutus. He had only recently joined the group and had no previous experience of reading, let alone performing in, plays of any kind, but the way in which his voice went lower and quieter the angrier the character became was absolutely chilling – quite unlike the histrionics one usually hears. Afterwards, he commented: 'some *real* drop in!'; Shakespeare's language 'allows it [the emotion] to come out'; '*I* had some language I wanted to bring out!' [*laughter*], and then later 'when the voice go low, there ain't gonna be no more talking . . . then the physicalness comes out . . . and I don't even recall what I done . . . I feel so bad afterwards.' Those sitting around or acting with him recognized the truth of the body language. The vet playing Brutus commented, 'I was watching your eyes and waiting for them to switch' (i.e. to jump out of the way if necessary). I would not have wanted to meet him in a dark alley in that mood either, though he was an immensely warm, intelligent and generous person that afternoon.

I give below some of the drop in from this exercise, with the associated lines from *Julius Caesar* (4.2.73–87). It is important to remember that the line, the 'feed', is first spoken by the facilitator, and repeated by the actor, then the vet's military experience is brought into play through the facilitator asking a question and again repeating the feed. Finally, the actor

speaks the line again through the lens and added intensity of that remembered experience. Occasionally the feed is again repeated if the facilitator feels that there is somewhere more to go with the line.

BRUTUS: Did not great Julius bleed? – *what does blood smell like on the streets?* Did not great Julius bleed?

Shall we now / Contaminate our fingers with base bribes? – *what does it feel like when a civilian makes money and you're making shit?* Shall we now / Contaminate our fingers with base bribes?

I had rather be a dog – *what was the mangiest dog you ever had to put down?* I had rather be a dog . . .

CASSIUS: You forget yourself / To hedge me in. – *What happens when you get pushed into a corner?* You forget yourself / To hedge me in.

I am a soldier I – *Are you proud of your service?* I am a soldier I

BRUTUS: Go to – *Is 'go to' fancy Elizabethan for 'fuck you'?* Go to.

What I saw was not the first time those particular actors had performed that scene, but they all agreed that they had gone further with it than they had managed previously. Not all the drop in necessarily hits the mark, but with the speed at which the session goes, that does not matter. A few of the questions are bound to resonate, and most do – with those sitting round as well as with the actor. The effect was to concretize Shakespeare's images (the dog, for instance), and, I would argue, to build metaphors. The vets' experiences serve as metaphors for those of the characters, and vice versa. A metaphor is a strangely powerful rhetorical device since it both *is* the thing being described, while being simultaneously quite different. And in this case, it gives the actors, and those watching, the chance to triangulate their experience with that of the character. This in turn encourages them to voice their own stories, in their own time and their own ways – to share them with the group (who clearly now, that afternoon, already knew them) but also with me. As one of the facilitators remarked, 'when it does come out, it no longer belongs to you, it belongs to the group; it takes the burden off'.

And Shakespeare's words fascinated these vets, whether or not they felt they fully understood them. That is partly the mystique of Shakespeare: the sense that he is 'difficult' and therefore 'not for the likes of me'. I have witnessed the same feelings of pride, achievement, even amazement in being able to speak and perform this language amongst poorly educated prisoners, and 10-year-old primary school students in tough areas of East London. One of the participants, a black Viet Nam veteran, put it this way: 'trying to understand what I'm saying . . . enjoying hearing and seeing; for me to stand up there . . . I may not understand, but really enjoying it', something he demonstrated by convincingly delivering one of Friar Lawrence's speeches as a southern Baptist minister.

For the project's actor-facilitators, it was something to do with breath and rhythm: the idea familiar from the work of Cicely Berry that the iambic pentameter is a heartbeat, and that the rhythm of the verse based on that underlying meter drives you forward to a different place, thus counteracting the stuck-ness of PTSD. This is perhaps the reason, too, for the intense pace of the process. I am not convinced of this particular explanation and have argued elsewhere about Shakespeare's subversion of the iambic metre through rhythms created by his use of rhetoric, and choice of word forms and sounds.[16] But, either way, there was no waiting for ponderous explanations of meaning, such as mars most people's educational experience of Shakespeare, but a driving through the lines, concentrating on conjuring up the images, and therefore the *feelings* that might be associated with them. It was certainly feelings that these ex-soldiers needed to access; one with severe clinical depression explained, 'I wanted to explore the language. Acting out helps me access the emotions; often I feel muted.' Later, having performed and loved the 'escalation' of Posthumus's fury with the runaway Lord on the battlefield in *Cymbeline*, he observed: 'what kept me coming back [to the group] was acting; it's theatre; it's safe. In the military, emotion is feminized and the effective [emotional] palette is "happy" or "angry"'. He felt that acting was enabling him to be more 'aware', and also 'to *modulate* emotion'.

I came away both elated and deeply moved. I felt privileged that this group of men had been so willing to talk in my presence about their trauma and their previous inability to express themselves. They had clearly found in this acting group the camaraderie, the familial support of the serving unit, which ex-military so commonly lose on demob. These are the feelings that Shakespeare demonstrates for good in the 'band of brothers' phrase in *Henry V*, and for ill in *Othello*, where no-one suspects the loyal and 'honest' Iago, everyone's friend, of the slightest wrongdoing. But, I wondered, did it have to be Shakespeare? Could the same effectiveness be claimed for any other artistic or communal activity – dance, hip hop, drawing, creative writing, on the one hand, or gardening or working with animals on the other? Given the opportunity, different individuals are likely to gravitate towards different types of activity.[17] And, of course, it is not new. To paraphrase the title of Murray Cox's book, *Shakespeare came to Broadmoor* (the UK's top-security mental institution) in 1989.[18] Group therapy was pioneered by Dr Tom Harrison at Hollymoor/Northfield Hospital in Birmingham in the 1940s: 'everyone was expected to take part in an activity which they were encouraged to plan'; these could be basic tasks like cleaning the ward, or they could involve the 'concept of the "intelligent story". One that has relevance, reveals underlying laws, and themes, that governs behaviour and that is congruent with human experience.' Either way, 'this process of reflective interpretation of activity enabled the

---

[16] Ros King, *Shakespeare: A Beginner's Guide* (Oxford, 2011), pp. 135–42.

[17] Inspired by the art of Winston Churchill, President George W. Bush has himself produced more than sixty portraits of veterans, celebrating their valour, although he does seem to be trying (perhaps failing) to explain something to himself: '[r]arely do I run into a vet who says, "You caused this to happen to me," . . . [t]hey go out of their way to make sure that their ole commander-in-chief understands that they understand the sacrifices they made.' See: www.voanews .com/a/president-george-bush-portraits-of-courage/ 3748579.html.

[18] Murray Cox, *Shakespeare Comes to Broadmoor: The Performance of Tragedy in a Secure Psychiatric Hospital* (London, 1992).

individual to redirect his energy and creativity towards the service of his group.'[19]

The aspect that I value most in Shakespeare is his capacity for ambiguity: his ability to weave variations on a theme within one play, and between one play and another; his facility with repetition and the building of metaphor that encourages reinterpretation and which allows readers and performers to learn from their own experience (not, as we used to be told, to be *taught* some moral lesson). The plays place before the eyes worlds to be imagined and triangulated with one's own. They are worlds which describe and evoke feelings, feelings that are like but not necessarily identical with one's own, and which can be further triangulated by those sitting around watching and listening. It is these features, I contend, that lend themselves to Shakespearian-themed therapeutic and educational programmes around the world. We need to bottle it, as they say, and use it more widely.

## POSTSCRIPT: ARMISTICE DAY, 2018

One hundred years after the end of World War I, acknowledgement of the traumatic effects of war on the mental health of survivors is beginning to creep into church memorial services. The third stanza of the winning entry in the Jubilate Hymns WW1 Centenary hymn-writing competition calls for 'Ease for the troubled mind / In endless conflict caught, / Each soul that cannot find / The peace beyond all thought'.[20] Perhaps, in the next hundred years, we can remember not only the soldiers who die but all those who survive, and their families, who are never quite the same again.

---

[19] Tom Harrison, lecture on the Hollymoor/Northfield experiments for the Sutherland Trust, 16 November 2001, www.sutherlandtrust.org.uk/wp-content/uploads/2014/02/9/01.11.16.pdf.

[20] Words by Ally Barret, to 'Love Divine' by John Ireland.

# WAR WITHOUT SHAKESPEARE: READING SHAKESPEARIAN ABSENCE, 1642–1649

## EOIN PRICE

Shakespeare wrote in the shadow of war. His plays deal with the historical conflicts of medieval England and ancient Rome but they were written during the French Wars of Religion, the Anglo-Spanish War, the Nine Years' War in Ireland, and other significant pan-European conflicts.[1] In death, Shakespeare has only become more tightly entangled with the history of international conflict. Michael Dobson has argued that the Seven Years' War helped accelerate the elevation of Shakespeare to the status of national icon.[2] Sarah Valladares has shown how the early-nineteenth-century Peninsular War provided the backdrop to the Covent Garden productions of J. P. Kemble, and the Shakespeare lectures of Samuel Taylor Coleridge.[3] Douglas Lanier has written about the commemoration of the tercentenary of Shakespeare's birth in the American Civil War, Ton Hoenselaars about the reception of Shakespeare in World War I-era France, and Jésus Tronch about how *Hamlet* came to represent the sense of ineffectuality and irresolution experienced during the Spanish Civil War.[4] In World War II, Shakespeare's plays were used, to contrasting effects, in a wide range of geographical locations: Ryuta Minami has written about Shakespeare in wartime Japan, Tibor Egervari about Shakespeare performances in Auschwitz, and Tina Krontiris on Shakespeare in occupied Greece.[5] Shakespeare was regularly invoked in the Cold War, too, as shown by Erica Sheen's study of airlift-era Berlin, and Krystyna Kujawinska Courtney's work on Shakespeare in Communist Poland.[6] More recent conflicts, such as the so-called 'War on Terror', have inspired further uses of Shakespeare.[7] This is hardly an exhaustive list, as the contributors to this issue demonstrate.

Whether we like to think of Shakespeare as a largely benign dispenser of cultural and political wisdom, or as the vanguard of English colonial expansion (and, in that sense, then, a product of war), there's

---

[1] On Shakespeare and the French Wars of Religion, see Gillian Woods, *Shakespeare's Unreformed Fictions* (Oxford, 2013), pp. 58–89. On Shakespeare and the Anglo-Spanish War, see Nick de Somogyi, *Shakespeare and the Theatre of War* (Aldershot, 1998), p. 132. On Shakespeare and the Irish wars, see Andrew Murphy, 'Shakespeare's Irish history', *Literature and History* 5 (1996), 38–59.

[2] Michael Dobson, *The Making of the National Poet: Shakespeare, Adaptation, and Authorship, 1660–1769* (Oxford, 1992), p. 227.

[3] Sarah Valladares, *Staging the Peninsular War: English Theatres, 1807–1815* (Abingdon, 2015), pp. 59–106.

[4] Douglas M. Lanier, 'Commemorating Shakespeare in America, 1864', in *Celebrating Shakespeare: Commemoration and Cultural Memory*, ed. Clara Calvo and Coppélia Kahn (Cambridge, 2015), pp. 140–60; Ton Hoenselaars, 'Great War Shakespeare: somewhere in France, 1914-1919', *Actes des congrès de la Société française Shakespeare* 33 (2015); Jésus Tronch, 'Hamletism in the Spanish Civil War, 1936–39', *Critical Survey* 30 (2018), 115–32.

[5] See the contributors to *Shakespeare and the Second World War: Memory, Culture, Identity*, ed. Irena R. Makaryk and Marissa McHugh (Toronto, 2012).

[6] See the contributors to *Shakespeare in Cold War Europe: Conflict, Commemoration, Celebration*, ed. Erica Sheen and Isabel Karremann (Basingstoke, 2015).

[7] For Shakespeare and the War on Terror, see Graham Holderness and Brian Loughrey, '"Rudely interrupted": Shakespeare and terrorism', *Critical Survey* 19 (2007), 107–23; David Coleman, 'Ireland and Islam: *Henry V* and the "War on Terror"', *Shakespeare* 4 (2008), 169–80.

no denying his abundance. But was it ever thus? The focus of this article is a war from which Shakespeare was curiously absent: the English Civil War of the mid seventeenth century. Shakespeare, of course, was dead by then, although that's never been much of an impediment. We are used to Shakespeare being at the centre of everything, but his plays seem to have played a reduced role at this crucial juncture in his nation's history. In this article, I will begin by thinking about how and why Shakespeare came to occupy a relatively marginal position, before turning to the writers who took his place in the print marketplace, focusing particularly on the Beaumont and Fletcher Folio of 1647. This hugely important but comparatively understudied book engages with the vexed politics of the Civil War in strikingly complex forms. While Shakespeare is often a vehicle for meaning in periods of conflict, at this time it was the plays of Beaumont and Fletcher that played the largest part on the paper stage.[8] My interest in this article, then, is why Shakespeare, so often celebrated for his ability to speak for the time, seems consigned to silence, and what it means that Beaumont and Fletcher, now confined to the margins of the canon, took centre-stage.

Shakespeare was not printed at all during England's decade of internecine conflict. Adam G. Hooks notes that 'virtually the same number of Shakespearean playbooks were published between 1623 and the Restoration in 1660 than had appeared in the 1590s'.[9] This observation about the general decline in the publication of Shakespeare's plays is instructive, but it does not account for the absence of newly printed material alone. As Table 1 shows, several Shakespeare editions appeared in the decade leading up to the Civil War, including the second edition of the Shakespeare Folio and a first edition of Shakespeare and Fletcher's *The Two Noble Kinsmen*. This is hardly the height of Shakespeare's print popularity, but nor does it obviously portend a fifteen-year hiatus in Shakespearian publication. Yet, as Table 2 demonstrates, it was not until 1655 that a publisher issued a new edition of a Shakespeare text (the 1652 edition of *The Merchant of Venice* is a reissue of the 1637 edition, with a new title page). Lukas Erne and Adam Hooks are among scholars who have shown that stationers sought to market Shakespeare's texts in

relation to the new political climate of the 1650s; this arguably makes the absence of Shakespeare editions in the 1640s all the more curious.[10] Shakespearian publication was not at its most prolific in the early years of the Restoration either, but, even then, the 1660s witnessed a significant new Shakespeare edition: the third Folio of 1663 and a reissued Folio of 1664 which included *Pericles* and six other plays now viewed as apocryphal. Emma Depledge has observed that these Folio editions 'suggest that Shakespeare was deemed to be vendible in the 1660s'.[11] So why was he not in the 1640s?

Depledge argues that, rather than disappearing from the cultural consciousness, Shakespeare's plays appeared in new genres in the 1640s, in response to the theatrical ban which made performing a risky, illegal business.[12] Shakespeare's plays circulated in abbreviated form, as drolls (short playlets) and play-ballads, and in commonplace books and anthologies. Diane Purkiss observes that Royalists regularly used Shakespearian tragedy to lampoon Oliver Cromwell in political pamphlets of the Civil War era.[13] Laura Estill has shown that both Royalists and Parliamentarians excerpted Shakespeare in manuscript miscellanies around this time.[14] Shakespeare continued to be read, used and, perhaps, even performed during the English Civil War, even if his plays were not being printed. To this list of caveats

---

[8] On the interregnum as a 'paper stage', see Rachel Willie, *Staging the Revolution: Drama, Reinvention and History, 1647–72* (Manchester, 2015), pp. 25–51.

[9] Adam G. Hooks, *Selling Shakespeare: Biography, Bibliography, and the Book Trade* (Cambridge, 2016), pp. 133–4.

[10] Lukas Erne, *Shakespeare and the Book Trade* (Cambridge, 2013), pp. 130–4; Adam G. Hooks, 'Royalist Shakespeare: publishers, politics, and the appropriation of *The Rape of Lucrece* (1655)', in *Canonising Shakespeare: Stationers and the Book Trade, 1640–1740*, ed. Emma Depledge and Peter Kirwan (Cambridge, 2017), pp. 26–37.

[11] Emma Depledge, *Shakespeare's Rise to Cultural Prominence: Politics, Print and Alteration, 1640–1700* (Cambridge, 2018), p. 41.

[12] Depledge, *Shakespeare's Rise*, pp. 13–38.

[13] Diane Purkiss, *Literature, Gender and Politics During the English Civil War* (Cambridge, 2005), p. 136.

[14] Laura Estill, *Dramatic Extracts in Seventeenth-Century Manuscripts: Watching, Reading, Changing Plays* (Lanham, MD, 2015), pp. 77–114.

Table 1

| Date | Text | Edition Number |
|------|------|----------------|
| 1632 | *1 Henry IV* | 9 |
| 1632 | *Comedies and Tragedies* | 2 |
| 1634 | *Richard II* | 8 |
| 1634 | *Richard III* | 10 |
| 1634 | *The Two Noble Kinsmen* | 1 |
| 1635 | *Pericles* | 5 |
| 1637 | *Romeo and Juliet* | 7 |
| 1637 | *The Merchant of Venice* | 5 |
| 1639 | *Hamlet* | 7 |
| 1640 | *1 Henry IV* | 10 |
| 1640 | *Poems* | 2 |

Table 2

| Date | Text | Edition Number |
|------|------|----------------|
| 1652 | *The Merchant of Venice* | 5 |
| 1655 | *King Lear* | 5 |
| 1655 | *Othello* | 5 |
| 1655 | *The Rape of Lucrece* | 9 |

we must also add that the Civil War apparently had a broader, negative effect on playbook publication. Alan Farmer and Zachary Lesser write that, from 1641 to 1649, the number of plays published dropped to 'levels not seen since the 1580s', whereas the 1630s had seen 'the highest edition totals of the entire early modern period'.[15] In such circumstances, the lack of Shakespeare publications may not be a surprise. But while the Civil War was a slow time for playbook publication more generally, and for Shakespeare especially, it was a boom period for the publication of Beaumont and Fletcher, the two authors controversially credited with the authorship of the plays in the 1647 Folio.

In an illuminating article, Heidi Craig offers a finely nuanced investigation of playbook publication in Civil War England, addressing both the absence of printed Shakespeare and the rationale behind the publication of the Beaumont and Fletcher Folio.[16] Craig offers several reasons for the decline in Shakespearian publications,

including: a legal dispute between Mary Allot, the widow of the publisher of the second Folio, and his apprentice Andrew Crooke, which prevented the earlier publication of the third Folio; the deaths in 1640 and 1641 of John Norton and John Smethwick, two of the most likely publishers of Shakespeare; and the fact that Miles Fletcher and Richard Cotes, who each owned the rights to multiple Shakespeare plays, shifted their focus towards the publication of religious or political material. The lack of printed Shakespeare in the Civil War is not the result of a straightforward process: it was part practical, part economic, part bad luck (or, as I will go on to argue, for Shakespeare's later reputation, good luck). In addition to these factors, Craig argues that the Shakespeare market had reached saturation point; the theatre ban meant that publishers (and readers) were inclined to look for novelties. Shakespeare, then, may have seemed old, or, in David Scott Kastan's words, 'a time-bound literary figure, very much of his age'.[17] Even so, we might expect a writer who apparently evokes an earlier, less obviously troubled time, to appeal particularly to publishers with Royalist sensitivities; instead, Humphrey Moseley, the foremost purveyor of Royalist writing, and the man Kastan credits with no less than the invention of English literature, turned his attention elsewhere.[18]

In 1647, Moseley and Humphrey Robinson published a volume of thirty-four plays and one masque, none of which had been printed before. They called the volume *Comedies and Tragedies*

---

[15] Alan B. Farmer and Zachary Lesser, 'Canons and classics: publishing drama in Caroline England', in *Localizing Caroline Drama: Politics and Economics of the Early Modern Stage, 1625–1642* (Basingstoke, 2006), pp. 17–41; pp. 20–1.

[16] Heidi C. Craig, 'Missing Shakespeare, 1642–1660', *English Literary Renaissance* 49.1 (Winter 2019), 116–44.

[17] David Scott Kastan, *Shakespeare and the Book* (Cambridge, 2001), p. 84.

[18] David Scott Kastan, 'Humphrey Moseley and the invention of English literature', in *Agent of Change: Print Culture and Studies after Elizabeth L. Eisenstein*, ed. Sabrina Alcorn Baron, Eric N. Lindquist and Eleanor Shevlin (Amherst, MA, 2007), pp. 105–25.

*Written by* FRANCIS BEAVMONT and IOHN FLETCHER. Beaumont and Fletcher's plays were attractive partly because so many of them were unpublished; market saturation was not a problem. But the mere fact that they had never been printed cannot have been enough to convince these publishers to undertake the hazardous process of producing a large-scale edition. Moseley and Robinson must have been convinced of the appeal of the plays and the prestige of their authors. Indeed, Beaumont and Fletcher plays that had previously made it into print proved to be very successful: *Philaster* went through five editions from 1620 to 1639, and *The Maid's Tragedy* and *The Scornful Lady* each went through five editions in a near identical period. *A King and No King* was printed four times, *Cupid's Revenge* three, and *The Bloody Brother* two.[19] Even *The Knight of the Burning Pestle* and *The Faithful Shepherdess*, which were both initially marketed as theatrical flops, went on to have later success and made it into second and third editions respectively. In the years immediately before the closure of the theatres and the outbreak of war, several stationers published first editions of Fletcher plays, suggesting an anticipated demand for Fletcher in print several years before the Folio was published.[20] Moseley's interest in publishing a Folio of Beaumont and Fletcher plays may have begun around this time. In 1641, the Lord Chamberlain issued a warrant preventing the publication of sixty King's Men plays; R. C. Bald, in a claim more recently endorsed by Lukas Erne, suggested that the King's Men made this move to block Moseley, before agreeing terms with him in 1646.[21]

Predictably, then, Moseley was keen to market the plays of the Beaumont and Fletcher Folio as new, but at the same time he also traded on their oldness. The title page of the volume emphasizes a double claim: the plays are '[n]ever printed before' but also supposedly 'now published by the Authors Originall Copies'.[22] This paradoxical desire to hark back to the '[o]riginall' while also bringing forth the truly new is characteristic of the book's fraught relationship with the apparently better days of the previous decades, the troubled times of the Civil War, and the uncertain future. Moseley reiterates many of these claims in his prefatory address, repeatedly locating the book's vendibility in its newness (the volume, he says, is 'entirely New') while also recounting, in brief, the lives of the now long-deceased authors (A4v). Fletcher died twenty-two years before the book was published; Beaumont died the same year as Shakespeare, thirty-one years before the 1647 volume. Moseley figures the plays in the book as popular, familiar, successful, redolent of brighter days, but also new, fresh and urgent: not crusty relics but texts capable of speaking to and for the times. In the first of his two paratextual addresses, the playwright and one-time Fletcher collaborator James Shirley presses the point even further, situating the plays of the Folio explicitly in the context of the Civil War, arguing not only that they are peculiarly apposite but that their new printed form makes them even

---

[19] Thomas Walkley published editions of *Philaster* in 1620 and 1622; Richard Hawkins published editions of the play in 1628 and 1634. William Leake published an edition in 1639. Richard Higenbotham published the first edition of *The Maid's Tragedy* in 1619; further editions followed in 1622 (for Francis Constable), 1630 (for Hawkins), 1638 (for Henry Shepherd) and 1641 (for Leake). Miles Partrich published editions of *The Scornful Lady* in 1616 and 1625; Thomas Jones published an edition in 1630; Augustine Matthews in 1635; and Robert Wilson in 1639. Walkley published *A King and No King* in 1619 and 1625, Hawkins published a version in 1631, and Leake published the 1639 edition. *Cupid's Revenge* was first published in 1615 by Josias Harrison and then in 1630 by Thomas Jones and 1635 by Matthews. Thomas Allott and John Crooke published the first edition of *The Bloody Brother* in 1639; a second edition followed in 1640, published by Leonard Lichfield, printer to the University of Oxford.

[20] John Waterson and John Benson published *The Elder Brother* in 1637; Waterson published *Monsieur Thomas* in 1639; William Cooke and Andrew Crooke published *Wit Without Money* in 1639 and *Night Walker* in 1640. In the same year, Lichfield published *Rule a Wife and Have a Wife*.

[21] R. C. Bald, *Bibliographical Studies in the Beaumont and Fletcher Folio of 1647* (Oxford, 1938), pp. 5–10; Lukas Erne, *Shakespeare as Literary Dramatist*, 2nd edn (Cambridge, 2013), pp. 174–5.

[22] Francis Beaumont and John Fletcher, *Comedies and Tragedies* (London, 1647). Subsequent references to this edition are cited parenthetically.

more important and powerful than they were when they were performed:

[a]nd now Reader in this *Tragicall Age* where the *Theater* hath been so much out-acted, congratulate thy owne happinesse that in this silence of the Stage, thou hast a liberty to reade these inimitable Playes, to dwell and converse in these immortall Groves, which were only shewd our Fathers in a conjuring glasse, as suddenly removed as represented, the Landscrap is now brought home by this optick, and the Presse thought too pregnant before shall be now look'd upon as greatest Benefactor to Englishmen, that must *acknowledge* all the felicity of *witt* and *words* to this Derivation.

(A3r–v)

Shirley encourages his readers to see the plays anew, through the 'optick' of the book and not the 'conjuring glasse' of the pre-Civil-War stage. In the '*Tragicall Age*' of Civil War, Beaumont and Fletcher, rather than Shakespeare, are proffered as the playwrights most beneficial to the nation.

Shakespeare, though, is not entirely absent from the collection. He is present in echoes and even direct allusions. Jitka Štollová notes that the Beaumont and Fletcher volume is 'modelled on its 1623 precursor', sharing several typographical features such as the double column arrangement and the use of pica roman type.[23] Erne alerts us to more correspondences: like the 1623 Folio, the Beaumont and Fletcher collection confines itself only to dramatic material; it features thirty-four plays, a similar number to the Shakespeare Folio, which contains thirty-six, and it makes similar claims about the authority of its texts.[24] The imagery of the 1623 book influenced the compilers of the 1647 volume in other ways too, as detailed by Jeffrey Masten in his discussion of authorship and patriarchal rhetoric.[25] The two volumes also share the same dedicatee. The 1623 Folio was dedicated to William and Philip Herbert; the 1647 volume was dedicated to Philip alone, as William had died, although he is mentioned as the '(now glorified) *Brother*' (A2r).[26] The dedication, which contains ten signatories, all members of the King's Men, makes a point of connecting the Herberts with the 1623 Folio, calling them '[p]*atrons to the flowing*

compositions of the then expired sweet Swan of Avon SHAKESPEARE' (A2v). Shakespeare's name, mediated through Ben Jonson's commendatory poem, is used to confer authority on the Beaumont and Fletcher collection.

Although Shakespeare's name appears in several of the volume's encomiastic poems, to help consolidate Beaumont and Fletcher's literary credentials, the use of his name is not straightforward. The Royalist poet Sir John Denham lists Fletcher alongside Shakespeare and Jonson in 'the Triumvirate of wit' (B1v), but some other comparisons treat Shakespeare a little less favourably. For example, George Buck – not to be confused with the long since deceased former Master of the Revels – puts Fletcher ahead of Shakespeare, George Chapman and 'applauded Ben' (C3r), while a poem by the Anglo-Welsh historian James Howell places Fletcher ahead of his rivals as the writer most valuable during the 'tragedy' of the Civil War era. Howell imagines that, had 'grim *BEN*' lived in the 1640s, he would 'rage' against the injustice of the time, while Shakespeare and George Chapman would have 'grown madd, and torn / Their gentle *Sock*' (B4r). Howell means to praise Jonson, Shakespeare and Chapman for what he imagines would be their righteous fury, but his description of the angry trio makes them sound impotent in their rage. In contrast, Howell confers power on Fletcher: '[r]are *FLETCHER'S quill*' would have 'soar'd up to the sky, / And drawn down Gods to see the tragedy'. Quite how Fletcher's plays are supposed to enact this miracle is unclear but, even though he is himself long since dead, Fletcher is configured as useful and relevant

---

[23] Jitka Štollová, '"This silence of the stage": the play of format and paratext in the Beaumont and Fletcher Folio', *Review of English Studies* 68 (2016), 507–23; p. 514.

[24] Erne, *Literary*, p. 174.

[25] Jeffrey Masten, *Textual Intercourse: Collaboration, Authorship, and Sexualities in Renaissance Drama* (Cambridge, 1997), p. 121.

[26] On the choice of the Herbert brothers as a dedicatee to the 1623 folio, see Sonia Massai, 'Edward Blount, the Herberts, and the First Folio', in *Shakespeare's Stationers: Studies in Cultural Bibliography*, ed. Marta Straznicky (Philadelphia, PA, 2012), pp. 132–46.

in a way that other great writers of the seventeenth century are not.

But where Howell's criticism of Shakespeare comes in the form of a backhanded compliment, other poets offer more bracing critiques of Shakespeare, in their attempts to emphasize the importance of Beaumont and Fletcher. In a posthumously published piece, the Royalist poet William Cartwright claims that Shakespeare was comparatively 'dull' to Fletcher:

> Shakespeare to thee was dull, whose best jest lyes
> I'th Ladies questions, and the Fooles replyes;
> Old fashion'd wit, which walkt from town to town
> In turn'd Hose, which our fathers call'd the Clown;
> Whose wit out nice times would obseannesse call,
> And which made Bawdry passe for Comicall:
> Nature was all his Art, thy veine was free
> As his, but without his scurillity;
> From whom mirth came unforc'd, no jest perplex,
> But without labour cleane, chast, and unvext.
>
> (D2v)

Shakespeare is here associated with '[o]ld fashion'd wit' and out-of-date clothing. His plays are scurrilous and his humour is, by implication, forced. Rather curiously, given the smuttiness of many of the plays in the Beaumont and Fletcher volume, Cartwright seems to think Beaumont and Fletcher plays are 'cleane, chast, and unvext'.[27] I will return to the veracity of the claims made by the commendatory poets later in this article, but for now it should suffice to note that Cartwright and his Royalist-supporting companions are keen to present Shakespeare as unfashionable and somehow ill-suited to the gravity of the occasion of war. In another poem, John Birkenhead, who would in time become the editor of the Royalist newsbook *Mercurius Publicus*, writes that:

> *Shakespear* was early up, and went so drest
> As for those *dawning hours* he knew was best;
> But when the Sun shone forth, [Beaumont and
>     Fletcher] thought fit
> To weare just Robes, and leave off Trunk-hose-Wit.
>
> (E3v)

Like Cartwright, Birkenhead figures Shakespeare as comically unfashionable, both in the sense that

his humour is old-fashioned and in the sense that his unfashionableness is the butt of the Royalist jokes. Beaumont and Fletcher, on the other hand, wear 'just Robes' rather than the inappropriate '[t]runk-hose' of an older time. Their plays are properly fit for the circumstances of Civil War. The implication is not that Shakespeare is a republican writer (although we know his plays were sometimes read as such) but that he is comparatively stale or inconsequential, unable to reform the ills of the day or restore former glories.[28] To the Royalist creators of the 1647 Folio, Beaumont and Fletcher were ripe for the time and more easily used for their political purpose. It is to their project that I now turn.

The Beaumont and Fletcher Folio was a collective effort, but scholars generally agree that Moseley was the driving force behind the volume (even if there is a certain irony to the critical elision of the book's other publisher, Humphrey Robinson). Moseley was well known as a Royalist sympathizer; Lois Potter describes him as a specialist in 'subversion for the polite reader'.[29] In the 1640s, he published a series of books by Royalist writers such as John Suckling, Edmund Waller, William Davenant, John Denham, Richard Fanshawe and James Shirley, which David Norbrook says 'evoked the world of the 1630s'.[30] Margaret Ezell adds that Moseley's publications sought to foster 'a literary and cultural community banding together in the face of national

[27] In his study of Shakespeare's sexual imagery, Eric Partridge acknowledges that Beaumont and Fletcher equal Shakespeare for smut, if nothing else: see *Shakespeare's Bawdy* (London, 1947), p. 53.

[28] The fullest study of Shakespeare's engagement with republican thought is Andrew Hadfield's *Shakespeare and Republicanism* (Cambridge, 2005). For examples of stationers marketing Shakespeare's plays in a republican context, see Erne, *Book Trade*, pp. 130–4; Kirk Melnikoff, 'Nicholas Ling's Republican *Hamlet* (1603)', in *Shakespeare's Stationers*, pp. 95–111.

[29] Lois Potter, *Secret Rites and Secret Writing: Royalist Literature, 1641–1660* (Cambridge, 1989), p. 19.

[30] David Norbrook, *Writing the English Republic: Poetry, Rhetoric and Politics, 1627–1660* (Cambridge, 2001), p. 159.

"tragedy"'.[31] But Moseley did not limit himself to the publication of professed Royalists. In 1645, he published an edition of John Milton poems in which, in Warren Chernaik's words, Milton was 'transformed against his will into a royalist'.[32] The book's title page, which situates Milton in relation to Henry Lawes, '[g]entleman of the KINGS Chappel, and one of His MAIESTIES Private Musick', is just one prominent example of how Moseley sought to frame Milton.[33] Nobody would claim, though, that Moseley's publication of these poems meant Milton was a Royalist. So how successfully did the producers of the Beaumont and Fletcher Folio present its deceased subjects as Royalist?[34]

One thing is for sure: Moseley and his contributors, who counted among them many of the most prominent Royalist voices of the time, were not subtle. Marcus Nevitt calls the volume the 'assertion of a collective royalist identity'; Trevor Ross goes further still in claiming that the volume was 'symbolically avenging Parliament's closure of the theatres'; Nicholas McDowell tops them all by declaring it 'a mass act of writerly resistance to the supposed cultural barbarity of the recently victorious Parliamentary party'.[35] The paratexts abound with references to royal imagery. G. Hills calls Fletcher the 'King of Poets' (F1v); John Harris describes Fletcher as the 'sole Monarch' and 'abs'lute Soveraign' (F4v); and Thomas Peyton, the former MP turned Royalist activist, says that praising Fletcher is a risky business that 'might raise a discontent / Between the Muses and the ___' (A2v).

The commendatory poems also routinely praise Beaumont and Fletcher for their wit: Shirley calls Fletcher 'the best wit ever trod on our English stage' (A3v); Aston Cockaine praised his plays as 'lasting Monuments of natural wit' (A4v); and George Lisle admires Beaumont and Fletcher as 'Two Potent Witts' (B1r). Of course, it was nothing new to praise a writer for their wit. Indeed, the poems appended to the 1623 Shakespeare Folio similarly sought to present their author as a paragon of wit. Jonson's poem 'To the Reader' singles out Shakespeare's 'wit' as one of his key characteristics; John Heminges and Henry

Condell note that Shakespeare's 'wit can no more be hid, then it could be lost'; Jonson's longer commendatory poem 'To the memory of my beloued' praises Shakespeare's wit and contrasts him with the 'antiquated' Aristophanes, Terence and Plautus; and Leonard Digges describes the Folio as a 'wit-fraught Booke'.[36] But the use of the word 'wit' in the Beaumont and Fletcher Folio carried with it a much more pronounced political charge. As McDowell notes, 'wit' had become a Cavalier code-word in the Civil War as 'royalists sought to claim a monopoly of literary and linguistic talent over a Parliamentary opposition and government that they represented as stereotypically Puritan and thus as grim, philistine, and deeply hostile to the arts'.[37] This newer understanding of wit exposed the older vision of wittiness to political scrutiny. Just as Jonson presented ancient comic

---

[31] Margaret J. M. Ezell, *The Oxford English Literary History*: Volume 5: *1645–1714: The Later Seventeenth Century* (Oxford, 2017), pp. 41–53; p. 43.

[32] Warren Chernaik, 'Books as monuments: the politics of consolidation', *Yearbook of English Studies* 21 (1991), 207–17.

[33] John Milton, *Poems* (London, 1645).

[34] The authorship of the plays in the 1647 Folio is contested, but the other writers thought to have been involved in their authorship were also dead by this point. Nathan Field died in 1620, William Rowley in 1626, Thomas Middleton in 1627, John Webster in 1634, John Ford in 1639, and Philip Massinger (whose role in the plays of the volume is considerably greater than Beaumont's) in 1640. Author attributions taken from Martin Wiggins and Catherine Richardson, *British Drama, 1533–1642: A Catalogue*, 10 vols. (Oxford, 2012– ), vols. 6–8.

[35] Marcus Nevitt, 'Restoration theatre and Interregnum Royalism: the Cavalier rivalry of John Denham and William Davenant', in *Sir John Denham (1614/15–1669) Reassessed: The State's Poet*, ed. Philip Major (London, 2016), pp. 52–74; p. 69; Trevor Ross, *The Making of the English Literary Canon: From the Middle Ages to the Late Eighteenth Century* (Montreal, 1998), p. 134; Nicholas McDowell, *Poetry and Allegiance in the English Civil Wars: Marvell and the Causes of Wit* (Oxford, 2008), p. 19. See also Ann Baynes Coiro, 'Reading', in *Early Modern Theatricality*, ed. Henry S. Turner (Oxford, 2013), pp. 534–55; p. 543.

[36] William Shakespeare, *Comedies, Histories and Tragedies* (London, 1623), A1v, A2v, A4v, B2r.

[37] McDowell, *Poetry and Allegiance*, p. 8.

writers as 'antiquated' to highlight Shakespeare's commercial relevance, so the 1647 encomiasts configured Shakespeare as outdated to prop up the image of Beaumont and Fletcher as vendible Royalist icons. For many of the volume's contributors, Beaumont and Fletcher's supposed wit could bring about what they saw as much-needed political change. The Cavalier poet Alexander Brome says that the plays 'bring exploded witt againe in fashion', causing a '[r]eformation' (F3r); Roger L'Estrange, the future Restoration press censor, calls the book a 'balsame' to the troubled times (C1r); and William Habington invokes Fletcher to help cure a country 'in the worst scaene of Time' (B3v). These images contrast with the earlier description of an impotently enraged Shakespeare.

So far, so Royalist, but the politics of both Royalism and reading are knotty and uncertain. The Civil War caused divided loyalties. Ezell observes that the dramatist and translator Thomas May wrote a commendatory poem to James Shirley's Humphrey Moseley-published 1646 edition of poetry, even though, by this time, May had joined the Parliamentary cause.[38] Sabrina Baron notes that Milton, assuredly not a Royalist, had Royalist connections: his brother served in the King's army, and his Oxfordshire in-laws were also Royalists.[39] Moseley, as Milton's publisher, marketed the poems to appeal to Royalists, but he would hardly complain if the book was bought by Parliamentarians, and he had no qualms about publishing Milton's material. Christopher D'Addario reminds us that 'just because a work was produced by a "royalist" does not mean it was only read by "royalists" or even in a royalist manner'.[40] It is perfectly possible to read the plays of the Beaumont and Fletcher Folio without endorsing the reams of prefatory Royalist rhetoric. Indeed, Katrin Beushausen is right to point out that a number of the poems 'steer away from ... politicisation ... and focus on the plays themselves', promising above all an enjoyable reading experience.[41] We might expect the Cavalier poet Robert Herrick to write something explicitly Royalist, for example, but his offering focuses on the beauty and variety of Fletcher's plays.

It is possible, then, that some readers discarded or rejected the Royalist packaging of the 1647 Folio. Despite the prefatory claims, Beaumont and Fletcher are not necessarily an obvious vehicle for Royalism. To end, I want to think about some of the ways in which the volume might even undermine its goals or open up the possibility of alternative readings. Jeffrey Masten has argued that the contributors apply contradictory models of authorship: some poets figure the book as a 'kingdome' and others view Beaumont and Fletcher as 'Consul-Poets', thus registering different kinds of political systems. 'This is the story of a volume', Masten writes, 'and perhaps a nation, that could not make up its mind(s)'.[42] I want to take this further still, making more visible the different ways in which the Royalist publication strategy activates conflicting, even directly divergent, political readings. Sandra Clark suggests that 'at certain moments in the seventeenth century [Beaumont and Fletcher's] plays were closely identified with royalist values; but that it is not clear that the point of first production was one of these'.[43] I would add that, in spite of Moseley's attempts, it is not clear that 1647 was one of these either.

Consider, for example, the vexed politics of the book's dedication. In 1623, when he was a dedicatee to the Shakespeare Folio, Philip Herbert was the Earl of Montgomery; by 1647 he had taken an additional title, Earl of Pembroke, from his deceased brother. But that is not all that had changed.[44] In the intervening years, Herbert had a troubled relationship with the English monarch. A favourite of James I, whom

[38] Ezell, 1645–1714, p. 42.
[39] Sabrina A. Baron, 'Licensing readers, licensing authorities in seventeenth-century England', in Books and Readers in Early Modern England: Material Texts, ed. Jennifer Andersen and Elizabeth Sauer (Philadelphia, PA, 2012), pp. 217–42; p. 226.
[40] Christopher D'Addario, Exile and Journey in Seventeenth-Century Literature (Cambridge, 2007), p. 61.
[41] Katrin Beushausen, Theatre and the English Public from Reformation to Republic (Cambridge, 2018), p. 219.
[42] Masten, Textual Intercourse, p. 151.
[43] Sandra Clark, The Plays of Beaumont and Fletcher: Sexual Themes and Dramatic Representation (Oxford, 1994), p. 15.
[44] I am indebted to David L. Smith's Oxford Dictionary of National Biography entry for the following information.

he served as a Gentleman of His Majesty's Bedchamber, Herbert had a trickier time with Charles I, and became even more alienated from court after disagreeing with the king about the 1639–40 negotiations with the Scots. In 1641 he was removed from his position as Lord Chamberlain. From 1642, he became a moderate Parliamentarian; Andrew Hopper has shown that Herbert prevaricated and groomed contacts on both sides of the war as he attempted to negotiate the strongest possible position.[45] This kind of vacillation was not uncommon, but in time it made him the subject of Royalist propaganda which figured him as an illiterate, unintelligent, drunken cuckold. In the Restoration, John Aubrey described him as the product of incest.[46] The decision to dedicate the 1647 volume to Herbert may have inspired all kinds of conflicting thoughts within the minds of its readers. It looks like an attempt to hark back to the happier days when Herbert was a royal favourite, but this attempt to restore a lost past is obviously – and perhaps for some readers, Royalist or otherwise, painfully – futile. The dedication might look like a failed attempt to curry favour with a man who, in his actions, did not have the Royalist cause firmly at heart. This may not have been a consideration for all readers, but it could be as well said to weaken as to bolster the strength of the volume's Royalist credentials.

Opportunities for devious or counterintuitive readings of the prefaces also abound. As we have seen, many of the poems display strongly Royalist convictions, but these strengths can become weaknesses; if a reader finds unexpected ironies in staunchly Royalist passages, they can undermine the entire enterprise. The final lines of the volume's penultimate poem, Shirley's second contribution to the prefatory material, may serve as an example:

> But let him live and let me prophesie,
> As I goe Swan-like out, Our Peace is nigh;
> A Balme unto the wounded Age I sing,
> And nothing now is wanting but the King.
>
> (G1v)

Scholars routinely (and reasonably) read this as Shirley hopefully imaging a peaceful restoration,

for Charles I. Masten describes it as a 'second coming . . . a projected moment of "Peace" (imagined in the midst of war)'; Štollová sees it as a much-needed 'message of hope' at a dire moment for the Royalists.[47] The implication, of course, is that the 'wanting' King will return from his enforced absence. Fletcher (and Shirley, through his prophecy) set the scene for his arrival; the poem ends with the conditions primed for his glorious entrance. This is, if you'll excuse the tongue-twister, surely Shirley's intention. But the phrasing and syntax invite a less optimistic and generous alternative reading. For many people at the time, regardless of their allegiance, King Charles had been found 'wanting', lacking the necessary skills to be a successful ruler. In this reading, he is wanting *because* he is wanting; the prospect of a sudden transformation, as Shirley desires, looks not only impossible but undesirable.

Finally, there are the plays themselves, which frequently resist their Royalist marketing. Philip J. Finkelpearl has helped to argue against the long-held belief that, as Coleridge had it, Beaumont and Fletcher are 'servile jure divino royalists', a belief presumably rooted in the 1647 Folio prefaces.[48] But old habits die hard, and it is always worth restating the political sophistication of Beaumont and Fletcher plays. Several of the prefatory poems offer miniature readings of specific plays (usually, it has to be said, ones not actually published in the 1647 Folio). In one such poem, Henry Howard, sixth Duke of Norfolk, gives an idiosyncratic, Royalist account of *A King and No King*. In his

---

[45] Andrew Hopper, *Turncoats and Renegadoes: Changing Sides in the English Civil Wars* (Oxford, 2012), p. 22.

[46] Margaret P. Hannay, Noel J. Kinnamon and Michael Brennan, 'Introduction', in *The Collected Works of Mary Sidney Herbert, Countess of Pembroke*, 2 vols. (Oxford, 1998), vol. 1, p. 10. See also John Aubrey, *Brief Lives*, ed. Richard Barber [1975] (London, 1982), p. 139.

[47] Masten, *Textual Intercourse*, p. 150; Štollová, '"This silence"', p. 518.

[48] Philip J. Finkelpearl, *Court and Country Politics in the Plays of Beaumont and Fletcher* (Princeton, NJ, 1990); Roberta Florence Brinkley, ed., *Coleridge on the Seventeenth Century* (Durham, NC, 1955), p. 658.

vision of the play, Arbaces is a returning war hero who 'saved his peoples dangers by his own' (A1v) and defeated his rival without the assistance 'of any *Mirmydon*'. Howard's reading of the play entails focusing on the pre-play narrative at the expense of what actually happens in the play. *A King and No King* begins with Arbaces's triumph but, as the action progresses, he becomes increasingly tyrannical. The play ends, in typically tragicomic fashion, with an astonishing about-turn; Arbaces learns that he is an illegitimate ruler who has no inherited right to the throne. What follows is a remarkable, complicated political rearrangement in which Arbaces is removed from power, because he is not the King, and then returned to power, because he marries Panthea, the heir to the throne. But he is no longer the supreme ruler. Zachary Lesser has argued that the play imagines a new form of government in which the royally born Panthea rules with the non-royal Arbaces.[49] None of this sits very easily with Howard's version of events; nor does it feel particularly conducive to a Royalist interpretation. It is surely possible to read the play in Royalist terms, but it is telling that Howard sidesteps the thorniest issues.

Elsewhere in the volume, the Cavalier poet Richard Lovelace provides a similarly Royalist negotiation of *Valentinian*, a Roman tragedy which is, in fact, part of the 1647 Folio. Valentinian is a corrupt ruler who is assassinated by a subject who becomes Emperor but who shows signs of corruption and is assassinated in turn. Fletcher reflects at length on the morality of resistance and the duty of subjects to their monarch. Gordon McMullan has shown that these issues would have felt very topical to the play's earliest audiences, but they would have felt even more pertinent to readers in 1647.[50] Lovelace focuses his attention on 'brave' (B2v) Aetius, the loyal subject who hopes to reform Valentinian through wise counsel but who is betrayed by Maximus, who thinks, with Aetius gone, it will be easier to kill Valentinian. By centring Aetius, Lovelace can laud loyal service while also criticizing the tyrannical Valentinian, 'the costliest Monarch' (B2v). But, as with Howard, Lovelace ignores aspects of the

play that might trouble his political convictions. In the final act, the usurper Maximus is killed by Eudoxa, Valentinian's widow. Where we might expect blame, we have praise. Affranius, a high-ranking military official, declares her 'righteous' (5.8.111); and Sempronius, a senator, calls her a 'saint' (5.8.116) and 'our protector' (5.8.117).[51] Killing Maximus, a usurper, is different from killing Valentinian, a legitimate ruler, but Eudoxa's actions complicate the picture considerably, demonstrating that, at least in some circumstances, violent resistance may be appropriate. Again, it is possible to read the final scene of *Valentinian* in Royalist terms, but it is notable that Lovelace does not try. Later, in the Restoration, the Earl of Rochester adapted the play, cutting the final act entirely, suggesting unease about the play's politics. That Rochester thought he had to make considerable changes to make it do what he wants it to do is a reminder of the play's unruly power.

That Beaumont and Fletcher's plays were co-opted to a Royalist cause does not mean that their plays were Royalist, any more than Shakespeare's co-option by campaigners for Brexit means that Shakespeare would have opposed the EU. Shakespeare's ambiguity, which enables diverse groups to adapt him to suit their own purposes, is one of the qualities we most frequently celebrate. Some critics will attribute this to Shakespeare's unique universality which renders him readily available to all circumstances, but there is reason to be sceptical of this conclusion. After all, when Restoration dramatists brought Shakespeare back to prominence, a little over a decade after the publication of the Beaumont and Fletcher Folio, they did not think of him as universal. On the contrary, Shakespeare was a writer in need of rehabilitation.

---

[49] Zachary Lesser, 'Mixed government and mixed marriage in *A King and No King*: Henry Neville reads Beaumont and Fletcher', *ELH* 69 (2002), 947–77; p. 964.

[50] For a reading of the play's Jacobean political context, see Gordon McMullan, *The Politics of Unease in the Plays of John Fletcher* (Amherst, MA, 1994), pp. 95–9.

[51] John Fletcher, *Valentinian*, in *Four Jacobean Sex Tragedies*, ed. Martin Wiggins (Oxford, 1998), pp. 233–328.

As we have seen, Shakespeare did not fit the 1640s, according at least to several of the most important literary influencers of the decade; and when the theatres reopened, Shakespeare's stock was not especially high. But the absence of newly printed Shakespeare texts in the English Civil War may have led to Shakespeare's later print success. The lull in the printing of Shakespeare playbooks during the war years solved the problem of Shakespearian saturation. Moreover, the sense that Shakespeare did not quite suit the culture of mid-seventeenth-century England may have helped him flourish again in the Restoration, as dramatists set about the process of making Shakespeare 'fit', to adopt Sandra Clark's phrase.[52] Shakespeare offered a challenge to a new generation of theatremakers, who adapted him to suit changing aesthetic tastes, enabling a process of adaptation and appropriation which has continued into the present day. Ironically, the canonization of Shakespeare was probably aided by his print absence during the troubled years of Civil War.

Beaumont and Fletcher's plays have not had the same sustained success, but they too have offered themselves up for political interpretation at moments of cultural crisis, and scholars could benefit from paying them more attention. Moseley's printing of the Beaumont and Fletcher Folio is an early example of the appropriation of Jacobean drama. Rather than telling us anything particular about Beaumont and Fletcher's political affinities, it instead suggests the rich ambiguities of their plays. At the same time, the fact that Moseley did not try to use Shakespeare for the Royalist cause does not mean that Shakespeare could not have been used, or that he was associated with republicanism. His print absence was arguably a result of his previous print abundance. Shakespeare, Jonson and Chapman each had a print presence when the Civil War began; but they brought with them a set of associations which may have made it seem that they were harder to co-opt to a Royalist cause. Beaumont and Fletcher's plays, many of which had never been printed, were ripe for use. Of course, politics was not the only concern, and practical issues also dictated Moseley's strategy: had he had access to thirty-four unpublished Middleton plays, he may have printed them as a folio. But he didn't. He had Beaumont, Fletcher and the unnamed collaborators of what was to become the 1647 Folio. It was their plays more than anyone else's that came to define the time, just not necessarily in the way that Moseley had hoped.

---

[52] Sandra Clark, ed., *Shakespeare Made Fit: Restoration Adaptations of Shakespeare* (London, 1997).

# ANTIC DISPOSITIONS: SHAKESPEARE, WAR AND CABARET

## IRENA R. MAKARYK

Writing for the *New York Times* in 1981, Frank Rich began his witty review of a production of *Shakespeare's Cabaret* with the following: '[a]s theater lyricists go, William Shakespeare is hard to beat. He may even be better than Lorenz Hart.'[1] Hart was, of course, the lyricist half of the famous American songwriting team of Rodgers and Hart, contributing to such well-known compositions as 'Blue Moon' and 'Bewitched, Bothered and Bewildered'. The pairing of Shakespeare with cabaret, formerly infrequent and considered rather cheeky, is now commonplace. Shakespeare's anniversary year of 2016 harvested a particularly large bumper crop. Just a few examples will suffice to give a flavour of these productions. At the British Library, Spymonkey, described in promotional material as the 'greatest clowns working in Britain today', presented an evening of 'genius comedy', 'a cabaret with a hilarious and joyful mash-up of clown and Shakespeare'.[2] The Cambridge Arts Theatre reprised what the *Independent* described as 'one of the best things to come out of the RSC': a 'comic concoction of hilarious sketches and show-stopping numbers'.[3] On the other side of the pond, Chicago's Shakespeare Theatre celebrated with *Shakespeare Tonight!*, 'a captivating marriage of Shakespeare and cabaret'.[4] Still farther afield, The Puzzle Collective's *Shakespeare Cosplay Cabaret* urged Australians to 'get ready for a night of music, dancing, circus, slam poetry, Shakespeare and superheroes!'[5]

As these descriptions suggest, the notion of cabaret is now generally associated with soufflé-light diversions that cleverly bring together the 'high' and the 'low', and thus appeal even to those who don't particularly care for the Bard. But how can such a genre function in wartime or in the horror of its aftermath? What purposes might it serve? This article maps out some of the connections between the characteristics and strategies of the early avant-garde cabaret and its subsequent use when married with Shakespeare – not for the purposes of light entertainment, distraction, or of morale-boosting propaganda, but as direct engagement with – and, indeed, reflection of – the madness of war. In this approach, I take my cue from Kenneth Burke's late-1930s essay, 'War, response, and contradiction'.[6] Burke takes as his point of departure a debate between Malcolm Cowley and Archibald MacLeish that unfolded on the pages of the *New Republic* concerning two broad ways in which art may approach the subject of war. The first, championed by Cowley, are works that

---

[1] *Shakespeare Cabaret* was conceived by Lance Mulcahy, who also wrote the music. The production was directed by John Driver and opened at the Bijou Theater, 209 West 45th Street, in New York. See www.nytimes.com/1981/01/22/theater/revue-music-of-the-present-in-shakespeare-s-cabaret.html.

[2] See www.bl.uk/events/late-at-the-library-spymonkeys-shakespeare-cabaret.

[3] See www.cambridgeartstheatre.com/show/shakespeare-revue.

[4] See www.chicagoshakes.com/plays_and_events/tonight.

[5] www.facebook.com/events/987853034692649.

[6] Kenneth Burke, 'War, response, and contradiction', in *The Philosophy of Literary Form* [1941] (Baton Rouge, LA, 1967), pp. 234-57.

emphasize feelings of horror, repugnancy and hatred. These, Burke contends, are 'extremely militaristic attitudes' that may easily be turned inside out; indeed, they 'might well provide the firmest basis upon which the "heroism" of a new war could be erected'.[7] Instead, Burke upholds the position of MacLeish who argued that the depiction of a 'human' war – that is, a work that deals with the totality of the experience of war, not just its horror – is more 'socially wholesome' and the 'soundest deterrent to war'. In the words of MacLeish, such works contain 'neither morality, nor text, nor lesson'.[8] This second, more complex, way, Burke suggests, combats tribal instincts. Taking this argument further, I propose that, in today's world, the Hamlet-esque 'antic disposition' of cabaret – its grotesque, satirical, adversarial, yet playful and intelligent nature – may be one of the few ways to respond critically and with authenticity to war, fake news, and the madness of their strongman adherents.

Originating in Bohemian Paris in the last quarter of the nineteenth century, cabaret originally functioned as an intimate venue for avant-garde artists, intellectuals, writers and their friends to exchange and to debate ideas, smoke, drink, recite poetry, and perform songs, sketches, improvisations, avant-garde dramatic works, and, usually, eat. They created and performed for each other and directly to each other in an often raucous performance space that was the centre of heady experimentation. Satirically attacking topical issues in culture, morals, and politics, and lampooning authority in its various guises and places, the cabaretists of the late nineteenth and early twentieth centuries created an alternative space to that of traditional, established theatres. Dissent was their leitmotif; conventional thinking, their target. Combining 'intimacy and hostility', 'participation and provocation', laughter and utopian hopes, they shadowed the fragmentation of the world and its imminent upheaval in World War I.[9]

Rather than inhabiting or growing into a specific hide-bound genre, early cabaret displayed a number of salient features that would continue to figure throughout the following decades and beyond: satire, parody, song, improvisation, topicality and playful impudence. It also engaged in a mutually influential and constantly evolving dynamic with other popular entertainments. At the turn of the last century, that meant drawing from vaudeville, circus, puppet shows, carnival and music hall. Reclaiming the importance of this genre of small forms[10] for theatre history, scholars such as Harold Segel, Laurence Senelick[11] and, particularly, Lisa Appignanesi, have exhaustively described and analysed the origins, dissemination and later offshoots of cabaret, a fact which makes extended discussion of its history unnecessary here. As they have shown, the cabaret gave birth to some of the most electrifying innovations in twentieth-century performance art. It provided 'the earliest podium for the expressionists, the Dadaists, the futurists; it was a congenial forum for experiments in shadowgraphy, puppetry, free-form skits, jazz rhythms, literary parody, "naturalistic" songs, "bruitistic" litanies, agitprop, dance-pantomime, and political satire'.[12]

Cabaret's rapid cultural acceptance and subsequent peregrinations from Paris to Petrograd and beyond revealed its inclination to shape-shifting, as each country introduced its own distinctive tonalities and accents to the genre, though everywhere it tended to draw its participants from peripheral groups whose outlook remained ironic.[13] In Germany and Austria, for example, some of cabaret's playfulness morphed into more serious political

---

[7] Burke, 'War, response, contradiction', p. 239.

[8] Burke, 'War, response, contradiction', pp. 239–40.

[9] Lisa Appignanesi, *The Cabaret* [1975] (New Haven, CT, 1984), p. 6.

[10] The German term is 'Kleinkunst'; the Russian, 'Theatre of Miniatures'; the Ukrainian, 'Theatre of Small Forms'.

[11] Harold B. Segel, *Turn-of-the-Century Cabaret: Paris, Barcelona, Berlin, Munich, Vienna, Cracow, Moscow, St. Petersburg, Zurich* (New York, 1987); Laurence Senelick, ed., *Cabaret Performance*, Volume 1: *Europe 1890–1920 – Songs, Sketches, Monologues, Memoirs* (New York, 1989); Laurence Senelick, ed., *Cabaret Performance*, Volume 2: *Europe 1920–1940* (Baltimore, MD, 1993).

[12] Senelick, ed., *Cabaret* 1, p. 9.

[13] Senelick, ed., *Cabaret* 2, p. xiii.

and aggressive humour, and took on the name of *Kabarett*. There, the presiding genius was the spirit of the clown who anarchically scoffed at everything with simultaneously joyful and derisive laughter.[14] In this vein, the inimitable Munich clown Kurt Valentin, wildly popular with audiences, deeply influenced the work of Bertolt Brecht. Erwin Piscator, too, fell under the spell of the cabaret in the 1920s. In Zurich, the Dadaist Cabaret Voltaire was a haven for those who opposed war: international artists and writers, some of whom had been eyewitnesses of the destruction; others, who presciently escaped before the devastation began. Safely in Switzerland, they engaged in anti-logical experiments employing outrageous costumes, masks and dance, aimed at freeing up the imagination from the constraints imposed by tradition and convention. In Budapest and Prague, the cabaret scooped up nationalist sentiment with its desire to overthrow the dominance of German culture. In Poland, though less strident, it mocked both smug conservatives and Young Poland modernists. In imperial Russia, the cabaret leaned more heavily towards the theatrical; some of the best-known cabarets presented a large dollop of mini-plays, skits and tableaux.

Topical, improvisational, impertinent, fluid in content and adaptable in form, the cabaret was the 'perfect medium for hard times'.[15] As Appignanesi has observed, its initially small size endowed the cabaret with a certain status of independence, while its potency derived in large part from the dynamic, and sometimes volatile, relationship between performers and spectators, whose roles could be reversed at any moment. Such a porous demarcation line between audience and performer held out the continual expectation and encouragement of experimentation, enhanced by improvisation with its possibility of an immediate response to 'hot' current events. Song endured as a central component of the cabaret and as another powerful democratic weapon with which to ridicule authority and hypocrisy – at times, it even served as a call to action, to protest, and criticism.[16]

In the confused, violent years of world war, civil war and revolution that ultimately brought an end to the Russian empire, cabaret strategies attracted into its creative vortex many extraordinary talents – among them, the directors Nikolai Evreinov, Vsevolod Meyerhold and Les Kurbas (Figure 11). Still the least well known of these, Kurbas was an actor, director, playwright, translator, pedagogue, theorist, filmmaker and musician. He created the foundations for twentieth-century Ukrainian theatre and film, influencing hundreds of actors, directors and designers. He also first introduced Shakespeare to the Ukrainian stage in 1920.

The delayed introduction of the Bard needs a brief explanation, since the state of Ukrainian culture under imperial Russian rule is still not widely known. In the nineteenth century, a series of tsarist decrees and memoranda crippled Ukrainian culture. At the height of the prohibitions, during the reign of Alexander II (1855–81), all theatre performances were banned; all Ukrainian books in print were removed from the shelves of libraries; and the translation of all foreign texts, including the Bible and Shakespeare, was strictly forbidden.[17] Even Ukrainian folk songs, when publicly performed, had to be sung in Russian. At the century's end, many restrictions remained in place, including limitations on subject matter and genre. Upper- and middle-class characters were required to speak Russian; peasants and children, Ukrainian. Such constraints led to the development both of national stereotypes (the

---

[14] Appignanesi, *Cabaret*, p. 40.

[15] Appignanesi, *Cabaret*, p. 205. Great Britain generally remained immune to the attractions of avant-garde cabaret, particularly of the more 'acid' variety. Appignanesi speculates that the presence of more democratic institutions in the UK tended to diffuse the sharpest of political satire (p. 208).

[16] Appignanesi, *Cabaret*, p. 2.

[17] On the tsarist decrees, see Valerian Revutsky, 'The Act of Ems (1876) and its effect on Ukrainian theatre', *Nationalities Papers* 5 (1977), 67–77; and Roman Solchanyk, 'Mykhailo Drahomanov and the Ems Ukase: a note on the Ukrainian question at the 1878 International Literary Congress in Paris', *Harvard Ukrainian Studies* 1 (1977), 225–9.

11  Les Kurbas in 1919. Volodymyr Hrycyn / Yosyp Hirniak Archives, New York. Courtesy of Virlana Tkacz.

Ukrainian equivalent of the stage Irishman) and generic ones: sentimental and melodramatic plays with obligatory musical and dance numbers featuring large choirs dressed in folkloric costume. Even after the 1905 Revolution, some of the strictest edicts, though relaxed, were not revoked. Full liberty for the Ukrainian theatre (however brief) was to come, paradoxically, only with the chaos of war and revolution.

Despite the upheaval caused by the cataclysmic events of that time, euphoria dominated both in the world of art and in the world of state-building. Finally, artists could have direct, unmediated access to the texts, genres and forms that hitherto had been prohibited, and which, in turn, they hoped, would inspire the creation of a new art, new modes and forms of expression and representation. Sharing this enthusiasm was the charismatic Les Kurbas (1887–1937). Born in Western Ukraine, educated in Vienna, and well versed in the traditions of world theatre, Kurbas spearheaded a theatrical renaissance which at first centred on the staging of the classics – not as an end in itself, but rather as part of the process of national and cultural self-discovery through dialogue and debate with

foreignness. A life-long voracious reader and polymath, he was deeply influenced by the ideas and the works of a plethora of thinkers, artists and creators, from Henri Bergson and Edmund Gordon Craig to Arnold Schönberg, Paul Cézanne, D. W. Griffith and Albert Einstein. He was also inspired by the cabaret.

Just as he arrived in Vienna in 1907 to pursue his university studies in philosophy and philology, the famous Fledermaus ('Bat') cabaret was founded.[18] Multicultural Vienna was a 'natural' for cabaret, with its strong national traditions of music, theatre and tart comedy. Kurbas became a frequenter of the Fledermaus, the 'in' place of the time, which featured the highly praised sketches, monologues and poems of Peter Altenberg. Described by one scholar as a 'most notorious drunk and arch bohemian, flâneur and lover of prostitutes',[19] Altenberg was also the central figure of café culture and of the cabaret scene, not just in Vienna but, arguably, in

---

[18]  Or, rather, re-founded. It had a brief, earlier, life as Nachtlicht ('Nightlight', founded in 1906).
[19]  Appignanesi, *Cabaret*, p. 52.

all of Austria. He memorably insisted the cabaret was 'the art of doing small things in the theater the way really big things are done'[20] – that is, cabaret was not insignificant or minor in purpose but, rather, it was theatre reduced to its essential components. This quintessence of theatre, as it was embodied in the cabaret form and developed by Altenberg and another famous cabaretist, Frank Wedekind, was among the important early influences on Kurbas.

Moving from Western Ukraine to Kiev in 1916, Kurbas encountered a robust cabaret culture which flourished in the basements of hotels, restaurants and derelict buildings. These locales were filled with artists from various national groups, many of them arriving in droves during the civil war, hoping to escape the hunger and chaos that ruled in Russia. Among them were Nikolai Evreinov, who scandalously linked theatre as spectacle with the scaffold, and Konstantin Mardzhanov, the creator of the Bi-Ba-Bo cabaret in Petrograd, which he transformed into the Crooked Jimmie in Kiev. New cabarets were constantly springing up; among the plethora of such venues was the Harlequin Mini-Theatre founded by a group of artists that included the future filmmakers Grigorii Kozintsev and Sergei Yutkevich. Kurbas himself became a cabaretist at the Art Cave, organized by Ukrainian and Russian poets, and by actors whom he headed. There, evenings of avant-garde poetry, revolution-themed works, music, mini-theatrical shows and skits were performed.[21]

The collapse of the tsarist empire had finally enabled aesthetic experimentation and released bottled-up political satire. The appeal of Shakespeare's *Macbeth* in this anti-monarchical revolutionary period is self-evident. Despite the anarchy and extreme deprivations of civil war that caused some of his actors to pass out from hunger, Kurbas and his company prepared their first Shakespeare production with both trepidation and jubilation, finally staging the play on 20 August 1920.[22] It was a fairly straightforward, if sardonic, interpretation of a play that Kurbas continued to contemplate, mining its depths in two other redactions and eventually coming, in 1924,

to create a third, radical re-interpretation using cabaret strategies with his newly minted company, the Berezil Artistic Association.[23]

Opening on 2 April 1924, two years after the creation of the Soviet Union and a few weeks after the death of Lenin, this was a tragi-farcical *Macbeth* – one unlike any other seen before anywhere in the old Russian empire – or, for that matter, in Western Europe. Anticipating a backlash from his spectators, Kurbas explained in interviews published in advance of the production that the revival of a pseudo-classical Shakespeare was 'formally impossible and, in essence, unnecessary'; instead, he insisted, Shakespeare must be 'refracted by the prism of the contemporary revolutionary world-view'.[24] I have examined this remarkable production in detail elsewhere;[25] here, I will focus primarily on those features which link it back to one of its significant progenitors: cabaret.

The stage was painted black. Decorative scenery was rejected and replaced by enormous movable

---

[20] Peter Altenberg, *Bilderbögen des kleinen Lebens* (Berlin, 1908). Quoted in Segel, *Turn-of-the-Century Cabaret*, p. 198.

[21] On the ferment in Kiev's theatre scene, see Hanna Veselovska, 'Kyiv's multicultural theatrical life, 1917-1926', in *Modernism in Kyiv: Jubilant Experimentation*, ed. Irena R. Makaryk and Virlana Tkacz (Toronto, 2010), pp. 243–74.

[22] On this and other Shakespeare productions in early Soviet Ukraine, see Irena R. Makaryk, *Shakespeare in the Undiscovered Bourn: Les Kurbas, Ukrainian Modernism, and early Soviet cultural politics* (Toronto, 2004).

[23] The Berezil, which takes its name from the archaic Ukrainian name for the month of March (i.e, spring, renewal, revolution, energy), was founded in 1922.

[24] On the production of *Macbeth* by the Fourth Studio of the Berezil Artistic Association, see 'Do postanovky Makbeta v maisterni M.O.B.', *Bil'shovyk* (Kiev) 3 (1924), 6 – an unsigned article, probably written by Stepan Bondarchuk.

[25] See Chapter 2, 'Tilting at da Vinci: Kurbas's 1924 *Macbeth*', in Makaryk, *Shakespeare in the Undiscovered Bourn*, pp. 65–112. The significance of this production was reiterated again and again by critics, actors and scholars of the time. See, for example, I[akiv] S [avchenko] – 'Shekspir dybom [Shakespeare upside-down]', *Bil'shovyk* (Kiev), 76 (1924), 6 – who predicted that many separate scholarly studies would, and should, be written about each scene of this production.

bright green screens of stretched canvas on which giant modernist red block letters announced the locality of each scene. Going a step beyond Craig's idea of self-supporting screens, Kurbas had 'living' screens form an essential part of the dramatic action, even serving as a kind of character. Raised or lowered when needed at the sound of a gong, the screens sometimes indicated the simultaneity of the action in different parts of Scotland; at others they underscored the emotions of the lead actors, emphasized tension, and even interfered in the action. Props, too, acquired their own life, flying down or up, as need be. The musical score also surprised with its jarring mixture of Anatolii Butskyi's contemporary atonal creations, Ukrainian folk songs, excerpts from Pietro Mascagni's *Cavalleria Rusticana* and a Schubert military march.

The porous boundary between stage and auditorium, fiction and reality, was consistently underscored. Most of the actors were dressed in contemporary workmen's clothes with stylized medieval accessories, suggesting the simultaneity of time past and time present. After a gong rang out announcing each sequence, the work lights came on and the actors entered as themselves, each at his or her own pace, occasionally greeting the audience. Only then did they engage in their roles. In effect, the actors presented a series of isolated, discrete 'numbers', as in a cabaret performance. Repeated throughout the production, such an 'engagement' and 'disengagement' with a role drew attention to the broader notion of theatricality. Suspending traditional drama's fluidity of action, the cabaret tactic of discontinuity invited the audience to interrogate its expectations of theatrical conventions both on stage and in life. Focusing on the skill and labour of the actor, the strategy encouraged a cerebral response to the play on both sides of the footlights, since the actors – as in cabaret – were required to be both performers and spectators to each other, as well as to the audience.[26]

The political and philosophical arc of the production echoed the cabaret attitude, provocatively addressing the audience as complicit collaborator in the events through an ironic, parodic 'commentary', at the centre of which was the Porter, here renamed the Fool. He usurped the primacy and the focal position in the play traditionally assumed by Macbeth. Like the jeering, disdainful Viennese cabaret clowns, Kurbas's Fool mocked political, religious and moral pretensions in three separate, extensive appearances resembling cabaret mini-plays that punctuated the intervals between the acts of Shakespeare's play. The central organizing principle of the whole production was a montage of contrasts and analogues that emphasized the themes of hypocrisy, cycles of violence and destruction, and their consequences.

During the first interval, actor Amvrosii Buchma (Figure 12) was dressed in fool's cap and motley clothing with gaudy, overstated make-up: a white face, crimson lips and a large bulbous nose which, combined with his exaggerated gestures, linked him to circus clowns, silent film and Dada. The allusions to the Harrowing of Hell plays in Shakespeare's Porter scene were literalized: pitchfork-carrying devils suddenly appeared on each side of the stage. When the Porter–Fool threatened them with his fist, they lifted up their heads and were 'transformed' into a cardinal and a Jesuit priest by the simple trick of flicking back their cowls on which had been painted grotesque, gaping faces. Organ music solemnly announced the end of this episode that marked the world of *Macbeth* as hellish, hypocritical, fantastical and mad. Clerical authority was mocked with aggressive buffoonery, part of the production's continuum of subversion that included the opening scene in which outrageously 'witchy' witches, bathed in an eerie violet light, entered bearing liturgical censers traditionally used by priests to purify a sacred space (Figure 13). Not only were the witches shockingly appropriating the gestures and tools of clerics but they also seemed to be endowed with mysterious powers, suggested by

---

[26] Valentyna Zabolotna, *Aktors'ke mystetstvo Ukrainy* [*The Actor's Art in Ukraine*] *(1922–1927)* (Kiev, 1992), p. 53. Zabolotna was Buchma's granddaughter.

12  Amvrosii Buchma as the Porter–Fool in Les Kurbas's 1924 *Macbeth*. Courtesy of The Shevchenko Theatre Museum (Kharkiv, Ukraine), formerly the Berezil Theatre.

13  Macbeth (Ivan Marianenko) with the witches in Les Kurbas's 1924 *Macbeth*. Courtesy of The Shevchenko Theatre Museum (Kharkiv, Ukraine), formerly the Berezil Theatre.

the fact that they were electrically wired. The Porter was visually and thematically connected to the witches. His nose, also wired, occasionally lit up, drawing attention to his clownish proboscis and mingling the audience's feelings of horror with laughter.

Upon his first entrance, the Porter–Fool cavorted across the stage using wild, unpredictable acrobatic leaps and grotesque dance steps. As in cabaret, he made impromptu speeches to the audience, interspersed with carefully rehearsed satirical couplets on topical social and political issues gleaned from the morning's newspapers. These were created by fellow actor Stepan Bondarchuk who was tasked with reading all the latest news and transforming juicy stories into punchy couplets. Each evening brought fresh comments and jokes about current events, religious superstitions and even backstage theatrical disputes, thus transforming the stage into a kind of cabaret revue which blurred the vicious political landscape of Scotland with that of volatile contemporary Soviet Ukraine. Explaining the significance of the use of such tools to members of his directorial lab, Kurbas insisted that such mini-plays were to be created only when they contributed to the themes of the original play.[27] In this case, the contemporary references were conceived as analogues of the historically distant references to Jesuitical equivocation and hypocrisy. History and contemporaneity, fiction and reality were conflated in a simultaneity of time and space. Through cabaret strategies, Shakespeare became their contemporary.

In his second appearance, in the fourth act, the Fool entered as a peasant-reaper, singing a traditional Ukrainian harvest song and miming the act of mowing the whole stage as if it were a field. As he methodically did so, he clipped away shards of stage light. With each movement, the stage visibly darkened. Seemingly overcome with fatigue from his hard work, he approached the members of the audience who sat on bleachers in front of him, and engaged in spontaneous exchanges with them, occasionally asking someone for a smoke. The futility of revolutionary political change, the enormous human cost of the recent bloody events (including the consequences of eleven changes of government in Kiev), and the common man's compliance out of fear and inertia, were brought home by the unexpected disjunction between the folk song – with its theme of the pleasures of seasonal bounty – and the symbolic destruction wrought by the Grim Reaper – Fool who indiscriminately and unemotionally destroyed the light of hope, the light of life. This sequence moved the action of the tragedy away from the great figures who committed violent deeds to those who lived within the world of the strongman's creation: the common man, unable to shape events, afraid, and perhaps even unwilling to be disturbed by what he could not change. In essence, this scene brought to the foreground the collusion of the thanes in Scotland's tragedy: their inaction that led to the murder of Lady Macduff, her family and the unnamed many others of the play.

The Fool's third and last appearance, which occurred in the final moments of the play when Macduff comes out carrying the head of Macbeth, caused a major scandal. Here, Kurbas looked into the future, a future built on a society's acceptance of violence as the central tool of change. Still wearing his Fool's make-up (the mocking, grinning face), Buchma came in costumed as a bishop. He then crowned Malcolm to the music of an organ whose solemnity was ironically undercut by the delicate sounds of the piccolo and the coarser sound of the harmonium. Just as he did so, a new pretender approached, killed the kneeling Malcolm, and seized the crown. Without pause, the Fool–Bishop once again chanted the same phrase: 'there is no power, but from God'. As the new King was about to arise, a new pretender murdered him, and the ritual was repeated once again. Unmoved by all, only folly survived the madness of the moral wasteland of a state founded

---

[27] Kurbas to his directorial lab, cited in 'Do postanovky *Makbeta* v maisterni M.O.B'.

in violence and dominated by a series of identically self-interested strongmen. Such an explosive political conclusion to the play directly attacked the legitimacy of those in power through the provocative strategies of cabaret coupled with the potency of a world classic. With this final scene, the production gave the lie to the newly developing Soviet narratives that mythologized and aggrandized the Revolution and its aftermath. Using satire, grotesque, exaggeration, clowning and discontinuity, Kurbas made the Fool the central figure of the tragedy. Only he, as the embodiment of folly, could survive the viciousness of the Scottish world, a world that resembled the contemporary moment, in which Lenin's death, rather than bringing a halt to violence, instead unleashed a series of new power struggles. The production thus raised troubling questions about the consequences of bloody exchanges of power as the basis for a new society. It looked both backwards and forwards in time, bringing together medieval Scotland and the very recent past, and even seeming eerily to predict the Stalinist terror to come.

Rather than a 'safe' production that confirmed classical ways of presenting Shakespeare, or a rousing propaganda piece that presented a clear ideological message, the 1924 *Macbeth* attempted, in its yoking of the power of the classic with the strategies of cabaret, an examination of the ethics and the consequences of war, violence and revolution. Such a powerful analysis could only be achieved with the use of a classic whose radical revision would provide a salutary shock to its audiences. Indeed, the fallout from, and polemical debates about, the production continued to reverberate throughout Kiev for weeks and months to come,[28] for, as Simon Barker has pointed out, '[a] Shakespeare read provocatively for uncertainties, hesitations and contradictions – and against the smoothing narratives of war and nation ... is a very unsettling experience indeed'.[29]

Standing at the point of origin of avant-garde Ukrainian Shakespeare, Kurbas's 1924 *Macbeth* is an iconic production that remains deeply embedded in Ukrainian theatrical history not only because of its far-reaching investigation of

theatrical practices (here only touched upon), but also because it was rooted in the fertile ground of a cultural renaissance – one which gave rise to a whole spectrum of wild and jubilant experimentation.[30] But Kurbas's dark version of the Scottish play literally had grave consequences for its creator, who was arrested in 1933 and executed, in 1937, on the personal orders of Stalin.[31] Acerbic cabaret fared little better.

Suppressed for nearly seventy years, cabaret's legacy was restored with the fall of the USSR in 1991, which ushered in another period of cultural efflorescence. Growing up at the end of the millennium, young urban Ukrainians felt finally liberated from Soviet censorship and from the requirement of serving the state. Like the avant-garde of the 1910s and 1920s, at first they turned to pure aesthetics as a way of showing their rejection of politics and of the endemic corruption that had characterized both the Soviet period and its aftermath. And, like Kurbas and his contemporaries, this generation reached out into the wider world, no longer experiencing the need to be defined as 'Ukrainian', but simply as artists.[32]

Among the most provocative of the many inheritors of the cabaret's legacy are the Dakh Daughters, created in 2012 in Kiev. Their 'freak

---

[28] Vasyl' Vasyl'ko, 'Shchodennyk [Diary]', 3 April 1924, p. 124. Vasyl'ko's unpublished diary is an invaluable source for a study of theatre of this period and particularly of the work of Kurbas. Vasyl' Vasyl'ko papers, Ukrainian State Museum of Theatre, Music and Film (Kiev), inv. 10369.

[29] Simon Barker, *War and Nation in the Theatre of Shakespeare and His Contemporaries* (Edinburgh, 2007), p. 28.

[30] See Makaryk and Tkacz, eds., *Modernism in Kyiv*, on the vast range of experiments in various disciplines, including graphic design, dance, poetry, theatre, visual art and music.

[31] Kurbas was charged with a list of violations including ignoring the building of socialism, directing Ukrainian theatre towards nationalist goals, creating incomprehensible formalist productions and – most improbably – conspiring to overthrow the government.

[32] Maria Sonevytsky, 'The freak cabaret on the Revolution stage: on the ambivalent politics of femininity, rurality, and nationalism in Ukrainian popular music', *Journal of Popular Music Studies* 28 (2016), 291–314; p. 294.

14 The Dakh Daughters and their 'freak cabaret'.

cabaret', growing out of a project aimed at ruth-lessly testing the borders of theatre and music, was inspired by early Parisian cabaret.[33] Made up of seven professional actors, musicians and dan-cers who play fifteen different instruments and sing in different languages and dialects, the women are made-up to look like actresses from the silent-film era: white faces, smoky eyes, blood-red lips (Figure 14). Their performance pieces draw from a variety of traditions, includ-ing Dada, the avant-garde, silent film and the early cabaret. They also borrow lyrics from authors they find inspiring, among them Shakespeare, Taras Shevchenko and Joseph Brodsky, as well as 'low' poets such as Charles Bukowski, described by one source as 'the king of the underground', thanks to his antics and deliberately clownish performances.[34]

The group's name is important in signalling their primary connection to theatre: they are first and foremost 'daughters' of the theatre; more specifically, they are all actresses from the small, independent (non-commercial), experi-mental Dakh Centre for Contemporary Arts, run by its creator, artistic director and producer Vlad Troitsky. His Dakh Theatre has developed a mixture of ritual, masks, dance, mime, drum-ming and haunting music to tackle a wide-ran-ging theatrical repertoire, including adaptations of Gogol, Dostoyevsky, Pirandello, Sophocles, Sarah Kane, Marius von Mayenburg, Martin McDonagh and Shakespeare (*Richard II, King Lear* and *Macbeth*).[35]

---

[33] Sonevytsky, 'The freak cabaret', p. 307, n. 3.
[34] A. Debritto, *Charles Bukowski, King of the Underground: From Obscurity to Literary Icon* (Palgrave Macmillan, 2013), p. 6.
[35] See the Dakh website: http://dax.com.ua. A flavour of the ritualistic, trance-like atmosphere created by the Dakh style is well described in Lyn Gardner's review in the *Guardian* (3

Like the Dadaists of the Zurich-based Cabaret Voltaire of the 1910s, the Dakh Daughters' stance is adversarial. They want to negate the entrenched spirit of corrupt politics and belligerent attitudes. The multi-instrumentalists – Nina Haretska, Ruslana Khazipova (Perkalaba), Tanya Havrylyuk (Tanya Tanya), Solomia Melnyk, Anna Nikitina, Natalia Hanalevych and Natalia Zozul (Zo) – explain their intention as being to open up 'a space on the border of theatre and music' and to cross 'all possible limits in genres and styles'.[36] Their ultimate goal is 'life-affirming performance about love, freedom and beauty which, at the end of the day' – they optimistically claim – 'will save the world'.[37] They create life at its highest pitch: shifting in rhythm, dynamic, boisterous, outrageous. From cabaret, the group inherits the transgression of generic and cultural boundaries, the emphasis on song and/as performance, the defiant humour, satirical edge, spectacle and dissent. Bizarre and hyper-energized, centred in contemporary hipster counterculture, their freak cabaret returns us to the concept of the antic in the *OED*'s many definitions: grotesque gesture, dress, shape, movement, fantastical clowning and theatrical representation.

The band's first hit song, 'Rozy/Donbass' ('Roses/Donbass'), viewed by 1.5 million viewers on YouTube, opens with the ponderous chanting of the first quatrain of Shakespeare's Sonnet 35 in which the speaker insists upon the flawed nature of all existence – human, natural and cosmic:

> No more be griev'd at that which thou hast done:
> Roses have thorns, and silver fountains mud;
> Clouds and eclipses stain both moon and sun,
> And loathsome canker lives in sweetest bud.

Their embrace of the imperfect nature of humanity reflects the band's avowed apolitical, though firmly anti-establishment, stance. Combining Shakespeare's words with those of a Ukrainian folk song (about a woman going mushroom picking), a punk spirit, rap rhythms and percussive sounds, the Dakh Daughters' collage is punctuated throughout with the raspy, shouted-out repetition of the word 'Donbass'.

'Roses/Donbass', the song's title, refers to the way in which the city of Donbass in Eastern Ukraine had been mythologized during the Soviet period as a city of a million roses, one for each inhabitant. It was, in fact, the industrial region of Eastern Ukraine, the centre of steel and coal production, and the stronghold of the then president Victor Yanukovych. Going further back, its history is more sinister: it was also the area that, arguably, suffered most from the Holodomor, the mass starvation during the famine of 1932–3. The menacingly chanted refrain of 'Donbass', part of the aggressive cabaret style, looked backward in time, reshaping history with cabaret madness. In retrospect, it was also as uncannily predictive as Kurbas's 1924 *Macbeth*.[38] The song, it must be emphasized, was written *before* the occupation of Crimea and the invasion of Eastern Ukraine. Indeed, the Daughters had publicly insisted on their rejection of the political in favour of an art-for-art stance, or what musicologist Maria Sonevytsky has called 'the privilege of political ambivalence'.[39] When the song was created, in 2012, Donbass was undergoing a wide-ranging renaissance that included the opening of riverside cafés, bars, clubs, opera, theatre, a new soccer stadium and a state-of-the-art international airport.

In late 2013, the Dakh Daughters brought their freak cabaret to the makeshift stage of the Euromaidan – the locus in central Kiev for the massive protests against the government of president Yanukovych, and the place where, shortly thereafter, presidential snipers fired at and killed nearly seventy unarmed citizens. Here, their cabaret strategies, reinterpreted by the many

---

February 2007) of *Prolog Macbeth*: 'more like hallucination than theatre'. See http://dax.com.ua/en/press/article3040.
36  See www.go2kiev.com/view/dakh.html. To date, the Dakh Daughters have performed in the Netherlands, Switzerland, Portugal, Slovakia, Norway, Austria, Germany, Estonia, Belgium, Poland, France, Russia, Brazil and throughout Ukraine.
37  www.go2kiev.com/view/dakh.html.
38  Sonevytsky, 'The freak cabaret', p. 291.
39  Sonevytsky, 'The freak cabaret', p. 292.

hundreds of thousands of demonstrators disillusioned with power and tired of corruption, acquired a darker resonance – one that was cemented after the invasion and the war which followed. It is now a song that is both indelibly stained with the fact of war and also serves as a kind of anthem for disenchanted youth. Analysing the Dakh Daughters' achievements, playwright Natalia Antonova has observed that the band 'does not establish an unattainable ideal for the audience to follow, it invites the audience to participate in the drama, in the fun. It sinks its pearly white teeth into politics, then spits it out, and turns it into something unexpectedly beautiful in the process.'[40]

Since 2014, the war in Eastern Ukraine has taken more than 10,000 lives, and displaced many more; it has broken apart families and created new socio-political fissures. Within this tragic framework, cabaret may be considered useless: it neither solves issues nor takes sides. With its galvanizing mix of the lyrical and the aggressive, the ugly and the beautiful, the funny and the touching, the intellectual and the irrational, cabaret, like Hamlet's antic disposition, is an oblique, wild and whirling form that points to and reflects the madness of the world. Like MacLeish's second way of dealing with war, cabaret offers neither morality, nor text, nor lesson – just the complexity of the human.

---

[40] Natalia Antonova, 'Jamala, the Dakh Daughters, and Ukraine's new femininity', July 2016, www.wdw.nl/en/review/desk/jamala_the_dakh_daughters_and_ukraine_s_new_femininity.

# THE COMEDY OF *HAMLET* IN NAZI-OCCUPIED WARSAW: AN EXPLORATION OF LUBITSCH'S *TO BE OR NOT TO BE* (1942)

## REIKO OYA[1]

### 'AGAINST A SEA OF TROUBLES'

In March 1942, Bosley Crowther, the film critic for the *New York Times*, was dismayed to see the premiere of Ernst Lubitsch's comedy film, *To Be or Not to Be*, which featured a troupe of Polish actors outmanoeuvring the dumb Gestapo and successfully saving the Polish underground. The egomaniacal star couple of the Polski Theatre, Joseph and Maria Tura, were played by the vaudeville and radio entertainer Jack Benny and the 'queen' of screwball comedy, Carole Lombard. Crowther resented that the film director made 'a spy-thriller of fantastic design amid the ruins and frightful oppressions of Nazi-invaded Warsaw', adding that '[t]o say it is callous and macabre is understating the case'.[2] The film's mixture of comedy and tragedy perplexed many other critics, who complained that 'a farce set against the agonies of bombed Warsaw, is in the poorest of tastes'.[3] Comedic representation of the Nazi oppression was not new in Hollywood: Charlie Chaplin had used satiric laughter to great effect in the stirring denunciation of Adolf Hitler in *The Great Dictator*. Somewhat inconsistently, Crowther raved about Chaplin's work when it was released in October 1940, stating that the 'tragicomic' film is 'a truly superb accomplishment by a truly great artist – and, from one point of view, perhaps the most significant film ever produced'.[4]

As a matter of fact, the war situation significantly worsened for the Allies between the two releases. Occupying Kiev, besieging Moscow and wrecking Yugoslavia, the seemingly unstoppable Nazis started the systematic killing of Polish Jews under a secret programme to be known as 'Operation Reinhardt' in January 1942, establishing concentration and extermination camps at Bełżec, Sobibór and Treblinka. It is sobering to think that, when the film's protagonist Joseph Tura impersonated a Nazi colonel (known as 'Concentration Camp Ehrhardt') and quipped, 'Ha, ha. Yes, yes. We do the concentrating and the Poles do the camping', the Holocaust was actually accelerating in Poland. America's relationship to the war in Europe also changed. When *The Great Dictator* premiered, isolationist sentiments were still strong and the film 'could be laughed at with disinterested appreciation'.[5] The United States finally entered

[1] I would like to thank Ann Thompson, Maddalena Pennacchia, Matthew Hanley, Yuji Kaneko and Nick Midgley for their pertinent and constructive comments on the early versions of this chapter. I am also grateful to the anonymous reviewers for their generous attention to the manuscript.

[2] Bosley Crowther, 'The screen', *New York Times*, 7 March 1942.

[3] C. A. Lejeune, '*The films*', *Observer*, 3 May 1942. Peter Barnes gives a summary and analysis of contemporary reviews of the film in the BFI Film Classics volume *To Be or Not to Be* (London, 2002), pp. 46–51.

[4] Bosley Crowther, '*The Great Dictator*', *New York Times*, 16 October 1940.

[5] Cited in Gerd Gemünden, *Continental Strangers: German Exile Cinema, 1933–1951* (New York, 2014), p. 80.

the war in December 1941 in response to the Japanese empire's surprise attack on Pearl Harbor, and the situation changed almost overnight. Shot in late 1941 and released in March 1942, *To Be or Not to Be* came into being at a troublous time indeed, when Hitler was no longer a laughing matter.

By the spring of 1942, anti-Nazi films were actually 'working up fresh steam for box office' in America as producers and distributors hoped that the audience's pre-war 'apathy' towards Hitler's dictatorship would 'be replaced by active interest under changed conditions now existing'.[6] Among them, Lubitsch's take on the Nazis was highly idiosyncratic: while other films portrayed SS officers as stereotypical movie villains, he lampooned them and their 'Führer' by using such standard comedy tropes as disguise, impersonation and repetition. The director explained his conception of Nazi evil in his reply to Crowther:

I admit that I have not resorted to methods usually employed in pictures, novels and plays to signify Nazi terror. No actual torture chamber is photographed, no flogging is shown, no close-up of excited Nazis using their whip and rolling their eyes in lust. My Nazis are different; they passed that stage long ago. Brutality, flogging and torturing have become their daily routine. They talk about it with the same ease as a salesman referring to the sale of a handbag. Their humor is built around concentration camps, around the sufferings of their victims.[7]

Admittedly, *To Be or Not to Be* was produced before the Wannsee conference and, even at the time of the film's release, Lubitsch, like the rest of the world, had yet to know the full horror of the Holocaust, which would only come to light after the surrender of Nazi Germany in May 1945. This, however, only underlines the prophetic insight of the director, whose view on the Nazis remained exactly the same when he wrote to his biographer Herman G. Weinberg in 1947: '[d]espite being farcical, it [*To Be or Not to Be*] was a truer picture of Naziism [*sic*] than was shown in most novels, magazine stories, and pictures which dealt with the same subject'.[8] Indeed, Lubitsch's emphasis on the

Nazis' 'banality of evil' notably anticipated Hannah Arendt's observation about Adolf Eichmann, one of the prime organizers of the Holocaust, when he was tried for 'crimes against humanity' by the District Court of Jerusalem in 1961.[9] The director's total commitment to the comedy film sets him apart even from Chaplin, who regretted having made *The Great Dictator* when the atrocities of the Nazis were laid bare after the war ('Had I known of the actual horrors of the German concentration camps, I could not have made *The Great Dictator*; I could not have made fun of the homicidal insanity of the Nazis').[10] Lubitsch defended *To Be or Not to Be* against hostile critics repeatedly, and never disavowed the Nazi travesty until his premature death aged 55 in 1947.[11]

In *To Be or Not to Be*, Crowther noted an indecorous, and immoral, juxtaposition not simply of comedy and profound tragedy, but also of fiction and real life. *The Great Dictator* was located in a fictional 'Tomania' ruled by 'Adenoid Hynkel', while Lubitsch's 'fantastic comedy' was set against 'a background of contemporary woe'. The year 1941 had already seen a flurry of films (such as Edward H. Griffith's *One Night in Lisbon* and Henry Hathaway's *Sundown*) that were set against a World War II backdrop. To Crowther, *To Be or Not to Be* was yet another example of this unacceptable confusion of opposites:

It is time some one justified this tendency ... to use the world's current misery as a backdrop for artificial

---

6 *The Hollywood Reporter*, 20 February 1942. Anti-Nazi films released in the USA in 1942 include *All Through the Night*, *Dangerously They Live*, *Desperate Journey*, *Mister V* (a.k.a. '*Pimpernel*' *Smith*), *Joan of Paris*, *Paris Calling*, *Nazi Agent*, *The Invaders* (a.k.a. *49th Parallel*) and *Pied Piper*.

7 Ernst Lubitsch, 'Mr. Lubitsch takes the floor for rebuttal', *New York Times*, 29 March 1942.

8 Herman G. Weinberg, *Lubitsch Touch: A Critical Study* [1968], 3rd edn (New York, 1977), p. 287.

9 Hannah Arendt, *Eichmann in Jerusalem: A Report on the Banality of Evil* (New York, 1963).

10 Charles Chaplin, *My Autobiography* (London, 1964), p. 426.

11 See his reply to Crowther, cited above, and his letter to the reviewer for the *Philadelphia Inquirer* (Mildred Martin), cited in Weinberg, *Lubitsch Touch*, pp. 246–7.

shows . . . It is time some one gave an explanation for this disregard of sensibility. There is certainly no artistic warrant for such a shocking confusion of realism and romance as is especially notable in *To Be or Not to Be*. And you'd think that the feelings of most persons would be completely outraged by a picture which airily banters within the wretched confines of Nazi-invaded Warsaw.[12]

Crowther's resentment was echoed by many reviewers, who censured Lubitsch's 'surprising choice' of occupied Warsaw as the setting for his comedy, saying, 'Hitler in Ruritania, yes, but the Gestapo in Poland, no'.[13] *To Be or Not to Be* certainly encompasses tragedy and comedy, and reality and fiction. Even those who were mostly positive about the film were shocked that it 'makes laughing matters of corpses and killings, with moments of high comedy, of satire, and – occasionally – of stunning realism'.[14] What Crowther and other critics did not quite realize was that the film is also *about* the different theatrical genres and different registers of truth. Lubitsch carefully scripted these apparent opposites in the film to resist the Nazi terror.

## LUBITSCH THE SHAKESPEARIAN

Ernst Lubitsch was born in 1892 into an Ashkenazi Jewish family in Berlin. He turned his back on his father's prosperous tailoring business to pursue a career in theatre. In 1910, he called upon Victor Arnold, a foremost stage comedian and character actor and a close associate of Max Reinhardt. Lubitsch's audition piece with Arnold was Shylock's powerful lines:

He hath disgraced me, and hindered me half a million; laughed at my losses, mocked at my gains, scorned my nation, thwarted my bargains, cooled my friends, heated mine enemies, and what's his reason? – I am a Jew. Hath not a Jew eyes? Hath not a Jew hands, organs, dimensions, senses, affections, passions; fed with the same food, hurt with the same weapons, subject to the same diseases, healed by the same means, warmed and cooled by the same winter and summer as a Christian is? If you prick us do we not bleed? If you tickle us do we not laugh? If you poison us do we not die? And if you wrong us shall we not revenge? If

we are like you in the rest, we will resemble you in that. If a Jew wrong a Christian, what is his humility? Revenge. If a Christian wrong a Jew, what should his sufferance be by Christian example? Why, revenge. The villainy you teach me I will execute, and it shall go hard but I will better the instruction.

(*The Merchant of Venice*, 3.1.50–68)

At the time, Reinhardt's enormously successful 1905 production of *The Merchant of Venice* was still playing at the Deutsches Theatre, with Jewish actor Rudolf Schildkraut playing a 'humanly convincing' Shylock to great acclaim.[15] The youthful Lubitsch did not quite reach the famed actor's artistic heights. As the director later jokingly reminisced, he delivered the speech 'as it was never played before – nor since, I hope – and I think he [Arnold] was a little frightened. He admitted, however, that I had possibilities.'[16] By 1911, the young novice actor found a place in Reinhardt's company at the Deutsches, where he stayed until 1918 and played such minor parts as Lancelot in *The Merchant of Venice*, the second gravedigger in *Hamlet*, and Peto in *Henry IV*. Meanwhile, he started working in cinema in 1913 as an actor, and later increasingly as a director. He directed popular silent comedies, including *Kohlhiesels Töchter* (*Kohlhiesel's Daughters*, 1920), an adaptation of *The Taming of the Shrew*, and *Romeo und Julia im Schnee* (*Romeo and Juliet in the Snow*, 1920), before scoring massive international success for historical spectacles such as *Madame DuBarry* (retitled

---

[12] Bosley Crowther, 'Against a Sea of Troubles', *New York Times*, 22 March 1942.

[13] 'To Be or Not to Be', *The Times*, 30 April 1942; Dilys Powell, 'The new films', *Sunday Times*, 3 May 1942. For similar statements, see, among others, John T. McManus, PM, 8 March 1942, in *Selected Film Criticism*, ed. Anthony Slide, 7 vols. (Metuchen, NJ, 1982–5), vol. 5, pp. 237–8; Lejeune, 'The films'; and the prize-winning letter from a reader (one Donald Jolly) entitled 'War background for comedy: a matter of taste?' *Picturegoer*, 8 August 1942.

[14] J[ames] S[helley] H[amilton], 'To Be or Not to Be', *National Board of Review Magazine* (1942), 5–6; p. 6.

[15] See Andrew G. Bonnell, *Shylock in Germany: Antisemitism and the German Theatre from the Enlightenment to the Nazis* (London, 2008), pp. 47–54.

[16] Cited in Scott Eyman, *Ernst Lubitsch: Laughter in Paradise* (Baltimore, MD, 1993), p. 31.

*Passion*, 1919) and *Anna Boleyn* (*Deception*, 1920). He relocated to Hollywood in 1922.

In America, Lubitsch achieved fame for his stylish comedies of manners and for his elegant 'touch', where the plot, the dialogue and the camera achieved great economy and sophistication by leaving out the mundane and the obvious.[17] Meanwhile, though Lubitsch did not quite cut it at Reinhardt's theatre, his love for Shakespeare endured. According to Gottfried Reinhardt, Max's son and a Lubitsch assistant, the director worked with various screenwriters but was actually '60 percent responsible' for virtually all the scripts he filmed,[18] and, in them, allusions to Shakespeare were a Lubitsch hallmark. Mark Antony's 'Friends, Romans, countrymen' (*Julius Caesar*, 3.2.74), for instance, appears both in *The Shop Around the Corner* (screenplay by Samson Raphaelson from a play by Nikolaus Laszlo, 1940) and *To Be or Not to Be* (screenplay by Edwin Justus Mayer from a story by Melchior Lengyel). In *Bluebeard's Eighth Wife* (1938), American multi-millionaire Michael Brandon (Gary Cooper) studies *The Taming of the Shrew* to win over his uncooperative eighth wife (Claudette Colbert), while in *Trouble in Paradise* (1932), Gaston Monescu (Herbert Marshall), a master thief masquerading as a baron, eagerly awaits a rendezvous with a (supposed) countess (Miriam Hopkins), asking the waiter, 'If Casanova suddenly turned out to be Romeo having supper with Juliet, who might become Cleopatra, how would you start?' There is another *Romeo and Juliet* reference in *One Hour with You* (1932), where a minor character, Adolph (Charles Ruggles), appears dressed as Romeo, in ruffles and tights. He is tricked by his valet into thinking he is attending a costume ball. Now he finds out the truth on the phone ('What? Romeo? You're coming as Romeo?' – 'Yes, Romeo. Of *Romeo and Juliet*. What? What? Not a costume party. Oh, oh. All right') and interrogates the servant:

ADOLPH Why did you tell me it was to be a costume party?
VALET Ah, monsieur. I did so want to see you in tights.

Adolph tries not to react, but his nervous blink betrays his inner panic. Indeed, Shakespeare was a talisman to Lubitsch, and his plays were conjured up even when their contribution to the film's plot-line was flimsy. In *To Be or Not to Be*, however, Shakespeare's Danish prince and his Jewish moneylender played a vital part in Lubitsch's fight against the Nazi oppression.

## 'SEIN ODER NICHTSEIN': HITLER'S HAMLET

It is not a little alarming to know that Hamlet's dilemma about 'To be, or not to be' was given its 'Final Solution' in Hitler's militaristic writings and speeches. Hitler used the phrase 'Sein oder Nichtsein', the customary German rendition of 'To be, or not to be' since the time of Christoph Martin Wieland and August Wilhelm Schlegel, from his election campaign on 5 March 1932 right up to his final New Year's message to German soldiers on 1 January 1945.[19] In his autobiographical writing *Mein Kampf* (*My Struggle*, 1925/6) alone, the phrase was used six times to promulgate his idea of the life-or-death battle. His description of the outbreak of World War I is typical:

[t]he fight for freedom had broken out on an unparalleled scale in the history of the world. From the moment that Fate took the helm in hand the conviction grew among the mass of the people that now it was not a question of deciding the destinies of Austria or Serbia but that the very existence [Sein oder Nichtsein] of the German nation itself was at stake ... I believed that it was not a case of Austria fighting to get satisfaction from Serbia but rather a case of Germany fighting for her own existence – the German nation for its own to-be-or-not-to-be, for its freedom and for its future.[20]

---

[17] The phrase 'Lubitsch touch' was made famous by Weinberg's 1968 book with that title.
[18] Cited in Eyman, *Ernst Lubitsch*, p. 179.
[19] Wolfgang Mieder, *The Politics of Proverbs: From Traditional Wisdom to Proverbial Stereotypes* (Madison, WI, 1997), p. 20. Mieder helpfully lists the 'Sein oder Nichtsein' citations in Hitler's writings and speeches.
[20] Adolf Hitler, *Mein Kampf*, trans. James Murphy [1939] (London, 1942), p. 99.

The phrase 'Sein oder Nichtsein' is idiomatic in German, and the citations in *Mein Kampf* might not directly refer to Shakespeare's *Hamlet*, even though Hitler actually regarded the English playwright as 'far superior to even Goethe and Schiller'.[21] The dictator's reference is significant all the same. As Karl Kraus observed in his 1933 anti-Nazi polemic, *Die Dritte Walpurgisnacht* (*The Third Night of Walpurgis*), Hitler's rise to power entailed an 'Aufbruch der Phrase zur Tat' ('a change from cliché to action'), where popular idioms were perverted into calls for war.[22] The dictator utilized the hackneyed Shakespearian phrase to hammer his point home and make it a reality.

In Hitler's formulation, 'To be, or not to be' was no longer a question, as 'Sein' was obviously the only feasible choice and Germans must single-mindedly struggle for their existence through military actions. This departs from Hamlet's musings completely. To Shakespeare's prince, 'to be' is to patiently 'suffer' life's hardships, while 'not to be', which to him seems more desirable at first, is 'to take arms' against them and die in fighting the inevitable losing battle. In the end, the 'dread of something after death' deconstructs the binary of suffering and action, and 'enterprises of great pith and moment' lose 'the name of action' (*Hamlet*, 3.1.58–90). The dictator used Hamlet's line just to pursue his very own political and military goals.

Hitler similarly exploited the familiar idiom to formulate his theory of war propaganda. Germany was waging war 'for its very existence' and its propaganda should solely 'strengthen the fighting spirit in that struggle and help it to victory':

when nations are fighting for their existence on this earth, when the question of 'to be or not to be' has to be answered, then all humane and aesthetic considerations must be set aside; for these ideals do not exist of themselves somewhere in the air but are the product of man's creative imagination and disappear when he disappears.[23]

Hitler argued that humanism and aesthetics 'are characteristic of only a small number of nations, or rather of races' (such as the Jews, one might surmise), and that '[h]umane and aesthetic ideals will disappear from the inhabited earth when those races disappear which are the creators and standard-bearers of them'.[24] He advocated a 'systematically one-sided attitude towards every problem that has to be dealt with'. Propaganda 'must not investigate the truth objectively' but 'present only that aspect of the truth which is favourable to its own side'.[25] War propaganda underplays inconvenient truths and reduces real-world complexities to a stark black-and-white situation. Once again, people are not given any choice.

Portraying the Polish underground movement in *To Be or Not to Be*, Lubitsch included three shots of *Mein Kampf* in display windows at which resistance fighters hurl stones (Figures 15 and 16).[26] He might not have been reacting specifically to the six Hamletian citations in *Mein Kampf*: the director did not like reading books, to begin with, and was unlikely to have pored over the dictator's pernicious, and badly written, tome. Nonetheless, Hitler's Manichean worldview must have been all too familiar to the German-born Jewish director. *To Be or Not to Be* challenged the dictator's military agenda in the contested site of the Shakespearian quotation, and championed the 'humane and aesthetic ideals' which the Nazi propaganda machine tried to quash. After all, Crowther made a pretty good point when he complained that 'Hamlet's most famous soliloquy was a positive declaration when compared to the jangled moods and baffling humors of Ernst Lubitsch's new film'.[27] By echoing, or even outdoing, Hamlet's ambivalence and procrastination, Lubitsch's Polish comedy resisted

---

[21] Timothy W. Ryback, *Hitler's Private Library: The Books that Shaped His Life* (London, 2009), pp. xi–xii.

[22] Cited in Mieder, *The Politics of Proverbs*, p. 12.

[23] Hitler, *Mein Kampf*, p. 106.

[24] Hitler, *Mein Kampf*, pp. 106–7.

[25] Hitler, *Mein Kampf*, p. 109.

[26] The connection between the Hamlet quotations in *Mein Kampf* and *To Be or Not to Be* has been largely overlooked in critical literature, a notable exception being a single paragraph in Stephen Tifft's insightful study, 'Miming the Führer: *To Be or Not to Be* and the mechanisms of outrage', *Yale Journal of Criticism* 5 (1991), 1–40; p. 5.

[27] Crowther, 'The screen'.

15 and 16 (below). Poles throw stones at Hitler's *Mein Kampf*. *To Be or Not to Be* by Ernst Lubitsch. © United Artists / Photofest.

16 *To Be or Not to Be* by Ernst Lubitsch. © United Artists / Photofest.

any quick resolution of contradictions and thereby defied the false dilemma between 'to be' and 'not to be' that Hitler had posed.

## LUBITSCH'S 'STRUGGLE'

Lubitsch was among Hitler's pet hates. In his Weimar cinema days, Lubitsch scored immense success by playing a series of racially typed Jewish bunglers. Thanks to these youthful exploits, he had the dubious honour of having his face featured in a Nazi propaganda poster with the legend 'The Archetypal Jew' in 1935.[28] His German citizenship was revoked, alongside that of other naturalized Jews who were deemed 'dangerous to the state', the same year.[29] *The Merry Widow* (1934) was banned in Germany 'on account of its director', and his name was included in the 'black list' of some sixty Hollywood personalities released by the Nazi Propaganda Ministry in 1938.[30] Lubitsch also secured a place in Fritz Hippler's anti-Semitic propaganda film *Der Ewige Jude* (*The Eternal Jew*, 1940), alongside such other 'foreign' German Jewish artists as 'the Jewish theatre director Max Reinhardt', 'the Jewish film director Richard Oswald' and 'the Jew Peter Lorre in the role of a child murderer' in Fritz Lang's *M* (1931). It shows newsreel footage of Lubitsch's visit to Berlin back in 1932, with a cynical voiceover: '[t]he Jew Ernst Lubitsch was hailed as a German film producer'.[31]

Being a member of the Hollywood Anti-Nazi League (1936) and subsequently of the European Film Fund (1939–), which supported German film artists stranded in France, Lubitsch was acutely aware of the tragic turn of events in Europe. In *To Be or Not to Be*, he opposed Hitler's heinous ideology not by bringing a direct indictment but rather by staging a sabotage. The film starts in Warsaw just before the Nazi invasion. The Polski company are rehearsing a new play, *Gestapo*, during the day and performing *Hamlet* in the evening. Meanwhile, the beautiful star of the company, Maria Tura, is arranging a clandestine meeting with an audience member, Polish military aviator Sobinski (Robert Stack), instructing him to visit her dressing room when her jealous husband is

intoning Hamlet's soliloquy, 'To be, or not to be'. As a result, Joseph Tura's big scene is wrecked by the dashing Polish patriot, who gets up from his seat in the second row and noisily walks out as soon as the famous soliloquy starts (Figure 17). The monologue is performed on three occasions in the film and is ruined in the same way every single time. Mladen Dolar gives an incisive analysis of Lubitsch's response to the most famous 'question' in the history of theatre:

[w]hat does comedy do with the question? *To Be or Not to Be* provides the brilliant answer: walk out on it. Three times there is Hamlet's monologue, and each time a guy walks out on it. Walk out on the question. To be or not to be? Sorry, I have to see my mistress … The answer to the question refuses the terms of the question and walks out, thereby answering not in the terms of the alternative, which seems to be exhaustive and exclusive – to be or not to be? – covering all possible entities and eventualities, squeezing them into the straitjacket of two clear-cut options.[32]

Exactly. It is, however, also worth noting that, for the film director, the 'straitjacket' was not really of Shakespeare's making. Lubitsch was addressing Hitler's reductive version of the 'question' which would lead to the 'Final Solution' in January 1942 at the Wannsee conference. He outstripped it by eliding the 'two clear-cut options' altogether.

The juxtaposition of reality and fiction that enraged Crowther is related to the question of 'to be' and 'not to be'. The Polish authorities ban the Polski's *Gestapo* show in a last-ditch attempt to placate Hitler. The Germans anyway invade Poland soon afterwards, and the Polski actors find themselves performing the censored play in real life

---

[28] Gemünden, *Continental Strangers*, p. 81.

[29] Eyman, *Ernst Lubitsch*, p. 232.

[30] Ben Urwand, *The Collaboration: Hollywood's Pact with Hitler* (Cambridge, MA, 2013), pp. 142–5.

[31] *The Eternal Jew* mistakenly cites Chaplin as a Jewish artist, probably misled by his role as a Jewish barber in *The Great Dictator*.

[32] Mladen Dolar, 'To be or not to be? No, thank you', in *Lubitsch Can't Wait: A Collection of Ten Philosophical Discussions on Ernst Lubitsch's Film Comedy*, ed. Ivana Novak (New York, 2014), pp. 111–29; p. 123.

17  Sobinski walks out on Joseph Tura's soliloquy. *To Be or Not to Be* by Ernst Lubitsch. © United Artists / Photofest.

to fool the Gestapo and save the Polish resistance. Lubitsch purposely mixed life and art in this metatheatrical film. While rehearsing *Gestapo*, theatre director Dobosh questions the authenticity of actor Bronski's Hitler make-up:

DOBOSH Who made you up?
MAKEUP MAN I did, Mr. Dobosh. What's wrong with it?

DOBOSH I don't know. It's not convincing. To me, he's just a man with a little moustache.
BRONSKI But so was Hitler.
DOBOSH Wait, it's not just the moustache. It's . . . I don't know. I just can't smell Hitler in him.
GREENBERG I can.
DOBOSH I know! I know! That picture! That's what he should look like!

BRONSKI But that picture was taken of me.
DOBOSH Then the picture's wrong, too.

The picture portrays an actor portraying Hitler, but to Dobosh, it is 'real'. In this way, 'real' Hitler was equated to his shadow's shadow. In the spy-thriller plot that follows, representation incessantly changes places with reality, and the Polish actors playing Gestapo for real are often indistinguishable from, or even more 'real' than, the real Gestapo officers. Joseph Tura, for instance, first poses as Colonel Ehrhardt to meet German spy Professor Siletsky. He next impersonates Siletsky to confront the real Ehrhardt. In the second meeting, Tura naturally mimics the mannerism of Siletsky he had observed in the first meeting. Much less naturally, the 'real' Ehrhardt also echoes the mannerism of Tura's 'fake' Ehrhardt.

Ehrhardt gives the most controversial line in the film during this second meeting. Totally unaware that the 'Siletsky' in front of him is Joseph Tura, Ehrhardt pans the narcissistic player's Shakespearian acting in his face, saying, 'What he did to Shakespeare, we are doing now to Poland.' The equation of a ham actor's butchering of a play with annihilation of millions of lives is shocking even from the mouth of the Nazi colonel. Even worse, the joke (almost) tricks the audience into sympathizing with a Nazi and laughing at the expense of a Pole, Tura's Hamlet acting being actually atrocious.[33] Ehrhardt's line was singled out for censure not only by hostile critics such as Crowther but by Lubitsch's close friends, including the film's producer Alexander Korda, Billy Wilder and the director's then-wife Sania, all of whom suggested eliminating the line after a private preview. According to director and screenwriter Walter Reisch, who was also present, Lubitsch was 'absolutely aghast' at the friends' suggestion and 'his proverbial humor froze up and nothing could thaw it out'.[34] The director adamantly refused to cut the line. The black, shock humour was his means for exposing the enormity and absurdity of the crimes committed by the Nazis. Even more importantly, he empowered the puny actors to outwit the perilous enemy by precisely blurring the line between Poland's brutal reality

and the Polski's theatrical illusion, between 'to be' and 'not to be'.

## WHICH THE JEW?

Lubitsch gave a firm personal commitment to To Be or Not to Be. The first shot of the film shows a shop sign in Warsaw bearing a Polish-flavoured version of his family name ('Lubinski'). After the Nazi invasion, it is shown again in the piles of rubble, giving eyewitness testimony to the devastation wrought by the German bombing raids. In the film, Felix Bressart, a Jewish émigré from East Prussia, played Polski actor Greenberg, who is a stand-in for Lubitsch. Greenberg, the only clearly marked Jewish character in the film, is a strenuous defender of laughter. Rehearsing Gestapo, the Hitler actor Bronski enlarges his part by inserting an unscripted gag line ('Heil myself').[35] The director is enraged:

DOBOSH That's not in the script!
BRONSKI But, Mr. Dobosh, please.
DOBOSH That's not in the script, Mr. Bronski.
BRONSKI But it'll get a laugh.
DOBOSH I don't want a laugh here. How many times have I told you not to add any lines? I want . . .
GREENBERG You want my opinion, Mr. Dobosh?
DOBOSH No, Mr. Greenberg, I don't want your opinion.
GREENBERG All right, then let me give you my reaction.
A laugh is nothing to be sneezed at.
DOBOSH Folks, I want everybody to understand this. This is a serious play, a realistic drama . . .

As if to preclude Crowther's criticism, Greenberg defends the vital importance of comedy and laughter ('A laugh is nothing to be sneezed at'). Lubitsch also scripted in a Crowther-style preaching ('This is

---

[33] Tifft gives an incisive analysis of the 'promiscuous' aims and effects of Ehrhardt's line in 'Miming the Führer', pp. 3–11, to which I am indebted.

[34] 'An interview with Walter Reisch', in Weinberg, Lubitsch Touch, pp. 244–5.

[35] The phrase 'Heil myself' is memorably reused in the 'Springtime for Hitler' number in Mel Brooks's The Producers (1967). Brooks also remade Lubitsch's To Be or Not to Be in 1983.

a serious play, a realistic drama') and then cut it short by having Maria Tura enter in a figure-hugging silk gown. She intends to wear this absurdly sexy number in a concentration camp scene:

DOBOSH It is a document of Nazi Ger ... Is that what you're wearing in the concentration camp?
MARIA TURA Don't you think it's pretty?
DOBOSH That's just it.
MARIA TURA Well, why not? I think it's a tremendous contrast. Think of me being flogged in the darkness. I scream, the lights go on ... and the audience sees me on the floor in this gorgeous dress.

To Maria's proposal, which Crowther would certainly denounce as 'callous and macabre', Greenberg responds, 'That's a terrific laugh', upholding comedy in the face of dire disaster once again.

After arriving in Hollywood, Lubitsch specialized almost exclusively in comedies – the only exception being the 1932 anti-war film, *Broken Lullaby* (a.k.a. *The Man I Killed*) – and it was only natural for him to plead for laughter and joviality even in the middle of the international crisis. He wrote in 1943:

[t]here's a revolution on in the world. Is laughter to depart? Is gracious and graceful living, wit and the jocund interplay, the amusing warfare of man and woman all to vanish? Must I weep for the world that was and not be permitted to re-create it? Devoutly I hope not. For then I should not desire to make more films. I should be content to die.[36]

As far as *To Be or Not to Be* was concerned, however, laughter had a more specific political, or even subversive, undertone. According to Melchior Lengyel, who co-wrote the film, 'Nazis and Fascists are essentially humorless creatures': 'Hitler, as well as his stooge Mussolini, invariably stare[s] out into the world with puffed-up arrogance and furious faces. Democracy, on the other hand, smiles even in danger.' Lubitsch, along with other 'members of this brave detachment', was 'fighting with the weapons of laughter against Nazi fascism'.[37]

Like Lubitsch back in the Deutsches Theatre days, Greenberg is a perennial bit-part actor, and his ambition is to give Shylock's famous speech, which was the film director's audition piece. It is noteworthy in this context that, probably due to the ambivalence of values found in Shakespeare's text, performances of *The Merchant of Venice* decreased significantly in Germany under the Third Reich, and that Shylock's plea for common humanity was cut in Rainer Schlösser's sanitized version dedicated to Joseph Goebbels in 1940.[38] In the backstage of the Polski's *Hamlet* show, Greenberg confides in his sympathetic friend, Bronski the Hitler impersonator (of all people), about his dream of playing Shylock one day:

The Rialto scene. Shakespeare must have thought of me when he wrote this. It's me. 'Have I not eyes? Have I not hands, organs, senses, dimensions, affections, passions? Fed with the same food, hurt with the same weapons, subject to the same diseases? If you prick us, do we not bleed? If you tickle us, do we not laugh? If you poison us – do we not die?'

Here, Lubitsch replaced 'I' for 'a Jew' in Shakespeare's original ('Hath not a Jew eyes? Hath not a Jew hands, organs, dimensions, senses, affections, passions ... '). The substitution was so subtle and discreet that it was not noticed by reviewers and critics until Gerd Gemünden raised the issue in 2003.[39] Admittedly, Lubitsch's approach to Shakespeare was neither scholastic nor even accurate. To begin with, there is little reason to call *The Merchant of Venice* Act 3 Scene 1 'the Rialto scene'; he probably confused it with Act 1 Scene 3, where Shylock recalls how '[i]n the Rialto you [Antonio] rated me / About my

---

36 Cited in Eyman, *Ernst Lubitsch*, p. 289.
37 Melchior Lengyel, 'You cannot outwit wit', *Variety*, 1 April 1942.
38 See Bonnell, *Shylock in Germany*, pp. 145–7, 223–6.
39 Gerd Gemünden, 'Space out of joint: Ernst Lubitsch's *To Be or Not to Be*', *New German Critique* 89 (2003), 59–80; pp. 72–3. See also his *Continental Strangers*, pp. 90–4.

moneys and my usances' (1.3.106–7). His use of the
'To be, or not to be' monologue neglects the order
of events in Shakespeare's *Hamlet*, too. As
a *Picturegoer* reader shrewdly observed, 'if Hamlet
is making his "To be or not to be" soliloquy,
Ophelia [played by Maria Tura] must be waiting
in the wings to make her entrance immediately
afterwards and not entertaining young officers in
her dressing room'.[40] Nonetheless, Greenberg's
'misquotation' of Shylock's lines was deliberate
and highly strategic. This spear-carrier of the
Polski is clearly Jewish, his surname (for
Ashkenazi Yiddish Grinberg) being among the
most common anglicized Jewish names, but the
word 'Jew' is omitted not only from his Shylock
speech but also from the whole of the film, where
the actor and his colleagues are 'Poles' ostensibly
fighting for a 'Polish', not Jewish, cause. Like
Bressart, lead actor Jack Benny was Jewish, but
his character Joseph Tura is (in his own words)
'that great, great Polish actor' and patriot ('I'm
a good Pole. I love my country and my slippers!';
'Long live Poland!').

Gemünden argues that the omission of the
word 'Jew' from Greenberg's lines highlights 'a
censoring of "the one who cannot be named"'
and shows that 'Hollywood increasingly forced
Jews to camouflage their ethnic and religious
identity in the 1930s'.[41] Censorship is indeed
among the film's foremost concerns – it was
almost retitled '*Censor Forbids*' at one stage – but
there seem to be other motives behind the film's
excision of the crucial word. Like the 'To be, or
not to be' monologue, Shylock's speech is
repeated three times in the film, with subtle
inflections. By the time of Greenberg's third
recitation, the real Hitler has arrived in Warsaw
and the Polski actors are trying to flee Poland.
They don the Gestapo get-ups yet again and
infiltrate the Polski Theatre, where the Nazis
are having a celebratory event. After Hitler enters
the auditorium, Greenberg bursts from the bath-
room and gives Shylock's speech in front of the
'Führer' (once again, Bronski in disguise) and an
assortment of real and theatrical Nazi officers
(Figure 18):

JOSEPH TURA [disguised as a Nazi officer]: How did you
get here?
GREENBERG I was born here.
JOSEPH TURA What made you decide to die?
GREENBERG Him.
JOSEPH TURA What do you want from the Führer?
GREENBERG What does he want from us? What does he
want from Poland? Why all this? Why? Why? Aren't
we human? Have we not eyes? Have we not hands,
organs, senses, dimensions, affections, passions; fed
with the same food, hurt with the same weapons,
subject to the same diseases, healed by the same
means, cooled and warmed by the same winter and
summer? If you prick us, do we not bleed? If you
tickle us, do we not laugh? If you poison us, do we
not die? If you wrong us, shall we not revenge!

The first exchange ('How did you get here?' – 'I
was born here') assimilates Jews into their native
Poland, when indeed the Polish nationalist movement was in itself 'furiously antisemitic' long
before the outbreak of World War II.[42]
Shylock's assertion of his ethnic identity ('I am
a Jew', *The Merchant of Venice*, 3.1.54) is omitted
and replaced by 'Aren't we human?'. The phrase
'a Jew' in the following lines is replaced by 'we'
(rather than 'I', as in Greenberg's first delivery),
and his comparison 'as a Christian is' (3.1.59) is
omitted. In this way, 'the Jewish Question' is
transformed into a 'Polish Question', with Poles
and Jews united in the name of humanity, irrespective of race and religion.

After the standout performance, Greenberg is
arrested by 'Lieutenants Lange and Schneider',

40 R. J. Dean, 'We should worry', *Picturegoer*, 19
September 1942.
41 Gemünden, *Continental Strangers*, p. 94. For the avoidance of
the word 'Jew' in the film, see also Joel Rosenberg,
'Shylock's revenge: the doubly vanished Jew in Ernst
Lubitsch's *To Be or Not to Be*', *Prooftexts* 16 (1996), 209–44.
For the place of Jewish actors and characters in Hollywood
films, see, among others, Lester D. Friedman, *Hollywood's
Image of the Jew* (New York, 1982); Alan Carr, *Hollywood and
Anti-Semitism: A Cultural History up to World War II*
(Cambridge, 2001).
42 Przemysław Wielgosz, 'Poland's nationalists are burying
their antisemitic past – this is dangerous', *Guardian*,
6 May 2018.

18 Greenberg recites Shylock's lines to Bronski's 'Führer'. *To Be or Not to Be* by Ernst Lubitsch. Courtesy George Eastman Museum.

who are of course Polski actors in disguise. Greenberg should, therefore, be absolutely safe but, actually, this is the last time for the audience to see him: he is nowhere to be seen when the troupe escape Poland and arrive in 'the country of William Shakespeare' (Figure 19). Lubitsch does not give any explanation about the disconcerting disappearance of the Shylock actor. His Polski colleagues are blissfully oblivious of him once they hit Britain. Contemporary reviewers did not notice the anomaly, either.[43] Lubitsch was famous for his clever handling of what the audience sees and does not see on screen, but Greenberg's disappearance was probably the director's subtlest 'touch', quietly pointing to the fate of the Jews and Poles under the Hitler regime. Rebutting Crowther's criticism, Lubitsch once remarked: 'I was tired of the two established, recognized recipes: drama with comedy relief and comedy with dramatic relief. I had made up my mind to make a picture with no attempt to relieve anybody from anything at any time.'[44] That is exactly what he did in *To Be or Not to Be*, where the tragedy of millions of Jewish and non-Jewish Holocaust victims was inscribed in the apparently happy ending of the madcap comedy.

It is worth noting that Greenberg, who is the film's standard-bearer for laughter, repeatedly talks about 'a laugh' and 'a terrific laugh' but does not laugh at all. To the melancholic actor, and to Lubitsch, 'a laugh is nothing to be sneezed at', not a laughing matter, but is something worth staking his life on. Lubitsch added Greenberg's final line ('If you wrong us, shall we not revenge!') at the production stage – it was not included in the script.[45] This testifies to the see-thing anger against Nazi brutality that underpinned Lubitsch's Shakespearian comedy once again.

---

43 As far as I can trace, Joel Rosenberg's 1996 article, 'Shylock's revenge', was the first to discuss the disappearance of Greenberg.
44 Lubitsch, 'Rebuttal'.
45 Gemünden, *Continental Strangers*, p. 93.

19 The Polski actors (minus Greenberg) arrive in Britain. *To Be or Not to Be* by Ernst Lubitsch. © United Artists / Photofest.

## EPILOGUE: HITLER'S 'CAMP' BOOK

After suffering major health scares and a few heart attacks, Lubitsch pieced together his final film, *Cluny Brown* (1946), in which he revisited some of the issues raised in *To Be or Not to Be*. In this romantic comedy, Czech resistance fighter Adam Belinski (Charles Boyer) emigrates to England in 1938. He is a great lover of Shakespeare – he recites John of Gaunt's 'sceptered isle' piece (*Richard II*, 2.1.40–50) and Portia's 'quality of mercy' lines (*The Merchant of Venice*, 4.1.181–2) whenever he makes a toast to his bemused English hosts, who apparently cannot identify the sources. It was a light-hearted, and lightweight, swan song from the ailing director, who seems to have made a conscious effort to blur the link between it and *To Be or Not to Be*: in Margery Sharp's novel *Cluny Brown*, on which the film was based, Belinski was a *Polish* resistance fighter.[46] Still, Lubitsch could not resist sniping at the man and the book he loathed yet again. In a dialogue which is not in Sharp's story, Belinski explains the imminent war to the well-intentioned but extremely politically unaware Sir Henry Carmel:

---

[46] Margery Sharp, *Cluny Brown* (Boston, MA, 1944).

SIR HENRY I say, this talk about war is all poppycock, isn't it?

BELINSKI No, Sir Henry. I know Hitler.

SIR HENRY Oh, yes, he's written a book, hasn't he?

BELINSKI Yes.

SIR HENRY Big success, isn't it?

BELINSKI Very big.

SIR HENRY Then what more does he want? Why doesn't he lie down and keep quiet?

BELINSKI Well, if you really want to know, Sir Henry, read the book.

SIR HENRY Sort of an outdoor book, isn't it? What's it called? Oh, yes, *My Camp*.

BELINSKI Yes. It's a kind of an outdoor book. The old German idea of sport. Not your kind of sport. Sir Henry, there will be war. It's inevitable.

This brings us back to the 'we do the concentrating and the Poles do the camping' line in *To Be or Not to Be*. Lubitsch was not being funny when he filmed this joke. He was squarely pointing at Hitler's *Mein Kampf* as the true source of the 'callous and macabre' camping exploits in Poland. *To Be or Not to Be* was certainly a comedy film, but Lubitsch's anger was very real.

# THE LION AND THE LAMB: *HAMLET* IN LONDON DURING WORLD WAR II

## ZOLTÁN MÁRKUS

In Humphrey Jennings's wartime documentary, *A Diary for Timothy* (shot between September 1944 and January 1945, eventually released in 1946), Hamlet makes a surprising appearance. Written by E. M. Forster and narrated by Michael Redgrave, the film is addressed to an infant, Timothy James Jenkins, who was born on the fifth anniversary of the beginning of World War II. It depicts the world – more precisely, end-of-the-war Britain – into which little Timothy was born. Towards the middle of the film, after a loud bang of a preventatively exploded landmine, the film's narrator invites the viewers to visit London: 'and suppose you went up to London; London in November looks a nice, quiet place, but you'd find things are chancy here, too, and the bad's so mixed with the good, you never know what's coming ... '.[1] As an illustration of chancy life in London, we can take a quick glimpse at the façade of the Haymarket Theatre and quickly find ourselves in the midst of Act 5, Scene 1, of a stage production of Shakespeare's tragedy, as the Gravedigger's words swim in, ' ... that day that our last King Hamlet overcame Fortinbras'. Hamlet, played by John Gielgud,[2] enquires, '[h]ow long is that since?'; the response, of course, is, '[c]annot you tell that? Every fool can tell that. It was that very day that young Hamlet was born – he that is mad and sent to England.' After the somewhat worn-out joke about England where Hamlet's madness is 'no great matter' since 'there the men are as mad as he', the scene changes back to wartime London. Both the reference to Hamlet's birth in a film

celebrating the arrival of little Timothy, and the joking yet community-building allusion to mad England, clearly indicate that the brief scene has been purposefully selected to serve Timothy's education. In fact, two more times do we return to the Haymarket within this brief sequence of the film – both times the Gravedigger scene appears astonishingly topical as it both humorously and defiantly reflects on the hardship and destruction the war has inflicted on London.

Film historians usually celebrate Jennings's film as a thought-provoking documentary both chronicling and commemorating the end of the war in Britain; they particularly praise its cutting-edge narrative techniques as well as its virtuoso editing. As Lindsay Anderson puts it, '[n]ational tragedies and personal tragedies, individual happinesses and particular beauties are woven together in a design of the utmost complexity'.[3] The film's few critics, on the other hand, find fault with its arguably lukewarm and complicit ideological stance. Its most vociferous detractor, film critic Andrew Britton, states that '[a]t one level, of course, the

---

[1] Humphrey Jennings, *A Diary for Timothy*, in *The Complete Humphrey Jennings*, 3 vol. DVD/Blu-ray edition (BFI, 2012–13), vol. 3.

[2] The Haymarket production of *Hamlet* opened on 13 October 1944. It was directed by George Rylands. Beside John Gielgud's Hamlet, George Woodbridge played the first Gravedigger, and Francis Lister, Horatio.

[3] Lindsay Anderson, 'Only connect: some aspects of the work of Humphrey Jennings', *Sight and Sound* 23 (1954), 181–6; p. 186.

whole point of the film is that it is the business of Timothy, the beaming bourgeois baby to whom the diary is addressed, to make sure that peace was worth fighting for'. On the other hand, according to Britton, 'the investment in imagining the future as a sort of prolongation of the war is unmistakable: by 1944, war has become for Jennings the glue which holds Britain together'. In Jennings's film, Britton claims, '[t]he war is experienced, and re-created, as a solemn national pageant in which, war being war, death naturally figures'.[4] Britton finds the film quotation of the Haymarket *Hamlet* particularly problematic: 'the production, starring John Gielgud, is represented as taking place in contemporary London so as to naturalize the sequence in terms of the documentary convention'. Britton quotes Hamlet – '"Dost thou think Alexander looked o' this fashion i' the earth?" / "E'en so." / "And smelt so? pah!"' – and concludes:

[i]n the midst of all the spurious uplift about Timothy, salvation, and the fragile promise of fresh young life, Hamlet's 'pah!' tells us where *A Diary of Timothy* actually stands. At a moment when one might have thought that an artist with socialist sympathies would be pondering what might be made of the massive defeat of the European right, Jennings recalls the past, and anticipates the coming period from a position of total nihilism.[5]

Of course, the quoted passage with the emphatic 'pah!' never appears in the documentary: Britton suggests that, by quoting *Hamlet* in his film, Jennings also appropriates the play's ideology, which – according to Britton – is 'a position of total nihilism'.

A more recent critique of the film agrees that, by including Gielgud's *Hamlet* production, Jennings subordinated his documentary's ideological concerns to those of *Hamlet*. Alessandra Marzola warns us that, this way, Jennings has decided 'to disrupt the compactness of what had been conceived as an uplifting narrative with this Shakespearean outburst. In spite of its brevity, Jennings's six-minute *Hamlet* works crucially and subversively upon the 40-minute long *A Diary for Timothy* and affects the viewers' response both to previous and subsequent sequences which become

"Hamletized" in the process'.[6] Both critics of *A Diary for Timothy* claim that Jennings has 'Hamletized' his documentary to detrimental results. But what exactly did the process of 'Hamletizing' mean in 1944/5? In other words, what did *Hamlet* mean to Jennings and his contemporaries? And does what *Hamlet* meant to Jennings and his contemporaries mean the same to Jennings's critics or us?

\*\*\*

Recalling the first day of World War II, John Gielgud describes a telling change in his schedule of plays for the fall 1939 season:

I remember that on the day war broke out I had started rehearsals for *Rebecca*, Daphne du Maurier's play, in which I was to star with Celia Johnson. Michel St-Denis was next door at the Queen's Theatre rehearsing *The Cherry Orchard*, with Edith Evans and Ronald Squire, and we all met in the pub during the lunch break. I had decided not to go on with *Rebecca* and I told them why: 'It's a commercial play, very good for peace-time, but I don't think it's the right thing to do now. Perhaps I can go back to the Old Vic for a bit and do something classical.' It was Guthrie, I think, who suggested that we should do *Lear*.[7]

Behind Gielgud's decision to swap the 'commercial' *Rebecca* for the 'right' play by a classical author, preferably Shakespeare, there lies a somewhat cliché understanding of Shakespeare's expected function in war-stricken London. Commercial plays are for 'peace-time'; in times of trouble, however, one should roll out the 'classics' – most

---

[4] Andrew Britton, 'Their finest hour: Humphrey Jennings and the British imperial myth of World War II', *CineAction!* 18 (1989), repr. in *Britton on Film*, ed. Barry Keith Grant (Detroit, MI, 2009), pp. 302–13; p. 309.

[5] Britton, 'Their finest hour', p. 311.

[6] Alessandra Marzola, 'Negotiating the memory of the "People's War": Hamlet and the ghosts of welfare in *A Diary for Timothy* by Humphrey Jennings (1944–45)', in *Shakespeare and Conflict: A European Perspective*, ed. Carla Dente and Sara Soncini (Basingstoke, 2013), 132–44; p. 132.

[7] John Gielgud with John Miller and John Powell, *Gielgud: An Actor and His Time* [1979] (New York, 1980), p. 130.

of all, Shakespeare. During war, Shakespeare ought to become the principal author in the theatres of London, even if his plays might be financially less profitable than more contemporary and less weighty works, such as the play-version of du Maurier's highly successful novel of the previous year. The subordination of commercial imperatives to 'right things' also entails a spatial move from the home of Mammon, the West End, to the home of Shakespeare, the Old Vic.

On several counts, however, these implied expectations of Shakespeare's role proved to be off the mark in the first phases of World War II. When the war broke out, theatres were shut down in London for a short while, but then gradually re-opened again. The first theatres to re-open, however, did not produce Shakespeare but, rather, revivals of long-running revue shows (Windmill: *Revuedeville*; Little Theatre: *Herbert Farjeon's Little Revue*), and the new productions were not Shakespeare plays either, but J. B. Priestley's *Music at Night* (Westminster Theatre) and a revue titled *The Little Dog Laughed* (Palladium).[8] Moreover, when Shakespeare was eventually put on stage again during the 'Phoney War' or 'Sitzkrieg', it did not happen first at the Old Vic but at other commercial ventures: a modern-dress *Julius Caesar* produced by Henry Cass opened at the Embassy Theatre at the end of November 1939 and Donald Wolfit launched his first London Shakespeare season at the Kingsway in February 1940.[9] The *King Lear* production at the Old Vic mentioned by Gielgud opened only on 15 April 1940 (followed by *The Tempest* at the end of May). In other words, the Bard was not at all dominant in London at the beginning of the war. And when his plays were eventually put on stage, they did serve commercial purposes, as much as anything else.

Gielgud's implied expectations for Shakespeare's wartime role were clearly modelled on Shakespeare's reception in the previous World War, during which Shakespeare was frequently utilized as a direct propaganda device.[10] World War II, however, was a significantly different affair from the 'Great War'. One of the differences crucial to the reception of Shakespeare in London was

the population's increasing suspicion of chauvinistic propaganda after (and as a result of) World War I. The inglorious early history of the British propaganda ministry, the Ministry of Information (set up in September 1939 and discontinued right after the end of the war), reflected the general public's detestation of jingoism: 'Public Failure Number One' and 'Ministry of Aggravation' were only two of its popular nicknames.[11] Even representatives of traditionally more gung-ho theatrical genres such as cabarets, revues and vaudevilles refrained from excessive exploitations of nationalism. Charles B. Cochran, the highly popular showman of the Great War, made it clear when discussing his preparations for a new revue in November 1939 that '[t]here will be no Jingo note or flag waving about the show', because it seemed to him 'out of keeping with the general sentiment'. 'This is not a Jingo war', he emphasized.[12] Chauvinistic appropriations of Shakespeare, in other words, would not find much popularity in London at the beginning of the war.

The authorities' improvisatory regulations and the insecurity of the general situation might explain

---

[8] J. C. Trewin, *The Theatre since 1900* (London, 1951), pp. 255–6; 'Over the footlights', *Theatre World* 32 (1939), p. 171. *Music at Night* was 'new' to Londoners only; it had already been produced at the Malvern Festival in 1938.

[9] The dates of first nights of Shakespeare productions in my work are, for the most part, based on J. P. Wearing's *The London Stage, 1930–1939* and *The London Stage, 1940–1949* (London, 1990 and 1991, respectively).

[10] See G. D. Kew, 'Shakespeare and the Great War' (unpublished MA dissertation, University of Birmingham, 1977); Balz Engler, 'Shakespeare in the trenches', *Shakespeare Survey* 44 (Cambridge, 1992), 105–11; L. J. Collins, *Theatre at War: 1914–18* (London, 1998).

[11] Mariel Grant, *Propaganda and the Role of the State in Inter-War Britain* (Oxford, 1994), p. 2. About the Ministry of Information, see also Michael Balfour, *Propaganda in War 1929–1945: Organisations, Policies and Publics in Britain and Germany* (London, 1979); Marion Yass, *This Is Your War: Home Front Propaganda in the Second World War* (London, 1983).

[12] 'Charles B. Cochran discusses the theatre in war time', *Theatre World* 32 (1939), p. 174.

why some theatres, especially the 'serious' ones, were rather hesitant to open up again. In contrast, music halls and variety theatres resumed their activities relatively quickly. On one end of the spectrum, the companies of the Old Vic moved out of London prior to the Blitz. By the time their theatre building was badly hit in the spring of 1941, they had already found a hospitable base at the Victoria Theatre in Burnley, Lancashire, and had launched several tours in Northern England and South Wales. On the other hand, the Windmill variety theatre, for example, not only did not leave London but took pride in its dependability of serving the public. Their famous slogan boasted that 'we never closed' (which waggish patrons tended to change into the apparently similarly truthful 'we never clothed').[13] As Harold Hobson somewhat resentfully observes, 'the most interesting thing about the theatre during the war is this contrast between the courage of the frivolous and the cowardice of the serious theatre'.[14]

Hobson, however, oversimplifies the issue. As to the Old Vic and Sadler's Wells, the decision to leave their London headquarters for tours in the 'provinces' aimed at not only physical but also financial survival. The annual *Report on recent activities of the Old Vic* demonstrates that the company's finances were in a disastrous state at the beginning of the war. In an unprecedented move, the government came to the rescue in 1940 by offering financial support for the tours: the Council for the Encouragement of Music and the Arts (better known as CEMA, founded in January 1940: as the predecessor of the Arts Council of Great Britain, it was in charge of providing entertainment to civilians) supported the Old Vic's tours to the so-called 'reception areas' in the countryside to which Londoners were evacuated. On the other hand, the Entertainments National Service Association (ENSA, an acronym frequently deciphered as 'Every Night Something Awful', with the chief task of bringing the arts to the military) financed the ballet and opera companies' visits to garrison theatres.

In his report of 1940/1, Tyrone Guthrie emphasizes the noble effects of the move:

[t]ours to places, which in twenty-five years have had no professional entertainment other than 'the pictures' and exceedingly cheap Vaudeville, have been made financially possible by the assistance of the C.E.M.A. . . ., the medium through which the British Treasury, for the first time since the Tudors, has made manifest a belief that Art in general, and the art of the theatre in particular, is not merely a graceful amenity but a necessity to a great nation which considers itself, and wishes to be considered, civilized.[15]

Understandably, Guthrie does not focus on the 'negative' outcome of abandoning the metropolis but on the 'positive' results of residing in the provinces. He emphasizes the role of theatre as a 'civilizing' vehicle of a 'great nation'. Whether due to concerns for physical or financial survival, or due to the lofty determination to bring the arts to the masses in the country as a kind of 'National' theatre, the Old Vic withdrew from London in the fall of 1940 and did not return on a permanent basis until 1944.

J. C. Trewin remarks that 'London was by now a touring date', and, as such, it became a 'provincial city'.[16] Although, from the point of view of the Old Vic's wartime activities, this observation might ring true, from a more general perspective it is hardly justifiable. The air-raids and the occasional waves of evacuations notwithstanding, London throughout the war remained a large metropolis and the power centre of not only the United Kingdom but an empire of half a billion people. In addition to the Old Vic's occasional visits, even when their headquarters were moved from the city, it was primarily two producers, Donald Wolfit and Robert Atkins, who put Shakespeare's plays on the London stage during the war years.

---

[13] Simon Trussler, *The Cambridge Illustrated History of British Theatre* (Cambridge, 1994), p. 301.

[14] Harold Hobson, *Theatre in Britain: A Personal View* (Oxford, 1984), p. 126.

[15] Tyrone Guthrie, 'The Old Vic and Sadler's Wells: 1940–1941', in *Report on Recent Activities of The Old Vic and Sadler's Wells Companies* (Burnley, 1941), p. 4.

[16] J. C. Trewin, *Shakespeare on the English Stage: 1900–1964* (London, 1964), pp. 188, 189.

The quality and the reception of these productions were rather uneven, in the same way as Shakespeare's mass appeal also fluctuated in the course of the war.

When the bombing raids of the London Blitz began in earnest in September 1940, the theatres were forced to close down again because of the mandatory night-time black-out. Similarly to the fate of other theatre companies, Donald Wolfit's theatre troupe found its predicament going from bad to worse: the bombs were falling relentlessly; their planned autumn tour had to be cancelled; several men from the group had been drafted; and now the theatres were shutting down. In a last-ditch effort to survive, Wolfit followed the example of Myra Hess's lunchtime piano recitals at the National Gallery and launched his 'Lunch Time Shakespeare' series at the Strand Theatre. Starting in October 1940, he and his players performed one-hour-long Shakespeare programmes of short scenes, soliloquies and songs – altogether, more than 100 times. For the low price of only 1 shilling, the audience could enjoy Wolfit's theatrical 'Shakespeare quotations'.

The heroism of this enterprise was repeatedly emphasized in contemporary sources. The headline of an article in the *Sunday Express* reads, 'Dared to put on Shakespeare in bombed London' and opens with the lines: 'Donald Wolfit, thirty-eight-year-old actor-manager, wanted to put on a programme either so exciting or so amusing that it would make his audience forget war. He chose scenes from Shakespeare and launched the boldest experiment of the wartime theatre.'[17] The article prompts that Wolfit is doubly bold: firstly, because he dares to play in 'bombed London', and secondly, because he dares to play 'Shakespeare'. Apparently, both were equally audacious endeavours in London at the beginning of World War II.

Wolfit argues that he picked scenes from Shakespeare because they were the 'right entertainment for the lives people are living in London now'. He further explains: 'Shakespeare represents more than anything else the fighting spirit of the country. Only the best is good enough for people who are striving and enduring as Londoners are

today'.[18] But if Shakespeare was simply 'the best' and the 'right entertainment' of the people, why was it such a bold act to perform him?

Whether it was risky for the box office to play Shakespeare or not, performing in the city with the constant threat of air-raids was obviously a courageous act. Wolfit's lunchtime Shakespeare series quickly became part of the 'finest hour' myth. One weekly newspaper in 1944, for instance, recalls the enterprise with great enthusiasm:

When London was reeling under the worst blows of the *Luftwaffe*, Wolfit lightened the intellectual black-out which dropped over the capital ... Actors and audience alike braved the bombs and the barrage to speak or hear again the rich, unforgettable rhythms, to feast colour-starved eyes on the bright velvets and brocades of other days. Bombs destroyed the dressing-rooms, blew away costumes, covered the stage with debris, but the performance went on. Civil Servants, typists, journalists, factory workers and students all packed themselves eagerly into that oasis of light and entertainment.[19]

In 1945, *What's On* stated that 'Londoners will remember with gratitude [Wolfit's] pioneer work at the Strand Theatre during the height of the 1940 blitz, when his lunchtime performances gave weary war-workers the chance to mitigate the ominous sounds of the War with the world's greatest poetry.'[20] In the records of Wolfit's company, a similar sentiment is registered:

If for nothing else, the work of the company will long be remembered for their season of Lunch Time Shakespeare at the Strand Theatre London, in 1940, when every other legitimate theatre was closed. Playing for a token salary of 3 pounds per week, the nucleus of the company gave performances during the worst of the blitz to approximately 400 people every day, who drew inspiration from

---

[17] 'Dared to put on Shakespeare in bombed London', *Sunday Express*, 27 October 1940.
[18] 'Dared to put on Shakespeare'.
[19] 'Donald Wolfit – greatest actor since Henry Irving', *News Review*, 3 August 1944.
[20] 'Donald Wolfit: Shakespeare's ambassador', *What's On*, 10 August 1945.

the mighty verse and the songs and sonnets of a free England.[21]

All of these quotes suggest that Wolfit was triumphant on both fronts: on the one hand, as the only 'legitimate' theatre open, his company played even when bombs were falling on the city; on the other, he played Shakespeare to masses of people who 'drew inspiration' from the Bard.

That this 'finest hour' narrative was, to some extent, an artificially generated myth can be inferred from the notes of someone who actually visited a performance of this series of Lunchtime Shakespeare. A representative of the nation-wide anthropological field project 'Mass-Observation' sat in on a performance on 15 October 1940. Mass-Observation was started by Charles Madge, Tom Harrisson and Humphrey Jennings in 1937: based on the work of dozens of full-time observers ('investigators') and thousands of volunteers, it was an ambitious anthropological programme surveying numerous aspects of British everyday life. Its 'investigator', L. E. (Len England), filed the following report about the Lunch Time Shakespeare performance he saw:

Under the auspices of the Council for the Encouragement of Music and Arts, Donald Wolfit, Rosalind Iden, and company, are giving extracts from Shakespeare, daily at one, at the Strand Theatre; admission one shilling.

Inv. [investigator] arrived at twenty to one, and went in the stalls; there were no programmes and no attendants. At that time there was only one person there, though some were in the bar at the back where light lunches and refreshments were being served. By the time the programme started, there were about 50 people in the cinema [sic], equal numbers of men and women. Inv. would say that not more than half came from offices, though the purpose of the lunch hour time was to enable office workers to get there. Some came late, and some left early.

The announcement of what scenes were being shown was made by an Elizabethan page. Scenery was of the simplest, chairs and a few draped tables.

Extracts were as follows:

1. Chorus from Henry IV [sic]; prologues to Acts 1 and 4. Applause 7 seconds afterwards.
2. Twelfth Night. The Orsino Scenes, Act 1, Scene 1, ('If music be the food of love') and a later scene where he

dispatches Viola ('Patience on a monument'). Included the singing of 'Come Away, Death'
3. Three songs   'Who is Sylvia, where is she'
                 'Oh, Mistress Mine'
                 'Blow, blow, thou winter wind'

Applause 15 secs

4. Hamlet. The nunnery scene, Hamlet's scene with Gertrude, and then a short scene with Hamlet and Fortinbras (obviously added for its mentions of war with the Polack, but completely confusing the audience by having no connection with the rest of the scenes).

Applause 7 seconds

The applause shows that the three short songs were very much more popular than the long scenes from Hamlet, and inv. felt that the audience was bored with these scenes – there are many long speeches which depend considerably on their context to other scenes for effect. Also, throughout the whole show, there was not one joke made, not one comic scene chosen.[22]

Granting that one occasion is not enough to draw generalizations and that the shortcomings of the 'investigator' must have influenced his findings, we might risk the following conclusions nevertheless: since the CEMA supported the programme, Wolfit and Co. were protected against losses and that was why they could afford charging only 1 shilling. Moreover, the attendance of only 50 people questions the proud claim of the company that 'approximately 400 people' saw the shows 'every day'. And, finally, the fact that the audience was occasionally 'bored' and would have preferred more songs indicates that the majority of the people present did not always 'draw inspiration' from the performance or the Bard. Similarly to Wilson Knight's *This Sceptred Isle* project, and the various quotations of the Shakespearian 'patriotic oldies' in the papers and on the wireless, Wolfit also invoked Shakespeare as a propaganda device. His intentions sounded lofty

---

[21] 'Eight years of actor management, 1937–45: a record of the productions of Advance Players Association Ltd.', p. 4.

[22] Mass Observation Archive, Topic Collection: Live Entertainment, 3/K, *Theatre Reports* (MOA: TC 16/3/K). I thank the Trustees of the Mass Obervation Archive, University of Sussex, for granting me permission to quote this report.

enough, but his propagandistic results appear to have been half-baked at best.

\*\*\*

Shakespeare was not a frequently played author in London at the beginning of the war, but, by 1944, he had returned to the London stage with a vengeance. One of the obvious reasons for a Shakespeare revival by 1944 must have been that the city became less threatened by air-raids and thus became sufficiently safe for theatre companies (such as the Old Vic, for instance) to return and play there on a regular basis. This argument seems convincing enough, although it is worth bearing in mind, on the one hand, that Donald Wolfit had proven that it was possible to provide theatrical entertainment under dangerous conditions, and, on the other, that rocket attacks were still a rather disruptive element of everyday life in London in 1944. In my view, there is an equally important reason for the 'rediscovery' and evident popularity of Shakespeare in the city by the end of the war: as the victorious outcome of the war was increasingly inevitable, and as unsettling political and social insecurities and self-doubts were gradually overcome, Shakespeare was once again evoked as a cultural icon that symbolized a prideful national/nationalistic tradition and unity.

A quick look at *Hamlet* productions in wartime London well illustrates this argument. Whereas the 1930s could be labelled as a '*Hamlet* decade' in British theatrical history, the war years up to 1944 saw only Donald Wolfit's stage revivals of the play. A renewed academic interest in *Hamlet* in the 1930s went hand-in-hand with a theatrical renaissance of the play. John Gielgud, for one, played the role in four different productions in this decade. His first Hamlet was put on stage in the 1929/30 season at the Old Vic (transferred to the Queens in May 1930). His second effort in the title role took place in 1934 at the New Theatre; this production had the longest run in London since Henry Irving's *Hamlet* in 1874.[23] After playing Hamlet in New York in 1936,[24] his third London Hamlet was put on stage at the Lyceum in the summer of

1939: this production was also performed at Kronborg Castle in Elsinore, Denmark, between 7 and 15 July 1939.

Apart from Gielgud's *Hamlet*s, two other productions of this play were particularly significant in the 1930s. In the 1936/7 season, Laurence Olivier played the Prince at the Old Vic. This production, directed by Tyrone Guthrie, was also a great success and was noted for having played the Shakespearian text in its entirety: each performance started at 7 p.m. and ran until almost 11:30. This *Hamlet*, furthermore, was the first to be invited to Elsinore, two years before Gielgud's 1939 production. Tyrone Guthrie directed another milestone production of this particular play in October 1938 at the Old Vic: this was a modern-dress production that also offered the play in its entirety; Alec Guinness played the title role – he was only 24 years old.

After a great decade, there was a virtual dearth of *Hamlet* productions in London in the first years of World War II. It was only Donald Wolfit who produced this play, which, moreover, had very short runs: in 1940, he played it in eight performances; in 1941, in one performance; and in 1942, in sixteen performances.[25] These endeavours, however, were rather unsuccessful, both artistically and financially. As a reviewer of his 1942 revival of *Hamlet* remarked: '[i]n more spacious theatrical times than these Mr. Donald Wolfit might be well advised to leave Hamlet alone. It is a part which he plays creditably but not memorably.'[26]

[23] See James Agate's review about this production in Stanley Wells, ed., *Shakespeare in the Theatre: An Anthology of Criticism* (Oxford, 1997), pp. 210–15, as well as James Agate, *Brief Chronicles: A Survey of the Plays of Shakespeare and the Elizabethans in Actual Performance* (London, 1943), pp. 264–9. Gielgud's 1934 production had 155 performances, whereas Irving's production was played 200 times. See John A. Mills, *Hamlet on Stage: The Great Tradition* (London, 1985), p. 216.

[24] About this production, see Rosamond Gilder, *John Gielgud's 'Hamlet': With Notes on Costume, Scenery and Stage Business by John Gielgud* (New York, 1937).

[25] These figures are based on Wearing, *1940–1949*.

[26] 'Strand Theatre: Hamlet', *The Times*, 21 January 1942.

The memory of Gielgud's, Guinness's and Olivier's Hamlets clearly overshadowed Wolfit's artistically less consequential efforts.

The year 1944, therefore, meant a turning point: in this year, no less than three *Hamlet* productions opened in London. Donald Wolfit started a new run of the play at the Scala (this production reached seventeen performances, which was his longest run of *Hamlet* during the war). In February 1944, furthermore, Tyrone Guthrie directed another innovative production: this time a distinguished Australian ballet dancer, Robert Helpmann, played the Prince of Denmark. Helpmann had already danced the role of Hamlet (in 1942, he had choreographed and danced the title role to Tchaikovsky's music), but it was the first time that he actually played the theatrical part. As a reviewer noted, the twenty-minute ballet was 'an extension of possibly ten seconds of delirium in the mind of the dying Hamlet. It was not Shakespeare, though most of the characters were there.'[27]

Guthrie's 1944 stage production was generally well received, although the majority of the reviews found Helpmann's Hamlet insubstantial. *The Times*, for instance, noted that 'Mr. Robert Helpmann's Hamlet, though clear and pointed, is much too light',[28] whereas James Agate observed that '[t]he trouble with this production is that Mr. Helpmann is not a great actor, but a charming one who reduces Hamlet to the size of figures in a canvas by James Pryde'.[29]

Out of the three *Hamlet* productions in 1944, Gielgud's staging was celebrated as the most successful. In a general overview of the development of British theatre in the first half of the twentieth century, Muriel St Clare Byrne devotes special attention to the 1944 Haymarket production of *Hamlet*. Byrne finds this a watershed production, describing it as follows:

[i]t was expertly designed, staged and lit: it was played by a distinguished cast, headed by the leading Shakespeare actor of the day; and it was produced by George Rylands, an English scholar and University lecturer, Fellow and bursar of his college, and director and trustee of the Arts Theatre at Cambridge. The lion and the lamb lying down together was in itself a portent – the theatre and scholarship, professional and amateur, the commercial theatre and state-aided Shakespeare.[30]

Byrne celebrates the production as a symbol of unity, emphasizing that it was created through the joint efforts of 'theatre and scholarship, professional and amateur', as well as, since the production was financially supported by the CEMA, of 'the commercial theatre and state-aided Shakespeare'. This line of argument is further bolstered when she adds that, '[n]or was this all: The production had already played to packed houses on its provincial tour, and in London the playgoing public, during the V2 bombing, in the last year of the Second World War, kept it running until August 1945'.[31]

After an extensive tour of the country – dashing through Manchester, Glasgow, Liverpool, Leeds, Bristol, Bournemouth, Cambridge, Derby and Oxford – the production starring Gielgud in the title role opened at the Haymarket Theatre on 13 October 1944. This was a greatly celebrated *Hamlet* with a high-powered cast: next to Gielgud's Hamlet, Leslie Banks played Claudius; Miles Malleson, Polonius; Leon Quartermaine, the Ghost; Marian Spencer, Gertrude; and Peggy Ashcroft, Ophelia. The production reached 106 performances. Horace Horsnell of the *Tatler and Bystander* reminded his readers that the role of Hamlet 'has been played in London during the past few months by such well-known actors as Donald Wolfit and Robert Helpmann; but Mr. Gielgud's

---

[27] 'Audience argued', *The Star*, 20 May 1942. About the setting and choreography of both the ballet and the theatrical production, see Leslie Hurry, *Settings and Costumes for Sadler's Wells Ballet's 'Hamlet'* (1942), *'Le Lac des Cygnes'* and the Old Vic 'Hamlet' (1944) (London, 1946).

[28] 'New Theatre: Hamlet', *The Times*, 12 February 1944.

[29] James Agate, 'Hamlet at the New-II', *Sunday Times*, 20 February 1944.

[30] Muriel St. Clare Byrne, 'Fifty years of Shakespearian productions: 1898–1948', *Shakespeare Survey 2* (Cambridge, 1949), 1–20; p. 18.

[31] Byrne, 'Fifty years', p. 18.

performance is likely to remain unrivalled'.[32] Ivor Brown also emphasized that '[t]his is the kind of Shakespeare I, for one, want, with neither actor nor producer attempting to steal the show, but a partnership of all the talents in service of the poet and his play'.[33] As in Muriel St Clare Byrne's comments, Brown also appreciated the stage producers' united efforts in the service of the Bard and his play.

James Agate titled his review of this production 'A great Hamlet', and began his praise of Gielgud's achievement by stating:

Hamlet is not a young man's part. Consider how ill it becomes a stripling to hold forth on the life after death, the propriety of suicide, the nature of man, the exuberance or restraint of matrons, the actor's art, the Creator's 'large discourse'. But Mr. Gielgud could not be of a better age; he is at the height of his powers; the conjunction is marvellously happy.[34]

Agate's acclaim of a mature Hamlet (Gielgud was 40 years old in 1944) ran against theories that had interpreted the Prince of Denmark as an adolescent 'stripling': imagining Hamlet as an experienced grown-up clearly entailed a defence mechanism against critical attitudes that had found Hamlet immature and lacking in proper judgement. While praising Gielgud's theatrical maturity, therefore, Agate also revealed his own interpretation of the Prince as a sober and wise hero.

Agate thus continued his praise of Gielgud's achievement: 'Mr. Gielgud is now completely and authoritatively master of this tremendous part. He is, we feel, this generation's rightful tenant of this "monstrous Gothic castle of a poem".' By quoting a well-known metaphor by Charles E. Montague, Agate declared Gielgud's 1944 Hamlet to be his best. And he went even further: '[i]n short, I hold that this is, and is likely to remain, the best Hamlet of our time'. Muriel St Clare Byrne agreed; her thoughts after having praised Gielgud's Haymarket Hamlet as a symbol of unity are quite illuminating:

[t]he tradition is there, and it's our own. As in the history of our literature, we have borrowed from abroad, and been enriched by our borrowing, turning it into 'blood and nourishment'. We have not thrown over our past; we have gone on, in the light of modern knowledge and modern technical developments in theatrical art which have modified but not fundamentally altered our taste.[35]

Byrne's rhetorical division between 'us' and 'them' recalls John Middleton Murry's appropriation of Hamlet a few years before; her distancing herself from radical and foreign innovations such as those of Komisarjevsky's echoes John Dover Wilson's objections against foreigners' disparaging views on the English Hamlet tradition, and her reference to Shakespeare as 'the romantic playwright' rehabilitates a tradition rooted in Romanticism that was severely criticized at the end of the previous war.

After finishing his London season, Gielgud went on a five-month tour under the aegis of the ENSA to perform to British troops serving in India and the Middle East. I find it significant that the Shakespeare play selected to entertain the troops and the local population was not a light-hearted Shakespearian comedy or a patriotic classic such as Henry V; it was Hamlet. Gielgud played the title role and he directed as well. The lion and the lamb lay down together one more time: Gielgud's very last performance ever as Hamlet took place at a matinee show in Cairo, Egypt.

As to the appropriation of Gielgud's Hamlet in A Diary for Timothy, we can now confirm that Humphrey Jennings's critics are right: Jennings does Hamletize his film. At the same time, it would be incorrect to call Jennings's quotation of the stage production 'disruptive' adaptation: the appearance of Hamlet (and Hamlet) in the documentary does not cause a destructive 'Shakespearean outburst' and does certainly not advocate or embrace 'a position of total nihilism'. The Hamlet with which Jennings Hamletizes his documentary has been thoroughly Englishized. As such, it functions as a perfect vehicle for defining and historicizing Englishness both in Jennings's film and in the Haymarket Theatre.

---

[32] Horace Horsnell, 'The theatre', Tatler and Bystander, 8 November 1944.

[33] Ivor Brown, 'Theatre and life', Observer, 15 October 1944.

[34] James Agate, 'A great Hamlet', Sunday Times, 22 October 1944.

[35] Byrne, 'Fifty years', p. 19.

# DIVIDING TO CONQUER OR JOINING THE RESISTERS: SHAKESPEARE'S LADY ANNE (AND WOOLF'S *THREE GUINEAS*) IN THE WAKE OF #METOO

## DIANA E. HENDERSON[1]

'Shakespeare and war' was the conference topic: this time, for once, I really did not intend to speak about gender. The world thought otherwise.

In October 2017, Hollywood producer Harvey Weinstein (once wittily hailed by Tom Stoppard as *Shakespeare in Love*'s 'only begetter, Mr. H. W.')[2] was accused of multiple sexual assaults. The weeks and months that followed saw countless women testifying to similar experiences of assault, harassment and silencing. Using the hashtag #MeToo to circulate their stories on social media, those who had endured isolated, isolating acts of violence found the power to speak and – at last – be heard. Dams burst: soon, other powerful sexual abusers were named, and male, trans and gender-nonconforming witnesses added their voices to the chorus. I began this article during those months, as exposure of assaults and misogynist backlash vied for public attention, even as gendered faultlines among those regarded as 'progressive' (already exacerbated in the USA by the 2016 presidential campaign) fractured further.

The early political effectiveness of #MeToo derived from its combination of the raw affective power of individual accounts and, through the sheer number of stories quickly told and recirculated, the ability to connect the extraordinary with the ordinary: those who had endured the predatory prurience of Hollywood's rich and famous had their traumatic encounters echoed across nations, classes and in countless everyday contexts. Those

(especially men) who were not familiar with the disheartening statistics began to notice, some bristling, others discovering that they knew more survivors of sexual assault than they had imagined – and that such widespread violence was normative.

As Simone de Beauvoir long ago recognized in *The Second Sex*, it is obviously bizarre that we should continue to regard the majority human population as a minority or tokenized 'other': in part, this has resulted from dividing, alongside other legitimate social distinctions, the ordinary from the extraordinary woman, and then dismissing the former, or creating rhetorical and social war between those thus categorized. Imagining oneself as the exceptional figure in dramatic fictions likewise comes at a cost. Thus, over the decades, I have been increasingly interested in the representation of more 'ordinary' women in Shakespeare's plays, at least as considered in terms of behaviour rather than social status: the Heros rather than the Beatrices, the way the Biancas have been set against the Katherinas. Building on the loyalty pressures that Adrienne Rich perceived within regimes of

---

[1] In memory of Barbara Hodgdon and Christy Desmet.

[2] 1998 Golden Globe Awards ceremony, broadcast live on 24 January 1999; in retrospect, screenplay winner Stoppard's seemingly innocuous off-colour joke about being asked to 'wrap up' (for UK listeners, the equivalent of 'zip up your fly') right before the quip about Weinstein demonstrates the unpredictability of our words in historical time.

'compulsory heterosexuality',[3] which remain espe-cially powerful for married women, I shall ulti-mately return to a strangely pertinent 'real-life' example of dividing to conquer from the late 1930s. That instance enmeshed gender, war, lit-erary criticism and a dash of Shakespeare, a decade before de Beauvoir published her lengthy analysis: it is Q. D. Leavis's scathing attack on Virginia Woolf's feminist anti-war tract *Three Guineas* – an attack which, not coincidentally, borrows its title from Shakespeare's *Richard II*.

But it is not only such rhetorical salvos or other divide-and-conquer behaviours among women that explain why many women experience the world as a battlefield. As the 2018 Nobel Peace Prize committee recognized, rape as a weapon of terror in war endures, and femicide remains a leading cause of premature death in 'peacetime' worldwide.[4] Given the importance of social media not only in spurring the #MeToo movement (and the Women's March before it) but also in creating new networks of Shakespeare scholarship, when considering my topic I solicited input there as well. Amidst the responses, Ellen MacKay's for-mulation best captured what this moment calls for: the analysis of 'war as a condition', a state of mind and body transcending borders and battlefields.

It is only most obvious that we are encountering the effects of war in the history plays. Transcending the First Folio categorization of comedies, trage-dies and histories, Shakespeare's corpus provides another relevant throughline: warrior men really *do* cause particular trouble for women. This is just as true in *Much Ado About Nothing* and *Othello* as when battle scenes are part of the play. And it is true even – or especially – when the war seems to be over.[5] Building on Patricia Cahill's insight that there are traumatic effects of war in early modern drama still to be explored, that awareness led me to think differently about those medieval women represented in early modern history plays who have long haunted my imagination, putting them in dialogue with female characters in other genres who are sexually slandered, to see the intersections anew.[6] Sexual assault's traumatic power to disrupt conventional boundaries and one's sense of

spacetime provides the extreme case, but the slip-page between rhetorical and embodied violence, both during and in the aftermath of war, haunts other gendered performances as well.

\*\*\*

All of which leads me back to a single troubling scene in *Richard III*, and the much maligned, often dismissed, figure of Lady Anne Neville. In this notorious early encounter, usually called

---

[3] Adrienne Rich, 'Compulsory heterosexuality and lesbian existence (1980)', in *Blood, Bread, and Poetry: Selected Prose 1979–1985* (New York, 1986), pp. 23–75.

[4] 'The Nobel Peace Prize for 2018', 5 October 2018, www.nobelprize.org/prizes/peace/2018/press-release; 'Femicide across Europe: Cost Action IS-1206', www.femicide.net. I use the word to describe gender-based murder of women, as attributed to Diana Russell in sociological research, although she herself cited Carol Orlock as its inventor in the 1976 *Crimes Against Women: Proceedings of the International Tribunal*, ed. Diana Russell and Nicole Van de Venn (Berkeley, 1990), p. 104.

[5] These truths are not confined to Shakespeare's drama – as I completed this article, two US veterans with records of sexual assault carried out horrific murders: the killing of two women in a Tallahassee, Florida, yoga studio by someone previously arrested on charges of battery against women and with an online track-record of 'incel' misogyny (2 November 2018; see www.nytimes.com/2018/11/03/us/yoga-studio-shooting-florida.html); and a mass shooting in Thousand Oaks, California, by a marine whose prior acts of violent anger were not deemed dangerous enough to warrant his being placed in custody. In the latter case, reports of PTSD have been supplemented by a female coach from his high school whom he attacked prior to joining the marines (7 November 2018; see www.bbc.com/news/world-us-canada-46150847 and http://losangeles.cbslocal.com/2018/11/08/thousand-oaks-gunman-high-school-coach-assault).

[6] See Patricia A. Cahill, *Unto the Breach: Martial Formations, Historical Trauma, and the Early Modern Stage* (Oxford, 2008), p. 209. On royal women (and especially Isabeau de Bavière's significance), see D. E. Henderson, 'What's past is prologue: Shakespeare's history and the modern performance of *Henry V*' in Henderson, *Collaborations with the Past: Reshaping Shakespeare Across Time and Media* (Ithaca, NY, 2006), pp. 202–58. On the sexually slandered 'ordinary' woman, see Henderson, 'Mind the gaps: the ear, the eye, and the senses of a woman in *Much Ado About Nothing*', in *Knowing Shakespeare: Senses, Embodiment, and Cognition*, ed. Lowell Gallagher and Shankar Raman (Baskingstoke, 2010), pp. 192–215.

a 'wooing' or 'seduction' scene, Richard of Gloucester isolates a war widow and war orphan – by which I mean the orphan of her actual father Warwick the Kingmaker (Richard Neville the Younger), though Shakespeare presents her grieving for her father-in-law, the dead King Henry VI, whose body accompanies her onstage and which she is attempting to have interred.

During the first months of #MeToo, a professor of Shakespeare (serendipitously from the University of Warwick) appeared on the Russell Brand podcast series *Under the Skin*. In addressing the episode's topic 'Shakespeare and power!', Tony Howard provided a normative synopsis of the scene's function, a significant portion of which is here transcribed:

[Richard III] is a figure who is kind of the dark shadow inside all of us. His only compulsion is to achieve power, and to humiliate as many human beings in the process as he can. And the way Shakespeare . . . shows that is to give him at the start of the play a pirouette through certain kinds of relationships. So, he . . . [approaches] a woman called Lady Anne whose husband he's murdered, and he woos her over a coffin. And at the beginning of that she is full of anger and hatred; by the end of it he's been successful in seducing her, and it's kind of showing off what willpower can actually achieve if it's totally focused. So, as a result of that, we know that he's going to be very successful, he's going to achieve anything he wants. He's going to stamp over a dozen bodies at least, and in fact . . . Shakespeare then shocks us by having him stamp over the bodies of children – because we can all say, okay look, we kind of empathize with the trickster, the jester, even the devilish character. We know he's acting out terrible impulses which we feel, and we get an ejection of pleasure, from feeling we can criticize it, but we're also along there with him. But when it comes to killing children . . . it's wrenching your guts, and you're forced to decide how far I'm going to go along with this.[7]

This podcast consciously attempts to reach a wider audience, something academics urgently need to do, and features a scholar who has supported progressive projects such as the Multicultural Shakespeare Project and the Black and Asian Shakespeare Performance DataBase. His comments are quite

reasonable and reflect the consensus reading of this scene within its larger narrative context. However, in the wake of #MeToo, I want to reflect on Act 1, Scene 2 a bit differently, and, as a first step, ask that we notice where his pronouns shift.

I would draw a distinction between commissioning the murder of small children as being a worse act – with which I think 'we' surely all do agree – and the assumption that *that* is the moment when 'you' start to feel the pleasure is past. Because, for all the deeply ironic amusement one can take in the wit of Richard (or Iago for that matter) plotting villainy *before* the victims begin to suffer, I have never been able to participate unambivalently in the 'we' finding 'an ejection of pleasure' in Anne's manipulation. And Shakespeare's bravura treatment of two types of war within the scene constitutes a large part of the reason: he shows us the physical evidence of war's murderous violence on the stage and perverts even the ability to grieve for the dead; and he juxtaposes this with Richard's rhetorical invocation of love-as-a-battlefield, an inheritance from medieval romance and Petrarchan verse which provides a staple of Shakespeare's erotic play, helping him incorporate lyric poetry within an embodied, conflict-based, social art form.

These patterns culminate in Richard's faux attempt to reprise the war quite literally, as he draws his sword to let Anne avenge her dead relatives and simultaneously literalizes the familiar imagery of the ladylove as murderous in refusing the suffering poet-lover. The inclusion of several unusually detailed stage directions in the First Folio reinforces this climax through gestures already signalled within the dialogue. First, '[s]*he looks scornfully at him*', prompting his verbal confirmation, '[t]each not thy lip such scorn, for it was made / For kissing, lady, not for such contempt'.[8]

---

7  I have lightly edited out filler phrases. First broadcast 23 December 2017, cited from www.youtube.com/watch?v=nSPWz8zw-1I (timecode 3:20ff – however, timecode varies on different sites and versions of the podcast).

8  William Shakespeare, *Richard III*, ed. James R. Siemon (London, 2009), 1.2.173 SD, 1.2.174–5. Subsequent citations refer to this edition and are given in the text.

Then Richard 'lend[s]' his sword, kneels and reveals his breast 'naked to the deadly stroke':

If thy revengeful heart cannot forgive,
Lo, here I lend thee this sharp-pointed sword,
Which if thou please to hide in this true breast
And let the soul forth that adoreth thee,
I lay it naked to the deadly stroke
And humbly beg the death upon my knee.

*He [kneels and] lays his breast open, she offers at
[it] with his sword.*
(1.2.176–81 and SD following)

As Anne stands above him, now literally holding the power to kill him with his weapon of war, he toys with her reluctance to perpetuate the bloody feud; moreover, he does so by shifting responsibility – not only for his current abjection but for his past war crimes as well – to her physical appearance:

Nay, do not pause; for I did kill King Henry,
But 'twas thy beauty that provoked me.
Nay, now dispatch; 'twas I that stabbed young Edward,
But 'twas thy heavenly face that set me on.

*She falls the sword.*
(1.2.182–5 and SD following)

Literalizing a metaphor often satirizes the connection between its component parts, but here it is the *inability* of the (supposed) ladylove to physicalize, to use a sword murderously, that heralds the ultimate degradation of Anne.

Looking across Shakespeare's dramatic genres illuminates his particular choices here, for he repeatedly envisions or presents the dagger or sword threatening a man's breast at moments when male bonds are in crisis. Two such instances have been frequently performed in recent years: one occurs during the climactic Act 4 trial scene of *The Merchant of Venice*, in which Shylock prepares his knife to cut Antonio while 'the clerk' unravels Shylock's revenge; the other takes place in *Julius Caesar*, with *its* Act 4 breast-bearing by Cassius as he argues with Brutus in their camp of war. In each of these cases, the refusal to shed blood marks the restoration of the normative social order, albeit uneasily. Status differences matter: male

friendships are restored in each instance, but in the former case at the expense of the 'alien' who chose to take up the knife of his own volition; in the latter scene, the brothers-in-law reaffirm both personal and political bonds as battle looms.[9] Chronologically prior to those re-gendered, genre-challenging re-citations, Shakespeare created the scene with Lady Anne which presages Shylock's humiliation without his volition and Brutus's refusal of violence without the satisfaction of authentic intimacy restored. When a woman holds the sword, the war is not over. This exchange gives the lie not only to what actually happened in battle, but also to Richard's and the play's profession of a difference between wartime and peacetime. Rather than its being deemed a demonstration that the social order has been restored or that her hope to inspire contrition is justified, Anne's refusal to kill becomes proof that she is a weak, expendable 'relict'. To put it more strongly: this is the culmination of the gaslighting of Lady Anne.

'Gaslighting' is a half-century-old term whose etymology derives from Patrick Hamilton's eponymous 1938 play (made widely famous by the 1944 George Cukor film), and is defined in the *OED* as '[t]he action or process of manipulating a person by psychological means into questioning his or her own sanity'; from the 1960s, it appears in the scholarship of clinical psychology as well as in popular culture, but it has gained more political currency with the rise of social media. In the psychiatric literature, it now describes 'events that range from the denial by an abuser that previous abusive incidents ever occurred up to the staging of bizarre events by the abuser with the intention of

---

9 For more on these scenes in recent performance, see D. E. Henderson, 'Hard hearts resounding now: anatomizing race, resistance and community in *The Merchant of Venice* and *Julius Caesar*', forthcoming in *Cahiers Élisabéthains* (2019). Seneca's *Hippolytus* has been cited as a precedent for the Lady Anne scene, despite the reversal of gender roles and the equally glaring distinction that the passion there is unfeigned.

disorienting the victim'; this is the sense in which I apply the term here.[10] Early in their exchange, Anne uncovers the physical wounds on the King's murdered corpse as incontrovertible evidence, only to have Richard shift registers and replace her sensory knowledge with inherited scripts about love's wounds. Richard Loncraine's 1995 film starring Ian McKellen and Kristin Scott Thomas takes Shakespeare a step farther: it replaces Henry's body with her dead husband's, thus implicitly sexualizing Anne's revelation even before Richard does so.

Even without such an alteration, however, the playtext does its objectifying work in performance. In our era, when most people encounter Shakespeare via screens and gravitate to the most immediately accessible, it seems all the more valuable for scholars to enlarge and historicize that digital corpus, at the same time making visible the techniques (including shot selection, as well as line delivery) that shape audience reception. For that reason, I turn to 1960's *An Age of Kings* as illustrative of an inherited performance tradition for the Lady Anne scene, within a series important both as a groundbreaking event in television history and in elevating the two tetralogies as Shakespeare's canonical English histories. Wikipedia thus describes the fifteen-part series: '[a]t the time, the show was the most ambitious Shakespearean television adaptation ever made, and was a critical and commercial success in both the UK and the US', adding that '[t]he series was a huge success, with an average viewing audience of three million in the UK'. In the USA, it became the first public-television hit serial (even before the formal establishment of PBS), launching the ongoing tradition of importing British 'masterpieces'. That many Shakespeare scholars, as well as the general populace, now are unfamiliar with one of the most influential television versions of its day says less about the shows than about the rocky transition from broadcast to the digital for major institutions such as the BBC.[11]

Predictably, large segments of Shakespeare's playtexts are significantly edited or cut, including

within the relevant episode 14 ('The dangerous brother'); half of Anne's opening speech is gone, as are approximately seventy other lines in their exchange (that is, a bit more than a third). However, the gaslighting segment of *Richard III* 1.2 remains nearly verbatim, including the sequence cited earlier.[12] As Paul Daneham's Richard rhetorically makes the war deaths of Anne's loved ones her fault, he is on his knees with his back to the low-angled camera; we look over his shoulder at the anguished face of Jill Dixon's Anne in a (standard) medium long shot holding his sword towards his breast, and us. The camera slowly closes in to a medium shot as he alternates admission of his violent actions (first towards King Henry, as in the Folio ordering) and his profession of love as motivation, causing her to pause rather than plunge the weapon into his

---

[10] Whilst knowing its flaws, I draw on Wikipedia as the most capacious accessible reference guide: http://en.wikipedia.org/wiki/Gaslighting#cite_note-Dorpat1996-3.

[11] http://en.wikipedia.org/wiki/An_Age_of_Kings. The BBC series was directed by Michael Hayes and broadcast in the UK in 1960, the USA in 1961, and several other European and Commonwealth countries then or subsequently. Until fairly recently, one had to go to the BFI to view these BBC shows; this was my experience when first working on its *Henry V*, and still true when Emma Smith's 2007 essay on the series went to press. The BBC finally released the series on DVD in 2009, once YouTube made it virtually impossible to control access. I again cite Wikipedia, for the same reason of interest in popular received tradition; moreover, in this case, the entry draws primarily from two key scholarly articles focusing on the series: Patricia Lennox, 'Henry VI: a television history in four parts', in *Henry VI: Critical Essays*, ed. Thomas A. Pendleton (London, 2001), pp. 235–52; and Emma Smith, 'Shakespeare serialized: *An Age of Kings*', in *The Cambridge Companion to Shakespeare and Popular Culture*, ed. Robert Shaughnessy (Cambridge, 2007), pp. 134–49. On the series' importance in the history of US public television, and despite its misspelling of Judi Dench's first name, see David Stewart, '"An Age of Kings": an import becomes public TV's first hit', 21 December 1998, http://current.org/1998/12/an-age-of-kings-an-import-becomes-public-tvs-first-hit. See also Patricia Lennox, 'An age of kings and the "normal American"', *Shakespeare Survey 61* (Cambridge, 2008), 181–98.

[12] *Shakespeare's An Age of Kings* (BBC Video; Warner Home Videos, 2009). The Lady Anne scene begins at timecode 8:20.

chest. Increasing the intensity, Daneham then shakes his head and forcefully cries, '[n]ay, now dispatch!' (my exclamation point) before she again braces to push on; ''twas I that stabbed your Edward', at which point he drops to a whisper for ''twas thy heavenly face that set me on'. The aural rollercoaster does its work: with her eyes still focused on him with a pained expression, she slowly lowers the sword, then looks further downward as she lets it drop. It is at this moment that a high-angle reaction shot reveals Richard's face in time to see him, hands parting his coat at his breast, using his eyes alone to glance down at the sword and back up at her face before articulating slowly, deliberately, his sinister double-bind: '[t]ake up the sword again' (pause, eyes back down at sword, then eyes sweeping up again for) 'or take up [pause, eyes widened, eyebrows raised, whisper-hissing] me' (1.2.186). Never has self-debasement been more obviously strategic – and fraudulent.

Isolated in her #MeToo moment, Anne turns away from his relentless stare, her face again revealed as she hesitantly stammers '[a]rise, dissembler', before recovering her poise and walking forward to medium close-up at 'though I wish thy death, / I will not be thy executioner' (1.2.187–8). Unmoved in response to her command, but then threatened with her upstaging his absurd alternatives (as well as his on-camera visibility), Richard jumps up, grabbing the sword, and lunges forward from behind her, pointing the sword at his own stomach for '[t]hen bid me kill myself, and I will do it' (1.2.189). The camera shot jumps as Anne does: accompanying her squeaking gasp, Richard reoccupies the foreground as she desperately turns towards him in horror. He is now closer to the camera than she, and first viewed in profile (revealing his ludicrous stage nose, making the preposterousness of this as 'seduction' more overt even as his violence overwhelms her). Daneham's Richard visually as well as rhetorically frames her now, with his face on one side of the shot, his hand on the other, and the sword poised between, and beneath her face, as she near-sobs 'I have already', her eyes as well as spirits again downcast (1.2.190). Having achieved equal stature and both spatial and psychological dominance, he turns his face back towards her (away from our gaze) as, calmly, condescendingly, he delivers the *coup de grâce* for dismissing what women say: '[t]hat was in thy rage' (1.2.190 – he even intrudes upon her verse line). In Richard's rhetoric, emotion legitimates his murders, while emotion silences Anne's speech.

Forty lines later, Richard's famous 36-line soliloquy retrospectively re-frames the encounter, both celebrating his 'conquest' and revealing his exploitative plan ('Was ever woman in this humour wooed? / Was ever woman in this humour won? / I'll have her, but I will not keep her long', 1.2.230–2); yet already, in the sequence analysed above, Lady Anne has – as Virginia Woolf would later describe Lady Bradshaw's submission to her husband's will in *Mrs Dalloway* – 'gone under'.[13] And with the camerawork's assistance, as in *An Age of Kings*, when a performer such as Paul Daneham relishes his part (just as Laurence Olivier had a few years prior)[14] it is hard to resist Shakespeare's brazen juxtaposition of normative rhetoric with a set of tableaux that expose both it and its victim simultaneously. Yet I do so, refusing any longer to collaborate with the premise that requires we refuse empathy to this less-than-extraordinary woman in order to enjoy that 'ejection of pleasure' which follows from aligning (even temporarily, as fantasy) with the bad boy's deceit. I think instead of the psychological legacy of her easy dismissal, as I imagine the alternatives absent from Shakespeare's scene – including anything like the truth of the historical Anne Neville's particular situation.

For, without going down the Richard III Society rabbit-hole, as a dramaturg I am interested as well in what the fifteenth-century known facts might provide, to triangulate the text and the received performance tradition: could they help

---

[13] Virginia Woolf, *Mrs. Dalloway* [1925] (San Diego, 1981), p. 100.

[14] Olivier's 1955 (US 1956) television/film version notably cut the soliloquy's third line after adding much more physicality, including his repeated enclosure of Claire Bloom's Anne, culminating with their two kisses.

reanimate the scene in a less misogynistic key, or at least help reveal its biased fictionality? Ironically, as Kavita Mudan Finn observes in her study of narratives about the Plantagenet queens consort, historian Michael Hicks's authoritative biography of Anne Neville begins with a lengthy excursis analysing Shakespeare's scene, not those facts – hardly inspiring confidence that the subsequent account will escape its legacies.[15] Yet, that said, Amy Licence's subsequent Neville biography (appearing a year after Finn's book) likewise begins 'Act One, Scene Two' before describing Loncraine's film version, in order to emphasize both the distance of present performance from Shakespeare's early modern one, and his from the historical facts.[16] As such, she anticipates my emphasis here, and provides a salutary reminder (as does Finn's entire book) that it is not the presence but the treatment of the materials that creates a particular legacy. Furthermore, both Hicks and Licence describe in detail not only the relevant facts – which are few – but also now-alien contexts, which are suggestive. Thus, while the outline of events may well be familiar to Shakespeare scholars, it seems worth recapping the history from a different angle, with Anne Neville's story at the centre.

Born on 11 June 1456 at Warwick Castle to Richard Neville the Younger and Anne Beauchamp (for whose marriage a papal dispensation was required, due to the church's extensive consanguinity laws),[17] Anne was the second surviving child, five years younger than her sister Isabel. As a descendant of many of the kingdom's most ancient families (including the Despensers and Montagus), Anne grew up in a world that presumed her family's entitlement beyond the individual life, and those assumptions likewise informed the thinking of their servants, including the historians of the time.[18] Through quite good luck in his marriage, relatives' deaths and consequent inheritances, her father (known to us as Warwick the Kingmaker) became the richest baron in the land.

The reliable written record of Anne's encounters with Richard Plantagenet, her first cousin once removed, begins in 1465, when he and the two Neville daughters were placed at the same table for the investiture of George Neville, their great-uncle (and Richard's uncle) as Archbishop of York. She was aged 9 at the time, Richard four years older. That same year, a major ceremony marked the reburial of her grandfather Richard, Earl of Salisbury, and uncle Thomas Neville, both of whom died at the Battle of Wakefield in 1460 – as had Richard's older brother Edmund, Earl of Rutland, and his father the Duke of York (although those corpses would not be reburied until 1476). They were all children of war.

In 1464, Edward IV had opposed the betrothal of Anne's sister Isabel to his and Richard's brother George, Duke of Clarence (nevertheless, they would eventually wed in 1469). The Burgundian chronicler Waurin claimed that a marriage was likewise planned for Anne and Richard, but Hicks dismisses the account, saying it is 'unsubstantiated and appears unlikely' (p. 65). Be that as it may, the fatherless Richard was brought up in Warwick's household for the next three years: 1465–8.

Subsequent years were complicated for all involved: in 1469, the rebellion against Edward IV led by Warwick and Clarence went awry; Isabel miscarried on a ship off Calais when conditions forbade her landing. At that point, Anne became a political pawn in her father's desperate alliance with his former enemy, the Lancastrian Queen Margaret, and as a result Anne, now aged 14, was betrothed on 25 July 1470 to Margaret's son Prince Edward, aged 17. If they had previously encountered each other at all, it was as small children, but their parents desperately needed to perform an alliance, and the children became their signifiers: '[t]he crown of England was the

---

[15] Michael Hicks, *Anne Neville: Queen to Richard III* (Stroud, 2006), pp. 13-17; Kavita Mudan Finn, *The Last Plantagenet Consorts: Gender, Genre, and Historiography, 1440–1627* (New York, 2012), pp. 13-14.

[16] Amy Licence, *Anne Neville: Richard III's Tragic Queen* (Stroud, 2013), pp. 9-11.

[17] Hicks, *Anne Neville*, p. 47.

[18] Hicks, *Anne Neville*, pp. 40-1.

objective for both parties'.[19] Unfortunately for Warwick's time-sensitive plans to use his new son-in-law as a royal figurehead, Anne and Edward's common ancestry back to John of Gaunt again violated the consanguinity rules and thus required a papal dispensation.[20] Bureaucratic mistakes ensued, and consequently it was not until 13 December 1470 at Amboise that Anne and Edward were wed; presumably the marriage was also consummated. Less than six months later, Edward would be dead.

In other words, the marital relationship that Shakespeare presents Anne as grieving was at the most a yearlong romance, at the least a political alliance involving no affection whatsoever. By contrast (and without contestation), as a girl she had known Richard. As for her father-in-law Henry VI, whose 'Readeption' of the throne her own father's invasion had managed that September, Anne had 'probably last encountered' him in 1460, when she was a very small child.[21] Furthermore, Warwick's subsequent assumption of the actual power and rule on Henry's behalf would prove fatal to him and perilous to Anne. By the time she, her mother, Edward and Margaret were able to sail back from France to England, her brother-in-law Clarence had switched sides again, joining his once-and-future king and brother Edward in Yorkshire. Anne landed in Weymouth the day before her father would die fighting against them – and an army led by their brother Richard – at the Battle of Barnet on 14 April 1471. Her mother fleeing to sanctuary, Anne was thus virtually orphaned and left with 'no choice what to do': she was part of Queen Margaret's entourage and accompanied her to Tewkesbury, where, on 4 May, in or soon after his first battle, her new husband was likewise killed. Adding insult to injury, she was 'personally dowerless': the marriage had brought her nothing but war dead.[22]

Hicks hypothesizes Anne's post-Tewkesbury feelings, including 'trauma at the bloodshed, and undoubtedly also concern for her own safety and for her own future. What was to befall her was far from clear' (p. 105). Although the teenage widow was in theory a *femme sole*, she had 'no means to

exercise her theoretical independence'; due to entails and her mother's retreat (she who would outlive them all, dying in 1492), Anne 'had only her expectations of inheritance to sustain her and to attract a male protector' (p. 103). These were the fifteenth-century realities, perhaps aggravated by the restoration of King Edward IV, whose behaviour with women seeking their rightful inheritances would today earn him the label of sexual predator.[23] And thus, after relying upon and citing an authoritative historian's factual account at some length, I again find myself balking at some of his seemingly reasonable conclusions. For example, that when Edward pardoned Anne, '[h]e could do no less. The Wars of the Roses were not waged against women. None were slain in battle, only three attainted as traitors by parliament'. No war waged against women – despite noting that Anne's mother complained that the King would not let her leave sanctuary;[24] that Anne was placed in Clarence's care (he whose latest allegiance-shift led to her father's death and her own misfortunes); and that these wars essentially erased the independence of a girl who grew up with extraordinary status, making her another 'ordinary' woman needing a man.

How apt then – true or not – that rumours circulated of Anne being kept as a scullery maid in Clarence's household, or that she 'allowed [Richard] to whisk her away to sanctuary' (p. 108) and a second marriage. Or that the form of compensatory choice Hicks ultimately accords her

---

[19] Hicks, *Anne Neville*, p. 82.
[20] Hicks, *Anne Neville*, pp. 85-6.
[21] Hicks, *Anne Neville*, p. 99.
[22] Hicks, *Anne Neville*, pp. 94, 105.
[23] Hicks, *Anne Neville* (p. 104) describes the inheritance struggles of 'the king's future bedfellows' Eleanor Butler, Dame Elizabeth Gray and Dame Margaret Lucy, though the label used for Edward is mine. (Jane Shore is the more famous mistress for early modern literary scholars.) Additionally, Finn notes that these were tricky times for royal women, with Malory's *Morte d'Arthur* providing 'an encapsulation of the anxieties surrounding the representation of queens in the late 1460s' (p. 8).
[24] Hicks, *Anne Neville*, pp. 102, 104.

is marital; he writes of her second marriage to Richard that '[i]f Anne was undoubtedly a victim, she was not helpless ... [making a] self-conscious decision not to remain where she was [and] not to become a nun ... It was her decision to marry, far within the prohibited degrees. There can have been few fifteen-year-old ladies, let alone princesses, who chose their marriage partners for themselves. Anne did' (p. 111). Rhetorically, this is impressive; as an indication of how patriarchal rule and the results of warfare limit women's notions of choice, it is depressingly accurate. As Finn observes, '[a]ll women, even queens, were made to conform to predetermined outlines' (p. 17). Thus, even without Shakespeare's alterations, the limited landscape for privileged Lady Anne remains haunting: imagine (if one dares) what it was like for those without her social rank.

So, given the historical record, the dramatic text and performance tradition, how do we treat Shakespeare's Lady Anne now? There are a number of common strategies. James R. Siemon in his Arden 3 introduction notes the late-eighteenth-century move to attribute responsibility for her fate to Anne's weak 'character', specifically her 'vanity', and those assumptions have hardly disappeared, although close readings such as Linda Charnes's in *Notorious Identity* strive to complicate them.[25] Thus, in the 2016 Norton introduction, Stephen Greenblatt still states flatly that 'Anne is shallow, corruptible, naively ambitious, and, above all, frightened' before adding the crucial point: that 'the scene's theatrical power rests less upon a depiction of her character than upon the spectacle of Richard's restless aggression transformed' into rhetoric.[26] Inverting the historian's emphasis on the family dynasty more than the individual life when trying to understand late medieval aristocracy, most 21st-century readers still build on the previous centuries' psychological vocabulary and judgements. As Finn emphasizes, this leads to anachronistic readings striving to find (or, as here, being dismissive when not finding) what we would regard as female agency (p. 2; on Anne, see pp. 163–5).

Another frequent and related strategy is to read Shakespeare's Lady Anne scene as a prelude to others with the royal women, especially the later stand-off in which Richard again attempts to acquire a wife. In the podcast cited earlier, for example, Professor Howard describes Richard as 'having to replay that seduction scene' with Queen Elizabeth (Woodville), 'doing the same thing, using the same words' (timecode 5:20ff.) as he attempts to marry her daughter ... and failing. The implication is that the later scene bookends and somehow redeems guiltily immoral responses to the earlier encounter. Elizabeth Woodville's successful deferral of Richard's suit becomes a mirroring rebuttal, which in a sense it is – although there is also a significant difference when the erotic target is not present and the words are *not* literally 'the same'. Moreover, the later scene hardly helps Shakespeare's by-then dead Queen Anne, and again perpetuates an antithesis between the extraordinary and the weakly ordinary woman who succumbs. Nor, in the fourth act, does Anne's own retrospective description help the matter, when she colludes in blaming her 'woman's heart' (4.1.78). Granted, Anne does break through the ghostly glass ceiling, joining an otherwise male chorus of apparitions as the penultimate voice encouraging Richard to '[d]espair and die' (5.3.163),[27] but that is far from a survivor's story or consolation to living women. So, although scholars as interlocutors of Shakespeare usually

---

[25] Siemon, ed., *Richard III*, pp. 13–14; Linda Charnes, *Notorious Identity: Materializing the Subject in Shakespeare* (Cambridge, MA, 1995), pp. 38–51.

[26] Stephen Greenblatt, Walter Cohen, Suzanne Gossett *et al.*, eds., *The Norton Shakespeare*, 3rd edn (New York, 2016), p. 561.

[27] The folio, unlike the quartos, does not even accord her the status of 'Queen', retaining the initial 'Lady' as her title. Cahill's *Unto the Breach* focuses on the Act 5 scene's unusual split staging in her complementary analysis, noting that 'to read *Richard III* as such a reparative history is to neglect the play's extraordinary staging of a traumatic past whose haunting temporality persists despite the play's desire to disavow it' (p. 210).

decry the removal of speeches and scenes from their larger narrative context, here I want to forestall any narrative movement across the playtext to find satisfaction and closure.[28]

In such resistance, I join others influenced by feminist film and performance theory, and am attempting thereby to do something slightly more complicated than just 'reading against the grain'. Taking a cue (as ever) from Barbara Hodgdon's playful opening to a classic book about endings in the histories, in which she emphasizes a production's primarily female casting of Richmond's army as resisting the text's conclusion, I refuse closing an opening: call it bookending in reverse.[29] In her 2018 British Shakespeare Association keynote address on the uses of *Romeo and Juliet* in Deepa Mehta's film *Water*, Courtney Lehmann similarly drew on feminist film theory and counter-cinematic techniques to highlight the cost of viewing Shakespeare's narrative arcs as inevitable – specifically, in effacing violence against women.[30] In Lady Anne's case, too, we might want to experiment with counter-disciplinary, or at least anti-linear, reading practices in order to resist forgetting what we have actually witnessed – especially if doing so allows us to see why some readers (including some of our students) are alienated from Shakespeare not because they *don't* 'get it', but because they do. So, wilfully refusing the forms of fulfilment the playwright prompts in Acts 4 and 5, let us linger a bit longer with the uncomfortable encounter.

It is worth recalling, as does Siemon, citing the following passage,[31] that the scene's first stand-off with swords occurs between men:

RICHARD: Villains, set down the corse, or by Saint Paul,
　　I'll make a corse of him that disobeys.
GENTLEMAN: My lord, stand back and let the coffin pass.
RICHARD: Unmannered dog, stand thou when
　　I command!
　　*Advance thy halberd higher than my breast,*
　　Or by Saint Paul I'll strike thee to my foot
　　And spurn upon thee, beggar, for thy boldness.
　　　　　　　　　　　　(1.2.36–42; emphasis added)

As Siemon observes, 'Fresh from pronouncing himself physically disempowered, Richard proves prodigiously powerful when he – alone, lame, with a withered arm and a single sword – halts a heavily armed procession and disarms a halberdier whose weapon points at his chest'. Attending to the men in the cortège helps remind us that 'others also fall before Richard's onslaught, and not because they are immoral, vain or female': the language of social distinction, 'of hierarchy and religion', allows Richard to stop the men even with a weapon drawn against his breast.[32] So Anne is clearly not alone in *not* using the sword, nor is her attention to bodily wounds the sole 'cause' for Richard's subsequent swordplay, any more than her beauty actually caused Lancastrian deaths. The gaslight stops dimming.

Yet, for all that, Siemon's analysis is so valuable precisely because it is so hard for us to see – especially in performance. Often this is because the followers themselves are removed, as in the Olivier/Bloom or McKellen/Scott Thomas encounters. In *An Age of Kings*, the highlighted line and associated action are cut. But even when present and presenting arms, we may forget the Gentleman because he is so quickly silenced, the hierarchies of birth and service are no longer visible to most watchers – and, ultimately, because Shakespeare so relentlessly focuses in on Richard versus Anne. In this regard, the halberd-bearer heralds not only potential violence but the way those victimized or with less social status can

---

28 For this reason, I do not elaborate on Shakespeare's departure from the historical record in collapsing Anne's thirteen-year marriage to Richard, erasing her maternity and her son Edward's sudden death in 1584, eleven months before her own.
29 See her description of the curtain call for Adrian Noble's 1988 *Plantagenets* at the RSC in Barbara Hodgdon, *The End Crowns All: Closure and Contradiction in Shakespeare's History* (Princeton, NJ, 1991), p. 3.
30 Courtney Lehmann, 'An élan of the soul? Toward a feminist counter-cinema in Deepa Mehta's *Water*', as delivered at the British Shakespeare Association, Belfast, 14-16 June 2018; I thank the author for sharing the text of her work-in-progress with me.
31 Siemon, ed., *Richard III*, p. 14.
32 Siemon, ed., *Richard III*, p. 14.

become, as Kim Solga puts it, invisible in plain sight.[33] Making that process matter in performance provides one way to foreground Anne's desperate situation as well.

As the functionaries of the social order become (or remain) silenced, attention turns to the flesh, and a form of he-said/she-said debate between two entitled yet conventionally disempowered bodies. Therefore, I want at least to gesture at what actors' bodies are showing us *now*, including and beyond those obvious differences suggested by the casting of actresses and modern perspectives on disability. One of the more outrageous ways of conveying 1.2's submerged shock potential occurs in Thomas Ostermeier's *Richard III* starring Lars Eidinger, performed across Europe and in New York, 2015–17.[34] During the gaslighting sequence, the actor strips naked slowly and matter-of-factly, speaking in plaintive tones before kneeling by the coffin and placing the sword to his breast. His audaciousness forces Anne (Jenny König) to look away repeatedly before succumbing to the temptation also facing the audience. His only remaining 'clothing' is the sling holding his prosthetic hump on his shoulder, and a leather band ringing his face. By revealing the taut actor's body behind the costume and grotesque movements and by emphasizing the (seeming) pathos in his voice, his seductiveness gains a measure of disturbing credibility.

When the Ostermeier *Richard* was performed at the Barbican in February 2017, Michael Billington complained: 'but why soften the play's political bite at such a crucial time?'[35] His premise hinges upon whether one includes embodied gender relations within the boundaries of the political – which, given the timing of his blog, seems an odd category to exclude. The previous grotesquery of Eidinger's movements contrasted with the beauty of his form when seemingly vulnerable makes Anne's inaction and his sinister use of power in appearing naked all the more compelling, and far too familiar a form of manipulation for those who have experienced sexual violence.

A more layered use of bodies anchors Judith Buchanan's 'Silents now' *Richard III*, a collaborative project in which Frank Benson's 1910 film fragments are supplemented with several actors reading at the side of the screen and three dancers performing in front of it.[36] This multimedia performance historicizes and complicates simultaneously. As in the Ostermeier production, the dancing Richard transforms himself from ungainly to able-bodied – indeed, aesthetically beautiful – before our eyes, thereby deconstructing disability, but, of course, with other consequences. And, in balletic form, *both* performers' hyper-able bodies also help elide visually the perversity of Anne's representation. Buchanan reports that the film's incompleteness, and requisite condensation of the verbal script, made replicating the Anne scene in Benson's film (which does retain the halberdier and quite an entourage throughout) all the more 'disquieting',[37] even as her project admirably aimed to bring the historical into the present, making the arcane film archive accessible through aestheticized collage.

Age provides a third aspect of embodiment that can be (and has been) used to effect. The historical

---

33 Kim Solga, *Violence Against Women in Early Modern Performance: Invisible Acts* (Basingstoke, 2009), pp. 1-28, reviews much of the performance theory canon through the lens of its applicability to 'in/visible' acts of violence against women on the early modern stage, amongst which I would place Richard's treatment of Anne. This silencing of bystanders, who might in our modern world be potential allies, complements her analysis.

34 My source was the Avignon Festival's recording; thanks to Robert Shaughnessy for directing me to it: www.youtube.com/watch?v=kifdmhDUe98.

35 Michael Billington, 'We're in crisis – so why has Ostermeier stripped Richard III of politics?', www.theguardian.com/stage/2017/feb/17/ostermeier-richard-iii-politics-thomas-barbican-lars-eidinger.

36 See her account in *Collaborating with the Dead: Revivifying Frank Benson's* Richard III: www.york.ac.uk/digital-editions/collaborating-with-the-dead; a short video including some of the Lady Anne dance scene appears at http://silents-now.co.uk/home/workshops/workshops-with-creative-collaborators.

37 Correspondence initiated via the private 'Shakespeare Friends' Facebook group, 8 June 2018. My thanks to her for describing and documenting process as well as product, and to Lisa Starks for maintaining that Facebook group.

Anne and Richard's youthful marriage – they were both still in their teens – contrasts nicely with middle-aged Al Pacino's conscious search for a much younger Anne in his 'making of' film *Looking for Richard* (1996) – looking as well for a plausible way to explain its grotesque power dynamics to a modern audience. A 30+-year age gap was still not enough to provide Winona Ryder with Anne's motivation, however, and her suggestion that they consult a scholar triggers a remarkable on-camera explosion of indignation from co-director Frederic Kimball. Watching this older man rail uncontrollably at the reasonable request of a young actress surrounded by men is both more poignant and funnier to watch two decades later, given Ryder's subsequent rocky career and survival: fortunately in this instance, Pacino plays a more active bystander than the halberdier in intervening, and Ryder's eye-rolling sign of resistance lives on now as a GIF, perhaps outlasting the career success of Kevin Spacey (here, Buckingham).

Young Winona foreshadows a more thoroughgoing young remake: Mike Lew's theatrical spinoff set in a contemporary high school, *Teenage Dick* (2018, premiering at the Public Theater in New York).[38] This version takes seriously the challenge of casting a disabled Richard (it was written for an actor with cerebral palsy), and makes the treatment of Anne more focal, explicitly commenting on Shakespeare's subordination of Anne's story to Richard's. The stark treatment of Anne's fate, including both victimization and added narrative authority, emphasizes the ongoing problems of women's contested control over their own bodies and the power of social media shaming. Debuting during a summer when a legally marginalized case of such harassment exploded into mass murder, this adaptation's choices make all too much sense.[39] Here is yet another indicator that the boundaries and even the temporal sequencing between war and peacetime can appear tenuous indeed to those under threat – including the threats appearing as misogynist rhetoric that so often spiral into physical violence against women.

\*\*\*

The inextricable involvement of headline violence with this latest treatment of Anne leads me not to closure but back to an even more fraught political moment in 1938, when Virginia Woolf felt compelled to articulate some of these very patterns and directly connect antifascism with pacifist feminism, in a tract she knew would alienate many readers. Alas that it has become prophetic, and remains urgent. Amidst government fears of imminent bombing by Germany and as she and her sister Vanessa tried to dissuade the latter's son Julian Bell from going to fight in Spain, Woolf self-published her thoughts in the form of a letter of response to an anti-war advocate's request for a donation. She first distinguishes *his* societal power as a full-fledged member of the bourgeoisie from *her* gendered limitations as merely one of the 'daughters of educated men' who was raised before women's suffrage or widespread access to higher education; she then turns to the consequences of that social exclusion, and to competing requests for support from a women's college and a women's professional organization. All three will eventually be given their guinea, upon certain strong conditions. The imaginary letter format indicates the care with which Woolf frames her bolder assertions, anticipating that she will encounter hostility.

Citing dismissive and bullying newspaper accounts about women in male-dominated professions, she turns to Shakespeare to construct an analogy between resisting such misogyny and fighting fascism abroad.

---

[38] I thank the playwright for sharing his script with me, and Louise Geddes for her response to its New York performance.

[39] On 28 June 2018, five Maryland newspaper employees were murdered by a man who in 2011 was found guilty of harassing a female high school classmate on Facebook; later he sued that newspaper unsuccessfully for reporting the facts. When the police chief 'was asked by reporters how the suspect was able to buy a 12-gauge shotgun despite having been found guilty of harassment', he replied: 'only those convicted of serious crimes and certain misdemeanours were banned from buying guns in Maryland'. See *BBC News*, 'Newspaper shooting suspect "barricaded exit"', 29 June 2018, www.bbc.co.uk/news/world-us-canada -44661778.

Given the topic, *Julius Caesar* makes sense, although it is typical of Woolf to choose – and obliquely at that – Brutus's problematic metaphor of the serpent's egg. She finds in the newspapers:

something which, if it spreads, may poison both sexes equally. There, in those quotations, is the egg of the very same worm that we know under other names in other countries. There we have in embryo the creature, Dictator as we call him when he is Italian or German, who believes that he has the right, whether given by God, Nature, sex or race is immaterial, to dictate to other human beings how they shall live; what they shall do . . . [a]nd he is here among us, raising his ugly head, spitting his poison, small still, curled up like a caterpillar on a leaf, but in the heart of England . . . And is not the woman who has to breathe that poison and to fight that insect, secretly and without arms, in her office, fighting the Fascist or the Nazi as surely as those who fight him with arms in the limelight of publicity?[40]

The logical inference is that scotching combative rhetoric, which trivializes others and creates hostile work environments, is intrinsically part of the anti-war effort, albeit at the caterpillar stage. At the same time, that invocation of Brutus's embryonic serpent allows an interpretive space of doubt, leaving it to the reader to decide whether impending violence can in any way be averted. Three critical responses to Woolf's work provide a disheartening coda that nevertheless reinforces the ongoing importance of her attempt, as well as of resisting certain easy divisions among women and the continued diminishment of sexual violence's effects.

One was spoken by fellow writer and friend E. M. Forster, two months after Woolf's 1941 suicide during the Blitz, in which he belittles her 'extreme Feminism' as 'unreasonable' and 'old-fashioned', indeed a remnant from '[h]er suffragette youth' 'when men kissed girls to distract them from wanting the vote'.[41] Deeming such forced kisses a matter of the past, he at least acknowledges that young women, rather than an 'elderly man' like himself, would be the best judges of *Three Guineas*. But his assumptions that feminism is *passé* and part of an older woman's tendency 'to keep on grumbling', as well as his resort to stereotypes (Woolf as radical suffragette?), remain all too familiar.

Alas that the most famous instance of a young(er) woman taking up Forster's challenge remains that of 31-year-old Q. D. Leavis – Queenie to her friends – in an eleven-page diatribe that never even addresses Woolf's anti-war argument. Leavis instead targets Woolf's self-labelling as a 'daughter of educated men', recasting it as exclusionary – what would now be called being an 'elite'. Because she is not a working professional, Leavis argues, Woolf is not only unqualified to speak on social issues but is essentially a social parasite – motivating Leavis's quotation from *Richard II* 2.3 within her title: 'Caterpillars of the Commonwealth unite!'[42]

Hers is a less ambiguous use of Shakespearian animal imagery, for little in that play leads one to regard Bushy or Bagot with much greater respect than Bolingbroke articulates, or to mourn them as lost butterflies. Rather, Leavis simply weaponizes Shakespeare as part of her rhetorical arsenal aimed squarely *ad feminam*. To call this an uncharitable reading is an understatement, despite the measure of truth in some of her barbs. She entirely omits, for example, Woolf's co-creation and maintenance of the Hogarth Press, as well as her work as a reviewing journalist. Nor was Leavis a disinterested reviewer or so very unentitled herself. Having attended the Latymer School and Girton College, in her early twenties she married her 30-something tutor F. R., who co-founded the famous journal *Scrutiny*, in which her attack appears.[43]

For many years I avoided this review, just as I avoided thinking much about the Lady Anne scene: call it empathetic self-protection. When I did ultimately read Leavis's essay, I found it

---

[40] Virginia Woolf, *Three Guineas* [1938] (New York, 1966), p. 97.

[41] Laura Marcus, 'Woolf's feminism and feminism's Woolf', in *The Cambridge Companion to Virginia Woolf*, ed. Sue Roe and Susan Sellers (Cambridge, 2000), pp. 209–44, pp. 226–7.

[42] Q. D. Leavis, 'Caterpillars of the Commonwealth unite!', *Scrutiny* 7 (1938), 203–14.

[43] 'Q. D. Leavis', The Leavis Society, www.leavissociety.com /q-d-leavis/index.html. For a fuller (and thus fairer) account of the journal's importance for its time and English studies, see Francis Mulhern, *The Moment of 'Scrutiny'* (London, 1979).

even more disturbing than anticipated, not only for its misogyny but for its rhetorical, projected use of racism: her line that Woolf's refusal of direct argument 'affects' Leavis 'like Nazi dialectic without Nazi conviction' still shocks, as does the vitriol with which she, a Jewish woman estranged from her family for marrying a gentile, accuses the gentile who married a Jew of making 'a weapon of feminine inconsequence'.[44] But, more than anything, it saddens me to read that the fundamental reason for Leavis's fury circles back to a perceived threat within her gender identification itself, and her consequent desire to be among the extraordinary women who must dissociate from others, in order, she hopes, to be 'accepted as intellectual equals by intelligent men (and so ultimately by the men who run the institutions and professions)' – a societal condition she furthermore argues is as it should be, premised on the greater disciplinary abilities of men.[45] Her accompanying conviction that university-style argumentation is superior to all other forms of thinking and writing remains uncomfortably familiar. The final sad irony here is that, as the Leavis Society website notes, Q. D. 'never' received 'any formal recognition' from those professions with which she so enthusiastically aligned herself.[46]

The ugliness of this weaponized rhetoric also creeps into Woolf's response to Leavis's review, though in more typically veiled fashion – and inaccurately, imagining that 'the professors of Eng. Lit. at Cambridge' must be 'poor old strumpets'.[47] But, of course, at the end of the day, Woolf's reputation has more than survived, and perhaps her awareness of her own and others' mixed feelings still can provide a valuable model for those struggling to write, with reviews and audiences in mind. Her gratitude to those who did read Three Guineas charitably is striking – all the more so given one more event that summer, between the book's publication and Leavis's review: the death of her beloved nephew in the Spanish Civil War.[48] Holding onto the pacifism which Julian Bell himself had earlier advocated before feeling compelled to oppose Franco on the battlefield, Virginia and Vanessa persuaded him to join the ambulance corps instead, but this did not protect him from a fatal

wound. No more would being in the photographic corps protect my own mother's similarly aged brother seven years later, while her future husband was slogging through the D-Day campaign from which he would return, damaged but alive. Even now, the ironies, as well as the boundaries, of war continue to overflow the measure, and the grieving of women for those they loved, killed by war, is too often drowned out in the weaponized rhetoric, including Shakespeare's, that silences or trivializes.

The final negative response to Three Guineas brings such rhetoric into the twenty-first century, and recalls Shakespeare's Richard dismissing Anne's words with '[t]hat was in thy rage': it is Theodore Dalrymple's 'The Rage of Virginia Woolf', first published in 2002 in City Journal (published by the Manhattan Institute, a conservative think tank).[49] Dubbing the book 'a locus classicus of self-pity and victimhood as a genre in itself', he proceeds for seventeen pages to wilfully misread, selectively quote, and dismiss both her facts and fictions, concluding that 'the very signature of her mind' was (with no apparent self-irony at his echoing her satire on Sir William Bradshaw in Mrs Dalloway) 'a self-pitying lack of proportion' (p. 8). Thus concludes a paragraph that begins by dismissing 'the extent and gravity' of the 'sexual abuse that she was alleged to have suffered as a child' (p. 8). He quotes part of the Three Guineas passage cited earlier (as well as one of Leavis's barbs) to conclude that '[h]er inability to distinguish metaphor from the literal truth is unremitting' (p. 13); he thereby misrepresents as incomprehension her attempt to enlarge the scope of what is 'deadly' beyond battle. Woolf scholars have, of course, rebutted the slanders and misrepresentations of her work here; what remains is the vitriol projected onto the object of

44 Leavis, 'Caterpillars', p. 204.
45 Leavis, 'Caterpillars', p. 205. 46 'Q. D. Leavis', as above.
47 See The Letters of Virginia Woolf, ed. Nigel Nicolson and Joanne Trautmann, 6 vols. (London, 1977-80), vol. 6, p. 271.
48 Nicolson and Trautmann, eds., Letters, vol. 6, pp. 250, 268.
49 Cited from www.city-journal.org/html/rage-virginia-woolf-12371.html; subsequent references are in-text and use hard-copy pagination.

his own vitriol, even sixty years after her death. For a woman writing, attempting to connect the ordinary with the extraordinary seems still to strike a nerve, as does a woman expressing any form of anger in her resistance. Thus the self-surveillance, the gaslighting and the silencing continue. And so, thinking of the lost possibilities of sisterhood, the reSisters who could not, and the forces that continue to divide us, I conclude simply: here's to Lady Anne, and all those who struggle to embody and remember those ordinary, unheroic casualties of war – and 'peace'.

# THE *HOMELAND* OF *CORIOLANUS*: WAR HOMECOMINGS BETWEEN SHAKESPEARE'S STAGE AND CURRENT COMPLEX TV

## CHRISTINA WALD

The motif of the soldier returning from war itself returns throughout Shakespeare's plays. Tragedies like *Richard III*, *Othello* and *Macbeth* use the delicate moment of homecoming as the starting point for violent escalation, and when a post-war plot follows the comedy pattern, as in *Much Ado About Nothing*, the reintegration of the returnee retains a destructive dimension. Shakespeare's late tragedy *Coriolanus* asks what happens when the returnee cannot be reintegrated into the civil society he defended in war and ultimately turns against his home. Shakespeare's dramatization of the (self-)destructive potential of the war returnee has had an intense cultural afterlife, especially during times of national crisis.[1] This afterlife includes, I will argue, the 'complex' TV series *Homeland*, in which the Coriolanus figure negotiates the international crisis instigated by terrorism and post-9/11 warfare.[2] Over seven seasons to date, since its premiere in 2011, the award-winning TV series has provoked controversy over its stance towards these wars and their implications for civil society, because its script is modelled closely on actual political developments and has often sought to anticipate them.[3] The debate has been fuelled by *Homeland*'s ideological ambiguity, which corresponds to the notorious ambiguity of Shakespeare's *Coriolanus* and its appropriations across the political spectrum.[4]

*Homeland* transforms the war homecoming of Coriolanus for its own medium and genre to fit in with the political thriller and serial-TV narrative format. Here, the US Marine Nicholas Brody returns home after being held captive by Al Qaeda in Iraq and Syria for eight years. Like

[1] As Cathy Shrank has summarized for the British context: '[t]hat interpretations of *Coriolanus* have been – almost without exception – politicized is as true for modern productions and critical appraisals as for seventeenth- and early-eighteenth-century adaptations. Almost every constitutional crisis in post-Restoration Britain prompted a rewriting of the play.' See Cathy Shrank, 'Civility and the city in *Coriolanus*', *Shakespeare Quarterly* 54 (2003), 406–23; p. 406.

[2] For the seminal definition of 'complex TV', a term that has replaced the earlier label 'quality TV', see Jason Mittell, *Complex TV: The Poetics of Contemporary Television Storytelling* (New York, 2015). *Homeland* is produced by Fox 21 Television Studios and broadcast in the USA on the cable channel Showtime. Its dissemination worldwide happens via national TV channels (e.g. Channel 4 in the UK), on-demand streaming services, and DVD/Blu-ray. The series was developed by Howard Gordon and Alex Gansa and is loosely based on the two-season Israeli series *Hatufim* (*Prisoners of War*), written and directed by Gideon Raff, who also co-produces and partly co-wrote the American version.

[3] See Frank Kelleter, 'Five ways of looking at popular seriality', in *Media of Serial Narrative*, ed. Frank Kelleter (Columbus, OH, 2017), pp. 7–36, for a general account of authentication strategies in current TV series.

[4] On the contested role of *Homeland* in sociocultural communication regarding various aspects of post-9/11 warfare, see Lindsay Steenberg and Yvonne Tasker, '"Pledge allegiance": gendered surveillance, crime television, and *Homeland*', *Cinema Journal* 54 (2015), 132–8; Diane Negra and Jorie Lagerwey, 'Analyzing *Homeland*: introduction', *Cinema Journal* 54 (2015), 126–31; Alex Bevan, 'The national body, women, and mental health in *Homeland*', *Cinema Journal* 54 (2015), 145–51; James Castonguay, 'Fictions and terror: complexity, complicity and insecurity in *Homeland*', *Cinema Journal* 54 (2015), 139–45; Lars Koch, '"I – I'm just making sure we don't get hit again": Serientext und Weltbezug in der TV-Serie Homeland', INDES: Zeitschrift für Politik und Gesellschaft 4 (2014), 42–54. Mittell suggests that 'any attempt to account for *Homeland*'s political meanings must remain open and unfinished until the series concludes, as it has demonstrated a willingness to revisit and revise its politics quite drastically' (*Complex TV*, p. 345).

Coriolanus, Brody is selected to be a politician because of his merits and his symbolic importance for the defence of the homeland: first he becomes a Congressman, then a promising candidate for Vice President and, in the eyes of some, the best possible future candidate for President. The next steps of Shakespeare's tragedy – the accusation of treason and the return as avenger – follow the thriller genre as it overlaps with this transition from soldier to politician. Right at the beginning of the series, CIA agent Carrie Mathison receives a tip that an American prisoner of war has defected while in captivity and is now part of an Islamist terror cell, planning an attack on the USA. Viewers are invited to share Mathison's detective work by scrutinizing Brody's potential attack on the homeland in an investigation which always verges on paranoia. The series therefore draws its basic narrative tension and hermeneutic pleasure from the questions of whether Brody is a traitor and terrorist, whether the American war hero has secretly become an enemy soldier, whether he is pursuing vengeance, and what could have motivated such a need for revenge. When his terrorist intentions are confirmed, the series, like the final act of *Coriolanus*, focuses on the question of whether appeals to his humanity can prevent him from attacking the homeland, as appeals to his patriotism are fruitless. These patterns are repeated in escalating variants through the serial structure – for example, in episodes that show Brody's activities as a double agent. In the third season, Brody is finally, like Coriolanus, executed for treason by war opponents whom he still claims to serve, and his homeland's commemoration of his sacrifice is even more problematic than in Shakespeare's play.

Despite these parallels, however, the writing and production teams of *Homeland* have never explicitly referenced Shakespeare, and the show has not directly evoked *Coriolanus* (or any other Shakespeare play) as an intertext either. Unlike the British and American versions of the political series *House of Cards*, for example, whose writers and actors pointed out that Shakespeare's *Richard III* was a central source of inspiration, and which repeatedly refers to Shakespeare through quotes and allusions, *Homeland*'s marketing has not drawn on Shakespeare's cultural capital. It is, if at all, an 'unmarked adaptation', to use a term which Douglas M. Lanier has recently proposed.[5] This constellation raises the foundational question for the study of Shakespearian afterlives of how we, as early modern scholars, measure and prove Shakespeare's influence on other artists. Do we need direct intertextual references, comments by writers themselves, or other material that proves their knowledge of Shakespeare's plays? Can we assume a more indirect cultural influence of his plays on modern culture? Should we avoid the risk of obsessive readings that detect Shakespearian traces in later works simply because we are so familiar with his oeuvre, or should we acknowledge that intertextual relations are created by readers as much as by authors? Should cultural analysis abstain from assuming 'influence' and instead simply discuss correspondences, since they might tell us something about comparable cultural moments?

The existing models to account for uncertain Shakespearian returns can generally be divided into models that assume cultural influence (which scholars uncover and explicate) and models that instead emphasize the scholar's own work of bringing historically distant texts together, irrespective of their intertextual relation. A prominent example of the first model is Marjorie Garber's work, which accounts for Shakespeare's 'uncanny modernity' by arguing that 'the plays, and the high regard for Shakespeare in the centuries following his death, have *created* … "modern" types as much as they have paralleled or predicted them'.[6] According to Garber, 'Shakespeare has scripted many of the ideas that we think of as "naturally" our own',[7]

---

5 Douglas M. Lanier, 'Shakespeare / not Shakespeare: afterword', in *Shakespeare / Not Shakespeare*, ed. Christy Desmet, Natalie Loper and Jim Casey (Basingstoke, 2017), pp. 293–306; p. 300.
6 Marjorie Garber, *Shakespeare After All* (New York, 2004), p. 776.
7 Marjorie Garber, *Shakespeare and Modern Culture* (New York, 2008), p. viii.

including *Coriolanus* as a paradigm for the uneasy transition from soldier to politician that is also at stake in *Homeland*.[8] Stanley Cavell, Elisabeth Bronfen and Graham Holderness, among many others, have offered models to compare Shakespearian texts to later, non-Shakespearian ones. Cavell sees Shakespeare's plays as a 'subtext' of Hollywood movies of the 1930s and 1940s coming together in a cultural conversation.[9] Bronfen has modified Cavell's method by connecting it to Stephen Greenblatt's new historicist concept of the circulation of social energies. In 'cross-mappings', she explores figures of thought shared by the texts as a heuristic practice that assumes a survival of Shakespearian energies, but does not seek to find intertextual evidence.[10] Holderness proposes a term that he takes from particle physics – 'collision' – and uses it to describe his comparison of Shakespearian and non-Shakespearian cultural products, which 'in their mutual impact generate an observable and meaningful pattern'.[11] Among these patterns, Holderness identifies 'a generic cultural formation' of the first decades of the new millennium, which he names 'the *Coriolanus* myth'[12] – a pattern into which, with some qualifications, *Homeland* can be placed, too.[13] The rewards of these alternative methods are remarkably similar not only in that conversations, cross-mappings and collisions produce insightful comparative readings, but also in that post-fidelity adaptation studies have long demonstrated that Shakespearian plays and their reworkings are mutually transformative when read in relation to one another.

## LOOPS OF TURNING AND RETURNING

I will revisit this methodological question after my own comparative reading, which hopes to provide new insights into the serialized process of war homecoming in both the early modern tragedy and the 21st-century serial thriller. *Homeland*'s exposition of the problematic war returnee figure centres on the metaphor of 'turning', and the conceptual spectrum between 'turning' and 'returning' provides a productive lens for Shakespeare's play,

too. The pilot episode of *Homeland* begins with letters randomly appearing and disappearing to show briefly the term 'homeland'. It introduces an ephemeral construction of home, threatened with obliteration. The first image of the series is a panorama shot of Baghdad with an explanatory caption, the letters of which do not disappear. Yet Baghdad is not the homeland of the title, but the external threat against which the USA must be defended. Accordingly, the plot is set in motion through intelligence information which warns of 'an imminent attack on US soil'. The first thirty seconds of the pilot thus define the self in opposition to the other: the concept of 'homeland' is introduced visually and narratively through the threatening other, which is constitutive but always also potentially destabilizing for the definition of the self – a common poststructuralist, psychoanalytic and postcolonial concept, which here acts as a narrative engine.

This constitutive interdependence of self and other requires a clear dividing line, but, in the minutes that follow, *Homeland* clarifies that this front line in global post-9/11 warfare is neither

---

[8] Garber, *Shakespeare After All*, pp. 776–7.
[9] Stanley Cavell, *Pursuits of Happiness* (Cambridge, 2003), p. 144.
[10] Elisabeth Bronfen, *Crossmappings: On Visual Culture* (London, 2018), p. 2.
[11] Graham Holderness, *Tales from Shakespeare: Creative Collisions* (Cambridge, 2014), p. 18.
[12] Holderness, *Tales from Shakespeare*, p. 89.
[13] I do not fully agree with Holderness's description of this myth as 'a peculiarly contemporary realisation of the classic man of war' (*Tales from Shakespeare*, p. 116), in which 'war is a matter of human agency, and its outcome is dependent on the courage and hardihood of an individual combatant' (p. 124). By contrast, I will argue that the respective *Coriolanus* characters are indicative of the failure of such notions of individual strength. Nonetheless, Holderness's reading of Shakespeare's text and Fiennes's film version 'in collision with' Kathryn Bigelow's post-9/11 *The Hurt Locker* (2009) and Sam Mendes's James Bond thriller *Skyfall* (2012) is relevant for my argument, because *Homeland* generically draws on, and has in turn influenced, post-9/11 films as much as the spy-thriller genre. See also Ronan Hatfull, '"Thou art my warrior": questions of allegiance and power in *Coriolanus* and *Homeland*', https://notyouwill.wordpress.com/tag/coriolanus.

territorially determinable nor clearly marked in terms of the identity of its protagonist. At CIA headquarters, a video of the previous night's military operation is shown, in which US soldiers in Afghanistan storm a cluster of wanted terrorists around Abu Nazir. The soldiers come across a locked, hidden interior room in which they suspect a high-ranking enemy is hiding. They find a figure whose physical condition and pose match this idea: a figure who is iconographically similar to the images of Saddam Hussein when found and captured in 2004 as part of Operation Red Dawn. The enigmatic figure, who first speaks in Arabic, identifies himself as one of their own: 'I am an American.' This moment of surprise is expressed by the Deputy Director of the National Counter-Terrorism Center, David Estes, in the phrase: 'turns out he is one of ours'. Although Estes proudly proclaims, 'because of you, an American hero is coming home', the return of the presumed dead is potentially destabilizing for the homeland, as the following minutes show, in another twist that dedicates special attention to the word 'turn'. Because of the information provided by an Iraqi informant, Carrie Mathison suspects that Brody has been 'turned'. In conversation with her supervisor, Saul Berenson, she presents her theory:

SAUL What were his exact words, please?
CARRIE 'An American prisoner of war has been turned.'
SAUL He said this in English?
CARRIE Yes. He whispered it into my ear right before the guards pulled me away.
SAUL And when he used the expression 'turned' –
CARRIE He meant turned – working for Abu Nazir.

Brody's return is a mystery: he comes back, but does he also come home? Does he still feel as though he belongs to the USA or has he been turned around and now plans to attack his homeland? So, is his return not a homecoming but a *Heimsuchung* – an attack on the homeland that is all the more devastating and uncanny (*unheimlich*) because it is secretly carried out by one considered American, 'one of ours'? For the later plot, the central question will be whether the soldier-turned-enemy can be turned again into an

American soldier who could serve as a double agent. This tension only increases when it is revealed that Brody converted to Islam while in captivity and secretly keeps practising his new religion after his return. Turning, turning back, or turning further, reversing and repenting, converting, coming back and actually coming home – this interplay between movements of turn and return grants the series numerous cliffhangers and turning points and is one of the themes repeated-with-variation typical of the serial form.

A reading of the exposition and plot of *Coriolanus* shows how the negotiation of self and enemy in the tragedy is made newly readable through *Homeland*'s focus on turns and returns. *Homeland*'s dramaturgy of excessively serialized loops of (re)turning also helps to uncover the more moderate serialized structure of Shakespeare's tragedy, which so far has rarely been discussed. Like the series, the opening of the tragedy – in which the word 'home' occurs more frequently than in any other Shakespearian drama[14] – presents a homeland under attack: while an armed uprising of the plebeians threatens the inner peace, the outer borders of Rome are attacked by the Volscians. Caius Martius has an ambivalent role in this double threat: even before his first appearance, he is identified by the insurgent plebeians as the 'chief enemy to the people' (1.1.6–7), but, at the same time, other plebeians point out how indispensable Martius is to Rome in wars against external enemies.[15] The third scene, in which Martius's mother and wife are waiting for his return from the latest war against the Volsces, allows the audience insight into Coriolanus's socialization. Already in his youth, '[when] he was but tender-bodied' (1.3.5–6), Volumnia sent him off to a savage war, from which he returned triumphant. Volumnia presents Coriolanus's first victorious return as a second birth, as an initiation into heroic-militant masculinity built on the serialization of leaving and

---

[14] See note 172 in William Shakespeare, *Coriolanus*, ed. R. B. Parker (Oxford, 1994), p. 342.
[15] All *Coriolanus* quotations refer to the Arden 3 edition, ed. Peter Holland (London, 2013).

returning to the homeland: '[t]o a cruel war I sent him, from whence he returned, his brows bound with oak. I tell thee, daughter, I sprang not more in joy at first hearing he was a man-child than now in first seeing he had proved himself a man' (1.3.13–17). This serialization is typical of the aristocratic warrior striving for fame at home by fighting abroad. Leslie Kurke's description of this phenomenon in Greek antiquity as a 'loop of nostos' fits Shakespeare's drama of the Roman warrior, too, which dramatizes this loop of turning away from the homeland and returning to it as a spiral of political and psychological escalation.[16]

As in *Homeland*'s initial scenario, the following scenes stage a crisis in the battle for Corioles, when the return of the hero is in doubt in several ways. Martius, on his own, pursues the Volscians into Corioles as the city gates close behind him. After the noise and agitation, there is a moment of silence on the stage which makes the leader's absence palpable. A Roman soldier comments, '[s]ee they have shut him in' (1.4.49), and is certain that Martius will not survive this suicide mission: '[h]e is himself alone / To answer all the city' (1.4.55–6). Like Brody, Caius Martius becomes a war hero believed dead. At the gates of Corioles, the Roman general Titus Lartius gives a glorifying eulogy and defines him, in the spirit of his name 'Martius', indicating Mars, the ancestor of Rome, as a superhuman, god-like Roman fighter:

Thou wast a soldier
Even to Cato's wish, not fierce and terrible
Only in strokes, but with thy grim looks and
The thunder-like percussion of thy sounds
Thou mad'st thine enemies shake, as if the world
Were feverous and did tremble.

(1.4.60–5)

Contrary to this praise presented in the past tense – completed, and thus politically secure – Caius Martius returns unexpectedly from the city gates as a 'thing of blood' (2.2.107), as Cominius will describe him later, as a bloody something that fights its way out of the gates. This imagery continues the war-as-rebirth metaphor of Volumnia's speech and

stages the loop of nostos as loop of (near-/alleged) death in war and the rebirth of war homecoming.[17] Upon his serialized returns to the stage space from combat off-stage, Martius is not immediately identifiable as one of Rome's own, as in the case of Brody's return. Thus, Lartius says 'O, 'tis Martius' (1.4.65) because he did not recognize him directly. Two scenes later, Martius returns from another battle even more disfigured. This time Cominius asks,

[w]ho's yonder
That does appear as he were flayed? O gods
He has the stamp of Martius, and I have
Beforetime seen him thus.

(1.6.21–24)

This image of the monstrous, bloody warrior figure is also significant in terms of the serialized distortion of his identity. As Peter Holland has noted, '[h]e has the stamp of Martius' can mean that he looks like Martius, but it can also mean that he looks like one of Martius's victims, indicating that he must be a - Volscian.[18] This ambiguity of belonging is taken up again two lines later when the blood covering Martius is described as clothing, stressing that it is unclear whether it is his blood or that of his opponent: it is unclear whose uniform Martius wears.[19]

The moment of return from the opponent's territory in *Coriolanus* thus involves a similar challenge to that in *Homeland*, because it is about the processes that distinguish one's own from the other, the fellow citizen from the enemy. This

---

[16] Leslie Kurke, *The Traffic in Praise: Pindar and the Poetics of Social Economy* (Ithaca, NY, 1991), pp. 15–17.

[17] See Janet Adelman, *Suffocating Mothers: Fantasies of Maternal Origin in Shakespeare's Plays* (New York, 1992), p. 152.

[18] See *Coriolanus*, p. 198, n. 23.

[19] 'MARTIUS. Come I too late? / COMINIUS. Ay, if you come not in the blood of others, / But mantled in your own' (1.6.28–9). As Robert N. Watson observes, two scenes later, the blood is also presented as a mask, again questioning the identity of Coriolanus ('Coriolanus and the "common part"', *Shakespeare Survey* 69 (Cambridge, 2016), 181–97; p. 187): 'CORIOLANUS. Alone I fought in your Corioles' walls / And made what work I pleased. 'Tis not my blood / Wherein thou seest me masked' (1.8.9–11).

distinction is not just an epistemic challenge for those left behind, but also a physical and psychological test for the soldier, who must maintain his identity while away, in order to return intact and readable. As critics have pointed out, Shakespeare's drama questions the uncompromising affiliation with Rome even before the reputed capture of Coriolanus, because the enormous importance of the Volscian leader Tullus Aufidius for the protagonist's identity is emphasized from the first scene onwards in Caius Martius's famous comments, 'were I any thing but what I am, / I would wish me only he' (1.1.226–7). Martius privileges this identificatory antagonism even above his national affiliation and allegiance in battle:

> [w]ere half to half the world by th'ears and he
> Upon my party, I'd revolt to make
> Only my wars with him.
>
> (1.1.228–30)[20]

The commitment to a close bond with the enemy right at the beginning of the drama is all the more remarkable as it is Shakespeare's own invention: in Plutarch's biography, Aufidius is first mentioned after Coriolanus's banishment. The exposition of *Coriolanus* thus opens up dramaturgic possibilities similar to the beginning of *Homeland*, as both stage the tension created by the potential alienation of the self through war and the possible turning of the self into the enemy on return.

Close ties to the war and the enemy make the soldier a problematic returnee figure. Shakespeare's tragedy shows Coriolanus already having trouble at the ceremony immediately after the battle, and above all upon his return to Rome at the consul appointment ritual. The deteriorating appointment ceremony is presented in a dramaturgy of serialization, which leads to an extension of the play's climax and peripety. Stretched over five scenes (2.2 to 3.3), the ceremony is structured by repeated movements of turning to the people, turning his back on them, and returning to them. For the Globe plays, such an extension or dispersion has been described by Bernard Beckerman as a 'climactic plateau' and an 'accumulation of [the] effect' of recognition and reversal.[21] In *Coriolanus*, this accumulation of

climactic moments and turning points is formed as loops of turning and returning, resulting in a dramaturgic spiral of political escalation. Menenius and Volumnia repeatedly demand Coriolanus's return to the marketplace to save the appointment ceremony ('You must return and mend it', 3.2.27; 'Return to th' tribunes … / Repent what you spoke', 3.2.37–8). Even though Coriolanus reluctantly promises to 'return consul' (3.2.136) when he goes back to the marketplace a fourth time, he cannot carry out the required U-turn in his attitude, which he, in yet another 'being turned' metaphor, describes as humiliatingly emasculating:

> My throat of war be turned,
> Which choired with my drum, into a pipe
> Small as an eunuch or the virgin voice
> That babies lull asleep!
>
> (3.2.113–16)

As a culmination of the political conflict, Coriolanus is banned from Rome under penalty of death. Famously, his curse – in which he exiles his exilers – announces, '[d]espising / For you the city, thus I turn my back. / There is a world elsewhere' (3.3.132–4). Coriolanus's attempt to once again turn the turning point, thus creating a 'peripety-atop-peripety',[22] is part of a strategy of re-empowerment, as the now grammatically active formulation of his turn away emphasizes.

His banishment of the people is on the one hand a megalomaniac presumption, implying that Coriolanus considers himself Rome. On the other hand, this presumption is not without foundation, for until this turning point Coriolanus has been repeatedly praised as the epitome of *Romanitas* for his extraordinary fighting power, courage, loyalty,

---

20 See James Kuzner, 'Unbuilding the city: *Coriolanus* and the birth of Republican Rome', *Shakespeare Quarterly* 58 (2007), 174–99; p. 189; Holderness, *Tales from Shakespeare*, pp. 97–8.

21 Bernhard Beckerman, *Shakespeare at the Globe: 1599–1609* (New York, 1962), pp. 42, 41.

22 Kenneth Burke, '*Coriolanus* and the Delights of Faction', *The Hudson Review*, 19 (1966), 185–202; p. 191.

honesty and readiness for self-sacrifice.[23] Through the references to Rome's mythic origins,[24] Coriolanus is presented as 'the quintessential Roman subject, the national ego-ideal that common soldiers are supposed to imitate but can never equal', as Coppélia Kahn has put it.[25] However, the returned war hero cannot be integrated into Rome's civil society. As Andreas Höfele has shown, Coriolanus stands for the mythical origin of Rome, as defined by its combat powers.[26] In historical Rome with its republican structures, Coriolanus is a dangerous contaminant who, according to the tribunes, must be removed. This removal trajectory is cast in the metaphor of the body politic, which is implicated in the play's conceptual spinning movement.

## THE SLIPPERY TURNS OF THE BODY POLITIC

The metaphor of the body politic, which the play employs from its first scene onwards,[27] is evoked in the dispute between plebeians and patricians immediately before Coriolanus's exile, to declare him a pathogenic foreign body that must be destroyed or excluded:

SICINIUS He's a disease that must be cut away . . .
BRUTUS [to the Citizens:] Pursue him to his house and
    pluck him thence,
  Lest his infection, being of catching nature,
  Spread further.

                                        (3.1.296, 309–12)

Against this image of control and expulsion – the immune reaction of the state body to germs – Menenius emphasizes Coriolanus's belonging and the unnaturalness of such a process, which he sees not as a cure, but as self-destruction. Thus, he characterizes the action of the tribunes as an autoimmune reaction, one which aims to heal the diseased body by fighting the alleged contaminant, but which in fact damages its own cells.

After his exile, Coriolanus conceives a plan of revenge which translates the autoimmune response that Menenius described into a counter-strategy:

originally responsible for the defence of Rome's social body, Coriolanus now turns against his homeland, which he calls 'my cankered country' (4.5.93), presenting his attack as a healing destruction. It remains unclear in which role Coriolanus

---

[23] Jane Kingsley-Smith, *Shakespeare's Drama of Exile* (New York, 2003), p. 138. The people by no means measure up to this ideal, and Coriolanus therefore calls them 'barbarians' (3.1.239). See also Francis Barker, 'Nationalism, nomadism and belonging in Europe: *Coriolanus*', in *Shakespeare and National Culture*, ed. John J. Joughin (Manchester, 1997), pp. 233–66; p. 250.

[24] Genealogically, the foundational relevance of bravery and courage for Rome can be deduced from the legend of the city's origins. Romulus, the son of Mars, founded Rome and defended its holy walls for the first time by murdering his own twin brother Remus. On its maternal side, Rome has a sacral-animal genealogy: born of the Vestal Virgin Rhea Silvia, the abandoned twins were nursed by a wolf. Coriolanus's mother Volumnia sees herself as a reincarnation of this founding myth as she embodies both the biological mother, the Vestal Virgin and the wet nurse, the wolf. On the one hand, she emphasizes Coriolanus's direct origin from her womb and, metaphorically, from the motherly matrix of Rome, but she also calls Rome 'dear nurse' (5.3.110), claiming that Coriolanus's Roman fighting power springs from her nurture: '[t]hy [Coriolanus'] valiantness was mine, thou suck'st it from me' (3.2.130). This wording equates Volumnia with Rome in a number of ways, as it invokes the terms that resonate in 'Rome'/'Roma': both the Greek *rhome* ('force') and the Latin *ruma* ('breast', 'teat'). See Gianluca Solla, 'Brudermord (Plutarch)', in *Rom Rückwärts: Europäische Übertragungsschicksale*, ed. Judith Kasper and Cornelia Wild (Paderborn, 2015), pp. 21–5; p. 25.

[25] Coppélia Kahn, *Roman Shakespeare* (London, 1997), p. 152.

[26] Andreas Höfele, *Stage, Stake and Scaffold: Humans and Animals in Shakespeare's Theatre* (New York, 2011), pp. 107–9.

[27] However, the first scene also already shows how the metaphor is led to its catachrestic limit as the hierarchical body metaphor for the Republic of Rome no longer works and is politically exploited in order to sedate the people. The body politic metaphor in *Coriolanus* has been discussed intensely; for the political dimensions, see Barker, 'Nationalism'; Adelman, *Suffocating Mothers*; Zvi Jagendorf, 'Coriolanus: body politic and private parts', *Shakespeare Quarterly* 41 (1990), 455–69; Bradley J. Irish, 'Coriolanus and the poetics of disgust', *Shakespeare Survey* 69 (Cambridge, 2016), 198–215; as well as Eve Rachele Sanders, 'The body of the actor in *Coriolanus*', *Shakespeare Quarterly* 57 (2006), 387–412, on the metatheatrical dimension of the play's concern with embodiment.

casts himself in this return to Rome's mythical origins: is he Remus, who breaks through Rome's walls? Or does he see himself as the successor to Romulus, the founder of Rome?[28] Does he, as a destructive new founder, unite the twin brothers in a single figure? Such a twin configuration seems to be what Coriolanus is aiming for in his search for a new identity in yet another rebirth and baptism by war. He wants to conquer Rome in order to bear its name, as his erstwhile comrade Cominius reports:

'Coriolanus'
He would not answer to, forbade all names.
He was a kind of nothing, titleless,
Till he had forged himself a name o'th' fire
Of burning Rome.

(5.1.11–15)

It remains unclear what name the nameless would carry after a victory over the homeland, but perhaps he would combine the contradictory names of Rome's defender and its destroyer in a 'political oxymoron, a pointed self-contradiction': Caius Martius Coriolanus Romanus.[29]

Jacques Derrida has made the concept of the autoimmune reaction fruitful for the discussion of current international (counter)terrorism as dramatized in *Homeland*, which provides a special perspective on Shakespeare's early modern drama.[30] In particular, Derrida is interested in the collective psychic component of such an autoimmune reaction and the removal of a clear dividing line between self and other, between defender and attacker, which is also central to Shakespeare's tragedy.[31] It is astonishing that – unlike in North's Plutarch, which details the military threat[32] – Rome is staged as defenceless against the returnee's attack without indicating specific reasons for this helplessness. A fight against Coriolanus and his army is not even considered:

MENENIUS We are all undone, unless
    The noble man have mercy.
COMINIUS You [the tribunes, the people] have brought
    A trembling upon Rome such as was never
    S'incapable of help.
    . . . Desperation

Is all the policy, strength and defence
That Rome can make against them.

(4.6.113–14, 124–6, 134–6)

The drama stages an unsubstantiated vulnerability, a helplessness and despair that appears as psychological shock – or, in the immunological metaphor of Derrida, as the inability to immunize the self against the self.

For the moment before Rome's self-destruction, Shakespeare reverts to the body politic metaphor from North's Plutarch translation. Plutarch describes the Romans as 'so fainte harted, so mistrustfull, and lothe besides to make warres' that 'they properly ressembled the bodyes paralyticke . . . losed of their limmes and members: as those which through the palsey have lost all their sence and feeling'.[33] In Plutarch's imagery, Rome suffers a paralysis of the body politic, because the soldiers, the limbs, can no longer register and pass on sensations to the head. Shakespeare transfers Plutarch's diagnosis of the disconnected body politic metonymically to Menenius as representative of

---

28 See Watson, 'Coriolanus and the "common part"', p. 194.
29 Garber, *After All*, p. 797.
30 For a discussion of *Homeland* in the light of Derrida's notion of autoimmunity, see Grant Farred, '"An American has been turned": thinking autoimmunity through *Homeland*', *Derrida Today* 7 (2014), 59–78.
31 For an alternative reading of *Coriolanus* in view of Derrida's concept of autoimmunity, see Maurizio Calbi, 'States of exception: auto-immunity and the body politic in Shakespeare's *Coriolanus*', in *Questioning Bodies in Shakespeare's Rome*, ed. Maria Del Sapio Garbero, Nancy Isenberg and Maddalena Pennacchia (Goettingen, 2010), pp. 77–94.
32 Here Coriolanus's 'whole armie (which was marvelous great, and very forward to service)' is described, and its complex military strategy is explained – see Geoffrey Bullough, *Narrative and Dramatic Sources of Shakespeare*, 8 vols. (London and New York, 1964), vol. 5, p. 532. This strategy aims at military annexation or destruction of the Roman allies as well as at the domestic destabilization of Rome through targeted attacks on plebeian estates. By contrast, Shakespeare's play does not detail or make plausible the military threat posed by Coriolanus.
33 Bullough, *Narrative and Dramatic Sources*, vol. 5, p. 535.

# CHRISTINA WALD

Rome when he is ridiculed by the Volscians before his appeal for clemency to Coriolanus:

I WATCHMAN You are a Roman, are you?
MENENIUS I am as thy general is.
I WATCHMAN Then you should hate Rome, as he does.
Can you, when you have pushed out your gates the very defender of them and in a violent popular ignorance given your enemy your shield, think to front his revenges with the easy groans of old women, the virginal palms of your daughters or with the palsied intercession of such a decayed dotant as you seem to be?

(5.2.37–46)

Here, the guard explains to Menenius that his personal paralysis and that of the Roman body politic are the result of an autoimmune reaction. Their own shield has become an enemy by the '[a]ll strange illogical logic' described by Derrida, 'by which a living being can … destroy … the very thing within it that is supposed to protect it against the other, to immunize it against the aggressive intrusion of the other'.[34]

This abolition of the dividing line between self and other, between defender and aggressor, is repeatedly reflected in the drama and shows that the military crisis is also an epistemic and psychic one: how can the self be defined if the binaries friend/foe, inside/outside, no longer apply? Derrida points out that the self-attack of the autoimmune response is also an attack on the very notion of 'self':

For what I call the autoimmune consists not only in harming or ruining oneself, indeed in destroying one's own protections, and in doing so oneself, committing suicide or threatening to do so, but, more seriously still, and through this, in threatening the I [*moz*] or the self [*soi*], the *ego* or the *autos,* ipseity itself, compromising the immunity of the *autos* itself: it consists not only in compromising oneself [*s'auto-entamer*] but in compromising the self, the *autos* – and thus ipseity. It consists not only in committing suicide but in compromising *sui-* or *self-*referentiality, the *self or sui-* of suicide itself. Autoimmunity is more or less suicidal, but, more seriously still, it threatens always to rob suicide itself of its meaning and supposed integrity.[35]

Autoimmunity not only injures the self, but also plunges the question of the self into an epistemic

and psychological crisis: in this sense, too, it is 'self-murder'.

In yet another turning metaphor, this crisis of the self and the associated crisis of national belonging are manifested in Coriolanus's only longer soliloquy. He opens the speech with 'O world, thy slippery turns' (4.4.12) to deplore the treacherous changes of fate, especially the transformation of political loyalties that drives him into the arms of the adversary. The 'slippery turns' self-reflexively comments on the genre of tragedy, as it evokes the spinning wheel of Fortuna, which shapes the *de casibus* tragedies of the medieval tradition. At the end of this speech, Coriolanus confesses: '[m]y birthplace hate I, and my love's upon / This enemy town' (4.4.23–4). In the language of *Homeland*, one could clearly state: 'a Roman soldier has been turned'. Or should one say 'has turned', because in the earlier banishment speech he emphasized his own agency ('I turn my back')? This wavering of the tragic protagonist between a position of helplessness, his passivity in the face of overpowering fate, and his autonomous activity is characteristic of Shakespeare's late tragedies of restitution, in which the force of fate as the engine of tragedy becomes doubtful and the protagonists' responsibility for their actions is explored.[36]

In addition to these questions about the tragedy form and the relation between external control and the protagonist's self-responsibility, the imagined

---

[34] Jacques Derrida, *Rogues: Two Essays on Reason* (Stanford, CA, 2005), p. 123.

[35] Derrida, *Rogues*, p. 45; emphasis in original.

[36] Andreas Mahler, '"There is restitution, no end of restitution, only not for us": experimental tragedy and the early modern subject in *Julius Caesar*', in *Julius Caesar: New Critical Essays*, ed. Horst Zander (New York, 2005), pp. 181–95. As Emma Smith has argued, 'Shakespeare's final tragedy performs that inscrutability Hamlet talks about, debating and deferring the notion and location of personality and individual agency' – see 'Character in Shakespearean tragedy', in *The Oxford Handbook of Shakespearean Tragedy*, ed. Michael Neill (Oxford, 2016), pp. 89–99; p. 98. The constant deferral of insight into the protagonist's identity and agency is used in the serial-thriller format of *Homeland* to keep audiences engaged while postponing the answers they are looking for.

loop of slippery turns has implications for the final, professedly unequivocal confession of Coriolanus's soliloquy: '[m]y birthplace hate I, and my love's upon / This enemy town'. Which birthplace is Coriolanus speaking of here? As discussed earlier, the encounter with the enemy outside of Rome became the site of Coriolanus's rebirth as a young war hero. This rebirth following a near-death experience has been repeated in a series of battles, including the war for Corioles, which led to a new name for the born-again Caius Martius. Is his hatred then for Rome or is it for Corioles, Antium, the sphere of the Volscians? And whom does he love? '[M]y love's upon / This enemy town': the first scene already titles Coriolanus as an enemy of the people, and in the banishment scene he eloquently marks his turn away from Rome, because he now identifies Rome with his domestic enemies. The terms 'enemy town' and 'birthplace' thus become ambiguous and might even refer to the same place, be it Rome or a Volscian city, to describe an ambivalent love/ hate relationship and unstable loyalty. The 'slippery turns' thus mark the fluid referentiality of the central concepts of war and war homecoming, that of the 'homeland' and its constitutive, hostile other.

This complex constellation of self and other, and the dissolution of a concept of homeland, are central to the reconfiguration of the Coriolanus motif in *Homeland*. Here, in the finale of the first season, the autoimmune reaction offers a concrete model for the execution of the attack on the homeland, which is planned as Brody's suicide bombing of the ruling elite of the USA, into which he is about to ascend: following the assassination of a politician, all accompanying politicians, including the Vice President and senior CIA staff, are escorted to a bunker. Despite setting off alarms with the suicide vest hidden under his military uniform, Brody is able to pass through security checks due to the state of emergency. Confined and isolated in a situation and place designed to provide immunity and security, he can now strike the USA at its core. The narrative stages the logic of the autoimmune reaction: only

when the immune system is ramped up is destruction set in motion, so that Brody, as the supposed defender of the body politic, is able to attack it.

As in *Coriolanus*, the autoimmune logic is used as political justification by the soldier who has turned against his home. Brody sees his attack as a cure for the USA, because he considers the political leaders as internal enemies. Just as Coriolanus is associated with the founding myth of Rome, including fratricide, with his planned assassination of his brother-turned-enemy, Brody places himself in a historical-mythical genealogy of the defence and re-founding of the USA (itself modelled on Rome in a *translatio imperii*). In the penultimate episode of the first season, he is sent by his terrorist network to Gettysburg to receive the suicide vest. There he stands for a long time, lost in thought at the site of the decisive battle of the American Civil War – allegedly decided by Joshua Chamberlain's unexpected and very risky manoeuvre. Chamberlain explained his readiness for self-sacrifice was a contribution to 'defend[ing] the national existence against treachery'.[37] In Brody's confessional video, in which he wears his Marine uniform and presents himself as a soldier within his family's tradition, Brody follows the same argument. He places his planned attack in the tradition of the American Civil War, as a defence of the USA from internal enemies who have betrayed American values by ordering drone strikes on civilian targets in Syria and then publicly denied responsibility for the deaths of young pupils. His autoimmune attack pursues a defensive, patriotic project of political restitution:

I was held captive for more than eight years. I was beaten, I was tortured, and I was subjected to long periods of total isolation. People will say I was broken, I was brainwashed. People will say that I was turned into a terrorist, taught to hate my country. I love my country. What I am is a Marine, like my father before me and his father before him. And as a Marine, I swore an oath to defend the United

---

[37] In a letter to the Governor of Maine, as cited in Alice Rains Trulock, *In the Hands of Providence: Joshua L. Chamberlain and the American Civil War* (Chapel Hill, NC, 1992), p. 8.

States of America against enemies both foreign and domestic. My action this day is against such domestic enemies – the vice president and members of his national security team, who I know to be liars and war criminals responsible for atrocities they were never held accountable for. This is about justice for 82 children whose deaths were never acknowledged and whose murder is a stain on the soul of this nation.

In contrast to Coriolanus in his 'slippery turns' soliloquy, Brody emphasizes his own responsibility in his address to the public. In a private conversation, however, Brody tries to justify his actions to his oblivious son by emphasizing the identity-changing impact of war in imagery akin to 'the slippery turns' of the wheel of fortune: 'all wars turn everything upside down. Everything and everyone.' The episode visualizes this rhetorical loop of (re)turning when Brody's daughter Dana attaches a mini camera to his car's steering wheel and viewers see rotating recorded images of Brody. The video footage is shown as part of the daughter's detective work, in which she attempts to interpret her father's peculiar behaviour prior to his suicide bombing. Suspense is thus increased as to whether Brody will turn back, be turned back, and genuinely come home in a conclusion of his prolonged turn/return movement.

## TURNING BACK, RE-TURNING, IMPOSSIBLE HOMECOMINGS

This question of a possible averting of the acute-threat scenario through the avenger's 're-turn', the undoing of his having (been) turned, determines the final act of Shakespeare's tragedy and the last two episodes of *Homeland*'s first season. In both cases, a request for protection from the soldier's own family is decisive; the issue of national affiliation is renegotiated through family affiliation. In *Coriolanus*, the body politic metaphor is re-envisioned as physical bond between mother and son when Volumnia equates her womb with the motherly matrix of Rome (5.3.122–5). Coriolanus recoils from this destruction of his origin, but as the further process shows, the alternative scenario of a complete homecoming, the return to the womb of the mother/

land, is just as destructive if the regressive scheme is followed to its logical end. After Volumnia persuades Coriolanus to agree to the peace treaty with Rome, she is celebrated on her triumphant return to Rome as mother of the people, as 'patroness, the life of Rome' (5.5.1), because she now embodies her son, whom she has metaphorically re-incorporated. The rhetorical imagery that gives expression to this re-incorporation phantasm condenses essential aspects of the returnee problem:

SENATOR Unshout the noise that banished Martius,
  Repeal him with the welcome of his mother.

(5.5.4–5)

The demand '[r]epeal him' has a complex meaning: on the one hand, it means that Coriolanus is to be recalled from exile, that he is called again. This is a delicate, if not impossible, undertaking, as the first line has emphasized with the 'impossible task' of unshouting,[38] and in fact, in contrast to Plutarch, Shakespeare's Romans do not plan on calling Coriolanus home. On the other hand, the condensed phrase 'repeal him' instead of 'repeal his banishment' (or, as in Plutarch, 'to repeale the condemnation and exile of Martius')[39] allows that the revocation refers not only to his exile, but also to Coriolanus himself. In this reading, Coriolanus would be undone by the victorious homecoming of his mother, reversed in an inversion of his birth by Volumnia, who has now metaphorically re-incorporated her son. The image of the unnatural destruction of one's mother and one's own motherland is thus replaced by a no less unnatural image of an identity-destroying return to the womb. The rhetoric of the disintegrating returnee finds its physical manifestation in the catastrophic final scene, as Coriolanus comes back from Rome and is executed as a traitor by the Volscians, who demand to 'tear him to pieces' (5.6.121).[40]

---

[38] See *Coriolanus*, p. 399, n. 4.

[39] Bullough, *Narrative and Dramatic Sources*, vol. 5, p. 533.

[40] This paragraph corresponds to my more extended argument in Christina Wald, '"And here remain with your uncertainty": Paradoxien des Raumes in Shakespeares Hikesie-Tragödie *Coriolanus*', in *Flucht und Szene*, ed. Bettine Menke and Juliane Vogel (Berlin, 2018), pp. 140–66.

The plea for protection in *Homeland* is likewise transferred to female figures, namely to the agent Mathison, who, like Volumnia, can be considered the embodiment of the state, and who, in keeping with one of Volumnia's strategies, encourages Brody's children to add weight to the supplication. She urges Brody's daughter to call her father in the bunker and persuade him to come home. Dana is not aware of any competitive situation with any other family, and even Mathison, despite her prophetic/paranoid intuition, cannot imagine that she is setting Dana in opposition to an unknown son of Brody's. However, viewers have discovered through multiple flashbacks that Brody's political revenge plan has a family core. During Brody's captivity, which at this time resembles a domestic community with the prominent terrorist Abu Nazir, he becomes the teacher and confidant of Nazir's young son Issa, who is increasingly presented as Brody's foster-son. The series here offers a plot element that unfolds Volumnia's image of Coriolanus's alternate family in the ranks of the opponent ('[t]his fellow had a Volscian to his mother, / His wife is in Corioles and his child / Like him by chance', 5.3.178–80). In this family constellation, Brody is gendered female: the position of Issa's patriarchal, authoritarian, often absent father is occupied by Abu Nazir, while Brody's role is presented as that of the indulgent, loving mother. His role as mother is visually highlighted in the scene of war atrocity: after the bombing of a school that turns out to have been a US drone strike, Brody searches for Issa among the wounded, mutilated and dead children, and eventually carries his corpse from the ruins. In this apocalyptic scenario of destruction and suffering, Brody appears in a *pietà* pose with the dead Issa, whose name is the Arabic form of 'Jesus'. This intimate moment of intense grief remains Brody's secret, yet the viewers witness it through flashbacks.[41]

This slow-motion scene and its silent use of the *pietà*'s pathos formula, which through the portrayal of a physical movement intends to trigger the corresponding mental movement in viewers, has so far remained the most politically radical moment of *Homeland*'s controversial stance towards post-9/11

warfare.[42] The substitute and blended family, with ambiguous gender, sexual, religious and national affiliations, is not presented as an unholy alliance but as a place of relative happiness, especially compared to Brody's Christian, American, heterosexual, nuclear suburban family with its traditional role allocation, into which he cannot reintegrate, and which is visually staged as a prison.[43] As the 'sentimental core' of the pathos formula of the *pietà*,[44] the gesture of mourning for the death of an innocent child invites us to feel empathy for the terrorists as the terrorized. And yet the scene remains politically ambivalent: while it is an invitation to empathize with the enemy and can be seen as a religiously reinforced

---

[41] The fact that Brody's American son is called 'Chris' emphasizes on the one hand the competition between the families, but, on the other hand, also invites a connection, because only the conflation of the two sons results in 'Jesus Christ'. In the Israeli original *Hatufim*, the Muslim foster-son is older and does not die, but instead eventually returns with the Jewish prisoner of war to Israel. Although some names were retained, such as the name of the daughter, Dana, *Homeland* replaces *Hatufim*'s Ismael with Issa – a notable change, as the name of Ishmael, Abraham's first-born son, ancestor of the Arabs and Islamic prophet, emphasizes the original kinship between Israelites and Arabs, while Jesus, as a Muslim prophet, can be read both as a uniting and a dividing figure between Islam and Christianity.

[42] See Mittell, *Complex TV*, p. 342: '[b]y dramatizing a drone strike, visualizing the deaths of innocent children, and having a sympathetic, white American character empathize with the Arab victims, *Homeland* offers dramatic fuel for a dissenting view against American military action that was typically found only on the extreme anti-war left and never on mainstream television'.

[43] As Albrecht Koschorke has shown, imaginations of the Holy Family in any case 'do not occur in the realm of naturalistic gender relations. Rather, they belong to a *logic of spirituality*, a logic whose essential quality is the *absence of sexuality* and in which customary gender attributions fail. Built into the imagined order of Christianity is also the possibility of transcending and exchanging sexual identities' – see *The Holy Family and its Legacy: Religious Imagination from the Gospels to Star Wars*, trans. Thomas Dunlap (New York, 2003), p. 12.

[44] Warburg contrasts 'antiquarische Schale' ('antique shell') and 'sentimentalen Kern' ('sentimental core') in the original German version of 'Theatrical costumes for the interludes of 1589'. See Aby Warburg, *Gesammelte Schriften*, ed. Horst Bredekamp and Michael Diers, 7 vols. to date (Berlin, 1998– ), vol. 7, pp. 422–38; p. 438.

critique of American post-9/11 warfare, which was described by George W. Bush as a Christian-motivated 'crusade' against Islamist terrorism,[45] it is also a problematic appropriation that makes the Muslim child only grievable as quasi-Christ(ian), thus strengthening a Christian–Western–American hegemonic claim on empathy.

In *Coriolanus*, the *pietà* moment is a noted absence. Critics have shown that – unlike in *King Lear*, for example – there is no moment of maternal/parental grief or insight into Volumnia's complicity in her son's death, though the relationship between Volumnia and Coriolanus bears features of the Maria–Jesus constellation, with an absent father figure, metaphorically equated with the war god Mars, and Volumnia's re-incorporation of Rome's founding mother, the Vestal Rhea Silvia, as well as her dual role as her son's mother and bride. As Kahn argues: 'Shakespeare supplies no *pietà,* allows his Romans no realization that Volumnia's imprint on her son results in his death. That death will change nothing.'[46] The same applies to the death of the tragic protagonist Brody: he also dies a sacrificial death for his homeland far from home and without the knowledge of his family or the American public. The sacrifice of his life for the good of his country has no ideological or practical consequences for the further course of post-9/11 warfare, nor for the comprehension of the homeland and its adequate defence. The earlier scene of overwhelming grief for a Muslim Jesus figure, however, allows Brody and the viewers the *pietà* moment of insight into their own complicity in this suffering through their implication in the military project of defending the homeland far from its territorial borders. While *Homeland*'s plot makes Brody's grief for Issa the engine of his revenge on the USA and thus the continuation of war, the *pietà* scene and its affect structure break through the cycle of violence and retaliation portrayed in Shakespeare's tragedy and the television series. For an extended moment, it lets audiences imagine a different, potentially not tragic, homecoming for the returnee from war, a recognition and acknowledgement of his changes as well as the changes in his homeland: a suspension of the violent loops of turning.

The shifting loyalties and unclear affiliation of the homecoming soldier speak to the methodological challenge of tracing the uncertain return of *Coriolanus* in *Homeland*, one of the many examples of how 'the genealogy of adaptations is often nebulous and spectrally intertextual, a web of meaning waiting to be made out of convergences and unthought relations that continue to be created and identified across multiple spaces and times'.[47] Any attempt at identifying and exploring such a genealogy will not only have to take into account the Shakespearian text (itself unstable, as manuscript studies have amply shown), but also stagings, adaptations, remediations and allusions that together constitute the cultural imaginary of *Coriolanus* on which *Homeland* may have drawn. Particular film and stage versions are likely links, such as Ralph Fiennes's 2011 film adaptation, which emphasizes Coriolanus's traumatization and has striking iconographic similarities to *Homeland*,[48] and Ivo van Hove's influential staging, shown internationally since 2007, which, like *Homeland*, addresses the role of the media in political debate and the undemocratic influence of the elite.[49] Among these potential linking elements is also the BBC series *Spooks* (2003–11), which, like

[45] In his speech of 16 September 2001, shortly after the attacks on the World Trade Center. Although Bush subsequently renounced this label after receiving strong criticism, the political discourse on the War on Terror remained religiously semanticized.

[46] Kahn, *Roman Shakespeare*, p. 158.

[47] Daniel Fischlin, 'Introduction: outerSpeares: Shakespeare, intermedia, and the limits of adaptation', in *OuterSpeares: Shakespeare, Intermedia, and the Limits of Adaptation*, ed. Daniel Fischlin (Toronto, 2014), pp. 3–50; p. 25.

[48] See Ronan Hatfull's account of such parallels in '"Thou art my warrior"'.

[49] Ivo van Hove's production of *Coriolanus* is part of the performance of *Romeinse Tragedies* by the Toneelgroep Amsterdam. Also of interest is the staging by James Hirsch at the Old Globe Theatre in San Diego in 1988, in which Coriolanus corresponded to Oliver North, an American Marine who illegally sold American arms to Muslim extremists in Iran, calling this venture 'patriotic' because he used the profits to support a right-wing group in Nicaragua. See Peter Holland's introduction to *Coriolanus*, p. 102.

*Homeland*, depicts the secret intelligence agency's work to safeguard the nation. In a strikingly similar scenario to Brody's failed suicide attack, in the episode 'Diana' (2005), a former MI5 employee triggers a state of emergency in order to attack the royal family at their retreat. The chief of operations describes this attack as 'the Coriolanus nightmare. The greatest fighter in your army turns against you and tries to destroy everything you stand for.'[50] This potential link between *Coriolanus, Spooks* and *Homeland* is also manifested in the cast, as Raza Jaffrey plays MI5 agent Zafar Younis in this episode and, in the fourth season of *Homeland*, Pakistani Lieutenant Colonel Aasar Khan, who metamorphoses into Brody when holding the desperate Mathison (by then the mother of Brody's daughter, born after his execution) in his arms, in a second *pietà* moment. Brody's posthumous return continues the Christian semantization, now featuring Brody as a resurrected Christ-like martyr questioned by the overjoyed but doubtful Mathison. His consoling *pietà* gesture is suddenly transformed,

however, into yet another menacing return of the presumed dead, when Mathison begins to fear the revenge of this revenant. Eventually, the scene resolves as a drug-induced hallucination by the mentally unstable Mathison, and Brody is transformed back into the Pakistani Lieutenant puzzled by Mathison's bliss of reunion turned panic. The series thus continues its *unheimliche* loops of turning and returning beyond the death of the homecoming soldier. It fits the eerie and haunting quality of the returnee figure that a series called *Spooks* provides a possible but elusive connection between Coriolanus and Brody. In this light, the shapeshifting, spectral comeback of the soldier with unclear affiliations offers a meta-adaptive comment on the uncertainties involved in the return of Shakespeare's Coriolanus to this particular 21st-century homeland.

---

[50] Thanks to Sylvia Mieszkowski for the reference to *Spooks*.

# SCHOLARLY METHOD, TRUTH AND EVIDENCE IN SHAKESPEARIAN TEXTUAL STUDIES

## GABRIEL EGAN

There is a conflict within Shakespeare studies about seemingly new methods that count things in the plays and poems, or about the plays and poems. In this article, I will argue that methods employing numbers are nothing new in Shakespeare studies, so we should be used to them; fears that a kind of numerology is invading the discipline are mistaken. And I will argue that the conflicts really arise not over the understanding of numbers but over the understanding of words. I will offer practical advice on how those unfamiliar with this area of Shakespearian research may distinguish reliable from unreliable investigations, taking in aspects of probability, best practices in using digital texts and tools, and the need to demonstrate any new method's power to make discriminations we care about.

\*\*\*

### AVERAGE NOT TYPICAL

There are plenty of things still to be discovered just by counting certain features in Shakespeare's plays, often with results that surprise even scholars who are deeply familiar with the works. Asked to approximate the average number of words in a Shakespearian speech – where a speech is defined as all the words between one speech prefix and the next – many experts will confidently guess between 15 and 30 words. A guess in this range would be reasonably accurate as an average for plays right across Shakespeare's career, as Table 3

shows. In these calculations, we count the number of words spoken in the play and divide that total by the number of speeches in the play, giving the average number of words per speech. *The Two Gentlemen of Verona* has the lowest average, at 18 words per speech, and *Richard II* has the highest at 37. Within this range, there is no obvious pattern over time or by genre or by authorship (sole versus co-authored).

Can we say, then, that a guess of 15–30 words is about right, in that most Shakespearian speeches fall within this range? No, we cannot. In fact, we cannot even say that most speeches fall in the range 18–37 words, which is the full range from the play with the lowest average speech length (*The Two Gentlemen of Verona*) to the play with the highest (*Richard II*). In fact, most Shakespearian speeches are much shorter than this, having fewer than 10 words. How come most speeches are so far below the average? Surely by the word 'average' we mean to convey something about what is typical in a set of data like these?

This apparent paradox comes about because we are being casual with language. When used in isolation, the word 'average' is usually taken to denote what is properly called 'the mean', which in this case is the number of spoken words in a Shakespeare play divided by the number of speeches in the play. The mean-average (as I shall call it) is not typical of the speeches in the play because there are a great many short speeches (of fewer than 10 words) and a small number of long speeches (of more than 35 words). The few

Table 3 Mean-average Lengths (in Words) of Speeches in Shakespeare's Plays

| Play | Mean | Play | Mean |
|------|------|------|------|
| Two Gentlemen | 18 (lowest) | Caesar | 22 |
| Shrew | 22 | As You Like It | 25 |
| 2 Henry VI | 28 | Hamlet | 23 |
| 3 Henry VI | 26 | Twelfth Night | 20 |
| Titus | 32 | Troilus | 22 |
| Richard III | 24 | Measure | 22 |
| Errors | 23 | Othello | 21 |
| Love's Labours Lost | 19 | All's Well | 23 |
| Richard II | 37 (highest) | Timon | 20 |
| Romeo | 26 | Macbeth | 22 |
| Midsummer | 30 | Antony | 19 |
| King John | 36 | Pericles | 32 |
| Merchant | 30 | Coriolanus | 23 |
| 1 Henry IV | 30 | Winter's Tale | 32 |
| Merry Wives | 19 | Lear Q | 28 |
| 2 Henry IV | 27 | Lear F | 22 |
| Much Ado | 20 | Cymbeline | 28 |
| Henry V | 32 | Tempest | 23 |
| | | Two Noble Kinsmen | 26 |
| | | Henry VIII | 31 |

long speeches have an effect on the mean-average that is disproportionate to how rare they are. The same phenomenon happens with data for household wealth: in a mean-average calculation, the stratospheric wealth of a tiny minority of individuals – the Bill Gateses and Warren Buffets – is effectively spread amongst everyone and drags the result higher than it would be if we confined ourselves to typical people. So too with speeches: the few exceptionally long ones make the mean-average higher than that of a typical speech. A second kind of imprecision is that I did not indicate what I mean by a 'word': does 'Never, never, never, never, never' count as one word or five? Being precise, we should say that this speech is five 'word tokens' but only one 'word type', and here we are concerned with tokens.

For data such as speech lengths and wealth, the mean-average is unrepresentative of the typical case.

There are two other kinds of average that are designed to capture representativeness: the median-average and the mode-average. The median-average is the typical value in the sense that if we place all the speeches in order of length, from lowest to highest, it is the length of the speech in the middle of that ordered list. For wealth, the median-average is the value chosen so that half of all households have less than that amount of wealth and half have more. For speeches, the median-average is the length chosen so that half of all speeches are shorter than this and half are longer.

The mode-average captures typicalness by putting the data into ranked categories, so that, for example, we count how many one-word speeches there are, how many two-word speeches, how many three-word speeches, and so on until we have counted all the speeches. Then we see how many speeches we have in each category, and the mode-average is the category that contains the greatest number of them. Figure 20 shows the results for *Hamlet*, and in its general shape it is typical of all Shakespeare's plays: there are few one- or two-word speeches, a lot of speeches a little longer than that (giving a peak on the left side of the graph), and a long tail to the right showing small and diminishing numbers for the longest lengths of speech. With *Hamlet*, it is clear that there are more four-word speeches than speeches of any other length, so four is the mode-average.

Table 4 shows the mode-average for all Shakespeare's plays in chronological order, and in it a startling pattern is obvious. Where the mean-average data had no discernible pattern, the mode-average data show that the speech-length most favoured by Shakespeare was about 9 words up to around 1599, and then suddenly it dropped to about 4 words, and stayed that way for the rest of his career. These numbers are my counts made in independent replication of the results reported by Hartmut Ilsemann who made this amazing discovery;[1] there will be more to say on replication of others' results shortly.

---

[1] Hartmut Ilsemann, 'Some statistical observations on speech lengths in Shakespeare's plays', *Shakespeare Jahrbuch* 141 (2005), 158–68.

Table 4 Mode-average Lengths (in Words) of Speeches in Shakespeare's Plays

| Play | Mode | Play | Mode |
|---|---|---|---|
| Two Gentlemen | 8 | Caesar | 4 |
| Shrew | 9 | As You Like It | 5=9 |
| 2 Henry VI | 9 | Hamlet | 4 |
| 3 Henry VI | 9 | Twelfth Night | 4 |
| Titus | 9 | Troilus | 4 |
| Richard III | 8 | Measure | 4 |
| Errors | 9 | Othello | 4 |
| Love's Labours Lost | 9 | All's Well | 4 |
| Richard II | 9 | Timon | 4 |
| Romeo | 9 | Macbeth | 4 |
| Midsummer | 9 | Antony | 4 |
| King John | 8=9 | Pericles | 6 |
| Merchant | 7=9 | Coriolanus | 4 |
| 1 Henry IV | 9 | Winter's Tale | 4 |
| Merry Wives | 8 | Lear Q | 6 |
| 2 Henry IV | 6 | Lear F | 4 |
| Much Ado | 9 | Cymbeline | 4 |
| Henry V | 4 | Tempest | 4 |
| | | Two Noble Kinsmen | 4 |
| | | Henry VIII | 3=4 |

What happened in 1599? 'The obvious reason', wrote Ilsemann about this pattern he discovered, 'must be the opening of the Globe Theatre in the same year. The first assumption that comes to mind is the spatial dimension of the stage, which would have prompted a shift from monological to dialogical action, and included a higher speed.'[2] But as Ilsemann acknowledged, the stage of the company's previous home, the Theatre in Shoreditch, was probably about the same size and shape as the new one at the Globe, so he wondered whether moving to the Globe changed Shakespeare's style because previously 'the playwright had to produce texts to be performed at various localities'.[3] But this idea is also difficult to reconcile with the theatre-historical evidence. As Alan Somerset showed, Shakespeare's company toured more often and more widely in the 1600s than they did in the 1590s,[4] so the need to produce plays to be performed in various locations

increased rather than decreased after the move to the Globe. The move to the Globe is the most prominent change in Shakespeare's professional career around 1599, but it is not clear how it might have caused him to prefer shorter speeches.

For our purposes in an article about method, we may leave this puzzle unsolved and pursue the question of just how Somerset came up with his surprising claim about an increase in touring when Shakespeare's men became the King's Men. He counted the evidence. G. E. Bentley's *The Profession of Player in Shakespeare's Time, 1590–1642* (1984) suggested that playing companies on tour were routinely denied permission to play (four times out of five),[5] but by making his own counts from a wider survey of evidence, Somerset came to the opposite conclusion: nineteen times out of twenty they were allowed to play.[6] Correcting Bentley's counts of various phenomena has become something of a cottage industry in Shakespeare studies. In *The Profession of Dramatist in Shakespeare's Time, 1590–1642* (1971), Bentley claimed that about half of all plays of Shakespeare's time were collaboratively written.[7] In a Ph.D. awarded in 2017, Paul Brown cited Helen Hirschfeld, Gordon McMullan, Philip C. McGuire, A. R. Braunmuller and Brian Vickers all repeating this claim from Bentley's book, but from his own counting and using our best knowledge of who wrote what, Brown found that in fact only about a quarter, not a half, of all plays were collaboratively written.[8]

Historians of the book count things too. Lukas Erne's *Shakespeare and the Book Trade* (2013) put

---

[2] Ilsemann, 'Some statistical observations', p. 162.

[3] Ilsemann, 'Some statistical observations', p. 163.

[4] Alan Somerset, '"How chances it they travel?": provincial touring, playing places, and the King's Men', *Shakespeare Survey 47* (Cambridge, 1994), 45–60; p. 53.

[5] Gerald Eades Bentley, *The Profession of Player in Shakespeare's Time, 1590–1642* (Princeton, NJ, 1984), pp. 177–84.

[6] Somerset, '"How chances it they travel?", p. 50.

[7] Gerald Eades Bentley, *The Profession of Dramatist in Shakespeare's Time, 1590–1642* (Princeton, NJ, 1971), p. 199.

[8] Paul Brown, 'Early modern theatre people and their social networks' (unpublished doctoral thesis, De Montfort University, 2017), pp. 170–84.

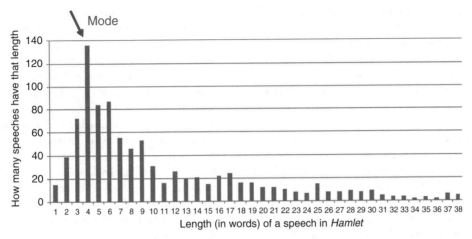

20 Length (in words) of a speech in *Hamlet*.

beyond doubt his claim that Shakespeare was by far the most successful writer of printed plays of his time, and for decades afterwards.[9] But there is no new primary evidence in Erne's book: He had the brilliant idea of counting the existing primary evidence, which any previous investigator could have counted but nobody actually did. That is, Erne turned existing data into new knowledge. Just how to count things can be a point of contention, of course. Does the 1623 Folio count as one edition of Shakespeare or thirty-six editions? Erne's counts have the significant merit of not being idiosyncratic, since he tallied editions the same way that Alan Farmer and Zachary Lesser did in their articles in *Shakespeare Quarterly* in 2005, showing that, contrary to Peter W. M. Blayney's influential claim, printed plays were an important and lucrative part of the early publishing industry.[10]

Counting things is nothing new in Shakespeare studies: theatre and book historians have been doing it for decades. Why then are the new computational-stylistics methods so widely reviled by some people? There seems to be a strict limit on the kinds of numerical operations some Shakespearians will countenance. Addition, subtraction, multiplication and division raise no hackles. Erne's book uses the word 'average' twenty-eight times in the first fifty-five pages – a mean-average of more than one every two

pages – but he never uses the words 'mean' or 'median' or 'mode'. Farmer and Lesser deployed a median-average when, for the reason we saw about the shape of a distribution (a left-side hump and a long right-side tail), a mean-average would be misleading, and they took the trouble to school Blayney on the difference between different kinds of average when his critique appeared to misrepresent their work.[11]

\*\*\*

WORDS, NUMBERS, SYMBOLS

Even the four basic arithmetic operations of addition, subtraction, multiplication and division can

[9] Lukas Erne, *Shakespeare and the Book Trade* (Cambridge, 2013).

[10] Peter W. M. Blayney, 'The publication of playbooks', in *A New History of Early English Drama*, ed. John D. Cox and David Scott Kastan (New York, 1997), pp. 383–422; Alan B. Farmer and Zachary Lesser, 'The popularity of playbooks revisited', *Shakespeare Quarterly* 56 (2005), 1–32; Peter W. M. Blayney, 'The alleged popularity of playbooks', *Shakespeare Quarterly* 56 (2005), 33–50; Alan B. Farmer and Zachary Lesser, 'The structures of popularity in the early modern book trade', *Shakespeare Quarterly* 56 (2005), 206–13.

[11] Farmer and Lesser, 'Popularity', pp. 24–5; 'Structures', p. 207, n. 7.

trip us up, since – and this is not sufficiently widely recognized – the intricacies in mathematics are at least as much verbal as numerical. In *Shakespeare's Fight with the Pirates* (1917), A. W. Pollard observed that, among the early editions of Shakespeare's *Richard II*, the 'second quarto has been found to add about 180 per cent. of new errors to those originally made [in the first edition], so that it is nearly three times as incorrect'.[12] The key word here is 'add'. The Q2 edition added to the errors in the play by adding another 180 per cent to the body of errors in Q1. In a recent survey of scholarship on stylometric analysis of early modern drama, Jeffrey Kahan wrote of Pollard's *Shakespeare's Fight with the Pirates* that '[p]erhaps the biggest fantasy in the text is its confident use of statistics. Pollard writes, for example, that there are 180% more errors in the Q1 of *Richard II* than in Q2. He states that this difference amounts to Q2 being "three times as incorrect as Q1". Three times the initial number is not an increase of 180%; it is an increase of 300%.'[13] There are two errors in this remark by Kahan. The first is that he has Q1 and Q2 around the wrong way. That is a venial slip that we can overlook, but we cannot overlook Kahan's inability to make sense of a simple English sentence. Pollard correctly claimed that Q2 added a further 180% (almost twice as many again) to the stock of errors in Q1, nearly tripling the errors. But Kahan misunderstood Pollard to be claiming that Q2 ended up with 180% of the errors in Q1. There are a great many misreadings and misunderstandings of this kind in Kahan's review, and they arise not because of Kahan's innumeracy but because of his illiteracy.

When mathematical notations are used in studies about Shakespeare, this presents an obstacle to readers who cannot remember, or never learnt, what those mathematical symbols denote. The mathematical symbols could be written out longhand as words to convey the same thing, since mathematical notation is merely a shorthand employed by specialists when communicating with one another. In *A Brief History of Time* (1988), Stephen Hawking reported that, in the planning of the work, '[s]omeone told me that each equation I included in the book would halve the sales'.[14] This is a sly joke on Hawking's part, since that sentence is itself a statement of the principle of exponential decay. If we suppose world sales of 10 million copies – the book's actual world sales in its first twenty years – then the falling off that would have been caused by each additional equation is given by the value of 10 million divided by two raised to the power of the number of equations in the book. On a plot in which the $x$ axis shows the number of equations and the $y$ axis shows the resulting world sales, Figure 21 depicts the exponential decay expressed in Hawking's sentence. This kind of falling-off governs many things, such as the rate at which unstable atoms undergo radioactive decay and the rate at which hot things get cold. By presenting this equation in words, Hawking exemplified the very procedure he needed to adopt. Mathematics is about language as much as it is about numbers.

Why then do mathematicians use symbolic notations rather than words to convey the expressions and equations they are concerned with? Each discipline is entitled to its own shorthand conventions, of course. Hawking put himself to the trouble of using words in place of symbols because he wanted to convey his ideas to readers beyond his own discipline. Earlier, I quoted and adopted Pollard's use of the notation Q1 and Q2 to refer to the first and second quarto-format editions of a play. This notation is convenient for tracing the family trees of publications because, in Shakespeare's time, a subsequent edition of any book was most commonly printed from the immediately preceding edition, so that an exemplar of Q1 was the printer's copy for Q2, and an exemplar of Q2 was the printer's copy for Q3, and so on. This convenience justifies experts stretching a point and using this convention even for editions, such as the 1595 first edition of *Richard Duke of York / 3 Henry VI*, printed not in quarto but in octavo format. E. K. Chambers fully understood this when he published his 'Table of

[12] A. W. Pollard, *Shakespeare's Fight with the Pirates and the Problems of the Transmission of His Text* (London, 1917), p. 71.

[13] Jeffrey Kahan, '"I'll tell you what mine author says": a brief history of stylometrics', *English Literary History* 82 (2015), 815–44; p. 823.

[14] Stephen Hawking, *A Brief History of Time: From the Big Bang to Black Holes*, intro. Carl Sagan (London, 1988), p. ix.

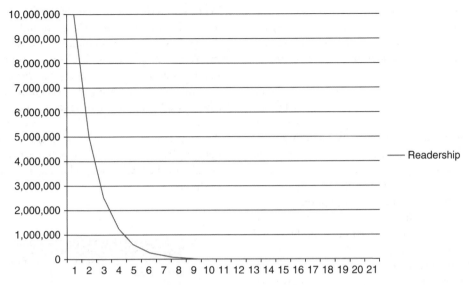

Figure 21 '... each equation I included in the book would halve the sales'.

Quartos', identifying the '*3 Hen. VI*. Q1' of 1595.[15] Aside from being more concise than words, symbolic notations invoke commonly agreed underlying definitions that need not be repeated each time they are used. Employing $\bar{x}$ to stand for mean-average and $\tilde{x}$ to stand for median-average, the mathematician expects the reader to appreciate the difference between these two types of average. That is, the symbolic notation is also a kind of readerly competence check. It is incumbent upon humanists who wish to use mathematical methods without adopting mathematical notations to express in words the differences – as between mean, mode and median – that are implicit in the symbols.

\*\*\*

## WHAT TO LOOK FOR IN STUDIES USING MATHEMATICS

The increasing use of mathematics in Shakespeare studies is creating an unwelcome divide between those who do it and those who think they have trouble understanding it, so I here offer a guide to sceptical reading of studies in computational stylistics.

This guide uses just three headings for the kinds of thing that should ring anyone's mental alarm bells when reading studies whose mathematics they do not understand: probability, replication and validation.

Probability is the measure of how likely it is an event will occur – not an event that has occurred but an event that will or might occur. Probability has nothing to say about past events, only future ones. If we read that there is a 1% probability that Thomas Kyd wrote the play *Edward III*, we should be aware that this assertion is nothing like the assertion that there is a 1% probability that Italy is going to leave the European Union. Kyd either did or did not write the play, and in its strict sense probability has nothing to say on such a matter. Yet claims of this type about probability are frequently heard in courtrooms, as when an expert witness testifies that there is a 1% probability that the DNA found at the crime scene belongs to someone other than the accused. The key to making sense of such a claim is understanding what kind of simile it constructs. The idea is that, if we

---

[15] E. K. Chambers, *William Shakespeare: A Study of Facts and Problems*, 2 vols. (Oxford, 1930), vol. 2, p. 394.

had a large number of cases to consider – say, 10,000 cases – then in 1% of them (100 cases) the DNA evidence that seems so damningly to incriminate the accused would in fact come from someone else.

The proposition that no real effect is being observed in our data is conventionally called the 'null hypothesis', meaning the hypothesis that nothing interesting is going on. We start by assuming that the counting we did to get our data is not measuring anything meaningful at all: the numbers are just random. The key question is: how unusual can our data get before that assumption becomes untenable? How much of a pattern do we need to see before we abandon the null hypothesis and assume that something other than random variation is producing the data we have? To help with this, there are a number of calculations we can make – such as Fisher's exact test, Student's $t$-test, and the chi-squared test – that are able to specify just how often unlikely results will come about purely by chance. We feed into these calculations the results of our counting and they will tell us how often we should expect to get those results when the null hypothesis is true and nothing interesting is going on. If the results that we have found will come up by chance only once in a billion years of investigating, then we perhaps should abandon the null hypothesis that nothing interesting is going on and assume instead that something beyond mere chance is driving our results.

Suppose that we have counted the frequency at which a couple of features – verse lines with feminine endings and verse lines that rhyme – appear in the first two acts of a play (see Table 5). We do not know who wrote the play, but we have a few candidates in mind. We do not know whether the play was sole-authored or co-written, and we wonder whether the rates of feminine endings and rhyme can at least help us decide that. Looking at the numbers, what strikes us is the asymmetry: Act 1 seems to have lots of feminine endings and little rhyme, while Act 2 seems to have few feminine endings and lots of rhyme. Our null hypothesis is that there is no real association, no 'contingency', underlying these numbers. That is, our null hypothesis is that the proportions of feminine endings and rhyme do not vary significantly between the rows, do not vary significantly between Act 1 and Act 2. If the numbers in the two columns vary significantly by row, then we have found a contingency between the columns and the rows – we have found a dependency between the variable 'verse style' and the variable 'division', showing that they are not independent variables but somehow are linked. We will not have established how these variables are linked, only that they are linked.

| verse style / division | Feminine Endings (% of lines) | Rhyme (% of lines) |
|---|---|---|
| Act 1 | 31 | 10 |
| Act 2 | 7 | 65 |

Table 5

Tests such as Fisher's exact test, Student's $t$-test and the chi-squared test allow us to ask how often we should expect to see these results when the null hypothesis is true. That is, if there is no underlying dependency influencing the numbers, just chance variation, how rare is this asymmetry we find in the numbers? These tests are widely misused, and the first common mistake – aside from neglecting to mention the null hypothesis at all – is choosing an improper null hypothesis, such as 'Act 1 and Act 2 are by the same author.' These tests have no power to comment on such a hypothesis because it contains a set of additional assumptions that we have no information about, such as the assumption that writers are consistent in their rates of feminine endings and rhyme. There may be any number of reasons other than authorship that explain Act 1 and Act 2 being so asymmetrical regarding these features. Maybe Act 1 consists almost entirely of verse dialogue (giving opportunities for feminine endings) and no songs (which tend to cause rhyme), while Act 2 contains mainly prose dialogue (so few opportunities for feminine endings) and lots of songs (which tend to cause rhyme). Fisher's exact test, Student's *t*-test and the chi-squared test have nothing to say on such matters: they can only comment on how often we would get this asymmetry by chance alone when nothing else is driving the difference. These tests may tell us that the asymmetry in our results is rare, tempting us to reject the null hypothesis, but if we chose an improper null hypothesis in the first place – such as the null hypothesis that the two texts are by the same author – then we will leap to a false conclusion when we reject it.

The second common error is inverting the meaning of the results of the test, so that instead of telling us how often we would get those results when the null hypothesis is true, the result is assumed to be telling us how likely it is that the null hypothesis is true. This is a logical fallacy. A test that tells us what to expect about the universe if we assume that something (the null hypothesis) is true cannot at the same time also be a comment on whether that something is true. Assuming that the null hypothesis is true is a premise in these tests and cannot also be a conclusion from that premise. It is traditional to reject the null hypothesis when the frequency with which chance would produce our results is low. In social sciences, a traditional cut-off is 1-time-in-20 (probability $p < 0.05$), at which point the results are said to be statistically significant. This is the most pernicious of all fallacies. There is nothing magical about a 1-in-20 probability.

Events rarer than 1-in-20 happen all the time. We may take two six-sided dice, one red and one white, and list all the possible outcomes of rolling them at the same time. The list will begin with 'red 1, white 1' and 'red 1, white 2', proceeding through all the combinations up to 'red 6, white 5' and 'red 6, white 6'. Our null hypothesis is that each die is fair in the sense that each of its six faces is equally likely – one-sixth likely – to be uppermost after we shake and roll the die. There are 36 possible combinations in all, and we may give each of 36 people 1 prediction of the outcome before we roll the dice. Each prediction has a 1-in-36 chance of coming

true (in the sense of being the combination we roll), and expressed as a decimal this is about 0.028. That number is much smaller than the 1-in-20 (0.05) probability at which results are traditionally (but falsely) said to become statistically significant.

We roll the dice and 1 of the 36 predictions we made comes true: someone had the 'winning' combination. Should the person possessing this correct prediction assign statistical significance to its correctness? Should this person conclude that 0.028, 1-in-36, is the likelihood that the null hypothesis is true and therefore, since their 'win' had so low a likelihood of occurring by chance, conclude that the dice are probably loaded? Of course not, in both cases. Before we rolled the dice, it was utterly predictable that an outcome with a 1-in-36 likelihood of happening was about to happen, and it did indeed happen at that likelihood. To take a more extreme example, every week someone wins the United Kingdom's National Lottery at odds of about 1-in-10-million. This does not mean that the National Lottery is unfair and the winner must have cheated. It is utterly predictable that somebody will win each week with a ticket that had just a 1-in-10-million chance of being the winning ticket. This is utterly predictable because 10 million tickets are sold each week. A *p*-value on its own – no matter how small – tells us nothing without additional information about the wider context in which it emerged. Yet exactly this faulty reasoning disfigures much scholarship in the field of computational stylistics.

This problem with probability is, at ground, one not of mathematics but of words and logic, involving the correct expression in words of a null hypothesis and the correct understanding of the consequences of abandoning it. A brilliant illustration of how tests such as Fisher's exact test and the chi-squared test have been misused in the analysis of First Folio compositor studies appears in Pervez Rizvi's recent article 'The use of spellings for compositor attribution in the First Folio' (2016).[16]

---

[16] Pervez Rizvi, 'The use of spellings for compositor attribution in the First Folio', *Papers of the Bibliographical Society of America* 110 (2016), 1–53.

Arguing *reductio ad absurdum*, Rizvi was able repeatedly to show that the standard statistical tests that have been used in compositor identification would attribute significance to the differences in spellings between divisions of the text that he made entirely at random. This article is the reason that the *New Oxford Shakespeare* (2016–17) does not rely on compositor identification for the arguments it makes about the early editions of Shakespeare. An illustration of the wider misuse of statistics, and especially the ubiquitous but meaningless $p < 0.05$ threshold, is given in John P. A. Ioannidis's much-cited article on 'Why most published research findings are false' (2005).[17]

Ioannidis's article takes us to the second consideration in sceptical reading, the problem of replication. It is a basic tenet of science that studies should be replicable: using the same conditions as those described in the experiment, the same or closely similar results should be obtained. Hartmut Ilsemann claimed in 2005 that the mode-average length of Shakespearian speeches suddenly dropped from about 9 words to about 4 around 1599, and because this is a straightforward claim I was able to independently replicate his results using the digital texts of the Oxford Complete Works edition of 1986–7 and three dozen lines of programming code.[18] Ioannidis showed that the replication of results is rarely possible with most scientific publications.

The situation is even worse in our field of Shakespeare studies because often the replication cannot be attempted. The most common reason is that the author relies on a dataset to which no one else has access. In the late 1990s, Donald W. Foster claimed that a database he had constructed called SHAXICON, which mapped Shakespeare's rare-word usage by dramatic character and date of composition, 'strongly supported' his belief that Shakespeare wrote the poem 'A funeral elegy for William Peter'.[19] No one has been able to replicate Foster's investigations because he has not made SHAXICON available to anyone, or even given a detailed description of what it does. The same problem besets the studies of Brian Vickers and his collaborator Marcus Dahl: although their database's contents have been loosely described,[20] no other

investigators have seen it, so it is impossible to confirm just what is in it.[21] Aside from the dataset from which a study's counts are drawn, replication of a complex investigation requires that the original investigators describe in full the technical details of what they did, and alongside this verbal account the publication should include any software source code used so that others can check whether this software really does what its creators think it does.

The databases Literature Online (LION) and Early English Books Online Text Creation Partnership (EEBO-TCP) are available to most investigators, and when studies are based on those databases it is possible for other investigators to check the claims that are being made. There are reasons why an investigator might find the LION and EEBO-TCP texts unsuited to her methods, most commonly because they are in original spelling and hence likely to upset counts based on the automated searching for particular strings of characters representing words. It is reasonable to take texts from these sources and first regularize the spelling, for example using the Variant Detector (VARD) software developed at the University of Lancaster, but if one does that it is then good practice to make the regularized texts available to everyone else. After all, there is more than one way to regularize early modern spelling, and

[17] John P. A. Ioannidis, 'Why most published research findings are false', *PLoS Medicine* 2 (2005), 696–701.

[18] *Shakespeare Survey* does not publish computer programs, so the source code used for this replication is available from the author's personal website (www.gabrielegan.com) alongside the metadata for the present article.

[19] Donald W. Foster, 'A Funeral Elegy: W[illiam] S[hakespeare]'s "best-speaking witnesses"', *PMLA* 111 (1996), 1080–1105; p. 1088.

[20] Brian Vickers, 'Thomas Kyd: secret sharer', *TLS* 5481 (2008), 13–15; 'The marriage of philology and informatics', *British Academy Review* 14 (2009), 41–4; 'Disintegrated: did Thomas Middleton really adapt *Macbeth*?', *TLS* 5591 (2010), 14–15; 'Identifying Shakespeare's additions to *The Spanish Tragedy* (1602): a new(er) approach', *Shakespeare* 8 (2012), 13–43.

[21] Gabriel Egan, 'The limitations of Vickers's trigram tests', in *The New Oxford Shakespeare: Authorship Companion*, ed. Gary Taylor and Gabriel Egan (Oxford, 2017), pp. 60–6.

for proper replication others will need to know just how it was done.

Replication is a high ideal, but even without it there is another kind of healthy scepticism about its own truth claims that any study can embody. If someone claims to have found a method of distinguishing authorship by measuring some feature of the text, this itself is a readily testable claim. Using the thousands of digital texts available to us, the validation of the new method would involve simply setting it to work on texts for which we already know the true author and then counting how often the method was able to identify this person correctly. Without validation, or with only a few validation runs, there is simply no way to tell whether the new method really is capable of distinguishing authorship. There should at least be tens, and preferably hundreds or thousands, of validation runs, and at the end of them the study should give a percentage figure for how often the new method got its authorship attribution correct when applied to the known cases. In general, a correctness figure of less than 90 per cent is hardly worth anyone's attention, since the best methods we currently have point to the correct authors about 95 per cent of the time, when given sufficiently large samples to work on. The same principle applies to studies that claim to quantify aspects of style such as genre, or to identify the date of a work's composition. We have hundreds of works for which we already agree the genres and dates, and the new methods must be shown, in rigorous tests, to come in the great majority of cases to the same widely accepted conclusions that we have already reached by other methods. This is perhaps the easiest kind of scepticism to commit to memory: if they did not validate their method, it is not valid.

\* \* \*

This account of scholarly method in Shakespeare studies has engaged with mathematics only so far as the elementary arithmetic operators and measures, such as the three kinds of average: the mean, the median and the mode. I hope to have shown that, when using even these simplest of mathematical procedures, investigators need to exercise caution in order to provide an adequate verbal account of what was done and why the results should be accepted by other specialists. I hope also to have provided some guidance for those trying to discriminate between good and bad scholarly practices in this field. When we move beyond these simple mathematical operations to more complex ones, such as calculating standard deviation, variance, and Shannon entropy, or applying data reduction with methods such as principal component analysis, the majority of Shakespearians have little hope of following the detail. Why does the threshold of comprehension fall just here, at $+$, $-$, $\times$, $\div$ and syllogistic logic? What is it about the more complex operations that makes Shakespearians so uncomfortable? The simplest answer is probably correct: this threshold corresponds to the level at which most Shakespearians ceased to study mathematics in their formal education. It is unhelpful to excoriate the profession for its collective lack of advanced mathematical ability. But it should be as much a source of embarrassment to admit that one is innumerate as to admit that one is illiterate, rather than (as now) innumeracy being almost a badge of honour for some humanist scholars. Since even the most elementary arithmetic operators and measures – the ones most Shakespearians are comfortable with – are quite capable of misleading us, we need to move forward collectively and slowly.

# BEAUTIFUL POLECATS: THE LIVING AND THE DEAD IN *JULIUS CAESAR*

## LISA HOPKINS[1]

Dr Johnson said that a pun was Shakespeare's fatal Cleopatra. I want to argue that puns are, appropriately enough, at work with particular vigour in a play about one of Cleopatra's lovers. *Julius Caesar* features a series of puns very early on, starting with the Cobbler's '[a] trade, sir, that I hope I may use with a safe conscience, which is indeed, sir, a mender of bad soles' (1.1.13–14),[2] and followed by his retort to Flavius – '[n]ay I beseech you, sir, be not out with me: yet if you be out, sir, I can mend you' (1.1.16–17) – and finally by '[t]ruly, sir, all that I live by, is with the awl' (1.1.22). Julius Caesar himself is also the subject of a pun in *Hamlet*, when Polonius says, 'I did enact Julius Caesar. I was killed i'th'Capitol. Brutus killed me' (3.2.99–100), to which Hamlet replies: '[i]t was a brute part of him to kill so capital a calf there' (3.2.101–2). The prince's joke is an opportunist one, but Lisa S. Starks-Estes implies that in fact it homes in on an important concern in *Julius Caesar* when she refers to 'Caesar, the sacrificial "calf" that Hamlet jokingly calls him in his exchange with Polonius'.[3] Moreover, the epigraph page of Linda Woodbridge and Edward Berry's *True Rites and Maimed Rites* shows that 'true rites' comes from *Julius Caesar* and 'maimed rites' from *Hamlet*,[4] further suggesting a more than merely chronological connection between the two plays. In this article, I shall argue that puns in *Julius Caesar* are not just wordplay, but can help us understand the central mystery of the play, which is why it kills off its main character halfway through. I shall consider first the sense of doubleness which accrues to Caesar, arguing that it is articulated through wordplay, which is, I shall suggest, a recurring feature of the relationship between the Latin language and native speakers of English. I then go on to explore what happens if the names of some of the play's characters are heard as puns, and to suggest that this allows us to see some of the ways in which *Julius Caesar* is not solely about the politics of ancient Rome but also about those of Shakespeare's England, particularly its religious politics, since the duality of Caesar is echoed by the splitting of Christianity into Protestantism and Catholicism. Caesar might have been a figure of divinity – this is the issue at stake in the opening scene of the play – but instead he becomes a figure for the impossibility of any certainty about divinity.

---

[1] With thanks to Domenico Lovascio, Matt Steggle, Kate Wilkinson and the anonymous reader of the article.

[2] All quotations from *Julius Caesar* are taken from William Shakespeare, *Julius Caesar*, ed. David Daniell [1998] (London, 2017); further references will be given in the text. For an exploration of the religious resonances of this particular line, see, for instance, Maurice Hunt, 'Cobbling souls in Shakespeare's *Julius Caesar*', in *Shakespeare's Christianity: The Protestant and Catholic Poetics of 'Julius Caesar', 'Macbeth', and 'Hamlet'*, ed. Beatrice Batson (Waco, TX, 2006), pp. 111–29; pp. 112–13.

[3] Lisa S. Starks-Estes, '*Julius Caesar*, Ovidian transformation and the martyred body on the early modern stage', in *Julius Caesar: A Critical Reader*, ed. Andrew James Hartley (London, 2016), pp. 103–24; p. 112.

[4] Linda Woodbridge and Edward Berry, eds., *True Rites and Maimed Rites: Ritual and Anti-Ritual in Shakespeare and His Age* (Urbana, IL, 1992).

In making my case, I shall hope to show that *Julius Caesar* does indeed have something strongly in common with *Hamlet*, in that both are centrally concerned with the relationship between the living and the dead. Horst Zander notes that '[i]t has become a convention in scholarship to discuss the two Caesars in the play, the private man and the political, public institution of "Caesar"'.[5] There are different ways of understanding the doubleness of Caesar: David Kaula calls *Julius Caesar* a play 'much concerned with contrasting images of Caesar, the would-be monarch of Rome and founder of the universal empire that later evolved into the universal church',[6] and John E. Curran notes that '[a]s a political phenomenon, Caesar was most often placed in one of two overly simplistic categories: tradition had labelled him either a Worthy or a Tyrant'.[7] However, I shall suggest that the play breaks into two because there really are two Caesars, a living and a dead. *Julius Caesar* is in one sense a study of the effects of being killed on a character, for in being assassinated Caesar becomes a god: Mark Rose argues that 'the assassination was not the end of Caesarism but effectively the beginning'.[8] The way that Shakespeare links the living and the dead in *Julius Caesar* is, I shall argue, the same way that he does in *Hamlet*, which is through playing on the word 'like'.

For anyone in the UK who received a classical education, Caesar himself is likely to be remembered in connection with a species of wordplay, a quatrain of dog Latin:

> Caesar adsum iam forte
> Brutus aderat
> Caesar sic in omnibus
> Brutus sic inat.

The eager young student of the classics may be puzzled to discover that this yields no sense, but as soon as she or he thinks of it not as a separate language but as mispronounced and misspelt English, a meaning of sorts appears:

> Caesar had some jam for tea
> Brutus had a rat
> Caesar sick in omnibus
> Brutus sick in 'at.

This feeble jest (remembered by me from the 1970s and by my mother from the 1950s) is clearly twentieth-century, since the omnibus joke would have been impossible earlier,[9] but Shakespeare shows us something not dissimilar in *The Merry Wives of Windsor*:

EVANS Peace your tattlings! – What is 'fair', William?
WILLIAM '*Pulcher*'.
MISTRESS QUICKLY Polecats? There are fairer things than polecats, sure.

(4.1.23–6)

Mistress Quickly simply does not understand Latin; the author of 'Caesar adsum iam forte' did, but they both achieve the same effect as both identify and cling fast to examples of the kind of incidental similarity of sound which is known to language teachers as a 'false friend'.

The processes of Latin learning are directly glanced at in *Julius Caesar* when Cicero says that 'men may construe things after their fashion / Clean from the purpose of the things themselves' (1.3.34–5). The Arden 3's note says of 'construe' that 'appropriate to this Roman story, the word had associations for Elizabethans of Latin lessons' (1.3.34 n), and a cognate form of the same verb is used again when Titinius, apostrophizing the dead Cassius, says: '[a]las, thou hast misconstrued everything' (5.3.84). There may also be a glance at the teaching of classical languages when Caska says: 'but for mine own part, it was Greek to me' (1.2.282–3). The primary meaning of Caska's

---

[5] Horst Zander, '*Julius Caesar* and the critical legacy', in *Julius Caesar: New Critical Essays*, ed. Horst Zander (London, 2005), pp. 3–55; p. 7.

[6] David Kaula, '"Let us be sacrificers": religious motifs in *Julius Caesar*', *Shakespeare Studies* 14 (1981), 197–24; p. 198.

[7] John E. Curran, Jr, 'What should be in that Caesar: the question of Julius Caesar's greatness', in Hartley, ed., *Critical Reader*, pp. 153–74; p. 155.

[8] Mark Rose, 'Conjuring Caesar: ceremony, history, and authority in 1599', in Woodbridge and Berry, eds., *True Rites*, pp. 256–69; p. 263.

[9] It is found in 'Nigel Molesworth's' (Geoffrey Willans's) *Down with Skool*, first published in London in 1953, but it is not clear if it originates there.

remark clearly pertains to the difference between those ancient Romans who could speak Greek and those who could not, but there is also a secondary layer of applicability centring on the existence of such a divide in Shakespeare's time too, with Shakespeare himself dismissed by his fellow play-wright Ben Jonson as having small Latin and less Greek while others of his contemporaries, most notably George Chapman, published translations of long Greek texts. Caska is an ancient Roman, but for this one moment he could be speaking as an Elizabethan, and articulating the probable situation of many members of the audience, not to mention that of the playwright: they know a bit of Latin, certainly enough to identify it as such if not always to construe it, but Greek is Greek to them.

For schoolchildren both in Shakespeare's day and more recently, the process of learning the Latin language was inseparable from learning about Roman history and its principal personal-ities: Latin was *about* Caesar, Brutus, Cassius and Cicero, especially since Miranda Fay Thomas notes 'T. N. Baldwin's weight of evidence that Cicero's *De Officiis* was a set text in Elizabethan grammar schools',[10] and when Cicero pops up briefly in *Julius Caesar* many of those in Shakespeare's origi-nal audience would have remembered their schooldays. When Henry V promises his men that their names will become familiar in men's mouths as household words, he is describing what was, in educated households, already the case for the characters of *Julius Caesar*. It would not there-fore be particularly surprising if those names were played with in Shakespeare's day in something of the same way as they are in 'Caesar adsum iam forte'. In this article, I want to explore some of what happens to *Julius Caesar* as a play if we, like Mistress Quickly, start hearing words and names as connoting things other than what they denote in Latin.

*Julius Caesar* offers abundant evidence of word-play and quips, and although there is nothing in the play quite as silly as the schoolboy doggerel I quoted earlier, there are things which are not far off it. David Daniell in his Arden edition of the play notes that:

Ben Jonson's remark in his *Timber* . . . has set off much discussion . . . :

Many times hee fell into those things, could not escape laughter: As when hee said in the person of *Caesar*, one speaking to him; *Caesar thou dost me wrong*. Hee replyed: *Caesar did never wrong, but with just cause*: and such like, which were ridiculous.[11]

The text of *Julius Caesar* as we have it has: '[k]now, Caesar doth not wrong, nor without cause / Will he be satisfied' (3.1.47–8), but this may of course represent a later revision. If it does, and if Shakespeare did indeed originally write 'Caesar did never wrong, but with just cause', was it through inattention, as Jonson seems to imply, or could it have been a deliberate paradox, perhaps designed to reveal something about Caesar's vision of himself?[12] Perhaps, though, the line simply showcases the slipperiness of rhetoric *per se*, and perhaps it does so because rhetoric lies at the heart of *Julius Caesar*. The play stages two battles, one of words between Mark Antony and Brutus, and one of swords between the armies of Antony and Octavius and those of Brutus and Cassius, but actually the second one merely confirms the win-ner of the first in his victory. Even if the fortunes of war had turned out differently, nothing that hap-pened at Philippi could have undone what had already happened in the pulpit in Rome. This is a play about the power of words, but it is also one which shows us that words may be only loosely connected to actions and things, and if it did ori-ginally contain the line 'Caesar did never wrong

[10] Miranda Fay Thomas, 'Political acts and political acting: Roman gesture and *Julius Caesar*', *Early Modern Literary Studies* special issue 25 (2016), p. 14.

[11] Daniell, ed., *Julius Caesar*, p. 136. See Ben Jonson, *Explorata, or Discoveries*, in *The Cambridge Edition of the Works of Ben Jonson*, ed. David Bevington, Martin Butler and Ian Donaldson, 7 vols. (Cambridge, 2012), vol. 7, pp. 499–596; p. 522.

[12] Perhaps I feel differently from Jonson as I write this in 2017 because I have just seen two productions of *Julius Caesar* which both had photographs of Donald Trump in their programmes, and Trump is surely capable of saying (or more probably tweeting) that he never does wrong but with just cause.

but with just cause' then it would have been no bad expression of that dangerous disconnect between words and facts.

In his Arden edition of the play, David Daniell notes that '[e]arly studies of imagery in Shakespeare usually expressed puzzlement that there was so little in *Julius Caesar*',[13] but there are several plays on names and words, starting with the cobbler's jokes and moving on to Cassius's bitter

> [n]ow is it Rome indeed, and room enough,
> When there is in it but one only man.
>
> (1.2.155–6)

This couplet depends on the standard early modern pronunciation of 'Rome' as 'room', but it also testifies to a willingness to take the iconic name of Rome and play with it. Daniell remarks on the importance in *Julius Caesar* of an 'emphasis on the efficacy of names',[14] and Zander, noting that 'the titular character appears in only three scenes out of a total of eighteen' but that 'Caesar's name occurs 219 times in the play, whereas Brutus' is mentioned only 134', observes that this is part of a wider pattern, for 'Shakespeare made more allusions to Caesar in his works than to any other historical man.'[15] In *Julius Caesar* itself, the most obvious example of this interest in names is the case of Cinna the Poet, who dies because of his name. When he is first introduced, he is detached from the action in terms of plot, but connected to it through atmosphere and imagery:

> I dreamt tonight that I did feast with Caesar,
> And things unluckily charge my fantasy.
> I have no will to wander forth of doors,
> Yet something leads me forth.
>
> (3.3.1–4)

When he tells the crowd that '[t]ruly, my name is Cinna' (3.3.27), he apparently has no idea of the probable result, but the audience surely does. His frenzied defence that 'I am Cinna the poet, I am Cinna the poet' (3.3.29) does nothing to help matters, because the play does not put much stock in poets:

> POET For shame, you generals, what do you mean?
> Love and be friends, as two such men should be,
> For I have seen more years, I'm sure, than ye.

> CASSIUS Ha, ha, how vildly doth this cynic rhyme.
>
> (4.3.128–31)

Cinna the poet dies because his name is Cinna. But could it be that the play is indulging in a spot of 'vild' rhyming on its own account, and might he also die because his name is Sinner? And, if so, might we perhaps notice that Brutus's name, as was often noted in Renaissance writings, contains a latent pun on Brute, and could Caesar even be Seizer? It has, after all, been suggested that both Marlowe and Shakespeare reduce the hero Aeneas to plain old Any-ass, a pun made explicit by Middleton and Dekker in *The Roaring Girl* ('though Aeneas made an ass of Dido, I will die to thee ere I do so'),[16] and the idea of a Caesar/Seizer pun seems to be implicit in Jonson's *Sejanus* when Sejanus says '[s]leep, / Voluptuous Caesar, and security / Seize on thy stupid powers'.[17] We know from the list of players that Shakespeare acted in *Sejanus*, and there might even be a sly glance at him when one of the charges made against Cremutius Cordus is 'thou praisest Brutus, and affirmst / That "Cassius was the last of all the Romans"' (3.391–2), though as Cremutius himself points out, lots of people wrote about Brutus and Cassius (3.411–13) and literary allusions are slippery things. Nevertheless, if Jonson was not above a pun on Roman names, it is hard to suppose that Shakespeare would have been so.

At first sight, *Julius Caesar* does not have much in common with the kind of medieval drama in which one might expect to find a character named Sinner. Critics have, though, found several points of similarity with both mystery plays and a more general medieval sensibility. Simon Barker

---

[13] Daniell, ed., *Julius Caesar*, p. 44.

[14] Daniell, ed., *Julius Caesar*, p. 45.

[15] Zander, '*Julius Caesar* and the critical legacy', pp. 6, 4.

[16] Thomas Middleton and Thomas Dekker, *The Roaring Girl*, ed. Paul A. Mulholland (Manchester, 1987), 3.2.59–60.

[17] Ben Jonson, *Sejanus*, ed. Philip J. Ayres (Manchester, 1990), 3.598–600. All further quotations from the play will be taken from this edition and reference will be given in the text.

speaks of 'a medieval Christian sense of the return of Caesar as a restless ghost',[18] suggesting that there is something potentially medieval inscribed within the very plot of the play; and, more specifically, Patrick Gray, noting that 'Shakespeare ... seems to draw inspiration for his departure from Plutarch from the conventional depiction of Julius Caesar's successor Augustus, as well as other tyrants such as Herod the Great, in medieval English mystery plays', observes that '"Caesar" in the mystery plays is typecast as a blustering, comically inadequate parody of Godhead' and says of Calpurnia's dream: '[a]s part of the plot, a neglected warning, it resembles the dream of Pilate's wife',[19] a subject found in one surviving mystery play and possibly originally present in more. In a similar vein, Lisa Starks-Estes suggests that '[t]he blazon of Christ's wounds is staged in the Towneley Cycle's *Last Judgement* ... Shakespeare draws from this tradition in *Julius Caesar* by staging Antony's blazon of Caesar's wounds.'[20] Steve Sohmer also argues for an echo of a specific set of mysteries – '[w]hen Shakespeare infused the text of *Julius Caesar* with markers to the liturgical calendar he was employing (or rediscovering) the established technique of the anonymous dramatist of the York Cycle' – and Hannibal Hamlin traces Decius's greeting 'Caesar, all hail' to Judas's words in the York cycle, compares Brutus staying awake and seeing the ghost to Jesus asking the disciples to watch in Gethsemane, and points out that it was 'a scene dramatized in the medieval cycle plays'.[21] *Julius Caesar*, then, seems to be indebted not only to Roman history but also to medieval mysteries, in which characters are often boldly and simply understood in terms of their moral status and eschatological destiny.

Moreover, *Julius Caesar* shares common ground with the mysteries in another way, too, for it is a play in which there are persistent glances at Christianity. Zander notes that '[s]cholars have ... quite frequently outlined the parallels between J. C. and J. C. – Julius Caesar and Jesus Christ – and have demonstrated that Shakespeare, too, seems to have had those parallels in mind'.[22] Antony says of the dead Caesar, '[h]ere is himself', with an obvious echo of *ecce homo*, and also refers to

'Caesar's three and thirty wounds' (5.1.52).[23] As many critics have noted, thirty-three was said to be Christ's age at the time of his death (and a change from the figure of twenty-three found in Appian), and the conspirators' sharing of wine at Philippi has something of the sense of a last supper; Hamlin notes, too, that Caesar's invitation to the conspirators to 'taste some wine' (2.2.126) is Shakespeare's invention and draws on the importance of wine as a symbol of betrayal.[24] Along similar lines, David Kaula notes that 'the dream of the statue is ... Shakespeare's invention. He may have found the idea for it in the medieval cult of the Holy Blood, which featured not only the proliferation of phials of Christ's blood but also stories about bleeding statues and paintings of Christ'; Kaula also suggests that 'Caesar becomes like the "banquet of most heavenly food", the "most godly and heavenly feast" described in the Anglican Communion Service', and says of the conspirators that '[o]utwardly they behave as Caesar's disciples; actually they are his mockers and betrayers'.[25] There is also a suggestion of the numinous when Brutus orders of the dead Cassius: '[c]ome therefore, and to Thasus send his body' (5.3.104). Arden 3's note on this line observes that 'F has "*Tharsus*", assimilating to Tarsus in Asia

---

[18] Simon Barker, '"It's an actor, boss. Unarmed": the rhetoric of Julius Caesar', in Zander, ed., *Caesar: New Critical Essays*, pp. 227–39; p. 234.

[19] Patrick Gray, 'Caesar as comic Antichrist: Shakespeare's *Julius Caesar* and the medieval English stage tyrant', *Comparative Drama* 50 (2016), 1–31; pp. 1, 2, 13.

[20] Starks-Estes, 'Ovidian transformation', p. 114.

[21] Steve Sohmer, *Shakespeare's Mystery Play* (Manchester, 1999), p. 71; Hannibal Hamlin, *The Bible in Shakespeare* (Oxford, 2013), pp. 187, 196.

[22] Zander, '*Julius Caesar* and the critical legacy', p. 4.

[23] At the production at the Crucible Theatre, Sheffield, in 2017, Eliot Cowan's Antony flung open the coffin and propped up the 'corpse' (Jonathan Hyde's Caesar, breathing through holes specially cut into the coffin); down the road in Stratford-upon-Avon, however, Andrew Woodall's Caesar, already too heavy for his fellow actors to carry offstage and having to be taken down through the trap, was not brought back on for this moment.

[24] Hamlin, *The Bible in Shakespeare*, p. 188.

[25] Kaula, '"Let us be sacrificers"', pp. 204, 207, 209.

Minor, the birthplace of St Paul', and Cassius, whose sight was ever thick, is not an impossible analogue for the apostle finally understanding a truth about a dead man with claims to divine status. Finally, Brutus calling his companions to a renewal of the battle says ''Tis three o'clock' (5.3.109), the hour at which Christ supposedly died.

Both the echoes of medieval drama and the allusions to Christianity are, however, obviously anachronistic, albeit in different ways. Firstly, although Dante put Brutus, Cassius and Judas in the same circle of hell, Caesar lived before Christ. Secondly, and more importantly, Shakespeare's own world was very different from that represented in medieval drama, which predated the fissuring of Christianity into two competing confessions. Kaula notes that 'now and then [the] characters forget they are ancient Romans rather than Elizabethans and speak of angels, devils, hell, doomsday, and other ingredients of the Christian cosmos', as when Trebonius says that '[m]en, wives and children stare, cry out and run, / As it were doomsday' (3.1.97–8), but in doing so they also inevitably speak of how the Christian world has become divided against itself. Kaula also observes of the decorating of Caesar's images that '[w]hat these details imply is a practice like the one condemned in the official Elizabethan homily *Against perill of idolatrie, and superfluous decking of churches*, the "popish" practice of venerating images of Christ and the saints and embellishing them with paint, jewels, and clothing', and he notes of Cassius's anti-Caesar remarks that 'another place in sixteenth-century literature where such comments and images appear, and appear quite extensively, is in the Protestant attacks on the Pope'. Indeed, he argues that 'in his claim to supreme spiritual authority as *pontifex maximus* (a title North translates as "chief Bishop of Rome"), Caesar and not St. Peter was actually the first pope and provided the model for his ecclesiastical successors'.[26] The play opens with the question '[i]s this a holiday?', and in so doing touches on two questions of overwhelming importance for Shakespeare's original audience: what *was* holy, and what *did* deserve a 'holiday'? Mark Rose notes that 'the tribune Marullus sounds strikingly like an indignant Puritan calling sinners to repent',[27] and Kaula suggests that the behaviour of the crowd around Caesar's body would also have reminded the audience of their own society: 'Antony is describing something the members of Shakespeare's audience could have witnessed in their own city: the avid quest for relics by the followers of Catholic missionary priests executed at Tyburn.'[28] The audiences of medieval mysteries saw a simple, clear-cut contest between Christianity and some very bad, but fortunately also comic, pagans; early modern audiences of *Julius Caesar* saw and heard things which would have reminded them of radically different and completely incompatible understandings of Christianity.

The context of the competition between the two confessions significantly complicates the potential identification of Julius Caesar with Jesus Christ. The atmosphere of religious and political extremism might even mean that Caesar suggests not Christ but his polar opposite: Domenico Lovascio notes the insistent accruing of herpetological imagery to early modern figurings of Caesar;[29] the idea of the snake had obvious resonance in the context of biblical narrative and drama, but it works to align Caesar with the devil rather than with Jesus. Or perhaps both are hinted at: Patrick Gray, noting that '[b]y the twentieth century, the problem of the "two Caesars" was well-established', suggests that 'the story of Caesar's rise and fall lends itself by nature to an intertextual typology of Christ and Antichrist'.[30] In this reading, Caesar both *does* and does *not* look like Christ, becoming a figure of uncanny duality whose power derives from the very closeness with which he mimics what he is not. As Gray himself also notes, 'Antony's

---

[26] Kaula, '"Let us be sacrificers"', pp. 197, 198, 200, 202.

[27] Rose, 'Conjuring Caesar', p. 256.

[28] Kaula, '"Let us be sacrificers"', p. 205.

[29] Domenico Lovascio, 'Re-writing Julius Caesar as a national villain in early modern English drama', *English Literary Renaissance* (2017), 1–33; pp. 6–10, 28–9.

[30] Gray, 'Caesar as comic Antichrist', pp. 2, 11.

presentation of Caesar's wounds closely resembles ... the story of Christ's Resurrection, but undermined and ironized', while Hamlin compares Caesar's failure to swim (again Shakespeare's invention) to Jesus walking on the water, and Lisa Starks-Estes suggests that 'Shakespeare exposes the pagan roots of Christianity by conflating mythology with the sacred': for her, '[b]y staging the creation of Julius Caesar as a martyr within a play highly inflected with Ovidian intertexts ... Shakespeare not only discloses the process by which bodies are made sacred, but also he underscores the connection between Christianity and its pagan past'.[31] Finally, Jack Heller suggests that there is a motif of failed sacraments in the play, for which one possible explanation might be that Caesar is *not* Christ.[32] If Caesar were Christ, sinners would be saved; but he is not so they are not, and Cinna dies.

In staging what amounts to an alternative life of Christ, Shakespeare builds on the example set by Marlowe in *The Jew of Malta*. Paulina Kewes notes that '[i]n *Julius Caesar* Shakespeare drew on Marlowe's translation of Lucan's Book I', and Lisa Starks-Estes observes that, '[f]ollowing Marlowe's lead, Shakespeare exploits the potential of Ovid on the stage in various ways', particularly when, '[i]n *Julius Caesar*, Shakespeare grafts Ovidian myths of Actaeon, Orpheus and Julius Caesar himself onto his source material from Plutarch, thereby exploring connections between theatre, myth and religious rites'.[33] For Starks-Estes, Antony's description of Caesar's corpse 'is inflected with the myth of Actaeon': 'Shakespeare changes the number of Caesar's wounds from twenty-three in Plutarch to thirty-three in *Julius Caesar*, which may suggest another connection to Ovid's myth, as Actaeon famously has thirty-three hounds'; Actaeon, as I have explored elsewhere, was an important figure for Marlowe.[34] Marlowe, an alumnus of Corpus Christi College, shows a clear interest in both Caesar and the body of the Christ in his work, repeatedly evoking Caesar and Caesarism as well as translating Lucan, and offering in Barabas an inverted shadow of Christ in ways which, as I have again shown elsewhere, also drew on the mystery plays.[35] Shakespeare, as so often, is

less confrontational and less provocative than Marlowe, but in *Julius Caesar* he is, I suggest, drawing on the model provided by Barabas, down to the death-and-apparent-resurrection motif, just as the agonizing sense of spiritual uncertainty engendered by the play seems to owe something to *Doctor Faustus*. *Julius Caesar* also has a dimension absent from *The Jew of Malta*, though, for although Caesar is *not* Christ, he *is* himself, and to be Caesar is something in its own right – indeed, in Shakespeare's hands, it is two things.

Caesar's similarities and dissimilarities to both Christ and himself are negotiated in part by the play's obsession with the word 'like'. Barbara J. Baines remarks that, in Shakespeare's plays in general, 'often the action turns on a single word – "nothing" in *King Lear*, "indeed" in *Othello*, "done" in *Macbeth*, "boy" in *Coriolanus*, and "if" in *As You Like It*'; in *Julius Caesar* I suggest that word is 'like', which also figured in the title of another play of the same year, *As You Like It*.[36] We hear 'like' first when Cassius says that Caesar 'doth bestride the narrow world / Like a Colossus' (1.2.134–5). In a play which places so much emphasis on the fragility, and indeed potential disablement, of human bodies, including Caesar's, this strikes a rare note of aggrandizement, but in so doing it also draws attention to the fact that the

---

[31] Gray, 'Caesar as comic Antichrist', p. 17; Hamlin, *The Bible in Shakespeare*, p. 195; Starks-Estes, 'Ovidian transformation', pp. 110, 116.

[32] Jack Heller, '"Your statue spouting blood": *Julius Caesar*, the sacraments, and the fountain of life', in *Word and Rite: The Bible and Ceremony in Selected Shakespearean Works*, ed. Beatrice Batson (Newcastle-upon-Tyne, 2010), pp. 77–93; p. 80.

[33] Paulina Kewes, 'Julius Caesar in Jacobean England', *The Seventeenth Century* 17 (2002),155–86; p. 174; Starks-Estes, 'Ovidian transformation', p. 107.

[34] Starks-Estes, 'Ovidian transformation', p. 111; Lisa Hopkins, 'What's Actaeon to Aeneas? Marlowe's mythological mischief', *Marlowe Studies* 4 (2014), 49–62.

[35] Lisa Hopkins, 'Moving Marlowe: *The Jew of Malta* on the Caroline stage', *Marlowe Studies* 6 (2016), 1–16.

[36] Barbara J. Baines, '"That every like is not the same": the vicissitudes of language in Julius Caesar', in Zander, ed., *Caesar: New Critical Essays*, pp. 139–53; p. 139.

two things are *not* very like: Caesar may make the psychological impact of a Colossus, but his own ageing body, deaf in one ear and subject to epilepsy, does not in the least resemble the scale or substance of the Colossus, and Shakespeare has been at some pains to stress this. Though Miranda Fay Thomas notes that '*The Book of the Courtier* makes reference to Caesar "wearing a laurel wreath, in order to hide his baldness"', Shakespeare considerably bigs up the idea of Caesar's debility: Patrick Gray notes that 'Shakespeare is more disparaging about Caesar's epilepsy than Plutarch is' and also observes that Caesar's partial deafness 'is Shakespeare's own invention'.[37] The idea of deafness has obvious metaphorical force, but together with the stress on Caesar's epilepsy and poor swimming skills (another Shakespeare invention), it also seems designed to point up the ways in which this vulnerable man is *not* like a Colossus.

The word 'like' recurs when Cassius says 'it is meet / That noble minds keep ever with their likes' (1.2.309–10). Here 'likes' means people who are like the speaker – equals, peers or *confrères*. The idea of a mutual *liking* between such people might possibly be implicit, but it does not have to be there, and the passage also reminds us that 'like' does not have to be a simple adjective but can also function as a noun.[38] Later Brutus muses that:

[b]etween the acting of a dreadful thing
And the first motion, all the interim is
Like a phantasma or a hideous dream:
The genius and the mortal instruments
Are then in council, and the state of man,
Like to a little kingdom, suffers then
The nature of an insurrection.

(2.1.63–9)

In this passage 'like' is used (twice) more conventionally than in Cassius's words: the interim between thinking of something momentous and actually doing it is 'Like a phantasma or a hideous dream', and the state of man is 'Like to a little kingdom'. The repetition of the 'like' construction both connects these two ideas and exposes the difference between them, revealing that, though

individually both phrases are grammatically meek, the conjunction of the two is provocative. The second, the comparison between 'the state of man' and 'a little kingdom', is conventional and ostensibly conservative: it is, for example, the idea that underpins much domestic tragedy of the period, as when Alice Arden's murder of her husband is classed as 'petty treason', and is also to be found in much homiletic literature. But for readers and audiences of *Julius Caesar*, the moralizing force of the comparison is diluted by the fact that it has been both introduced by and compared with the idea of a dream, an idea whose importance is bolstered by the cumulative effect of Calpurnia's dream, Cinna the poet's dream, and Brutus's dream (unless, of course, it is real) of Caesar's ghost before Philippi. The fact that we are at this very moment poised between the conception of a major enterprise and its fulfilment invites us to regard the present as the dream or phantasma which Brutus labels it as, and potentially to connect that atmosphere of unreality to the supposed political truth of the second 'like' construction, in ways which might perhaps destabilize its aura of naturalness and certainty. That 'like' might unsettle apparent certainties rather than reinforce them is further suggested by the fact that the next use of the word also concerns a dream, when we hear how Calpurnia dreamed she saw Caesar's statue, '[w]hich, like a fountain with an hundred spouts, / Did run pure blood' (2.2.77–8). Again, the construction is conventional, but Calpurnia's use of it, like Brutus's, is tainted by at least a touch of the phantasmagoric as water turns into blood – perhaps with a potential rewriting of the idea of water turning into wine, but perhaps merely as a signifier of the unnatural and counterintuitive.

---

[37] Thomas, 'Political acts', p. 14; Gray, 'Caesar as comic Antichrist', pp. 3, 5.
[38] I follow *OED* (1) in terming it an adjective in most of the contexts in which it appears in this play, though it can also be an adverb, a preposition and a conjunction, and on rare occasions even a noun.

Two further uses of the word 'like' associate it not with dreams but with animals. As the climax of the play approaches, Antony accuses the conspirators:

> You showed your teeth like apes, and fawned like
>   hounds,
> And bowed like bondsmen, kissing Caesar's feet;
> Whilst damned Caska, like a cur, behind
> Struck Caesar in the neck. O you flatterers!
>
> (5.1.41–4)

There are four 'likes' here, and each works to diminish, and in most cases to dehumanize, the conspirators: they are 'like apes', 'like hounds', and 'like bondsmen', while Caska is singled out as 'like a cur'. The passage as a whole is further testimony (if we needed it) to Antony's facility with rhetoric, but it also reveals the power of 'like' to allow one character to shape how we perceive another, further underlining the ways in which 'like' may serve as an ideologically driven tool for representing people and things, rather than a simple, neutral way of telling truths about them.

Brutus too employs animal similes when he declares:

> [b]ut hollow men, like horses hot at hand,
> Make gallant show and promise of their mettle:
> But when they should endure the bloody spur,
> They fall their crests, and like deceitful jades
> Sink in the trial.
>
> (4.2.23–7)

For Brutus as well as for Antony, comparing an enemy to an animal proves a satisfying rhetorical move as he uses 'like' to build two similes comparing men to horses. However, not only is it too little, too late, but his ability to deploy language again lags behind Antony's: there is no inherent shame in being a horse, which is how he designates Antony and Octavius, whereas a dog is in Shakespeare always a problem animal. 'Like' may be a word of power, but it needs to be carefully and appropriately deployed.

Some uses of 'like' in the play are distinguished by the fact that a particular and ominous tonality accrues to them. Etymologically, 'like' derives from the Anglo-Saxon 'lych', a corpse, a meaning preserved in modern English in the phrase 'lych-gate', meaning the gate through which a corpse is carried into the churchyard: to be *like* something is to share a body with it. Shakespeare seems to remember this derivation in *Hamlet*, where Horatio tells the hero, 'I knew your father; / These hands are not more like' (1.2.211–12), making a mockery of Hamlet's own prophecy that his father was so special that 'I shall not look upon his like again' (1.2.187), since that is exactly what he is about to do. The idea of hands is doubly significant: not only does the simultaneous likeness and unlikeness between one's left hand and one's right lay bare the ways in which the 'lych' is both like and unlike the person, but it also potentially alludes to the common trope of dying as shaking hands. This image is traceable back to Greek funerary statuary, where the dead person is often shown shaking hands with a living friend, and is mentioned several times in early modern drama, for instance when Ferdinand in *The Duchess of Malfi* tells his sister: '[y]ou have shook hands with Reputation'.[39] Miranda Fay Thomas notes that '*Julius Caesar* contains three key scenes that involve a handshake to signify a binding promise',[40] but though that may indeed be what they signify, they are also suggestive of the iconography of death.

The idea of bodies clings to several of the uses of 'like' in *Julius Caesar*. Titinius says of Cassius that '[h]e lies not like the living' (5.3.58), and Lucilius prophesies of Brutus:

> [w]hen you do find him, or alive or dead,
> He will be found like Brutus, like himself.
>
> (5.4.24–5)

Both Cassius and Brutus are still recognizable as themselves in that both still look like themselves, but neither has life, without which all likeness is reduced to a hollow parody of itself. There is a similar idea of death in play when Antony laments:

> O world, thou wast the forest to this hart,
> And this indeed, O world, the heart of thee.

---

39 John Webster, *The Duchess of Malfi*, ed. John Russell Brown (Manchester, 1974), 3.2.134.
40 Thomas, 'Political acts', p. 4.

How like a deer, strucken by many princes,
Dost thou here lie?

(3.1.208–11)

There is already a pun here on hart/heart, and like (which is emphasized by the half-rhyme with 'lie') also functions in effect as a pun since it is the 'lych' of Caesar which lies 'like' a deer (with a third potential pun on 'dear'). Later, Antony declares: '[o]ver thy wounds now do I prophesy / (Which like dumb mouths do ope their ruby lips / To beg the voice and utterance of my tongue)' (3.1.259–61); here, once more, death lurks, since the wounds are what made Caesar a 'lych'.

Most suggestively, the play actually theorizes its own use of 'like' when Brutus says: '[t]hat every like is not the same, O Caesar, / The heart of Brutus earns to think upon' (2.2.128–9). Baines suggests that '[t]he "like", a form of metaphor, is not the same as that which it claims to be', but I think there is more than that at stake in these lines.[41] 'That every like is not the same' could conceivably remind us that Brutus's decision to assassinate Caesar was based not on certainties but on probabilities, that is on what *might* or was *like* to happen, and specifically on his fear that Caesar might be a seizer; however, 'like' here also seems to have something of the same register as the uses of 'like' which accrue to the Ghost in *Hamlet*, and its basic meaning would therefore seem to be that not all corpses are equal. Caesar's, in particular, is special, at least in this play, for Caesar, uniquely in Shakespeare's Roman plays, comes back as a ghost, which is both *like* his body and yet *not* his body. The focus on Caesar's body also chimes with a very odd detail found in Appian's account of Caesar's funeral, which is (in modern translation) that, after Antony's speech had whetted his hearers close to violence, 'someone raised above the bier a wax effigy of Caesar – the body itself, lying on its back on the bier, not being visible. The effigy was turned in every direction, by a mechanical device, and twenty-three wounds could be seen, savagely inflicted on every part of the body and on the face.'[42] Ernest Schanzer, noting amongst other things that Antony's word 'vesture' is also found in the 1578 translation of Appian by W. B. (possibly

William Barker), argues that Shakespeare used this as a source. If this is right, he would have found some suggestive details in it.[43] Appian declares that 'there were some that perswaded *Lucius Piso*, to whome *Caesar* had left his Testamente, that it should neyther be brought forthe, nor his body buryed openly, least it mighte breede some newe tumult in the Citie'; however, it was in fact displayed, and used by Antony as a prop to support his oratory: '[a]t euery of these words *Antonie* directed his countenance and hands to *Caesars* body, and with vehemencie of words opened the fact'. Antony also swore those who supported him to a rather striking oath: 'that all should keepe *Caesar* and *Caesars* body'. The curious suggestion of doubleness here, as if Caesar and Caesar's body were separate entities, is reinforced when 'one shewed out of the Litter the Image of *Caesar*, made of waxe, for hys body it selfe lying flat in the Litter, could not be seene. Hys picture was by a deuise turned about, and .xxiij. wounds wer shewed ouer al his body, and his face horrible to behold.'[44] The overall effect is to create a tension between the body itself and its simulacrum, which both represents the body and yet is not the body – which is, in short, the like of this 'lych'. This scene does not appear in Shakespeare, but there is something very like it when Antony uses Caesar's cloak as a substitute for his body. In Appian, before displaying the wax image, Antony had 'stripped the clothes from Caesar's body, raised them on a pole and waved them about', and had also 'turned and made a gesture towards the body of Caesar' every time he had listed one of his titles or qualities, which apparently authenticates the truth of Caesar's identity as 'sacrosanct', 'inviolate', 'father of his country', 'benefactor' and 'leader'. In *Julius Caesar*, too, he displays the robe, stopping to move the audience by recalling 'the first time ever Caesar put it on' (3.2.169), and Miranda Fay Thomas notes that '[t]he deictic "this"

---

41 Baines, '"That every like is not the same"', p. 144.
42 Appian, 'Caesar's funeral', trans. John Carter, www .livius.org/sources/content/appian/appian-caesars-funeral.
43 Ernest Schanzer, ed., *Shakespeare's Appian* (Liverpool, 1956), p. xxi.
44 Schanzer, ed., *Shakespeare's Appian*, pp. 35, 42–3, 45.

and the imperatives "look", "see", and "mark" all imply a gesture which Antony must deploy to point out specific wounds'.[45]

Antony's evocation of Caesar's body, modelled as it seems to be on Appian's description, exposes an uncertainty about what is and is not a real body, which chimes exactly with one of the issues which had fissured Christianity into two different confessions, one believing in transubstantiation and one believing in consubstantiation, and it also potentially comments on the political as well as the religious climate. In 1599, Elizabeth was 66, and Mark Rose, arguing that the play speaks to 'the way the crown penetrated the church', relates *Julius Caesar* to her age and childlessness, reading it as effectively a succession play in disguise.[46] The Queen's motto was '*semper eadem*' ('always the same'), but it was increasingly obvious that change was in fact bound to come when she finally died (as she did four years after the first production of *Julius Caesar*). When the Queen's own wax effigy was borne through the streets in 1603 as England waited for its new ruler to come from Scotland, it can rarely have been clearer that every like is not the same.

To conclude, then, I have suggested that not only is wordplay important in *Caesar* but that the puns perform work, particularly that on 'like' which consistently activates an idea of uncanniness and doubleness attaching to death. This culminates in the apparent reappearance of Caesar's body after Brutus and Cassius have shared wine, an obvious echo of the Christian story which forces together Rome's twin identities of classical past and Christian present. It also calls attention to the uniqueness of Caesar in being the only ghost in the Roman plays, and thus implicitly invites us to read him as a flawed type of Christ, in ways which both make him synecdochic of Rome's twin pasts as capital of the Roman empire and capital of the Catholic world, and also glance outwards from the stage to offer implicit comment on Shakespeare's own society. What did the Romans do for us? They gave us a cast of memorable characters and a language both alien and familiar, through which our greatest playwright was able to speak about things which were both like the world inhabited by his audience and yet also safely different from it.

---

[45] Thomas, 'Political acts', p. 22.

[46] Rose, 'Conjuring Caesar', pp. 265, 267. Peter Lake extends the idea of topicality to read the play as about Essex specifically in 'Shakespeare's *Julius Caesar* and the search for a usable (Christian?) past', in *Shakespeare and Early Modern Religion*, ed. David Loewenstein and Michael Witmore (Cambridge, 2015), pp. 111–30; p. 129.

# ANCIENT AESTHETICS AND CURRENT CONFLICTS: INDIAN *RASA* THEORY AND VISHAL BHARDWAJ'S *HAIDER* (2014)

## MELISSA CROTEAU

The aim of art is not to discover the nature of reality but to secure for us the highest experience of life.

(Mysore Hiriyanna, 'Indian aesthetics 2')[1]

On many levels, Shakespeare's *Hamlet* is a play about acting. When considering styles of theatrical performance, our eponymous Prince exhorts the players to perform their parts 'gently', with 'temperance' and 'smoothness', 'hold[ing] … a mirror up to nature' (3.2.5, 8, 22). This acting philosophy has been theorized and realized in diverse ways on stage and screen in the Eurocentric West, but it stands in stark contrast to one of the foremost ancient aesthetic theories of India – that of *rasa*, which refers to the emotion an audience member experiences during a performance, be it drama, dance, poetry or music. Simply put, *rasa* theory posits that all the acting in a performed narrative must focus on eliciting powerful emotion from the audience; thus, 'robustious' acting is frequently found on stage and screen in India, as is often noted by critics of Bollywood, or, more accurately, Indian popular cinema, which is not restricted to film made by the Mumbai-based industry.[2] Furthermore, *rasa* theory dictates that every theatrical work should be governed by one primary *rasa*, out of a group of eight designated emotions, which may appear in the piece but must serve to support the dominant *rasa*.[3] In 2014, Indian director Vishal Bhardwaj adapted *Hamlet* into the Hindi film *Haider*, transforming Shakespeare's 'rotten' state of Denmark into the beleaguered, divided North Indian state of Jammu and Kashmir in the turbulent 1990s. In *Haider*, Bhardwaj uses *rasa* aesthetics

powerfully to express the suffering of the mainly Muslim population of the Kashmir Valley at the hands of the occupying Indian military as well as Pakistani and home-grown militants.

Though *rasa* theory has not been widely used to analyse film, a few scholars have noted that it is, in fact, a vital shaping force in Indian popular cinema.[4] The earliest claim to this effect that I could find is in an article entitled 'What did Bharata mean by rasa?' written by S. S. Barlingay, a professor of philosophy at Poona University, which digs deeply into the ancient founding text of Indian aesthetic theory, the *Natyasastra* (*NS*), believed to have been written by a Brahmanic sage called Bharata some time between

---

[1] Mysore Hiriyanna, 'Indian aesthetics 2' [1951], in *Indian Philosophy in English: From Renaissance to Independence*, ed. N. Bhushan and J. L. Garfield (Oxford, 2011), pp. 207–18; p. 210.

[2] 'Bollywood' refers to Indian popular cinema that is made by the film industry based in Mumbai, and its films are predominantly made in the Hindi language. While the majority of the nearly 1,000 films produced in India annually are made by the Mumbai-based industry, there are strong film industries in other parts of the nation, such as a thriving Tamil-language industry in the South, and a unique Bengali industry based in Kolkata in the North-east. The term 'Bollywood' is sometimes used to describe all 'popular' – as opposed to 'art' – films produced by India; however, this is a misrepresentation of the diverse cinema produced by this incredibly heterogeneous country.

[3] Patrick Colm Hogan, 'Rasa theory and dharma theory: from *The Home and the World* to *Bandit Queen*', *Quarterly Review of Film and Video* 20 (2003), 37–52; p. 39.

[4] See, for example, Vijay Mishra, *Bollywood Cinema: Temples of Desire* (London, 2002), p. 50.

200 BCE and 200 CE. The title of this article alludes to the fact that arguments about the meaning and nuances of the lengthy and minutely detailed *NS* have been ongoing for about two millennia, as can be seen in the 2016 compilation *A Rasa Reader: Classical Indian Aesthetics*, which, at nearly 500 folio-sized pages, covers only the responses to Bharata's concept of *rasa* and is limited from the time of the *NS* to the year 1700.[5] In the conclusion of his careful analysis, Barlingay asserts: '[p]erhaps the nearest approach to "Rasa" would be a cinematographic film', which includes both aural and visual elements.[6] Alisha Ibkar, of Alighar Muslim University (coincidentally, the university attended by the character Haider in the film), strongly affirms that 'Indian cinema is completely based on Performance aesthetics. The depiction of *rasa* and channeling it to the audience is the quintessential aspect of Indian theatre and cinema. *Rasa* theory is the very essence of what makes Bollywood unique and eternal and it constitutes but the very structure and backbone of Indian cinema.'[7]

In addition, scholar Patrick Colm Hogan has used *rasa* theory in his cognitive theory-oriented work on Indian cinema and culture.[8] These scholars concur that *rasa* theory has an integral impact on Indian popular cinema; however, these academics, and scholars over the centuries, have not agreed on the basic definitions of a few key terms in the theory, to which we now turn.

## RASA THEORY: COMPLEXITY AND PARADOX

Before engaging in a *rasic* reading of Bhardwaj's *Haider*, we must delve into some of the complexities of *rasa* theory, as it is our specific approach that will govern the analysis. It has been particularly helpful to examine the work of philosophy, theatre history and aesthetics scholars to acquire an understanding of the *NS*'s theory of *rasa* as a contested field in which the meaning of the Sanskrit in the *NS* has been interpreted in various ways; then those readings were taken up and understood differently, etc. This article takes the perspective of S. S. Barlingay and Bharat

Gupt, a current classicist and theatre theorist at the University of Delhi, who both return to the Sanskrit of the *NS* and find that *rasa* theory applies most specifically to performed media, and not, as a great many have claimed, to poetry on the page. The importance of this point lies in the relationship between the *rasas* and the other elements of *Natya*, and their roles in the theatrical experience. Barlingay contends that the three main characteristics of *rasa* are: (a) it designates a staged or performed medium, (b) 'it is composite in nature', and (c) it essentially 'represents movement and is extended in time'.[9] These characteristics, of course, are found in cinema. It is helpful to understand that *rasa* more literally refers to 'juice and flavour', and 'flow' is one of its 'basic meanings'.[10] Therefore, the theoretical definition of *rasa* as an emotion experienced by the spectator of a performance carries with it the idea that the feelings evoked are a type of distillation, or 'pure' liquid essence, of one of the eight *rasas*. Plus, the 'flowing' nature of these *rasas* underscores that the experience of a *rasic* emotion is always a part of an open, creative process that begins with the emotion and message of the author/artist, which is communicated through the various elements of stage language, and finally received as *rasa* experienced by the spectator, who is a co-creator of the *rasa* as she interprets the performance for herself but shares experience of the *rasa* collectively with the actors and other spectators.

---

[5] Sheldon Pollock, trans. and ed., *A Rasa Reader: Classical Indian Aesthetics* (New York, 2016).

[6] S. S. Barlingay, 'What did Bharata mean by rasa?' *Indian Philosophical Quarterly* 8 (1981), 433–56; p. 452.

[7] Alisha Ibkar, 'The Natyasastra and Indian cinema: a study of the rasa theory as a cornerstone for Indian aesthetics', *International Journal of English Language and Translation Studies* 3 (2015), 80–87; p. 87.

[8] Hogan has used *rasa* theory effectively in his book *Understanding Indian Movies: Culture, Cognition, and Cinematic Imagination* (Austin, TX, 2008), and journal article 'Rasa theory and dharma theory'. Hogan also references Darius Cooper's book *The Cinema of Satyajit Ray: Between Tradition and Modernity* (Cambridge, 2000), which applies rasa theory to the work of the eminent Indian art cinema director.

[9] Barlingay, 'What did Bharata mean by rasa?' p. 452.

[10] Barlingay, 'What did Bharata mean by rasa?' p. 452.

Eminent Indian scholar Kapil Vatsyayan asserts that the 'worldview' of the *NS* 'proceeds through paradox: impersonality and intensity; the specific and the universal; the inner and the outer; the *bindu* (point) and its projection into infinite variety; stillness and movement; the physical body and its transcendence'.[11] Vatsyayan declares that '[t]he artistic experience [of *rasa*] is acausal and whole, a state of beatitude and bliss in the mind of the experiencer, the creator ... [*Rasa* is] the highly charged state of momentary freedom and emancipation which motivates, inspires creation ... [and] this experience ... facilitates an abstraction of life into its primary emotions and sentiments'.[12]

In this sense, *rasa* is intensely personal, but for the experiencer of *rasa*, the emotions are a 'meta-experience', detached and distanced from one's own life, as they are externally produced or channelled through a performance and shared with others.[13] It is this meta-experience which creates empathy in the spectator and allows her to experience pleasure and freedom, even when experiencing *rasic* emotions of sorrow or disgust. This has led some theorists to compare the *rasic* experience to Aristotle's notion of catharsis, and, indeed, there is a 'purgative' effect posited in the enjoyment of a 'universalized' emotion.[14] Finally, it is important to understand that one experiences *rasa*; it is not a mental or intellectual recognition, but rather is related to tasting a wonderful meal, something with which the *rasic* experience is often compared, a tradition starting with Bharata himself. Theatre practitioner and scholar Richard Schechner declares: '[r]asa is flavor, taste, the sensation one gets when food is perceived, brought within reach, touched, taken into the mouth, chewed, mixed, savored, and swallowed ... *Rasa* is sensuous, proximate, experiential.'[15] In plain terms, *rasa* is visceral, not cerebral.

In *rasa* theory, most pundits agree about the meaning of *rasa* and the idea that the *bhavas* ('emotions') evoke the *rasas* in the audience/experiencer. However, current scholars utilizing the theory, whether as an analytical lens or a practical tool for the theatre, tend to focus on the *sthayi bhavas* – usually translated as 'standing or dominant emotions' – as embodied by the *actors*, who then serve as the primary

conduit for *rasa*.[16] This view centres on acting styles or approaches that express emotion, which are a vital part of *rasa*, but not the whole picture. Gupt states clearly that '*bhava* is not to be taken simply as emotion, but as a psychological theory about the nature of emotions', which opens up the complexity of the term and leads us beyond the actor's expression into the larger arena of the theatrical experience.[17] Again, Barlingay and Gupt offer the most complete and helpful view on the subject, as they both return directly to the sixth chapter of the *NS*, which focuses on *rasa* theory, and lead us through the Sanskrit, rather than oversimplifying for an Anglophone or European audience, or presenting readings filtered through the *NS* interpretations of the highly influential tenth-century Shiavite Abhinavagupta and his successors.[18] Moreover, it is crucial to comprehend the larger significance of *Natya*, and how it participates in the communication of *bhavas*, to perceive its substantial connection to the specific elements of cinema. '*Natya*' refers to a combination of media, namely 'dance–theatre–music', and Barlingay concludes logically that Bharata's aesthetic theory is about the totality of 'stage language' and its effects (*rasas*). The *rasic* emotion is communicated to the experiencer/spectator by and through '[t]he set of actors *and environment*, and the acting and the bodily expression, *the direction and the director* – all these form the material of the *Natya* language' (my emphasis).[19] Gupt also quotes the *NS* passage summarizing what is included in *Natya*, and contends that the word *abhinaya* in the list, usually translated simply as 'acting',

[11] Quoted in Susan L. Schwartz, *Rasa: Performing the Divine in India* (New York, 2004), p. 14.

[12] Schwartz, *Rasa*, p. 14.

[13] See Barlingay, 'What did Bharata mean by rasa?' p. 444.

[14] See Bharat Gupt, *Dramatic Concepts: Greek and Indian: A Study of the 'Poetics' and the 'Natyasastra'* (Delhi, 1994), pp. 271–3.

[15] Richard Schechner, 'Rasaesthetics', *The Drama Review* 45 (2001), 27–50; p. 29.

[16] See Hogan, *Understanding*, p. 107; and Schechner, 'Rasaesthetics', p. 29.

[17] Gupt, *Dramatic Concepts*, p. 86.

[18] See Schechner, 'Rasaesthetics', p. 28.

[19] Barlingay, 'What did Bharata mean by rasa?' p. 443.

'may be taken as acting in common parlance, but for Bharata ... it represents *the whole gamut of visual and aural semiotics*' in the staging of a performance (my emphasis).[20] It is also significant that three of the eleven elements in the *Natya* description refer to music – song, instruments and *svara* (breathing, sound or musical notes) – which 'cover[s] all the literary and musical content of a performance text'; the 'theatre-house' appears on the list as well.[21]

With the full meaning of *Natya* in mind, it is not difficult to identify the analogues between the language of the stage and the language of cinema. Much has been theorized regarding the semiotics of film, and, with its focus on the spectator's experience, apparatus theory lines up very well with *rasa* theory. This study will endeavour, however, to interact more directly with *rasa* theory, rather than to filter it through later Western concepts. Therefore, what are the visual and aural signifiers that communicate *rasa*? Clearly, this is done powerfully by all the elements of *mise-en-scène*: setting, the human figure, lighting and frame composition.[22] The use of the term 'mise-en-scène', imported from the theatre into film studies, illustrates film's inheritance from that ancient art and represents the move of this study, among others, to apply theatrical aesthetic theory to cinema. The 'theatre-house', a part of *Natya*, can be compared meaningfully to frame composition, as it is analogous to the shape and boundaries of the stage, but it could also be expanded to refer to the material conditions of spectatorship, i.e. where, when and how one is viewing the performed text. Sound is another element that is imperative to film and to *Natya*, with its emphasis on music as a storytelling device and interpreter and instigator of emotion. In film, there are three types of sound to consider – dialogue, sound effects and music – and these three work together to evoke intense emotional responses. Indian popular cinema is known particularly, of course, for its vivid use of music that does not conform to the construction of 'reality' expected in most Western film. Concomitant with music is cinematography, especially in Indian film. Camera movement and the use of various lenses and filters create the perspective and tone of a shot, and patterns established cinematographically help define characters and

establish mood, which are paramount in the maintaining of one primary *rasa* throughout a film. Editing, perhaps, has the least direct connection to *rasa* theory, as it does not exist *per se* in the theatre. Nonetheless, editing is a pivotal element of visual semiotics in film and, therefore, can be a potent communicator of emotion, as Kuleshov's and Eisenstein's work proved in the first half of the twentieth century. Editing can be broken down into the three elements of collage (the placement of shots next to one another), tempo (shot length and transitions) and timing (the coordination of cutting with other aural and visual elements).[23] As observed in techniques such as juxtapositional editing, quick-cutting (short shot lengths), lap dissolves, and cuts coinciding with major sound effects, editing frequently evokes *rasic* effects in an audience.[24]

As previously stated, Bharata identifies eight *rasas* in the *Natyasastra*, which are listed in Table 6 with their translations.

As pointed out by Hogan and Jones, Indian films are most commonly dominated by the *rasas* of romance (*shringara*) and sorrow/pathos (*karuna*).[25]

Table 6

| Rasa | Emotion |
| --- | --- |
| Shringara | Love in union and separation |
| Hasya | Humour |
| Karuna | Pathos, sorrow, compassion, grief |
| Raudra | Anger, wrath |
| Vira | Heroism |
| Bhayanaka | Fear/panic |
| Bibhatsa | Distaste/recoil/disgust |
| Abdhuta | Wonderment/surprise |

[20] Gupt, *Dramatic Concepts*, p. 86.
[21] Gupt, *Dramatic Concepts*, p. 87.
[22] Maria Pramaggiore and Tom Wallis, *Film: A Critical Introduction*, 2nd edn (New York, 2008), p. 88.
[23] Pramaggiore and Wallis, *Film*, p. 199.
[24] Schwartz, *Rasa*, p. 15.
[25] See Hogan, 'Rasa theory', p. 40; and Matthew Jones, 'Bollywood, rasa and Indian cinema: misconceptions, meanings and *Millionaire*', *Visual Anthropology* 23 (2010), 33–43; p. 39.

Not surprisingly, Vishal Bhardwaj's *Haider* is governed by *karuna* – the *rasa* of sorrow, pity and grief – from start to finish, an emotional landscape that is undergirded by the *rasas* of disgust (*bibhatsa*), as represented by the extreme, grisly violence in the film, and romance, which, as in the case of Hamlet and Ophelia (here Haider and Arshia), increases the pathos of the narrative. In her book *Rasa: Performing the Divine in India* (2004), Schwartz lists the colours and deities associated with each of the eight *rasas*. Importantly, *karuna* is associated with the colour of doves or pigeons, a hue ranging from dull white to warm, pinkish grey, to deeper shades of grey; and it is connected to Yama, the god of death, king of ghosts, and the 'moral judge and punisher whose assistants [monsters and demons] torture the wicked in hell'.[26] Depictions of Yama are dominated by red and black colours, and he is related to Rudra and Agni, the gods of terrifying wrath (bringing both disease and healing) and fire, respectively. These colours and motifs appear prominently in *Haider*. Dove-colour is particularly apposite for this tale of lost and betrayed familial and romantic love; it is the colour of sadness and melancholy, of a muted world, and of twilight, that liminal moment between day and night, life and death, being and not being. The red and black colours that accompany rage, bloodshed and destruction feature predominantly in the latter half of the film, in which Haider seeks to kill his uncle, Khurram, who is responsible for his father's death at the hands of pro-Indian government militia. Throughout *Haider*, *karuna* is evoked vividly through *mise-en-scène*, particularly in the cold, harsh, awe-inspiring terrain of the valley of Kashmir, nestled into the soaring Himalayas. It is a dramatic landscape, to say the least, and the film opens in the dying season of fall and moves into a snowy winter. A frosty grey mist blankets the valley throughout *Haider*, which can be seen in nearly every exterior long-shot in the film.

## ROTTEN/ROMANTIC KASHMIR

Kashmir typically has been used very differently in Hindi cinema, as a magnificent and exotic backdrop for romantic passion. Rachel Dwyer and Divia Patel identify Kashmir as a 'specific chronotope of

romance' in Indian cinema, and note that the 'traditional paradise of Urdu literature is associated with that of Kashmir'.[27] Consequently, after the first use of the region in Raj Kapoor's *Barsaat* (*Rain*, 1949), 'Kashmir featured as a location for romance for several decades, until the political situation made shooting there almost impossible' in the late 1980s.[28] One element that has been highlighted particularly in the romantic Kashmiri landscape is water (e.g. rivers and waterfalls), which is frequently used as a symbol for eroticism in Indian film, leading to the practice of using spring and the rainy season to express romantic love: 'spring for love in union and the rainy season for love in separation'.[29] Tellingly, Bhardwaj has chosen the opposite seasons for *Haider*: autumn and winter, where snow serves as a substitute for rain in marking the doomed love of Haider and Arshia, who, unlike Hamlet and Ophelia, have one beautiful scene of union in the typical Bollywood 'log cabin' romantic chronotope.[30] Bhardwaj's choice to set *Haider* in the heart of Indian cinema's celebrated romantic landscape, following its decline into a terrifying police state, highlights Bhardwaj's message in *Haider*. Like Akira Kurosawa in his twentieth-century Shakespeare adaptations, Bhardwaj makes a brave statement in *Haider* condemning the appalling corruption and gruesome violence perpetrated by official authorities in his own nation, as well as militants from within and outside the country. After years of encroaching Indian government control over the majority Muslim region, Kashmir erupted in violence after the blatant rigging of Kashmiri elections in 1987, after which 'furious Kashmiri leaders went underground. Soon afterwards, the bombings, strikes, assassinations and stone-throwings began.'[31]

---

[26] Sukumari Battacharji, 'Yama', in *Encyclopedia of Religion*, 2nd edn, ed. Lindsay Jones (Basingstoke, 2005), p. 9868.

[27] Rachel Dwyer and Divia Patel, *Cinema India: The Visual Culture of Hindi Film* (London, 2002), p. 61.

[28] Dwyer and Patel, *Cinema India*, p. 61.

[29] Dwyer and Patel, *Cinema India*, p. 60.

[30] Dwyer and Patel, *Cinema India*, p. 70.

[31] William Dalrymple, 'Curfewed Night by Basharat Peer', 20 June 2010, www.theguardian.com/books/2010/jun/20/curfewed-night-basharat-peer-dalrymple.

In response, the Indian government militarized the state of Jammu and Kashmir, and used its troops, largely from outside the region, to perpetrate 'systematic torture' on the state's citizens, including 'a series of horrific rapes and atrocities' which 'radicalized a population who were vaguely pro-Pakistani' but previously not energized to act against Indian forces; however, the 'massacres of the early 1990s changed Kashmir forever: militant groups sprung up in every village'.[32] In *Imagining Kashmir* (2016), Patrick Colm Hogan describes Muslim citizens of the area being compelled to leave their homes and 'forced to pass before concealed informants for possible denunciation'.[33] If an individual was implicated in terrorist plots, without any further proof, he or she would be 'disappeared' into a 'camp' or a prison, tortured and, often, killed. Kashmir itself 'has been turned into a sort of prison, with a massive apparatus that dwarfs that of any actual prison'.[34] As one *Haider* reviewer observes: '[p]acked with perfidy, passion and *pathos, Hamlet* is seemingly the perfect canvas on which to project a fresh perspective of the reality of living in an open-air prison' (my emphasis).[35] Bhardwaj clearly saw in *Hamlet* a text that parallels the disintegration of a family with that of a state, and pursued this project to make a statement about the atrocities committed by the Indian government against the Muslim citizens in this region. To do this, he invited Kashmiri journalist Basharat Peer – who wrote *Curfewed Night* (2010), a 'searing memoir about the bloody struggle for justice in Kashmir' – to co-author the film's screenplay with him, and it shows.[36] Haider's father, the surgeon Hilaal Meer, 'disappears' in one of these 'crackdowns', in which a masked informer signals that Hilaal is involved in terrorism against the Indian government. In this case, the informer is Hilaal's own brother, Khurram, who represents Muslims who aid and abet the Indian forces in order to gain power and money. Since the troubles began in Kashmir, the subject of Muslim terrorism, by both Pakistani insurgents and local militia, has appeared in several Indian films, most notably in *Roja* (Mani Ratnam, 1992), *Mission Kashmir* (Vidhu Vinod Chopra, 2000) and *LOC: Kargil* (J. P. Dutta, 2003). In their article 'Hamlet–Haider*: from rotten Denmark to rotten Kashmir'

(2015), three Pakistani scholars aver that these Bollywood films kept 'the rotten Kashmir pot blazing': 'elements like war hysteria, fanatic patriotism and jingoism are thoroughly stimulated in the name of commercial entertainment'. Consequently, they praise *Haider* for not ignoring this 'shocking and terrible history, about which India knows slightly and cares even [less]'.[37] The *rasic* process is highlighted in their claim that the power of these Indian films lies in their ability to 'stimulate' *rasic* emotions such as heroism, fear and anger. Even in the most humanitarian of these films, *Roja*, the grotesque and deadly human rights abuses perpetrated by the Indian government are almost entirely absent. Bhardwaj must have recognized that 'revenge turns up frequently as a personal motive in Kashmir terrorist films',[38] and he decided to turn the tables in his Kashmiri narrative, using the revenge tragedy of *Hamlet* as a model for the revenge of the wronged Kashmiris.[39] *Haider*, as with a great many didactic performative works in India, employs the pathetic *rasa* to impart its ethical meaning and to stir audiences to think, and perhaps act, differently, by inspiring empathy towards the suffering Kashmiris.

[32] Dalrymple, 'Curfewed Night'.
[33] Patrick Colm Hogan, *Imagining Kashmir: Emplotment and Colonialism* (Lincoln, NE, 2016), p. 29.
[34] Hogan, *Imagining*, p. 29.
[35] Nandini Ramnath, 'Haider: desperately seeking Hamlet in the Valley of Kashmir', 2 October 2014, http://scroll.in/article/681740/haider-desperately-seeking-hamlet-in-the-valley-of-kashmir.
[36] Dalrymple, 'Curfewed Night'.
[37] Gohar Ayaz, Zia Ahmed and Ali Ammar, '*Hamlet–Haider*: from rotten Denmark to rotten Kashmir', *International Journal of English and Education* 4 (2015), 116–23; p. 117.
[38] Hogan, *Imagining*, p. 26.
[39] In her insightful review of *Haider*, Ramnath notes that at least two films have offered views of the Kashmiri crisis that are sympathetic to those suffering under India's police state: *Harud* (2010), directed by Aamir Bashir, who plays Liyaqat, the Laertes character in *Haider*; and *Valley of the Saints* (Musa Syeed, 2012), which also deals with environmental issues in Kashmir.

## HAIDER THROUGH THE LENS OF KARUNA

Indeed, *Haider* is set in a very specific milieu for a purpose, and, therefore, its thematic, stylistic and plot elements conform to the narrative of Kashmir in the 1990s, despite the fact that it is an adaptation of *Hamlet*. The commonalities mentioned above, including the dominant *rasa* of *karuna*, connect these two texts; however, their differences have inspired some critics to complain that the film works better as a tragic tale about Kashmir than as an adaptation of *Hamlet*, while others have griped that Bhardwaj 'invoked the Bard' too much and thus compromised what would have been a better film without Shakespeare.[40] The beauty or ugliness of the level of 'Bardiness' in *Haider* is surely in the eye of the beholder. Nevertheless, I believe Bhardwaj and Peer's screenplay weaves the elements of *Hamlet* into *Haider* quite adroitly and to great effect. *Haider* begins with white titles on a black screen announcing that we are in the Kashmiri city of Srinagar in 1995, expecting the audience to know that this was at the height of violence in the region. The first image in the film is of Dr Hilaal Meer, Haider's father, being shoved through claustrophobic grey stone alleys by Muslim terrorists with machine guns. The *mise-en-scène* strongly evokes the *karuna rasa*, as the shots are dominated by grey tones, lacking any warm colours (perhaps through use of a filter), and there is a pale, chilly grey light pervading these frames. We soon learn that Hilaal is being taken to a terrorist leader suffering from an infected appendix, and he agrees to operate on the man to prevent his death. Interstitial – one could say lyrical – shots of the landscape around Srinagar bridge between film sequences, starting here and running throughout the film, and these allow the audience to take a pause outside the narrative and soak in the atmosphere of sorrow and grief that pervades the countryside in Kashmir. Long and extreme long shots reveal the cold, misty terrain, marked by a muddy river and generally dreary environs, which seem both hostile and entrapping. Here at the beginning, we meet the true star of this narrative, Ghazala Meer, played by Tabu in the

Gertrude role, as she is teaching school children about what family is: 'brothers and sisters and fathers and mothers. It is unselfish acts and kindly sharing.' This ironic introduction warns us of the explosive unravelling of her family as the narrative unfolds. A little later, at home, Ghazala is unhappy when she helps her husband prepare to operate on the terrorist who is now in their attic. She takes a telephone call during the procedure, which we will later learn is from her brother-in-law, the crooked lawyer Khurram, who is complicit in the oppression of his Muslim neighbours. The next morning, there is a 'crackdown' in their village, and Hilaal is identified as a 'threat' to the Indian government by a masked man and whisked away roughly to an undisclosed location. He is 'disappeared', and his house is bombed to smithereens with a rocket launcher as Ghazala watches in horror. The couple's son, Haider, then comes up from Aligarh Muslim University, where he is studying Indian revolutionary poets of the colonial era, and begins to search for his father in camps and prisons. His search is emotionally presented to the audience through a montage of images of him going from camp to camp, prison to prison, rendered extraordinarily poignant by the film's first musical number, 'Jhelum' (after the river running through the valley), sung in plaintive, minor tones by the clear tenor of Arjit Singh. Along the way, we learn that many people are, like Haider, on arduous quests to find loved ones. At one point, as song lyrics declare 'Blood, blood, blood, blood has become the colour of time' and 'Blood is a molten ember', we see shots of bloody corpses heaped in the back of a government truck. For nearly four minutes of this song, there is no diegetic sound, only the melancholy voice of the singer narrating the region's tragedy. The montage ends with a shot of Haider in the grey gloaming, throwing pictures of his father's face he used in the search into a blazing fire. Here we see sorrow and anger, shades of *karuna*, Rudra and Agni. The images are enough to tell the story,

40 See Ayaz *et al.*, 'Hamlet–Haider'.

and the song radiates the *rasa* into the soul of the spectator.

Accompanying Haider on this journey is his dear childhood friend, Arshia, daughter of the head of the Jammu and Kashmir police in Srinagar, Parvez Lone. Arshia is a newspaper writer in the area and uses her press pass to gain access for them into the facilities that house prisoners. In *Haider*, Arshia evidently fills the role of the bosom confidant Horatio, as well as the thwarted love interest Ophelia. She is clearly in love with Haider, but he seems oblivious to her charms as he is obsessed with finding his father. Meanwhile, Parvez has been tasked with leading the efforts of the Indian government to further brutally subdue Muslim militants – a project called 'Operation Nightingale' – and co-opts Khurram to conscript his 'terrorist' clients into counter-insurgency militia forces. Khurram also runs for local political office in order to consolidate his power, although he tells Haider he is seeking office in order to find his beloved brother Hilaal. A fast-paced montage then rapidly shuttles the viewer between heated speeches at two Kashmiri political rallies, one featuring Khurram, and a press conference in Srinigar led by Captain Murthy of the Indian Army, who arrogantly tells the crowd that India is fighting for peace in the region against the 'enslavement to Pakistan', not against Kashmiris. Martial-sounding music featuring prominent drums heightens the tension of this sequence, which is punctuated with black-and-white footage of earlier revolts against Indian aggression. The *rasa* evoked by this precisely choreographed collage of imagery is that of disgust, primarily the disgust of the filmic narrator and the Kashmiris towards the deadly politics being played by the government and politicians; however, one can also see the disgust of the military industrial complex towards the Kashmiris, in the form of disrespect and dehumanization.[41]

As a bridging extreme long shot of the valley reveals that it is now bleakly snow-covered and blanketed with pale blue-grey mist, we are introduced to the 'ghost', Roohdaar, played by the ubiquitous Irrfan Khan, accompanied by pop-style instrumentation reminiscent of a Bond or *Mission: Impossible* film. He is thus coded as a mysterious but not malevolent operative. With a pronounced limp, dark sunglasses and dull white robe draping his entire figure, he is, indeed, phantasmal, reminding us of Yama, king of ghosts. We learn about his purpose after we see Haider kidnapped by Muslim militants and taken to a graveyard. Here, Roohdaar tells Haider that he has a message from his father: 'Revenge'. In a dark, grey-toned flashback, Roohdaar then unfolds the dolorous tale of Hilaal's incarceration, torture and eventual murder by Khurram's militia. Roohdaar claims to have been Hilaal's cellmate in prison, sharing in his sufferings, and announces to Haider that he vowed to become Hilaal's 'soul' and carry his message to his son. In the end, Haider is told where his father is buried, and, in an icy, misty graveyard, he weeps over his father's grave, driving the pathos home. It is at this point that Haider begins to behave as if he were insane, but always with a bit too much reason in his madness. His change is marked graphically by appearing next with a shaved head and a beard on his face in one of the most memorable scenes in the film, his 'to be, or not to be' analogue, in which he speaks to a crowd at Laal Chowk, a prominent market where politicians give stump speeches. He wears a rope around his neck tied in a noose and talks into its frayed end, beginning: 'Do we exist or do we not? If we do, then who are we? If not, then where are we?' The speech is markedly aimed at the identity and situation of Kashmiris, who are colonized in the North by Pakistan and China, and by India everywhere else in the state. The scene is primarily shot with a chaotic hand-held camera, often in extreme close-ups where the bumping and canting create a sickly vertigo. Haider chants with rap-style delivery: 'There is no law; there is no order. Whose laws? Whose order? Made on order, law and order. India! Pakistan! A game on the border'. And here there is a cut to an extremely low-angle medium long shot of Haider, distorted by a wide-angle lens. 'India clings to us. Pakistan leeches on. What of us?

---

[41] See Hogan, *Imagining*, pp. 31–2.

What do we want?' The crowd chants, 'Freedom!' Underscoring the complexity of that concept in Kashmir, Haider responds: 'Freedom from this side; freedom from that side. We will be free!' As he sings ironically, 'A world better than the world, our India / We are her children', Khurram, who is in the crowd, calls out to him 'Mother!' trying to communicate that his mother is there and wishes to speak to him; however, the syntax of this exchange firmly establishes that Ghazala embodies the riven relationship between India and the Kashmiris. Pathos, disgust and anger are evoked in this scene as Haider rails against the system that has caught them all in an inescapable, mortiferous trap.

It is at this juncture, perhaps surprisingly, that Bhardwaj treats us to that ineluctable Bollywood romance montage, as Arshia is the only one with whom Haider can share Roohdaar's message and his own confusion, though he does confront his mother with a photo of the dead Hilaal, leading swiftly to the announcement of Ghazala and Khurram's wedding. Bhardwaj falls back on the romantic Kashmiri 'log cabin' trope long used in Indian popular cinema, which 'features as a space offering ... privacy, allowing the audience the pleasure of imagining complete solitude and remoteness'.[42] Finally, the *shringara* (romantic love) *rasa* is the focus, and this montage, with its beautiful love song 'Khul Kabhi Toh', sung by the dulcet voice of Arjit Singh, depicts the union of these lovers remarkably graphically for an Indian film. The montage begins with the two playing in heavily falling snow, then moves into the dark interior of a log cabin with only the golden light of the fire illuminating parts of their entwined bodies. This overwhelming moment of warmth and intimacy ends with Haider weeping in sorrow and holding a gun to his head (see Michael Almereyda's *Hamlet*, 2000). We are swiftly ushered back into the cold world of *karuna*, which is all the more jolting following our romantic escape.

At Ghazala and Khurram's wedding, Haider plans a special finale: he will shoot the groom. We see him hiding the pistol he will use, creating suspense. However, it is also here that we are given the flamboyant spectacle of Haider's 'Nightingale' song and dance sequence, the equivalent of the *Mousetrap* play. Haider's donning of a large, red bird-beak-shaped hat throughout the festivities leading up to the performance reveals that he knows his uncle is collaborating with Operation Nightingale. In the elaborate performance, featuring a group of male dancers wearing light grey and red-clothed puppets representing Ghazala, Khurram and Hilaal, Haider sings an allegorical song about two birds – his mother (a nightingale) and father. The male was poisoned by 'a falcon of bad intention', who then imprisoned and killed the male bird. In the dramatic finale of the song, a giant black puppet representing the falcon emerges onto the 'stage' of the Martrand Sun Temple, where the performance is taking place, and when he turns around, we see the falcon is truly a satanic red demon. Haider is visibly seething with anger as he sings of his father's demise, and ends the song by pointing at Ghazala and Khurram in a full shot from Haider's perspective, shifting focus from his hand to the perpetrators' faces, so the blame lands where our eyes do. The cinematography in this impressive Bollywood number is characteristically elaborate, but even more baroque than most, featuring sweeping crane shots, bird's-eye long shots from above, and extreme low angles leading to exaggerated wide-angle shots with Haider's angry face and movements in the foreground and distorted backgrounds. The giant black and red falcon/demon puppet is a *coup de théâtre*, and Haider wipes prominent red and black paint in stripes on his face during the performance; these colours connect with both the imagery of Yama and the *rasa* of *raudra* (anger).

This act of aggression is the climax that sets the falling action in motion. Haider, like Hamlet, balks from shooting Khurram when he is at prayer. He is caught by Parvez, who gives Haider to his idiot sons, Salman and Salman (after the action star Salman Khan), to kill. Salman and Salman, our Rosencrantz and Guildenstern, end up being brutally murdered by

---

[42] Dwyer and Patel, *Cinema India*, p. 70.

Haider, who savagely bashes each of their heads in with rocks in the open snowy, mist-bound landscape. Haider, at this point, believes he has no choice but to join the insurgency and cross over to Pakistan, so he plans to meet Roohdaar's men in the graveyard where he first met his father's 'soul'. On the way, he cannot resist stopping one last time in the dark, shadowy ruins of his home, where he encounters his mother and they play out a version of the 'closet scene', in which Haider confronts his mother with her guilt, but she explains that she had no idea that Khurram was a government informant when she told him of the terrorist in their attic. Haider insists he must leave but she begs for him to shoot her, ending her 'agony'; at that moment, Parvez arrives to kill Haider, but Haider is quicker on the draw. Arshia falls apart emotionally after her father's death, as we see her, in a dull white gown, unravelling the yarn of a blood-red scarf she had given to her father and wrapping herself in it. She is trapped in this inescapable web of violence and finally shoots herself in the head. Haider flees to the graveyard, and there encounters Roohdaar's men cheerfully digging graves in the snowy ground, enclosed by misty forest and grey skies. What follows is the most excessive and delightful version of the grave-digging scene ever filmed; it is a Bollywood *tour de force*, with the three diggers singing jovially of life and death in a rock-style song rhythmically matched to the striking of their shovels in the cold graves. As they cry, 'Not twilight or sunset / Just darkness, only darkness' in the dove-coloured setting, the smooth crane shot flies fluidly above the men then pulls closer to them at an odd, slightly canted eye-level shot in which the skeletal, black branches of the trees in the background finally come into focus behind them. It is a masterful song and 'dance' number that provides some much-needed levity before the horror that is to come. Despite its drab colour, this is the most self-conscious, over-the-top use of music and choreography in the film, because there is no excuse for it in the narrative, as there is in the wedding scene; thus, it is not characteristic of Bhardwaj's work, which tends to avoid flashy Bollywood numbers in general and any musical interludes that are not seamlessly integrated into the narrative fabric. One

can see this in his other Shakespeare adaptations, *Maqbool* (2003) and *Omkara* (2006), as well as his non-Bardic work, such as *Kaminey* (2009) and *Rangoon* (2017). Bhardwaj chose Shakespeare's gravedigger scene to launch into a flight of fancy, and it does bring humour, strangely, while maintaining the *karuna rasa* in its *mise-en-scène* and its lyrics. When the song concludes, there is a rather interesting on-the-nose translation of Shakespeare's gravedigger scene between the men and Haider, but it is the 'So Jao' gravedigger number that dazzles, even if as a guilty pleasure in this *karunic* (my word) environment.

From this point on, the tragedy escalates apace. Haider, hiding in the dark house adjacent to the graveyard, spots Arshia's funeral procession, and he and her brother Liyaqat fight, resulting in the latter's death. Khurram and his militia arrive, coming at the house armed to the teeth with machine guns, grenades and a rocket launcher. The full-scale battle that erupts in the snowy graveyard is shot in a stylistic combination of a 1980s Hollywood action movie and a shoot-out in a classic Western: quick cutting between jerky hand-held shots of individual fighters, intermittent slow-motion shots to dramatize action and gore, high-angle extreme long shots over the bloody, body-strewn graveyard, and occasional silent pauses to ratchet up the tension. When the scene abruptly shifts to a quiet shot of the back of a white SUV stopping on a road, we are startled to see Roohdaar and Ghazala in the vehicle. Wearing a red hijab, a long black wrap, and no make-up, she looks in the depths of despair as she exits the SUV and walks silently up to Khurram directly after he has launched a rocket into the now-collapsed and smouldering house where Haider remains. Khurram begrudgingly grants her a chance to bring Haider around, so she enters the half-incinerated, gloomy house as her bloody son stumbles down the stairs to meet her and they clasp on to each other for dear life. Needless to say, this is the most heart-breaking, pathos-inducing moment in the film, intensified by the dark shadows surrounding them and the flashes of deep scarlet in his blood and her hijab, captured so poignantly by a shot/reverse-shot series of hand-held extreme close-ups, each shot containing both heads so we sense their intimacy as we feel their grief. There is no music on the soundtrack as they exchange their final words; the silence between the dialogue augments the despondence. As Haider tells her of his drive for vengeance, a tearful Ghazala expresses what we know to be true: 'Revenge begets revenge. Revenge does not set us free.' As Haider still refuses to surrender, Ghazala walks slowly out of the dark house into the grey, snowy graveyard, stopping at its edge, just in front of Khurram and what is left of his soldiers. Music creeps back into the scene here in deep, weeping cello notes, as Ghazala, in super-slow motion, calmly throws off her long black wrap in a medium long shot from behind her. Diegetic sound has disappeared as there is a cut to a high-angle long shot above her, showing the soldiers turning to run from her in slow motion, then a shot of Khurram yelling and running towards her. The music is now moving in a quick pattern of three ascending notes repeating over and over, building the suspense as we finally see the source of the response: Ghazala is wearing a suicide vest containing eight grenades and her hand is on the pull trigger. The close-up on the vest moves up her body into a bird's-eye crane shot looking down on her as she raises her head to gaze at the grey sky as if in silent prayer, the camera mimicking the movement of a soul rising after death. A high-pitched violin note is sustained as she pulls the trigger in an extreme close-up on her hand, which still bears the red circle of her wedding paint. In a moment, it is over. Diegetic sound returns, cruelly, with the tinkling sounds of the pins leaving the grenades and the massive explosion. Chaotic hand-held shots show Haider stumbling through the black smoke towards a pile of dark grey ashes and body parts, crying 'Mother!' When Haider spots Khurram crawling on the ground, his legs having been blown off below the knee, Haider lurches towards his uncle with a crazed look. As he hovers over Khurram holding a pistol to his uncle's head, the camera captures him in a series of chaotic,

jerky canted-angle close-ups, which move between him and Khurram's blackened face; Haider hears his father's voice in his head telling him to avenge Hilaal's murder, and then his mother's voice layered on top of that saying that 'freedom lies beyond revenge'. This cacophony is accompanied by the same three quickly ascending violin notes in a loop, rising in volume with the tension. This is the most melodramatic moment in an unapologetic melodrama, and, in my opinion, Bhardwaj has earned it. Haider suddenly throws the gun away, cueing the abrupt cessation of the ascending notes, leaving one quietly sustained high pitch. Haider rises and limps off, crazed and blood-stained, moving away from the graveyard as his uncle begs for a mercy killing. The final shot of the film is a high-angle extreme long shot revealing the chilling carnage of the scene: broken, bloody bodies strewn everywhere, smoke and fire, a true hellscape. This image strikingly reflects the gods of Yama, Rudra and Agni, and the overwhelming grief and loss of the *karuna rasa* is palpable. Haider passes through the gate and back into the world as the screen fades to black. Hamlet lives to die another day.

Outside the diegetic world, Bhardwaj ends the film with white titles on black screens announcing that there is now 'relative peace' in Kashmir and that the Indian Army saved thousands of civilian lives there during the disastrous floods in 2014, but a melancholy song sung by a plaintive female voice haunts us in the soundtrack, intensifying the feelings of grief and sorrow even as we are told that there is hope. Savouring this mix of sorrow and pleasure is at the core of *rasa* theory; we experience the pure pathos of the *rasa* while taking joy in the aural and visual artistry of the film (and, for Shakespearians, taking delight in the departures from and translations of our beloved *Hamlet*). This article has attempted to demonstrate that the most significant concept in Indian aesthetics, *rasa* theory, can be a fruitful and revelatory tool for analysing cinematic texts. Bhardwaj's *Haider* provides a lucid and stimulating illustration of this as it compellingly evokes empathy and introspection through *rasas*, in true paradoxical fashion. As for the message of the film, tragically, violence in Kashmir continues on all sides of the conflict. A *New York Times* article in late 2016 declared that Kashmir was 'paralyzed by an "adored" band of militants',[43] and so the tragedy continues, but now it also affects those of us who have been moved by our experience of the *karuna rasa* through Bhardwaj's film to care about the people who call that beautiful, violence-plagued valley of Kashmir home.

---

[43] Geeta Anand and Hari Kumar, 'Kashmir is paralyzed by an "adored" band of militants', 14 November 2016, www .nytimes.com/2016/11/15/world/asia/kashmir-india-pakistan-militants.html.

# FAILURE TO THRIVE

## ELIZABETH MAZZOLA

The baby 'puts one and one together and begins to see that the answer is one, and not two'.

(D. W. Winnicott, *Collected Papers*[1])

There are good breasts and bad ones, Melanie Klein proposes: mothers who nourish and mothers who thwart their offspring – those who hear a child's cries and respond accordingly, and those who prompt cries, or punish them and walk away.[2] Shakespeare takes pains to describe mothers of both stripes on his stage, setting the gentle but helpless figures of Lady Macduff and Hermione against Lady Macbeth and Volumnia, fierce women steeped in blood.[3] Some mothers want to see their children grow and flourish, but alongside them the playwright places mothers who appear instead to wish their children ill. More ambiguously, less brutally, some mothers on Shakespeare's stage simply let their children go. Lear's desire for his daughter's nursery thus pushes him in harm's way, given how the infant is only tentatively embraced by his mother in so many of Shakespeare's plays.

Part of this article seeks to uncover the likenesses between the very different kinds of mothers depicted on Shakespeare's stage. If intimacy can be cruel, cruelty is usually intimate, and so perhaps the radiant Hermione's warmth in *The Winter's Tale* is just as punishing as the violence Lady Macbeth promises she would visit upon the imagined child in her arms (1.7.54–8): although we are told that, after her son Mamillius dies, he is buried in the very same tomb with the mother who collapses upon hearing of his sudden death (3.2.145, 195), Hermione's miraculous resurrection sixteen years later leaves Mamillius in the dust,

[1] D. W. Winnicott, 'Transitional objects and transitional phenomena', *International Journal of Psychoanalysis* 34 (1953), 89–97; repr. in *Collected Papers: From Paediatrics to Psychoanalysis* (London, 2000), p. 268.

[2] Melanie Klein, *The Psycho-analysis of Children*, trans. Alix Strachey (London, 2011), p. 206.

[3] In a discussion of nineteenth-century British literature, Josephine McDonagh argues that it is around these two kinds of figures – the mother, 'the inculcator of civil values', and her opposite, the 'barbaric infanticidal woman' – that 'visions of social life revolve'. See 'Infanticidal mothers and dead babies: women's voices on political economy and population', *Barcelona English Language and Literature Studies* 7 (1996), 11–20; p. 12. Early modern representations of mothers and maidens are just as equivocal, however. For a treatment of Shakespeare's Ophelia as fair maiden and aborting mother, see Erik Bruun, '"As your daughter may conceive": a note on the fair Ophelia', *Hamlet Studies* 15.1–2 (1993), 93–9. Bruun argues that many of the herbs and flowers Ophelia mentions in the speech before she drowns herself could bring on miscarriages and were well-known abortifacients. For a related discussion of Ophelia's flowers, as well as the claim that her grief at Polonius's death may also stem from mourning for the child she's been forced to abort, see Robert Parker and Brian Painter, 'Ophelia's flowers again', *Notes & Queries* 41.1 (1994), 42–3. As Parker and Painter point out, the referent of Ophelia's song is unclear: 'He is dead and gone, lady; / He is dead and gone; / At his head a grass-green turf / At his heels a stone" (4.2.28–31). For more details about child death and Shakespeare, see also Stephanie Chamberlain, 'Fantasizing infanticide: Lady Macbeth and the murdering mother in early modern England', *College Literature* 32.3 (2005), 72–91. That the dangerous mother is a myth promulgated by early modern writers as a way to conceal the violence patriarchy wreaks on families in general and women in particular is investigated by Frances Dolan in *Dangerous Familiars: Representations of Domestic Crime in England 1550–1700* (Ithaca, 1994): see 159–70 for specific reference to *The Winter's Tale*. Along similar lines, one might also recall that, while Solomon and Abraham are prepared to murder children in the Hebrew Bible, the Hebrew midwives are depicted as routinely saving babies from death.

his return unbidden by the magic that recalls his mother to life and to their family. Lady Macbeth's invented child remains unhurt, in contrast, not dead or even merely forgotten, because he has never been born.[4]

Perhaps good breasts and bad breasts are harder to differentiate than Klein proposes, something I explore below. But another part of this article analyses the variety of attributes of the children who are loved or cast aside by Shakespeare's mothers. I am especially interested in the cherished children uneasily attached to Lady Macbeth and Hermione. On the surface, at least, the differences between these children are hard to discern, and their standing – their importance as heirs, their relation to their fathers, the array of deep feelings they inspire in their mothers – equally unclear. Uncertainty about the future or one's duty or one's status can take a roughly human form in the shape of the child in one's arms, a shape that is anxious, yielding, tenacious, clawing. The result is that – just as there are good breasts and bad ones, caring mothers and cold ones – there are worthy objects of maternal care and unworthy ones in Shakespeare's stories: children who come into being or learn to belong, and other ones – unsightly, grotesque or somehow malformed – who don't belong, who refuse the process or are repudiated by it.[5]

Four theories about maternal feelings drive this discussion. The first comes from anthropologist Nancy Scheper-Hughes, whose study of infant mortality in rural Brazil discovered a region where great emotion maxes out, leaving children to die and mothers to grieve. Even in less reduced settings, however, the nursery's contests over restricted resources of affection, attention, time and food often involve 'small wars' which alter landscapes and uproot families.[6] Still, violence there is not as common as desertion or attrition or, on the part of the infant, some more subtle failure to thrive. This insight is underscored by the work of contemporary philosophers and neuroscientists, although they might have us think about what Scheper-Hughes calls this 'political economy of emotions' in a different way. Arguing that emotions are 'genetically hard-

wired, reflex-like responses', Joseph LeDoux, for instance, describes emotion as 'subserved by neural circuits in the brain', a model which roots feeling alongside thought but also reminds us of a necessary limit on how many neurons are fired, whether a small war is being waged or a big one. Viewing feeling as unfolding along nerves and cells and prompted by assorted stimuli, such claims imagine a ceiling on whatever emotions can be stirred in someone or stimulated in another – a fixed number of impulses that can be mixed, repressed or unleashed. What this also means is that, if reason must be calculating, it is not always cold; warmth can flood, but it too must be measured. Scheper-Hughes's and LeDoux's frameworks for analysing maternal care are important to, but also modified by, the insights of poets and playwrights who explore the sad fact that feelings generated between two people don't always match up, even in the nursery. Certainly, the bond between children

---

[4] All references to Shakespeare's plays are to the Norton edition, prepared by Stephen Greenblatt, Walter Cohen, Jean E. Howard, Katharine Eisaman Maus, Gordon McMullan and Suzanne Gossett (New York, 2015).

[5] The subject is clearly taboo even in Bakhtin's picture of the carnival in *Rabelais and his World*. Except for miscarriage and abortion, which 'challenge and modify [his] cyclical theory of the body', '[a]ll other in-and-outpourings are celebrated as testaments to the corporeal openness by which the body transgresses the boundaries between itself and the world'. See Sally Minogue and Andrew Palmer, "Confronting the abject: women and dead babies in modern English fiction', *Journal of Modern Literature* 29.3 (2008), 103–25; pp. 105, 103.

[6] In 'A genealogy of genocide', Nancy Scheper-Hughes examines the ways contemporary societies regularly carry out relatively peaceful assaults on their weakest and most vulnerable members – especially the sick, aged and dying – making use of careful decision-making and elaborate institutions such as the nursing home and other places of dedicated neglect to put certain people out of the way: *Modern Psychoanalysis* 28.2 (2003), 167–97. Scheper-Hughes's discussion of the political economy of emotions at work in the ways we delegate care and outsource attention is richly developed in an earlier study of infant mortality, *Death Without Weeping: The Violence of Everyday Life* (California, 1989), as well as in 'Life boat ethics', in *Gender in Cross-Cultural Perspective*, ed. Caroline Brettell and Carolyn Sargent (Englewood Cliffs, NJ, 1993), pp. 31–7.

and their caregivers is inevitably a lopsided one, proximity mostly exposing how much is given, how little is shared.[7] With these three approaches in mind, we might better understand why references to the much-loved Mamillius's weakening health are scant in *The Winter's Tale*, as well as the reasons why his death occurs offstage, and his burial place is located offsite. The status of the child to whom Lady Macbeth has given suck, we might remember, is even more famously shadowy.[8] Yet Shakespeare cares a great deal about the indifference shown to these children, and he takes pains to offer an additional explanation for it, this one revolving around their appearance or behaviour, how they stand or see things or what they say, whether they cling to mothers or avoid them, seek their love or refuse to budge. So the fourth principle is that the nursery is a literary setting in which children actively participate in relationships with their caregivers.

Of course, all children deserve a chance at life, and so it shouldn't matter how overlooked or cruelly neglected children differ from ones who are loved and kept alive. But storytellers like Shakespeare sometimes tip the balance in one way or another. In his assorted pictures of children as dolls (see *Macbeth*, 3.4.103) or 'a changeling' rolled up in a blanket (*The Winter's Tale*, 3.3.109), as hungry mouths or still forms, we are invited to separate a 'very pretty bairn' (*The Winter's Tale*, 3.3.68) from a 'birth-strangled babe' (*Macbeth*, 4.1.130), the child easy to love deliberately put next to the one easier to shun. But the presence of so many unlovely examples on Shakespeare's stage also makes us wonder exactly where nature ends and culture begins – in the baby's smile, or in the mother's? And what makes the nursery such a charged and dangerous place, where attachments are firmly established or sometimes fatally broken?

\*\*\*

Judging himself a 'rogue and peasant slave', unformed and accordingly unloved (*Hamlet*, 2.2.527), an unhappy prince proceeds to make analogous ontological distinctions about other characters in Shakespeare's *Hamlet*, regularly

[7] Ruth Leys finds fault with what she calls neuroscientist Joseph LeDoux's 'Basic Emotions Paradigm', but his model has found its way into a variety of contemporary views on the biological underpinnings of interior life, perhaps in concert with the increasing medicalization of people at every stage of their lives. See Joseph LeDoux, *The Emotional Brain: The Mysterious Underpinnings of Emotional Life* (New York, 1996), esp. p. 438; and Leys, 'The turn to affect: a critique', *Critical Inquiry* 37 (2007), 434–72. For a more recent and specific consideration of the biology behind maternal feeling, see Pam Belluck, 'Pregnancy changes the brain in ways that may help mothering', which reports that scientists at The Institute of Human Development have uncovered how hormone surges in pregnancy cause '"pruning" which streamline[s] certain brain areas to be more efficient at mothering skills': www.nytimes.com/2016/12/19/health/pregnancy-brain-change.html?. According to this research, grey matter loss registered in brain scans of women who had given birth might 'represent a beneficial process of maturation or specialization', as well as indicate hormonal or neurological differences that illustrate biological rather than cultural definitions of motherhood. Scheper-Hughes's investigations of impoverished mothers encourage us to wonder, however, whether any 'pruning' depicted in the brain scans of these women might illustrate changes 'beneficial' to *other* children under the mother's care.

Many literary writers play with such pruning, but they also can have a wider view of attachment, too. In *Romantic Intimacy* (Stanford, 2013), Nancy Yousef explores Wordsworth's poems depicting encounters with beggars, in which, she argues, '"intimacy" crystallizes a tension between sharing and enclosing as opposed imaginations of relational possibilities' (1). We might add Wordsworth's Lucy poems to Yousef's explorations of encounters with unlovable strangers. Still, the ways that British women writers at this same time imagined the household and its parent–child relationships tend to be more direct about the imbalances involved, even when the ties are more tender and loving or more obviously eroticized. Consider Mary Shelley's Victor Frankenstein's monstrous offspring, or Charlotte Bronte's Bertha Mason, lodged in the same household as Rochester's beloved Jane Eyre. If Bertha is a figure for Jane's unruly desires, she is also a drag on Rochester's abilities to satisfy them. Such examples help persuade us of McDonagh's conclusion that motherhood's 'positioning' as a metaphor for cultural reproduction needs 'resisting and unpacking' (17).

[8] An important part of Scheper-Hughes's 1989 agenda is analysing Western assumptions about 'universal' maternal feelings, as articulated by Sara Ruddick, *Maternal Thinking: Towards a Politics of Peace* (Boston, MA, 1995), and Nancy Chodorow, *The Reproduction of Mothering: Psychoanalysis and the Sociology of Gender* (Berkeley, 1999), pp. 401–3, 408.

indicting the fleshy, patchy or unredeemed as sub-standard, criminal or false. The shabby Claudius is nothing like the Herculean figure of his father, for instance (3.4.52–70), and Hamlet's mother Gertrude's body is similarly marked by "eyes without feeling / feeling without sight, / Ears without hands or eyes" (3.4.78–80). Such ill-formed beings are rejected as defective, lewd and beastly, not even good enough to think with;[9] but Hamlet's disparagement of his mother is also a way to explain the reasons for his self-doubt and rationalize the possibility of his non-being, for if Gertrude's marriage to Claudius erases Hamlet's father, it also cancels the deformed child they had together.

Yet the disgust such ambiguous figures elicit (even in themselves) is merely one of several points on a wide spectrum of feelings sparked by the baby who requires ongoing care, a complicated collection of emotions which must be provoked and then sorted in order for newborn creatures to anchor themselves in the world. Whether the spectrum's furthest reaches are marked by homicidal rage or cool neglect seems unclear in Shakespeare's plays, however, and it is equally unclear whether the more familiar regions of tenderness or solicitude, or merely benign interest – like the curiosity which encourages a shepherd to unwrap the abandoned baby Perdita, bundled like a Christmas present in *The Winter's Tale*, 3.3.67 (this bundle is 'pretty' like a present, too, betraying no signs of cold or hunger, making no demands on the recipient) – begins in love, laughter or some grudging acknowledgement of likeness or pained want.[10] The castaway Perdita, whose status as lost thing is fixed by her name, is a curious exception to the rules which typically spell out how a child's survival is grounded in attachment and safety, guaranteed by a snug place in the home.[11] Instead, Perdita's singularity, beauty, isolation and detachment are repeatedly linked as a way to ennoble and rescue her and divide her from the nursery. Perdita's story also suggests that feelings about babies need to find safe harbour in the world outside the home, that a mother's love must be part of the larger world to really make a difference, and that maternal feelings belong to a realm organized by many cares but still limited in its resources – the nursery's borders therefore permeable, changing and always political.

Uncertainties about available resources and competing attachments assert themselves almost immediately in *The Winter's Tale*, when Leontes, unable to persuade his boyhood friend Polixenes to prolong his visit to Sicilia, asks his wife Hermione to try her luck, and she is quickly able to extract

---

In their eco-critical reading 'Filicide in Euripedes' *Medea*: a biopoetic approach', Maria Mackay and Arlene Allen investigate how the wicked mother's slaughter of her sons with Jason makes evolutionary sense, given the ways a new husband might prefer his own children with Medea anyway – she's still thinking like a mother when she murders her sons, just not like a mother of these two particular boys: *Helios* 41.1 (2014), 59–86. Indeed, being kind with cruelty, pulling the weak out of the way of the strong or favoured, might align the mother's instincts with those of nature (74).

[9] I refashion here Levi-Strauss's claim that animals serve as things good to eat as well as 'good to think with', but also draw on Julia Lupton's discussion of Caliban in 'Creature Caliban' in *Shakespeare Quarterly* 51.1 (2000), 1–23. Insisting on this character's humanity, Lupton argues that 'Caliban's creatureliness may also *exceed* the increasingly troubled solutions of secular humanism in its historicist variants, pointing to a new universalism defined by a cosmopolitical community of differences rather than by an exclusive set of national markers' (4).

[10] See a recent account of a child abuse case in Oklahoma, where the murdered child 'looked like a skeleton' (13 Dec. 2016, Crimesider Staff / *CBS News*), or Adrienne Rich's opening to *Of Woman Born,* which discloses an equally wrenching story of a woman who murdered several of her children. Alongside this brief account, Rich includes one of her own journal entries, in which she raises the question: 'How shall I learn to absorb the violence and make explicit only the caring?' See *Of Woman Born: Motherhood as Experience and Institution* (New York, 1976), pp. 24, 22. The desperate straits of parents in all of these cases seem strangely established by the violence they (would) enact on their offspring: the children are represented both as victims and as sources of stress, problems that need to be solved and another injury to a parent already overburdened.

[11] Dolan reminds us about the shepherd's assertion that the abandoned Perdita is the unwanted child of a poor gentlewoman (*Dangerous Familiars*, p. 159) and nicely comments on the continued references to the baby as 'lost', rather than as the target of violence and object of deliberate neglect by members of the Sicilian court (167).

Polixenes's agreement to stay. Describing her success here, the Queen likens the happy outcome to the good fortune of her betrothal, stating that 'I have spoken to th' purpose twice. / The one for ever earned a royal husband; / Th' other, for some while a friend' (1.2.107–9). Other people become prizes in this discursive system, tools of will, appendages that indicate one's strength or skill, and saying or extracting 'yes' become the same thing in Hermione's hands, a view that conflates a supplicant with a benefactor and renders granting a wish the same as expressing one. But we are already aware that the Sicilian economy is a fragile one when we overhear the servants of Leontes and Polixenes trading compliments at the very start of the play. Acknowledging Bohemia's gratitude for Sicilian hospitality, Polixenes's servant Archidamus tells Camillo that when the Sicilian court returns the visit, Leontes and his royal entourage will be offered 'sleepy drinks' in order to mask the defects of Bohemian courtesies; these drinks, Archidamus claims, will keep his guests' senses 'unintelligent of our insufficience' (1.1.12–13). The relationship between intimates is pictured here as something that relies on drugs, silence, cheating and unconsciousness, their tie also prolonging this debilitated state. If infants are likewise vulnerable to the narcotic charms of the mothers who nurse them, the people in Archidamus's care, he wryly comments, 'though they cannot praise us, as little accuse us' (1.1.13–14). What makes things grow in this landscape ironically causes them to stumble, and the nursery's pleasures are rewritten as toxic when indifference or insufficiency can stand for watery love.

The reference to sleepy drinks is only the first of many challenges to Hermione's mothering in *The Winter's Tale*. In his rage at her success with his friend, Leontes mutters he is glad Hermione hasn't nursed Mamillius (2.1.58), the soporifics supplied to unwitting guests withheld from a royal heir. Moreover, in her few scenes with the boy, Hermione deliberately measures her time with Mamillius, telling her attendants to remove him at the start of Act 2, Scene 1: 'Take the boy to you', she explains: 'he so troubles me' (2.1.1–2). She quickly returns to her child, but in the meantime we see him carefully distinguishing between mother-substitutes, indicating a knowledge of 'blue noses' and 'black brows' (2.1.9–16) and showing that he's not only expert at evaluating replacements for his mother but also, like Hamlet, skilled in ranking their shortcomings. Hermione is just as discriminating. As we observe in her dealings with her husband and his friend, Hermione's affections are designed to be won or earned, carefully apportioned rather than lavished freely. Later in this brief scene, Mamillius will tell his mother a story rather than beg one from her, additional evidence that he's the one from whom things are extracted rather than the other way around. Rarely is the tender, gracious Hermione presented as generously bestowing things – more often she is collecting them. And, each time, the connection is petitioned for, the deserving performed, the return perfunctory: you are either my 'prisoner' or my 'guest', as Hermione informs Polixenes (1.2.53–4).

The baby daughter to whom Hermione gives birth in prison after Leontes's jealous accusations of adultery appears unmarked by such rules organizing attachment, however, and this is what spares Perdita from her father's wrath. Hermione's attendant Paulina explains the logic to the jailer guarding the Queen when Paulina initially applies for the baby's release: 'You need not fear it, sir', Paulina explains:

> This child was prisoner to the womb, and is
> By law and process of great nature thence
> Freed and enfranchised, not a party to
> The anger of the King, nor guilty of –
> If any be – the trespass of the Queen.
>
> (2.2.62–6)

Paulina hopes to guarantee the baby's safety through summoning the jailer's sense of justice, or taking for granted her parents' indifference, helping the baby escape its home, a prison where birth only means doom. But she is also pointing to a cognitive process a child must pass through in order to survive, be loved, or perhaps be merely seen, something particularly important in two of Shakespeare's plays – *Macbeth* is the other example –

where babies are briefly tended but also not breast-fed.

What Paulina's speech illustrates is the way it is not breast milk or 'sleepy drinks' but careful argument and ritual display which establish a child's place in the family. After persuading the jailer to release Perdita to her, Paulina returns to court where she asks Leontes to entertain the idea of a resemblance between him and the silent infant she puts in front of him (the Latin *in-fant* means 'not' 'speaking'), pointing out his own indelible features in the newborn daughter he has refused to hold. Placed on the ground, the child does not move or cry; it not only elicits no warmth but also summons no attention or commentary. Partly this is because Paulina forbids anyone else to pick the baby up: 'For ever / Unvenerable be thy hands if thou / Tak'st up the princess by that forced baseness / Which he has put upon't!' (2.3.77–80), she says – anyone else's care in this case damaging, if the child has not yet been officially claimed and redeemed from 'baseness' by its father. Yet establishing a tie is also complicated by the need for correct timing, obtaining the listener's ear, detecting some openness to review the claim, as well as the downgrading of rival ties. The psychoanalyst D. W. Winnicott's calculations about the way the child absorbs the mother's abundant love also preclude too many people from coming together in the nursery, and we see the same curtailing of affection when the ladies surrounding Mamillius tease him with mention of his sibling's impending birth. This restriction is enacted again when Perdita's relationship with her mother is suppressed by Paulina in order that a tie with Leontes can be achieved. The newborn's link to a mother accused of adultery would endanger it, so linking it to the father instead is a way to verify the child's ambiguous humanity and spare the 'bastard' or 'brat' from a rash consignment to the trash.

The first thing Paulina does in this scene is get Leontes to look. 'It is yours', Paulina insists:

And, might we lay th' old proverb to your charge,
So like you, 'tis the worse. Behold, my lords,
Although the print be little, the whole matter

And copy of the father: eye, nose, lip,
the trick of's frown, his forehead, nay, the valley,
The pretty dimples of his chin and cheek,
his smiles, The very mould and frame of hand, nail,
  finger.

(2.3.97–103)

The King here is reduced to a collection of tiny features, an array of small body parts that make him less a father than another version of the baby, and both of them relatively equal in their incapacities – parent and child fashioned from a limited stock of possibilities and 'humbled to meaner forms' rather than 'reared to worship', the way Leontes prefers to elevate subjects like the loyal servant Camillo (1.2.316). Although the superficial resemblance is supposed to be a guide to and sign of a deeper tie, it leaves little else to imagine. The relationship between parents and children is chiefly rhetorical, in other words. It not only begins with a persuasive act but consists of many more. Caliban, as Julia Reinhard Lupton observes, is denied such sympathy in *The Tempest* and thus remains stuck, his development arrested; but, unlike the imagined infant in Lady Macbeth's arms, Caliban is not easily negated.[12] Caught between animality and human glory, occupying the grey area between an alien being and a son, he is neither kin nor kind, able to groan and curse but not to love or smile. Perdita's fate is happier. She will replace a missing sheep in the pastoral place she comes to inhabit and then assumes the role of a rural shepherdess in Bohemia. If a Sicilian future has been saved by her banishment, it has also been pushed away, the work of reproduction rewarded but also relocated

---

[12] Lupton comments on the way the term 'creature' implies an always-unfinished state, the possibility of metamorphosis ongoing, 'its tense forever imperfect' ('Creature Caliban', p. 1). In some cases, this state of continued unfolding goes the other way or becomes suspended, however, and results in the non-being which seems to characterize Caliban's existence. As Lupton explains, the term 'marks the radical separation of creation and Creator. This separation can in turn articulate any number of cuts or divisions: between world and God; between all living things and those that are inert, inanimate, or elemental; between human beings and "the other creatures" over which they have been given rule' (see 1–3).

elsewhere.[13] Perdita's humanity itself is attested by her plasticity and capacity to take root on her own, even in forbidding settings, the *rebirth* associated with spring offering the child a more fruitful network of associations and emotions than the bare facts surrounding her birth.

\*\*\*

Like clay which no one presses into matter, Caliban in contrast will persist in a failed state. It's curious, though, how his lumpen form is ascribed in *The Tempest* to his deformed spirit, rather than to Prospero's cruelty or neglect or lacklustre parenting skills. Shakespeare frequently absolves parents of their links to failed children. In *As You Like It*, for instance, Oliver's cruelty is self-begotten, even if his brother Orlando's innate nobility is passed down from a loving father. Lear's disinheritance of his ungrateful daughters is similarly explained to us by a servant who blandly observes that all women turn to monsters (3.7.106). It becomes the children's fault if they dry up and die or, like Caliban, curse their fates. Even Mamillius is presented as withering apart from his mother, and taken from us without our noticing. Using Sicilian accounting methods, the boy apparently puts one and one together and concludes, along with Winnicott, 'that the answer is one'. Mamillius then goes quiet and disappears, as if to correct a surplus and undo the process that gave him life and ensured his footing. He appears dejected rather than rejected, and de-forms himself rather than grows up:

> He straight declined, dropped, took it deeply,
> Fastened and fixed the shame on't himself,
> Threw off his spirit, his appetite, his sleep,
> And downright languished.
>
> (2.3.14–17)

Next to a new baby, a rival mass, Mamillius lets go, willing himself out of being in his solitude, fear, self-interest and love.

In her 1989 study *Death Without Weeping*, Scheper-Hughes explored the unusually high rates of infant mortality in rural Brazil – where statistics reveal infant deaths cancelling out nearly 40 per cent of all births – and uncovers a similar explanatory apparatus for the loss of young children and set of feelings behind it. Investigating the nature of maternal love and child death over a twenty-year period, Scheper-Hughes considers the chances for a child's staying alive as hedged by the 'everyday violence' of 'chronic scarcity and loss', where hunger and doubt regularly reshape the outlines of a 'small and tormented human community' (14–15), pushing some children away to die and sparing others. What are the effects of such violence on 'the ability to love', and what are the reasons behind this calculus of attachment and sacrifice, Scheper-Hughes asks. She goes on to explain how some children's failure to grow, to eat or drink, their inability to walk or meet the gaze of another, is construed by their mothers as a preference to die. Afflicted by *doenca de crianca* ('doomed child syndrome') or *fraqueza* ('wasting'), the sickly children are called ghost babies, stunted by hunger and therefore judged to be unearthly beings who didn't want to be born, angels who more properly belong in heaven, displaced creatures who have no business – and therefore no traction – on earth. This conclusion about wrongful life and inevitable death is drawn by the mothers themselves, not by the anthropologist, although, as Scheper-Hughes also illustrates, the apprehension that a child doesn't want to live is often exactly

---

[13] See Lee Edelman's refusal of the future typically embodied by literary representations of a child in *No Future: Queer Theory and the Death Drive* (Durham, 2004). I thank my colleague Vaclav Paris for this reference, as well as for the reference to Sebastião Salgado's disturbing photographs of children in rural Brazil. Also see Anca Parvulescu, 'Reproduction and queer theory: between Lee Edelman's *No Future* and J. H. Coetzee's *Slow Man*', *PMLA* 132,1 (2017), 86–100. Parvulescu wisely reminds us that the regular work of reproduction involves both men and women in ways other than child-bearing and child-rearing, and cites Scheper-Hughes's most recent work on the global trafficking of human organs as an example. For a useful reading of Lady Macbeth's rejection of a reproductive body for the hard body of the witch, see Diane Purkiss, "Body crimes: the witches, Lady Macbeth and the relics', in *Female Transgression in Early Modern Britain: Literary and Historical Explorations*, ed. Richard Hillman and Pauline Ruberry-Blanc (London, 2014), pp. 29–50.

what consigns him or her to a short and painful life. Its gums ripped from her nipple, Lady Macbeth's murdered baby is also starving, we might recall. David Daube writes eloquently that the wish never to have been born is 'more sophisticated' and 'more radical' than the wish for suicide because it 'involve[s] a good deal of reflection on the past and some even on the phenomenon of being', and the recurrent deaths of the tiny beings Scheper-Hughes tells us about provide a stark and wrenching example, the youngest members of society offering its most searing indictment, their innocence of the world a hard-won experience.[14]

The feelings of repulsion or indifference mothers feel towards a doomed baby are thus prompted by the feelings of rejection or disinterest which the child himself seems to evince, the display the child makes of his own lack of investment in the pointless project of staying alive. What causes these babies to be morose and unresponsive and cut off from their families also appears to render them inhuman – not only a bad investment of scarce resources but also a trap, a dangerous diversion of already struggling love and time and hope. Such children are poisonous to households as well as to themselves: what gives them life makes them sick, and what pushes them into the world pulls them back out. Equally tragic is the way their loss leaves their families intact.

The examples with which Scheper-Hughes supplies us shatter the model of 'reproductive futurism' recently challenged by queer theorist Lee Edelman, who resists the idea of the redemptive possibility revolving around the figure of the child.[15] Such examples also explode whatever cherished ideas we hold about the security of the nursery and limitless warmth assumed to be safely confined within. But Scheper-Hughes's extraordinarily detailed investigation of these doomed children and the families who bury them takes care not to blame mothers for failing to care for, or even to seem to want, such children. These mothers' motives are calculating, but not cold or heartless[16] as the anthropologist explains, her reluctance to pass judgment coming from respect for her subjects and witnessing of the severity of their

impoverished state, living day to day in a place where work can't be found, hunger rages and medical help is faraway, deficient and expensive. The future is bleak for those who manage to grow up in a world of regular terrors and tiny coffins, and so the doomed child's reasons make sense to everyone else in the difficult world they share. It would likewise be wrong to think the child is unloved or unwanted or a victim of abuse, as Scheper-Hughes also emphasizes. A 'selective neglect', we learn, 'is not motivated by anger, hate, or aggression toward the small baby'.[17] Instead, a careful attention is at work, both parent and child negotiating the steps that pull towards life or death. Salgado's haunting image of one such doomed child (Figure 22) shows us a seemingly contented baby, comfortably nestled among flowers, his crib a cozy coffin, his eyes jewels that sparkle and blankly stare.[18] The child is beautiful, and it's hard to look away. But his gaze is also a refusal. As Scheper-Hughes explains, the child has fallen off the standard track marked by milestones such as gaining weight or smiling, sitting up or standing, sucking or lifting one's head, grabbing for a finger, and therefore fails to receive the associated affections rewarded for meeting these developmental goals. Lupton's account of

---

[14] For another perspective on the reflections of such doomed beings, see David Daube, 'Black hole', *Rechtshistorisches Journal* (1983), 177–93 (p. 177). Daube's work is cited by Scheper-Hughes, *Death Without Weeping*.

[15] See Parvulescu, 'Reproduction and queer theory', p. 86.

[16] My phrasing here is inspired by Deborah Nelson's 2017 paper 'In defense of coldness', presented at the The City College of New York's 28 April 2017 Rifkind Center's Interdisciplinary Forum on 'Emotional Politics', organized by Mikhal Dekel and Andreas Killen. In *Tough Enough: Arbus, Arendt, Didion, McCarthy, Sontag, Weil* (Chicago, 2017), Nelson elaborates her account of the unsentimentality in the works of contemporary women writers, particularly their refusal of the feelings which anaesthetize, provide false comfort, or pretend to supply watery relief.

[17] Scheper-Hughes, *Death Without Weeping*, p. 315.

[18] For a helpful overview of Salgado's work and range of concerns, see 'The salt of the earth: Sebastião Salgado's own way of seeing. That's how the light gets in', https: gerryco23 .wordpress.com/2015/08/01/the-salt-of-the-earth-sebastiao-salgados-own-way-of-seeing.

22 Sebastião Salgado's image of a child, from *Other Americas* (1986). © Sebastião Salgado / Contact Press Images, courtesy of the artist.

the creature Caliban's inchoate state makes use of a similar set of signs, the mechanisms for belonging to the world relying on a perceived desire to belong, a wish for reciprocity, a desire that's easily registered by another body.[19] Traversing the gap between doomed creatures and viable ones in order to leave behind permanently what Scheper-Hughes calls a 'precarious ontological status' (366–7) requires acquiring the tools for having a future, including being able to give love or express hate, as well as knowing the difference between the two. Failing to satisfy these tests, 'ghost babies' seem to fail at being human.

The quivering thing at the heart of David Lynch's 1977 film *Eraserhead* (replayed in the 1980 *Elephant Man*, where the fleshy mass has the heart of Romeo and tragic soul of Hamlet) is also the curse which pollutes Thebes in *Oedipus Rex*, the miscarried child condemned to live, his survival dooming him and the rest of his world. This mass also describes the rotting brother's corpse in *Antigone*, strung between two worlds, baggage that remains deadly for those who say they love him, such that Polyneices's sister is executed for acknowledging him and curses those who, in

contrast, can sever their ties. Other lives pile up behind Oedipus and Polyneices: unable to gain a legitimate foothold among the living, these 'wrongful' lives block the passage for other beings. Yet, as Daube also reminds us, Oedipus doesn't want to die so much as discover the conditions of his birth, as if that could remedy them.[20] Many other stories revolve around the premise of a grotesque figure doomed primarily by being born. Such a tainted object is doubled in *Medea*, where the mother takes care to dispose of two sons, cutting her ties with her adulterous husband but also making room for a more vital set of connections should she be able to marry and mother again. These ill-fated or misbegotten children come to stand for reasons for loving or hating in the worlds we occupy, even if they also take the brunt of our decisions; they serve as signs of our ability to throw

---

[19] An interesting analogue is offered by Nancy L. Segal and Satoshi Zanakawa, 'Does breast milk have a sex bias?' in the New York Times: www.nytimes.com/2017/01/21/opinion/sunday/does-breast-milk-have-a-sex-bias.html.

[20] For a related discussion, see David Daube, 'Dividing a child in antiquity', *California Law Review* 54 (1966), 1630–7.

off an 'unusable' future or, conversely, to put ourselves inside a world able to manage on its own.[21]

Sometimes, we know that these tainted things might love or live and grow, but feel that their human worth is unclear. The mother told to murder Oedipus is unable to kill her child; but in giving the baby to a shepherd, Jocasta consigns Oedipus to a worse fate, and her misguided love for the cursed child – an aborted abortion – is emphasized by her incestuous ties to him years later: never, apparently, has she been able to love Oedipus properly or let him go or extricate herself from the damage he will cause. Such abjected things are still vital, as Oedipus' tragedy proves – his abiding connections toxic, inevitable, uncanny.[22] Connections to others are not enough to make one safely human, however. Apparently, one also needs a mother who will push her child far away and sever its ties to the place where it was born.

\*\*\*

Making the determination to love a child requires time, certain linguistic tools and sufficient material resources:[23] Coriolanus's mother Volumnia's ferocious claim that the breasts of Hecuba are no lovelier than Hector's forehead spitting blood (1.3.39–43) is shared against the background of a Rome besieged by grain shortages. Not all babies will survive on Shakespeare's stage, and the Macbeths' imagined child is even denied a proper burial. Actually, *Macbeth* unfolds in an especially impoverished setting not unlike the ravaged conditions of Shakespeare's London, regularly torn by famine and plague, filled with beggars and vagrants and those made homeless by land reform, a setting where want and hunger ruled. The procedure for obtaining care in such environs, even from one's mother, could therefore be uncertain, and thorny are the thresholds parents must cross in choosing to consign their offspring to the nursery or to the grave, as older stories also record. Not only are playwrights like Euripides and Sophocles similarly interested in this setting, but so are biblical writers who show us patriarchs nearly pushed over the edge in regions of hard choices and uncertain provisions: Solomon pronouncing justice over the

body of the baby he'd slice in two (Kings 3.16–27), Abraham initiating his covenant with Yahweh by nearly murdering his son (Genesis 22).[24] Ancient cultures and early modern ones take shape as safe spaces for unwanted babies, offering a provisional theory about the good things they promise, the reasons for not murdering them.

---

[21] I borrow the phrase 'unusable future' from Jonathan Baldo who, in '"A rooted sorrow": Scotland's unusable past', explores how James I traded a Scottish legacy for an English one when he assumed the throne upon Elizabeth I's death: *Macbeth: New Critical Essays*, ed. Nick Moschovakis (London, 2008), pp. 88–103.

[22] Cognitive science does not tell us why Jocasta holds on to the child she's been told to murder. But it might account for the way the baby ends up replacing her husband: in one way or another, the family will be eradicated, the normal lines of descent twisted, the nervous system's coordinates still fixed. The play, exposing the limits of such circuitry, invites us to think about which person is better off dead. The Tanakh describes the mothers who entertain such thoughts as harlots; Toni Morrison envisions the mother who contemplates this sacrifice as a tragic heroic figure in *Beloved*. Raymond Carver's 1988 short story 'Popular mechanics' offers another meditation on the theme.

[23] Alexandra Sacks explores the phenomenon of matrescence – or the process of becoming a mother – as a specific neurobiological experience, with no reference to the larger cultural or physical environment, the setting in which raging hormones play out. See 'The birth of a mother', www.nytimes.com/2017/05/08/well/family/the-birth-of-a-mother.html. In addition, the focus of Sacks's discussion is entirely on feeling uncertain about oneself, not about the new being in one's care.

[24] In Tanakh, Kings 3.16–28, we are told the story of two prostitutes who claim the same child after another child dies during the night when one of the women accidentally 'lay on it'. According to one of these women, the other 'arose in the night and took my son from my side while your maidservant was asleep, and laid him in her bosom; and she laid her dead son in my bosom'. It is striking how a narrative of jealous want is also marked by carelessness, sleep, indifference, as well as the fact that it is a living child which is more important than *one's own* child. Scheper-Hughes (*Death Without Weeping*) also recounts this story (408) as a parable of limited resources. We might also consider another story of failed childcare in the blind Isaac's dealings with the twins Jacob and Esau, whose distinguishing features can be crudely copied to fool the old man out of a single blessing.

Such stories also spell out the ways feelings in the nursery are at once primal and cultural, prompted by cries and caresses but also shaped by the encouragement and resources of the larger world. A recent article in the *New York Times* describes how scientists have similarly located maternal feeling in a more extensive web of resources and limits, exploring how breast milk distinguishes girls from boys by supplying a richer product to male children, so that a caregiver's love is attached to a baby only as deeply as it is affixed to the resources afforded by a particular environment. For parallel reasons, the mothers Scheper-Hughes describes do not breast-feed their children because poverty makes them doubt their ability to nourish; regular ruin teaches them to withhold a cheap and readily available antidote to thirst, to see their good breasts as bad breasts, and view their babies' mouths as closed. Shakespeare's mothers likewise ignore perceptions which might bind them to children and sidestep the pressures offered by nearness in space, susceptibility to voice or breath, the touch of a hand or the shape of a nose, even though these are things Paulina mentions to Leontes, rewards Hermione links with being a bride. Instead, it is the features of the larger environment which are shown to organize maternal responses, the nursery in *The Winter's Tale* nestled inside a wider landscape marked by jails and tombs and rough seas, as well as 'more remote and desert' places (3.1.176).

Maybe for this reason appraisals are so 'crucial to emotions', as cognitive philosopher Jesse Prinz (*The Emotional Construction of Morals*) notes, such evaluations embodied by and shaped within a person rooted to a particular world. Sometimes these appraisals hit a sturdy wall or one that gives way, and what Prinz calls the 'small emotional repertoire' of feelings with which we are 'innately furnished' not only restricts *what* we can feel but necessarily also limits *when* and *where* we can feel it.[25] Shakespeare correspondingly illustrates how feelings are spent or saved, apportioned, invested, postponed and redirected: in competition with other feelings, emotions are inevitably reduced, straitened and reorganized when they are expressed. Lady Macbeth's imagined murder of her child unfolds in an especially forbidding world of food shortages and starless nights where horses eat each other, banquets lack sauce, and fires need to be lit repeatedly in spaces where the lights have gone out. 'Who would have thought the old man to have had so much blood in him?' (5.1.33–4), Lady Macbeth exclaims after Duncan's murder, amazed because the rest of the economy in Scotland is so clearly strained, her husband wearing borrowed robes and honoured with another noble's title. Second-best beds are prominent in Shakespeare's imagination, but we also see feelings recycled, doubled-up, handed down or redistributed because of scarcity or need.[26]

---

[25] See Jesse Prinz, *The Emotional Construction of Morals* (Oxford, 2007), pp. 65–7. In 'The emotional basis of moral judgments', *Philosophical Explorations* 9.1 (2006), 29–43, Prinz emphasizes how cognition is shaped by nonrational information such as smells and appearances. One implication is that any kind of appraisal about where to put our feelings is rooted in a particular setting, with other choices and examples available for reference or counterclaims, as Prinz notes: 'Emotions co-occur with moral judgments, influence moral judgments, are sufficient for moral judgments, and are necessary for moral judgments, because moral judgments are constituted by emotional dispositions' (36). At the same time, he argues for a non-cognitive basis of emotions, claiming that cognitive theories 'put emotions too high up on the phylogenetic and ontogenetic scale' (*Emotional Construction*, p. 57). Prinz's work on the way sentiments motivate thought sees our dispositions as strangely walled in, impervious, however: he isolates emotional life in the way that rationalists might want to close off thought. Examples which trouble his theory include the complicated responsibilities of caregivers required to have maternal feelings for children in their care who are also required to relinquish those feelings for their own children. Another example could be found in the parent who grieves less over the death of a daughter than over a son, because this person's country observes the one-child rule. Prinz also fails to consider the ways feelings can change over time – how a helping of Viagra or the onset of puberty or menopause, or a food shortage or influx of cash, might alter a person's judgement from one day to the next. And how influential are emotions upon judgements when our obligation to act – as when we watch a play – is lessened?

[26] Lady Macduff's colloquy with her son is an example of the broken, emptied nest, in contrast, as I explore more fully below. Shakespeare's stage is crowded with such examples of failed maternal feeling, and although the Queen in *Richard II* likens her woe to a 'prodigy' or monstrous birth, and calls

That this economy imagines tenderness as a *trade-off* is clear in the way Lady Macbeth's child is only mentioned when she describes her affection as measured by her deadly embrace. 'I have given suck, and know / How tender 'tis to love the babe that milks me' (1.7.54–5), she says, representing motherhood by referring to the relinquishing of a duty, converting all other feelings into the contracted ones obligation supplies. All of the experiences and emotions connected with motherhood are transformed here into a picture of forgoing what one loves, and the child itself is set aside in the process of being held or cared for, aborted by being born. The welfare state in Scotland which Shakespeare maps out also rules out sharing – just as Duncan's inauguration plans for his son obviate a more equitable distribution of spoils. Another mouth to feed puts stress on an already-burdened system, and so Lady Macbeth withholds love from the baby she tenderly holds.[27] There is no larger order to supplement or enrich things, no network of others to help bestow care or grant favours. Her child is accordingly depicted as something personal, limited to her, reserved for her body, contained and constrained by her feelings, its existence only verified by her holding of it. The baby is not an heir or merely something which his father has seen, and, nameless, he does not cry. Winnicott's maths makes this one-sidedness clear, as does a theatre which later shows us Lady Macbeth's sleepwalking form, where she acts and we feel, she murders and we mourn. In a world stripped of luxuries, Macbeth's witches remain desperate inhabitants of a ravaged place unrewarded by success. The impoverished setting in the play resembles the harsh landscape Scheper-Hughes describes, yet if a few people survive in *Macbeth*, families don't; although Fleance escapes the men who murder his father, Siward is left to mourn his son.[28] In their fleeting appearances and unmourned deaths, these children expose the family for what it really is, a flimsy shelter against need, cold and violence.

\*\*\*

Older stories take mother love as anything but a given, but Solomon's sentences in the Hebrew Bible also aim to explain why some mothers will lose out in stories of child-love and child-rearing. The father-figure proposes killing the child whom two mothers claim because neither of these mothers has held the child tightly: one would have him murdered and the other willingly parts from him, mothering rendered as passive, an end-product rather than a point of origin, and finally a consequence of a patriarch opting not to draw blood. Just as we see in *Oedipus'* account of the ambivalent Jocasta, motherhood becomes something unnatural, a potential danger to children. If we can locate maternal instincts in these narratives, they are just as routinely thwarted, circumstantial and subject to change.

That the attachment process is protracted, the negotiations complex and the influence of outside forces curiously important is also indicated by the work of Japanese roboticist Masahiro Mori, who in

herself 'a gasping new-delivered mother' (2.2.64), there are others on hand to tend gardens and oversee growth in a battered England in that play. The nurse in *Romeo and Juliet* refers to her dead child Susan: 'She was too good for me' (1.3.21–2).

[27] See Katherine Knowles, 'Appetite and ambition: the influence of hunger in *Macbeth*', *Early English Studies* 2 (2009), 1–20. William Carroll's *Fat King, Lean Beggar* (Ithaca, NY, 1996) does not describe *Macbeth*, and only mentions *Lear's* imagery of poverty rather than any encounters with actual poor people. Linda Woodbridge's *Vagrancy and Homelessness and English Renaissance Literature* (Urbana, IL, 2001) supplies a rich account of homelessness and poverty, but does not mention *Macbeth*. Steve Mentz and Craig Dionne's anthology *Rogues and Early Modern English Culture* (Ann Arbor, 2006) supplies additional information, as does Ross Douthat, 'The post-familial election', New York Times, 11 Nov. 2016: www.nytimes.com/2016/11/06/opinion/sunday/the-post-familial-election.html. Douthat examines the modern-day phenomenon of the scarcity of family ties, commenting that 'families have grown more attenuated: fewer and later marriages, fewer and later-born children, fewer brothers and sisters and cousins, more people living for longer and longer stretches on their own'.

[28] See Knowles, 'Noble imps: doomed heirs', in *Shakespeare's Boys: A Cultural History* (Basingstoke, 2014), for a discussion of the precarious state of heirs and first-born sons 'whose childishness contrasts with their dynastic significance' (16). These sons demand their inheritance while also expressing a wish to be perceived as individuals (14).

1970 coined the phrase 'uncanny valley' to describe how inanimate objects such as dolls or robots win affection or summon the impulses of caregivers by displaying signs of human-ness. Especially useful is the way Mori's model suggests how, alongside feelings of attachment prompted by certain features in a baby or replica of one, other feelings take shape, such that the neurons which fire *about* someone else might start to fire *for* this creature, sometimes with love, sometimes without. Mori's spectrum envisions a region where connections come together or fall apart, for this 'uncanny valley' is situated alongside hills and mountains, places of real bonding positioned next to flat spaces, areas of indifference or neutrality giving way to desire and tenderness or subsiding to hate.[29] Nearness and recognition can tilt the balance in one way or another, but so can time, money or the lack of competing objects – the outlines of a doll traced by moonlight might be alarming or reassuring, depending on what other comforts a child can see or sense nearby. As Scheper-Hughes reminds us, the 'anthropomorphization of the fetus, neonate, infant, and baby is everywhere subject to cultural "nomination", but it is always a "courtesy" anthropomorphization. For it will be many months before the infant can display an undoubtedly "human" smile, and years will pass before she can turn a "twitch" into a meaningful wink.'[30] Just as hope or want can extend such 'courtesy', nerves can be bent or pushed to register discomfort or bestow love.

Whether human-ness means softness, passivity, vitality or the ability to reciprocate feelings is not entirely clear in Mori's study, however. What he reports is that dolls with sufficiently lifelike features can spark tenderness, but, should a doll veer too close, or move, or twitch (instead of 'meaningfully wink'), opposite feelings are produced. Five toes, a bright smile, clear skin can be enticing, persuasive, reassuring, but sometimes the effect is eerie or off-putting instead: a talking doll or walking zombie easily crosses the line; a stuffed animal with protruding eyes that sees but does not tell might pass muster. Mori's model includes the way we dread the robot whose battery never runs down or won't turn off. At certain junctures, the tiny creature in one's arms is endangered, but at other times this thing might appear dangerous itself. Indeed, the asymmetry between caregiver and object which Nancy Yousef describes in *Romantic Intimacy* can sometimes be craved, or even provide relief. Explaining the sad fate of the gorilla Harambe, much loved and carefully tended until he was shot to death by his keepers, Nathan Heller helps us understand the uncanny valley as the terrifying place where we encounter the 'limits of our moral reach'.[31] Unable to discern whether Harambe's interest in a little boy who had scaled the Cincinnati Zoo's fencing and entered the gorilla's pen was human or inhuman – his devotion tender or deadly – the animal's keepers decided they could no longer read their ties to a creature they had named and whose birthdays they'd celebrated, determining instead that the spectrum of feeling in the uncanny valley could be reshuffled and the map of the world correspondingly reset.[32]

---

[29] Masahiro Mori, 'The uncanny valley', *Energy* 7,4 (1970), 33–4. According to Mori, 'as robots appear more humanlike, our sense of their familiarity increases until we come to a valley' (33), where we encounter instead a 'sense of strangeness' if, for instance, the robot's hands are cold or lack soft tissue (34). In this valley, Mori puts corpses, zombies, prosthetic hands, mannequins, as well as a laughing human face when the distortion of muscles has been slowed down. For additional details, see Christopher H. Ramey, 'An inventory of reported characteristics for home computers, robots, and human beings: applications for android science and the uncanny valley', in *Proceedings of the ICCS/CogSci-2006 Long Symposium: Toward Social Mechanisms of Android Science, July 2006, Vancouver, Canada*, pp. 21–5. The author would like to acknowledge Ramey's extraordinarily generous assistance in supplying me with a copy of this article.

[30] Mori, 'The uncanny valley', p. 413.

[31] Nathan Heller, 'Not our kind', *The New Yorker*, 28 November 2016. Heller points out that 'Harambe', in Swahili, means 'pulling together'. The online version is entitled 'If animals have rights, should robots?': www.newyorker.com/magazine/2016/11/28/if-animals-have-rights-should-robots. I also want to acknowledge the advice of Mark Rodriquez, who helped me think about Harambe's life and death more deeply.

[32] Leys explores this emphasis on 'pre-conscious' or 'non-conscious', 'inhuman' or 'pre-subjective' forces and the

In revealing similar limits to empathy or caps on our capacity to feel for a monster like Oedipus or mourner like Antigone, Sophocles' theatre shrewdly measures how we ascertain resemblance, belonging, pity and fear. We see Oedipus' eyes gouged out, for instance, but merely hear about Jocasta's strangled cries, and the wounded hero Philoctetes's oozing, smelly foot has no impact on the sympathy we bestow, although disgust at the infected limb keeps his countrymen away for ten years. Indeed, the playwright's theory of emotional appraisals and moral judgements centres around the ways these sentiments are aroused not in our bodies, but by the bodies of others.[33]

\*\*\*

So what Solomonic wisdom explains Lady Macbeth's clasp of the smiling baby she'd murder, or the death of Leontes's son and recovery of his daughter in *The Winter's Tale*? Does Mori's theory of the 'uncanny valley' only describe how a caregiver might feel towards something, or can it also account for what she needs to do with those feelings? Scheper-Hughes's model of maternal attachment and detachment implies that the landscape of the nursery widens or narrows depending on a range of cultural pressures, including the availability of material resources, employment opportunities, the existence of other siblings, and a ready, safe milk supply. We can conclude that, in many cases, what imperils one child might be exactly what enables another one to flourish; what leads one mother to withhold milk also encourages her to save it for another child, one judged less likely to die. We can also imagine that, despite what the greeting-card industry or parenting magazines tell us, feelings about children cannot expand exponentially: maternal love is renewable, but not always sustainable.[34] Indeed, Scheper-Hughes's researches underscore the fact that maternal love is *always* limited. No matter how many children they bear, as she was surprised to discover, Brazilian mothers from all social classes end up with three or four living children. Maybe this is because the numbers of neurons are already fixed, their connections able to change but never to expand

continually, the circuitry reliable but also ultimately unyielding. Drawing on this kind of circuitry, Othello says it's better to decide that Desdemona is cheating rather than continue to wonder about her love (3.3.341); with the same ceiling in mind, Hamlet tells his mother she cannot love his father and his father's brother at the same time (3.4.54); Leontes's first rush of affection for the daughter he banished sixteen years earlier is based on Perdita's resemblance to her mother, a woman at that point long presumed dead (5.1.222). Shakespeare's families can only bear a carefully restricted weight, in other words. For this reason, Lear's daughters Goneril and Regan fight over his kingdom even as they seek to reduce the number of their father's retainers, and, in *Macbeth*, while Donalbain and Malcolm both escape after their father's death, only Malcolm returns to Scotland. If sibling pairs like Oliver and Orlando, and Laertes and Ophelia, contradict the example of singletons in the bulk of Shakespeare's plays, resources are nonetheless restricted in both cases: Ophelia drowns herself, and Oliver dumps his estate on Orlando.

The unfolding of tragedy and comedy alike on Shakespeare's stage teaches his audience that getting born and growing up never take place in a vacuum, even in the nursery, along with the

widespread scholarly conclusion that reason and rationality are overvalued, along with the claim that affects are independent of and prior to ideology ('The turn to affect', pp. 434–7). She challenges the premise of a complete separation between the affect system and meaning or cognition (443), the reductive thinking in which something can only be 'fully conscious' or 'corporeal', rather than somewhere in-between (457). Both Prinz's work and Leys's critique of it have been enormously useful to my thinking, but I also want to mention the contributions of members of the 2015–16 Rifkind Center Seminar on Emotions.

[33] Perhaps something similar happens when we judge refugees undeserving of a place in our country because they've already lost a space: a homeland is never represented by gates that open up, only by those which shut down or block off. See Seyla Benhabib, *The Rights of Others: Aliens, Refugees, and Citizens* (Cambridge, 2004).

[34] I borrow this distinction from my City College colleague Chad Jenkins.

fact that these achievements are produced by discrete set of decisions and activities which could go
awry at any point, given the logistics surrounding
geography, care and provisions which enable any
attachment to unfold. Just as nature is subject to
change and influence, emotions must be parcelled
out the way Duncan rewards his men, extracting
the honours and dreams and ambitions of one and
foisting or shoe-horning them onto the other.
*Macbeth* and *The Winter's Tale* make explicit this
need for redistribution: Leontes worries that there
are not enough rewards to go around in the same
way Macbeth does, and both Leontes and Lady
Macbeth fantasize about murdering their offspring – Leontes pronouncing death for the newborn: 'The bastard-brains with these my proper
hands / Shall I dash out (2.3.140–1); and Lady
Macbeth promising 'I would, while it was smiling
in my face, / Have plucked my nipple from his
boneless gums / And dashed the brains out'
(1.7.56–8). Yet Leontes pronounces death on the
newborn because he prefers to dwell in a perfect
past where the mother's love is reserved for him,
whereas Lady Macbeth hurls herself into the future
in planning her husband's ascent, remembering no
past worth saving or set of rival ties. We could see
Lady Macbeth and Leontes as versions of the terrorist and the nativist, the person who wants to
storm borders and overturn tradition the inverse
of the person locked inside, only consoled by
tradition.[35] But both of these characters are stuck
in the uncanny valley, tied to corpses and statues,
and fearing dreams or sleeping figures, the touch of
others in this murky space.

The daughter Perdita survives in *The Winter's
Tale* not only because she is a replacement for
Mamillius in a world where riches must be carefully weighed and measured, but also because she
escapes the nursery and experiences the 'selfsame
sun' outside its walls (4.4.32). Maybe Mamillius is
old enough to conclude that it would be better had
he not been born. Perdita, taken from her mother
before she has been weaned, is awarded priority
because she has no needs, the child whose drain on
the household economy is negligible now getting
a chance to survive. Mamillius's status, in contrast,

remains ambivalent, probably because he remains
stranded *inside* the home for so long. The young
Prince is first described as an 'unspeakable comfort'
(1.1.29) at the start of *The Winter's Tale*, 'a gentleman of the greatest promise' (1.1.30–31) as well as
a 'kernel' and 'sweet villain', a 'calf' and copy and
a collop (138), unmade or dehumanized in the
process of assuming a likeness, thwarted in his
efforts to belong. In stark contrast is the 'thriving
issue' Perdita, who starts as a 'prisoner'. Quickly
'freed and enfranchis'd' (2.2.63), and then determined to look much like a king (97–101), her
equivocal status as something real because she can
be cast off continues to hold: Hermione faints upon
hearing of Mamillius's death, but not upon hearing
of Perdita's banishment, and when Leontes retracts
his charges against Hermione upon learning that
his son is dead, he says nothing at all about recalling
Perdita (3.2.147–68). Out of his hands, she is out of
his thoughts, and the ambivalence which often
surrounds the newborn is externalized, projected
outside and sent away with the banished baby, so
that, after Perdita is shipwrecked in Bohemia, her
rescuers display a similar uncertainty. When a bear
eats her attendant, the terrors of child-bearing are
exposed as real and unmanageable but also short-
lived, and the bear quickly disappears along with
the person it consumed, the demons of the nursery
exposed and exorcised in one sitting. When child-
bearing gets severed from child-forswearing, the
anthropomorphization which Scheper-Hughes

---

[35] Knowles's comment that, in *Macbeth*, inherited monarchy
will replace the election of leaders seems germane ('Noble
imps', p. 45): 'the realization that future kingship will depend
on patrilineal succession rather than personal achievement is
the driving force behind Macbeth's increasing desperation'.
This is the nexus at which the nationalist and terrorist anxieties find relief, where there are no outsiders to alter the
course of history, no other legitimacy other than that offered
by blood. See, too, Parvulescu's description of the 'queer
man' who seems to resemble Leontes because he 'does not
imagine a good life. He knows no compassion, no sentimentality, no love. He hates birthdays' ('Reproduction and queer
theory', p. 86). In contrast is the figure of Dickens's Scrooge
who, as Parvulescu notes, is finally inserted into a 'normative,
reproductive family unit' (86).

describes can be successfully carried out by strangers, and the safety of the child no longer put in doubt.

A more severe accounting process governs the exchanges in *Macbeth* – the baby whom Lady Macbeth would murder traded for one who's never been born. Later, the 'trembling' bundle of nerves which Macbeth sees in the young soldier before him and derides as 'the baby of a girl' (3.4.105–6)[36] is transformed into Siward's son, the figure of a youthful warrior ready to die because he can kill, and worthy of love because he can die.[37] The 'baby of a girl' might be a doll or a young girl, a fetish object or the child able to calm herself with one – a failed person, that is, or a growing one. But *The Winter's Tale* makes clear that the girl who can make a home wherever she is is better-off than the son sacrificed by Siward (or young Mamillius overlooked by everyone else in his household) and relegated to a mound of bodies which mark where Scotland renews itself. That it's so hard to tell whether Macbeth is describing a little girl or her toy is Shakespeare's point, I think, because the relationship between girl and doll makes them indistinguishable, cherished and loved by, dependent on, and bound to each other. This is a picture of attachment that refashions or rewires each being into the other in a *canny* valley where two creatures come together in delight and similitude. The reunion of Perdita and her mother in *The Winter's Tale* offers a parody of this place, where the daughter recovers her rightful role by seeing herself in the image of her mother as a statue.

Beside the equivocal examples of 'the baby of a girl' in *Macbeth* and the replica Perdita ultimately offers of a stone, we have few other happy survivors of the nursery on Shakespeare's stage. 'Untimely ripped' from his mother's womb (5.10, 15–16), Macduff escapes her loving clutches to cause her death, and his heir later disowns his father before he is horribly murdered by Macbeth's assassins, the 'unusable' future's main task here being to wipe out an unusable past.[38] Before he dies, Macduff's son calls out his father's abandonment and detects his mother's lying (4.2.37), rejecting the conditions of his birth along with his helplessness, and asking

to be heard as someone with his own claims, able to be seen as well as to refuse likeness. Macduff's son imagines his mother with another man (4.2.61–2) and views all husbands and fathers as either murdered or murderers, hangsmen or on the gallows. His dying words to his mother instruct her to 'run away' from the fouled nest they have occupied together, exposing the nursery as a slaughterhouse, a place of blood and cold.

'Given how dangerous or ambivalent love always is, why should we think that it is any less so between a mother and her children?', Scheper-Hughes asks, inviting us to disown or at least qualify a sentiment we prefer to cherish.[39] One keeps seeking in Shakespeare's stories of restoration and renewal some picture of attachment, a bond that shuts out death – something other than the bundle washed ashore in Bohemia in *The Winter's Tale* and

---

36 Some editors describe Macbeth as here referring to a doll; others propose Macbeth is referring instead to a female infant or young girl. See R. C. Bald, 'Macbeth's "baby of a girl"', *The Shakespeare Association Bulletin* 24.3 (1949), 220–2. A discussion of Siward's son is offered by Karl F. Zender, 'The death of young Siward: providential order and tragic loss in *Macbeth*', *Texas Studies in Literature and Language* 17.2 (1975), 415–25.

37 This is what makes so harrowing and obnoxious the ending to Clint Eastwood's Oscar-winning *Million Dollar Baby* (Warner Brothers, 2004), recently listed as one of the top ten films of the twenty-first century by the *New York Times*. The boxing coach, played by Eastwood, leans in to whisper (in Gaelic) to the bedridden young woman (Hilary Swank) that she is 'my darling, my blood', after telling her he will honour her wishes and disconnect her from the breathing machine to which she's hooked up after a disastrous beating in the ring. He becomes her father at the moment he ends her life, and accepts his kinship when he helps her breathe her last. Disability-rights advocates protested that the movie poorly represented rehabilitative outcomes for spinal-cord injuries; to those very real complaints, I'd add the dismal picture of what acknowledging paternity entails, or looks forward to. Wes Davis makes a similar point about paternity's tangled claims when he notes that Yeats, whose poem 'The lake isle of Innesfree' supplies the source for Eastwood's character's term of endearment, didn't write his poems in Irish: www.nytimes.com/2005/02/26/opinion/fighting-words.html.

38 See Knowles on this scene ('Noble imps', p. 54).

39 Scheper-Hughes, *Death Without Weeping*, p. 353.

rescued by a shepherd and a clown. Leontes's embrace of Hermione's stony form at the end of the play, much like the child's clutch of an unloving doll, is an ambiguous solution, as is the image of the uncanny valley we find in the graveyard where Hamlet cradles Yorick's skull. Some things, Shakespeare shows us, are pulled out of this place of love and death; other things, like the children Brazilian mothers mourn, are forced there to wait to die. Mamillius seems to choose to go to this place himself. Maybe Mamillius's brief life flashes by in the winter's tale we overhear him start to tell Hermione in Act 1, shortly before his death, which occurs while no one else is looking. The boy recounts a story of a man who dwelt alone by a churchyard, letting us into the lonely place the child so often inhabits in Shakespeare's plays, an elaborate tomb also designed to contain a mother's loving embrace.

# TIPPETT'S *TEMPEST*: SHAKESPEARE IN *THE KNOT GARDEN*

## MICHAEL GRAHAM

The British composer Michael Tippett (1905–98) has gained a reputation as 'the most literary composer since Wagner', owing to his propensity to exhibit his literary credentials 'conspicuously and apparently self-consciously'.[1] In her list of 'the most exceptional of [Tippett's] literary "gods"', Suzanne Robinson rightly includes Goethe, Jung, Yeats and T. S. Eliot.[2] The absence of Shakespeare from Robinson's list is somewhat surprising, however, given the vital influence of this playwright's work on Tippett's life, music and aesthetics. Tippett's abundant admiration for Shakespeare is apparent in his copious writings. In one essay, 'Some categories of judgement in modern music', for example, he positions Shakespeare alongside Beethoven as one of the two essential creators of art 'in the humanistic tradition' within which Tippett himself avowedly operates: 'I call this the Shakespeare–Beethoven archetype.'[3] Elsewhere, he describes Shakespeare as 'absolutely universal … an enormous cauldron who we pour things into and take things out of'.[4] Robinson herself suggests that Tippett moreover felt a keen personal connection with Shakespeare's work, writing that Shakespeare functioned as a crucial 'amulet' for Tippett 'on a lifetime's journey fraught with "all the insecurity, incoherence, incompleteness and relativity of our everyday life"'.[5]

Like his great friend and counterpart, Benjamin Britten, Tippett drew on *A Midsummer Night's Dream* for inspiration with one of his operas, *The Midsummer Marriage* (1955). As Ian Kemp notes, Tippett's first opera similarly features 'two pairs of lovers in a magic wood … interweaves fantasy and reality, and … capitalizes on the idea that "midsummer madness" signifies a willingness to accept the workings of the imagination.[6] Of all Shakespeare's plays, however, Tippett was seemingly most fascinated by *The Tempest*, since he repeatedly engaged with this work in his music and writings over a three-decade stretch. In 1962, Tippett composed incidental music for a production of *The Tempest* at the Old Vic, a project that additionally resulted in *Songs for Ariel* for high voice and piano. He worked on his *Tempest* opera between 1966 and 1969, and *The Knot Garden* premiered at Covent Garden on 2 December 1970. *Songs for Dov*, a composition for tenor and chamber orchestra which

---

1   Suzanne Robinson, 'Introduction', in *Michael Tippett: Music and Literature*, ed. Suzanne Robinson (Farnham, 2002), pp. 1–20; p. 1. See also Irene Morra, 'Tippett, verse drama, and *King Priam*', in *Twentieth-Century British Authors and the Rise of Opera in Britain* (Aldershot, 2007), pp. 11–20.

2   Robinson, 'Introduction', p. 1.

3   Michael Tippett, 'Some categories of judgement in modern music', in *Music of the Angels: Essays and Sketchbooks of Michael Tippett*, ed. Meirion Bowen (London, 1980), pp. 44–8; p. 46. For brevity, future citations of Tippett's work will use his surname only.

4   Tippett, quoted in Meirion Bowen, *Michael Tippett* (London, 1982), p. 71.

5   Robinson, 'Introduction', p. 14. The Tippett quote is taken from 'Towards the condition of music', in *Tippett on Music*, ed. Meirion Bowen (Oxford, 1995), pp. 7–15; p. 13.

6   Ian Kemp, *Tippett: The Composer and His Music* (London, 1984), p. 217.

chronicles the further adventures of the Ariel character from *The Knot Garden*, also debuted during this year. Prospero's masque in *The Tempest* provides lines for a reconciliatory chorus in Tippett's fourth opera, *The Ice Break* (1977): '[s]pring come to you at the farthest / In the very end of harvest' (4.1.114–15). In 1995, Tippett came out of a three-year retirement to write *Caliban's Song*, his final composition, for inclusion in his *Tempest* suite for the Purcell tercentenary.

According to Tippett's biographer, Meirion Bowen, *The Knot Garden* represents 'the climax of [Tippett's] fascination with Shakespeare'.[7] The opera's epigraph, which reveals its focus on people attempting to achieve individuation, is taken from *All's Well That Ends Well*: 'simply the thing I am / Shall make me live' (4.3.272–3). *The Tempest*, however, is the central reference point in a work built out of a typically vast tangle of literary and musical allusions. Tippett significantly alters *The Tempest*'s plot and text, placing quotations of Shakespeare's verse next to a variety of other references as well as his own distinctive idiolect. Nevertheless, the play's themes and structure remain integral to the opera and its outcomes. Tippett was drawn particularly to *The Tempest*'s ruminations on the granting of forgiveness, which he felt were especially relevant to his own nihilistic, violent age. *The Tempest*, according to Tippett, poses the question of 'who does the forgiving?' for a society in which 'the Christian religion is becoming less and less all-powerful'.[8] He writes further that Shakespeare's late comedies 'are the best models' of a 'dramatic tradition where personal relations are considered for themselves alone, and are arranged in a kind of pattern or as a kind of dance', since they explore 'every avenue of possible forgiveness and reconciliation, amongst individuals at war with each other'.[9] Ultimately, *The Tempest* demonstrates how 'love and forgiveness, set in opposition to power, are able to transcend the absolute nature of power' – a description which also neatly summarizes *The Knot Garden*'s fundamental conclusions.[10]

Following the mythological settings and characters of *The Midsummer Marriage* and *King Priam*

(1962), *The Knot Garden* was the first of Tippett's operas to be set in modern times and feature distinctively modern people (albeit with numerous Shakespearian and classical resonances). The opera, in the composer's words, offers an examination of 'what sort of world we live in now and how we may behave in it'.[11] *The Knot Garden*'s basic scenario means that it also has a strong claim to be considered the most overtly psychoanalytic of all *Tempest* adaptations, even bearing in mind the extensive exploration of the play along these lines by scholars and practitioners over the past century. It depicts an extended group therapy session led by Mangus, a psychoanalyst and self-styled Prospero figure who is attempting to assist several individuals struggling with identity and relationship crises. Thea (a gardener and Mangus's primary analysand) and Faber (a civil engineer) are a married couple experiencing difficulties owing to Faber's philandering and Thea's consequent remoteness.[12] The timid adolescent Flora, their adopted daughter and one of the objects of Faber's indiscriminate desire. Mel and Dov are a gay couple – a black writer and white musician, respectively – who separate over the course of the opera. Denise is a self-righteous freedom fighter recently disfigured through torture, who eventually couples up with Mel.

*The Knot Garden*'s eponymous setting is a surreal, responsive space, which functions primarily as a psychological metaphor. The 'garden', for example, is most active in Act 2 ('Labyrinth'), when 'it is in total disarray and the maze in operation',

---

7 Bowen, ed., *Tippett on Music*, p. 71.

8 Tippett, 'Dreams of power, dreams of love', in Bowen, ed., *Tippett on Music*, pp. 220–7; p. 221.

9 Tippett, 'Dreams', p. 221. Tippett cites Chekhov's *The Cherry Orchard*, Shaw's *Heartbreak House* and Albee's *Who's Afraid of Virginia Woolf?* as typical modern examples of this genre.

10 Tippett, 'Dreams', p. 221.

11 Tippett, 'Preface', in Bowen, ed., *Tippett on Music*, pp. vii–ix; p. viii.

12 Thea's name associates her with Theia, a Greek goddess of the Moon. Perhaps, then, Thea might also be linked with Sycorax from *The Tempest*, a fearsome female figure who was 'so strong / That could control the moon' (5.1.269–70).

throwing the characters into swift, intense encounters with each other.[13] At the end of this act, when there is a tender duet between Dov and Flora, a rose garden then magically appears. Tippett might have taken inspiration for *The Knot Garden*'s title and location from *Love's Labour's Lost*, in which the King of Navarre's 'curious-knotted garden' (1.1.228–9) is a key symbolic feature. Louis Adrian Montrose suggests that Navarre's garden represents both 'self-entrapment' and 'transcendence', along with the 'labyrinthine self-deceptions of the misguided wits which effloresce within its confines' – a description that applies perfectly well to this opera.[14] Virginia Mason Vaughan and Alden T. Vaughan further observe how the idea of a psychological labyrinth is integral to *The Knot Garden*'s parent work, which contains several references to mazes and manoeuvrings. In the final act of *The Tempest*, for example, Alonso proclaims '[t]his is as strange a maze as e'er men trod' (5.1.242), while the first four acts of the play conclude with invitations to move: '[c]ome, follow' (1.2.501), '[l]ead the way' (2.2.163), '[f]ollow, I pray you' (3.3.109) and '[f]ollow, and do me service' (4.1.258). According to Vaughan and Vaughan, it is only once the characters' 'physical and psychological journeys through the island's maze have ended' that they are finally able to group together and leave for home.[15]

*The Knot Garden*, then – to borrow Frank Dauster's assessment of Borges's contemporaneous labyrinth stories – emulates *The Tempest* by presenting 'a series of individuals who are seeking, essentially, the centre of their individual labyrinths'.[16] Tippett's garden is the equivalent of Shakespeare's island: by moving through its labyrinthine form, his modern characters are able to work through their assorted personal and interpersonal problems and regain a sense of agency and empathy, in order to re-enter and renegotiate the outside world. In fact, the action of *The Knot Garden*'s final act moves on to a peculiar version of Prospero's island, when Mangus organizes an improvised group performance of scenes from *The Tempest* as a therapeutic exercise. During these faltering, farcical

'charades', Mangus plays Prospero, Flora plays Miranda, Faber plays Ferdinand, Dov plays Ariel, Mel plays Caliban, and Thea and Denise observe. Ultimately, the disidentification and enforced interaction required by this 'play within a play' (or 'opera within an opera') results in the most profound personal and collective breakthroughs for several of the characters, including the analyst himself.

## 'PROSPERO'S A FAKE': MANGUS–FREUD–SCHOENBERG

[We] gang up into groups or congregations and elect a leader, on whom to project the notion of a centre, and who will speak as falconer to falcon, as teacher to disciple, as God to creature. And I mean not only a social or political leader. It happens everywhere, great or small; for instance in the world of sport; and, I am afraid, even in the world of psychoanalytic therapy, and certainly in the world of music.

(Tippett, 'What do we perceive in modern art?')[17]

*The Knot Garden* begins, predictably enough, with a tempest (although this would appear to be a collective psychological squall, rather than a literal one), and Mangus the psychoanalyst lying on a couch 'as a still point in a whirling storm'.[18] Mangus's name aligns him with Prospero, recalling 'the Renaissance *magus*, the seer who sought to

---

[13] Tippett, *The Knot Garden* (libretto) (London, 1969), p. 3.
[14] Louis Adrian Montrose, '"Folly, in wisdom hatch'd": the exemplary comedy of *Love's Labour's Lost*', *Comparative Drama* 11 (1977), 146–70; pp. 150–6.
[15] William Shakespeare, *The Tempest*, ed. Virginia Mason Vaughan and Alden T. Vaughan (London, 1999), p. 17.
[16] Frank Dauster, 'Notes on Borges's labyrinths', *Hispanic Review* 30 (1962), 142–8; p. 142. The idea of people seeking individuation through a labyrinth is similarly integral to Britten's *A Midsummer Night's Dream*, which is based on what 'may be the ultimate literary labyrinth' (Harold Bloom, *Bloom's Literary Themes: The Labyrinth* (New York, 2009), p. xv). See also Maurice Hunt, 'Individuation in *A Midsummer Night's Dream*', *South Central Review* 3 (1986), 1–13.
[17] Tippett, 'What do we perceive in modern art?', in *Moving into Aquarius* (St Albans, 1974), pp. 85–93; p. 87.
[18] Tippett, *Knot Garden*, p. 5.

23 *The Knot Garden*, 1.1, 'It's clear I'm Prospero' (Mangus). Musical examples from the score of *The Knot Garden* by Michael Tippett reproduced by permission of Schott Music Ltd.

improve the world through his magical art'.[19] His saviour complex and pretensions to Prospero-esque omnipotence are further apparent from his opening lines, which he delivers to the audience:

MANGUS So, if I dream,
It's clear I'm Prospero:
Man of power.
He put them all to rights.

(*The Knot Garden*, 1.1)

During this opening gambit, the orchestra follows Mangus's vocal movements, perhaps indicating that he does hold a certain level of 'power'. Yet his self-absorption and hubris are emphasized musically by extended, jumpy melismas, which are especially prominent and ridiculous when he sings 'Pro-spe-e-ro-o-ho-ho-ho-ho-ho-ho-ho' (see Figure 23). Mangus ends the scene in 'a pose of self-satisfaction', after the couch seemingly disappears at his command.[20]

Tippett observes that, in *The Tempest*, 'Prospero stands in for God: he, possessing complete magical powers, can do everything, and in the end, he can demand the act of contrition that results in forgiveness and the possibility of leaving the island to return once more to civilization.'[21] Mangus, who describes himself as a 'priest-magician' (1.6), would like to perform the same role for his patients, by acting as a God substitute in a godless world, and

using his 'magic powers' to help them reach a point of reconciliation. His attitude is understandable, since, as Bruce Fink notes, psychoanalysis has 'taken over the former role of confession for many and prayer/atonement for others, situating the analyst in [a] God-like position . . . fit to deliberate on all questions of normal and abnormal, right and wrong, good and bad'.[22] Mangus would appear to be Tippett's caricature of a Freudian 'ego psychologist', a figure whom Fink describes as a 'judgmental, all-knowing Other'.[23] The Jungian composer had little time for Freudian analytical approaches, believing them to be inadequate: '[w]ithout in any way belittling Freud, I know that I cannot abide entirely in his therapeutic examination of the collective primitive in us . . . Some of us are driven by other agonies to a deeper analysis, [where] we meet on the labyrinthine paths of the collective unconscious.'[24]

Intriguingly, Mangus's main musical association is a twelve-note 'Tempest' motif beginning on the

[19] Kemp, *Tippett: The Composer and His Music*, p. 407.
[20] Tippett, *Knot Garden*, p. 5. [21] Tippett, 'Dreams', p. 221.
[22] Bruce Fink, *The Lacanian Subject: Between Language and Jouissance* (Princeton, NJ, 1995), p. 88.
[23] Fink, *Lacanian Subject*, p. xiii.
[24] Tippett, 'What I believe', in *Music of the Angels*, pp. 49–56; p. 51.

# THE KNOT GARDEN

## ACT I

### Confrontation

MICHAEL TIPPETT

24 *The Knot Garden*, 1.1, opening twelve-note 'Tempest' motif.

note B, which opens the opera (see Figure 24). Tippett dismissed Schoenberg's serialism as 'alphabetic',[25] so the appearance of a dodecaphonic pattern at the very beginning of *The Knot Garden* is something of a surprise, perhaps even implying that the rest of the opera will follow suit. The motif is in fact the opera's central musical building block, governing everything from surface features to underlying structure. Many of *The Knot Garden*'s most significant moments are in B or closely related keys, while transformations of the motif are heard at 'tempestuous' points, often being used to initiate and break up action. The motif features particularly prominently at the beginning of the Act 2 'Labyrinth' section, and between the characters' duets in this act. Arguably, the continual reappearance of this musical pattern could indicate Mangus's mastery over *The Knot Garden*'s events. Its manipulation and breakdown over the course of the opera, however, might more feasibly signify

Mangus's waning influence and shaky grasp on proceedings.

In his essay 'What do we perceive in modern art?', Tippett actually expresses a tempered admiration for Schoenberg, describing him as the composer who 'experienced [the] dislocation of centre most courageously, consistently, and sensitively':

[Schoenberg] wished to give order to the centre of these centreless musical notes, that is the twelve equal semitones of the equal tempered octave, by arranging them for the purposes of each composition into a subjectively chosen alphabetical row, which is to be constantly repeated. This is what I would call Schoenberg's fundamentalism, absolutely justified for himself but which he failed to justify rationally to the general satisfaction of his peers.[26]

---

[25] Tippett, *Those Twentieth Century Blues* (London, 1991), p. 274.
[26] Tippett, 'Modern art', p. 87.

204

Significantly, Tippett elsewhere aligns Schoenberg with Freud, portraying them both as flawed revolutionaries: '[l]ike Freud, [Schoenberg] was an idealist driven by a demon. Like Freud his demon drove him down a road of over-simplification, towards a dogma – the law of the twelve-tone system ... That [their students] induced in [them] a God-the-father attitude is equally apparent.'[27] The pairing of Mangus with a Schoenbergian tone row, then, would appear to be something of a pointed Tippettian joke. He immediately undermines his hubristic Freudian analyst, who is attempting to 'give order' to his 'centreless' patients, by aligning him with a composer whom Tippett similarly regarded as innovative, egotistical and fundamentally wrong.

Being a Freudian ego analyst, Mangus almost inevitably falls into the trap of 'counter-transference', which occurs when the analyst abandons neutrality, and instead

gets caught up in the ... game of comparing him or herself with his or her analysands, sizing their discourse up in terms of his or her own. 'Are they ahead of me or behind me in their comprehension of what is going on here in the analytic setting or elsewhere? Are they submissive to my wishes? Do I have any control over the situation? Do I have the upper hand?'[28]

If such competitive feelings are not put to one side, then analysands will grow to resent their analyst, attempt to disprove his or her theories (as Thea does with Mangus), and eventually reveal them to be 'an ordinary person like the analysand, who is not always right and who may even turn out to be dumber than the analysand'.[29]

In Act 3 of *The Knot Garden*, when Mangus self-indulgently plays Prospero, the 'man of power', in his favourite play, he does in fact inadvertently subject himself to the same process as his patients, and shows himself to be as 'dumb' as them. The first *Tempest* charade sees Mangus-Prospero and Flora-Miranda exploring the island, training Mel-Caliban, and freeing Dov-Ariel. The charades then veer off-course for the first time, with Dov-Ariel attacking Mel-Caliban, apparently in retribution for Ariel's enslavement by Sycorax, but actually

because of Dov's simmering resentment towards Mel.

MANGUS-PROSPERO Caliban and Ariel;
   Mine to command;
   Theirs to be grateful.
   *(Using the wand he splits open the tree. With a whoop Dov-Ariel rushes out and flings himself on Mel-Caliban who is knocked off his precarious balance)*
DOV-ARIEL Your filthy mother Sycorax is dead;
   But you're alive alright.
   I've waited centuries for this. *(He belabours Mel-Caliban)*
FLORA-MIRANDA O father, help, help!
MANGUS-PROSPERO *(Hauling Dov-Ariel off)* Stop: what's this?
DOV-ARIEL Hands off, I do but play my part
MEL-CALIBAN O no: you went beyond the script.
DOV-ARIEL As I shall always do.
MANGUS-PROSPERO Control yourselves: obey!
                    *(The Knot Garden, 3.2)*

Following this charade, Thea notes how, in this strange, improvised *Tempest*, '[s]cenes turn in the hand / Beyond [Mangus-Prospero's] book / When played by persons' (3.3). After the second charade, in which Mel-Caliban attempts to rape Flora-Miranda, much to Denise's distress, an increasingly irate Thea asks 'what are you Mangus? / Man of power? / Or dabbler: pimp: voyeur?' (3.5).

A few scenes later, Mangus's initial poise and superiority disintegrate completely. The final *Tempest* charade depicts a mock trial of Dov-Ariel and Mel-Caliban, and concludes with Mangus-Prospero freeing Dov-Ariel but angrily reasserting his authority over Mel-Caliban, who is mocked by Dov-Ariel. By this point in the charade, the line between play and reality has become increasingly blurred.

---

[27] Tippett, 'Moving into Aquarius', in *Aquarius*, pp. 35–42; p. 37.

[28] Fink, *Lacanian Subject*, p. 86.

[29] Fink, *Lacanian Subject*, p. 88. Freud's most famous case of counter-transference was with 'Dora' (Ida Bauer). For further details, see Sigmund Freud, *A Case of Hysteria (Dora)*, trans. Anthea Bell (Oxford, 2013).

# MICHAEL GRAHAM

MEL-CALIBAN *(Quoting with exaggerated rhetoric)*
This Island's mine, by Sycorax my mother.
And I am all the subjects which you have,
Which first was mine own King'.
MANGUS-PROSPERO King is too much.
You would usurp my place?
Inferior!
Back to the penitentiary or the school.
FLORA-MIRANDA *(Crying out)*. Father, for pity's sake!
All, all are free!
DOV-ARIEL *(Dancing around Mel-Caliban provocatively to taunt him)*
Ca – ca – Caliban
*(Wolf whistling)* (Whew, whew)
Was a bad man
(Whew, whew)
And never forget it,
Sang Ariel, for
I'm the king of the castle
I'm the king of the castle . . .

*(The Knot Garden, 3.8)*

Mangus, having lost control once again, angrily breaks character, dismisses his play and moves towards the footlights to address the audience. His ensuing speech mirrors the moment in *The Tempest* when Prospero renounces his books, the source of his knowledge. It furthermore references Lear's line 'I am a very foolish, fond old man' *(King Lear, 4.1.58)*, spoken when the old King has succumbed to madness but obtained a greater degree of clarity about his own predicament and the state of humanity. In Kemp's words, by this point, Mangus-Prospero has realized that he 'is like everyone else: he too has reached an impasse. With [a] startling admission of arrogance and futility, Mangus's universe collapses like a pack of cards.'[30]

MANGUS Enough! Enough!
We look in the abyss.
Lust for Caliban will not save us.
Prospero's a fake, we all know that;
And perhaps the island's due to sink into the sea.
Now that I break my staff and drown my book
DOV, MEL, FABER 'Full fathom five, thy father lies'
VOICES OFF STAGE *(Spoken)* 'Ding-dong, Ding-dong'
MANGUS *(Spoken)* I'm but a foolish, fond old man,
Just like the rest of you,
Whistling to keep my pecker up . . .

*(The Knot Garden, 3.9)*

Tippett musically depicts Mangus's 'collapsing universe' by combining a few pointed quotations from throughout the opera. Short, bombastic references to Mangus's twelve-note 'Tempest' theme accompany his dismissal of the charades and 'I'm but a foolish, fond old man' (see Figures 25 and 26), while tritely magical celesta, xylophone and trumpet music taken from when Mangus was pretending to conjure the island at the beginning of Act 3 underscores 'Prospero's a fake.'

Tippett notes that 'Mangus is not without success in sorting out the difficulties of the six other personalities on stage.' 'But', he asks, 'are the successes, if that's what we dare call them, of the [opera's] denouement really the product of Mangus's manipulation?' According to the composer, the answer is only 'partially'.[31] *The Knot Garden*'s characters are indebted to Mangus for putting them 'on the island', as it were, and (mis)guiding them through their individual and collective psychological labyrinths. Granted, the patients reach a point of resolution primarily through communicating with each other in the guise of their Shakespearian alter egos, and Mangus offers little in the way of diagnosis or tangible assistance. Yet he is the one who came up with the idea of the *Tempest* charade, and the psychological wellbeing of several of his patients does improve because of it – his influence over the other characters therefore cannot be discounted completely. In particular, despite Thea's considerable misgivings about his methods, Mangus manages to engineer a reunion between her and Faber, and Thea declares herself 'no more afraid' (3.7) following the successful resumption of her marriage.

Nevertheless, following the mismanaged and meandering *Tempest* charade, certain of Mangus's patients, and especially Mangus himself, begin to understand that his authority is arbitrary and his 'power' illusory. By *The Knot Garden*'s conclusion, the posturing psychoanalyst is left looking 'foolish' rather than grandiose. Like so many other Prosperos from this era, he ends his *Tempest* in fragile, pensive

---

30 Kemp, *Tippett: The Composer and His Music*, p. 411.
31 Tippett, 'Dreams', p. 221.

206

25 *The Knot Garden*, 3.9, 'Enough! Enough!' (Mangus).

26 *The Knot Garden*, 3.9, 'I'm but a foolish, fond old man' (Mangus).

mood. While *The Knot Garden* might not contain the radical postcolonial sentiments of several of its *Tempest* cousins from this period, Mangus's late, humble expression of inadequacy means that the opera can certainly be considered part of the trend in mid-twentieth-century *Tempest* criticism and performance for questioning Prospero's traditionally understood supremacy and genius.[32]

## 'I'M A TWO-WAY MAN': DOV–ARIEL–TIPPETT

Kemp ponders whether Mangus is something of a self-portrait for Tippett, and if *The Knot Garden*, like *The Tempest*, might therefore be interpreted as 'an allegory about the creative artist'.[33] Arguably, by questioning Mangus-Prospero's influence and usefulness, Tippett casts doubt on his own privileged position as an artist – to use his phrase, 'one who creates order out of chaos'.[34] Inspired by Hölderlin's elegy 'Bread and wine', a recurring question for Tippett during his career was 'what are poets for in a barren age?':

Throughout history, society has recognised that certain men [*sic*] possess [a] gift and has accorded them a special place. But if such men [*sic*] – poets if you like – are honoured, are the products of their imagination of any real value to the society which honours them? Or are we, particularly at this present point in our history, deluding ourselves that this may be so?[35]

According to Tippett, his treatment of Mangus demonstrates how, in the later twentieth century, 'the romantic notion of the creative artist as someone who can solve mankind's problems, dies hard'.[36]

Another creative artist in *The Knot Garden*, however, stands out as an even more strikingly autobiographical creation. Tippett admitted that Dov, 'the [gay] musician who expresses heart-break' was a highly personal character for him: '[t]he question is often posed to me: with which of your operatic characters do you most identify? The assumed answer is usually Mangus [... but] for me, an identification with Dov ... has always seemed close'.[37] It is possible that Dov's relationship with

Mel parallels Tippett's own 'tempestuous' affair with the painter Wilfred Franks during the 1930s.[38] Tippett, like Dov, was left bereft and sought psychoanalytic assistance after Franks, who was uncomfortable with homosexuality, jilted him to marry a woman.[39]

Dov's psychological upset stems chiefly from confusion over his gender and sexuality, and a consideration of the character arguably offers much insight into Tippett's own uncertainty over such issues, particularly during his younger years. Tippett labels Dov as 'sexually ambivalent' or 'bisexual', although on the evidence of *The Knot Garden* it seems that Dov is attracted only to men. Here, however, Tippett might not be using 'bisexual' in its modern sense, to indicate Dov's sexual preference. Rather, he seems to be referring to Dov's gender, or 'emotional make-up', as he puts it.[40] In the final scene of *The Knot Garden*'s first act, Dov admits to considerable insecurity about his gender identity, describing himself as 'a two-way man' (1.13). Then, in the final scene of Act 2, when Flora reveals to Dov that 'Sometimes I dream I am a boy / Who dies for love / And then I am a girl again', he responds pointedly, 'Yes, I understand' (2.9). Dov's musicality, sexuality and gender queerness are emphasized through his continual alignment with Ariel, *The Tempest*'s singing, sexually metamorphic sprite. At one point, Faber crudely makes plain the implications of this association

---

[32] For a discussion of contemporary postcolonial versions of *The Tempest*, see Rob Nixon, 'Caribbean and African appropriations of *The Tempest*', *Critical Inquiry* 13 (1987), 557–78.

[33] Kemp, *Tippett: The Composer and His Music*, p. 413. Bowen writes in the second edition of *Michael Tippett* (London, 1997) that Tippett's house, 'Nocketts', 'occasionally resembled the psychological knot garden of his eponymous opera, wherein one encountered a changing kaleidoscope of marital tensions and sexual proclivities, the host finding it difficult to resist playing Mangus' (p. 49).

[34] Tippett, 'Poets in a barren age', in *Aquarius*, pp. 148–56; p. 148.

[35] Tippett, 'Poets', p. 148. [36] Tippett, 'Dreams', p. 220.

[37] Tippett, 'Dreams', p. 221. [38] Tippett, *Blues*, p. 61.

[39] See Tippett, *Blues*, pp. 57–62.

[40] Tippett, 'Dov's journey', in *Music of the Angels*, pp. 236–8; p. 237.

when he remarks crudely how 'Ariel was fairy' (1.12) before unceremoniously attempting to seduce Dov.

Dov's post-*Knot Garden* journey further underlines his gender fluidity. *Songs for Dov* follows him through his '*Wanderjahre*': in Tippett's words, 'those years of illusion and disillusionment, innocence and experience, which we all pass through to reach what maturity we may'.[41] In the second song of this cycle, Dov conducts imaginary conversations with Ariel ('the girl-boy', as he puts it) and Mignon ('the boy-girl') from Goethe's novel *Wilhelm Meisters Lehrjahre* (1795), and wonders whether he too should pursue a life of music, free from gender constraints. Mignon, in the words of Terence Cave, is a circus performer, a 'child woman who insists on dressing as a boy, is partly aphasic but is capable of eloquent expression through song'.[42] Like Ariel, she therefore embodies musicianship, 'gender ambiguity, acrobatics ... [and] deference to a saviour and protector'.[43] In *Wilhelm Meisters Lehrjahre*, Mignon is referred to as 'zwitterhaft' ('hermaphroditic'), and criticism in the early twentieth century assumed that she was of indeterminate sex, although more recent readings present her less deterministically as a precursor to 'the modern challenge to a crudely sex-based antithesis of "male" and "female"'.[44]

As a homosexual and artist in mid-twentieth-century British society, Tippett apparently considered himself something of a 'two-way man': a 'hermaphroditic' Ariel–Mignon figure, in a psychological sense. Robinson notes how the prevailing view in Tippett's culture was that gender and sexuality were tightly bound together, and the composer constantly had to grapple with 'the problem of masculinity in a society that associated homosexuality with effeminacy'.[45] Iain Stannard further points out the ongoing stereotypical 'overlap between homosexuality and musicality as forms of deviancy which are open to feminization'.[46] Tippett was well aware of such assumptions, and, to a certain extent, his own views reflect these wider opinions on homosexuality, musicality and gender. According to Stannard, 'Tippett saw [psychological] hermaphrodism as enforced to some

degree by social conceptions of the artist and ... the homosexual too.'[47] His letters, for instance, 'frequently return to the notion of a union between masculine and feminine sides in his psyche'.[48] In one, Tippett professes that he 'can't help feeling that there's a somewhat special psychological balance for people like ourselves' – that is to say, homosexuals.[49] In another, he writes that, since 'artistic creation is so often ... polarised as feminine, as against the pure disembodied abstract intellect ... it's hardly any wonder if artists turn out hermaphroditic in temperament from time to time'.[50]

Arguably, Tippett's opinions about gender-suspect artists and the bipartite homosexual brain do simply reflect common contemporary clichés around gender and sexuality. Stannard suggests, however, that Tippett found 'theories of [psychological] hermaphrodism ... inadequate', and that he was dissatisfied by the 'relatively clear-cut acceptance of two stereotypical gender types'.[51] 'I'm beginning to doubt the absolute claims of what is called normal psychology', Tippett writes at one point: '[l]ife is just a bit more mysterious'.[52]

---

[41] Tippett, 'Dreams', p. 224.

[42] Terence Cave, *Mignon's Afterlives: Crossing Cultures from Goethe to the Twenty-First Century* (New York, 2011), p. 1.

[43] Cave, *Mignon's Afterlives*, p. 235.

[44] Cave, *Mignon's Afterlives*, p. 242.

[45] Suzanne Robinson, '"Coming out to oneself": encodings of homosexual identity from the First String Quartet to *The Heart's Assurance*', in *The Cambridge Companion to Michael Tippett*, ed. Kenneth Gloag and Nicholas Jones (Cambridge, 2013), pp. 86–102; p. 96.

[46] Iain Stannard, 'Hermaphrodism and the masculine body: Tippett's aesthetic views in a gendered context', in *Masculinity and Western Musical Practice*, ed. Ian Biddle and Kirsten Gibson (Farnham, 2009), pp. 279–304; p. 281.

[47] Stannard, 'Hermaphrodism', p. 280.

[48] Stannard, 'Hermaphrodism', p. 280.

[49] Tippett, letter to Francesca Allinson, 16 September 1943, in *Selected Letters of Michael Tippett*, ed. Thomas Schuttenhelm (London, 2005), p. 110.

[50] Tippett, letter to Douglas Newton, 22 May 1943, in Schuttenhelm, ed., *Selected Letters*, p. 151.

[51] Stannard, 'Hermaphrodism', pp. 287–8.

[52] Tippett, letter to Francesca Allinson, 16 September 1943, in Schuttenhelm, ed., *Selected Letters*, p. 110.

Stannard therefore proposes that Tippett's musical works 'act as a discursive field in which some of [his] concerns [about gender] are played out'.[53] *The Knot Garden*, arguably Tippett's most autobiographical work, appears to offer one such challenge to received wisdom, with an exploration of the vagaries of gender and sexuality via a youthful musician who attempts to move beyond the boundaries of standard identity (in part through engagement with Shakespeare), but whose efforts to do so cause him considerable emotional distress.

Dov – and, by association, Ariel – can perhaps be regarded as a heroic figure within *The Knot Garden*, albeit not in a traditionally 'masculine' sense. Since Tippett sides with these characters by emphasizing the especial importance of music to the pursuit of collective psychological wellbeing. Tippett writes that, ultimately, in the opera, 'acts of forgiveness, of reconciliation, are ... effected through the magic influence of music, not through the manifestations of Mangus's power, however well intended'.[54] *The Knot Garden* therefore follows *The Tempest*, and a 'tradition that stretches from Shakespeare to the present, in which music, or poetry allied with music, acts as agency for those special moments – acts of contrition, acts of forgiveness, submission to love – where the drama needs to be focused, clarified, intensified'.[55] Important examples of redemptive, diegetic musical interruptions in *The Knot Garden*'s dramaturgy include a cathartic blues ensemble in Act 1, a consolatory Schubert duet between Dov and Flora in Act 2, Dov's subsequent whimsical song 'I was born in a big town', and Dov-Ariel's 'Come unto these yellow sands' during the closing moments of Act 3. Dov, as the chief agent of music in the opera, is therefore arguably its most special character.

## FLORA: MIRANDA IN WONDERLAND

Flora, Dov's Act 2 duet partner, is another quietly radical presence within *The Knot Garden*. At the beginning of *The Knot Garden*, is another quietly is a sensitive and frustrated girl, poised on the verge of adulthood but frightened by and resistant to this impending change, primarily because of her adoptive father's lecherous behaviour towards her. Flora's name indicates her youth and virginity, along with her close relationship with her adoptive mother, Thea the gardener. In Act 1, when Dov and Mel surprise Flora by careering onstage 'in character' as Ariel and Caliban respectively, Flora joins in their play-acting, pretending to be Alice in Wonderland. Almost immediately, however, she berates herself for assuming a childlike identity.

FLORA *(Involuntarily; spoken with a tiny voice like a stage Alice)*
'I'm sure I'm very sorry'
*(Passionately with a slight tremor in her voice)*
O, do stop play-acting;
I'm real somewhere; I'm Flora.

(*The Knot Garden*, 1.9)

This brief alignment of Flora with Alice is further indicative of her personality, life stage and gender construction. Flora, like Alice, is beginning to express a desire for subjectivity, and, in the words of Carina Garland, is at 'the border between states'.[56]

Flora's main literary link, however, is not to Alice, but to Miranda from *The Tempest*, whom she plays in the Act 3 charade and whose budding sense of agency closely mirrors her own. At the end of *The Tempest*, one wonders how Miranda's journey will continue: whether she will become a subservient wife and mother to Ferdinand, or if her father's teachings, along with her own forthright personality and initiative, will make her an exceptional woman.[57] Her rebuke of Ferdinand during their chess game indicates the latter, although her immediate promise to call his cheating 'fair play' (5.1.175) because she loves him suggests the former. There seems to be no such confusion over Flora's future by the end of *The Knot*

---

53  Stannard, 'Hermaphrodism', p. 286.
54  Tippett, 'Dreams', p. 223. 55 Tippett, 'Dreams', p. 221.
56  Carina Garland, 'Curious appetites: food, desire, gender and subjectivity in Lewis Carroll's Alice texts', *The Lion and the Unicorn* 32 (2008), 22–39; p. 23.
57  For a discussion of Miranda's unique education, see Hiewon Shin, 'Single parenting, homeschooling: Prospero, Caliban, Miranda', *Studies in English Literature, 1500–1900* 48 (2008), 373–93.

27 *The Knot Garden*, 2.6, Flora rejects Faber.

*Garden*, however. When Faber and Flora recreate *The Tempest*'s chess scene in the third charade, she defiantly and definitively rejects the patriarchal oppression that he embodies:

FLORA-MIRANDA (*Quoting with exaggerated rhetoric: a caricature of false innocence*) 'Sweet Lord you play me false!'
FABER-FERDINAND (*Quoting with exaggerated rhetoric: a caricature of false charm*)
'No my dearest love,
I would not for the world'
FLORA-MIRANDA Oh yes you would.
False: false.
Dov-Ariel, lend me your wings.
I'm free: I'm free. (*She runs off. Dov-Ariel follows*)
(*The Knot Garden*, 3.6)

Notably, Flora's accusations and concomitant statement of liberation are accompanied by Faber's jaunty, haphazard trumpet theme (see Figure 27). Her confident ownership of this music demonstrates that she is no longer defined by her tormentor's attempts at sexual domination, and can now stand up to him as an equal. Faber, the middle-aged would-be 'playboy', is meanwhile rudely confronted by his delusions of youth and charisma. Perhaps the alignment of Faber with Ferdinand also sheds some doubt on the sincerity of the latter's intentions in *The Tempest*. Ferdinand, after all, has similarly eyed '[f]ull many a lady ...

with best regard' (3.1.39–40), and seems particularly drawn to Miranda for her inexperience, since he says to her that he will marry her if she is 'a virgin, / And [her] affection not gone forth' (1.2.447–8).

Through the unusual vehicle of *The Tempest* charades, then, Flora finally overcomes her fear of adulthood, and becomes ready to face her own 'brave new world' of identity construction. The audience is left with no idea where she will go from here: her possibilities are boundless. By the end of *The Knot Garden*, Flora is perhaps no longer Miranda but Ariel, set free from the bonds of her previous existence to start a new life of self-definition. While Miranda arguably remains trapped by patriarchal structure in *The Tempest*, being transferred seamlessly from Prospero to Ferdinand, Flora emphatically escapes such strictures during *The Knot Garden*'s final moments. She is, in some ways, the anti-Miranda.

## 'WE SENSE THE MAGIC NET': JUNGIAN SHAKESPEARE

T. S. Eliot, whom Tippett regarded as his 'spiritual and artistic mentor',[58] describes in one of his lectures how, in Shakespeare's works, 'a hidden and

---

[58] Tippett, *Blues*, p. 188.

mysterious pattern of reality emerges as from a palimpsest'.[59] According to Robinson,

[t]he very substantial achievement of Shakespeare, in Eliot's mind, was 'to see *through* the ordinary classified emotion of our active life into a world of emotion and feeling beyond, of which I am not ordinarily aware'. Shakespeare's genius lay in his perception of humanity and such skill as to have unveiled 'these strange lands of more than natural darkness and more than solar light'.[60]

If Eliot understood Shakespeare in this quasi-mystical fashion, then it is reasonable to assume that Tippett did too, particularly when one considers the evidence of his *Tempest* opera. During the finale of *The Knot Garden*, to quote Paul Driver, 'the transcendent shadows and glints through the confused doings of the modern men and women presented, and takes them dimly by surprise. A clear perception of its significance is not permitted them; they are merely to be bewildered by it into a provisional and partial cognisance of broader scope to their lives.'[61]

After Mangus's 'Prospero's a fake' speech initially breaks the fourth wall, all of the other characters except Thea and Faber join him to address the audience and offer a lesson from Tippett about how humanity might best progress. Tippett admired the sentiment of The Beatles' 'All you need is love' (1967),[62] and in a moment reminiscent of that song's message, the *Knot Garden*'s ensemble call for a rejection of self-absorption in favour of compassion and engagement with others

ALL If, for a timid moment
　We submit to love,
　Exit from the inner cage,
　Turn each to each to all

(*The Knot Garden*, 3.9)

The vocal writing for this moment is highly illustrative (see Figure 28). One at a time, the characters begin singing long notes on 'If', building to a dissonant crescendo before suddenly stopping and singing the remainder of the first two lines in quiet unison. Initially, they are accompanied by swooping strings, before the orchestra drops out and delicate woodwind joins them on 'for a timid moment'.

Musically, then, there is a move from loud, grating individuality – notably underpinned by a B-minor chord that by now carries a well-established link to psychological tempestuousness – to tentative, homorhythmic close harmony. An increase in volume and an expansion from a tight cluster chord to a chord spanning two octaves aurally exemplifies the characters 'opening up' to love. A B pedal note supports them, perhaps indicating that a collective, faltering psychological realization is occurring at this point. This move from jarring dissonance to something approaching unified consonance is then repeated for the next two lines, when the characters exit their inner cage of psychological individualism and 'turn' (in a musical, emotional and literal sense) to each other as one.

Following this 'turn', Dov briefly quotes Tippett's 1962 setting of Ariel's song inviting Ferdinand to love and dance, 'Come unto these yellow sands', which encapsulates the conclusion's most vital themes of music, empathy and forgiveness. The characters then acknowledge their artificial surroundings, 'within this theatre, upon this stage' (3.9), echoing Shakespeare's meta-theatrical reference to 'the great globe' (4.1.153) in Prospero's 'Our revels now are ended', which Mangus will soon quote from when all of the characters eventually leave the stage and the world of the knot garden 'dissolves'. Next, the title of Goethe's poem *The Magic Net* is

[59] T. S. Eliot, 'Shakespeare as poet and dramatist', first lecture manuscript, Houghton Library, Harvard, p. 10, quoted in Suzanne Robinson, 'The pattern from the palimpest: convergences of Eliot, Tippett, and Shakespeare', in *T. S. Eliot's Orchestra: Critical Essays on Poetry and Music*, ed. John Xiros Cooper (New York, 2000), 149–78; p. 155. For an exploration of Eliot's influence on Tippett, see Oliver Soden, 'Tippett and Eliot', *Tempo* 67 (2013), 28–53.
[60] Robinson, 'Pattern', p. 155. The Eliot quote is taken from 'Poet and dramatist', p. 11.
[61] Paul Driver, '*The Knot Garden*', in *Michael Tippett, O. M.: A Celebration*, ed. Geraint Lewis (Tunbridge Wells, 1980), pp. 155–60; pp. 155–6.
[62] Tippett, 'Art and man', in *Music of the Angels*, pp. 28–33; p. 28.

28  *The Knot Garden*, 3.9, 'If, for a timid moment . . .'.

referenced; according to Tippett, this allusion provides *The Knot Garden* with 'its most fundamental metaphor':[63]

ONE AFTER THE OTHER Here, here, here, here, here
ALL We sense the magic net
   That holds us veined
   Each to each to all
DOV 'Come unto these yellow sands'

(*The Knot Garden*, 3.9)

What, though, is this half-glimpsed, transcendental, and 'fundamental' 'magic net' that, in Tippett's account, might transform humanity? A potential answer lies in a 1974 postscript that the composer provides for the second edition of his book *Moving into Aquarius*. This essay almost perfectly summarizes *The Knot Garden*'s concerns and

conclusions, and offers a succinct distillation of Tippett's inspirations and aesthetics, containing a typically idiosyncratic mix of social commentary, technological fear and New Age optimism, interspersed with references to Brecht, Mozart, Goethe, Shakespeare, Blake and Jung. Tippett initially notes how modern society is struggling to deal with what he calls 'the religious problem' – that is to say, a post-Holocaust loss of faith:

[n]ot only is there now no longer any miracle of divine intervention at the request of private prayer, even if accompanied by the most steadfast faith and exemplary righteousness, but there is also no true Christian satisfaction any more to be drawn from

[63] Tippett, *Blues*, p. 84.

28 (cont.)

the pleasure of divine reward as the price of divine retribution . . . If we cannot make God, that is to say our particular 'local' righteousness, any longer an alibi for the brutalities we use against an alien righteousness; and if no received religion or ideology that we know can dispense with the claim to exclusivity of such righteousness, then our state might seem desperate. The way forward might seem like universal anarchy and despair.[64]

'And yet', Tippett writes, citing people's capacity for joy and love even in the concentration camps, 'humanity *cannot* go out; it *must* go on'.[65] He then quotes Caliban's 'Be not afeard . . . ' speech, which is 'sung . . . out of [Caliban's] darkness', as evidence of humanity's capacity to dream and 'dream again', even in the face of great oppression.[66] After this reference to *The Tempest*, Tippett moves on to discuss 'the same rich vein of dreams' in Jung, specifically in a letter of Jung's from 1929:

[w]e live in the age of the decline of Christianity, when the metaphysical premises of morality are collapsing . . . That's why the young are experimenting like young dogs. They want to live experimentally, with no historical premises. That causes reactions in the unconscious, restlessness, and longing for the fulfilment of the times. (This is called 'Chiliasm'.) When the confusion is at its height a new revelation comes, i.e. at the beginning of the fourth month of world history.[67]

In Tippett's interpretation, this letter means that 'at the year 2000 AD the 2,000-year world "month" of Pisces – shall we say, of ideological purity and fratricide – [will go] over gradually into the "month" of Aquarius – shall we say, of compassion and attempted union of the opposites'.[68]

In *The Knot Garden*, Tippett foreshadows his later essay by presenting dreaming and psychological exploration, inspired by *The Tempest* and Jung, as the solution to modern humanity's current crisis. *The Knot Garden*'s finale offers a tentative Jungian moment of 'compassion and attempted union', with the sensed 'magic net' a clear metaphor for the Collective Unconscious, which can apparently provide guidance, understanding and togetherness for modern individuals feeling disorientated in a violent, godless world. This moment of collective

psychological eucatastrophe might be regarded as a Jungian '*cision*, [a] cut that . . . eject[s] a prior state of existence and chart[s] a new series of possible futures'.[69] Kiernan Ryan argues that such 'visionary utopianism' is also a crucial feature of much of Shakespeare's work, especially at moments in *The Tempest* such as Gonzalo's Commonwealth dream (2.1.137–57) and Prospero's 'Our revels now are ended' speech (4.1.148–58).[70] *The Knot Garden*'s unashamedly transcendental ending therefore seems to follow its Shakespearian model by illustrating, in Ryan's words, a 'battle between utopian possibility and dystopian reality'.[71]

Despite his apparent pessimism about the worth of creative artists, then, the concluding moments of *The Knot Garden* suggest that Tippett, as Edward Venn puts it, 'retains his faith that art will transcend it all'.[72] Contrary to the composer's own assertions, *The Knot Garden* does not lay to rest 'any lingering belief that humanist art could achieve that moral power over and within humanity which religious

---

[64] Tippett, 'Postscript', in *Aquarius*, pp. 163–7; pp. 164–5.

[65] Tippett, 'Postscript', p. 166. [66] Tippett, 'Postscript', p. 166.

[67] C. G. Jung, letter to Walter Robert Corti, 12 September 1929, quoted in Tippett, 'Postscript', p. 167.

[68] Tippett, 'Postscript', pp. 166–7.

[69] S. J. McGrath, 'Sexuation in Jung and Lacan', *International Journal of Jungian Studies* 2 (2010), pp. 1–20; p. 5.

[70] See Kiernan Ryan, *Shakespeare's Universality* (London, 2015), pp. 43–50.

[71] Ryan, *Universality*, p. 43. This split is even more pronounced in Tippett's final opera, *New Year*, which is set across the two worlds of 'Somewhere Today' (dystopia) and 'Nowhere Tomorrow' (utopia). According to Philip Brett, a utopian impulse is also a distinctive feature of Britten's work, since Britten's operas 'offer not only a rigorous critique of the past but possibly also the vision of a differently organized reality for the future'. See Jennifer Doctor, Judith LeGrove, Paul Banks, Heather Wiebe and Philip Brett, 'Britten, (Edward) Benjamin', *Grove Music Online*, https://doi.org/10.1093/gmo/9781561592630.article.6435. Brett's comment suggests unexplored points of Shakespearian comparison between Tippett and his more famous counterpart.

[72] Edward Venn, 'Idealism and ideology in Tippett's writings', in *Music and Literature*, pp. 35–59; p. 44.

art, and, indeed, traditional religion itself had failed to engender'.[73] Rather, as Wilfred Mellers notes, the opera actually implies that 'supreme art like that of Shakespeare may sometimes do for us what religion did for earlier epochs',[74] since it is a curious encounter with *The Tempest* that ultimately allows *The Knot Garden*'s bewildered, warring characters to glimpse the transcendental truth of the Collective Unconscious and, in Tippett's phrase, 'move into Aquarius'.

---

[73] Tippett, 'Postscript', p. 163.

[74] Wilfred Mellers, 'Tippett at the millennium: a personal memoir', in *Tippett Studies*, ed. David Clarke (Cambridge, 1999), pp. 186–99; p. 194.

# TAUTOLOGICAL CHARACTER: *TROILUS AND CRESSIDA* AND THE PROBLEMS OF PERSONATION

## SAMUEL FALLON

In the first act of *Troilus and Cressida*, Aeneas pays a visit to the Greek camp, looking for a king whom he claims not to know by sight. 'Is this great Agamemnon's tent I pray you?' he asks (1.3.215). A few lines later, he tries again: 'How may / A stranger to those most imperial looks / Know them from eyes of other mortals?'(1.3.222–4). It is a timely question, one that introduces a vein of comic irony to what has been – to this point – a dourly serious scene, anchored by Ulysses' famous account of the decline of 'degree'. 'The specialty of rule', he had warned, 'hath been neglected', and now Aeneas had arrived to prove the point (1.3.77). It is not quite clear whether Aeneas' uncertainty is genuine; Agamemnon, for one, is not convinced. The joke is on the Greek King either way: the implication of the question is that his 'most imperial looks' are not, in fact, particularly distinguished, or at least that they are *indistinguishable* from those of the 'other mortals' in the Greek tents. And if we take Aeneas seriously – if he is genuinely confused – the effect is even more unsettling: if 'high and mighty Agamemnon' (1.3.230) cannot be recognized, who in the play can?

Aeneas' encounter with Agamemnon is easy to overlook – it is peripheral to the main plot, with Aeneas coming merely to deliver a message – but it reflects a pervasive uncertainty about the status of *Troilus*'s persons: about their solidity and security as individuals, their ability to be identified, distinguished, remembered, 'known'. This uncertainty is woven deeply into the world of the play. It lies behind the Trojan deliberations on

the doubtful 'worth' or 'value' of Helen, the 'pearl, / Whose price hath launched above a thousand ships' (2.2.80–1); it shadows, too, the uneasy self-consciousness of Troilus and Cressida, who imagine themselves as proleptic allegories of constancy and unfaithfulness. The remoteness, and the seeming instability, of these characters has long troubled the play's critics. 'We do not know what the characters are like', wrote John Bayley some decades ago, 'because there is neither time nor occasion to find out, and for the same reason they have no idea of themselves'.[1] These are characters 'etiolated', as Linda Charnes's influential reading has it, 'by their own citationality'; 'weary', in the words of Heather James, 'of their status as tropes'.[2] The play's characters, this line of criticism suggests, are compromised by the overdetermining presence of the long literary tradition behind them, a tradition felt as a 'textual psychosis' that forecloses the integral selfhood that we have come to expect of dramatic characters.[3] On this view, *Troilus and Cressida*'s widely remarked 'ugliness' reflects the mimetic deficiency of a play that advertises itself, in a preface to the second state

---

[1] John Bayley, 'Time and the Trojans', *Essays in Criticism* 25 (1975), 55–73; p. 60.

[2] Linda Charnes, *Notorious Identity: Materializing the Subject in Shakespeare* (Cambridge, MA, 1993), p. 84; Heather James, *Shakespeare's Troy: Drama, Politics, and the Translation of Empire* (Cambridge, 1997), p. 98.

[3] Carol Cook, 'Unbodied figures of desire', *Theatre Journal* 38 (1986), 34–52; p. 50.

of the first quarto, as 'never staled with the stage'.[4] It is thus no surprise that René Girard would diagnose in *Troilus* a 'pessimism' rooted in a 'distrust for mimetic behavior in general and theater in particular'.[5] The problem with characters like Agamemnon, it seems, is that they never escape their textual origins.

But Girard's argument is in fact quite different. In his view, the play's characters are afflicted by a surplus rather than a deficiency of mimetic energy. Indeed, despite the suggestion that it was never performed, *Troilus* is a laboratory of theatrical forms: it is filled with scenes of voyeuristic spectatorship, of antic mimicry, of pageantry and display, and in this sense, as Girard observes, it 'puts the mimetic disease on stage'.[6] The disease runs deeper than explicit metadrama. In Girard's account, mimetic effects ground the basic modes of social function (and dysfunction) in the play: the reciprocal gestures of lovers, but also the imitative desire behind Pandarus's voyeurism; the exemplarity that supports the system of military rank, but also the 'pale and bloodless emulation' that slowly corrupts the Greek army (1.3.134). Mimesis in these forms operates as an insidious force of 'undifferentiation', collapsing the system of degree on which, as Ulysses famously argues, the social order and all of its hierarchical distinctions depend. When Ulysses reports Patroclus's parodic impressions of the Greek generals – 'Sometimes, great Agamemnon, / Thy topless deputation he puts on' (1.3.151–2) – the capacity of mimetic theatricality to blur lines, to render even the King worryingly indistinct, becomes especially clear: here the performative methods of character find themselves at odds with the integrity of the play's persons. In such moments, we might suspect that the stability of *Troilus*'s characters is threatened by nothing so much as the mimetic forms that bring them to life.

The influence of Girardian theory has waned since its height in the 1980s and 1990s, when Girard's own *A Theater of Envy* cast Shakespeare as a precocious modern, a writer who grasped ahead of his time the mimetic desire that, for Girard, came to define the nineteenth-century novel.[7] The 'neomimetic approach' seemed

especially fertile for drama, pointing up as it did the intersections between imitation as theatrical practice and emulation as psychosocial complex.[8] But while more recent criticism has attended closely to the techniques of mimesis on stage, it has largely left Girard's theory of mimetic subjectivity behind. This article brings them back into contact, recovering Girard's mimetic theory by positioning it within and against the history of 'personation', the term that emerged in the seventeenth century as the name for imitative performance. As we will see, early modern personation discloses a set of concerns that closely mirror Girard's, for it encourages us to conceive of persons – both onstage and off – as figures of theatrical mimesis.

This article's particular interest, then, lies in how *Troilus and Cressida* frames the *person* as a dramatic and as a social category: the 'key category', as Anthony Dawson and Paul Yachnin argue, in early modern 'theatrical performance and the pleasures it provides'.[9] In what follows, I focus on two

---

[4] Shakespeare, *Troilus and Cressida* [1998], The Arden Shakespeare, Third Series (London, 2006), p. 120. For a survey of the negative aesthetic judgements that *Troilus* has tended to provoke, see David Baker, *On Demand: Writing for the Market in Early Modern England* (Stanford, 2010), pp. 68–74.

[5] René Girard, *A Theater of Envy: William Shakespeare* (New York, 1991), p. 159.

[6] Girard, *A Theater of Envy*, p. 159. Girard's chapters on the play in *A Theater of Envy* build on his earlier essay 'The politics of desire in Troilus and Cressida', in *Shakespeare and the Question of Theory*, ed. Patricia Parker and Geoffrey Hartman (New York, 1985), pp. 187–207.

[7] Girard, *A Theater of Envy*, p. 6.

[8] Girard calls his method 'neomimetic' in order to distinguish it from 'the old pap of "mimetic realism," a supposedly separate artistic mimesis with its conflictual sting removed' (*Theater of Envy*, p. 5). For an especially insightful Girardian reading of *Troilus and Cressida*, see Eric Mallin, 'Emulous factions and the collapse of chivalry: *Troilus and Cressida*', *Representations* 29 (1990), 145–79, which situates the play alongside the Essex rebellion as a representation of the decline of the chivalric ideal amid court factionalism.

[9] Anthony B. Dawson and Paul Yachnin, *The Culture of Playgoing in Shakespeare's England: A Collaborative Debate* (Cambridge, 2001), p. 7. See also Yachnin, 'Personations: *The Taming of the Shrew* and the limits of theoretical

competing and overlapping logics of individuation. One is the logic of mimetic performance: 'The Elizabethans', write Dawson and Yachnin, 'understood "person" to mean an embodied character, a real fiction, a body always and completely interwoven with mind in the performing of a role'.[10] The other, reflected in the play's fascination with scenes of naming, is the system of difference and degree that separates persons from each other, conferring on them the distinctness on which individuality depends.[11] The tension between these two modes went to the heart of early modern ideas of personhood and dramatic character, with the concept of personation emerging precisely at their intersection – and *Troilus and Cressida* staging their collision. What appears as a crisis of undifferentiation, I will argue, is at root a conflict between the play's twin logics of individuation. This conflict in turn reveals a paradox at the heart of the mimetic approach, which depends on the very distinctions that the mimetic self, in its extreme form, renders null. From this perspective, Girard's preoccupation with *Troilus* registers its troubling implications for his model of the mimetic self – a model that the play both exemplifies and explodes.

## MAKING DISTINCT

In *An Apologie for Actors* (1611), a treatise published two years after *Troilus and Cressida*'s first quarto, Thomas Heywood conjured a scene of the same Trojan heroes in order to argue the aesthetic power and moral force of the stage. Unlike poetry (which, he wrote, can describe images but not present them to the eye) and portraiture (which can show images but not 'action, passion, motion, or any other gesture'), plays deliver living beings – 'a *Hector* all besmered in blood, trampling vpon the bulkes of Kinges' or a '*Troylus* returning from the field in the sight of his father *Priam*, as if man and horse euen from the steeds rough fetlockes to the plume in the champions helmet had bene together plunged into a purple Ocean'.[12] Heywood's examples are well chosen: on the one hand, they are indisputably

heroic and hence fit vehicles of moral instruction; on the other, their status as legends heightens the thrill of theatrical embodiment. 'Oh', he declares, 'these were sights to make an *Alexander*'.[13]

When he wrote the *Apologie*, Heywood likely had in mind his own Trojan play, *The Iron Age*. His vivid descriptions of gory battle are, after all, a poor fit for *Troilus and Cressida*, which offers little of the action that Heywood seems to relish. The difference is clear enough in Shakespeare's version of the scene sketched above: Trojan warriors returning from battle. As Hector and Troilus and their peers cross the stage silently, attention focuses on Cressida and Pandarus, who observe them from above:

CRESSIDA Who's that?
PANDARUS That's Antenor. He has a shrewd wit, I can tell you, and he's man good enough. He's one o'th' soundest judgements in Troy whosoever, and a proper man of person.

. . .

*Enter Helenus passing by [below]*
CRESSIDA Who's that?
PANDARUS That's Helenus. I marvel where Troilus is. That's Helenus. I think he went not forth today. That's Helenus.

. . .

*Enter Troilus passing by [below]*
CRESSIDA What sneaking fellow comes yonder?

---

criticism', *Early Modern Literary Studies* 2 (1996), 1–31. On character and Shakespearian drama, see Paul Yachnin and Jessica Slights, eds., *Shakespeare and Character Theory, History, Performance and Theatrical Persons* (New York, 2009).

[10] Dawson and Yachnin, *Culture of Playgoing*, p. 3.

[11] My concern is thus less with subjective interiority, a topic much addressed in Shakespeare criticism, than with persons viewed from without, as objects of recognition, identification and evaluation – though I will also suggest that the internalization of these dynamics ultimately constitutes an important part of the play's wrestling with personation. The key study of interiority and early modern drama remains Katharine Eisaman Maus, *Inwardness and Theater in the English Renaissance* (Chicago, 1995), a response in part to new historicist and cultural materialist critiques of the subject, most notably Catherine Belsey, *The Subject of Tragedy: Identity and Difference in Renaissance Drama* (London, 1985).

[12] Thomas Heywood, *An Apologie for Actors* (London, 1611), sigs. B3v–B4r.

[13] Heywood, *Apologie*, sig. B4r.

PANDARUS Where? Yonder? That's Deiphobus.—'Tis
Troilus! There's a man, niece, h'm? Brave Troilus, the
prince of chivalry!

(1.2.185–9, 214–17, 223–6)

Cressida's exchange with Pandarus introduces the vein of curious irony that runs through *Troilus*, an irony realized in the regular deflation of its famous heroes. Here that deflation takes the form of generic displacement, with military heroes cast into a world of romantic comedy and epic praise – the 'prince of chivalry' – put to the work of erotic advertisement: this Troilus is not a sight to make an Alexander but rather to draw a blush from Cressida. Even more deflating is the surprising fact that these heroes need to be *introduced* – that Cressida apparently does not recognize them. For her, names facilitate the evaluative judgements that typically follow them: once named, Antenor can be commended for his sound judgement and Troilus for his bravery. But, of course, Cressida's questions and Pandarus's answers also serve the audience; they perform the stage business of putting names to faces. If this is a practical necessity in a play whose cast is filled with similarly dressed soldiers, it is also slightly awkward. In Heywood's sketch, Hector and Troilus hardly need to be named; in Shakespeare's play, we could not recognize them otherwise.

Names, it turns out, are more than a momentary concern in the play. Cressida's repeated question – 'Who's that?' – in fact becomes something of a refrain, a periodic reminder of the opacity of so many of *Troilus*'s characters. 'Who's there?' ask Patroclus and Achilles, fifteen lines apart, when they meet a roving Thersites (2.3.22, 37). 'See, ho! Who is that there?' asks Paris, struggling to make out a face in the night (4.1.1). When Aeneas comes knocking for Cressida, who must be delivered to the Greeks, Pandarus answers the door: 'Who's there? What's the matter? Will you beat down the door?' (4.2.45–6). Aeneas asks a version of the question in searching for Agamemnon early in the play; so too, during a later visit to the Trojan camp, does Agamemnon when he glimpses Troilus: 'What Trojan is that same that looks so heavy?' (4.6.97). Hector puts it most directly in the same scene: 'The worthiest of them', he instructs

Ajax, 'tell me name by name' (4.7.44). If there is an echo, in these moments, of the opening of *Hamlet*, the force here is less mystery than ironic deflation: no one is distinct enough to be clearly seen. The insistence with which the question returns, then, reminds us that names are needed to get anything done in this world. They are what allow enemies to be measured up and prospective lovers scouted. They consolidate the persons who bear them, bringing them into significance, rendering them knowable. Hence the comparative evaluations that so often follow: 'the worthiest of them', 'a proper man of person', 'good enough'.

The indexical register of these exchanges points to the power of names, in Saul Kripke's account, to 'fix a referent'. For Kripke, a proper name depends on an 'initial baptism' that establishes a stable relation of reference, a relation sustained through a causal chain that links one speaker to the next.[14] *Troilus and Cressida* doesn't offer baptism properly speaking, but the ostensive form of its recurring question (who's *that*?) recalls the generative force of baptism, re-grounding for new audiences the relation between name and referent.[15] The nearest thing to an exception comes when Achilles, on meeting Hector, calls on the gods to name the fatal wound he plans to inflict:

Tell me, you heavens, in which part of his body
Shall I destroy him – whether there, or there, or there –
That I may give the local wound a name,
And make distinct the very breach whereout
Hector's great spirit flew? Answer me, heavens!

(4.7.126–130)

---

14 Saul A. Kripke, *Naming and Necessity* [1972](Cambridge, MA, 1980), esp. pp. 96–7 and 135–40. Kripke's 'causalist' approach opposed 'descriptive' theories of proper names, which held that a name is an abbreviated description of its referent (and hence that, to be functional, a name's speaker must be associated with a uniquely identifying description or cluster of descriptions).

15 The phenomenon of 'multiple grounding' plays a central role in later developments of the causalist theory. See, for instance, Gareth Evans, 'The causal theory of names', *Proceedings of the Aristotelian Society* Supplementary Volume, 47 (1973), 187–208; and Michael Devitt, 'Should proper names still be problematic?' in *On Reference*, ed. Andrea Bianchi (Oxford, 2015), pp. 108–43; p. 123.

Achilles' taunt makes clear how much depends on the conferral of a name. Naming Hector's injury would seem to certify it, to make it official; it would open up the possibility of fame, a reward (or punishment) that can attach only to a unique and durable referent. Here the power to differentiate and specify – to 'make distinct' – acquires an almost magical aspect, reflected in Achilles' apparent sense that naming the wound will actually bring it into being. (That his own heel would become the stuff of legend ironizes Achilles' bluster without diminishing the sense of naming's uncanny power.) The act of naming hence works as a source of superstition – such that, when Hector needles Menelaus about Helen, Menelaus stops him short: 'Name her not now, sir. She's a deadly theme' (4.7.65).

To the extent that all of this is metadramatic scaffolding – an aid for playgoers tracking a large cast of similar characters – it is vaguely embarrassing, a reminder of the theatre's reduction of its persons, however renowned, to ordinary bodies. An actor settling into a role, suggests Bert States, is caught in 'a contest for possession in which the actor-character teeters constantly on the verge of catastrophe – that is, of becoming one of us'.[16] States's example is Hamlet, a character whose canonicity subjects each new performance to the scepticism of audiences who declare the lead actor 'too squat, or too tall, not right for the role'.[17] On the early modern stage, this awkwardness was particularly pronounced in history plays, where, as Brian Walsh suggests, the actor's body reveals the irreversible absence of heroes of the past: 'The living breathing body on stage disrupts rather than effects continuity and thus highlights how the temporality of drama forces audiences into an awareness that the actual past is always irrecoverable.'[18] The tension between actor's body and character's person was perhaps even sharper for Hector and Achilles, whose legends transcended national history. They were, as Heather James argues, palimpsests layered by their long literary afterlives, and if this tradition came with its own indignities – a gradual downward migration from epic to romance, satire and cheap-print ballad – embodiment at times feels like the crowning one, forcing famous names into unrecognizable bodies.[19]

Such deflation is a theatrical problem, but it is also a diegetic one: the opacity of identity underscores a pervasive sense within the playworld that the available forms of individuation and distinction are at risk. For Ulysses, indeed, their disintegration (the breakdown of what he calls 'degree') is a sickness at the heart of the Greek ranks. Degree, Girard writes, is the 'differential principle' on which a whole structure of 'rank, distinction, discrimination, hierarchy' rests, and its destabilization – or more precisely, as David Bevington suggests, its revelation as a relative rather than an objectively ordered structure – suggests the collapse of difference itself.[20] Without difference, the prerogatives 'of age, crowns, sceptres, laurels' can no longer 'stand in authentic place' (1.3.107–8). And so the failure of degree precipitates that of social norms and ultimately of moral value: 'right and wrong', says Ulysses, 'Should lose their names, and so should justice too' (1.3.116, 118). It is telling that he describes this moral breakdown as a loss of *names*: for Ulysses, nothing is real without the distinguishing force of identification. Nothing, we might add, and no one.

For the Greeks, the breakdown of degree has a distinctly theatrical flavour. As Ulysses warns the generals, Achilles has confined himself to his tents, where Patroclus 'with ridiculous and awkward action / Which, slanderer, he "imitation" calls / ... pageants us' (1.3.149–51). Ulysses complains that Patroclus's performances – strutting pompously

---

[16] Bert O. States, *Great Reckonings in Little Rooms: On the Phenomenology of Theater* (Berkeley, 1985), p. 121.

[17] States, *Great Reckonings*, p. 120. States continues with an observation that might apply to the Homeric heroes as well as Hamlet: 'So we have the impression of a stranger speaking Hamlet's lines; the real Hamlet instantly retreats to literature, becomes a mouthed text floating in and out as the actor finds him in certain phrases and loses him in others.'

[18] Brian Walsh, *Shakespeare, the Queen's Men, and the Elizabethan Performance of History* (Cambridge, 2009), p. 26.

[19] Heather James, *Shakespeare's Troy: Drama, Politics, and the Translation of Empire* (Cambridge, 1997), esp. pp. 1–2, 85–118.

[20] See David Bevington's introduction to the Arden 3 *Troilus and Cressida*, p. 74.

as Agamemnon, mimicking the palsied age of Nestor – push to 'the extremest ends / Of parallels' (1.3.167–8) – that is, they slanderously pass off exaggeration as likeness. But the danger comes less from parodic excess than from Patroclus's 'act[ing] thy greatness', as Ulysses describes it to the King, in the first place (1.3.158). Imitation crosses boundaries; it encroaches on the individual prerogatives of whomever it touches. Playing someone suggests that his person can be put on. Hence Achilles' responses to the miniature dramas he watches: 'Excellent! 'tis Agamemnon right' (1.3.164). This duplicative aspect of imitation is felt more broadly as a surge of Girardian mimetic rivalry. Nestor points out the dynamic, observing that 'in the imitation of these twain [Achilles and Patroclus] . . . many are infect', and that Ajax, in particular, now 'keeps his tent like' Achilles (1.3.185–7, 190). The resulting mimetic crisis, Girard argues, unfolds as a spiralling process of undifferentiation, an erosion of the forms that preserve hierarchical distinction.

The play's obsessive returns to scenes of naming can thus begin to seem symptomatic: an attempt to rescue individuation from a world in which it is disintegrating. The Greek army's crisis of degree is not the only example. Cressida's and Pandarus's attempts to name and thereby distinguish the Trojan soldiers seem to be equally doomed. Just before the pageant of returning heroes, Pandarus and Cressida debate the merits of the city's leading princes:

PANDARUS . . . Troilus is the better man of the two.
CRESSIDA O Jupiter! There's no comparison.
PANDARUS What, not between Troilus and Hector? Do you know a man if you see him?
CRESSIDA Ay, if I ever saw him before and knew him.
PANDARUS Well, I say Troilus is Troilus.
CRESSIDA Then you say as I say, for I am sure He is not Hector.
PANDARUS No, nor Hector is not Troilus, in some degrees.
CRESSIDA 'Tis just to each of them: he is himself.
(1.2.58–68)

Cressida's tone is gently teasing; she is concealing for the moment her love for Troilus, pretending to favour Hector instead. There is 'no comparison', in

this sense, because Hector is so clearly superior. Yet the literal sense of Cressida's response lingers, suggesting not merely a rejection of this particular comparison but a more general refusal of the kinds of distinctions that Pandarus wants to draw. Naming, suggests Wittgenstein, is 'preparatory to the use of a word'. 'But what', he asks, 'is it preparation *for*?'[21] In this case, we might say it is preparation for the particular language game of evaluation, a game that demands the fixing of referents, to which particular descriptions – *brave, proper, admirable* – can be assigned. But that descriptive vocabulary is worryingly shrunken, and the comparisons they should articulate hard to enforce. None of the play's characters seems distinct enough to stand up to evaluation, and in its place Pandarus can offer only tautology. Troilus may not be Hector, but neither Cressida nor Pandarus can say exactly what distinguishes one from the other. The most that can be said of either is that 'he is himself'.

## PERSONATION

When distinctions fail in this way, the consequences can be serious: the breakdown of authority in the Greek camp, for instance, or the unnerving ease, later in the play, with which Diomedes replaces Troilus as Cressida's lover. More broadly, difference is what secures the play's persons – what ensures that they can be recognized as individuals. Two centuries after Shakespeare, William Hazlitt would worry that a gradual refinement of manners culminating in an 'insipid sameness' had ruined contemporary drama. 'There can be no great refinement of character', he wrote, 'where there is no distinction of persons'. In erasing difference, he argued, the modern habit of 'abstraction' threatened the 'essentially concrete and individual power' proper to 'dramatic poetry'.[22] Although

---

[21] Ludwig Wittgenstein, *Philosophical Investigations*, 3rd edn, trans. G. E. M. Anscombe (New York, 1968), § 26.
[22] William Hazlitt, 'On modern comedy' [1813], in *Selected Writings*, ed. Jon Cook (Oxford, 1991), p. 106; and 'Modern tragedy' [1820], p. 110.

Hazlitt's assessment is tethered to the sensibilities of the nineteenth-century stage, his account of dramatic personhood has proven a durable one – and one that lurks behind later readings of *Troilus*'s characters, whose felt 'etiolation' reflects their status as more types than selves. A similar worry emerges in Girard's discussion of character. 'Most of us', he argues, 'want characters to belong only to well differentiated species, unrelated to one another; if they are mixed together, it becomes too confusing and everything turns *monstrous*.' But whereas Hazlitt worries over the ascendance of a habit of generalizing abstraction, Girard locates the threat to differentiated character in the operations of 'mimetic interaction' – a force that works in Shakespearian drama to galvanize 'the "deconstruction" of separate essences'.[23] *Troilus*'s persons, and their constitutive distinctness, are on this account undone by the corrosive likeness of emulation.

Shakespeare's contemporaries were no less concerned than Girard about the 'separate essences' who populated their plays. *Character* is arguably the wrong word – only later would it acquire the modern sense of 'imagined person' – and yet accounts of early modern playgoing foreground the persons encountered on the stage. Thomas Nashe, writing in 1592, described the thrill of watching Shakespeare's Talbot 'triumphe againe on the Stage, and haue his bones newe embalmed with the teares of ten thousand spectators ... who, in the Tragedian that represents his person, imagine they behold him fresh bleeding'.[24] Nashe's 'person' is, as Dawson has written, a decidedly ambiguous term – one that 'bespeaks the impossibility of splitting body from self or self from role'.[25] Two decades after Nashe, however, in a similar account of theatrical charisma, Heywood would attempt to split them:

[W]hat English blood seeing the person of any bold English man presented and doth not hugge his fame, and hunnye at his valor, pursuing him in his enterprise with his best wishes, and as beeing wrapt in contemplation, offers to him in his hart all prosperous performance, as if the Personater were the man Personated, so bewitching a thing is liuely and well spirited action, that it hath power to new mold the harts of spectators

and fashion them to the shape of any noble and notable attempt[?][26]

Heywood's text is the central document in the emergence, at the turn of the seventeenth century, of *personation* as a conceptual framework for dramatic character. According to Andrew Gurr, the term 'was called into being by the same developments' that by 1600 had rendered 'characterisation ... the chief requisite of the successful player'.[27] For Heywood, personation indeed seems to have been rooted in a concept of imitative likeness: character succeeds when the 'Personater' is able to resemble the 'man Personated' so persuasively that it is 'as if' they were in fact the same person. His prescriptions emphasize verisimilar performance, urging actors (like Hamlet to the players) to avoid 'overacting trickes', and 'any impudent or forced motion in any part of the body'. Instead, an actor should 'qualifie euery thing according to the nature of the person personated'.[28]

But the emergence of *personation* as a term of dramatic art was neither automatic nor total. In the last decades of the sixteenth century, it found wide usage as a more encompassing label for the (often textual) mediation of persons. While 'to personate' could mean to *impersonate*, to adopt a false identity, it didn't require a sense of deception: when the 1616 lexicon *An English expositor* gave the definition 'To represent the person of another', it allowed both for role-playing and fraudulence.[29] At its broadest, the

---

[23] Girard, *Theater of Envy*, p. 156.

[24] Thomas Nashe, *The Works of Thomas Nashe*, ed. Ronald B. McKerrow, 5 vols. (London, 1903), vol. 1, p. 212.

[25] Anthony Dawson, 'Performance and participation: Desdemona, Foucault, and the actor's body', in *Shakespeare, Theory and Performance*, ed. James C. Bulman (New York, 1995), pp. 31–47; p. 34.

[26] Heywood, *Apologie*, sig. B4r.

[27] Andrew Gurr, *The Shakespearean Stage, 1574–1642*, 3rd edn (Cambridge, 1992), p. 100.

[28] Heywood, *Apologie*, sig. C4r.

[29] John Bullokar, *An English expositor teaching the interpretation of the hardest words vsed in our language. With sundry explications, descriptions, and discourses* (London, 1616), sig. M1r.

term referred to almost any form of representation – to standing in for, or symbolizing, something or someone. Often it referred to personification: George Puttenham translated *prosopopoeia* in 1589 as 'the Counterfait in personation'.[30] More simply, it could refer to the acts of designating, identifying and naming, as when Nashe describes his nemesis Gabriel Harvey 'personat[ing] this man and that man, calling him *my good friend Maister Doctour* at euery word'.[31] As this example suggests, the emergence of the word owes something to the explosion of satire in the 1580s and 1590s, where this nominative mode – the singling out of individuals – became a key rhetorical strategy.[32] Stretching across all of these, personation offered a category capacious enough to include the many forms by which persons could be rendered susceptible to discourse.

When it migrated into the theatre, personation retained this variety, including the nominative function that governed many of its uses. John Marston's *Antonio and Mellida*, probably performed in 1599, offers its earliest recorded usage as a term of dramatic art: 'Whom', one of Marston's characters asks of another in the Induction, 'do you personate?' But while this question reflects the imperative of nominative identification – the answer names, for the benefit of the audience, the character being played – it also registers a concern for representational likeness: 'Faith, we can say our parts', insists another character, 'but we are ignorant in what mould we must cast our actors'.[33] The fact that theatrical personation could refer to mere role-playing, to disguise, to symbolic representation and (particularly in masques) to personification allegories explains its numerous and contradictory critical appropriations.[34] It also suggests something important about the term's implicit force: even as it consolidated around the concern for imitative performance evinced in Heywood's *Apologie, personation* was also emerging as a catch-all term for different ways to fashion persons. In this sense, mimetic playing could be understood as the particularly theatrical technique by which persons are made.

The idea that mimetic playing brings persons into being helps explain a further expansion of the concept in the ensuing decades. Writing in

*Leviathan* (1651), Thomas Hobbes turned to personation – now firmly tied to the theatre – in order to articulate a theory of personhood in general: '[A] Person', he wrote, 'is the same that an *Actor* is, both on the Stage and in common Conversation; and to *Personate* is to *Act*, or *Represent* himselfe, or an other'.[35] For Hobbes, persons are to be grasped by analogy to performance and understood as a species of character. Just as a theatrical person comes into being through representation, so too do ordinary persons; indeed, being a person means being represented before a public audience, whether on stage or 'in common Conversation'.[36] Hobbes offered the most striking version of this

---

[30] George Puttenham, *The Arte of English Poesie*, in *Elizabethan Critical Essays*, ed. G. Gregory Smith, 2 vols. (Oxford, 1904), vol. 2, p. 170.
[31] Nashe, *Strange Newes*, in *Works*, vol. 1, p. 279.
[32] See, for instance, Robert Burton in *The Anatomy of Melancholy* (New York, 2001), who distinguishes satirists who 'generally tax vice' from 'such as personate, rail, scoff, calumniate, perstringe by name' (vol. 1, p. 343). On the rise of 'embodied writing' in the last decades of the sixteenth century, see Douglas Bruster, *Shakespeare and the Question of Culture: Early Modern Literature and the Cultural Turn* (Basingstoke, 2003), pp. 65–93.
[33] John Marston, *Antonio and Mellida*, ed. W. Reavley Gair (Manchester, 2004), Induction, lines 5, 3–4.
[34] Gurr's association of *personation* with mimetic characterization has been challenged by several scholars. Matthew Steggle, *War of the Theatres: The Poetics of Personation in the Age of Jonson* (Victoria, 1998), locates the term amid the fashion for *ad hominem* satirical drama; Robert Weimann and Douglas Bruster, *Shakespeare and the Power of Performance: Stage and Page in the Elizabethan Theatre* (Cambridge, 2008), pp. 139–59, use it to refer to teasingly self-aware or 'secretly open' performance, quite opposed to the deep characterization offered by Gurr; and Mary Jo Kietzmann, 'Will personified: Viola as actor-author in Twelfth Night', *Criticism* 45 (2012), 257–90, makes it the name for a mode of freely imaginative, 'explicitly non-mimetic' acting.
[35] Thomas Hobbes, *Leviathan* (London, 1985), Part I, Ch. 16, p. 217.
[36] The suggestion that all persons are represented has been a standing provocation to scholarship on *Leviathan*, partly because it seems at odds with Hobbes's distinction between 'artificial' and 'natural' persons. On the problems of representation that Hobbes's discussion of persons and personation raises, see Hannah Fenichel Pitkin, *The Concept of*

turn, but he was not the first to make it. Samuel Daniel had already tied personation to public comportment: although we cannot know what great men 'do within', the chorus of *Philotas* (1605) declares, 'Yet know we by th'euents, what plottes haue beene, / And how they all without do personate.'[37] A similar sense governs John Florio's use of the term in his 1603 edition of the *Essayes*, where it translates Montaigne on the cultivation of outward selves: '[W]hat person a man vndertakes to act, he doth ever therewithal personate his owne.'[38] In such usages, *personation* summons the stage to figure the presentations of self that, as Erving Goffman famously argued, constitute us as social beings.[39]

Naming, the previous section suggested, is one method of fashioning persons; mimetic personation can now be seen to be another. And if naming is a constant preoccupation in *Troilus*, personation is the method with the most powerful advocates within the play. Ulysses, in particular, insists on a view of persons as formed in and by their communication. Attempting to cajole Achilles out of seclusion, Ulysses reminds him:

> That no man is the lord of anything,
> Though in and of him there be much consisting,
> Till he communicate his parts to others.
> Nor doth he of himself know them for aught
> Till he behold them formèd in th'applause
> Where they're extended.
>
> (3.3.110–15)

As for Hobbes, the stage here is the organizing analogy for the presentation of self: Achilles, Ulysses advises, must communicate 'his parts' and recognize himself in 'th'applause' of his audience. But what is striking is the Greek general's suggestion that this performance is not merely public display – it is also how Achilles might come to know himself. Such knowledge comes from 'beholding' a detached and projected self, a self made legible through the reflecting gaze of others. There is thus a paradoxical circularity to Ulysses' advice: communicating one's parts is what enables one to grasp them and hence to perform them more ably.

This circularity is perhaps endemic to mimetic personation. For Heywood and Hobbes, persons are at once subjects and objects of mimetic performance. In the *Apologie*, Heywood suspends the *dramatis persona* between personater and personated, assigning no clear priority: if the personated is the model imitated by the personater, it is at the same time an effect projected by the personater. Characters on this account are strangely hard to locate: they are taken as pre-existent givens by the very process that also claims to bring them into being.[40] As Henry S. Turner argues, the theatrical metaphor that underlies Hobbes's definition of the 'person' hinges on a 'tautology of identity' that is 'the definitive gesture of mimesis: actor and character "bodied forth" in such a close coincidence of identity that the distinction between the real and the fictional is temporarily suspended, and may even become irrelevant'.[41] Thus Hobbes's person is both agent and effect of public personation: 'to *Personate* is to *Act*, or

---

*Representation* (Berkeley, 1967), pp. 14–37; and Marko Simendic, 'Hobbes on persona, personation, and representation: behind the mask of sovereignty' (unpublished Ph.D. dissertation, University of York, 2011).

[37] Samuel Daniel, *Certaine small poems lately printed with the tragedie of Philotas* (London, 1605), sig. B8r.

[38] Michel de Montaigne, *Essayes*, trans. John Florio (London, 1603), sig. D3v.

[39] Theatrical performance is also the guiding metaphor of Goffman's *The Presentation of Self in Everyday Life* (Garden City, 1959). 'The self . . . as a performed character', Goffman writes, 'is not an organic thing that has a specific location, whose fundamental fate is to be born, to mature, and to die; it is a dramatic effect arising diffusely from a scene that is presented, and the characteristic issue, the crucial concern, is whether it will be credited or discredited' (253).

[40] For a very different view of Heywood's treatise, see Weimann and Bruster, *Power of Performance*, 143–5, who emphasize the 'distinction' between personater and personated, a distinction that in their account links 'the two aspects of the performer' to 'the two modes and media of cultural production – writing and performing' (144).

[41] Henry S. Turner, *The Corporate Commonwealth: Pluralism and Political Fictions in England, 1516–1651* (Chicago, 2016), p. 222.

*Represent* himselfe'.[42] Perhaps the most fascinating example of this circularity is Sir Thomas Browne's exhortation in *Christian Morals*: 'Though the World be Histrionical, and most Men live Ironically, yet be thou what thou singly art, and personate only thyself.'[43] Here the mimetic impulse is fully internalized, and persons take shape as the products of their own reflexive acts of representation – as imitations of themselves.

It is this inward turn that emerges in Achilles' own version of the Ulyssean theory of self-communication. Having been warned by Ulysses that fame rusts when out of use, Achilles responds with an elaborate specular metaphor:

> This is not strange, Ulysses.
> The beauty that is borne here in the face
> The bearer knows not, but commends itself
> To others' eyes. Nor doth the eye itself,
> That most pure spirit of sense, behold itself,
> Not going from itself, but eye to eye opposed
> Salutes each other with each other's form.
> For speculation turns not to itself,
> Till it hath travelled and is mirrored there
> Where it may see itself. This is not strange at all.
>
> (3.3.97–106)

Even as Achilles here offers a concept of selfhood rooted in social reflection – acknowledging the 'others' eyes' on which the 'bearer' of beauty depends – he seems to retreat from it. The 'others' whom he evokes are gradually crowded out by the speech's obsessive returns to self-regard. 'Speculation' might travel, but its destination will be nowhere other than '[w]here it may see itself'. Personation thus turns out to be a closed circle, the projection of a personated for the benefit of the personater. The circling rhythms of the speech themselves seem to write Ulysses – and indeed everyone other than Achilles – out of the exchange: the recursive syntax of phrases like 'eye to eye opposed' and 'each other with each other' turn Achilles back onto himself. The recursive turn is especially clear in the book-ending repetition of 'This is not strange'; in the first instance, *this* refers to Ulysses' arguments about reflection, but by

the second it refers reflexively to Achilles' own words.[44] The self-referring momentum of the speech is registered most powerfully in the hammering repetition of the passage's key word: *itself*.

Achilles' circling solipsism marks both the logical end and the breaking point of mimetic personation. If names in *Troilus* are tools of distinction, invoked in order to differentiate and fix individuals, personation is a practice of similarity exemplified by the actor who simulates a character. Personation, that is, frames persons through likeness: likeness to others and, in its terminal form, to themselves. The tautological circularity that emerges in *Troilus* and in Hobbes alike thus expresses something like the mimetic ideal: a form of maximal resemblance in which personater and personated merge. By the same token, however, this circularity endangers the mimetic model, for it finally dissolves the distinctions – between personater and personated, between self and other – that enable it. *Troilus*'s uncertain and seemingly unstable characters find themselves caught in this cul-de-sac. In Girard's reading of this passage, Achilles evinces 'the paradox of the human self, the mysterious unity of self-centredness and other-centredness in all human beings', a combination that 'bin[ds] people inextricably to one another, even as it tears them apart internally and externally'. But where Girard sees self-centredness as the 'surrender to others [of] the modest degree of autonomy that could be ours' – as the narcissistic force that thrusts Achilles into the thicket of mimetic competition – the greater risk might be the opposite: that Achilles' self-

---

[42] On this point, see also Simendic, 'Hobbes on persona', p. 109, who argues that Hobbes 'saw no contradiction in defining a person both as represented and as representative. The rationale behind this rests on his views on the inseparability of a person as a human being and a persona that he or she "bears" or "sustains".'

[43] Sir Thomas Browne, *Christian Morals*, in *The Major Works*, ed. C. A. Patrides (New York, 1977), p. 463. Published posthumously in 1716, *Christian Morals* was one of Browne's last works.

[44] Achilles' insistence that '[t]his is not strange' might also be read as an emphatic denial of difference: 'This is nothing other than itself.'

speculation, by internalizing the mirroring presence of the other, will sever him from such relations altogether.[45]

Even as *Troilus* demonstrates the force of Girard's mimetic approach, that is, the play also unsettles it, producing characters who cannot distinguish themselves from each other or – even more worryingly – escape the circular logic of self-imitation. The play's multiple scenes of naming appear, in this light, as attempts to recover a sense of individual distinctness threatened by the undifferentiating pull of mimesis. In these scenes, the impulse is to specify and compare: knowing Troilus means knowing that, as Pandarus tells Cressida, 'Paris is dirt to him'; or that, as Ulysses tells Agamemnon, he is '[m]anly as Hector but more dangerous' (1.2.235; 4.6.107). But the most telling moments come when naming fails to deliver the satisfaction of difference: when, for instance, Cressida concludes of Troilus that 'he is himself'. Under the pressure of mimetic likeness, names are unable to individuate; they can no longer command meaningful, distinguishing predicates. The resulting tautologies are undifferentiation in another key: the grammatical symptom of a mimetic disease.

## TAUTOLOGICAL CHARACTER

In a recent book on the biopolitics of personhood, Roberto Esposito revisits the Roman concept of the *persona*, a term that 'refers both to mask and to face: image and substance, fiction and reality'. Personhood, he writes, 'came into being precisely at the point of transition – and divergence – from the first to the second': from the 'theatrical costume' to 'the individual who wore it'.[46] The resulting division, and the suture that binds it, lie at the root of what Esposito calls the *dispositif of the person*: the normative split between the (biological) body and the (artificial) person that governs and possesses it, as something both identical to and alienated from itself. In its path from character to self, this account of the person traces the same path as seventeenth-century personation. Indeed, it is no coincidence that Esposito locates the emergence of

the modern *dispositif* at just this moment – in the work of Hobbes and Locke, for whom persons are understood, respectively, as representing and as owning themselves. Such self-possession separates one from others even as it introduces internal division, 'assign[ing] to the subject the property – and therefore the objectification – of itself'.[47] Esposito's words here underscore the person's essentially tautological form. On the one hand, tautology frames the sense of internal difference that self-mastery and reflexivity demand: a person, writes Locke, is a being that 'can consider itself as itself'.[48] And yet, on the other, tautology seems to refuse the differentiation of self from self. Insisting instead on their identity, this 'most contradictory expression' seems ready to collapse the divide at the heart of both mimetic personation and its signal offshoot: the modern individual.[49]

Personhood, in Esposito's account, thus marks a striking internalization of the mimetic principle that orients Girard's account of social interaction. It establishes a new 'relation that precedes and determines all others: the relation of everyone with himself or herself in the form of personal

---

45  Girard, *Theater of Envy*, 147.

46  Roberto Esposito, *Third Person: Politics of Life and Philosophy of the Impersonal*, trans. Zakiya Hanafi (Cambridge, 2012), p. 74.

47  Esposito, *Third Person*, p. 83.

48  John Locke, *An Essay Concerning Human Understanding*, in *The Empiricists* (New York, 1974), p. 67. The emergence of reflexive selfhood is often taken as a signal feature of the rise of modernity; see, especially, Anthony Giddens, *Modernity and Self-Identity: Self and Society in the Late Modern Age* (Stanford, 1991), and Charles Taylor, *Sources of the Self: The Making of the Modern Identity* (Cambridge, 1989). Taylor argues, for instance, that modern selfhood is characterized by 'a turn to oneself in the first-person perspective – a turn to the self as a self', a 'reflexive language' that we might recognize as invoking the trope of self-predication (p. 176). Esposito, on the other hand, urges a turn from the first to the third person, which refuses the indexical perspective of the self-conscious self and hence 'separates the semantics of the person from its natural effect of separation' (*Third Person*, p. 14).

49  The phrase is Esposito's (*Third Person*, p. 83) characterization of his own description (quoted above) of the subject's 'objectification . . . of itself'.

identity'.[50] The sealing off of the individual – Esposito describes it as an 'immunizing' resistance to community – finds an echo in tautology's self-enclosing grammar, a grammar whose pervasive presence in *Troilus* tracks the anxious withdrawal of its characters from the social whole. The trope indeed seems to haunt the play. It drives the tragic energy of the play's final scenes: as Troilus steels himself to spy on Cressida's betrayal, he declares that 'I will not be myself, nor have cognition / Of what I feel' (5.2.64–5). And it sustains, too, a vein of cutting, sardonic humour: 'Ajax goes up and down the field', quips Thersites at one point, 'asking for himself' (3.3.37–8). In such twists of syntax – in sentences bent back on themselves – we can feel the ugliness of a play often thought to enact a distinctively modern sense of disenchantment. A guiding thread of criticism locates in *Troilus* a shift in the early modern epistemology of value, in which the notion of intrinsic worth gives way to what Hugh Grady calls 'the dynamics of autonomous reason, power, desire, and capital'.[51] That the central object of disputed value is Helen – whose 'worth' the war-weary Trojans famously debate – suggests the degree to which the play's persons are overtaken by the same scepticism. As Lars Engle argues, 'The ugliness many find in the play arises from the intensity with which it forces all its characters to partake of the same demystifying economy.'[52] Both possessing and possessed by themselves, *Troilus*'s characters are themselves ambiguous property. They might give themselves away too cheaply: 'Who shall be true to us', Cressida laments of women in love, 'When we are so unsecret to ourselves?' (3.2.121–2). Or they might, like Ajax, prove resistant to valuation altogether: 'They say he is a very man *per se*, / And stands alone' (1.2.15–16). Here tautology implies an isolation from recognition, from sympathy, even from articulation. Tautological characters thus embody the characteristic ambivalence with which *Troilus* approaches the idea of reflexive personhood: their reflexivity is always at risk of becoming a form of alienating withdrawal – or of devolving into sheer opacity.

Take the example of pride, the most contagious vice in the play and the most nakedly self-referential. Achilles is the most serious case, a character who

'speaks not to himself', we are told, 'but with a pride / That quarrels at self-breath' (2.3.169–70). He is hardly alone: indeed, the breakdown of degree is caused above all by pride's rampant spread. Ajax, reports Nestor, is also 'grown self-willed and bears his head / In such a rein, in full as proud a place / As broad Achilles' (1.3.188–90). The distinctive characteristic of pride is its reflexive turn, its exclusive regard for the self: *self-will, self-breath*. 'He that is proud', declares Agamemnon, 'eats up himself. Pride is his own glass, his own trumpet, his own chronicle – and whatever praises itself but in the deed devours the deed in the praise' (2.3.153–6). Reflexivity in this mode, however, leads to precisely the opposite of self-consciousness: it renders one opaque and incalculable not only to others, but also to oneself. If in Ajax the results are a comically doltish impenetrability – 'He's grown a very landfish', says Thersites, 'languageless, a monster' (3.3.255–6) – they are darker in Achilles, who declares, 'My mind is troubled, like a fountain stirred, / And I myself see not the bottom of it' (3.3.309–10). The consequences, as Ulysses warns Achilles, might be dire:

> The cry [of public opinion] went once on thee,
> And still it might, and yet it may again,
> If thou wouldst not entomb thyself alive
> And case thy reputation in thy tent.
>
> (3.3.178–81)

---

[50] Roberto Esposito, *Bios: Biopolitics and Philosophy*, trans. Timothy Campbell (Minneapolis, 2008), p. 66.

[51] Hugh Grady, *Shakespeare's Universal Wolf: Studies in Early Modern Reification* (Oxford, 1996), p. 60. On *Troilus* as negotiating the changing economic conditions of early modern England, see also Lars Engle, *Shakespearean Pragmatism: Market of His Time* (Chicago, 1993); William O. Scott, 'Risk, distrust, and ingratitude in Shakespeare's *Troilus and Cressida*', *Studies in English Literature, 1500–1900* 52 (2012), 345–62; and Baker, *On Demand*, pp. 62–92. For an argument, against Grady, that the play offers a positive account of value – no longer inherent but grounded in public opinion and collective labour – see Paul Yachnin, 'Populuxe and artisanal value in *Troilus and Cressida*', *Shakespeare Quarterly* 56 (2005), 306–27.

[52] Engle, *Shakespearean Pragmatism*, p. 163.

For Achilles, self-objectification promises a kind of social death, entombment within walls of his own making.

The self-regarding turn of pride thus risks a loss of external distinction. But fame and 'reputation' – the play's primary categories of distinction – generate their own forms of self-predication, evident in the many characters who uncannily anticipate their futures as epic legends. When Troilus urges the Trojans to continue fighting for Helen because their 'present courage may beat down our foes, / And fame in time to come canonize us' (2.2.200–1), this prospect of a canonized future self serves as a spur to action, a model to imitate and – in a paradox central to the discourse of personation – thereby bring into being. But proleptic self-awareness eventually proves paralysing for characters whose 'legendary status', as Charnes argues, 'threatens to crush their representational viability as "subjects".'[53]

This pressure weighs on no one so heavily as the play's lovers, whose courtship offers a case study of sorts in the distinguishing power of names. Their remarkable encounter in Act III, choreographed and mediated by Pandarus, hinges on an exchange that transforms 'Troilus' and 'Cressida' into allegorical signifiers:

TROILUS ...
    True swains in love shall in the world to come
    Approve their truth by Troilus. When their rhymes,
    Full of protest, of oath and big compare,
    Wants similes, truth tired with iteration –
    'As true as steel, as plantage to the moon,
    As sun to day, as turtle to her mate,
    As iron to adamant, as earth to th' centre' –
    Yet, after all comparisons of truth,
    As truth's authentic author to be cited,
    'As true as Troilus' shall crown up the verse
    And sanctify the numbers.

CRESSIDA  Prophet may you be!
    If I be false, or swerve a hair from truth,
    When time is old and hath forgot itself,
    When waterdrops have worn the stones of Troy
    And blind oblivion swallowed cities up,
    And mighty states characterless are grated
    To dusty nothing, yet let memory,
    From false to false among false maids in love

    Upbraid my falsehood! When they've said, 'as false
    As air, as water, wind, or sandy earth,
    As fox to lamb, or wolf to heifer's calf,
    Pard to the hind, or stepdame to her son',
    Yea, let them say, to stick the heart of falsehood,
    'As false as Cressid'.

(3.2.169–92)

It is no surprise – given the deep associations between naming and the concern for difference, distinction and degree – that Troilus and Cressida imagine their names evoked in a discourse of comparative evaluation, the superlative terms in the amplifying similes of future swains. Like Achilles and Menelaus, Troilus believes in the power of naming to enforce a particular reality, to fix the world as it is, by making himself a trope. Each of the lovers' speeches ends by turning its speaker into a predicate, rendering 'Troilus' and 'Cressida' the objects of their own sentences, the standards by which they measure themselves. Simile thus culminates in tautology: having contemplated other comparisons, the lovers become both tenor and vehicle – they are as true, and as false, as themselves.

The likeness of similes is, in another form, the likeness of mimetic performance – the verisimilar action of Heywood's personation. In this sense, reifying 'Troilus' and 'Cressida' as proleptic allegories turns them into objects for their own imitation, the selves whom they are compelled to personate. For Cressida, in particular, the logic of self-imitation seems inescapable: once her falseness is declared – no matter the counterfactual grammar – it seems to function as a pre-determining given. Her evident discomfort in the scene implicates the claustrophobic language of tautological selfhood:

TROILUS What offends you, lady?
CRESSIDA Sir, mine own company.
TROILUS You cannot shun yourself.
CRESSIDA Let me go and try.
    I have a kind of self resides with you –
    But an unkind self, that itself will leave
    To be another's fool. I would be gone.

(3.2.140–6)

---

[53]  Charnes, *Notorious Identity*, p. 418.

Cressida's frustration with 'mine own company' marks a rare moment of introspection; more often, we encounter the play's persons from without, through characters scrutinizing each other. Interiority, as we find it here, takes the form of self-division – the division of mimetic personation, which frames 'Cressida' as both the product and the controlling origin of her actions. Hence the shifting language of agency, the tension between the first person ('I would be gone') and the externalized self that 'will leave / To be another's fool'. And yet the rhetoric of division never produces the distinctions Cressida is after. Even as she grasps for otherness – the 'unkind self' that seeks to leave Troilus – she finds herself caught in the loop of self-sameness. As in Achilles' speech above, the very word *self* again becomes an isolating refrain, foreclosing Cressida's every attempt to shun her own company. Self-division here refuses the satisfactions of reflexivity; it can be felt only as a paralysing expression of the manifestly impossible.

For Troilus, the scene of Cressida's inevitable betrayal arrives as a test of his ability to know her. 'This is and is not Cressid', he tells Ulysses after watching her with Diomedes (5.2.149). The line reflects the urge to make sense by making distinctions, by separating Cressida from her 'unkind self'. But he is brought up short by the fact of her indivisible personhood:

> Within my soul there doth conduce a fight
> Of this strange nature, that a thing inseparate
> Divides more wider than the sky and earth,
> And yet the spacious breadth of this division
> Admits no orifex for a point as subtle
> As Ariachne's broken woof to enter.

> (5.2.150–5)

This is one way of articulating what a person is: capable of 'dividing' between constancy and inconstancy, love and betrayal, yet finally 'a thing inseparate' – that is, an *individual*. Troilus's instinct to separate Cressida from herself is the play's final return to naming as a generative, individuating, act; what Troilus wants is to authoritatively rename Cressida, to say what she is and is not. But the closure of tautological character refuses the possibility of this separation. To say with Pandarus that 'Troilus is Troilus' is to imagine him as immune to distinction and even to articulation, a thing defined by its irreducible solidity; to insist that Cressida 'is not Cressid', on the other hand, is to search for the possibility of self-division, to pursue distinction where none is finally possible. Whatever else she may be – and however vehemently Troilus insists otherwise – Cressida can only be '[a]s false as Cressid'.

Cressida in this sense marks the dead end of personation. Caught between two selves, divided but not finally separable, she emerges from the overcharged mimesis that Girard found so compelling, and so worrying, in *Troilus and Cressida*. Like Achilles and Ajax and Troilus, Cressida is a person when and insofar as she personates herself; like them, she offers a vision of personhood as a phenomenon produced by a mimetic logic turning in on itself. Persons on this model are essentially mimetic things, but their paradoxical effect is the disruption of the mimetic economies that the play sets in motion: they imitate not others but themselves. When character becomes tautology, then Agamemnon cannot be seen, Achilles cannot inspire, Helen's worth cannot be known, and Cressida can be watched by a host of spies and yet remain a mystery. The breakdown of the play's military and romantic plots thus reflects the paralysing withdrawal of characters who are removed from the possibility of meaningful action. For Girard, the resulting undifferentiation is the sign of the corrosive effects of emulous desire. If *Troilus* demonstrates the explanatory force of his model, however, we might also say that it short-circuits it: after all, once the mimetic principle is fully internalized, it is no longer an engine for social interaction at all. The play might thus seem to obsess Girard less because it exemplifies his mimetic approach than because it exposes that approach's limits.

This possibility lurks in the shadows of Girard's essays on *Troilus*, essays that repeatedly worry over the integrity of the play's characters. As Girard argues, the play works on our desire for characters who are 'well differentiated species': separate, distinct, self-sufficient. But where Girard sees a frustration of this desire – characters who fail to be 'separate essences' – I suggest that the play's crisis arises, on the contrary, in its satisfaction: in characters who are, in the end, all too separate from each other and, for that reason, resistant to meaningful differentiation. The trajectory of character in *Troilus and Cressida*, I have suggested, anticipates the shifts in mimetic personation that helped give rise to the modern discourse of personhood. But if this is so, the play offers little in the way of reassurance: its persons are profoundly unsettling. Their tautological closure might be construed as a form of protection, an immunizing resistance to the demands and impositions of others. Shakespeare is at pains to show just how debilitating such closure can be: for Cressida, it means wrestling with an 'unkind self' that one cannot disown – it means being at once alienated from and trapped within oneself. We may want characters to be separate essences, models of self-possession. But *Troilus and Cressida* suggests that individuality on these terms is a deeply uncertain proposition. In this play, being a 'thing inseparate' entails a resistance to the forms of differentiation that allow us to know each other, or to escape ourselves.

# 'RUDE WIND': *KING LEAR* – CANONICITY VERSUS PHYSICALITY

## PETER J. SMITH[1]

The titular quotation, 'rude wind', comes from the meeting of Albany and Goneril in Act 4 of *King Lear*. She remarks that she has 'been worth the whistling' (4.2.30). Registering her iniquity, he adopts her suffluent adage and both inflates and poisons it: '[o]h Goneril, / You are not worth the dust which the rude wind / Blows in your face' (4.2.30–2). Wind is associated with rudeness; rudeness in the sense of 'harsh', 'stormy', 'destructive', but also in the sense of 'unmannerly' or, as *OED* has it, 'offensively or deliberately discourteous' (*OED*, 4). *King Lear*'s wind, here and elsewhere, is rude in the sense that traditions of low comedy are rude, Bakhtinian billingsgate terms are rude, and schoolboy humour, seaside postcards and fart jokes are rude.

In what follows I propose that we should confront the canonical centrality of Shakespeare's putatively greatest play with an awareness of its physicality, somatology and even scatology. Such an approach seems, at first sight, to be both perverse and iconoclastic but it will reveal a way of exposing the play's insistent materiality and, in so doing, demonstrate the fallacy of readings which champion its metaphysical, philosophical or even theological status. Moreover, a reading that turns its attentions to the *waste*-fulness of the text may helpfully lead us away from the abstractions of theoretical approaches which, too frequently, sanitize, airbrush or euphemize the deprivations which feature so prominently at the heart of this devastating and devastated play.

It would be risking turning *King Lear* into *Carry On Shakespeare* to point out that it contains one of the most elemental fart jokes in the whole of Eng. Lit. –

'[b]low winds and crack your cheeks!' (3.2.1) – but it may well be that such flatulent readings serve, plosively and positively, to complicate what are by now almost jaded assumptions about the play's transcendent greatness. One small instance: note that in Albany's contemptuous salutation he speaks of 'dust'. Chaucer's 'The Pilgrim's Tale' is as dry as dust, and Harry Bailey interrupts him: '[t]hy drasty rymyng is nat worth a toord!' (7.930).[2] *Drast*, meaning 'shit', and dust are frequently mixed, right up until the nineteenth century and the invention of domestic sewerage systems. As late as 1865, Mr Boffin in Dickens's *Our Mutual Friend* is euphemistically collecting dust – that is, the mixture of ashes from fireplaces and horse dung which was used in the manufacture of bricks and road surfaces.[3] Bruce Thomas Boehrer insists that Ben Jonson, as an apprentice bricklayer, 'would have come into close contact with manure on a regular basis', and Kent's violent outburst in *King Lear* associates plastering with the lavatorial as he threatens to 'tread this unbolted villain [Oswald] into mortar and daub the wall of a jakes [that is, a toilet] with him' (2.2.64).[4]

---

[1] This article grew out of a public lecture given at the Rose Theatre in Kingston upon Thames in May 2015. I am grateful to Timo Uotinen and Richard Wilson for their hospitality, and to members of the audience for enlightening questions and comments. Ben Haworth and the anonymous reader for *Shakespeare Survey* made helpful suggestions.
[2] Quotations from Chaucer refer to *The Riverside Chaucer*, ed. Larry D. Benson (Oxford, 1988).
[3] Lee Jackson, *Dirty Old London* (New Haven, CT, 2014), p. 11.
[4] Bruce Thomas Boehrer, *The Fury of Men's Gullets: Ben Jonson and the Digestive Canal* (Philadelphia, PA, 1997), p. 154.

Later in the same scene, the Ajax / 'a jakes' pun reappears: '[n]one of these rogues and cowards / But Ajax is their fool' (2.2.122–3). Thus, not only is Albany's 'dust' probably faecal, but its destination is Goneril's face. Could it be that behind this throwaway detail lurks the notorious flatulence of *The Miller's Tale* – the 'thonder-dent' (i.e. thunder-clap) fart of Nicholas who lets one fly full into the face of the squeamish Absolon? Shakespeare's *Troilus and Cressida* draws its plot and character from Chaucer's narrative poem, while the prologue of *The Two Noble Kinsmen* pays tribute to 'Chaucer, of all admired' (line 13). The source of Shakespeare and Fletcher's play was *The Knight's Tale*; is it such a stretch to imagine Shakespeare reading that of the Miller which immediately follows?

But, before ruining *King Lear* by irreparably associating its magisterial substance with whoopee-cushion puerility, we must first acknowledge its supreme canonical reputation. In Dr Johnson's opinion, 'The Tragedy of Lear is deservedly celebrated among the dramas of Shakespeare. There is perhaps no play which keeps the attention so strongly fixed; which so much agitates our passions and interests our curiosity ... So powerful is the current of the poet's imagination that the mind which once ventures within it is hurried irresistibly along.'[5] Nearer our own time, for A. C. Bradley, the greatness of *King Lear* is indisputable: '*King Lear* has again and again been described as Shakespeare's greatest work, the best of his plays, the tragedy in which he exhibits most fully his multitudinous powers; and if we were doomed to lose all his dramas except one, probably the majority of those who know and appreciate him best would pronounce for keeping *King Lear*.'[6]

Published over a century ago, this opinion has enjoyed a long life and has hardened into something of a critical orthodoxy. Even the usually sceptical Jan Kott finds *King Lear* superior to other plays: '*King Lear* is still recognized as a masterpiece, beside which even *Macbeth* and *Hamlet* seem tame and pedestrian. *King Lear* is compared to Bach's *Mass in B Minor*, to Beethoven's *Fifth* and *Ninth* Symphonies, to Wagner's *Parsifal*, Michelangelo's *Last Judgement*, or Dante's *Purgatory* and *Inferno*.'[7] The same Dantesque comparison was made by Barbara Everett, who insisted on the eminence of the play: *King Lear* is 'our greatest tragedy, a *Divine Comedy* of the modern world'.[8]

Writing in 2004, Marjorie Garber registers this modernity in terms of the apocalypse of 9/11, proposing that the play addresses us from 'ground-zero – as, in a sense, it has always done'.[9] And, in the same year, Richard Wilson trounced the tradition of reading the apocalyptic ending in terms of a Christian deliverance. The deception practised on Gloucester and the King's extreme suffering function, he argues, to disabuse its audience about 'the concern of God, working of providence, influence of the planets, power of the Pope, decision of the king of France, or effect of the Armada over the cruelties suffered on stage'.[10] Romantic readings hint at the play's metaphysical aura, while more recent historicist ones suggest the play's omnipotence in its capacity to challenge systems of belief upon which Western Christendom has been predicated for over two millennia. However, in their albeit various ways, both approaches assume and reinforce the play's canonical centrality.

What could be more iconoclastic than to attack this play? The mischievously controversial critic, Terence Hawkes, who once told the *Guardian* that he would rather 'watch *The Bill* on TV than go out to see Shakespeare', knew exactly what he was doing when he attacked the reputation of Shakespeare's masterpiece.[11] Almost quarter of a century ago in an interview, he and James Wood (the paper's chief literary critic) had an argument about the greatness of Shakespeare. They took as their starting point Hawkes's recently published book on *King Lear*, in which we might

---

[5] R. W. Desai, ed., *Johnson on Shakespeare* (London, 1997), p. 183.

[6] A. C. Bradley, *Shakespearean Tragedy* [1904] (London, 1991), p. 243.

[7] Jan Kott, *Shakespeare Our Contemporary* [1965] (London, 1967), p. 100.

[8] Barbara Everett, *Young Hamlet* (Oxford, 1989), p. 59.

[9] William Baker and Kenneth Womack, eds., *The Facts on File Companion to Shakespeare* (New York, 2012), p. 1184.

[10] Baker and Womack, eds., *Companion*, p. 1187.

[11] 'Was Shakeseare really a genius?' *Guardian*, 8 March 1995, 10.

have expected him to say something laudatory about Shakespeare – he doesn't:

JAMES WOOD Professor Hawkes, in your new book, *King Lear* (published by Northcote House), you say that there has been much dispute over the years about whether *King Lear* is a 'masterpiece' and the logical extension of your position is that it may very well not be. But wouldn't you agree that even if we can't know if *Lear* is a masterpiece, the fact that we go back to it again and again suggests in itself some value.

TERENCE HAWKES But I want to know *who* goes back and in what circumstances . . . most people don't go home and take *King Lear* off the shelves; they watch TV. What directs people back to *King Lear* by and large is an education system which insists on having English at the core of its humanities programme, and Shakespeare at the core of English.[12]

This exchange typifies Hawkes's own version of the politics of literature and his scepticism towards the institutions which promote the circulation of High Culture. He insists on the necessity of literature's *political* intervention in the *status quo*: 'I don't want to say these texts are great because I want to allow historicism its full play . . . I believe in change in societies, and the idea that certain texts are the products of genius freezes change, because it appeals to a notion of transcendent values. I don't believe in that.' It is significant that Hawkes attempts to politicize *King Lear* because, while *Hamlet*'s reception dwelt on the political corruption of Elsinore and identified the Prince not merely as a revenger but as a political scourge, *King Lear* was often read as a retreat from politics.[13]

Hawkes's trademark mock-truculence insists on the material conditions of the play's consumption – in the theatre or the classroom. Underlined by its canonical centrality, *King Lear* is infused with a kind of cultural capital which precludes, argues Hawkes, any challenge to its continued circulation. In his review of Bruce Thomas Boehrer's *The Fury of Men's Gullets: Ben Jonson and the Digestive Canal*, published in 1998, Hawkes's concern with the scatological appears to satisfy this demand for a more material analysis, although he rightly points out that scatological or carnivalesque readings of canonical drama 'may be distasteful to a culture

which still peers at the Early Modern period through Victorian spectacles':

[n]evertheless, it raises a central issue in respect of the public theatres and their dramatists in a community over which ordure held such sway. London not only stank to high heaven as a result of its enormous problems of waste disposal, but the popular entertainments with which the theatres competed almost made a feature of confronting, involving and to some extent splattering their audience with blood, guts and general filth.[14]

Hawkes goes on to argue that the separation of theatre, on the one hand, and bear-baiting, on the other, 'with its savagery, spittle, blood, guts and faeces' 'would certainly not have made sense to the average member of an Early Modern audience'. Indeed, as he notes, such spaces as the Hope doubled as arenas for both bear-baiting and theatrical entertainments. Hawkes is concerned that sanitized, 'Victorian' readings of Jonson's plays too readily gloss over their rude materiality: 'Jonson's interest in bodily functions, his unrelenting pursuit of the links between the alimentary and the literary, his preoccupation with eating, evacuation, vomiting and the all-too-human stench that these disseminate are less shortcomings in need of explanation than dimensions of an art whose true contours we still fail accurately to discern.' Centrally here, Hawkes's insistence on scatological

---

[12] *Guardian*, 8 March 1995, 10.

[13] R. A. Foakes, *Hamlet versus Lear: Cultural Politics and Shakespeare's Art* (Cambridge, 1993), p. 45.

[14] Terence Hawkes, 'The Fury of Men's Gullets: Ben Jonson and the Digestive Canal by Bruce Thomas Boehrer', *London Review of Books*, 21 May 1998, p. 24. Recently, this prevailing view of urban pollution has been taken to task. In *Sanitation in Urban Britain, 1560–1700* (London, 2016), Leona J. Skelton challenges what she calls the 'chamber pot in the window' myth (p. 3). She asserts, contrary to stereotypes of the early modern city as knee-deep in faeces, that its population was determined to suppress noxious practices in an effort to combat miasma. Unfortunately, most of the cases she cites illustrate the breach rather than the observance of decontamination, and one wonders whether her sense of the lived experience of early modern citizenry isn't a little rose-tinted. See my review of this book in the *Journal of the History of Medicine and Allied Sciences* 72 (2017), 223–5.

materiality outweighs Boehrer's reliance upon anthropological theory: 'Boehrer's recourse to Deleuze and Guattari's theories of bodily space seems needlessly complicating.'[15]

From its beginnings, scatological criticism has been characterized by a wide variety of analytical approaches. For instance, Norbert Elias and David Inglis addressed the development of the modern faecal habitus in sociological terms, while Norman O. Brown discussed the excremental vision in terms of psychoanalysis, and Mary Douglas dealt with the anthropology of dirt.[16] Rose George's *The Big Necessity: Adventures in the World of Human Waste* explores sewage disposal and public hygiene from the point of view of sustainability and environmentalism, an endeavour anticipated during World War II by the Quaker and pacifist Reginald Reynolds.[17] John G. Bourke described various feculent rituals as long ago as 1891 in his encyclopaeedic *Scatalogic Rites of all Nations* (the title of which makes him sound like a shitty version of George Eliot's Dr Casaubon).[18] In literary studies, of course, Peter Stallybrass and Allon White's *The Politics and Poetics of Transgression* read sexual and scatological taboos in cultural materialist terms, while Gail Kern Paster's *The Body Embarrassed* typified the new historicist approach to somatic studies.[19]

Recent developments in waste studies are defiantly materialist, as a brief survey of the field over the last decade or so will illustrate. Jeff Persels and Russ Ganim are scatology's new-wave pioneers. In 2004, their *Fecal Matters in Early Modern Literature and Art* argued that, while sexuality 'has long been the darling of academic readers [scatology] still retains the power to make us blush, to provoke shame and embarrassment'. They go on: the contributors to this volume address 'unflinchingly ... the objective reality of the scatological as part and parcel of *material culture*'.[20] Three years later, Valerie Allen's *On Farting* analysed the systems of belief surrounding the complicated exegetic traditions leading to the variety of explanations of involuntary farting as found in the commentaries of Augustine and the classical medicine of Hippocrates and Galen.[21] Anal eruptions testify to post-lapsarian bodily disobedience

(which, incidentally, is also the cause of involuntary erections). Sophie Gee's *Making Waste* examined the underside (or backside) of a period more usually associated with the pioneering optics of Isaac Newton or the lucent architecture of Christopher Wren, both of whom illuminated the Enlightenment. By contrast, Gee dwells rather on the period's 'waste matter: excrement, snot, sweat, nail clippings, garbage, dead dogs'.[22] Perhaps surprisingly she proposes a literary antecedent in Milton, and especially the way he 'pays scrupulous attention to God's dregs and discards'.[23] The influence on Pope and Swift is undeniable and the latter certainly serves to ground this excremental vision in the mire of ubiquitous filth: 'Swift's is a worldly, temporal vocation, not heavenly and philosophically dense as Milton's is.'[24]

Martha Bayliss in *Sin and Filth in Medieval Culture* argued that what, in the modern world, is trivial, embarrassing, taboo or merely a topic of puerile humour was, in the pre- and early modern world, not simply the emblem for but 'the actual embodiment of the sin that made ... flesh impure and

---

[15] Hawkes, '*The Fury of Men's Gullets*', p. 24.

[16] Norbert Elias, *The Civilizing Process* [1939], 2 vols. (Oxford, 1969–82); David Inglis, *A Sociological History of Excretory Experience: Defecatory Manners and Toiletry Technologies* (Lampeter, 2000); Norman O. Brown, *Life Against Death: The Psychoanalytic Meaning of History* (Middletown, CT, 1959); Mary Douglas, *Purity and Danger: An Analysis of the Concept of Pollution and Taboo* [1966] (London, 2002).

[17] Rose George, *The Big Necessity: Adventures in the World of Human Waste* (London, 2008); Reginald Reynolds, *Cleanliness and Godliness* (London, 1943).

[18] John G. Bourke, *Scatalogic Rites of All Nations* (Washington, DC, 1891). The title page of the first edition warns 'Not for General Perusal'.

[19] Peter Stallybrass and Allon White, *The Politics and Poetics of Transgression* (London, 1986); Gail Kern Paster, *The Body Embarrassed: Drama and Disciplines of Shame in Early Modern England* (Ithaca, NY, 1993).

[20] Jeff Persels and Russ Ganim, eds., *Fecal Matters in Early Modern Literature and Art* (Abingdon, 2004), p. xiii; my emphasis.

[21] Valerie Allen, *On Farting: Language and Laughter in the Middle Ages* (Basingstoke, 2007).

[22] Sophie Gee, *Making Waste: Leftovers and the Eighteenth-Century Imagination* (Princeton, NJ, 2010), p. 91.

[23] Gee, *Making Waste*, p. 41. [24] Gee, *Making Waste*, p. 103.

corrupt'.[25] As she puts it: '[e]xcrement did not just *mean* sin; in medieval thought, it *was* sin, the material embodiment of corporeal corruptibility'.[26] Notice the reappearance of that word 'embodiment': Bayliss's criticism is refreshingly materialistic and shares with a lot of recent work on scatology a bracing suspicion of the abstractions and obfuscations of more rarefied literary theories. In this, she follows perhaps the most staunchly materialist of recent writers on scatology, Susan Signe Morrison.

Morrison's brilliant *Excrement in the Late Middle Ages* exemplifies the ethical dimensions of such an approach. There, she argues that literary theory too frequently dematerializes the body and abstracts the somatogenic inspiration of so much artistic endeavour. Corporeal experience is deodorized and its representation euphemized: 'material dirt itself demands investigation'.[27] She attacks poststructuralist linguistics, feminism and, especially, psychoanalysis, all of which have tended to theorize physical processes out of sight (and, we might add, smell): 'the recent critical debate about the history of the body has tended to avoid the topic of excrement. The stench of material flesh can be hidden by theoretical musings.'[28] Morrison's intensely somatic focus allows her to insist on the contiguity of the Middle Ages and the contemporary period. Rather than flush away what modernity condemns as disgusting, we must 'see ourselves in that threatening, filthy alterity'.[29] In this way we ought – metaphorically, anyway – to emulate the communal dumping of the medieval citizenry and so engage collectively in popular *solid*-ification, as it were, of biological democracy. The alternative is selfish individuation and the etiolating fragmentation of the body politic. As Morrison insightfully cautions us, the 'privatisation of excrement can [only] limit us and harm our planet'.[30]

In 2015, Morrison's *The Literature of Waste* was published, the logic of which is accumulative rather than analytic. It is in this amassing of material that the book demonstrates a salient feature that all the above studies share – that is, albeit articulated to differing degrees, a concern with the ubiquitous, indeed ineluctable, *materiality of lived experience*. For instance, the ninth chapter is deftly entitled, 'The

secret life of objects: the audacity of thingness and the poignancy of materiality'.[31] Here, she writes: '[d]ung leaves an ontological deposit, preventing us from seeing ourselves as wholly different'.[32]

An instance of this material focus can be seen in the work of Holly Dugan, for whom Hawkes's cocktail of the discharges of the Hope Theatre looms large. Dugan's approach is invigorated by what Morrison terms 'Thingness'. Of Jonson's *Bartholomew Fair*, Dugan writes:

the play's many references to the scent of livestock, pork, leather, tobacco, stale gingerbread, ale, farts, belches, sweat and urine conjure both the *material realm* of the fair and the stage. Like Smithfield market, the Hope, located to the south on Bankside, had its own uniquely foul stench, connected to that of the surrounding area: the aroma of the pike stews, soap-boiling yards, rose gardens, mud and the flooded polluted ditches of the surrounding area, were combined with the smells of the theatre – its structure ... and its occupants (the sweat, urine, belches, perfume of the actors, animals and crowd, along with the apples, oysters, ale and tobacco that they undoubtedly consumed inside). These scents, to name just a few of them, defined the smellscape of the Hope.[33]

These features often figure conspicuously in antitheatrical accounts and descriptions of London, and are, Dugan concludes, an important part of the understanding of 'the material conditions of London's theatrical entertainments'.[34] For Bruce Boehrer, it is Middleton as well as Jonson who

[25] Martha Bayliss, *Sin and Filth in Medieval Culture: The Devil in the Latrine* (New York, 2012), p. 7.
[26] Bayliss, *Sin and Filth*, p. 23.
[27] Susan Signe Morrison, *Excrement in the Late Middle Ages: Sacred Filth and Chaucer's Fecopoetics* (New York, 2008), p. 1.
[28] Morrison, *Excrement*, p. 4. [29] Morrison, *Excrement*, p. 158.
[30] Morrison, *Excrement*, p. 157.
[31] Susan Signe Morrison, *The Literature of Waste: Material Ecopoetics and Ethical Matter* (New York, 2015), p. 121.
[32] Morrison, *Waste*, p. 131.
[33] Holly Dugan, '"As dirty as Smithfield and as stinking every whit": the smell of the Hope Theatre', in *Shakespeare's Theatres and the Effects of Performance*, ed. Farah Karim-Cooper and Tiffany Stern (London, 2013), pp. 195–213; p. 204; my emphasis.
[34] Dugan, '"As dirty as Smithfield"', p. 213.

captures vividly 'early modern London's rapid urbanization and environmental degradation'.[35] Civic immorality, in Middleton's work, is symbolized by ordure: 'Middleton is able to depict the city so successfully as a site of moral turpitude because he also views it as a place of excrement.'[36] Jonson's faecal imagination is, in contrast, burdened with urban detritus in shockingly material terms: '[f]rom a jaundiced perspective [*The Devil is an Ass*] is the story of London itself, in little: the arrival of new goods, the growth of markets, the increase of desire and frenetic activity, all in the end reduced to sewage: the contents of a closestool, a shithouse, a prison'.[37] While Jonson and Middleton are readily construed in these scatological ways, Shakespeare's canonical centrality tends to discourage such an approach.

As Prince Hamlet remembers the nobility of his dead father, he notes how the King protected Gertrude from the buffeting air (quite the opposite of Albany and Goneril): 'so loving to my mother / That he might not beteem the winds of heaven / Visit her face too roughly' (1.2.140–2). Shakespeare's transcendental canonicity shields his reader, like Gertrude, too frequently from the buffeting of the playwright's flatulent materiality.[38] However *King Lear* typifies Shakespeare's contempt for the abstract. Shakespeare is bluntly, most of the time rudely, concrete, and it is this concreteness or materiality, especially in terms of physicality (what Bayliss called 'embodiment'), to which we must now turn.

Shakespeare's characters are continually validating what they say with what they organically are, habitually equating their speech with their bodies. At the beginning of *Richard II*, for example, Bolingbroke accuses Mowbray of lying. He threatens literally to make him eat his words – '[w]ith a foul traitor's name stuff I thy throat' (1.1.44) – and asserts that 'what I speak / My body shall make good' (1.1.36–7). At the opening of *Macbeth*, Duncan seizes upon the body's genuineness; physicality validates speech. Addressing the Bloody Sergeant, he remarks: '[s]o well thy words become thee as thy wounds; / They smack of honour both' (1.2.44–5). The Bloody Sergeant himself is unable to speak further, but his very body calls out for assistance: 'I cannot tell – / But I am faint; my gashes cry for help' (1.2.42–3).

Similarly, in his supremely understated incitement to riot, Mark Antony disclaims his oratorical skills and relocates them in the gaping cuts of the body in front of him:

> Show you sweet Caesar's wounds, poor poor dumb mouths,
> And bid them *speak for me*. But were I Brutus,
> And Brutus Antony, there were an Antony
> Would ruffle up your spirits, and put a tongue
> In every wound of Caesar, that should move
> The stones of Rome to rise and mutiny.
>
> (*Julius Caesar*, 3.2.220–5; my emphasis)

Previously in the same play, Casca has quite literally vocalized his political aspirations through his destructive dexterity: '[s]peak, hands, for me!' (3.1.76). Even the lowly Third Citizen in *Coriolanus* recognizes the irresistible rhetorical force of wounds. He asserts that they are unable to deny Coriolanus their voices, 'for if he show us his wounds and tell us his deeds, we are to put our tongues into those wounds and speak for them' (2.3.6). Edmund realizes the rhetorical importance of the wound. It is as if his false reports may be substantiated by corporeal evidence: '[s]ome blood drawn on me would beget opinion / Of my more fierce endeavour' (2.1.33–4). These wounds testify to dignity and even majesty, publicly displayed and heroic in stature (but note that Edmund's are fraudulent). In contrast to such ennobling damage, the body in *King Lear* is tested almost to destruction: gross, stinking, frail and, as it is forced towards ruin, beshitten.

Meeting Lear on the heath, Gloucester requests that he may kiss his sovereign's hand. Lear responds: '[l]et me wipe it first; it smells of mortality' (4.5.129). Although in *Titus Andronicus*, we see

---

[35] Bruce Boehrer, *Environmental Degradation in Jacobean Drama* (Cambridge, 2013), p. 39.

[36] Boehrer, *Degradation*, p. 39.   [37] Boehrer, *Degradation*, p. 61.

[38] The motif of wind blowing in the face was one Shakespeare also used in *Richard II*. The King asks Aumerle about Hereford's departure: 'what store of parting tears were shed?' Aumerle responds: '[f]aith, none for me, except the north-east wind, / Which then grew bitterly against our faces, / Awaked the sleeping rheum, and so by chance / Did grace our hollow parting with a tear' (1.4.5–9).

the aftermath of Lavinia's rape with her hands lopped off, her tongue cut out and her mouth issuing a fountain of blood, nowhere do we actually witness the procedures of physical torture in progress. Nowhere, that is, with the obscene exception of the blinding of Gloucester. The attention the playwright pays to the physical devastation of Gloucester's eyes is unique: '[o]ut, vile jelly! / Where is thy lustre now?' (3.7.81–2). With chilling irony, Shakespeare has Gloucester foresee his own punishment. As Regan interrogates him as to the reason he has sent the King to Dover, Gloucester replies: '[b]ecause I would not see thy cruel nails / Pluck out his poor old eyes' (3.7.54–5). It is at this point that the audience starts to flinch as we realize the torturous potential behind Goneril's earlier 'Pluck out his eyes!' (3.7.5). What William Ian Miller has called the 'blind world of *Lear*' leads directly to a prurient fascination with stink and the reek of corruption: '[t]here's hell, there's darkness, there is the sulphurous pit, burning, scalding, stench, consumption' (4.5.125).[39] In *King Lear*'s opening lines, the play's most perfidious character has successfully (but only temporarily) deodorized: of Edmund, Gloucester asks Kent, '[d]o you smell a fault?' (1.1.15). The incipient stench is there, albeit not yet manifest. As Miller puts it, '[t]he blind world of *Lear* is a world of hopelessness, randomness, moral chaos and despair. Only smell thrives, and that is why the atmosphere is so poisoned and depressingly frightening and filled with utter disgust with life.'[40] Like that of Poor Tom, the body in *King Lear* is 'grime[d] with filth' (2.2.172), foetid and faecal.

As Caroline Spurgeon notes, the body is the central image in *King Lear*, yet it is an agonized body 'in anguished movement, tugged, wrenched, beaten, pierced, stung, scourged, dislocated, flayed, gashed, scalded, tortured, and finally broken on the rack'.[41] Even the usually level-headed Albany threatens to dismember his wife, justifying his violence towards her in terms of his own sanguinary determinism: '[w]ere't my fitness / To let these hands obey my blood, / They are apt enough to dislocate and tear / Thy flesh and bones' (4.2.64–7). These moments illustrate the centrality of *King Lear*'s tortured body, the revelation of which the playwright stages most profoundly in Lear's tearing at his clothes in order to

join Poor Tom in his nakedness: 'thou art the thing itself; unaccommodated man is no more than a poor, bare, forked animal' (3.4.105). David Hillman pronounces *King Lear* to be 'the most painfully corporealized play among Shakespeare's works', and, during the play's most profound moments in the final scene, Lear attempts again to expose that corporeality: '[p]ray you, undo this button' (5.3.308).[42]

There is no need for theoretical abstractions, because Shakespeare sites his drama in the physicality of his scripts and the actors speaking them. The drama is concretized in front of us, in the flesh. Alexandra Harris insists on this physical certainty: '[t]hrough all the spouting, cracking, spilling, washing in Shakespeare's plays, the human body proves stubbornly solid'.[43] Kent's role as a messenger intersects with that of Oswald, whom Kent tripped and humiliated only a few days earlier in the presence of the King, and his challenge is phrased in suitably carnal terms: '[c]ome, I'll flesh ye' (2.2.45). Oswald reiterates this reference to human tissue when he describes the situation to Cornwall as 'the fleshment of this dread exploit' (2.2.121). It is as though the challenge has become incarnate.

*King Lear* illustrates the idea of corporeal verity. Edmund's realization of his political aspirations is intimately related to his physical attractiveness to the warring princesses. By choosing to sleep with one or other sister, he is able to fashion his own political advancement:

> To both these sisters have I sworn my love;
> Each jealous of the other, as the stung
> Are of the adder. Which one of them shall I take?
> Both? one? or neither?
>
> (5.1.55–8)

---

[39] William Ian Miller, *The Anatomy of Disgust* (Cambridge, MA, 1997), p. 76.

[40] Miller, *Anatomy*, p. 76.

[41] Caroline Spurgeon, *Shakespeare's Imagery and What it Tells Us* (Cambridge, 1935), p. 339.

[42] David Hillman, *Shakespeare's Entrails: Belief, Scepticism and the Interior of the Body* (Basingstoke, 2007), p. 120.

[43] Alexandra Harris, *Weatherland: Writers and Artists under English Skies* (London, 2015), p. 112.

While Edmund's physical assertiveness and Edgar's physical privation offer two extremes of somatic politics (one with and one without authority), Lear's movement from the former to the latter demonstrates the play's prurient obsession with histolysis. Unlike in *Hamlet* – where the flesh is 'too, too solid' (1.2.129), locking the Prince's transcendent spirit within the nutshell prison of Denmark – in *King Lear*, the flesh is mortified, decaying, rotting.[44] For Charles Lamb, this fleshly disintegration is intensified by the cussed buffeting of nature, particularly a wind which is both careless and promiscuous:

[o]n the stage we see nothing but corporal infirmities and weakness, the impotence of rage; while we read it, we see not Lear, but we are Lear, – we are in his mind, we are sustained by a grandeur which baffles the malice of daughters and storms; in the aberrations of his reason, we discover a mighty irregular power of reasoning, immethodized from the ordinary purposes of life, but exerting its powers, as the wind blows where it listeth, at will upon the corruptions and abuses of mankind.[45]

Stephen Greenblatt talks about the way in which the play, in spite of its several mentions of Jove or Apollo as well as the gods, is actually supremely naturalistic. There are no ghosts or witches as there are in *Richard III, Julius Caesar, Hamlet* or *Macbeth*. Cordelia is not a spirit and Lear's mistaking her for one is a symptom of his insanity. In the words of Greenblatt:

*King Lear* is haunted by a sense of rituals and beliefs that are no longer efficacious, that have been *emptied out*. The characters appeal again and again to the pagan gods, but the gods remain utterly silent. Nothing answers to human questions but human voices; nothing breeds about the heart but human desires; nothing inspires awe or terror but human suffering and human depravity. For all the invocation of the gods in *King Lear* it is clear that there are *no* devils.[46]

Greenblatt is talking about the competing religious positions surrounding the Jacobean cult of exorcism, and, while important, this is a tangential concern here. However, Greenblatt does insist on the play's secularism and his term '*emptied* out' is key

for this discussion, because it is clear that in the very first scene of this play, Lear is (intentionally or not) voiding his self, emptying himself out, evacuating himself. The division of the kingdom, together with its parcelling out, is a kind of self-division or fragmentation which drives a wedge between the King's two bodies. The Fool will later draw attention to this act of splitting by referring to the egg-shell and the peascod, both fissured and emptied (1.4.141, 182), and the clefting and voiding of Lear's reason is similarly figured: '[t]hou hast pared thy wit o'both sides and left nothing i'th'-middle' (1.4.168).

Lear's abdication is a kind of political enema, evacuating all monarchical power, and it happens so quickly we almost miss it. Lear's opening line is a command, '[a]ttend the lords of France and Burgundy, Gloucester' (1.1.33). Gloucester's response is immediate and submissive: 'I shall, my lord'. Fewer than 100 lines later, a similar command is issued: '[c]all France. Who stirs? Call Burgundy' (1.1.127). The impatient and anxious question, which itself splits Lear's decree in two, demonstrates the evacuation of his regal self. Within the space of just 7 lines, Kent refers to his King as 'Royal Lear' (1.1.140) and 'old man' (1.1.147). It is a metamorphosis of alacrity and degradation and it will lead, on the heath, to the violent confrontation of human and elemental.

Lear's linguistic impotence takes place in public: 'fie, fie, fie! Pah, pah!' (4.5.128), 'kill, kill, kill, kill, kill, kill!' (4.5.183), '[h]owl, howl, howl, howl!' (5.3.232) or '[n]ever, never, never, never, never' (5.3.284). Paradoxically, his moments of greatest eloquence are saved for the wind – rude, persistent and indifferent:

---

[44] For a fascinating consideration of *Hamlet* and claustrophobia, see Ian McEwan's comic novel, *Nutshell* (London, 2016).
[45] Jonathan Bate, ed., *The Romantics on Shakespeare* (Harmondsworth, 1992), p. 123.
[46] Stephen Greenblatt, *Shakespearian Negotiations: The Circulation of Social Energy in Renaissance England* (Berkeley, CA, 1988), p. 119.

You cataracts and hurricanoes, spout
Till you have drenched our steeples, drowned the
    cocks!
You sulph'rous and thought-executing fires,
Vaunt-couriers of oak-cleaving thunderbolts,
Singe my white head; and thou all-shaking thunder,
Strike flat the thick rotundity o'th'world!

                              (3.2.2–7)

The 'oak-cleaving thunderbolts' in *King Lear* are the natural heir/air to Nicholas's 'thonder-dent' fart; the lightning bolt, the flash of flame as the fart is combusted by Absolon's flaming coulter, a flare so bright that it nearly strikes the viewer blind: 'with the strook he was almoost yblent'.[47] Much virtue in that 'almoost'. In the comic universe of *The Miller's Tale*, the agony is temporary – unlike Gloucester's, the blindness is short-lived. In the anguished world of Shakespeare's play, by contrast, there is never relief. Nature, goddess of the wicked Edmund, protracts the agony well beyond breaking point: '[h]e hates him / That would upon the rack of this tough world / Stretch him out longer' (5.3.289–91). Harris underlines the symbiosis between violence in the natural world and that undergone by the protagonist himself: Shakespeare 'had dared to make no disctinction between the storm and the man who experiences it'. Lear, as we hear before we see him on the heath, is 'minded like the weather'.[48] As Ewan Fernie has recently argued of *King Lear*, '[h]uman self and physical world are interpenetrating in Shakespeare's play'.[49]

The language of the heath is the momentous rhetoric that qualifies *King Lear* as Shakespeare's most canonical tragedy – the most significant epic since the *Divine Comedy* – but this is a momentousness unabashed by cosmic flatulence: '[r]umble thy bellyful' (3.2.14). Lear's tempestuous outburst draws attention to the superfluity, the redundancy, the wastefulness of nature's destruction. Opposed to the 'thought-executing fires' and the 'oak-cleaving thunderbolts' is the 'white head' of 'a man / More sinned against than sinning' (3.2.59–60). It is an image of the impotence of humanity against the force not of the supernatural but of the *natural* – what Lear himself calls 'the enmity o'th'air' (2.2.398) – all the more cataclysmic for its ordinariness.

In its examination of the sufferings of the '[p]oor naked wretches' (3.4.28) against the 'pitiless' (3.4.29) and rude wind, Shakespeare's play collapses the distinctions between canonicity and physicality, folding each into the other. In its pervasive exploration of palpable weakness, hunger, waste and shit, the excruciating agony of *King Lear* demands that its very canonicity be registered in terms of embodiment.

---

[47] Benson, ed., *Chaucer*, p. 76.   [48] Harris, *Weatherland*, p. 233.
[49] Ewan Fernie, *Shakespeare for Freedom: Why the Plays Matter* (Cambridge, 2017), p. 240.

# CONTENT BUT ALSO UNWELL: DISTRIBUTED CHARACTER AND LANGUAGE IN *THE MERCHANT OF VENICE*

## ELENA PELLONE AND DAVID SCHALKWYK

Character, so central to eighteenth- and nineteenth-century appreciation of Shakespeare, fell out of favour in the mid twentieth century. This first occurred at the hands of the 'New Criticism'. L. C. Knights, in 'How many children had Lady Macbeth?', was instrumental in the classic shift of critical focus from the life and humanity of the fictional people in Shakespeare's plays (exemplified by A. C. Bradley)[1] to a view of the texts as elaborate poetic forms, to be read for their network of figurative structures and connections rather than for the psychology of their characters. The rise of structuralist, poststructuralist, new historicist and materialist theory and criticism in the 1980s took the New Critical aversion to character still further: the New Criticism, and its British counterparts in figures such as F. R. Leavis, Cleanth Brooks, L. C. Knights, Wilson Knight and Derek Traversi, were considered too entrapped by a belief in a common humanity, even if these critics eschewed Bradley's insistence that Shakespeare's characters were somehow real people, amenable to the same moral and psychological judgement.

The problem with character criticism for the new theory and politics was that it was both anachronistic and politically regressive. Historicist critics maintained (wrongly) that the idea of a subjective interiority did not exist before Shakespeare, and Marxists and poststructuralists held (also wrongly) that an interest in Shakespeare's characters necessitated a lack of attention to the broader ideological, social and political aspects of the plays. Recently, character is receiving renewed attention as a means to restore an ethical dimension to our interest in literature, and even a more nuanced concern with politics. Cognitive psychology has offered compelling reasons to revisit the question of a certain kind of constancy among all human beings, traditionally collected under the rubric of 'human nature', and disturbing political developments in the twenty-first century that seek to fracture any sense of human solidarity lead us to ask whether the idea of a common humanity might not be quite as regressive as critics and theorists have thought.

A recent anthology offers essays in what it terms 'the new character criticism', and its editors, Paul Yachnin and Jessica Slights, observe that 'Shakespeare's characters have continued to have a lively existence for theater practitioners, playgoers, students, and general readers.'[2] Indeed, they make the more forceful claim that 'character is the organizing principle of Shakespeare's plays – it organizes both the formal and ideological dimensions of the drama and is not organized by them – ... character is the principal bridge over which the emotional, cognitive, and political transactions of theater and literature pass between actors and playgoers or between written texts and readers'.[3]

---

[1] A. C. Bradley, *Shakespearean Tragedy: Lectures on Hamlet, Othello, King Lear Macbeth*, 3rd edn (Basingstoke, 1992).

[2] Paul Yachnin and Jessica Slights, eds., *Shakespeare and Character: Theory, History, Performance and Theatrical Persons* (London, 2009), p. 3.

[3] Yachnin and Slights, eds., *Shakespeare and Character*, pp. 6–7. See also the special issue on character in Shakespeare of *Shakespeare Studies* 40 (2012), guest edited by Michael Bristol.

In the light of nearly a century of anti-character prejudice, this is a provocative claim. But it is liable to upset only a coterie of academics who have become ensconced in an academy that, in its focus on professionalism and historicism, has grown ever more alienated from a world beyond archival research and the scholarly press.

This article, a collaboration between a theatre practitioner and an academic, seeks to reinvigorate scholarly enquiry into the nature of Shakespearian character, not as abstraction from the text, but as experienced in performance. We steer a path between the denigration of character as a critical concept by almost a century of Shakespeare criticism and the elevation of character as a unitary, centripetal force of performance and appreciation by the non-academic world of audiences, directors and actors. For Yachnin and Slights, character as organizing principle of Shakespeare's plays arises from a dialogical interaction through which ideological and ethical issues may be expressed and interchanged between figures whose psychological unity remains intact. Each character is a single and singular entity through which ideology is both expressed and contested. Talking about Shylock, they insist on the unity of his character, especially as expressed by the constant reference to him in the play as a dog or cur: 'there is no transcendence of ideology in the play. Even when he gets his day in court, just when he has the chance to make a public case for his injured fatherhood and manhood, Shylock is still a dog that lifts its leg, as it were, against the Venetian state.'[4] Although we agree that character is inescapable for our critical appreciation of the poetry, the structure, the plot, the ideology and the humanity of Shakespeare's plays, we disagree with both Yachnin and Slights and the common, popular notion beyond the academy that there is an inherent unity in the concept of character in Shakespeare.[5] This runs the risk of fetishizing character. We mean this in the technical sense of an object invested with excessive emotion and fantasy, without recognizing that such an object is in fact a product of *relationships*. Such relationships are obscured or forgotten in the very perception of character as fetish. The signal case of such fetishization is *Hamlet*, which, as Margreta de Grazia reminds us, has been almost universally reduced to Hamlet the character, whose ineffable mystery we continue, tirelessly, to try to pluck out.[6]

There are many other examples of this tendency to fetishize single characters. The list is long: Othello, Cleopatra, Macbeth, Ophelia, Lear, Richard III, Rosalind ... and, of course, Shylock. *The Merchant of Venice* has long been considered Shylock's play. Just as every actor would prefer to play Malvolio rather than Orsino in *Twelfth Night*, so Shylock has overwhelmed all the other characters, in the eyes of critics, actors and audiences. It used to be Portia. We could investigate this shift of sympathies, but the point remains that a single character has tended to dominate the play and its manifold relationships.

The key term here is relationships. For even the most character-driven readings and performances would not deny that a character is always established in relation to other characters. In responses, provocations, challenges, declarations, questions, denials, pleas. But the conception of character we are interrogating is assumed to accommodate such relationships from a position of singular integrity or identity: a character such as Shylock seems to be reactive and proactive in relation to others from a position of independent psychological repleteness; from this certain centre, he engages in the bond with Antonio, pleads for a recognition of his own humanity, is torn by his loyalty as a father,

---

[4] Yachnin and Slights, eds., *Shakespeare and Character*, pp. 11–12.
[5] For audiences, actors and directors, Shakespeare is synonymous with character as it is encapsulated by Alexander Pope's famous statement that: '[t]o this life and variety of Character we must add the wonderful Preservation of it; which is such throughout his plays that had all the Speeches been printed without the very names of the persons I believe one might have apply'd them with certainty to every speaker': Alexander Pope, 'Preface to Shakespeare', ed. Jack Lynch, http://andromeda.rutgers.edu/~jlynch/Texts/pope-shakespeare.html.
[6] Margreta de Grazia, *Hamlet without Hamlet* (Cambridge, 2007).

insists on the letter of the bond, and finally declares that he is content but also unwell at the verdict of the court. But is there such a centre? If so, where does it lie? How does an actor find and express it? And is there an essence that exists no matter what we do with it or who plays the part?

Audiences, actors, directors and theatre critics are now committed to the belief that a character like Shylock can be represented only by a great actor – one who offers a single, commanding embodiment of the facets of the figure we call 'Shylock'. Actors long to play Shylock; directors plot the play around such a major figure; audiences flock to *The Merchant of Venice* to see and hear celebrity actors: to Laurence Olivier at the Old Vic, Al Pacino on screen, F. Murray Abraham on Broadway, Patrick Stewart at the RSC, or Jonathan Pryce at Shakespeare's Globe. But what if Shylock's character were distributed among different actors?

Karin Coonrod's historic production of *The Merchant in Venice* in July 2016, staged for the first time in the Venetian Ghetto,[7] distributed the character in precisely this way by having five different actors play the part of Shylock – one in each scene in which he appears. Coonrod felt that five Shylocks would explore the representation and embodiment of the character in new ways:

I couldn't settle on a famous guy to play Shylock because in my head I could see what they would do ... what better way to truly investigate the *character* of Shylock, rather than a mere interpretation of Shylock, than by allowing all of us entrance into him ... This way the painful human nature of the character will be highlighted more than the individual performance of an actor.[8]

The key provocation here is Coonrod's desire to allow all of us entrance to Shylock, Jew and non-Jew, man and woman, father and mother, outsider and insider alike. The casting of five Shylocks began as an exploratory tool in development. And it remained, gathering layers of poetic implication. Shylock as everyman. As the outsider. As the slivers of self that are self-persecuting and incongruent. As all the nationalities, all the genders, all the humans, that have ever been displaced, considered 'alien',

been betrayed, and of all the hurt and complex parts of our soul that seek belonging and integration. Of our fractured self that seeks healing. But also retribution and revenge. Of a splintered mirror that reveals more than the individual who gazes in.

Such distribution of character, especially in Coonrod's hands, challenges a further commonplace of current criticism and theory: the rejection of the notion of a universal humanity that frequently manifests as a reflex revulsion. Thomas Newkirk, in 'Selfhood and the personal essay', remarks on the rigid exclusion of categories at particular moments of academic consensus: '[t]he capacity to self-monitor in matters of taste – to identify and resist the appeals of sentimentality – is part of the identity equipment of academics, particularly in the humanities ... It is a form of cultural capital, an ingrained preference for the ironic, distanced, critical, and complex that, as Bourdieu demonstrated, serves to establish class distinctions.'[9] The notion of a universal humanity has for the past four decades been excoriated by the academics Newkirk mentions, as precisely part of the 'identity equipment' of 'taste', although taste would itself be part of the category of concepts considered to be beyond the framework formed by the 'ironic, distanced, critical and complex'. It is excluded on multiple grounds: by an entrenched historicism, a more attenuated sense of political mission which used to see the universal as the refuge of that arch-scoundrel 'liberal humanism', and, ironically – for it borrows from the very Leavisian and Ricardian moral vocabulary that it

---

7 See Carol Rutter's review of the production, 'Shakespeare's *The Merchant of Venice* in and beyond the Ghetto', *Shakespeare Survey 70* (Cambridge, 2017), 79–88; and Shaul Bassi's account of the origins of the production, 'The Merchant in Venice: re-creating Shakespeare in the Ghetto' in the same issue (67–78).
8 Personal interview with EP (Venice, 8 July 2016); www.merchantinvenice.org; http://moked.it/international/2016/02/14/culture-shylock-gets-ready-to-land-in-venice.
9 Thomas Newkirk, 'Selfhood and the personal essay: a pragmatic defence', in *What Makes Writing Good? A Multiperspective*, ed. William Coles and James Vopat (Lexington, MA, 1985), pp. 33–53; p. 39.

attacks – its fellow traveller, 'sentimentality'. To speak for a universal humanity is to wallow in something completely foreign to a properly critical intellect: '[t]he author's rationality is in question, and so is the credibility of the argument. If you are the victim of a "sentimental" epithet, you have been excluded from the magic circle. It is as if your readers are too tough for you, and you are too much of a sissy for them'.[10] Newkirk quotes Richard Miller's argument that 'these judgments and preferences are not purely intellectual; they are experienced bodily as forms of discomfort, even revulsion'.[11] This is apposite for our argument. For the experience of the theatre as Coonrod presented it in the Venetian Ghetto was also not *purely intellectual*. It was experienced *bodily* by members of the audience, certainly as discomfort and revulsion at some points, but also as identification, in ways that could not be dismissed as mere sentimentality.

By splitting the 'character' of Shylock across five different actors in the Venetian Ghetto production, Coonrod thus evokes what Michael Bristol revives as Shylock's 'human condition' by extending the character from a single figure to multiple embodiments of such humanity, restoring a long-derided sense of the 'common humanity' of Shakespeare's characters and ourselves: '[f]or Shakespeare the idea of human nature appears tragically in the image of unaccommodated man the "poor bare forked animal" . . . Human fragility, "the thousand natural shocks that flesh is heir to" . . . is the common and natural condition of human personhood'.[12] A diversely refracted Shylock did not meet with universal approval. One prominent Shakespeare academic who saw the production observed that the experiment 'seemed to sacrifice any possibility of development in the play's most compelling character in order to make a fairly obvious political point about the way race is perceived'. To say this is to think of character in Shakespeare in a linear, teleological way – as something that 'develops', achieving completion only at the end after passing through successively progressive stages of mental and emotional expression in a continuous embodiment of a single self.

The five Shylocks of this production were not merely a bold experiment or a distracting gimmick, but rather revealed something crucial and often unnoticed about Shakespeare's uses of language in the creation and conceptualization of character.[13] That 'splitting the part and making literal the multifaceted and somehow irreconcilable personality of the character' emphasizes that the conception of five Shylocks, or indeed multiple Shylocks, is contained within the text itself.[14] The words through which character is constructed in Shakespeare (and it is always constructed, never given) suggest a character whose multiplicity resembles that of Montaigne's celebrated descriptions of a fragmented, even contradictory, selfhood:

[i]f I speak variously of myself, it is because I consider myself variously; all the contrarieties are there to be found in one corner or another; after one fashion or another: bashful, insolent; chaste, lustful; prating, silent; laborious, delicate; ingenious, heavy; melancholic, pleasant; lying, true; knowing, ignorant; liberal, covetous, and prodigal: I find all this in myself, more or less, according as I turn myself about; and whoever will sift himself to the bottom, will find in himself, and even in his own judgment, this volubility and discordance. I have nothing to say of myself entirely, simply, and solidly without mixture and confusion.[15]

Montaigne likens the descriptions of the self to the adoption of different theatrical roles: '[t]here is no description so hard, nor so profitable, as is the description of a man's own life. Yet must a man

---

[10] Suzanne Clark, 'Rhetoric, social construction, and gender: is it bad to be sentimental?', in *Writing Theory and Critical Theory*, ed. J. Clifford and J. Schlib (New York, 1994), pp. 96–108; p. 101.

[11] Newkirk, 'Selfhood', p. 39.

[12] Yachnin and Slights, eds., *Shakespeare and Character*, p. 23.

[13] See Rutter, '*Merchant*', p. 85, n. 10: 'letting us see Shylock in pieces, Shylock as a series of parts, Coonrod was doing something . . . ambiguous and radical. She was unsettling continuity, a fixed interpretation of the role, and ultimately the play.'

[14] Bassi, 'Merchant *in* Venice', p. 75.

[15] Michel de Montaigne, 'Of the inconstancy of our actions', in *Essays*, ed. J. I. M. Stewart, trans. John Florio (London, 1931), vol. 2, p. 1.

handsomely trimme-up, yea and dispose and range himselfe, to appear on the Theatre of the World.'[16]

In Shakespeare's theatrical construction of the self through what he would have known as 'personation', and we call character, the 'contrarieties' of self are distributed across its staged and verbal manifestations, even though the names that act as speech prefixes are embodied by a single actor. Coonrod's distribution of the role of Shylock across different actors in *The Merchant in Venice* made such distributed character much more apparent. Moreover, that move involved a paradox: the distribution of Shylock's character across differentiated bodies, singular and particular in size, shape, accent, nationality, race and gender, invited the recognition of an utterly unsentimental *universal* humanity. The universal was embodied through multiplied singularity.

When five actors play a single character, what exactly is distributed in a play that consists of nothing but lines of prose and verse? Obviously, those lines, with their speech prefixes of 'Shylock' or 'Jew'; yet, when those lines are distributed across different actors, this does not mean that each actor portrays an incomplete or fractured character: merely a *part* of a whole. The richness of the language with which Shakespeare draws his characters is akin to the range of different frequencies across the colour spectrum. But there is a danger that a single actor's interpretation and presentation of a character may obscure or obliterate some of the colours or combine them into the impression of white light.

Distributing the character across different actors means that each actor refracts what we might see as only white light in a *single* actor into the different hues and shades that are in fact the unrefracted components of that light. Each of these actors fills the lines with voice, expression, movement and the semiotics of the body in different ways, bringing out aspects of the text (and therefore of emotion, response, thought, provocation, reflection, rhythm) that are likely to have been attenuated or even negated in a totalizing performance by a single actor. In the distribution of Shylock across five actors, each prism renders apparent a particular coloured component of the white light, but is not reduced to that single component: it retains the full spectrum. Each actor embodies a full humanity; he or she is not a partial or truncated personation of such humanity.

The challenge actively to understand each embodiment as both a whole and as a part of a whole invites the viewer to identify with such a distributed Shylock in a range of possible ways – not only to participate actively in the process of understanding the continuity of character across different forms of embodiment, but also to recognize themselves in the representation. And that was Coonrod's ambition: to distribute the character of the 'Jew Shylock' in such a way that all of us might recognize ourselves in him and him in ourselves. This provocation, consciously to consider the construction of character, might seem similar to Brecht's *Verfremdungseffekt*, by which the familiar emotional engagement with a character is disturbed and suspended to challenge the audience to think politically, but it passes through a very different route. Rather than alienating the audience emotionally, Coonrod sought to forge a 'community of strangers' by exciting them to recognize, through the differences between actors communally creating a single character, a universality in which all are complicit: 'he is us'.[17] The distribution of character thus travels beyond the actors, into the body of the audience. The audience becomes a sea of Shylocks.

In a BBC interview, Howard Jacobson discussed the challenge for an audience: 'the idea put me off . . . because I want to retain sympathy for one person . . . for me retaining sympathy for Shylock is very important'. He praised Sorab Wadia, who played the first Shylock, as 'saucy, quick, agile . . . terrific'. But he and the interviewer referred to him, not by his name, but as 'the young Shylock' and 'the Indian actor' – 'I love the Indian actor' –thereby obfuscating the person behind the epithets.[18] And this is what we all do with character.

---

[16] Montaigne, 'Of exercise or practice', in *Essays*, vol. 3, p. 2.
[17] BBC World Service, 'The Merchant in Venice', 7 August 2016, www.bbc.co.uk/programmes/p04331nk.
[18] BBC, 'The Merchant in Venice'.

In Coonrod's words, Shylock was distributed across 'a young Zoroastrian man, an older Croatian man, an English woman, a middle-aged Venetian man and a middle-aged Jewish American man', each of them presenting 'the complexities of Shylock's character: successful merchant, strict disciplinarian father, wronged man, killer, foreigner, misunderstood, marginalized'.[19] Our default response tends to reduce an actor to a category, and indeed a character to an archetype, but this multi-casting resists being captured by labels – older, younger, woman, man, Indian, Jew. When there are five different Shylocks – differing in age, race, acting style, religious convictions, sexual preference, accent, gender, height, weight, hair colour, ear shape – we are propelled to see past all these 'characteristics' and confront the tendency to make arbitrary categorical difference a thoughtless tool of alienation. Diana Henderson notes of this distribution:

[b]y embodying Shylock diversely, the ways we do and don't find differences 'significant' really came through … we forget that four centuries mean that groups and religions and categories themselves don't have stable meanings, yet people often talk about characters as if we understand them using our modern categories (of gender, age, etc.). So the production really brought out those complexities in intelligent, moving and often disturbing ways.[20]

Distribution of character asks us to question whether differences are significant beyond our reflex responses.[21]

Leslie A. Fiedler claims that, through bad conscience, we persist in misremembering Shylock and all the stereotypes he embodies to expurgate Shakespeare 'by cancelling out or amending the meanings of the strangers at the heart of his plays'.[22] But Coonrod, challenging this tendency, reveals the complexity of the outsider as a fluid category: 'I opened up the character of Shylock to be played by five very different actors … [s]o the character of Shylock became Jewish *and* universal, an expression of every outsider living in a dominant and often cruel culture'.[23] We are invited to embrace the outsider at the heart of the play: 'to feel what burns, to open eyes to the light, to hear a cry and a call, to wonder at these stones and find a way of justice and mercy: a stand for

Judgement'.[24] The outsider is focused on Shylock 'the Jew', whose cruel persecution was heightened in the historic place of the Venetian Ghetto's imprisoning walls, with its memorial plaque commemorating those murdered in the shoah. And yet the outsider is simultaneously everyone. It is 'the Indian actor'. It is Portia. It is the servant. It is the pregnant moor. It is the melancholic merchant. It is any one from whom we arbitrarily distance ourselves through categories of identity and exclusion that in our minds remain static, immutable and unfractured.

The distribution of character recognizes that 'the stranger' extends to all parts of our fragmented selves, and to all the characters' yearning for connection in Shakespeare's play. Characters obsess about faraway things, with nostalgia and melancholy; about riches, about ships, about Belmont, about the moon:

[t]utto il tempo un po' come una fisarmonica questo spettacolo … it's opened and it's closed at the same time sui i sentimenti dei personaggi. Perché Antonio is sad, Bassanio è preoccupato per Portia, Shylock per la figlia, Jessica per Lorenzo, Lorenzo per l'amore di Jessica,

---

[19] https://www.broadwayworld.com/article/VIDEO-Justice-Ruth-Bader-Ginsberg-to-Preside-Over-Mock-Trial-As-Part-of-Venices-The-Shylock-Project-20160329/. and Kevin Coonrod, 'breaking the fourth wall: reinventing and resituating Shakespearean performance', Gardon College, unpublished.

[20] Diana E. Henderson, 'Hard hearts and coronets: anatomizing resistance and community with Shakespeare now', plenary lecture given at the European Shakespeare Research Association conference in Gdańsk, 27–30 July 2017.

[21] Sabine Schülting, discussing a dark and daring 1978 German production by George Tabori with multiple Shylocks, variously played by a cast of thirteen actors, notes that the effect was to blur binary oppositions, increase emotional impact, and show both the critical potential and disturbing effects of an adaptation. See Sabine Schülting, '"I am not bound to please thee with my answers": *The Merchant of Venice* on the post-war German stage', in *World-Wide Shakespeares: Local Appropriations in Film and Performance* (London, 2005), pp. 65–71; pp. 69–70.

[22] Leslie A. Fiedler, *The Stranger in Shakespeare* (London, 1973), p. 99.

[23] Kevin Coonrod, 'Foreword', in *Radical Revival as Adaptation: Theatre, Politics, Society*, ed. Jozefina Kompaoraly (London, 2017), p. v.

[24] Quotations taken from Coonrod's programme note, p. 7.

e Lancillotto fra due padroni ... tutti questi personaggi anche Salanio e Salarino sono sempre in preoccupazione per qualcosa.[25]

And this melancholy is never fully disclosed or satisfied. For, ultimately, at the heart of the play, and perhaps at the heart of human experience, we are all outsiders searching for a love and mercy that integrates us, but forever finding it elusive.

The first Shylock, in the scene in which Antonio and Bassanio engage over the bond, is played by Sorab Wadia – 'the Indian actor' – who was born in India to parents of Persian ethnicity and Zoroastrian religion, lives in New York, identifies as a Persian-Indian-American and is, in his own words: 'Actor & Singer. Also: pianist, photographer, traveller, polyglot, potter, hiker, knitter, cook, transcriptionist, animal lover, oenophile, secular humanist & wannabe farmer'.[26] His interpretation brought out the character's charisma and humour with wit and irony, rather than telegraphing the hatred and rancour signalled in Shylock's asides. His comic responsiveness was exemplified one night when he improvised playfully on the lines 'does a dog have money? Can a cur lend 3000 pounds?' as an actual dog wandered onto the open-air stage in the middle of his monologue, to send the audience into gales of laughter. The proposed contract for a pound of flesh to be cut off 'from whatever part pleases me' was expressed with infectious humour, making it a 'merry bond' indeed. His proffered hand seemed a genuine gesture of friendship – 'I would have your love.' A handshake would have been customary to complete business transactions in the Renaissance: 'among Christians a contract was sealed with a kiss or with a handshake, contracts with Jews were sealed with a bow, so that the bodies of the parties need not touch'.[27] Antonio, from fear of touching a 'polluted' Jewish body, rejects Shylock's offer of his hand and his love, ensuring that the only intimacy possible between them will be at knife's point. In the trial scene, when the knife is finally released from his chest, both Shylock and Antonio begin to laugh. Although this moment is played by Ned Eisenberg – the

fifth Shylock – it reprises the earlier moment of laughter when the first Shylock struck the bond. These echoes and iterations between the Shylocks seemed to occur organically. Wadia, reflecting on his performance, remarks: '[h]oly shit, that's Ned, it's a gesture Ned does and I'm using it, so obviously we are informing each other whether we know it or not and I love that we are. Working as an organism taking from each other even when we don't know we are taking from each other.'[28]

Although Wadia is a very different actor from the other Shylocks, and offers his own nuanced interpretation as the 'first-scene' Shylock, we understand that this Shylock does not exist solely to repeat a first-scene existence over and over. Nor is this Shylock capable of a different ending from Ned Eisenberg's 'trial-scene' Shylock. The distribution of lines allows the interpretation of character to change in each scene, yet the narrative remains shared. This first-scene Shylock can only be the last-scene Shylock after he has lost his daughter as the middle-scene Shylock. The casting of a different Shylock in every scene thus allows the audience to be fully invested in that moment of his existence as complete and contained within that moment: a character fully realized in a moment, but also changed from moment to moment.

The local Venetian actor, Adriano Iurissevich, an expert in *Commedia dell'arte* with an accomplished career, played the second Shylock. Having to act in English, which demands particular

---

[25] From an interview with Michele Guidi (Bassanio). 'All the time the play is a bit like a piano-accordion ... it's opened and closed at the same time with the feelings of the characters. Because Antonio is sad, Bassanio is concerned about Portia, Shylock for his daughter, Jessica for Lorenzo, Lorenzo for the love of Jessica, and Lancelot between two masters ... all these characters, even Salanio and Salarino, are always preoccupied with something.'
[26] See www.artisttrove.com/artist/340316836046495/Sorab%20Wadia.
[27] Richard Sennett, 'Fear of touching: the Jewish Ghetto in Renaissance Venice', in *Flesh and Stone: The Body and the City in Western Civilization* (New York 1994), p. 215.
[28] Interview with Sorab Wadia, unpublished documentary footage, Ted Hardin and Elizabeth Coffman, 2016.

verse and prose rhythms, was a challenge to him: 'you get to the maximum only in your own language because when you have to think of the words there is a problem, the words have to come by themselves'.[29] His Shylock did not have the sardonic wit of Wadia's but was full of sensitivity. He used his *Commedia* training to give physicality to the character and a different rhythm to the scene. Instead of a tyrannical father, we see an older man concerned for his daughter, sympathetic to his servant, and weary of a world full of painful intrusions from outsiders who hate him. He infused his interactions with compassion. For him, Shylock was 'very human, somebody in conflict who is feeling something bad is going on and they don't know what to do. Hesitation, conflict between love and hate, somebody who would like to be loved I think.'[30] The moment of farewell with Jessica became profoundly moving. Working in the spaces between the lines, it was filled with uncertainty, anxiety and premonition. The role of father was embodied in all its strength of attachment as well as its overbearing protectiveness.

The third Shylock was played by Jenni Lea Jones – an actress with an extraordinary singing voice that she affirms is her 'Welsh birthright'. In a play in which the absent mother is particularly remarkable, for Jones the casting of a female Shylock brought out the maternal aspects of the character: 'a parent losing a child is a huge thing . . . coming from a maternal perspective'.[31] Jones was struck by Shylock's humanity and complexity, feeling that his many aspects and facets rendered him Shakespeare's most complicated character, even more than Hamlet: 'a lot of people will say that this is an anti-semitic show, which I cannot believe in any way because Shakespeare has made this character so real and so complex; there is nothing to not like about him. [A c]ompletely rounded character on the stage . . . you understand why he behaves the way he behaves.'[32]

Jones's Shylock enters at the pivotal moment when the play becomes darker and more unhinged, a moment seamlessly matched by Coonrod in the timing, when the natural light fades and the electric light kicks in. Peter Ksander, the lighting director,

remarks: 'when we lose the actual sun there is a point where there are no shadows. Not even attached shadows, not even the ones that fall on your faces. And that is the moment we click into artificial light, our own sun, our own way of revealing.'[33] Jones gives two spine-chilling wails before she delivers the most famous monologue in the play – 'hath not a Jew eyes?' Kent Cartwright observes: 'the most powerful moment in the play, for me, was when, after the daughter-ducats episode, the female Shylock let out a prolonged, gut-wrenching howl of almost inexpressible pain, frustration, and anguish. With that feral cry the play pivoted and deepened emotionally for me.'[34] Jones delivers the speech, full of grief and agony, underscored by cello music. It is the lament of a mother who has lost her child. It is Medea. It is Rachel. It is the absent Leah. And it is a primal cry against all injustice.[35]

The fourth Shylock, Andrea Brugnera, takes up mid-scene from Jones, commencing the dialogue with Tubal who is played by Ned Eisenberg, the last Shylock. Brugnera, an Italian actor, has worked with and known Coonrod for sixteen years, from the birth of Compagnia Colombari in Orvieto, Umbria. Brugnera speaks little English, and embodies a range of physical *Commedia* expression. His Shylock was conveyed by strongly stylized gesture, which evoked a great deal of pathos. He was doubled with Lancillotto's blind father, Gobbo:

---

[29] Interview with Adriano Iurissevich, unpublished documentary footage, Ted Hardin and Elizabeth Coffman, 2016.
[30] Interview with Adriano Iurissevich.
[31] Interview with Jenni Lea Jones, unpublished documentary footage, Ted Hardin and Elizabeth Coffman, 2016.
[32] Interview with Jenni Lea Jones.
[33] Interview with Peter Ksander, unpublished audio, 2016.
[34] Personal email correspondence, 2016.
[35] In his commanding account of the genesis of *The Merchant in Venice*, Shaul Bassi, who conceived of and drove the project, remarks that 'no Jewish Shylock was allowed to usurp or supplant the suffering borne by the Jews who were deported from Venice. And yet the prolonged howl of anguish uttered by the woman Shylock allowed for both empathy with Jewish suffering and for a more generalized identification with persecuted minorities' ('Merchant *in* Venice', p. 75).

he was thus both the father who thinks he has lost a son and the father who has lost a daughter.

Brugnera felt that performing Shylock was like entering into the secret language of Shakespeare, and that the work was important because it was universal in time and space:

quello che mi sorprende è la potenza di questo personaggio di Shylock ... perché nello stereotipo, anche shakespeariano, è un personaggio chiuso in un ruolo ben definito – invece, moltiplicandolo o dividendolo frantumavo in cinque biologie diverse – in cinque bios diversi, degli attori diversi, di lingue diverse, di modi di vedere diversi – questo personaggio diventa tutti – non è soltanto Shylock – non è soltanto il popolo ebraico, non è soltanto l'ebreo errante – è l'umanità. E per me, credo che sia il personaggio più umano che incontrato – più umano con il pericolo di essere più inumano. Quindi e molto reale, è molto realistico.[36]

Ned Eisenberg, the final Shylock, brings us back to contemporary Stanislavski-based acting. He speaks with a New York accent and is precise and clear in his delivery. Eisenberg is the only Jewish actor who plays Shylock. He performed Tubal to Brugnera's emotional widower in the previous scene, offsetting Brugnera's pain with his own calculated, clinical provocation. Turning from Tubal into the final Shylock, Eisenberg brings a sense of wit and irony back to the part, echoing Wadia's delivery as the first Shylock. The doubling here in effect splits Shylock between cool, calculated menace and passionate betrayal, whilst imbuing the character he is about to play with an interior state of resolve that has moved beyond emotional reaction and self-pity. Eisenberg internalizes Tubal's role as provocateur, carrying it into the final scene. Brugnera plays Shylock along *Commedia* lines, in starker emotional colours, in contrast to Eisenberg's incredulous use of satirical humour combined with an intense demand for retribution. Eisenberg expresses his righteous anger with cool logic and a honed, single focus that is somewhat insane: 'I don't see him as a typical villain, I think he is somewhat insane by the end of the play as a result of what he has lost.'[37] As much as the sympathy of the play is with Shylock, the production still holds him accountable, simultaneously holding all of us

accountable, for our daily use of words of persecution, for our fear of the other, our thoughtless perpetuation of injustice, and our easy use of a term, 'mercy', without ability to show it.

In discussing the experience of playing part of a distributed character, Eisenberg notes: 'it's interesting to see how everyone plays it ... we have to coalesce with each other and create one character with five different interpretations'.[38] Wadia, the first Shylock, commented that he would have performed Shylock's 'hath not a Jew eyes?' monologue differently from Jenni Lea Jones's interpretation. Here, we see distribution of character is not a distribution of a specific interpretation, because in heightening a particular aspect of character, filtered through the response of an actor, the variations are innumerable. Such variability asks an audience to interrogate preconceptions of what character is: it exposes the erroneousness of the idea that something is 'not in character', since the quality of being human is in fact often revealed in inconsistency: 'whoever will look narrowly into his own bosom, will hardly find himself twice in the same condition. I give to my soul sometimes one face and sometimes another, according to the side I turn her to.'[39] Shylock remains Shylock in the multifaceted interpretation. And so we are asked to consider what it is exactly that makes him Shylock. The distribution of character destabilizes

---

[36] 'What surprises me is the power of this character Shylock ... because in the stereotype, even Shakespearian, he is a character closed in a well-defined role – instead, multiplying or splitting it into five different biologies – in five different bodies, different actors, of different languages, of different ways of seeing – this character becomes all – it is not only Shylock – it's not only the Jewish people, it's not only the wandering Jew – it is humanity. And for me, I believe it is the most human character encountered – the most human with the danger of being the most inhuman. So it is very real, it is very realistic.' Interview with Andrea Brugnera, unpublished documentary footage, Ted Hardin and Elizabeth Coffman, 2016.

[37] Interview with Ned Eisenberg, unpublished audio, 2016.

[38] Interview with Ned Eisenberg, unpublished.

[39] Montaigne, 'Exercise', 3.1.

the idea that something essential defines Shylock – that, as we queried earlier, there is an absolute centre to the character that can be expressed only by the centripetal interpretation of a single great actor. Simply, he is Shylock because he tells us he is – 'Shylock is my name' – but also because we accept that he is. The audience is essential in the endowment of his character. It is a collaborative process between them, the actor and the playwright: 'wear his words and wear his characters and be them and then let the audience get what it will from your performance'.[40]

The production was marked by a powerful sense of ensemble: just as character was not privileged as a centripetal idea, neither was performer. The actors came together at this moment in history to invite the audience into the play as guests and make it a sacred space.[41] Coonrod told the cast:

You will be meeting people, it's not like they are excised from the play, some people live here, look at the windows, you can see people looking out the windows ... It's very beautiful. This kind of play outside is a high level of guerrilla theatre ... This is what's exciting, is the extremity, ok? So it's like being in prison, but ... we are also involving the people, *tutti quelli che sono qui* ... it's up to you to be the angel, to say 'welcome to our play'. You! It's our party. This is your space ... Consecrated for our work. Together.[42]

All the performers were complicit in all the components of storytelling; they were scattered around the Ghetto always in sight of the audience, moving from watching to participating, a continuous mutability and movability of presence in space. They were dressed and undressed by 'black angels' – visible stage hands. For example, Elena Pellone (one of the authors of this piece) was robed in this way, changing from ensemble member into Nerissa, while Portia is similarly dressed and Lancillotto is purposefully disguised. In this recurring stage convention, actors moved fluidly into performance spaces – an indication of authentic representation as well as a signalling of the ways in which character must play a performance of self.

Nerissa now must be servant to Portia, just as Portia must be dutiful daughter to her father's will.

This fluid tapestry movement in the ensemble and the veil between the world of actors and the actor's world, always transparent in the moonlight, allowed a further engagement with Shylock not only as everyman, but also as a cog in corrupted social conventions, every moveable part both a willing participant and a victim of the system. When playing the bragging jacks, Portia, Nerissa and the servant Balzarina (conceived as female) are de-robed – released from one social convention – and re-robed as the 'Bragging Jacks', liberated and incarcerated in another social convention. And this moment of de-robing, of painting the canvas white in order to re-colour it in front of the audience, was a rippling motif in the play. A neutral mask is created and recreated as the Shylocks are liturgically dressed and undressed.

Both the specificity of Shylock's Jewishness and his shared humanity are embodied in this repeated ritual of the dressing and undressing. Dressing Shylock identically, in stone-coloured robes and yellow sashes, confirms a shared identity; but the ceremonial donning and doffing of this costume by actors of different age, race, gender and demeanour conveys both the distributed humanity and the multi-faceted nature of the character. It connects the character in a linear way to the Shylock embodied in the scenes before, yet also allows a cleansing of preconceived notions as the dressing simultaneously resets the character to a nascent state, or neutral form. It frees the audience from a tendency to allow powerful initial impressions to obliterate later nuances, or the telos of Shylock's end to

---

[40] Interview with Sorab Wadia.
[41] See Bassi's account of the significance of staging the play in the Venetian Ghetto: '*The Merchant in Venice* was predicated from the outset on a creative collision between the play and the place, in an attempt to see how two (early) modern myths could resonate with each other ... both *The Merchant* and the Ghetto are fundamentally ambivalent documents of Western civilization in having been both instruments of intolerance and catalysts for cultural transformation' ('Merchant *in* Venice', pp. 69–70).
[42] Discussion with the cast, unpublished audio.

overwrite, say, the poignancy, concern and loneliness of Shylock as father.

Paul Edmondson observes that '[w]atching the five Shylocks put on their robes to take up the role in their respective scenes made the production feel liturgical to me ... invoking the memories of the Ghetto itself, and paying full tribute to all Jews who have been persecuted'.[43] There are two moments in which the five Shylocks come together to form a chorus. This is distributed character as shared community. Moving slowly together, they begin a low keening sound, as the company, Greek-chorus-like, weave amongst them, mocking and abusing them in different languages – Italian, French, German, Spanish, English – shouting 'my daughter, my ducats, fled with a Christian', then gathering together, chanting 'why, all the boys in Venice follow him, crying his stones his daughter and his ducats', alternating between Italian and English. This builds to a climax until Jones turns and lets out her terrible, spine-chilling wail, the others resembling Rodin's *Les bourgeois de Calais*.

This moment marks both the chronological centre of the play and the heart of the interpretation. The choric moment integrates the persecuted, the persecutors and the audience: 'wherever this play is done, though there will be no ghetto, this wail is at the center ... it is almost like the wail of GOD at what we have done to ourselves ... there is the mystery, the ineffable, the theatrical gesture'.[44]

The doubling by actors playing Shylock as non-Jewish figures who persecuted him gave the distribution of character a further poetic resonance. In the trial scene, Elena Pellone as Nerissa disguised as the silent clerk, watching and notating all, became aware that the figures of persecution on the stage, who were played by actors who had also doubled as Shylocks, meant that the idea of nemesis deepened as figures of self become the assailants. Graziano was played by Wadia, the Doge by Jones, and the two imposing court officials by Brugnera and Iurissevich – all of them once Shylock. Wadia remarked of his split position: 'throw insults at my alter ego standing there literally on 180 degrees between two characters: the "villainous" Jew and

the most raging anti-semite'.[45] This combination of 'most raging anti-semite' and '"villainous" Jew' enables us as audience to consider that we are often our own worst enemy, as fragments of ourselves turn against us and persecute us. As Cartwright noted:

the logic, as far as I can see, was in the fact of the doubling, that major Venetian characters also doubled as Shylock. If the doubling here was meant to be thematic, then I walked away with the sense that we are perhaps all anti-semites and, simultaneously, all potential Shylocks. I'm not sure that I am quite comfortable with that formulation or even whether that is what the production meant to say, but that is one idea that lingers in my mind.[46]

Distributed character is therefore not defined solely by speech prefixes but distributes like a drop of wine through water to permeate all the facets of the play. Distribution becomes sharing. As each part is whole and simultaneously makes the whole, each role of persecutor and persecuted becomes part of a singular identity.

We began by stating that the distribution of character is embedded in Shakespeare's text, that the 'contrarieties' of self are distributed across the

---

[43] Personal email correspondence, 8 November 2016.

[44] Personal email correspondence, 21 August 2016. Marie Malherbe, a French artist working in the Ghetto, composed a poem – *A Midsummer Night's Scream – Un cri dans le Ghetto –* that responded to Shylock's wail as performing a healing ritual, which distributed that healing not only across all the absent people in the ghetto, but across the very stones of the Ghetto itself:

> Mercy Merci
> Colombari
> par votre farce libératrice
> le ghetto crie ses cicatrices
> et marche vers sa guérison.
> ('Mercy Thanks / Colombari / by your liberating farce / the ghetto laments it scars / and walks towards its healing.')

See www.artmajeur.com/fr/artist/mariemalherbe/blog/249382/a-midsummer-night-s-scream-un-cri-dans-le-ghetto.

[45] Unpublished documentary footage.

[46] Personal email correspondence, 8 October 2016.

character's staged and verbal manifestations. But the distribution of character across the five Shylocks, and their doubling as other, opposing characters, are embodied in the way Shakespeare distributes language between characters in the play. Each character speaks a language peculiar to him- or herself that bears their identity like a fingerprint. And this is true. But the relationships among characters – the way in which character is constituted out of relations, similarities and differences – are also informed by the way in which language is distributed across and through character, and is shared with the different members of the audience as words pass from one character to another, retaining their earlier sense but also resonating with a new sense and intonation.

This distribution is captured by Mikhail Bakhtin's notion of dialogism and heteroglossia – that all language in use is formulated as a response to someone else, and that even when we speak with our greatest individuality and distinctiveness our utterances are always filled with the voices, the intonations, and therefore the judgements and emotions, of others. Our voices are never wholly individual, wholly our own. Key words pass from mouth to mouth in the play; they are masticated and transferred, lobbed like a ball in a tennis match. The new word, imbued with its overtones, transforms our original notions. The greater ideas of the play resonate with each word's new overtones in this intense word game. Distribution of character by dividing in effect multiplies the possibilities and transforms into both an individual and a shared experience. Just as the character is distributed, the word signifying the whole in itself is, although individual, defined only by shared use, transformed through context and a new perception of meaning.

Let's look at two examples of Shakespeare's distribution of language. The first is the word 'content', which is used only six times. Antonio is 'content' to seal to the bond; Bassanio reads the injunction to 'be content' when he achieves Portia; and Jessica wishes Portia 'all heart's content'. In the trial scene, the final three usages pass noticeably

from Antonio to Portia to Shylock, linking the three of them in a painful triangle. Each use of the word means something different and yet contains within it all the meanings of its previous use, so that Shylock's final 'I am content' is almost a vomiting of words violently force-fed to him by the others. The second example is the word 'mercy'. Everyone knows this word in the voice of Portia, in the resonant, well-known tones of '[t]he quality of mercy is not strained'. We tend to think of 'mercy' as *her* word. Or at least as the word of the Christians. In fact, the first time we hear the word is in the opening line of Act 3, Scene 3. Shylock enters mid-argument – 'speak to me not of mercy' – and the word born in his mouth in actuality has just been passed to him offstage by Antonio. As it is passed, it changes its resonance through the negation: it signifies a lack of understanding, on the one hand, or a shared understanding too well that neither can offer the other mercy or be shown it. And the play has already shown us the meaning of Antonio's mercy: it is to spit on Shylock's gabardine, to refuse the friendship offered in the line 'I would have your love.' So 'speak to me not of mercy' also contains 'do not beguile me with a notion you know nothing of'. From there, the word is passed to his daughter Jessica, before it is reiterated by the Duke, and taken up by Portia in her famous speech. Mercy is moved cyclically until its last utterance, when Portia asks Antonio, 'what mercy can you show him?' The word that Antonio has initiated silently offstage returns to him. What has Antonio learnt of mercy? Not enough.

The last scene of the play was rewritten in Coonrod's production as a second moment of chorus, with the five Shylocks crashing through the fifth act to reiterate the courtroom monologue directly to the audience: 'you'll ask me why I'd rather have the weight of carrion flesh'. They have the final spoken words in the play, ending with the question 'are you answered?', spoken in repetition and directed at the audience. But this is not the last word of Coonrod's production of the *Merchant in Venice*. The word 'mercy' has one final journey. It breaks the confines of the play. It transcends and surrounds the actors and the audience in projections of light upon the Ghetto walls, in Hebrew, Italian and English. The walls literally speak:

the ending – the collective 'Are you answered?' – seemed powerful, although perhaps more for its confrontational quality than for any answer that we might make to the question. When Jessica throws up her arms and 'Merci', 'Misericordia', and the Hebrew 'Rakhamim' are flashed on the wall, I felt that the intention was not so much to reinstate Portia's position, as it were, as it was to say something like, mercy on all of us![47]

In these projections, Coonrod is making explicit something inherent in Shakespeare's distributed language. The quality of mercy is not strained. But neither is it restrained. It is shared. Mercy is not Portia's word. Coonrod's projections embody Shakespeare's challenge to us to make mercy our word. By challenging the fetishization of character, a reductive categorization of 'characteristics' and ownership over language as a divisive tool, we can experience a sense of character that is not held static in the idea of teleological repleteness. Through distributed character and language, Shakespeare and this production may just hold us all accountable individually, for what we are all in together.

To speak of 'what we are all in together' is to return to the issue of a universal humanity, and the ways in which a distribution of character may contribute to the visceral, embodied sharing of that notion across multiple differences. Such universality is not a 'core' essence that resides at the heart of every character, but rather a distribution of differences that, through their very multiplication, may strike each individual member of an audience as a point of human identification, and thereby attenuate received and habitual tendencies towards defining the self in terms of the exclusion of the other: '[e]very man beareth the whole stamp of human condition'.[48] This happens in Shakespeare in the way he writes what we call character, especially in the ways in which words and speech acts pass between speakers to infect them, as it were, with the resonant intonations of other uses. But it is especially powerful when the singularity of character is distributed across actors whose very distinctions and dissimilarities invite an embodied empathy that opens a view to the universal without the taint of sentimentality.

---

[47] Personal email correspondence with Kent Cartwright, 8 October 2016.
[48] Montaigne, 'Exercise', 3.2.

# AUTISTIC CULTURE, SHAKESPEARE THERAPY AND THE HUNTER HEARTBEAT METHOD

## SONYA FREEMAN LOFTIS

(Behavior is communication.)
(Not being able to talk is not the same as not having
anything to say.)
 (Julia Bascom, *Loud Hands: Autistic People, Speaking*)[1]

I pitied thee,
Took pains to make thee speak, taught thee each hour
One thing or other. When thou didst not, savage,
Know thine own meaning, but wouldst gabble like
A thing most brutish.

(*The Tempest*, 1.2.355–9)

Disability autobiography may be regarded as
a postcolonial – indeed, an anticolonial – phenomenon,
a form of autoethnography, as Mary Louise Pratt has
defined it: 'instances in which colonized subjects
undertake to represent themselves in ways that *engage
with* [read: contest] the colonizer's own terms'.

(Thomas Couser, *Signifying Bodies: Disability in
Contemporary Life Writing*)[2]

Cultural stereotypes about autistic spectrum disabilities collide with cultural expectations about performing Shakespeare. Shakespeare is about words and language (autistic people often struggle with communication).[3] Shakespeare is about strong emotion (autistic people may struggle to identify emotion and to express it in socially sanctioned ways). Shakespeare is about play and playing (autistic people, for the most part, do not play in ways that neurotypical [non-autistic] people recognize as 'play'). However, the reasons for this imagined tension between cultural stereotypes of autism and cultural conceptions of Shakespeare may be more deep-seated and disturbing than they initially appear. Harold Bloom has infamously

and bombastically claimed that Shakespeare invented the human.[4] The growing field of disability studies shows that autistic people face dehumanizing stereotypes and cultural practices – that autistic people may be falsely regarded as not-human or less-than-human because of mental disability.[5] Thus, multiple tropes converge to render the term 'autistic Shakespearian' an oxymoron. Under Bloom's schema, to claim to engage Shakespeare is to claim to be fully human: fully capable of communication, emotion and play.[6]

1 Julia Bascom, 'Quiet hands', in *Loud Hands: Autistic People, Speaking*, ed. Julia Bascom (Washington, DC, 2012), Kindle edition, p. 120.
2 Thomas Couser, *Signifying Bodies: Disability in Contemporary Life Writing* (Ann Arbor, 2009), pp. 7–8.
3 Psychologists define autism spectrum disorder as a diagnosis that includes difficulties with socialization and communication (communication skills range from nonverbal to talkative but awkward), a limited range of interests (the 'special interests' associated with the autism spectrum can include a wide variety of topics and subjects, and sensory integration issues (hyper- or hypo-sensitivity to light, sound, and touch). For an explanation of the *Diagnostic and Statistical Manual of Mental Disorders* (DSM) criteria, see Tony Atwood, *The Complete Guide to Asperger's Syndrome* (London, 2007), pp. 10–17.
4 Harold Bloom, *Shakespeare: The Invention of the Human* (New York, 1998).
5 For further discussion of dehumanizing autism stereotypes, see Stuart Murray, *Representing Autism: Culture, Narrative, Fascination* (Liverpool, 2008), pp. 1–26; Mark Osteen, ed., *Autism and Representation* (New York, 2008), pp. 1–48; Sonya Freeman Loftis, *Imagining Autism: Fiction and Stereotypes on the Spectrum* (Bloomington, IN, 2015), pp. 1–22.
6 I am not arguing that those who are incapable of communication, emotion and/or play are not fully human – far from

These imagined cultural tensions between the autistic subject's impairments and the performance of Shakespeare seem to inform some of the rhetoric undergirding and theoretical principles guiding the Hunter Heartbeat Method (HHM), a Shakespeare-based drama therapy for autistic children. Kelly Hunter, of the Royal Shakespeare Company, invented the programme a little over twenty years ago to provide social skills therapy for autistic children.[7] Using role-playing games built on plots, characters and lines from *The Tempest* and *A Midsummer Night's Dream*, the programme engages a variety of ages and the full breadth of the autism spectrum (ranging from nonverbal elementary-school-aged children to 'high-functioning' teenagers).[8] One of the programme's major goals is to improve the social and communication abilities of autistic youth, focusing on skills such as eye contact, body language and 'basic play'.[9] Paired one-on-one with adult actors who guide them through various games, autistic children are taught to imitate the facial expressions, vocal inflection and body language of neurotypical adults as they embody various Shakespearian characters.

There are multiple strengths to the HHM's approach. The practitioners of the HHM are enjoined to act with compassion and empathy towards the autistic children with whom they work, and the programme may encourage its neurotypical practitioners to build relationships with autistics, thus increasing autism awareness.[10] The HHM also teaches neurotypical educators to assume the competence of autistic children – this is a key tenet in working effectively with people with mental disabilities, since disability discrimination all too often begins with the assumption of the disabled subject's incompetence.[11] Because some autistic people are hypersensitive to sound and touch, the HHM allows for adaptations in activities that engage those senses: unlike some other autism therapies (such as Applied Behavior Analysis), Hunter's method encourages a respectful understanding of autistic sensory sensitivities.[12] Finally, there is some possibility for autistic collaboration in the construction of the games themselves:

practitioners are instructed to 'ensure that an enthusiastic suggestion from a child is greeted with equal enthusiasm from yourself and that you always try out their ideas'.[13]

But while the HHM has led to the development of new communication and social skills in some autistic children, the programme often employs rhetoric that casts the autistic subject as an incomplete human being waiting to be 'awakened' (read: civilized, humanized) by Shakespeare. Bringing Shakespeare to autistic children is a charitable impulse, but it also bears the impulse of the cultural colonizer. Charity, an ancient practice that has all too often proscribed the interaction between the able-bodied and the disabled, evokes the power of those who give (neurotypical adults), the vulnerability of those who receive (autistic children), and the cultural capital of that which is given (Shakespeare's language).[14] Indeed, the HHM

---

it. I am merely pointing out that various cultural stereotypes forward ableist definitions of the term 'human'.

7  For background information on the HHM, see Nisonger Center, 'Shakespeare & autism', http://nisonger.osu.edu /clinics-services/child/shakespeare-autism.

8  Functioning levels are controversial in the autism community for a variety of reasons. For more on the issues at stake, see Loftis, *Imagining Autism*, p. 9.

9  Nisonger Center, 'Shakespeare & autism', http://nisonger .osu.edu/clinics-services/child/shakespeare-autism.

10  See, for example, Robin Post's foreword to Kelly Hunter, *Shakespeare's Heartbeat: Drama Games for Children with Autism* (New York, 2015). Page numbers in subsequent citations of Hunter's book refer to the Kindle edition; the foreword is unpaginated. Post explains that she has learned a great deal through her work with the HHM: she feels that the programme's 'compassionate perspective has informed and impacted all areas of my teaching making me a more intentional and humanistic listener'.

11  As Post explains, 'another of Kelly's leadership strengths is an attitude and expectation that the children will be perfectly capable of doing whatever she asks of them'.

12  Applied Behavior Analysis (ABA) has long been controversial within the autism community. Some autistics have written about ABA experiences that could be classified as abuse. For example, see Bascom, 'Quiet hands', p. 120.

13  Hunter, *Shakespeare's Heartbeat*, p. 228.

14  For more on disability's long (and complex) relationship with charity, see Henri-Jacques Stiker, *A History of Disability*, trans. Willian Sayers (Ann Arbor, MI, 1999), pp. 65–90; Sharon

builds on larger cultural assumptions dictating that Shakespeare is a universal good, a panacea with the power to 'heal' and 'cure', thus translating Shakespeare's cultural capital into a symbol of the medical model's desire for a world without mental disability.

## SHAKESPEARE AND ACCESSIBILITY: THE FAILURE OF UNIVERSAL DESIGN

The HHM (like other forms of Shakespeare-based therapy) functions on beliefs that Shakespeare's language encapsulates and expresses the human experience and, therefore, that familiarity with Shakespeare is necessary in order to be a fully developed and 'healthy' human. Indeed, the programme is part of the growing phenomenon of therapy/charity Shakespeares that Ayanna Thompson has termed 'Shakespeare reform programs', Michael Jensen describes as 'Service Shakespeare', and Geoffrey Ridden calls 'Shakespeare as therapy': such programmes target a diverse collection of minority groups including prison inmates, at-risk youth, people who experience homelessness, and people with Alzheimer's disease.[15] The belief that Shakespeare's plays celebrate something quintessentially human is widespread, and Shakespeare therapy programmes gain prestige and power based on such claims. As Matt Kozusko has argued, 'Shakespeare for some time has served a secular need for sacralized texts ... the words are agreed to have a particular power ... first as a means of capturing something essential and timeless about an audience's lived reality, and second as a means of validating and guaranteeing the fundamental humanity of that audience.'[16] As Alan Sinfield has pointed out, the school classroom frequently engenders the belief that 'the plays reveal universal "human" values and qualities.'[17] Ironically, the cherished belief that Shakespeare's words contain something essentially human leads to the belief that to understand and appreciate Shakespeare's text therefore validates one's status as human.[18] When it comes to engaging Shakespeare's text, 'the pupil is being persuaded to internalize success or failure with particular and relative cultural codes as an absolute

judgement on her or his potential as a human being'.[19] Thus, Shakespeare becomes a matrix of social belonging, dictating, to some extent, who belongs to a particular 'human' society and who does not.[20] To lack Shakespeare is to be cast outside of the social circle (or, perhaps, to lack the proper attributes of humanity altogether). Because '[a] healthy public is one that both requires and celebrates the identifying markers of the human condition in its constituent members', to create a healthy body politic it becomes necessary to ensure that all members of the body politic have access to the 'healthy' and 'wholesome' texts of Shakespeare.[21]

This line of thinking has dangerous potential, particularly as it relates to those users of Shakespeare who have disabilities. From this logic (Shakespeare expresses the human and is therefore needed by all humans to validate their humanity) springs the belief that Shakespeare's language may have the ability to restore humanity where it is perceived to be lacking – the belief that Shakespeare's language might have the ability to

---

L. Snyder and David T. Mitchell, *Cultural Locations of Disability* (Chicago, 2006), pp. 37–68.

[15] See Ayanna Thompson, *Passing Strange: Shakespeare, Race, and Contemporary America* (Oxford, 2011), p. 121; as well as the following articles, all from *Borrowers and Lenders: The Journal of Shakespeare and Appropriation* 8 (2013): Michael P. Jensen, '"What service is here?": exploring service Shakespeare'; Geoffrey M. Ridden, 'The Bard's speech: making it better; Shakespeare and therapy in film'; Isabelle Schwartz-Gastine, 'Performing A Midsummer Night's Dream with the homeless (and others) in Paris'; Michael P. Jensen, '"You speak all your part at once, cues and all": reading Shakespeare with Alzheimer's Disease'.

[16] Matt Kozusko, 'Shakespeare and civic health', in *Disability, Health, and Happiness in the Shakespearean Body*, ed. Sujata Iyengar (New York, 2015), p. 109.

[17] Alan Sinfield, 'Give an account of Shakespeare and Education, showing why you think they are effective and what you have appreciated about them. Support your comments with precise references', in *Political Shakespeare: Essays in Cultural Materialism*, ed. Jonathan Dollimore and Alan Sinfield (Manchester, 1985), pp. 134–57; p. 138.

[18] Kozusko, 'Shakespeare and civic health', p. 114.

[19] Sinfield, 'Give an account', p. 136.

[20] Kozusko, 'Shakespeare and civic health', p. 109.

[21] Kozusko, 'Shakespeare and civic health', p. 109.

heal. Ableist agendas have long presented people with disabilities as less-than-people or not human.[22] Thus, that which may restore or enliven humanity in the dehumanized subject (Shakespeare) might be imagined to have the power to end disability (the power to heal or cure). A popular-culture faith in Shakespeare's potential to provide psychological, social and emotional healing is surprisingly common. Denise Albanese has examined 'the pedagogical imperative that has attached to Shakespeare in the twentieth century, which takes as its agenda that Shakespeare is ... good and good *for* you, if only you will learn to take it in properly ... such a stance is so naturalized as to go without acknowledgment'.[23] Ridden has argued that 'Shakespeare has become so prevalent and powerful ... as a shorthand to signal high culture that his name and his works can be invoked as therapeutic', and Thompson has examined the 'belief that personal reform can be achieved through Shakespearian study and performance'.[24] Historically, the medical model has presented disability as an individual problem in need of treatment and rehabilitation.[25] Combining the search for treatment with a need to restore a fundamentally missing human nature, Shakespeare therapy fuses the medical model's agenda that seeks to eliminate disability from society through treatment or cure with the belief that those with disabilities will not be restored to full humanity without treatment or cure. Via this schema, the medical model of disability appropriates Shakespeare's cultural capital. In using Shakespeare as a potential source of healing and treatment, therapies like the HHM exist in a complex matrix of ideologies in which Shakespeare's cultural currency is used to authorize the medical model of disability – a model that many disability rights activists have rejected as oppressive, dehumanizing and fundamentally colonial in its impulses and orientation.

The HHM also markets itself as a therapy programme based on beliefs that Shakespeare is universal and that therefore Shakespeare should be made accessible for all people (including people with mental disabilities). As Marjorie Garber has argued,

Shakespeare is 'the fantasy of originary cultural wholeness, the last vestige of universalism'.[26] Kelly Hunter explains her motives in establishing the programme as motives founded on Shakespeare's universality:

I was preoccupied with the notion that Shakespeare's plays have untapped powers, inaccessible to many people through traditional means of performance and I was deeply frustrated by the overused maxim that 'Shakespeare is for everyone'. I absolutely agreed in the universality of Shakespeare's plays but ... [f]or me it sounded lazy to just say Shakespeare belonged to the people – I wanted to test that out.[27]

In Shakespeare therapy, the belief that Shakespeare is universal results in the impetus *to make him universal*. If 'Shakespeare is for everyone' and yet there are minority groups who seem to lack access to Shakespeare, a colonial impulse is inspired: those who have Shakespeare must find a way to bring Shakespeare to those who are perceived to be without him.[28] In the case of disability communities, the question of Shakespeare's 'accessibility' therefore becomes key. If Shakespeare is universal, then Shakespearians are challenged to ensure that

---

[22] For more on the history of ableism, see Snyder and Mitchell, *Cultural Locations of Disability*, pp. 3–36.

[23] Denise Albanese, *Extramural Shakespeare* (New York, 2010), p. 142.

[24] Ridden, 'The Bard's speech'; Thompson, *Passing Strange*, p. 121.

[25] For more on the various models of disability, see Tom Shakespeare, *Disability Rights and Wrongs Revisited*, 2nd edn (New York, 2014), Kindle pp. 1–7.

[26] Marjorie Garber, 'Shakespeare as fetish', *Shakespeare Quarterly* 41 (1990), 241–50; p. 243.

[27] Hunter, *Shakespeare's Heartbeat*, p. 234.

[28] Albanese has described this kind of colonial impulse as 'bardic messianism' (*Extramural Shakespeare*, p. 128). Ayanna Thompson has argued that in Shakespeare reform programmes, 'the logic and rhetoric ... seem to tiptoe between a form of liberal humanism that espouses the benefits of learning for all, and a form of neo-colonialism that espouses the benefits of learning specific texts' (*Passing Strange*, p. 143). Thompson has further noted that Shakespeare reform programmes frequently 'approach issues of diversity without explicitly inviting critical dialogues about ... privilege, and power structures' (p. 138).

those with disabilities are able to have equal access to his work. Accessibility is a central tenet of the disability rights movement and is a desirable goal in a variety of contexts. In fact, one of the highly lauded goals of disability studies as a critical field is to achieve 'universal design': for everything (from built spaces to social structures) to be accessible to everyone (no matter what kind of body or mind they may have), all of the time.[29] As many disability scholars have noted, universal design is desirable in theory, but it is an unachievable goal in reality: it is impossible to design an environment that will equally accommodate everyone's needs simultaneously.[30] In a similar way, a project to make Shakespeare 'universal', 'accessible' and 'inclusive' must necessarily create a Shakespeare that meets the needs of many diverse groups – striving for a 'universal' Shakespeare is much like striving for universal design. The goal is unattainable: a version of Shakespeare that speaks to one audience may not communicate well with another, and no amount of translation, adaptation or accessibility is likely to create a Shakespeare that communicates equally well with all audiences and all cultures in all circumstances. As Christy Desmet and Robert Sawyer point out, the need to create a universal Shakespeare can only create different Shakespeares by splitting Shakespeare apart: '[p]aradoxically, Shakespeare's universality, his putative appeal to "audiences of all continents, races, and languages", is grounded in his fragmentation'.[31] In light of the failure of both universal design and universal Shakespeare, the HHM (and other Shakespeare-based therapies) ultimately adopt the opposite approach to making Shakespeare 'universal'. If Shakespeare cannot be made to meet the needs of a particular minority group, then the minority group must be changed (through therapy) to meet the majority groups' expectations of what Shakespeare should be: thus, the programme tries to change the autistic subject in order to meet the needs of a rigidly neurotypical conception of Shakespeare.[32] What begins as an impulse to bring Shakespeare to those with mental disabilities ultimately becomes the impetus to eliminate (to cure or treat) mental disabilities. Ironically, the endeavour to make Shakespeare accessible, universal and inclusive has led to the effort

to eliminate disabled diversity through the (presumably homogenizing) power of Shakespeare's text. The narratives we tell about Shakespeare being 'good for us' have both a persuasive and a dangerous cultural power: if observers are expecting a certain narrative (the narrative of Shakespeare being able to heal, psychologically, emotionally and socially, the disabled, oppressed and/or outcast), then users of Shakespeare may be overlooking other narratives (such as the need for social change).[33] In this way, Shakespeare's assumed complicity in and affirmation of the medical model of disability may draw attention away from the disability rights movement and its call for social equality for people with mental disabilities.

## WHAT IF SHAKESPEARE IS THE CURE? PASSING AND PERFORMING NEUROTYPICAL

Indeed, the HHM (vis-à-vis Shakespeare as cure) is firmly wedded to the medical model of disability: in overlooking the neurodiversity paradigm, the programme prioritizes treatment for autism over the need for social acceptance for autistic people. Traditionally, the medical model has focused on 'treatment' and 'cure' for people on the spectrum. However, the neurodiversity movement that has grown within the autism community works in

[29] For more on universal design, see Margaret Price, *Mad at School: Rhetorics of Mental Disability and Academic Life* (Ann Arbor, MI, 2011).
[30] To give a very basic example, if we add curb cuts (to accommodate people who use wheelchairs), it will make it more difficult for blind people who use canes to distinguish the street from the sidewalk. For further explanation of why it is impossible to achieve universal design, see Tom Shakespeare, *Disability Rights*, pp. 36–46.
[31] Christy Desmet and Robert Sawyer, *Harold Bloom's Shakespeare* (New York, 2001), p. 5.
[32] True accessibility would require neurotypical Shakespearians to change conceptions of what Shakespeare is and how it should be performed in order to meet the needs of autistic people.
[33] Kozusko, 'Shakespeare and civic health', pp. 121–2; Thompson, *Passing Strange*, pp. 134, 143; Albanese, *Extramural Shakespeare*, pp. 138–9.

tandem with the larger disability rights movement to oppose the medical model. Recognizing autistic behaviour as a difference rather than a deficit, the neurodiversity movement argues that such mental differences are a normal part of human diversity.[34] Espousing neurodiversity, members of the disability rights movement recognize autistic people as a cultural minority group who form a community with shared experiences and values.[35] Autistic activists and self-advocates point out that some autistic traits (memory skills, single-minded focus, honesty) can also be strengths. Autistic culture commonly celebrates autistic characteristics that psychologists consider to be deficits as sources of fulfilment and joy. For example, people on the autism spectrum often have 'special interests' (interests that are unusual in subject or depth) and engage in self-stimulatory behaviours (commonly known as 'stimming') such as pacing, rocking and hand-flapping.[36] Many autistic adults consider such characteristics to be a central part of self-identity; some people on the spectrum find special interests to be deeply fulfilling and enjoy engaging in stimming.[37] Rather than seeking a cure or a treatment for autism, the neurodiversity movement works for disability accommodations and social acceptance for autistic people. In other words, instead of trying to change the disabled child, the neurodiversity movement seeks to change societal attitudes towards disability. However, the practitioners of the HHM frequently seem out of touch with the concerns of the neurodiversity movement and of the autistic community, addressing autism in terms that evoke the medical model's focus on deficit, cure and treatment.

Despite the HHM's emphasis on providing a treatment for autism, it seems unlikely that Shakespeare is the 'cure' to neurodiversity and that children's neurology is being fundamentally changed by this ten-week programme: it is more likely that the programme is teaching autistic children the skills needed to pass as neurotypical. People with disabilities passing as non-disabled has a long history, and a great deal of critical ink has been spilt on the subject of 'passing' in the field of disability studies.[38] In the autism community, passing for neurotypical is

controversial for many of the same reasons that passing for straight is controversial in the LGBTQ community. As Ellen Samuels explains, '[l]ike racial, gender, and queer passing, the option of passing as nondisabled provides both a certain level of privilege and a profound sense of misrecognition and internal dissonance'.[39] Although those who pass as non-disabled may 'avoid the perceived stigma attached to a disabled identity', passing has significant costs: 'if ... disabled people pursue normalization too much, they risk denying limitations and pain for the comfort of others and may edge into the self-betrayal associated with passing'.[40] The consensus among autistic adults is that passing for neurotypical is often exhausting: spending long hours attempting to imitate neurotypical body language, dealing with environments that aggravate sensory sensitivities, and ignoring the need to stim can all cause

---

[34] See Nick Walker, 'Liberating ourselves from the pathology paradigm', in Bascom, ed., *Loud Hands*, Kindle p. 154.

[35] Joseph N. Straus, 'Autism as culture', in *The Disability Studies Reader*, 4th edn, ed. Lennard J. Davis (New York, 2013), Kindle pp. 451–75.

[36] For more on these topics, see Atwood, *Asperger's*, pp. 184–214.

[37] This focus on autistic identity is central to debates about autism and terminology. There is some disagreement in the autism community regarding preferred terminology, with some arguing that 'having autism' implies that autism is a disease or defect. Others claim the term 'autistic' as a statement of identity, while some prefer 'person with autism'. For more on the terminology debate, see Loftis, *Imagining Autism*, pp. 6–11. In this article, I have used the term 'autistic' consistently, as this is the terminology generally preferred in the neurodiversity movement.

[38] For a discussion of 'passing' in the disability community at large, see Simi Linton, *Claiming Disability: Knowledge and Identity* (New York, 1998), pp. 19–21; Ellen Samuels, 'My body, my closet: invisible disability and the limits of coming out', in *The Disability Studies Reader*, 4th edn, ed. Lennard J. Davis (New York, 2013), Kindle pp. 308–24; Ellen Samuels, 'Passing', in *Key Words in Disability Studies*, ed. Rachel Adams, Benjamin Reiss and David Serlin (New York, 2015), Kindle pp. 135–6.

[39] Samuels, 'My body, my closet', p. 313.

[40] John Swain and Colin Cameron, and Rosemarie Garland-Thomson, both qtd in Samuels, 'My body, my closet', p. 313.

frustration, fatigue and even physical pain.[41] Indeed, passing can also have a lasting psychological toll, since it may involve the public denial of identity (a decision not to be 'out' as autistic). In spite of the potential problems with passing, the HHM's focus on 'treating' autism may be promoting passing skills for autistic children rather than providing a fundamental change in neurology.

The HHM's rhetoric is clearly in line with the medical model: the programme's language side-steps the issue of autistic identity and unquestioningly forwards passing as a desirable goal for people with disabilities. A new study from the Ohio State University shows that the students involved in the programme are improving their social skills: '[a]n initial pilot study with 14 students with ASD yielded data indicating positive changes in the students' interpersonal skills, pragmatic language, and overall adaptive behavior after a ten-week intervention'.[42] In the analysis of these results, the 'deficit-based' assumptions of the Shakespeare-based therapy are clear: '[o]verall, the Heartbeat Method shows promise regarding the improvement of core deficits associated with autism spectrum disorder'.[43] The HHM is a 'minimal treatment dose' which only requires a 'once-weekly intervention'.[44] Although current medical consensus acknowledges that there is no 'cure' for autism, Shakespeare is being considered as a possible 'treatment', a way for society to change the social development of the autistic child: 'the research team is assessing the ability of these games to affect [sic] significant and long-term change to the core features of autism'.[45] In such statements, it is accepted without question that changing the 'core features of autism' is a desirable goal and that naturally everyone (including autistic people) should seek that goal. However, the medical model's focus on changing the individual means that people may ignore the need for larger social change – overlooking the role that society plays in disadvantaging those with cognitive differences.

Furthermore, the programme's Shakespeare-based games are teaching skills that autistic children can use to pass as neurotypical, thus transforming Shakespeare into a tool that 'normalizes' the

autistic subject – Shakespeare's text authorizes the HHM, lending cultural authority to the imperative to pass. Key games in the HHM focus on eliminating autistic body language and replacing it with neurotypical body language. For example, the 'lovers' magic trance' is a role-playing game loosely based on *The Tempest*, in which Ariel guides Ferdinand to Miranda. Hunter describes the lovers' magic trance as 'a key game providing the opportunity for the children to explore a smooth, flowing physical language, counteracting the awkward stiffness that they so often experience'.[46] This activity teaches children to mask autistic body language and to mimic neurotypical body movements. Like many of the games in the HHM, the game requires extensive eye focus and eye contact (Ferdinand and Miranda must maintain eye contact at the end of the sequence), as well as the ability to imitate neurotypical body language (the child imitates her neurotypical partner's movements as Ariel guides Ferdinand). In other words, the game teaches children how to 'look' neurotypical and rewards them for changing autistic body language. In fact, autistic movements only look 'awkward' and 'stiff' from a neurotypical perspective (stimming, based on the aesthetic pleasure of repetition and sensory appeals, can be seen as beautiful). Autistic body language is only disabling when people discriminate against those who display such body language. Clearly, there is a philosophical and ethical tension in questions of autistic passing. On the one hand, teaching autistic children to pass may teach them invaluable life skills that will help them to function in a world of neurotypical social expectations. On the other hand, teaching autistic

---

[41] For various autistic perspectives on passing for neurotypical, see Bascom, ed., *Loud Hands*.

[42] Marc J. Tasse, 'Epilogue', in Hunter, *Shakespeare's Heartbeat*, p. 240.

[43] Margaret H. Mehling, Marc J. Tasse and Robin Root, 'Shakespeare and autism: an exploratory evaluation of the Hunter Heartbeat Method', *Research and Practice in Intellectual and Developmental Disabilities* 4 (2017), 107–20; p. 118.

[44] Mehling *et al.*, 'Shakespeare and autism', p. 116.

[45] Post, 'Foreword'.

[46] Hunter, *Shakespeare's Heartbeat*, p. 165.

children to pass may not help to increase social acceptance for autistic identity and expression. In short, games such as the lovers' magic trance may teach children to hide autistic identity: the HHM, in its efforts to 'cure' autism, may simply forward passing for people with disabilities.

### 'THIS ISLAND'S MINE:' RESISTING THE COLONIZATION OF AUTISTIC CULTURE

One of the founding principles of the disability rights movement is the concept of disability as a source of identity and community: however, the rhetoric of the HHM prioritizes treatment over identity and/or community.[47] Although autistics also participate in face-to-face gatherings such as the annual Autreat, much of autistic culture is created and sustained via the internet: online interaction allows autistics to come together while avoiding the pitfalls of face-to-face socialization, the challenges of verbal vocalization, and the difficulties of unwelcoming sensory environments. In other words, the internet offers the ideal realm for autistic socialization, with a resultant explosion of online autistic communities (such as Wrong Planet) and advocacy organizations (such as the Autistic Self-Advocacy Network). Autistic blogging has reached the level of art form, with a large number of influential autistic activists gathering large followings on neurodiversity blogs. Over time, the autistic community has developed a unique culture of its own: '[w]ithin a medical model, autism is constructed by professionals – psychiatrists, psychologists, educators – in their articles, books, and clinical practices. Within a social model, autism is constructed by autistic people themselves through the culture they produce (including writing, art, and music), and its shared features give it cohesion and a distinctive identity.'[48]

As autistic activist Jim Sinclair explains:

[w]e have certain shared values in affirming the validity of our way of being. We have many common experiences both with the experience of autism itself, and with being autistic in a world of neurotypicals. We have a history of significant events experienced by our

community. We have a dynamic, constantly-evolving set of customs and rules growing out of our shared experiences and our common needs. We have certain terms, expressions, and in-jokes that are distinct to our community.[49]

One unique element of autistic culture is the celebration of stimming, an activity which is, in many ways, the autistic equivalent of neurotypical play.[50] Autistic activist Julia Bascom explains the pleasures of stimming:

flapping your hands *just so* amplifies everything you feel and thrusts it up into the air … [i]t takes a million different forms. A boy pacing by himself, flapping and humming and laughing. An 'interest' or obsession that is 'age appropriate' – or maybe one that is not. A shake of the fingers in front of the eyes, a monologue, an echolaliated phrase. All of these things autistic people are supposed to be ashamed of and stop doing? *They are how we communicate our joy.*[51]

Indeed, some autistic activists have argued that stimming, as a form of self-expression, is a uniquely autistic language.[52] That autistic children do not usually engage in activities that neurotypical people consider to be play (e.g. hobbies, games, pretend play) has been frequently noted.[53] That autistics might have their own ways to play (such as stimming) has been frequently overlooked.[54]

---

[47] For further discussion of disability identity and community, see Julia Miele Rodas, 'Identity', in Adams et al., eds., *Key Words*, Kindle pp. 103–5; Jeffrey A. Brune, 'Minority', in Adams et al., eds., *Key Words*, Kindle pp. 122–4.

[48] Straus, 'Autism as culture', p. 457.

[49] See Jim Sinclair, 'Autism Network International: the development of a community and its culture', in *Loud Hands*, p. 46.

[50] Neurotypical people also engage in stimming (but much less frequently and to very different effect). For example, there is not usually an imaginative element in neurotypical stimming.

[51] Julia Bascom, *The Obsessive Joy of Autism* (London, 2015).

[52] Amanda Baggs, 'In my language', 14 January 2007, www.youtube.com/watch?v=JnylM1hI2jc.

[53] See Nicola Shaughnessy's discussion in 'Curious incidents: pretend play, presence, and performance pedagogies in encounters with autism', in *Creativity and Community among Autism-Spectrum Youth*, ed. Peter Smagorinsky (New York, 2016), pp. 187–216.

[54] I am not trying to create a false binary between neurotypical and autistic forms of play. It is possible for autistic people to

In fact, one of the HHM's primary objectives is to teach autistic children how to 'play'; this objective seems to be based on our culture's commonly held misconception that autistic people have no prior existing culture (and, thus, forms of play) of their own. It is true that autistic children's refusal to play in socially sanctioned ways is often regarded as a symptom of pathology; the autistic child may demonstrate a '[l]ack of interest in toys, or pla[y] with them in an unusual way (e.g. lining up, spinning, opening/closing parts rather than playing with the toy as a whole)' and psychologists frequently cite a lack of 'pretend play' as a developmental deficit in autism.[55] (Notice, however, that the 'unusual' ways to play listed in the above example – lining up, spinning, opening/closing – are all examples of stimming. This tactile manipulation of objects, which actively engages the autistic imagination, is interpreted by the neurotypical observer as a lack of ability to be 'creative'.)[56] Anne McGuire describes 'the ways in which disabled children's play has been transformed by the field of developmental psychology as an instrument of surveillance, measurement, and evaluation'.[57] This cultural 'policing' of play suggests the level of scrutiny (and potential censure) to which autistic children may be subject. Autistic stimming and neurotypical play are somewhat analogous: stimming and pretend play are both pleasurable ways of spending leisure time; stimming, like pretend play, can actively evoke engagement with imagination.[58]

The HHM seems to be a part of the larger cultural discourse that seeks to police and limit autistic play and to encourage neurotypical play in its place.[59] According to Hunter, the therapy's 'ultimate aim no matter where the children are on the spectrum is for them to experience what a game *feels* like'.[60] Because play as a concept is neither ahistorical nor a-cultural, what is primarily being taught through the HHM is what play feels like, and is defined as, for and by neurotypical people. This strong emphasis on teaching neurotypical play appears throughout Kelly Hunter's book, *Shakespeare's Heartbeat*, which serves as the 'treatment manual' for the HHM. Hunter encourages practitioners to '[n]ever give up

on the child's ability to play' and wonders about the implications of researching play as a measurable result of the programme: '[i]t will be interesting to see how important the art of playfulness is within the findings of the research and whether in fact playfulness is deemed measurable at all. I've tried to convey the significance of playfulness within the games.'[61] In *Shakespeare's Heartbeat*, Hunter presents playfulness as central to the human experience. Since our culture often conceives of autistic children as children who fundamentally lack the ability to play, it is all too often believed that these children are therefore incapable of basic human attributes. Hunter sees the therapy as giving autistic children an opportunity that all children should have but that autistic children lack: 'all children with autism are indeed children and all children deserve the chance to play'.[62] This desire to teach play is based on a colonialist impulse – the idea is that neurotypical educators know how to play and that they can teach autistic children how to resemble them. Specifically, Shakespeare is the medium

---

engage in neurotypical forms of play and for neurotypical people to engage in autistic forms of play.

[55] Anne McGuire, *War on Autism: On the Cultural Logic of Normative Violence* (Ann Arbor, MI, 2016). This and all subsequent citations refer to the Kindle edition, which is unpaginated. See also Shaughnessy, 'Curious incidents', p. 191.

[56] Autistics are also frequently thought to lack imagination, although some researchers (and autistics) have disputed this. See Shaughnessy, 'Curious incidents', p. 209; Bruce Mills, 'Autism and the imagination', in Osteen, ed., *Autism and Representation*, pp. 117–32.

[57] McGuire, *War on Autism*.

[58] There is very little research on imagination and stimming. However, some autistic adults maintain that stimming can actively engage imagination. Stimming can also involve a 'pretend' element. However, since the imaginative element of stimming is usually internalized rather than externalized (in most cases, no narrative is vocalized), it may leave little evidence of what a neurotypical observer would recognize as 'play'.

[59] I am not arguing that children should be allowed to engage in activities that might be dangerous. However, most forms of stimming (like most forms of pretend play) are not dangerous or inherently harmful.

[60] Hunter, *Shakespeare's Heartbeat*, p. 24.

[61] Hunter, *Shakespeare's Heartbeat*, pp. 225, 238.

[62] Hunter, *Shakespeare's Heartbeat*, p. 239.

through which the HHM teaches neurotypical conceptions of play. Children are encouraged to speak a neurotypical language, to move through the world in neurotypical ways, to engage in neurotypical play – to adopt the culture of the neurotypical colonizer, who is charitably bringing Shakespeare (read: humanity) to autistics.

It is symbolically appropriate that one of the two plays used in the HHM is *The Tempest*, a play with a celebrated history of postcolonial performances and interpretations: Shakespeare's text (presented in the HHM in a series of games that focus on teaching language, imperialist impulses and cultural power dynamics) comes to symbolize the programme's colonization of the autistic subject. In the *Tempest* games, the slaves of the imperialist Prospero are central roles for the autistic children to focus on and learn to perform: '[t]hese first games use Caliban as a focus for the children' and '*The Tempest* games focus also on themes of liberty and imprisonment using the characters of Caliban and Ariel to provide a deeper means for the children to express themselves.'[63] The game of '[t]eaching Caliban to speak' has a multi-layered symbolic resonance in this context, since some of the autistic children who engage in the HHM are nonverbal (some may communicate by signing or typing but not by speaking). In this game, 'Caliban is gabbling, making noise with no language. He is moving around the circle on all fours, making a never-ending clamorous babble.'[64] Miranda says, '[m]y name is Miranda. Your name is Caliban', in an effort to get Caliban to speak his name.[65] The choice to engage children with a communication disability in a game about learning to speak is already symbolically laden, as playing the game may evoke the frustration that neurotypicals experience in attempting to communicate with autistics (and that autistics experience in attempting to communicate with neurotypicals). Furthermore, because verbal stimming is common among autistic children, practitioners may find it difficult to convince the child performing the role of Caliban to stop stimming and to switch over to neurotypical pretend play. As Hunter explains, '[a] few children enjoy the babbling so much that they wilfully refuse to stop, and if after a few attempts they can't move on from the

babbling, abandon the game'.[66] In Shakespeare's play, Miranda is unable to recognize that Caliban may have a prior language and culture of his own – although it is possible that what she calls 'gabble' is the language of his mother Sycorax (1.2.355–9). The HHM seems to function on the premise that autistic people have no prior language or culture that is unique to the autistic community. Just as Shakespeare's Miranda does not recognize Caliban's 'gabble' as a possible foreign tongue, the HHM does not recognize stimming as a possible mode of play and expression. Even more significantly, the passage alluded to from *The Tempest* may draw the attention of some participants and viewers to the colonial impulses underlying developmental psychology, the modern special education classroom and the HHM itself.

Although Shakespeare's text is not directly used in this particular game, Miranda's words from *The Tempest* may uncomfortably haunt the image of the neurotypical adult teaching the autistic child to speak. This is especially true when the autistic child plays Caliban and the neurotypical practitioner of the HHM plays Miranda:

I pitied thee,
Took pains to make thee speak, taught thee each hour
One thing or other. When thou didst not, savage,
Know thine own meaning, but wouldst gabble like
A thing most brutish, I endowed thy purposes
With words that made them known.

(1.2.355–60)

In this passage, not only is Miranda positioned as the able-bodied subject that gives magnanimously (and charitably) but also Caliban is positioned as both ungrateful and unknowing. Although Shakespeare's textual Caliban is probably more likely to be interpreted as racially Other (rather than disabled), the colonial impulse that polices the racialized body is bound up in the same cultural

---

[63] Hunter, *Shakespeare's Heartbeat*, pp. 121, 9.
[64] Hunter, *Shakespeare's Heartbeat*, p. 139.
[65] Hunter, *Shakespeare's Heartbeat*, p. 139.
[66] Hunter, *Shakespeare's Heartbeat*, p. 142.

logic that attempts to treat and cure the disabled body.[67] As McGuire argues, there is a connection between modern developmental psychology (the branch of the medical model that diagnoses and treats autism) and the history of colonialism:

[t]he developmental perspective dominated (and continues to dominate) colonial rule, particularly through ideologies spawned by evolutionism. Colonial dominance was/is maintained through the surveillance and policing of all bodies, the sharpening of the boundaries separating normal from abnormal development and the recognition that departures and deviations from 'normal' (and, thus, always and already white, male, able-bodied, heterosexual, and middle-classed) development represented somatic *pathologies*. Under colonial logic, people of color and indigenous people, queer, disabled and poor people ... became conceptually linked through their purported pathological deviance from the esteemed status of 'fully' developed human. The biomedical gaze that watches for and recognizes difference as pathology simultaneously inaugurates the necessity for biomedical/pedagogical interventions that aim to restore not simply health but also civility.[68]

In the colonial perspective, all Othered bodies are pathologized bodies that fail to reach 'the esteemed status of "fully" developed human'. And such less-than-human creatures create a demand for 'biomedical/pedagogical intervention' – a need that both Shakespeare's Miranda and the HHM try to meet. Miranda's effort to teach Caliban to speak stems from a charitable impulse ('I pitied thee'). Originally funded by charitable organizations, the HHM relies on the long-standing charity schema that has determined power structures between the able-bodied and the disabled for hundreds of years.[69] It is all too often a relationship founded on pity: a relationship in which people with disabilities are perceived as victims, and 'this victimization prompts the social dynamic in which the normals feel pity for the stigmatized and express their good intentions and well wishes – in other words, their disavowal of stigma – through charity, or at least through a charitable attitude which often comes across as patronizing'.[70] Miranda gives Caliban language. The HHM gives autistic children Shakespeare. The charity system highlights the superior social position of those who

give (neurotypicals) and the dispossessed position of those who receive (autistics). It also draws attention to the cultural power of that which is given through such acts of charity. Hunter's rhetoric describes autistic people as though they were 'asleep', unaware of their own lives and experiences: '[t]his lies at the heart of the work, the fundamental aim of which is to use Shakespeare as a means of waking the children up to their own lives'.[71] In *Shakespeare's Heartbeat*, Shakespeare is imagined as a life-giving force (the heartbeat) that will make autistic people fully alive – and fully human. In short, *The Tempest* games of the HHM subtly suggest the imperialist impulse at work between the neurotypical colonizer and the colonized autistic child.

## CONCLUSION: AUTISTIC WAYS TO PLAY

My students think that I read Shakespeare beautifully. (I know, because they often say so, with obvious delight and wonder, asking how they can learn to read it as well as I do.) Shakespeare's easy numbers flow from my lips readily and naturally, with the facility of long familiarity. I also know that, like all of the words that I speak, Shakespeare's lines bear the monotone timbre born of autism, that I speak Shakespeare's words with almost no outwardly discernible intonation or emotional expression. Given my students' responses, I am not convinced that this mode of speaking Shakespeare is inherently flawed – indeed, it could be seen as uniquely beautiful, an authentically autistic appropriation of Shakespeare's language. In our culture, disability is so often thought of as a deficit that very little thought is given to the possibility of 'disability as a generative and creative force'.[72] But my teaching of

---

[67] McGuire, *War on Autism*.  [68] McGuire, *War on Autism*.
[69] Hunter, *Shakespeare's Heartbeat*, p. 235.
[70] Jeffrey R. Wilson, 'The trouble with disability in Shakespeare Studies', *Disability Studies Quarterly* 37 (2017).
[71] Hunter, *Shakespeare's Heartbeat*, p. 155.
[72] I'm inspired here by the International Disability Film Festival's goal to 'celebrat[e] disability as a generative and creative force': see 'Superfest: The International Disability Film Festival', http://longmoreinstitute.sfsu.edu/Superfestfilm.

AUTISTIC CULTURE

Shakespeare clearly springs from mental disability, from a distinctively autistic experience of the world. And my teaching is both joyful and playful (just not in ways that are readily translatable to neurotypical definitions of 'joy' and 'play'). The HHM seems, on some fundamental levels, to assume that Shakespeare and disability are separate worlds – and that, if we could somehow unite these worlds, it would be a powerful and 'healing' unity. I can only hope that, as we continue to explore and experiment with the HHM, that we will not foreclose the possibility of explicitly autistic Shakespeares – that we will not shut down or invalidate autistic notions of what it means to play.

# THE SENECAN TRAGEDY OF FESTE
# IN *TWELFTH NIGHT*

## JUDITH ROSENHEIM†

His mind to him a kingdom is, and one full of such present
    joys that he finds contentment there. Outwardly he may be
        little better than a slave; but Epictetus was a slave outright and yet absolutely free: and so is Feste.[1]

A. C. Bradley here invokes Epictetus as a Greek source of the classical Stoicism that was exerting an increasing influence on the intellectual life of Renaissance England. Fostered by James Sanford's 1567 translation of Epictetus' *Enchiridion* into English as *The Manuell*,[2] this influence accommodates what Bradley's association of Epictetus with Feste can be seen to suggest: which is that the character Shakespeare has created in Feste is, like Epictetus, a Stoic. To be sure, the play nowhere calls Feste a Stoic, the closest he comes to that nomination being Sebastian's rebuke of him as a 'foolish Greek'.[3] Yet evidence assembled in the following pages will suggest that Bradley's insight is profoundly valid. For Feste's words and deeds will be seen to exhibit an array of Stoic meanings so pervasive, wide-ranging and evidently intended as to make this philosophy the defining element of his character.

While valid, however, Bradley's insight remains flawed. For Bradley sees Feste's Stoicism as making him, despite his servitude, happy. And while rightly assuming that Feste expects his Stoicism to make him happy, Bradley does not conjure with the play's representation of Feste's Stoic creed as disappointing his expectation by making him unhappy. As we shall see, it is by falsely defining his human nature that Feste's Stoicism makes him

unhappy. For, as falsified by its Stoic definition, Feste's nature becomes an ideal that he cannot achieve. And by exploiting Feste's failure for the purpose of insulting and injuring him, Malvolio incites him to the anger that transforms him from a Stoic into an avenger. It is by making him an avenger that Malvolio's insult and injury make him unhappy. But not only making him unhappy, Feste's quest for vengeance also makes him unfree. For, as a Stoic, Feste recognizes the vengeance he seeks against Malvolio as bound to recoil upon him – the recoil of his vengeance making it a compulsion to destroy not only Malvolio but himself as well. It is this self-destruction that Feste intimates in the song he sings about 'the wind and the rain' (5.1.390), it being his own exposure to these elements that Feste's song represents him as anticipating. For Feste's vengeance has caused him to forfeit the favour of his mistress, and, with that favour, the shelter of her house. Knowing these elements to be lethal, Feste sees the forfeiture that exposes him to them as effecting his death. And, in deriving from the Stoicism he had trusted to make him happy and free, Feste's death assumes a tragic meaning, as further emerges in the observation that the song invoking his death concludes the play.

---

[1] A. C. Bradley, 'Feste the Jester', in *A Miscellany* (London, 1929), p. 210.

[2] *The Manuell of Epictetus, Translated out of Greeke into English by Ja. Sanford* (London, 1567). Hereafter cited in the text.

[3] All Shakespeare quotations are cited from *The Riverside Shakespeare*, General Editor G. Blakemore Evans (Boston, 1974).

THE SENECAN TRAGEDY OF FESTE IN *TWELFTH NIGHT*

To say that Feste is a Stoic, however, is by no means to suggest that he does not think himself a Christian, as Feste suggests in appropriating the Pauline *topos* of the wise fool.[4] For, tutored by such Renaissance Neostoics as Justus Lipsius and Guillaume du Vair,[5] Feste can be expected to regard his Stoicism merely as a rational rendering of Christian truth. Nor does Shakespeare omit to grapple with Feste's Neostoic supposition, though demonstrating how he does so must be deferred to future work. It is rather with what the play regards as the true disparity between Feste's Stoicism and Christian truth that this article must deal, the foundation of this disparity being what Epictetus identifies in the first words of his *Manuell*, which distinguishes the things that are 'in us' from the things that are not 'in us', the things in us pertaining to our mind, whereas the things not in us pertain first and foremost to our 'Body': 'Of al things which are, some are in us, some are not. In us are Opinion, Endevor, Desire, Eschuing, & Briefly al that which is our worke. In us are not our Body, Possessions, Honours, Soverainties, and summarily al that which is not our worke' (Ch. 1). The importance of Epictetus' distinction lies in his sense that we can truly own only those things that are in us. For it is only these inner things that cannot be taken away from us. And, being inalienably ours, these inner things make us free – in contrast to externalities, which are servile because, as things 'not ours', they can be taken away: 'The things which are in us are free and franke by nature, and can not be prohibited, empeached, nor taken away. Such things as are not in us, bee servile, feeble, and may be prohibited, empeached, and taken away, as things unto other men belonging, and not ours' (Ch. 1). It is, furthermore, by teaching men to recognize what is and is not our own that Epictetus means to make them happy: 'If thou thinke onely the things thyne, which truly are thine, and the things other mennes, which truly are other mens, no man wyl constrayne thee, no man wyll hinder thee, thou shalt blame no body, thou shalt accuse no body, thou shalt do no thing against thy wyll' (Ch. 2). But, not only thus purporting to make men free and happy, claiming only

what is our own is also to make them good. For then, says Epictetus, 'no man shal hurte thee, and moreover, thou shalt have no enimy. For in nothing which is hurtefull thou canst not be persuaded" (Ch. 2). By referring what is in us to our minds and what is not in us to our bodies, Epictetus advises men that repudiating their bodies in favour of their minds is going to make them free, happy and good. And this expectation appears to inform what we learn of Feste when we meet him in 1.5. For, having disowned the body, Epictetus concludes that its 'death is not terrible' (Ch. 8). And this same dismissal of his body to the point of courting its death is what Feste has evidently been trying to implement prior to our meeting him in 1.5. For this scene begins by informing us that Feste has left Olivia's house, thereby abandoning the profession that supports the life of his body.

\*\*\*

Yet, contrary to his Neostoic expectation, Feste's attempt to repudiate his body transgresses the Christian definition of his nature, as stated by Thomas Aquinas to include not only his mind or soul but also his body: 'It belongs to the nature of man to be composed of soul, flesh, and bones.'[6] And making Thomas's definition of man's nature normatively Christian is what follows from Feste's attempt to deny it, which appears to be intimated in a seemingly vacuous question that Andrew puts to Toby in 1.3 – 'What is "*pourquoi*"? Do, or not do?' (1.3.91) – for these words can be seen to resonate with St Paul's sense of sin as setting enmity between his will, which expresses his mind or soul, and his deed, which expresses his body: 'For to wil

---

[4] See R. Chris Hassel, "'Man's estate": the festival of folly in *Twelfth Night*," in *Faith and Folly in Shakespeare's Romantic Comedies* (Athens, GA, 1980), pp. 172–3.
[5] See Justus Lipsius, *The Two Bookes of Constancie* [1584], trans. Sir John Stradling [1595], ed. with intro. Rudolf Kirk (New Brunswick, NJ, 1939), and Guillaume du Vair, *The Moral Philosophie of the Stoicks*, trans. Thomas James [1598], ed. with intro. and notes by Rudolf Kirk (New Brunswick, NJ, 1951).
[6] Thomas Aquinas, *Summa theologica*, Q, 75. Art. 4 (I.688).

is present with me: but I finde no meanes to per-forme that which is good. For I do not the good thing, which I wolde, but the euil, which I wolde not, that I do' (Romans 7.18–19).[7] And the word 'do', which Paul's observation of what he 'wolde' and 'wolde not' elides, is what *Andrew*'s 'Do, or not do' appears to invoke. As Paul sees sin to set 'Spirit against ... flesh' (Galatians 5.17), mind against body, and will against deed, so sin is what Feste commits in his mind's Stoic repudiation of his body, the sinfulness of this repudiation causing it to fail. So, as it is a part of his nature in its Christian – and thus true – definition, Feste cannot repudiate his body, as he shows in 1.5 by returning, under the pressure of bodily want, to reclaim the life-sustaining profession he had abandoned. Like Paul, Feste cannot do what he would do. But not only sinfully failing to do what he would do, Feste is also, like Paul, compelled to do what he would not do, in being incited by Malvolio's injurious insults to vengeance. For, quite apart from the Stoic threat of its recoil upon his body, vengeance is precisely what Paul declares Christian faith to prohibit: 'Dearly beloved, avenge not your selves, but give place unto wrath: for it is written, Vengeance is mine: I wil repaye, saith the Lord' (Romans 12.19). Nor is Feste's vengeance a merely venial trespass. For what Feste's vengeance expresses is a refusal to forgive Malvolio's injurious insults, this refusal flouting what Christ himself posits as the condition of his own forgiveness: 'Forgive us our dettes, as we also forgive our det-ters' (Matthew 6.12). Since it is by the forgiveness of his sins that man is saved, what Feste does in refusing to forgive Malvolio is to forfeit his own salvation, this forfeiture constituting the ultimate recoil of his vengeance upon himself. And in thus compelling him to forfeit his salvation, Feste's ven-geance can be seen to destroy both his body and his soul.

Yet, rather than sweeping to his revenge, Feste, not unlike Hamlet, requires the whole length of the play to wreak it. For, being Stoically aware that his vengeance must recoil upon him, Feste both desires and fears it, his fear launching him on a quest to achieve his vengeance by means that

will evade its recoil. The only effect of this quest, however, is to drag Feste relentlessly towards the vengeance he fears. For Feste's efforts meet with the repeated humiliation of failure, which so inten-sifies his lust for vengeance as finally to vanquish his inihibiting fear of its recoil. Feste is at last driven to destroy Malvolio by destroying himself, his self-immolation belying, as we shall see, the Stoic's possession of his mind by certifying him as mad.

\*\*\*

It is not Epictetus' *Manuell,* however, that explains how – far from making him happy, free and good – Feste's Stoicism imprisons him in the insane evil of vengeance. To grasp his descent into this hellish state, we must address the philosopher of the ancient world whose *Familiar Epistles* and *Moral Essays*[8] were the chief means of imprinting Stoic doctrine on the Renaissance: the Roman Seneca. Granted that the absence of their English transla-tion until 1614, coupled with T. S. Eliot's refusal to countenance their unmediated influence on Shakespeare,[9] have discouraged critics from enter-taining these works as a direct source of the Stoicism in Shakespeare's plays. Yet Feste's words and deeds will be seen as so pervasively Senecan as to warrant asserting the direct involvement of this philosopher in the Stoic formation of his character, and most suggestively in two of Feste's quirky adversions: the first being to Pythagoras' doctrine of the transmigration of souls,[10] by which Feste would force Malvolio to confess himself stupid;

---

7 All biblical citations are from *The Geneva Bible: A Facsimile of the 1560 Edition,* intro. Lloyd E. Berry (Madison, WI, 1969). Spelling has been minimally modernized.

8 Seneca, *Moral Essays,* 3 vols., Loeb Classical Library (Cambridge, MA, 1970). Seneca, *Ad Lucilium epistulae mor-ales,* with an English translation by Richard M. Gummere, 3 vols., Loeb Classical Library (Cambridge, MA). Quotations from both works hereafter cited in the text.

9 T. S. Eliot, 'Shakespeare and the stoicism of Seneca', in *Selected Essays* [1932] (New York, 1960), 109.

10 Though not attributed to Pythagoras, this doctrine is also described in *Shakespeare's Ovid Being Arthur Golding's Translation of The Metamorphoses* [1567], ed. W. H. D. Rouse (London, 1951), Book XV, lines 176–95.

the second being the 'whirligig' (5.1.376), or top, by which Feste would minimize his vengeance, and thus the severity of its recoil upon himself, by miniaturizing what Seneca magnifies as a cyclone. Speaking of conquerors who, in destroying others, destroy themselves, Seneca sees them as 'cyclones that whirl together what they have seized, but which are first whirled themselves and can for this reason rush on with all the greater force, having no control over themselves; hence, after causing such destruction to others, they feel in their own body the ruinous force which has enabled them to cause havoc to many' (*Ep.* 94.67 III.55).

Yet, not only a philosophical expounder of Stoicism, Seneca was also the author of tragedies, these tragedies being readily available to Shakespeare in translations that Thomas Newton collected and published in 1581 as *Seneca his Tenne Tragedies*.[11] And conjuring with Feste's vengeance requires us to recognize it as Senecan not only in its philosophic motivation but also in the character of its execution. For, as exhibited in Seneca's *Medea* and *Thyestes*, vengeance takes aim not at the body but rather at the mind, with Medea and Atreus crushing the minds of Jason and Thyestes by compelling them, through appalling self-revelations, to recognize the conquering power of their evil. This mind-crushing *anagnorisis* is what Medea achieves by murdering her child before the eyes of its father: 'Loe heare dost thou beholde thy wyfe?' (II *Med.* 98). This same recognition of Atreus' power to make him eat his own children is what Thyestes attests in confessing, 'I know my brother' (II *Thy.* 89). And it is by means of a similarly devastating self-revelation that Feste will crush the mind of Malvolio.

Yet, beyond the avenging evil of Medea and Atreus, what most relentlessly devastates the minds of Jason and Thyestes is the recognition that their own misdeeds have caused the disasters now overtaking them. And this same recognition of his own guilt is what Feste's self-revelation forces upon Malvolio. For Feste invokes Malvolio's reference to him as a 'barren rascal' (5.1.375), thereby identifying Malvolio's insults as inciting him to make the steward a still more abject

fool than Malvolio had made of him. As Medea and Atreus force Jason and Thyestes to recognize themselves as the authors of their suffering, so Feste forces Malvolio to recognize himself as the author of his suffering, this cruel recognition driving him to the wrathful cry for vengeance that attests the shattering of his mind.

Informing the Senecan nature of both Feste's Stoicism and his vengeance is Seneca's own suggestion of a deep continuity between these two parts of his oeuvre. For, whereas his Stoicism embraces reason while his tragedies exhibit the triumph of passion, Seneca himself observes that these elements of the mind 'do not dwell separate and distinct, but passion and reason are only the transformation of the mind toward the better or the worse' (*On Anger*, 1.8.3). And in his insightful study of *Renaissance Tragedy and the Senecan Tradition*,[12] Gordon Braden identifies the term of this continuity as the desire to dominate, the 'better' or 'worse' nature of this domination being merely a function of its direction. Whereas domination is rationally 'better' in its inward direction towards the self, which it subjugates to the reason of the cosmos, this same dominating impulse becomes passionately 'worse' in its outward direction against an injurious world. Braden thus recognizes Stoicism as but 'one manifestation of drives that, swerving in another direction, lead to the rage of Seneca's madmen' (30).

That 'better' and 'worse' should constitute contrary directions of an identical impulse is what Braden finds the Renaissance to have internalized: 'The Renaissance, almost without thinking about it, is open to that unity, to the level on which sage and madman can be seen as limiting versions of a single style of selfhood' (85). And, in turning Feste from Stoic into avenger, Shakespeare can be seen to participate in this

---

[11] *Seneca his Tenne tragedies*, trans. into English, ed. Thomas Newton [1581], intro. T. S. Eliot, 2 vols. (New York, 1967) – hereafter cited in the text.

[12] Gordon Braden, *Renaissance Tragedy and the Senecan Tradition* (New Haven, CT, 1985), pp. 5–27. Hereafter cited in the text.

same Renaissance consciousness of continuity between Seneca's inwardly better reason and his outwardly worse passion. But not only echoing Seneca's view of reason and passion as good and bad directions of the mind, Shakespeare is concerned in *Twelfth Night* to show how the tenets of Stoicism inevitably transform its better reason into worse passion. For Feste will acknowledge using his own rational words to incite or cause the passion for vengeance, therein adducing what we shall see as the Stoic equation of reason with causation. In using rational words to cause vengeance, Feste sees himself as giving them, all too easily, an outward direction that makes them wrong: 'A sentence is but a chev'ril glove to a good wit: how quickly the wrong side may be turned outward!' (3.1.11–13) – Feste here insinuating the turning outward of his words as vehicles of the reason he is transforming into passion. Since giving an account of this transformation requires me to describe the tenets impelling it, its description is what I must now attempt, begging the reader to consider what follows.

\*\*\*

Whereas Epictetus sees the things pertaining to men's minds as their own, Seneca more specifically defines what is truly man's 'own' (*Ep.* 41.7) as 'soul, and reason brought to perfection in the soul' (*Ep.* 41.8). And in thus defining man's 'peculiar property' (*Ep.* 41.8) as his rationally perfected soul or mind, Seneca is endowing him with high nobility. For, identifying reason as 'a common attribute of both gods and men' (*Ep.* 92.27; II.465), Seneca sees it as 'nothing else than a portion of the divine spirit set in a human body' (*Ep.* 66.12; II.9–11). Nor does Seneca view man's mortality as seriously hindering his kinship with divinity. For in declaring man to be 'like a god in all save his mortality' (*On Firmness*, 8.2), Seneca, like Epictetus, dismisses death as being 'no evil' (*Ep.* 82.9). And he does so by dismissing the future threat of death in favour of an emphasis upon life in the present. Disparaging the anticipation of evils to come, Seneca declares it 'madness ... to be tortured by the future' (*Ep.* 74.33; II.135).

Still Seneca regards man's kinship with divinity as a potential that he must labour to realize. For, whereas reason 'in the gods ... is perfected', in man it is merely 'capable of being perfected' (*Ep.* 92.27; II.465). And hindering that perfection were the passions associated with his body, which clouded his reason. It was therefore the Stoic's task to realize the divinity of his reason not by moderating his passions but rather by eradicating them as so many diseases of the soul, Seneca declaring that 'philosophers of our school reject the emotions' (*Ep.* 116.1; III.333) in the opinion that no 'half-way disease can be either wholesome or helpful' (*Ep.* 116.1; III. 333). And while the passions to be extirpated included love, especially as institutionalized in marriage, as well as the grief of bereavement, the primary passion to be uprooted was that of the body's lust for life. Indeed, Seneca disparages the desire to live to such an extent that he censures the Stoic's reluctance to die as sinning against the divine reason of the cosmos, thereby turning his death into the deserved fate of a criminal. Thus, it emerges that, to perfect his mind in the reason that makes it his 'peculiar property', man must make it his sole property by rejecting his body and its passions. For Seneca insists that '"nothing is a good, if it be composed of things that are distinct"; rather, 'the essential quality of each single good should be single' (*Ep.* 102 7; III.171–3). It is in the apathetic perfection of its singleness that man's reason becomes the defining element of his nature. And in thus reducing his essence to rational singleness, the Stoic, now thinking with a reason no different from cosmic reason, becomes a wise man or *sapiens*.

Having become man's 'peculiar property', perfect reason also becomes the source of his happiness. For, asserting that 'reason alone brings man to perfection', Seneca concludes that 'reason alone, when perfected, makes man happy' (*Ep.* 76.16; II.157); indeed, once it has become his single essential quality, reason emerges as 'man's only good, the only means by which he is made happy' (*Ep.* 76.16; II.157). And the Stoic estimation of man's reason – rather than his life – as the sole source of his happiness informs Feste's readiness to defect from the occupation that sustains his body.

How, then, was the Stoic to know that he had become a *sapiens*? By achieving a state of change-lessness that the Stoics called *constantia*, a term that was translated as both 'constancy' and 'firmness'. It was because the cosmos was stable and unchanging that the Stoic was likewise to be stable and unchan-ging, or constant. And it was because the cosmos was made stable and unchanging by its divine rea-son that the Stoic was to be made similarly constant by perfecting his human reason. For, as Seneca says, 'It is reason alone that is unchangeable, that holds fast to its decisions' (*Ep.* 66.32; II.23) – this unchangeable stability, constancy or firmness being regarded by Seneca as the highest of the Stoic virtues, for 'underlying them all is a single virtue – that which renders the soul straight and unswerving' (*Ep.* 66.13; II.11).

Attesting the virtuous changelessness or con-stancy of the Stoic *sapiens* was his ability 'to play the role of one man' (*Ep.* 120.22; III.395), even under the direst of circumstances – for

virtue is free, inviolable, unmoved, unshaken, so steeled against the blows of chance that she cannot be bent, much less broken. Facing the instruments of torture she holds her gaze unflinching, her expression changes not at all, whether a hard or a happy lot is shown her.

(*On Firmness*, 5.4–5)

As these words attest, the Stoic was to demonstrate his constancy not merely in his words but also, and primarily, in his deeds. For Seneca insists that

philosophy teaches us to act, not to speak; it exacts of every man that he should live according to his own standards, that his life should not be out of harmony with his words, and that, further, his inner life should be of one hue and not out of harmony with all his activities. This, I say, is the highest duty and the highest proof of Wisdom, – that deed and word should be in accord, that a man should be equal to himself under all conditions, and always the same.                    (*Ep.* 20.2; I.133–5)

And, being changelessness itself, the Stoic's firm-ness or constancy can never be lost, nor its virtue 'unlearned' (*Ep.* 50–8; I.335), the Stoic's 'steadfast-ness of soul' or constancy denoting 'a peace that is won for all time' (*Ep.* 78.16; II.191).

In making him constant, the Stoic's perfect reason was also to make him benevolent. For Seneca sees the rationality of the gods as making them unfai-lingly kind: 'And what reason have the gods for doing deeds of kindness? It is their nature. One who thinks that they are unwilling to do harm, is wrong; they *cannot* do harm' (*Ep.* 95.48–9; III.89). As the nature of the gods makes them kind, so this same nature in man is seen by Seneca to have 'engendered in us mutual affection, and made us prone to friendships' (*Ep.* 95.52; III.91), 'for human life is founded on kindness and concord, and is bound into an alliance for common help ... by mutual love' (*On Anger*, I.v.3). Yet Seneca also sees the gods as doing no harm only because they suffer no harm: 'They cannot receive or inflict injury; for doing harm is in the same category as suffering harm' (*Ep.* 95.49; III.89). And just as the gods cannot do harm because they cannot receive harm, so the rationally perfected Stoic likewise can-not do harm because he cannot receive harm. For Seneca insists that 'no wise man [which is to say, no rationally perfected and therefore constant Stoic] can receive either injury or insult' (*On Firmness*, ii.1). To be sure, Seneca does not deny that attempts will be made to injure and insult him. But, says Seneca, 'the invulnerable thing is not that which is not struck, but that which is not hurt; by this mark I will show you the wise man' (*On Firmness*, iii.3). Though struck, the wise man will not be hurt.

What attests him unhurt by insult or injury, moreover, is the wise man's ability to confront these assaults without anger: 'If he is a wise man, he is free from that anger which is aroused by the mere appearance of injury, and in no other way could he be free from the anger than by being free also from the injury, knowing that an injury can never be done to him' (On Firmness, ix.3). For while, as diseases of the soul, all passions disturb its rationality, anger is described by Seneca as 'the most hideous and frenzied of all the emotions' (*On Anger*, I.i.1). So far from rationality does Seneca place anger as to agree with those who define it as "'a temporary madness'": 'You have only to behold the aspect of those possessed by anger to know that they are insane' (*On Anger*, I.i.2–3). For, citing Aristotle's definition of anger as 'the desire to repay suffering' (*On Anger*, I.iii.3), Seneca observes that 'anger craves vengeance' (*On Anger*, I.vi.4). Yet, in craving vengeance, anger is seen by Seneca as 'giving no thought to itself if only it can hurt another, hurling itself upon the very point of the dagger, and eager for revenge though it may drag down the avenger along with it' (*On Anger*, I.i.1). It is by inciting a self-recoiling vengeance that anger is seen to denote madness. For only a madman would destroy his enemy at the cost of destroying himself.

It was in order to defend him against the injurious assaults of Fortune and thus against the anger that must inevitably cause him to crave an insanely self-immolating vengeance that Seneca tells his disciple Lucilius to 'gird yourself about with philosophy, an impregnable wall. Though it be assaulted by many engines, Fortune can find no passage into it. The soul stands on unassailable ground, if it has abandoned external things; it is independent in its own fortress' (*Ep.* 82.5; II.243). Yet the rational fortress that was to defend Feste against the injury and insult that must make him angry and thus vengeful is precisely what he has breached by inconstantly returning, under the pressure of bodily need, to the house he had abandoned. Even while becoming inconstant in his deed, however, Feste will be seen to assert constancy in words that profess his Stoic contempt of death. And by disdaining death in Stoic words that are belied by his deed, Feste validates a fault that, as Seneca admits, was often imputed to the Stoics: 'There is a very disgraceful charge often brought against our school, – that we deal with the words, and not with the deeds, of philosophy' (*Ep.* 24.15; I.175).

In its most significant effect, however, Feste's inconstancy exposes him to the insulting and injurious assaults of Fortune in the person of Malvolio. For, having become inconstant, Feste is no longer a wise man. And charging him with an unwisdom that he construes as stupidity, Malvolio now insults

Feste, the truth of that insult causing it both to strike and to hurt him, thereby inciting him to the anger that craves vengeance.

Thus, by demanding the surrender of his body, which, as a part of his nature, cannot be surrendered, Feste's Stoicism launches him on a quest for the insane triumph of a vengeance that destroys him body and soul. It is 1.5 that initiates the process of Feste's transformation from Stoic to avenger. And how this scene draws on the above-described principles of Stoicism to initiate this transformation is what we must now address, by observing their involvement in Feste's discourse with Maria, Olivia and Malvolio.

\*\*\*

Maria opens this scene by identifying Feste as having left Olivia's house, thereby deserting his occupation, which shortly turns out to be that of a fool: 'Nay, either tell me where thou hast been, or I will not open my lips so wide as a bristle may enter, in way of thy excuse. My lady will hang thee for thy absence' (1.5.1–4). In defecting from his profession, Feste can be seen to imitate Seneca's derogation of his own 'affairs' (*Ep.* 8.2; I.37) as directed to gaining the external possessions that he regards as unnecessary: 'None of our possessions is essential' (*Ep.* 25.4; I.185). Indeed, Seneca sees these possessions as preventing the Stoic from possessing the mind or soul that is his single 'peculiar property' (*Ep.* 41.8; I.277): 'We should belong to ourselves, if only these things did not belong to us' (*Ep.* 42.8; I.283). And informing Seneca's view of external possessions as unnecessary hindrances is his conviction that 'nature demands but little' (*Ep.* 17.9; I.113), even the little that nature demands serving only the body, which, as an alien 'weight' (*Ep.* 65.16; I.453) upon the soul, does not deserve the work required to support it: 'Work is not a good. Then what is a good? I say, the scorning of work. That is why I should rebuke men who toil to no purpose' (*Ep.* 31.4; I.223–5). Rather than concerning himself with the body, Seneca disdains even its want: 'Do you ask what is the cure for want? It is to make hunger satisfy hunger' (*Ep.* 110.19; III.277). And providing a still more effective remedy for hunger is death itself: 'If the utmost pinch of need arrives, [the Stoic] will quickly take leave of life and cease being a trouble to himself' (*Ep.* 17.9; I.115).

Beyond banishing want, however, death has the further benefit of obviating what Seneca regards as the most tormenting aspect of life: the fear of death: 'I shall die . . . I shall cease to run the risk of death' (*Ep.* 24.17; I.177). And this same Senecan approval of death for banishing the fear of death is what Feste's likewise evinces by way of deflecting Maria's warning that his mistress Olivia will hang him for his absence: 'Let her hang me! He that is well hang'd in this world needs to fear no colors (1.5.5–6) – 'colors' here being seen by the Riverside editors (note to line 6) as invoking 'collars', as the noose by which he will be hanged. Feste seems to be saying that once hanged, he will no longer fear being hanged. And reinforcing this Senecan meaning is his response to Maria's challenge that he 'Make that good' (1.5.7). For Feste now explains that he will not fear colors, because, being dead, 'He shall see none to fear' (1.5.8). It is as a Senecan Stoic that Feste professes to approve his own death as cancelling his fear of death.

Yet besides suggesting 'collars', Feste's 'colours' are aptly seen by the Riverside editors to suggest the colours of 'military standards' (note to line 12), as Maria suggests in observing that Feste has acquired his 'I fear no colours' 'In the wars' (1.5.12). It thus appears that Feste has been a soldier. And making this observation Stoically significant is the meaning that Seneca imparts to the soldier, who, in viewing himself as a small and therefore insignificant part of a larger army, symbolizes the Stoic condition of man in the cosmos. Rather than concerned with our individuality, the cosmos is seen by Seneca to regard us merely as 'parts of one great body' that 'comprises both god and man' (*Ep.* 95.52; III.91). Thus, it does not impugn the benevolence of the gods to see them as caring more for 'the whole human family' than for 'single persons' (*On Providence*, 3.1; I.15), or, by extension, for the wholeness of the cosmos. And this means that, rather than imputing evil to the suffering we necessarily endure as mere parts of this greater cosmic wholeness, we should 'refrain from chafing over whatever happens to [us], . . knowing that the very agencies that seem to bring harm are working for the preservation of the world, and are a part of the scheme for bringing to fulfillment the order of the universe and its functions' (*Ep.* 74.20; II.127). As the Stoic's self-subordination to the cosmos finds its symbol in the soldier, so the 'agencies' of cosmic wholeness are likened to his commander. Just as the commander of an army unhesitatingly yet irreproachably sacrifices the individual soldier to the success of his campaign, so the 'supreme commanders in the universe' act 'as guardians of the human race, even though they are sometimes unmindful of the individual' (*Ep.* 95.50; III.89). And just as the soldier obeys his commander in the knowledge that he plays a small part in a larger campaign that is good even if its success requires his death, so the Stoic likewise vows obedience to the cosmos regardless of how it disposes of him – 'for it is a bad soldier who grumbles when following his commander' (*Ep.* 108.9; III.229). Indeed, in making him a bad soldier, the Stoic's disinclination to die at the will of his cosmic commander makes him a criminal who deserves to die: 'I say that good men are willing that these things should happen and, if they are unwilling, that they deserve misfortune' (*On Providence*, 3.1; I.15). By suggesting that he has been a soldier, Feste's presence 'in the wars' proclaims his Stoic readiness to die at the command of his cosmic commander. Yet of course, Feste's inconstant return to Olivia's house shows him disinclined to die, thereby incurring the criminality that causes him to deserve his death. And it is with reference to this criminality that Maria equates the threat of his being 'turned away' with death by hanging: 'Yet you will be hang'd for being so long absent, or to be turn'd away – is not that as good as a hanging to you?' (1.5.16–18). Professing, however, to dismiss Maria's insistence that he confront his peril, Feste continues to disdain death in words that he means to charge with Stoic wit: 'Many a good hanging prevents a bad marriage, and for turning away, let summer bear it out' (1.5.19–20). Setting aside its meaning as a sexual quibble, Feste's suggestion that a 'good hanging prevents a bad marriage' invokes

Seneca's disdain for marriage as a passionate alliance that impedes the Stoic's rationality, as Feste further attests by observing to Cesario that Olivia 'will keep no fool ... till she be married, and fools are as like husbands as pilchers are to herrings, the husband's the bigger' (3.1.33–5). But, likewise Senecan, is Feste's observation that 'for turning away, let summer bear it out' (1.5.20) – Feste here suggesting that, as a season of warmth, summer will diminish the discomfort of his homelessness and is thus a good time to be turned away from Olivia's house. Yet, in thus identifying summer as the season now present, Feste is also declining to anticipate the future arrival of less clement weather, his focus on the present to the exclusion of the future reflecting Seneca's insistence that it is 'madness ... to be tortured by the future' (*Ep.* 74.33; II.135). In true Senecan fashion, Feste considers that the weather is fine now – that it must soon turn cold being none of his concern.

To the sensible Maria, however, Feste's professed readiness to die is mere folly. And determining to save Feste from his folly, Maria takes aim at the Stoically charged wit that is its merely verbal expression, to that end dereogating his claim to 'fear no colors' because he will not be alive to see them as 'A good lenten answer' (1.5.9) – which is to say, weak. It is plausibly the contradiction of Feste's Stoic words by his inconstant deed that contributes to their weakness. Yet particularly noteworthy is Feste's sense of this weakness as habitual: 'Well, God give them wisdom that have it; and those that are fools, let them use their talents' (1.5.14–15). For, just as Feste's colors suggests 'collars', so the Riverside editors observe (note to line 15) that his 'fools' bears an aural similarity to 'fowls', which, by adducing the fool's cockscomb, suggests that he is, like a fowl, stupid. And further invoking the suggestion of stupidity in 'fools' as 'fowls' is the tendency of 'talents' to suggest a fowl's 'talons' (note to line 15). For these 'talons' appear to invoke the dubious recourse to which fools of limited wit habitually resorted, which was to savage members of their audience by holding them up to ridicule. It is the 'impossible slanders' of such a 'dull fool' that Beatrice in *Much Ado About Nothing* adduces in observing that they cause men to 'laugh at him and beat him' (2.1.137–8, 142). Feste apparently suspects that, as such a 'dull fool', he too will slander men and be beaten, this suspicion likely influencing his decision to abscond from this profession. In thus disclosing a correspondence between his own diffidence and his Stoic creed, Feste subtly invites us to regard that creed as valorizing what he must otherwise view as a craven retreat from the world.

Yet, rather than alleviating Feste's diffidence, his Stoicism serves only to aggravate it. For having, by the inconstancy of his deed, forfeited the wisdom of his Stoic words, Feste renders them powerless to evade Maria's contempt for the readiness to be hanged that they profess. It is the lameness of his wit that Feste demonstrates in retreating from his resolution by being 'resolv'd on two points' (1.5.22–3), as Maria attests by supplying his well-worn punch-line, 'That if one break, the other will hold; or if both break, your gaskins fall' (1.5.24–5). Indeed, Feste's own gaskins appear metaphorically to have fallen. For, not unlike his Stoic pretension to disdain his bodily nature, Feste's gaskins conceal his bodily nature, their falling revealing that nature. By defeating the words that merely pretend to Stoic constancy, Maria forces Feste to let it go. Now admitting that he would prefer living to dying, Feste will beg his mistress to restore him to the post that sustains his body.

Needing his wit to stay him in this attempt, Feste anxiously invokes it as the divine reason within him: 'Wit, and't be thy will, put me into good fooling!' (1.5.32–3). Yet, aware of having forfeited the wisdom of his wit, Feste also adduces the *topos* of the Christian fool, who becomes wise in the forfeiture of wisdom – this unwisdom enabling him to 'pass for a wise man' (1.5.35). That he is not, however, a Stoic wise man is what Feste now appears to admit. For, in observing 'Better a witty fool than a foolish wit' (1.5.36), Feste seems to mean that he had rather save his life by being witty as an inconstant fool than forfeit it as a foolishly constant *sapiens*.

To gain Olivia's forgiveness, however, Feste must overcome her sense that, in addition to being a 'dry fool' (1.5.41), his defection has made him 'dishonest' (1.5.42). And in confronting these two challenges, Feste's wit falters. For he can think of no way to deal with these charges other than by unwittily suggesting that they are corrigible: Olivia should 'give the dry fool drink, then is the fool not dry' (1.5.44–5) and 'bid the dishonest man mend himself: if he mend, he is no longer dishonest (1.5.45–6). In suggesting that mending would make the dishonest man no longer dishonest, however, Feste appears to have run foul of a Stoic principle, as he now suggests by observing that, in failing to mend himself, the dishonest man should be mended by 'the botcher' (1.5.46–7). For while 'botcher' signifies a mender, to botch is also to ruin, as in Timon's suggestion that, in lacking his companionship, Apemantus would not mend but rather mar himself: "tis not well mended so, it is but botch'd' (*Timon*, 4.3.285). By invoking the mender as 'botcher', Feste appears to see his own mending as botching. For we have seen Seneca insist that 'nothing is a good, if it be composed of things that are distinct' (*Ep.* 102.7; III.171), the Stoic's reason making him good in being uncontaminated by such distinct things as the passions. Yet the uncontaminated purity of his reason that makes the Stoic a single man is what mending destroys, because, as Feste observes, mending involves patching one thing with another: 'Any thing that's mended is but patch'd' (1.5.47–8). As, in making something less than single, patching makes it not good, so the mending that patches Feste's dishonesty likewise makes him less than a single man and thus not good. And as it denotes both mending and fool, Feste's use of this term intimates the dubiety of his mending as a fool's errand that, by making him inconstant to his original defection, puts paid to the singleness that makes him a *sapiens*.

Beyond its futility, however, Feste's Stoic derogation of his mending may harbour something sinister. For Feste goes on to apply patching to both virtue and sin: 'Virtue that transgresses is but patch'd with sin, and sin that amends is but patch'd

with virtue' (1.5.48–9) – his apparent meaning being that the sin mended by the virtue that patches is no better than the virtue impaired by the sin that patches it, because both destroy the singleness of constancy. Yet by thus attributing an equal imperfection to all things patched, Feste is intimating something profoundly amoral in constancy itself. For Feste seems to be implying that the moral status of what a person decides to do is less important than that he remain constant to his decision, constancy being pursued for its own sake rather than for the sake of the good. And the amorality of Stoic constancy is what Feste is destined to express. For the Stoic shame he incurs in becoming inconstant to his defection from work is shortly to make him relentlessly constant to vengeance, in which Feste refuses the patching virtue of forgiveness that would have averted his soul's damnation.

Recalling himself to the task of reingratiating himself with Olivia, Feste now turns from his inconstancy to hers. By telling her that 'there is no true cuckold but calamity' (1.5.51–2), Feste informs her that she will prove unfaithful to her grief. For, as a passion, grief cannot command the rationality that makes it constant. Rather, borrowing Nashe's 'beauty's a flower' (1.5.52), with its implied 'that wrinkles will devour', Feste adduces the evanescence of Olivia's beauty as making her inconstant to her grief. But making Feste's meaning still more clearly Senecan is its suggestion that, since Olivia must be inconstant to her irrational grief, she might as well abandon it right away. For this same advice is what Seneca gives the sorrowing Lucilius in telling him to abandon grief willingly and 'as soon as possible', lest he endure the shame of merely growing 'weary of sorrowing': 'I should prefer you to abandon grief, rather than have grief abandon you' (*Ep.* 63.12; I.435). To grieve is thus to court inconstancy. And, as its irrationality makes grief inconstant, so its irrationality makes fools of those who indulge it. For, having cajoled Olivia into declaring that her brother's soul is 'in heaven' (1.5.69) – which is to say, in bliss – Feste challenges her mourning for him as the irrationality that turns her into a fool: 'The more fool, madonna, to mourn for your brother's soul, being in heaven. Take away the fool, gentlemen' (1.5.70–2).

Now approving Feste's wit, Olivia reinstates him by rhetorically asking Malvolio to approve what she herself apprehends as his mending: 'What think you of this fool, Malvolio? doth he not mend?' (1.5.73–4). Yet, unwilling to see Feste regain the favour of his mistress, Malvolio exploits the diseased passion for living implicit in the inconstancy of his mending to insult that mending as 'Infirmity': 'Yes, and shall do till the pangs of death shake him. Infirmity, that decays the wise, doth ever make the better fool' (1.5.75–7). Signalling the forfeiture of his wisdom, Feste's infirm or diseased passion can mend or 'better' him only as a fool. And, forced by the truth of Malvolio's insult to receive or internalize it, Feste now admits that he is 'no fox'. But most forcibly attesting that Feste has received Malvolio's insult is the anger he evinces in responding to it: 'God send you, sir, a speedy infirmity, for the better increasing your folly! Sir Toby will be sworn I am no fox, but he will not pass his word for sixpence that you are no fool' (1.5.78–81).

It is the unwisdom implicit in Feste's inconstancy that Malvolio now makes explicit by calling him a 'barren rascal' (1.5.84), able to be 'put down ... with an ordinary fool that has no more brain than a stone' (1.5.84–5). And, in thus insulting Feste, Malvolio also seeks to injure him. For Malvolio derogates Olivia's delight in Feste for the purpose of persuading her to dismiss him, thereby exposing him to 'the wind and the rain' that must shortly kill him. By seeking Feste's dismissal, Malvolio would force him to confront the very death he has been seeking to evade. But it is a death that Feste must Stoically see himself as deserving. For, just as the Stoic soldier who refuses to die deserves to be punished with death, so Feste's refusal to die like a Stoic must make him see himself as deserving the 'turning away' that Malvolio now advocates and that Maria has subtly criminalized by comparing it to death by hanging.

In thus causing Feste to see himself as deserving the 'turning away' that must kill him, Malvolio's injurious insult not only strikes him but also hurts him. For Malvolio triumphantly observes that his insult has reduced Feste to silence: 'Look you now, he's out of his guard already. Unless you laugh and minister occasion to him, he is gagg'd' (1.5.86–7). And by showing him in fact as a 'barren rascal', Feste's silence attests that he has received Malvolio's insult, thereby seeing himself to be exactly as Malvolio has described him. It thus emerges that Malvolio exploits Feste's Stoic idealism to insult and injure him for failures that its unrealizable demands have made inevitable. As, by receiving Malvolio's insulting assault on the inconstancy of his mending, Malvolio makes him angry, so his receiving of Malvolio's injuriously intended assault on his wit can only intensify Feste's anger. And as anger craves vengeance, vengeance is what Feste's anger now causes him to crave. Far from endowing him with a godlike benevolence that makes him a friend to other men, the unfulfillably Stoic demand that he repudiate his body incites Feste to the anger that is now to make him an avenger.

\*\*\*

Yet, fearing the recoil of this vengeance, and thus poised between craving and fear, Feste seeks a way of wreaking his vengeance that will enable him to evade its recoil, something he thinks he has discovered in the nighttime revels of Toby and Andrew in 2.3. For Feste will exploit these revels to foment a quarrel between Toby and Malvolio. By inciting Toby to anger, this quarrel causes him to crave vengeance. And exploiting Malvolio's ambitious expectation of greatness, Maria translates Toby's anger into a stratagem to achieve this vengeance, by dropping a letter in Malvolio's path that purports to contain a declaration of love from his mistress. Yet, in thus devising Toby's vengeance, Maria really serves Feste's vengeance, while absolving him, as he thinks, of its recoil. For Feste's Stoicism advises him that, though no deed is done in the absence of an external impression, which produces an impulse, it is not the one who impels a deed that is responsible for it, but rather the one who enacts it. And this is because, between being impelled to act and acting, there falls what the Stoics called the pause, the pause denoting, as

Seneca explains, the ability of man's reason to dominate his impulse by either giving or denying it his assent:[13]

Every living thing possessed of reason is inactive if it is not first stirred by some external impression; then the impulse comes, and finally assent confirms the impulse. Now what *assent* is, I shall explain. Suppose that I ought to take a walk: I do walk, but only after uttering the command to myself and approving this opinion of mine.

(*Ep.* 113.18; III.293)

Being able to give or deny his assent to an impulse makes every man responsible for the impulse to which he assents. Thus, while Feste can produce an external impression that produces an impulse to vengeance in Toby, it is Toby rather than Feste who is responsible for assenting to that impulse by avenging himself on Malvolio.

It is by encouraging the drunken 'caterwauling' of Toby and Andrew that Feste would foment Toby's quarrel with Malvolio, as Maria attests: 'What a caterwauling do you keep here! If my lady have not call'd up her steward Malvolio and bid him turn you out of doors, never trust me' (2.3.72–4). Loving Toby, and not wanting him to be turned out of doors, Maria urges him to hold his peace. Yet the rowdy behaviour that Maria would inhibit is just what Feste seeks to encourage: 'Beshrew me, the knight's in admirable fooling' (2.3.80). Again, Maria would silence them: 'For the love o'God, peace!' (2.3.85). But it is too late. Malvolio now enters to deliver his own just, if pompous, rebuke, which concludes by threatening Toby with expulsion from Olivia's house. Defying Malvolio's threat, Toby now sings a song that mocks his eviction: '"Farewell, dear heart, since I must needs be gone"' (2.3.102). Again Maria urges prudence – 'Nay, good Sir Toby' (2.3.103) – only to be again countermanded by Feste, who sings the second line of Toby's song, even though it associates his eviction with death: '"His eyes do show his days are almost done"' (2.3.104). It is, however, by impugning Toby's courage that Feste finally drives his oblique challenge of Malvolio's authority into open defiance:

SIR TO. [*Sings.*] 'Shall I bid him go?'
CLO. [*Sings.*] 'What and if you do?'
SIR TO. [*Sings.*] 'Shall I bid him go, and spare not?'
CLO. [*Sings.*] 'O no, no, no, no, you dare not'
SIR TO. [*To Clown.*] Out o' tune, sir! ye lie. [*To Malvolio.*]
Art any more than a steward? Dost thou think because thou art virtuous there shall be no more cakes and ale?

(2.3.109–16)

As Malvolio had tried to have Feste expelled from Olivia's house, thereby threatening him with death, so, by inciting Toby to defy Malvolio, Feste has caused him to incur this same threat of expulsion from Olivia's house that threatens death. As the threat of expulsion had incited Feste to anger with its craving for vengeance, so this same threat inspires this same anger and craving in Toby. Thus, it appears that Feste has inspired Toby to take the vengeance he fears to take, the vengeance that the clever Maria devises on his behalf.

Yet, rather than giving him satisfaction, Feste's proxy vengeance appears only to have engendered a bitterness that focuses on the words impelling it. Observing that words have two meanings, of which one is right and the other wrong, Feste observes a tendency for the wrong meaning to predominate: 'A sentence is but a chev'ril glove to a good wit: how quickly the wrong side may be turn'd outward!' (3.1.11–13). Why Feste thus attacks words, moreover, is suggested by such phrases as 'reason and discourse' (*Measure for Measure*, 1.2.185) and 'discourse of reason' (*Hamlet*, 1.2.150), which represent words as the vehicles of reason. For, as the vehicles of reason, words are causative, as Seneca observes in declaring 'cause' to be a term 'by which we mean reason'. And, in declaring that cause 'moulds matter and turns it in whatever direction it will, producing thereby various concrete results' (*Ep.* 65.2; I.445), Seneca can be seen to inform Feste's wish that his 'sister had had no name' (3.1.16–17). For, as he explains, 'her name's a word, and to dally with that word might make my sister wanton'

---

[13] Charlotte Stough, 'Stoic determinism and moral responsibility', in *The Stoics*, ed. John M. Rist (Berkeley, 1978), pp. 221–4.

(3.1.19–20). But the materially causative nature of rational words that is troubling Feste is the vengeance that his words have just incited in Toby. For, by using words to cause vengeance in Toby, Feste has redirected their reason outward, thereby transforming it into passion. And this is because, as incited by anger, vengeance is the height of irrationality, the irrationality of vengeance falsifying the rationality of the words that incite it, as Feste attests in regarding his words as 'so false, that I am loath to prove reason with them' (3.1.24–5). And, in seeing his vengeance-inciting words as falsifying their rationality, Feste also becomes, as he says, a 'corrupter of words' (3.1.36). For, by using them to incite vengeance, Feste has destroyed the rational goodness of his words, thereby destroying their Stoic integrity.

Having destroyed the Stoic integrity of his words, Feste has also destroyed the Stoic rationale for repudiating his body, as his changing attitude towards the money that supports its life appears to attest. For, notwithstanding that he 'impeticos', or pockets, the 'gratility' or 'little tip' (2.3.26) given him by Andrew 'for thy leman' (2.3.25), Feste had initially professed to neglect his body by refusing to accept handouts from his betters. Thus, when, in 2.3, Toby would pay Feste for singing a song – 'Come on, there is sixpence for you. Let's have a song' (2.3.31–2) – his offer being seconded by Andrew – 'There's a testril of me too. If one knight give a – ' (2.3.33–4) Feste interrupts that offer by way of refusing this money, even though it has been freely offered. For, not only seeing this money as insulting the Stoic integrity to which he pretends, Feste can also be seen to take offence at the smallness of the sums being offered him, which insult his integrity for virtually nothing. In 2.4, Orsino too would pay Feste for singing a song – 'There's for thy pains' (2.4.67) – only to have Feste demurringly tell him, 'No pains, sir, I take pleasure in singing, sir' (2.4.68). As earlier, he professes to prefer his Stoic self-sufficiency to Orsino's handout. Yet, when Orsino responds by offering to pay Feste's pleasure, Feste accepts his money – 'Truly, sir, and pleasure will be paid, one time or another' (2.4.70–1) – his acceptance in 2.4 being plausibly informed by his moral self-compromise in 2.3. Having used words to instigate vengeance, and thus forfeited the apathetic singleness that dispenses with the body and its passions, Feste now accepts money when it is offered.

Yet, regarding himself as demeaned by owning his body, Feste now seems determined to cover himself with shame. For 3.1 shows him not merely accepting the coin that Cesario offers him, but also asking her to double it, thereby crossing the line between accepting money and begging for it. And it is as a self-humiliating beggar that Feste offers to put the money he begs of Cesario to the unnatural breeding of usury: 'Would not a pair of these have bred, sir?' (3.1.49). For Feste derogates his usury by comparing it to the lustful union of Troilus with Cressida, his fostering of this union casting him in the base role of that arch-procurer, Pandarus: 'I would play Lord Pandarus of Phrygia, sir, to bring a Cressida to this Troilus' (3.1.51–2). What Feste's self-shaming here suggests is that he loathes himself, as he likewise suggests by now accepting the wretchedly small sums he had earlier refused. For, in calling the coin offered him by Cesario 'Cressida', Feste is invoking her eventual lapse from aristocratic status to abject beggar: 'The matter, I hope, is not great, sir – begging but a beggar: Cressida was a beggar' (3.1.54–5). As with the Cressida he begs, Feste sees himself as having lapsed from noble Stoic to beggar.

How Feste's self-debasement alienates him from his salvation is what Shakespeare appears to have allegorized through his dismissal of the disguised Viola in 3.1, and also through his own banishment by Sebastian in 4.1. Yet, passing over these meanings, as well as the doctrinal import in three important aspects of 4.2 – Malvolio's imprisonment, Feste's disguise, and Feste's insistence that Malvolio acknowledge himself to be mad – let us concentrate on how 4.2 shows Feste, now advancing towards the ownership of his vengeance by putting his own hand to it, assaults Malvolio's mind. Having incited Toby and Maria to prompt behaviours in Malvolio that indict him for madness, Feste has effectively licensed Toby to treat him like a madman by having him 'in a dark room, and bound' (3.4.135–6). And Feste now proposes to condition Malvolio's release from his dark prison on his admission of being mad, only to accomplish the precise opposite of the admission he had intended. For by causing Malvolio to be immured in darkness, Feste has walled him off from the world. And by thus depriving Malvolio of any reality external to himself, Feste has apparently turned his gaze inward towards the realm of his own mind, the realm to which his externally directed ambition had heretofore blinded him. Whereas Malvolio's ambitious expectation had disabled the judgement of his mind, he now claims his mind as an inalienable part of his essence. For, though helpless, friendless and desperately wanting to be released, Malvolio refuses to gratify Feste by confessing himself mad – his staunch defence of his sanity signifying his refusal to surrender his mind, just as Feste cannot surrender his body. On the contrary, what Malvolio now finds in his mind is a kingdom or fortress that empowers him to resist the imputation of madness by which Feste would take it away. Thus, rather than inducing him to the confession of madness that renounces the possession of his mind, the dark prison that has deprived Malvolio of everything other than his mind has caused him to possess it with utter certainty. And, in coming into an unswerving possession of his mind, Malvolio has achieved the constancy in adversity that defines him as a Stoic who, by possessing nothing else, possesses his own mind.

It is, moreover, through a Stoically associated recourse that Feste now reinforces our awareness of how far his cruelty reflects the continued rankling of Malvolio's charge that he is stupid. For, now deviously exploiting Malvolio's desire to prove his sanity, Feste interrogates him on Pythagoras' doctrine of the transmigration of souls, this doctrine assuming a Stoic significance in the recognition that Seneca himself for a time embraced it with 'ardent zeal' (*Ep.* 108.17; III.241). For, as aptly described by Seneca as lodging the souls of deceased human beings in the bodies of animals prior to their reassuming human form (*Ep.* 108.19; III.241),[14] this doctrine was seen by him to assuage the fear of 'our so-called death' by representing it

merely as 'a change of abode' (*Ep.* 108.20; III.243). Yet Feste here identifies these animal abodes of human souls as 'wild-foul' (4.2.50–1). And, in addition to observing that this doctrine provides for the humiliating descent of human beings from animals, Malvolio's agreeing attestation 'That the soul of our grandam might happily inhabit a bird' (4.2.52–3) also shows this doctrine providing for human descent from one particularly stupid bird: the woodcock – it being from this stupid bird that Feste would have Malvolio take his own descent.

Not only fostering Feste's representation of Malvolio as the scion of a stupid woodcock, Pythagoras' doctrine is seen by Seneca to impugn the eating of animal food by making men 'fearful of guilt and parricide, since they might be, without knowing it, attacking the soul of a parent and injuring it with knife or with teeth – if, as is possible, the related spirit be dwelling temporarily in this bit of flesh!' (*Ep.* 108.19; III.241–3). And when, repudiating this fear-inspiring doctrine, Malvolio implicitly denies the animal descent that provides for his stupidity, Feste takes this implied denial of his stupidity to prove him insane, and leaves him to languish in his dark prison: 'Fare thee well. Remain thou still in darkness. Thou shalt hold th'opinion of Pythagoras ere I will allow of thy wits, and fear to kill a woodcock lest thou dispossess the soul of thy grandam' (4.2.57–60).

Having failed, as Sir Topas, to break Malvolio's faith in his own sanity, Feste now launches a second assault on the steward's mind in his 'own voice' (4.2.66), thereby drawing still closer to owning his vengeance. Yet, faring no better than his first attempt to force the surrender of Malvolio's mind, Feste's deceiving voice produces a second unintended effect. For, having been humbled by his imprisonment to the recognition of being unloved and friendless, Malvolio comes to see himself as the Stoic sees himself: that is, as needing friends. And this Stoic frame of mind is what Malvolio attests in attempting to make a friend of

---

[14] In Rouse, ed., *Shakespeare's Ovid*, Book XV, lines 176–95.

Feste. In a new tone of civility that includes addressing him four times as 'good fool' (4.2.71, 85, 105, 109), Malvolio promises to repay Feste's kindness 'As I am a gentleman' (4.2.82). It thus appears that, in becoming a Stoic, Malvolio confirms not only his sanity but also the benevolence that qualifies him as a gentleman. And, thus ennobled by his new-found benevolence, Malvolio, for the first time in the play, engages our sympathy.

In thus ennobling himself as a Stoic, Malvolio has apparently assumed the identity surrendered by Feste. Yet, just as Malvolio appropriates a new identity, so it appears that Feste likewise does the same. And just as Malvolio appropriates Feste's identity, so Feste now appropriates Malvolio's identity. For Malvolio's very name has intimated the evil of his will, thereby associating him with that archetype of evil whom Toby had described as 'an emeny to mankind' (3.4.98). And, in shedding this demonic association in favour of Stoic benevolence, Malvolio bequeaths it to Feste. For, while purporting to exorcise the 'fiend' vexing Malvolio – 'Out, hyperbolical fiend! How vexest thou this man!' (4.2.25–6) – Feste cannot but prompt our recognition that the 'fiend' vexing Malvolio in 4.2 is none other than himself. And in representing his 'rage and his wrath' (4.2.127) as likening him to 'the old Vice' (4.2.124) who is son to the devil, Feste himself appropriates this demonic identity.

It is in the contrast of his debasing wrath with Malvolio's noble benevolence that Feste finds his most intolerable humiliation. For in turning Malvolio into a Stoic, Feste has endowed him with the nobility that he, Feste, has forfeited; this enraging recognition finally banishes his ability to fear the recoil of his vengeance. Come what may, he will reduce Malvolio from gentleman to 'goodman devil' (4.2.131). Having made Malvolio a Stoic, Feste means to make him, like himself, a failed Stoic. And in compelling him to demolish Malvolio's nobility, whatever the cost to himself, Feste's rage and wrath have finally driven him mad.

It is, thus, appropriate that what Feste exhibits in 5.1 is madness. For, being asked to read the letter he has helped Malvolio write, Feste malevolently imitates Malvolio's voice as that of a madman, his antics so far exasperating Olivia as to impel her to ask him, 'How now, art thou mad?' (5.1.293). Even in ordering Feste to 'read i' thy right wits' (5.1.297), Olivia cannot induce him to shed the voice of Malvolio's madness, thereby causing us to recognize that this insane voice has become his own. Thus, when Malvolio arrives on the scene to plead his wrongs, Feste has already impaired his standing with Olivia. And while Feste thus raves to Olivia's displeasure, Malvolio recounts his injuries with a dignity that impels her to make him 'the judge / Of thine own cause' (5.1.354–55). But, most ominously for Feste, Olivia addresses him in words that, even while branding him as a fool, convey pity: 'Alas, poor fool, how have they baffled thee!' (5.1.369). And by thus infuriating Feste to an uncontainable madness, Olivia's sympathy for Malvolio impels him to wreak his vengeance on the steward in the only way that will finally conquer him: that is, by forcing him to recognize Feste as the agent of his torment:

Why, 'some are born great, some achieve greatness, and some have greatness thrown upon them.' I was one, sir, in this interlude – one Sir Topas, sir, but that's all one. 'By the Lord, fool, I am not mad.' But do you remember? 'Madam, why laugh you at such a barren rascal? And you smile not, he's gagg'd.' And thus the whirligig of time brings in his revenges.  (5.1.370–7)

By thus citing the letter that had entrapped Malvolio, as well as his own anguished pleading with Feste in his disguise as Sir Topas, Feste reveals himself to his enemy as the one who has systematically exploited and punished his ambitious expectation of greatness. But, not only revealing himself as the destroyer of Malvolio's expectation, Feste also identifies his malice as payback for Malvolio's having insulted him as a 'barren rascal'. For, rather than the 'barren rascal' or stupid fool that Malvolio had taken him to be, Feste has shown himself clever enough to have made an even more abject fool of Malvolio than Malvolio had made of him. As Malvolio had exploited Feste's delusional – and thus inevitably failing – quest for an inner Stoic greatness to humiliate him, so Feste has used Malvolio's delusional – and thus inevitably failing – quest for an external greatness to humiliate him. As, in using the inevitable failure of Feste's delusional Stoicism to insult him, Malvolio had forced Feste to blame his humiliation on himself, so, in using Malvolio's delusional ambition to insult and injure him, Feste now forces Malvolio to blame his humiliation on himself. And as blaming himself had forced Feste to receive or internalize Malvolio's insults, thereby affirming their truth, so the recognition of having brought his misfortunes upon himself destroys the self-control through which Malvolio possesses his mind. Whereas 1.5 had shown Olivia instructing Malvolio that a gentleman displays his 'generous, guiltless, and ... free disposition' by taking 'those things for bird-bolts that you deem cannon-bullets' (1.5.91–3), recognizing himself as not 'guiltless' of his overthrow prevents Malvolio from taking Feste's 'cannon-bullets' for 'bird-bolts'. Rather as the accuracy of Malvolio's insults had incited Feste to the angry vengeance he is now wreaking, so the accuracy of Feste's insults goad Malvolio to the same self-abandoned rage that cries out for vengeance: 'I'll be reveng'd on the whole pack of you' (5.1.378). As Malvolio had driven Feste to vengeance, so Feste now drives Malvolio to vengeance. And as Malvolio had driven Feste to vengeance by driving him mad, so Feste drives Malvolio to vengeance by driving him mad. For, in demoting him to the plebian rank of 'goodman devil', Malvolio's angry cry for vengeance insinuates its recoil upon himself, by signalling that he is no longer fit to be Olivia's steward, and will thus be, like Feste, turned away from her house.

It thus appears that vengeance expels both Feste and Malvolio from Olivia's house, the grim effect of these expulsions being what Feste registers in the song he sings to conclude the play. Yet, rather than relating 'the wind and the rain' that he anticipates enduring to his vengeance, Feste's song appears to represent this recoiling vengeance as but the inevitable conclusion of a disastrous life. For the subject of the song that Feste sings is himself, beginning with the inception of his life as 'a little tiny boy' (5.1.389). Much like Jacques's seven stages of man, this song follows Feste's life from its initial stage of childhood to 'man's estate' (5.1.393), to coming 'alas, to wive' (5.1.397), and finally to coming in old age 'unto my beds' (5.1.401). What is common to these four stages of life, moreover, is the vice they all exhibit, which Feste sees himself as helpless to correct, their cumulative evils reinforcing his Stoic assertion in 1.5 that man cannot mend. For Feste obliquely represents his 'man's estate' as making him one of those 'knaves and thieves' against which 'men shut their gate' (5.1.395), just as his coming 'to wive' impeaches him for the 'swaggering' (5.1.399) that prevents him from thriving. And in observing of his old age that 'with toss-pots still had drunken heads' (5.1.403), Feste appears to represent drunkenness as its comparably persisting vice. In thus portraying his human condition as a sequence of incorrigible vices, Feste appears to be validating the vengeance he has just wreaked on Malvolio as likewise inevitable. For what Feste's vengeance attests above all is the impossibility of the ultimate mending that is forgiveness. What Feste appears to be saying in this song is that his Stoic ideology has rendered his vengeance an inevitability from whose deadly recoil nothing could have redeemed him – the only comfort emerging from his song being the Stoic suggestion that his death and damnation have been the common lot of man since that long distant time when 'the world begun' (5.1.405). Accepting his fate as that of an individual whom the Stoic cosmos deems unimportant, Feste ends the play by likewise deeming it unimportant: 'But that's all one, our play is done' (5.1.407). Thus concluding the play with his impending death, Feste endows it with tragic meaning, a meaning implicit in the recoil of a vengeance to which he has been compelled by the Stoicism he had trusted to set him free.

# SHAKESPEARE PERFORMANCES IN ENGLAND, 2018

## STEPHEN PURCELL, *London Productions*

Dividing this review into two sections for the first time this year made painfully evident just how much Shakespearian performance goes on in the capital. With Paul Prescott taking on reviewing duties for productions outside of London, and me confining myself to those performed within the bounds of the M25, we split the usual length of the *Survey* review equally between us. The smorgasbord of Shakespeare on offer within my geographical remit, combined with a particularly Shakespeare-heavy summer season at Shakespeare's Globe, meant that I ended up having to forgo a number of London-based productions: revivals were out, so I missed Filter's *A Midsummer Night's Dream* at the Lyric Hammersmith, and Jonathan Munby's *King Lear* in the West End; I was unable to attend a number of shows with shorter runs, such as Max Webster's *As You Like It* at Regent's Park and Paper Cinema's *Macbeth* at Battersea Arts Centre. This review would undoubtedly have been stronger and more representative of Shakespeare in London with their inclusion. Paul, of course, has also covered a handful of productions that ended up in London after opening elsewhere, not least the RSC's summer shows, which transferred to the Barbican in the autumn. These caveats aside, my full and stimulating year reviewing in London revealed some interesting tendencies in the capital's Shakespeare. Cross-casting in major roles and 50/50 gender splits in companies are now so usual as to be unremarkable; casts were generally racially diverse, and often disability-positive. All of these trends were especially evident at the Globe, where they are clearly now a matter of artistic policy. This also felt like a very political year in Shakespearian performance, with many productions

taking the opportunity to respond to the #metoo movement (the comedies in particular); Trump, Brexit and climate change were also in the mix, though perhaps to a lesser degree. I found myself especially struck by a tendency to rewrite or reframe Shakespearian plays, often in order to provide a more comforting or celebratory ending – I wonder if that, too, is a sign of the times.

## ALL'S WELL THAT ENDS WELL?

My reviewing year started at the Sam Wanamaker Playhouse, with the final Shakespearian production of Emma Rice's two-year tenure as the Globe's Artistic Director. The production was Caroline Byrne's *All's Well That Ends Well*, and it carried many of the hallmarks of Rice's artistic programme: a rewritten and restructured text, a folk-tale aesthetic, and a 50/50 gender split in the cast. The production's cross-gender casting allowed for some sharp commentary on gender performance. Imogen Doel's Paroles was a brilliant parody of toxic masculinity, swaggering, coldly charming and slightly predatory. His repartee about virginity with Helena (Ellora Torchia) was not an even-handed exchange between friends, but an intrusive attempt at seduction. It was funny but uncomfortable; when it became clear that Helena was not going to yield to him, he suddenly dropped his charming persona and became cold and aloof. The character's fragile pride had a powerful pay-off later on in the gulling sequence, as the Dumaine brothers and Bertram (all played by male actors) physically dominated the diminutive Paroles, baying laddishly at his humiliation. Paroles made a pitiful figure, blindfolded, his face streaked with black as if he had smeared his makeup with tears. This previously threatening character suddenly had his fragility exposed, sharing it for the first time with the audience. Bertram and the Dumaine brothers were turning against him in order to buttress their own sense of masculinity; in his cowardice, he had fallen short. The production's commentary on masculinity extended to the conventionally cast characters too: Bertram (Will Merrick) and Diana (Paige Carter) had a genuine sexual chemistry, and her willingness to go along with Helena's bed-trick seemed to be motivated by her anger that Bertram could have been so intimate with her while being unable to follow through on his promise of marriage. Left alone, she sounded angry as she said 'My mother told me just how he would woo' (4.2.70), prompting an audience laugh: she had thought better of him, and he had confirmed her worst fears. 'She says all men / Have the like oaths' (4.2.71–2), she continued, looking confrontationally at the laughers in the auditorium as if accusing the men there too.

For all this, the production was ultimately interested in reconciliation. Byrne and her dramaturg Annie Siddons had interposed a number of new, often wordless scenes, generally accompanied by music. The first, at the very start, was an image of death: Helena tending to the centre-stage tomb of the late Count Rossillion, as two ghoulish candle effigies of his death mask burned behind her. Before 2.3, a spell-like healing sequence showed the King (Nigel Cooke) descend into a candlelit bath inside the stage trap; magical chimes struck as Helena dropped in a powder and used her hands to swirl the water. Later, the Widow (Martina Laird) helped Helena into the same bath as she promised to restore the weary pilgrim to health. In both cases, the bath carried connotations of baptism and spiritual rebirth; the fact that Paroles's imprisonment was staged in the same part of the space suggested very strongly that his self-acceptance was a comparable process of renewal. Helena and Bertram's story, meanwhile, was reshaped to prefigure his change of heart in the final scene. On their first parting in 2.3, they almost kissed, but were maliciously interrupted by Paroles; later, another short scene was added in which Bertram read of Helena's apparent death and broke down in tears. Just before the final act, Diana and Mariana wound a scarf multiple times around Helena's waist to signify a pregnant belly, and upon their arrival at the King's court in 5.1, she was going into labour. This made sense of Diana's otherwise inexplicable delay in revealing the truth in the final scene: she was stalling as she waited for Helena to give birth, which would provide concrete proof of the consummation of Helena and Bertram's marriage. In a wonderful climactic moment, the central doors swung open to reveal Helena with her new-born child. The play concluded with a moving, wordless reconciliation between Helena and Bertram as the stage emptied. They consummated the kiss, at last, that had been interrupted so much earlier in the play, and she passed their baby to him. Finally, they each went to the two death-mask candles that had been burning since the start of the show and blew them out, symbolizing the play's movement from death to rebirth.

This emphasis on healing and renewal was shared by Cheek by Jowl's *Périclès, Prince de Tyr*, which visited the Barbican in April as part of its international tour. Directed by Declan Donnellan and performed by the company's French ensemble, the production reinvented *Pericles* as a play-within-a-play, the dreams of an unnamed hospital patient (Christophe Grégoire) recovering from a catastrophic illness that had left him bedbound and catatonic. All of the action took place within a startlingly blue modern hospital room; the production repeatedly switched between the fantasy of the inner play and the mundanities of the patient's real life, as his family and carers waited for him to recover. The patient took the role of Périclès and doubled in the smaller roles of Cléon and le Maître (Pander); while the title character's journey from trauma to recovery clearly mirrored the patient's own, the two minor characters seemed to represent repressed facets of the protagonist's personality, his weakness and his cruelty. The rest of the casting of the inner play drew entirely on characters present in the frame. These figures tended to be cast as roles that paralleled their 'real-life' relationship with the protagonist: his daughter (Valentine Catzéflis) as the daughters of Antiochus and Périclès; his wife (Camille Cayol) as the wives of the three characters played by the patient himself; the son-in-law as the outsiders who threatened the daughter characters (Antiochus, Léonin, Bout/ Boult and Lysimaque/Lysimachus); the doctor (Cécile Leterme) as the play's various helpers and healers, and the two nurses or orderlies as various minor characters and bystanders. The action of *Pericles* was thus strongly hinted to be a psychodrama in which the protagonist's unresolved issues – most notably, his possessiveness over his daughter and sexual resentment of his son-in-law – were played out.

The two frames intersected disorientingly throughout the production. Dialogue in the world of the frame was delivered in naturalistic mumbles, the quiet drone of a radio discussion programme in the background. With a snap of the lights and a change in the soundtrack, we would be switched suddenly into a world of high drama. The acting in the inner play was larger-than-life, leaning heavily on its myth-like qualities. All of the props were items from the hospital room: the patient's bed became Périclès's boat, his straitjacket the suit of armour. The patient emptied a bed pan over his head during the first storm scene, a metaphor for Périclès's powerlessness before overwhelming natural forces, and during his meeting with the fishermen they gave him a strip-wash, emphasizing his complete vulnerability. The sound design frequently suggested an underwater setting, implying a retreat into the protagonist's unconscious; indeed, sexual elements repeatedly crept into the fantasy scenes, Périclès and Thaïsa's dance to a gentle 1940s ballad, for example, starting out as a comical stag-and-deer courtship dance and quickly becoming borderline pornographic.

The frames began to converge towards the end, Lysimaque bringing Marina to Périclès's hospital bed where the latter lay catatonic, the medical staff functioning as medical attendants within both narratives at once. As Marina sang a snatch of the 1940s song to reawaken her father, the protagonist's wife stayed on the outside of the scene, patiently reading a magazine as we awaited Thaïsa's inevitable return. The narrative switched back into the inner narrative for Périclès's reunion with Thaïsa at Ephesus, and, as he took her hand, the lighting snapped back to the hospital frame even as the soundscape of waves and seagulls suggested we were still in Ephesus. The song from Pentapolis returned as the whole family were reunited, its lyrics coming poignantly into focus: 'J'attendrai / Le jour et la nuit, j'attendrai toujours / Ton retour' ('I will wait / Day and night, I will always await / Your return'). Happily dancing with Thaïsa, Périclès collapsed one last time and was guided back into his bed as the radio from the hospital frame faded back in. Now conscious and weeping, the patient looked around him in confusion as his wife and daughter embraced him.

If both of these productions shared a desire to find a unifying aesthetic tone in texts that might normally resist such a treatment, the same could not be said of Simon Dormandy's *Much Ado About Nothing* at the Rose Theatre, Kingston. Set in a modern luxury Sicilian hotel, the production opened with a tongue-in-cheek advertisement of the hotel's various amenities being interrupted by the news that Don Pedro was on his way; Leonato (David Rintoul), evidently the hotel owner, ordered an immediate shutdown, upon which an alarm blared, guests were evacuated and shutters descended. It soon became clear that Don Pedro (Peter Guinness) was a powerful Mafia boss. He arrived with an armed guard; the 'action' from which they had just returned was never explained, but it was clearly both illegal and violent. This Don Pedro expected (and largely commanded) unquestioning obedience from everyone around him. His easy assurances to Claudio that Hero would be his – before either Hero or her father had been consulted about the matter – exposed his unassailable sense of entitlement. This extended to Claudio too, played by Calam Lynch as a young misogynist prone to unpredictable outbursts of rage (he had no time for Beatrice's jesting, for example, snapping at her in

2.1). As Kate Lamb's Hero prepared for her marriage in 3.4, she seemed to be having a panic attack, displacing her anxieties about marrying a psychopath she barely knew onto her choice of wedding dress. Her fears were not unreasonable: there was a strong implication in the jilting scene that the women in this world were subject at all times to the threat of unexpected masculine violence. Claudio pushed Hero violently back towards her father; even Leonato pulled a gun on his daughter.

This deeply disturbing presentation of the play's power relationships was rather undercut by the production's take on the leading roles. As Benedick and Beatrice, John Hopkins and Mel Giedroyc were charming, funny and exuberant, refugees from a sunnier and more benevolent production. Both of the gulling scenes were played for belly laughs: 2.3 added Stewart Wright's Dogberry as the underling whom Benedick sends to fetch a book (2.3.3–4), creating new opportunities for comedy when Dogberry returned with the book later in the scene while Benedick was trying to stay hidden. For Beatrice's eavesdropping scene, the clowning was ratcheted up a notch, with Beatrice getting into a fight with an uncooperative sound and lighting console, and engaging in some deeply silly physical comedy (with the aid of a body double) under a trestle table. While this was very funny, it produced one of the first moments of real tonal uncertainty in the show. As Hero exited, she delivered the line 'Some Cupid kills with arrows, some with traps' (3.1.106) sadly, as if she felt the latter applied to her – she had been trapped by powerful men into consenting to a marriage she did not really want. Giedroyc played Beatrice's final soliloquy sincerely, and its last couplet had been altered, so that where Shakespeare's Beatrice believes in Benedick's merit 'better than reportingly' (3.1.116), this version of the character could only 'Confess it is a truth I can't deny'. This downbeat ending rang true for both characters, but was a sudden and somewhat jarring change of gear after the frothiness of the comedy that had preceded it.

As throughout, the performance ended on an uneven note. Claudio kicked off again as Benedick admitted he 'did think to have beaten thee' (5.4.108), squaring up to his former friend and offering a very tangible cudgelling; Benedick's 'Come, come, we are friends' (5.4.116) sounded more like an aspiration than an accurate description. Don Pedro was about to go offstage to execute his brother before Benedick suggested deferring punishment until 'tomorrow' (5.4.126), but as soon as Benedick was happily distracted by the dance, Don Pedro cocked his gun and walked off grimly anyway. The production had strongly hinted that Hero was trapped in a marriage she did not want, and that Claudio was an unreformed misogynist psychopath – but it ended on a celebratory note nonetheless. I could not help but feel something a bit more radical was in order here – a darker ending, perhaps, that acknowledged that the violent, unjust world in which the play had been set would go on doing its damage.

This was not an issue for Josie Rourke's *Measure for Measure*, which opened at the Donmar Warehouse in October. Rourke's adaptation – the last Shakespearian production of her seven-year stint as Artistic Director – complicated the problem of this 'problem play', asking what would happen to its ethical contours if the genders of its protagonists were switched. Thus, the production played through a very heavily cut version of the play twice, once in Renaissance dress with fairly conventional casting, and then a second time in modern dress with Angelo and Isabella switched, Isabella becoming the Duke's corrupt deputy and Angelo a young man entering a religious retreat called The Cloister (Figure 29).

The first half was a compelling (though largely unsurprising) rendering of the play's central storyline. Jack Lowden's Angelo was confident in his authority, casually turning his back on subjects whom he considered beneath his dignity to honour with undue attention. As he propositioned Hayley Atwell's Isabella, her dilemma felt horribly contemporary; there were audience gasps at 'Who will believe thee, Isabel?' (2.4.154). Atwell made a thoughtful, vulnerable Isabella, searching the audience for answers as she asked 'To whom should I complain?' (2.4.171); later, she would

29 *Measure for Measure*, 2.2 (second version), Donmar Warehouse, directed by Josie Rourke. Jack Lowden as Angelo and Hayley Atwell as Isabella. Photograph by Manuel Harlan.

scrutinize Mariana's face as she weighed up whether or not to kneel for Angelo's life, trying to read there what it was that was making Mariana plead for the man who had wronged them both so egregiously. When, in the closing lines of the first half, Nicholas Burns's coolly authoritarian Duke presented himself to Isabella as her future husband, she doubled over and screamed furiously at him. The lights blacked out, and the rear wall of the stage came to life in a psychedelic extravaganza of coloured light; when the lights came back up, Isabella was in modern dress, and the play began anew.

It was thus possible to read what followed as Isabella's own fantasy of revenge against the men who had trapped her. But, while the second half was evidently a replay of sorts, copying some of the staging of the first, it was not a straight swap. Deputy Isabella was a woman in a man's world:

where Adam McNamara's Provost had been meekly obedient to Angelo in the first half, for example, in the second half the same character was huffily insubordinate to his new boss, openly scornful of her authority. Novice Angelo, entering a retreat rather than making a lifetime vow, was also much more empowered than his Isabella counterpart. Where she had been nervous and fidgety in her first interview with the Deputy, he went into the equivalent scene with huge confidence, snatching her folder and mobile from her and handling her resistance with calm assurance. In their second meeting, where novice Isabella had been bullied and sexually assaulted, novice Angelo was *seduced*. In the first half, Deputy Angelo had sat on a downstage bench and pulled the petrified Isabella towards him, caressing her intimately while she flinched at the violation. This stage picture was mirrored with a twist in the second half, when Deputy Isabella approached the seated Angelo, lifting his hands to her body and awakening his sexual desire; once she had aroused him, she pulled away, enjoying her power to manipulate a young man into *choosing* to abandon his vow of chastity. For his part, novice Angelo seemed just as angry at his own weak will as he was at Isabella's indecent proposal, and repeated 'More than our brother is our chastity' (2.4.185) several times at the end of the scene almost as a mantra, desperate to convince himself.

The most striking difference was in the replacement of the first half's Mariana (Helena Wilson) with a male counterpart, Frederick (Ben Allen). Where Mariana had been an outcast in the power structures of Renaissance Vienna, her reputation ruined after her abandonment by Angelo, Frederick was, according to Rourke's edit, a 'merchant, whose cargo, some five years since, miscarried at sea'[1] – financially ruined, maybe, but not cast adrift in the same way. Like Mariana, Frederick's love for the Deputy was 'violent and unruly' (3.1.245), but this description has very different implications when it refers to a man's feelings about a woman. Frederick's sense of entitlement as a man in 2018 was of a different order from Mariana's – she had a certain legal dependence on Angelo, whereas he had merely an emotional claim on Isabella. There was something much uglier in this. In the second half, three men (the Duke, Angelo and Frederick) conspired to sexually entrap the only powerful woman in their society. Frederick and Angelo lost no time in publicly humiliating Deputy Isabella, sending what was presumably a video of her in the throes of orgasm to the mobile phones of virtually all the characters on stage; unsettlingly, there was scattered (though by no means unanimous) audience laughter at this moment.

*Measure for Measure* – in the context of this production, the title could be taken to imply that the two halves were somehow equal, the crimes of the two Deputies commensurate. Read through this lens, the production is open to charges of false equivalence: in a year in which the phrase 'believe women' resonated loudly across political discourse,

was it not irresponsible of Rourke to present a hypothetical scenario in which believing the only woman involved was precisely the wrong course of action? Some commentators found it inexcusable that, opening just days after the hearing into the sexual assault allegations against US Supreme Court nominee Brett Kavanaugh, the production staged a scene in which Deputy Isabella demonstrated to novice Angelo how easily she could pretend to be an emotional victim of sexual assault herself.[2] I was not so sure; it seemed to me that Rourke was offering the juxtaposition of the two halves in order to demonstrate how the gender-flipped scenario was not, in the end, comparable with the first. Switching the genders, I felt, *still* made the play a study of the insidious workings of patriarchy.

Over at the Young Vic, *Twelfth Night* was Kwame Kwei-Armah's first production as the theatre's new Artistic Director. Conceived by Kwei-Armah and composer Shaina Taub, and co-directed with Oskar Eustis, this musical adaptation of the play was a reimagining of the same team's 2016 Shakespeare in the Park production in New York. Where that production had celebrated its own home town, this one was reinvented as a tribute to London – especially, according to Kwei-Armah's programme notes, 'Caribbean culture, and the diversity that this city is so proud to represent'. Thus, a stunning *trompe l'oeil* set depicted a London street, primary-coloured terraced houses stretching off into the distance and international flag bunting criss-crossing the road. The Notting Hill carnival and its connotations of community and diversity were clearly being invoked: before the show, a group of more than twenty supernumeraries were dancing in the street, playing ball games, and handing out party food in the auditorium. This community chorus of non-

---

[1] *Measure for Measure*, ed. Josie Rourke (London and New York, 2018), p. 111.

[2] See, for example, Peter Kirwan, 'Measure for Measure @ The Donmar Warehouse', The Bardathon, 30 September 2018, http://blogs.nottingham.ac.uk/bardathon/2018/09/30/measure-for-measure-the-donmar-warehouse.

professionals – appropriately diverse in terms of age, ethnicity and body type – was apparently drawn from 'friends and neighbours' of the Young Vic.

While the production's spoken dialogue was generally from Shakespeare's play, Taub's songs were a much looser adaptation, modern in style and playfully intertextual. 'I've seen myself from both sides now', sang Gabrielle Brooks's Viola, with a nod to Joni Mitchell; the chorus listed the characters who were 'crazy in love', the melody briefly following Beyoncé's. 'Play On', the feel-good and funny opening number, emphasized the ways in which various characters were 'playing on' through their pain. Viola's 'willow cabin' speech was reinvented as a love song, 'If You Were My Beloved', which had such a powerful effect on Olivia (Natalie Dew) that she picked it up immediately after Viola's exit; the number concluded as a lovely trio between Orsino (Rupert Young), Olivia and Viola, each of them separately and privately expressing their unrequited love, in perfect harmony. Viola's sung soliloquy in 2.1 raised some of the questions that this production otherwise toyed with in only a rather jokey way; 'Is this costume getting me wrong', she asked, 'Or letting loose what's been in me all along?': 'Was the old me only a costume too? / Who am I besides how I look to you?' Indeed, Viola's motivation for remaining in disguise overlapped with the production's concern for the politics of representation: 'I feel so *seen* as a guy.' At the end, she reprised this song, explaining to Sebastian (Jyuddah Jaymes) that adopting his costume had given her strength but allowed her to recognize that 'Maybe the man I tried to be is the girl I always was.'

Where the songs in Shakespeare's text are about mortality and the slipping away of youth, here the focus shifted to something more straightforwardly joyful. 'O Mistress Mine' was replaced with a fun waltz, in which each character in turn – culminating, of course, with Malvolio – was told 'You're the worst' (Figure 30). This was a production very much on the side of 'cakes and ale': there was no real cruelty to Sir Toby's treatment of Malvolio here, which amounted to little more than shutting him in

a van for a few minutes. Malvolio was played by Gerard Carey as a gloriously vain caricature, hyper-British, prissy and moustached. As so often with this part, the party pooper turned out to be the most theatrically entertaining figure onstage: here, his conceited patter song 'Count Malvolio' slipped into a showstopping tap dance number that made my face ache from grinning. Where Shakespeare's play ends on a melancholic note, reminding us that 'the rain it raineth every day', Kwei-Armah and Taub's musical finished with a new song about the importance of empathy. Loose ends were easily dispensed with: upon learning that she had married not Cesario but Sebastian, Olivia simply shrugged and sang 'You're lovely and free / So, hey, that works for me', and there was little sense that Malvolio's pride had been very seriously wounded by the events of the play, his exiting vow of revenge replaced with a sniffy 'I hope you're all very happy together.' It would be easy to gripe that the production was a bit lightweight and uncomplicated, but ultimately it set out with a clear idea of what it wanted from Shakespeare – exuberance, inclusivity, diversity, popular appeal – and more than achieved it. A party of schoolchildren near me clearly loved it, erupting with a huge cheer as Viola and Orsino finally embraced, and one of them was visibly weeping with joy by the end. Shakespearian theatre could do a lot worse.

## POLITICAL TRAGEDIES

Another 2018 Shakespearian debut took place further along the South Bank. Nicholas Hytner's *Julius Caesar* was the second-ever production at the new Bridge Theatre, and the first Shakespearian one. With galleries encircling the acting area, and a large pit full of standing spectators, the Bridge had been reconfigured for this production into something closely resembling an Elizabethan public playhouse (though by the magic of modern technology, there were multiple platform stages that were raised and lowered as necessary). As the audience entered, a rock band was playing at a pro-Caesar rally, into which the standing spectators were co-opted as attendees. The band was charismatic and energetic, playing well-known songs like 'Eye of the Tiger' and

30 *Twelfth Night*, 2.3, Young Vic, directed by Kwame Kwei-Armah and Oskar Eustis. Melissa Allan as Feste, Gbemisola Ikumelo as Maria, Martyn Ellis as Sir Toby Belch, Gerard Carey as Malvolio, Silas Wyatt-Barke as Sir Andrew Aguecheek, and others. Photograph by Johan Persson.

'Seven Nation Army' (both songs with populist political connotations), and encouraging the audience to sing, dance and clap along. At one point, David Morrissey's Mark Antony came out to help whip up the crowd. This was then interrupted midflow by Flavius and Marullus. The sense of the audience's fun being ruined was palpable; encouraged by the band to boo the tribunes, many of the standing spectators obliged. Asked 'Knew you not Pompey?', a band member replied 'Pompey's dead!' before his bandmates joined in, in unison, 'Get over it!' as if it were a well-known political rejoinder ('You lost – get over it!' was, of course, a popular 'Leaver' riposte to 'Remoaners' following the 2016 Brexit referendum). In 1.2, David Calder's Caesar emerged onto a central platform to greet the crowd; he wore a leather jacket and a red baseball cap, which he tossed into the mob with a gigantic

smile. Despite the creative team's repeated insistences that they did not see Caesar as a Trump figure, the costume was clearly inviting the parallel, and this was augmented by the character's childish sense of his own exceptionalism, and his palpable enjoyment of his own myth.[3]

There was more than a hint of popular narratives about both Brexit and Trump here: Antony and Caesar as populist rabble-rousers versus an out-of-touch and complacent 'liberal elite'.[4] Ben

---

[3] See, for example, Nicholas Hytner's piece on the production for the *Guardian*, 25 January 2018, or Michelle Fairley's interview with the *Evening Standard*, 31 January 2018.

[4] This phrase was used in relation to Brutus in Matthew d'Ancona's essay for the programme; Hytner also wrote a piece for the *Guardian* referring to the conspirators as the 'liberal establishment' (see above).

Whishaw's Brutus was evidently a well-known intellectual, signing a copy of his book for a fan on his first appearance in 1.2; 2.1 was set in his study, the floor and desk strewn with well-thumbed paperbacks. This Brutus was very much the academic, delivering his lines with gestures that suggested precision and fine distinctions. He was a political theorist, an intellectual radical; as the assassination plot developed, he seemed both excited and nervous to be putting his theory into practice. His confidence that 'We shall be called purgers, not murderers' (2.1.180) seemed scarily naïve, his faith in the people's capacity and will-ingness to follow his reasoning horribly misguided. Both he and Michelle Fairley's Cassius seemed literally out of touch with the groundlings, speaking their soliloquies not direct to the audience but in a kind of self-reflexive limbo, as if they were debating themselves, or rehearsing their arguments.

Several key roles were re-gendered. There was a sexist dimension to Caesar's rejection of Cassius: 'Let me have *men* about me', he said, clearly intending her to hear, pausing slightly before adding ' . . . that are *fat*' (1.2.193). It was significant in this respect that four of the six conspirators who came to Brutus's house were women. When a female Cassius, speaking to a female Casca (Adjoa Andoh), referred to Caesar as 'A man no mightier than thyself or me / In personal action' (1.3.75–6), there was a sense that a point about gender inequality was being made. But these women also faced prejudice from their own side: there were strong hints that Brutus undervalued their advice on Cicero and on Antony in 2.1 at least in part because of their gender, and an undercurrent of sexism in the later quarrel scene between Brutus and Cassius. 'Shall I be frighted when a madwoman stares?' (4.2.94), he asked rhetorically during their argument, and even after their reconciliation he refused to listen to her warnings against marching to Philippi, insisting that 'Good reasons must of force give place to better' (4.2.255) with the air of an academic airing an abstract proposition. As Cassius allowed herself to be overruled – clearly against her own better

judgement – Trebonius (Abraham Popoola) sunk his head into his hands, despondently.

The production achieved a great deal of its impact from its immersive elements. For Caesar's assassination, the space was reconfigured as a gigantic flight of steps leading to Caesar's throne, the groundlings standing either side of it (Figure 31). The conspirators shot Caesar from the bottom of the steps, and those of us who were standing were immediately shouted at by the production's many supernumeraries, here playing security guards, to 'Get down!' Most of the crowd immediately obliged, crouching on the floor, though one or two conspicuously remained standing. The production's crowd-wranglers returned in other guises throughout the production, shouting interjections and goading spectators during the funeral speeches, herding several hundred of us to 'make a ring about the corpse of Caesar' (3.2.159), and shepherding us every which way in the ensuing chaos. The effect from within the crowd was utter confusion and not a little discomfort, bumping into one another and treading on toes; I imagine that, from the galleries, the effect must have been a spectacular image of political unrest. In the climactic battle scenes, we were herded aggressively once again, this time by soldiers carrying automatic weapons. Sudden flashes of light illuminated the darkness around us as gunfire and shouting broke out; smoke, the smell of gunpowder, and the sensation of an ash-like substance falling from above made it a truly multisensory experience. While I enjoyed the thrillingly realistic effects of this, I found myself troubled by the ethics of the production's deliberate encouragement of physical jostling and disorientation among its standing spectators, not least because I suspected that the effects of this were best appreciated from the galleries above (and, of course, via the NT Live broadcast). Coercing an audience so close to London Bridge into play-acting these scenarios only months after an actual terror attack in the same location also seemed more than a little insensitive.

The National Theatre staged four Shakespeare productions in 2018: Artistic Director Rufus Norris's *Macbeth*, Simon Godwin's *Antony and Cleopatra*, Justin Audibert's one-hour adaptation

31 *Julius Caesar*, 3.1, Bridge Theatre, directed by Nicholas Hytner. David Calder as Julius Caesar. Photograph by Manuel Harlan.

of *The Winter's Tale* for young audiences (directed by Ruth Mary Johnson) and Emily Lim's large-scale community production of *Pericles*. My schedule meant I was able to see only the first two in this list. Norris's *Macbeth*, his first Shakespeare at the theatre, was set in a murky post-apocalyptic wasteland in which the sun never shone. This seemed to be a world much like our own, perhaps a few years in our future, where civilization had fallen to ruin because of some unnamed catastrophic event. Characters wore ragged, dirty clothes that seemed to have been salvaged from another time: Macbeth's and Banquo's armour, for example, was improvised from scraps held together with parcel tape. The castle was little more than a ruin, Macbeth and his wife (Rory Kinnear and Anne-Marie Duff) living out of suitcases in a concrete bunker. Whenever Duncan's soldiers entered a scene, they gave an animalistic hoot to identify themselves, and all of them seemed to be armed with machetes. This was clearly a dangerous world, full of potential for ambush, invasion and cruelty: Malcolm (Parth Thakerar) made his first appearance following his rescue from captivity with his arm in a sling, his fingers bloodied and mangled as if by torture. The social collapse that had produced this world was evidently still in living memory. The two murderers (Alana Ramsey and Joshua Lacey), a down-on-their-luck twenty-something couple, reacted with cries of nostalgic delight when Macbeth offered them two unopened cans of pop as payment for the murder of Banquo; the woman opened hers immediately, while her partner fingered his as if it were a priceless piece of treasure. When she admitted to being 'one . . . / Whom the vile blows and buffets of the world / Have so incensed that I am reckless what / I do to spite the world' (3.1.109–12), it seemed to express the lurking danger of the society depicted: having lost nearly everything, almost everyone had become desensitized to violence. A thin line separated this pale imitation of civilization from complete lawlessness – Macbeth's worries about Duncan's murder were not religious but social in nature, and his anxiety that his 'Bloody instructions' might 'return / To plague th'inventor' (1.7.9–10) seemed entirely sensible. Another total collapse could be only one more betrayal away.

The production strongly suggested that whatever had happened to society had already deeply damaged our protagonists. In a subtle change to the standard text, Macbeth referred to his 'blackened deep desires' (1.4.51), implying damage and decay rather than innate evil. Lady Macbeth especially was evidently traumatized by the loss of their child, gasping with horror as she realized the necessity of calling upon the 'murd'ring ministers' (1.5.47) whose terrible effects she seemed to know first-hand. Later, when Macbeth urged her to 'Bring forth men-children only' (1.7.72), he tenderly stroked her womb and she nodded sadly at the implied memory. Their relationship deteriorated over the course of the play, Macbeth becoming hostile, sarcastic and cruel as she started to collapse. Moments before her death, we saw her contorted with guilt inside their bunker, as the stage revolved to show Macbeth outside, responding to the sound of her scream within as if trying to convince himself he was beyond caring – 'I have supped full with horrors' (5.5.13), he insisted, perhaps speaking for most of the characters in this production. But over the course of the speech in which he reacted to the news of her death, the stage revolved again, and he entered the room and cradled her corpse, his nihilism becoming legible as not an absence of emotion but a result of it. Later, his own final words were reinvented: on the verge of winning his climactic combat with Macduff, the witches cried 'Hold!', and Macbeth, distracted by them, was stabbed by his enemy, dying with a resigned 'Enough' (5.10.34).

Where Norris's *Macbeth* was unfairly savaged by the critics, Godwin's *Antony and Cleopatra* was a hit, garnering multiple five-star reviews and winning the 2018 *Evening Standard* Theatre Awards for Best Actress and Best Actor. The production opened with a tableau of the final scene, Cleopatra's body downstage, her handmaidens dead on the monument (Figure 32). Tunji Kasim's Caesar stood on the steps, speaking the eulogy to the title characters that concludes Shakespeare's play (5.2.350–60). At the bottom of the steps, a woman in military uniform – who we would later learn was Agrippa (Katy Stephens) – turned to the audience to object to this romanticized posthumous characterization with a vehement 'Nay'. Explaining that 'this dotage of our General's / O'erflowed the measure' (1.1.1–2), she went on to deliver Philo's opening speech in the past tense, concluding by inviting us to 'behold and see' (1.1.13). This was not an impartial observer; as she referred to Cleopatra in racist derogatory terms ('tawny front … gipsy's lust', 1.1.6,10), Agrippa indicated the corpse before her with contempt. The production was thus framed with narration that explicitly provoked the audience to make a judgement on the title characters, while distancing us from the unsympathetic reading given voice by Agrippa.

As this speech concluded, the set revolved to reveal a sun-drenched Alexandrian courtyard, ornate turquoise-tiled walls and sun loungers around a large ornamental pool. Cleopatra's body remained stationary on the forestage, her prone form recontextualized by the change of setting: no longer dead, now merely sunbathing on the floor, to be immediately awoken by the amorous Antony. Where Egypt was a space of luxury, curves and colour, Rome was square and flat, its walls a washed-out marble and its forms hard and unyielding. Ralph Fiennes's Antony seemed deeply uncomfortable in the latter, fidgeting in his chair while the composed, urbane Octavius sat easily in his. Comfortably at home in Alexandria, he was a fish out of water in Rome: a politician with the lolloping, shambolic air of a washed-up Boris Johnson, casually admitting to his drunken

32 *Antony and Cleopatra*, 5.2/Prologue, National Theatre, Olivier Theatre, directed by Simon Godwin. Various characters, including Sophie Okonedo as Cleopatra, Katy Stephens as Agrippa, Georgia Landers as Iras, Gloria Obianyo as Charmian, and Tunji Kasim as Caesar. Photograph by Johan Persson.

behaviour in Egypt with an apologetic tilt of a tumbler of brandy. Antony seemed almost always to have a drink in his hand, and Fiennes's performance hinted strongly at an addictive personality: he resolved to return to Cleopatra, admitting to the audience that 'i'th' East my pleasure lies' (2.3.38) with the weary but unapologetic air of a man who feels he has no agency in such a decision. And one could see why he wanted to return. Where many of his fellow Romans viewed him with undisguised scorn, Sophie Okonedo's Cleopatra worshipped him. His mythologized self-image was completely dependent on her for its sustainability – hence his fury when she failed to reflect it back to him. Okonedo's Cleopatra was also battling deep-seated insecurities, her theatrical flourishes and wry humour barely hiding a fidgety nervousness. Her anxieties that Antony might fail to return to her were urgent and real: at times, she seemed unsure of the depth of his love for her, and at others she seemed terrified by the prospect of his death (in 2.5, for example, she seemed to be expecting news of his death when the messenger arrived). At the end, as Antony died a slow, unheroic death, she continued to see something glorious.

Contrasting views of the title characters were embodied in the augmented roles of Agrippa and Octavia. Agrippa was the only professional woman in the distinctly masculine world of Rome. When Tim McMullan's slightly seedy Enobarbus delivered his rhapsodic description of Cleopatra in 2.2, Agrippa sat transfixed as she listened, her looks slowly darkening as she realized the extent of Cleopatra's magnetism. Her interjections – 'O, rare for Antony!', 'Rare Egyptian!' and 'Royal wench!' (2.2.212, 225, 233) – were clearly not intended as compliments, each becoming more disdainful than the last, and she concluded 'Now Antony / Must leave her utterly' (2.2.239–40) with a kind of Puritanical satisfaction. When Enobarbus demurred, explaining that 'Other women cloy / The appetites they feed, but she makes hungry / Where most she satisfies' (2.2.242–4), Agrippa visibly slumped, wounded at Enobarbus's implied dismissal of her own sexuality. Hannah Morrish's Octavia, meanwhile, was given an extended character arc by her inclusion in Caesar's

military party during the final two acts. If this ran the risk of making the campaign seem like her own vendetta against Antony, this was undercut by having her replace Dolabella in the final scene, bringing Antony's two wives face to face. Where one might have expected a scene of rivalry and recrimination (as in, for example, Dryden's imagining of the same scenario in *All for Love*), here it was touching for its understated compassion. Cleopatra was vulnerable and childlike, looking slightly lost, her legs dangling over the edge of her monument; she claimed, perhaps disingenuously, not to know who Octavia was. As Cleopatra described her lover in the most hyperbolically heroic terms, the central idea of the production came to a head:

CLEOPATRA Think you there was, or might be, such a man
As this I dreamt of?
OCTAVIA Gentle madam, no.

(5.2.92–3)

Neither woman was lying – both were describing, with sadness, their different perceptions of the dead man. Octavia seemed moved by her rival's expression of an overwhelming love that she had never felt herself.

SHAKESPEARE'S GLOBE

This year saw a number of landmark Shakespearian productions for artistic directors of London theatres. Perhaps the highest-profile debut was that of Michelle Terry, whose inaugural season as Artistic Director of Shakespeare's Globe opened in May. The controversy surrounding the departure of her predecessor Emma Rice meant that there was some pressure on Terry to prove that the Globe would not be retreating to a more conservative artistic programme. As it turned out, this was far from the case: Terry programmed a season that not only continued Rice's rule of a 50/50 gender split in (nearly) every cast, but was also radically actor-centred in a way that built on and extended the ensemble-based ethos established under the theatre's first Artistic Director, Mark Rylance. Thus, the first two shows of the season were performed by the same company of twelve actors, who had rehearsed them with two directors, Federay Holmes and Elle While. As many decisions as possible were made collaboratively in the rehearsal room, with no single individual in control.[5] The ensemble-based approach meant that actors were afforded the creative freedom to make new choices at each performance, so the productions as I saw them on Press Day may have been very different from the performances later in the run. Both productions were cast gender-, age- and race-blind (more or less), and performed on a bare stage without any set dressing or extensions to the thrust. Terry herself, an actor rather than a director, was a member of the ensemble, and while she took the lead role in *Hamlet*, she played a trio of much smaller roles in *As You Like It*. The ensemble comprised a mix of artists from the Globe's various eras, including actors who first played there under each of the three previous artistic directors, alongside some newcomers.

Ellan Parry's costumes for both productions were deliberately anachronistic, incorporating Elizabethan doublets, hoses, farthingales and ruffs, nineteenth-century frock coats and hats, and modern hoodies, woolly hats and sneakers. Parry's design was engaging with the Globe's own history, raiding its store of past costumes in the same way that the ensemble was assembling actors from across the various eras of the organization's history: at one point, for example, Jack Laskey's Rosalind wore the same outfit as Ganymede that Naomi Frederick, his co-star in the theatre's 2009 *As You Like It*, had worn then. In *As You Like It*, Pearce Quigley's Jaques was the most obviously anachronistic figure, wearing a modern black velvet suit and white trainers. Playing mischievously with the presence of the audience and ad-libbing in mockery of the text, he seemed a very liminal figure, on the edge not just of the exiled court but of the play itself. In *Hamlet*, meanwhile, the costumes set up a distinction between the characters from Elsinore and those from elsewhere: where Claudius's court and guards tended to wear Elizabethan clothing, Hamlet, Horatio and the Players seemed to have stepped straight out of the twenty-first century, as if Wittenberg and the theatre

represented a modern challenge to Elsinore's more archaic ways of thinking about one's place in the world. Significantly, Hamlet's own costume choices started to reach back in time as he began to embrace his role as revenger.

The productions' gender-blind casting tended to create an effect whereby the disjunction between actor and role slipped in and out of focus. In *As You Like It*, the gender-blind casting worked against the essentialism of the text, distancing the production from Rosalind's various generalizations about stereotypically masculine or feminine behaviour. Laskey's Rosalind was a gender-fluid figure, slipping from masculine to feminine throughout the show in a Russian doll of gender performances, a male actor playing a female character in an androgynous disguise as a boy-playing-a-woman, seductively unzipping a rose-embroidered cardigan as she urged Orlando (played here by Bettrys Jones, a female actor) to woo her. References to gender in both plays tended to provoke audible responses from spectators: when James Garnon's Claudius, for example, accused Terry's Hamlet of 'unmanly grief' (1.2.94), there was a darkly ironic murmur of audience laughter, and a similar sound could be heard as Hamlet himself declared with his female voice, 'frailty, thy name is woman!' (1.2.146). As a woman, Terry was able to embody Hamlet's more misogynistic moments without running the risk of appearing to endorse them; her Hamlet repeatedly invaded Ophelia's body and personal space in a sexually aggressive and sometimes downright violent way.

Terry's casting also helped to emphasize the character's youth and vulnerability. This was a Hamlet full of adolescent rage, with a petulant defiance of authority figures. He was already in a state of extreme emotion on his first appearance; all it took was to hear the word 'seems' from his mother to bring him to the point of tears, and his first speech was open and impassioned. Diminutive,

---

5 For details of this process, see Bridget Minamore, '"It's an eight-way tug of war!": Why has Shakespeare's Globe put everyone in charge?' *Guardian*, 16 May 2018.

and with a higher-pitched voice than most men, he looked tiny when he was left alone onstage, dwarfed by the architecture, physically withdrawn and unconfident, crying out 'God … God … ' (1.2.132) as if calling out for a benevolent, all-seeing figure whose existence he was beginning to question. He delivered most of the speech beginning 'O all you host of heaven' (1.5.92–110) – usually a soliloquy – with the Ghost still onstage, clinging to his father's arm and refusing to let him depart (Figure 33); Colin Hurley played the Ghost as an unusually human figure, shaking his head with sadness as his son got caught up in anger. Tellingly, it was only when Hamlet was distracted by his thoughts of his mother that he let go his hold, allowing his father's spirit to slink away unnoticed. Later, in 3.4, as Hamlet was tearing into Gertrude,

the Ghost re-entered and quietly embraced his son, draining him of his rage and making him go limp.

One of the most exciting aspects of these productions was their inclusive attitude towards disability. Deaf actor Nadia Nadarajah's use of sign language was incorporated beautifully into both productions. All her lines as Celia were signed, most of them without verbal speech, though Rosalind occasionally acted as her translator. Gestural by its nature, sign language is of course highly theatrical, and seeing Rosalind sign as she spoke emphasized just how physical many of Shakespeare's images are in this play ('I prithee, take the cork out of thy mouth, that I may drink thy tidings', 3.2.198–9). It was playful, too: when Celia mimed shooting an arrow in her description of Orlando as a hunter (3.2.240), Rosalind leapt across the stage so that she could be 'hit' by it

33 *Hamlet*, 1.5, Shakespeare's Globe, Globe Theatre, directed by Federay Holmes and Elle While. Colin Hurley as the Ghost and Michelle Terry as Hamlet. Photograph by Tristram Kenton.

34 *As You Like It*, 3.2, Shakespeare's Globe, Globe Theatre, directed by Federay Holmes and Elle While. Jack Laskey as Rosalind and Nadia Nadarajah as Celia. Photograph by Tristram Kenton.

(Figure 34). The use of sign language characterized numerous characters' relationships with Celia: Rosalind's near-constant signing with and for her cousin created a strong impression of their bond; her own father (Helen Schelsinger) was casual and half-hearted in his use of it; Oliver (Shubham Saraf), unable to converse with her upon their first meeting, attempted to learn it straight away, conveying their instant connection. The same was true in *Hamlet*, in which Nadarajah played Guildenstern. Rosencrantz (Quigley) served as Guildenstern's translator; Richard Katz's Polonius made awkward, inexpert attempts to sign despite evidently having no ability to do so (his sign for 'Hamlet' was a gesture of a crying toddler rubbing his eyes). Hamlet signed with his friends on their first meeting, but began to neglect to as he lost patience with them, and by 3.2 he was aggressively

forcing Guildenstern to lip-read him, even at one point grabbing his friend's face – prompting Horatio (Catrin Aaron) to turn away in disappointment.

One of the primary reasons to keep a production loose and unblocked in a space like the Globe is presumably to allow actors the space to react to the vagaries of audience response and outdoor performance. I am not sure, when I saw the productions on Press Day, that most of the cast yet had the necessary confidence to do this. James Garnon was a notable exception, responding to audience reactions as if they were simply part of the worlds of the plays. During his soliloquy as Claudius in 3.3, he seemed to be asking his questions of the spectators in the yard: 'but, O, what form of prayer / Can serve my turn?' he pleaded, before launching into an over-performed prayer of 'Forgive me my foul

299

murder!' (3.3.51–2). Unconvinced by his his-trionics, he dropped the act and quipped at the yard, 'That cannot be', pausing for laughter before explaining, 'since I am still possessed / Of those effects for which I did the murder' (3.3.53–4). Later, as a plane flew overhead, he yelled at it as if it represented his rapidly departing hopes of salva-tion. Terry seemed to be attempting something similar as Hamlet, pausing for a long time after 'Am I a coward?' (2.2.573), for example, as if awaiting an answer; she asked the question 'To be or not to be?' (3.1.58) to the audience very simply, and offered her answers almost conversationally. I got the impression that in both speeches she was aiming for, but not quite achieving, a more sincere back-and-forth between Hamlet and the auditor-ium, and it seems that later in the run she estab-lished this more fully. An account on Twitter of the 7 July performance noted that Terry used precisely these moments to make contact with one particular groundling, taking her hand as the spectator con-firmed with a 'yes' that Hamlet was 'a coward', and returning to the same woman later in the show to ask 'To be, or not to be?'[6] When the woman replied 'To be', Hamlet apparently confirmed with a wag of the finger, 'That is the question'; later in the speech, he referred back to her earlier accusation of cowardice as he explained, 'Thus conscience does make cowards of us all' (3.1.85).[7]

A similarly actor-centred approach underpinned the Globe's touring company. An ensemble of four experienced actors and four new graduates, this company rehearsed three plays – *The Merchant of Venice*, *The Taming of the Shrew* and *Twelfth Night* – under the same director, Brendan O'Hea. Like the main-house ensemble shows, these were cast age- and gender-blind, and performed on a bare stage. Perhaps the most radical aspect of this tour was its inclusion of a number of 'Voter's Choice' perfor-mances, in which the audience themselves would decide which of the three plays the company would perform. The costumes were, accordingly, designed to accommodate all three: a base of white tops, blue kilts and Doc Marten boots, on top of which various coats, cloaks and hats could be donned to sketch in particular characters. I saw

the second 'Voter's Choice' show at the Globe itself. At the start of the performance, two of the cast announced the format as an 'unprecedented' experiment in the history of the new Globe, jok-ingly admitting to being terrified. When they gave the titles of the three contenders, the huge audi-ence cheer as *Twelfth Night* was mentioned made it pretty clear how this particular vote was going to go. The choice was determined by the volume of cheering, and though *Merchant* and *Shrew* drew some impressive applause (and some boos), there was no competing with the Beatlemania-level hys-teria the audience offered for *Twelfth Night*; the floor and benches beneath me in the Middle Gallery literally shook from the noise and the foot-stamping. This was an exhilarating start, and it was hard for the production to live up to it. The per-formance was a perfectly good rendition of the play, but seemed to be coasting on the goodwill generated by the format rather than really exploit-ing the crowd's energy; with the exception of some nice moments from Steffan Cennydd's Viola and Sarah Finigan's Sir Andrew Aguecheek, there was a surprising absence of audience interaction and spontaneity.

I was somewhat unconvinced by the production's approach to its gender-blind casting. Where *As You Like It* and *Hamlet* had adopted costume and acting choices that played up the characters' performances of gender, this one seemed to be inviting us to think of gender as irrelevant to each character's identity. All the characters here were in androgynous cos-tumes, and many of them were cross-cast: Orsino and Sebastian were played by women, for example, and Viola by a man. But the plot of *Twelfth Night* hinges upon a number of characters misreading gender signifiers; asking the audience to be 'blind' to gender signifiers from the start, I felt, undermined the play's subversion of them, so that Viola's trans-gression of gender norms did not seem especially unusual. In *As You Like It*, Jones had adopted an exaggeratedly masculine swagger as Orlando, and

---

[6] @shaksper, 11.42 p.m., 7 July 2018.
[7] @shaksper, 11.49 p.m., 7 July 2018.

Laskey's Rosalind the restrained physical vocabulary of a woman who had been trained to perform a restrictive model of femininity, but had begun to break out of it. Here, by contrast, we were being invited not to notice gender in a play that demands the opposite.

The second half of Terry's opening season was structured around 'charting the journey of the character of Emilia through Shakespeare's work', namely through *Two Noble Kinsmen*, *The Winter's Tale* and *Othello*.[8] The climax to the season was a short run of Morgan Lloyd Malcolm's *Emilia*, a new play about the early modern poet Emilia Bassano in which the title character was portrayed as a black woman, a trailblazing proto-feminist and the unwilling inspiration for both the 'Dark Lady' of Shakespeare's sonnets and Emilia in *Othello*. As a season through-line, the theme was not entirely convincing: the implication that Shakespeare's various Emilias might have been based on Bassano is implausible when it comes to the very minor role in *The Winter's Tale* and the character who inherits her name from Boccaccio (via Chaucer) in *Two Noble Kinsmen*. Their namesake in *The Comedy of Errors* was excluded from the season for no apparent reason, and the theme was rephrased in the programme for *Love's Labour's Lost* to refer simply to 'the Dark Lady' so that Rosaline might be included. Nonetheless, the theme broadly signalled the season's interest in gender and racial equality, and made more sense to me after I had seen Nicole Charles's all-female production of Lloyd Malcolm's incendiary play than it had before.

The first of the Emilia plays, Barrie Rutter's *Two Noble Kinsmen*, was very much a piece of popular folk theatre. The pillars and tiring house of the Globe stage had been partially covered over with greenery, giving the theatre a May Day feel. An onstage band accompanied the action in a generally folky mode, slipping playfully into jazz and swing. As might be expected in Barrie Rutter's first post-Northern Broadsides production, Northern accents, rapid speech and direct audience address were very much in evidence. The production was full of song, dance and humorous set pieces, the 3.5 Morris dance a breathtakingly exciting moment

rather than the odd digression it can often seem to be. The dancers were clad in masks and multi-coloured rags, and Jos Vantyler's comically pedantic Schoolmaster stripped off his black cloak and hat to join them, revealing a brightly ribboned Green Man outfit. The dance itself was fast, funny, thrilling, even dangerous, punctuated throughout by bursts of applause and gasps of delight from the audience.

The production was exuberant rather than subtle, largely overlooking the queer and melancholy undertones that had been so central to Blanche McIntyre's 2016 RSC production. The characters of the main plot were played largely as folk-tale archetypes: little more than their colour-coded costumes distinguished Paul Stocker's Palamon from Bryan Dick's Arcite. With the carnival mood of the subplot predominating, the audience's laughter did much to ironize the play, pointing up the title characters' postures ('What a misery / It is to live abroad and everywhere!', 2.2.97–8), their childishness ('I saw her first!', 2.2.163) and their sudden U-turns (as, for example, when they disclaimed the bond they had expressed so insistently only moments earlier). This was a more forgiving production than the RSC's, though, and while it had fun at the expense of the male characters' sexism and sense of entitlement, there was no implication that it wanted to problematize the ending: Palamon and Emilia (Ellora Torchia) tentatively embraced and comforted one another as the play concluded, and Theseus (Jude Akuwudike) was allowed to retain his authority in the closing moments even as he gave voice to ideas that the audience had previously laughed at in ridicule ('the right o'th' lady / Did lie in you, for you first saw her and / Even then proclaimed your fancy', 5.6.116–18).

The subplot was the locus of more idiosyncratic, more fully human characters. The Doctor (Sue Devaney) was re-gendered as a female character, becoming an unapologetic champion of female

---

[8] Michelle Terry's introduction to the *Two Noble Kinsmen* programme.

sexuality; Jon Trenchard's Wooer was innocent and childlike, making the intensely problematic resolution to the subplot *slightly* less creepy than it can otherwise become. Francesca Mills brought immense physicality and energy to the role of the Jailer's Daughter. This is a role especially suited to the Globe, since so much of her speech is playable as direct address: Mills had the audience laughing warmly at her character's infatuation with Palamon, and when the departing Morris dancers left her alone onstage, one of them returning to strip her of her ribboned cloak before shutting the tiring house doors on her, the audience loudly vocalized their sympathy. Indeed, Mills's restricted height meant that the Morris dance sequence became a metaphor for the way in which various characters in this play 'pick up' the Jailer's Daughter and use her before discarding her again (she was quite literally thrown around the stage at one point). A figure at once of physical vulnerability and irrepressible energy, she ran away with the show.

The relationship between stage and audience was central, too, to Blanche McIntyre's *The Winter's Tale*. Will Keen's Leontes let the audience in on his descent into mad jealousy from the start, slowing down in the middle of the line 'Too hot, too hot' (1.2.110) as if he were moving from a benign observation of Hermione and Polixenes's behaviour to a realization of what that behaviour meant. 'To mingle friendship far', he began, pausing as if he were working out the answer, ' . . . is mingling *bloods*' (1.2.111). He was thinking in real time, sharing every leap with the audience, running it past us, almost as if asking us for assent. Later, as he explained that he had had 'Nor night nor day, no rest' (2.3.1), there was a chilling sense that we were witnessing the pivotal moments in his thinking – this was evidently the first moment that he realized he could not cope with the idea of Hermione's continued presence in his court, and that therefore (by his logic) she had to be killed. Sirine Saba's Paulina had a stage presence to rival his – fierce, vehement, speaking quickly but with great clarity, beating her chest and gesticulating emphatically. There was

something enormously timely, in the summer of 2018, about the conviction with which she spoke truth to power and defied the passive complicity of the attendant lords; in her confrontation with Leontes in 2.3, she dominated the centre of the stage, pushing him to the periphery with the force of her words. I wanted to applaud as she swept offstage.

The audience were called upon to bear witness throughout the play. At the start of the trial scene, Leontes stood at the lip of the small semi-circular thrust which had been added to the front of the stage, addressing us directly, looking insecure and vulnerable; when he demanded to 'be cleared / Of being tyrannous' (3.2.4–5), it was clear that it was not only Hermione on trial here. Moments later, the same spot became the location from which Priyanga Burford's Hermione defended herself, again making appeals to the whole playhouse. The scene was full of quick, powerful exchanges between the couple; once again, as she concluded that Leontes's impulsive abuse of due process was 'rigour, and not law' (3.2.113), I felt a thrill at the sheer topicality of her complaint. If it seemed too predictable in this context that Leontes would dismiss the Oracle's vindication of Hermione as 'fake news', the moment was brilliantly live. Leontes examined the scroll in silence for a few seconds, as Hermione moved over to him, ready to forgive and even to comfort him; he struggled against her attempts at physical contact, breaking away and moving to the centre of the stage to announce with horrible calmness, 'There is no truth at all i'th' oracle' (3.2.139). There was an audible murmur of shock through the audience.

In an interview in the programme, McIntyre indicated that she had aimed 'to bring Bohemia close to us, and push Sicilia away by contrast'. Accordingly, where the Sicilians were clothed in a variety of broadly historical costumes from different pre-modern cultures, the Bohemians wore modern dress; the sheep-shearing festival was a very 21st-century kind of party. Once again, the audience was treated as part of the fictional world of the play, warmly invited by Annette Badland's Old Shepherd to 'bear witness' to Florizel and

Perdita's engagement (4.4.382). The Bohemian characters interacted with spectators in a clownish register, the Old Shepherd and the Clown (Jordan Metcalfe) high-fiving the front row of the ground-lings upon discovering the gold, Autolycus (Becci Gemmell) entering through the audience and ad-libbing through her introductory song. Paradoxically, though, there was a reduced sense in the Bohemian scenes that the characters were actually in dialogue with the audience – as a loud helicopter circled above during one of the Clown/ Autolycus exchanges, for example, drowning out their audibility, neither performer felt empowered to address the distraction, ploughing through as if it were not happening.

The audience's role as witnesses came back into focus in the final scene. There was some audience laughter as Leontes began to scrutinize the life-like qualities of Hermione's statue, but this worked in the scene's favour: Paulina silenced the laughs by gesturing for quiet and rather sternly insisting to the whole auditorium,

> It is required
> You do awake your faith. Then, all stand still.
> Or those that think it is unlawful business
> I am about, let them depart.
>
> (5.3.94–7)

As a few groundlings began to chuckle at this last invitation, Leontes stepped forward to address them himself, ordering that 'No foot shall stir' (5.3.98). It was a lovely moment, simultaneously addressing the here-and-now of the playhouse and insisting on taking the play's climax seriously. At the end, as Leontes awkwardly attempted to pair up Camillo (Adrian Bower) and Paulina, the rigidity and distance between the couple's bodies formed a visual contrast to the warm embraces taking place on the other side of the stage. Though she was invited to 'Lead us from hence' (5.3.153), Paulina in fact stayed behind as the others exited, starting to walk offstage very slowly before segueing into the closing jig. In many ways, this was her play.

Claire van Kampen's *Othello* brought Mark Rylance back to the Globe for the first time since 2015, in his first Shakespearian role at the theatre since *Richard III* and *Twelfth Night* in 2012. Rylance played Iago as earnest and low-status, wearing a humble red cap and a slightly shabby uniform. This Iago was completely focused on his mark at all times, every word spoken with the aim of communicating his trustworthiness; he offered his fellow characters the most outrageous lies and violent suggestions in a low-key, throwaway manner as if they were perfectly unremarkable. I had been expecting Rylance to woo the audience's complicity as he had as Richard III, turning on us later in the play as he lost our support. As it turned out, he took a very different approach. He certainly used the old Rylance charm, playfully referring directly to playgoers (he indicated an example of 'a duteous and knee-crooking knave', for example, in the yard, at 1.1.45), and using his stutter to comic effect as if Iago were making the lines up as he spoke. But he tended to do this during his scenes with other characters, not in soliloquy. We, like Othello, Roderigo and Cassio, were his *marks*, not his allies. He turned on us in a heartbeat, frequently contemptuous, and made no attempt to win us over. He bluntly stated 'I hate the Moor' (1.3.378), and then left a confrontational pause, as if daring us to react. Having ensnared Othello, he scornfully observed that 'Thus credulous fools are caught' (4.1.43), as if he thought us just as credulous. Interestingly, quite a few lines from Iago's asides and soliloquies had been cut, rendering the character even more inscrutable than usual. There were only occasional hints as to what lay beneath: he warned André Holland's Othello against 'the green-eyed monster' (3.3.170) with a sudden, visceral intensity, as if he had momentarily forgotten his manipulation of Othello and had fallen into a sincere description of his own, all-consuming jealousy. Indeed, when Sheila Atim's Emilia later described jealousy as 'a monster / Begot upon itself, born on itself' (3.4.158–9), she seemed to be speaking from experience.

The production dealt in interesting ways with racial and sexual prejudice. With a racially diverse cast, including black actors as Cassio (Aaron Pierre) and Emilia, Othello's outsider status in this society was marked more by his American accent than by the colour of his skin (and it was noticeable that Rylance's own transatlantic drawl strategically shifted a little farther West in Iago's scenes with Othello). Having said this, the undercurrent of racism remained: despite heavy cuts to the text, characters continued to associate dark skin with sin. Emilia in particular seemed to have internalized this prejudice, hurling racialized insults at Othello in the final scene ('the blacker devil', 'her most filthy bargain', 5.2.140, 164); tellingly, one of these slurs was subsequently used against her by her own husband ('Filth, thou liest', 5.2.238). Iago's references in soliloquy to his suspicions of both Othello and Cassio with Emilia had been retained, so it was striking that the subjects of his sexual jealousy were all black. In this production, perhaps, Cyprus became a space in which the latent prejudices of the more egalitarian Venice were unleashed to destructive effect. All the most politically powerful figures in Venice were female: the Duke (here called the 'Doge') and both senators were played as women, setting up an interesting contrast with the regressive, male-dominated space of Cyprus. Indeed, the same actors who had played these women in Venice returned as courtesans in Cyprus. Jessica Warbeck's earnest and impassioned Desdemona seemed displaced and disempowered in Cyprus, while the silence of Atim's Emilia was striking precisely because of her evident poise and confidence. A female Lodovica (Badria Timimi) saying 'My lord, this would not be believed in Venice' (4.1.242) after Othello's first act of violence against his wife intensified this contrast.

The Globe audience's readiness to engage vocally with the performance made for some interesting effects. There was audible shock and sympathy as Cassio was made an example and stripped of his rank; there were gasps as Emilia resolved to steal Desdemona's handkerchief, and cries as Othello struck Desdemona. Despite Rylance's aloofness, there was also some audience laughter as Iago's cleverness revealed itself, and at the audacity of his manipulations. Having been largely contained within the fictional world over the first half of the play, Othello started to build up a closer relationship with the yard during his conversation with Iago in 3.3, playing various lines as direct address to the audience. But the audience's volubility had an interesting effect on both Othello and Cassio's direct address, in that both of them had to feign deafness to the audience's laughter at lines like 'This fellow's of exceeding honesty' (3.3.262) and 'I never knew a Florentine more kind and honest' (3.1.39). Rylance's Iago could respond to actual audience reactions, but these two could not.

The last Shakespearian production of the Globe's summer season, Nick Bagnall's *Love's Labour's Lost*, took place indoors in the Sam Wanamaker Playhouse. Though the programme framed it as 'the final play of the 2018 summer season to follow the Dark Lady through Shakespeare's canon', I am not sure this really came across – many of the lines about Rosaline's blackness had been cut, and where most of the season's Emilias had been played by actors of colour, Rosaline was played here by a white actor, Jade Williams. In any case, it was Kirsty Woodward's endearingly awkward Princess, not Rosaline, who was the focus of this production. The production opened with her entering through the darkened auditorium, carrying a single candle; once onstage, she pulled out a large trunk from which she unpacked a number of childhood toys. She wound a small music box, sounding a waltz; this brought to life both the band in the gallery and the ensemble onstage, who lit the chandeliers. Boyet (Charlotte Mills) interrupted this explosion of fantasy with the words, 'Madam, the King your father –', but the Princess refused to hear the end of the sentence, drumming noisily on the trunk and intensifying the retreat into make-believe: the music built to a crescendo, the ensemble waltzed with one another, and the Princess opened the large trunk to allow Paul Stocker's handsome King of Navarre to climb out of it. His crown looked like something from a child's dressing-up box, while his followers, Berowne (Dharmesh Patel) and Dumaine (Tom Kanji), resembled toy soldiers (Longueville and Maria were cut). The Princess, then, was avoiding the reality of her father's death by immersing herself in a fairytale world she associated with childhood.

From this point onwards, the general register of the production was big, silly and slapstick.

Many of the characters were unashamed caricatures – Nathaniel and Holofernes (Kanji and Stocker again), for example, doddering geriatrics in white wigs and wheelchairs like something out of a sketch show. Even the love poetry was played in an insincere, over-the-top register: when Berowne, the King and Dumaine spoke the odes to their loves in 4.3, each one was more overblown than the last, posing grotesquely and half-singing the lines to musical accompaniment. Jos Vantyler doubled as Armado and Moth, playing all the dialogues between these characters solo, alternating between the reedy, Northern-accented Moth and the larger-than-life, cartoonishly Spanish Armado. Vantyler's Armado was excessive in every respect, costumed and made-up as a kind of Elizabethan New Romantic, all lacy flounces, clattering beads and heavy eyeliner. At one point, he performed a duet of 'To All the Girls I've Loved Before', with Moth singing Willie Nelson's lines in a brilliant falsetto and Armado bursting with Hispanic virility as Julio Iglesias's part kicked in.

In the programme, Bagnall noted that he wanted to maintain a sense of the 'looming shadow of death hanging over the whole play', but aside from the beginning and end, I only registered one moment of darkness. This was when Rosaline rather callously reminded Katherine (Leaphia Darko) of the way in which Cupid had 'killed [her] sister' (5.2.13), and Katherine responded with tears and anger. It was significant that the exchange was interrupted by the Princess, who clumsily attempted to make light of it by declaring it 'a set of wit well played' (5.2.29); there was no room for rough edges in her fantasy world. But grief can be avoided for only so long. In a climax of mad brilliance in the Pageant of the Nine Worthies, Armado's gold-armoured Hector descended on wires from the heavens trap amid a shower of golden confetti; his brawl with Costard (Kanji) was interrupted not by a new arrival, but by Boyet, whose line closely followed her first: 'The King your father –' (5.2.712). This time, her sentence was cut short not by the Princess's refusal to hear the news, but by her completion of the sentence: 'Dead, for my life' (5.2.713). The Song of Spring and Winter turned out to be the same waltz that the music box had played at the start, and the Princess finally ushered her companions back into her toy box, closing the lid on them as the candles were once again extinguished. Perhaps the production suffered from the same problem as its protagonist, gliding casually past the play's darker elements; but perhaps this was the point. Maybe the production had deliberately been a little too overblown, too zany, too highly strung – the Princess could not sustain a retreat into a fairytale world that excluded the harsh reality of death. The text draws attention to the generic limits of comedy in its closing moments, and Berowne's insistence that 'Our wooing doth not end like an old play' (5.2.860) felt especially apt here.

As I write this in late December 2018, the United Kingdom is in a Brexit-induced meltdown. It is unclear whether Theresa May's premiership will survive Christmas and this week's instalment of low principles and high skulduggery feels like a fitting climax to a fractious and unhappy year. For months, the news has cycled remorselessly between Brexit, the rise of far-right populism across Europe and beyond, ever starker warnings of environmental collapse, and the latest inanities and outrages of the Trump administration. The *OED*'s word of the year was 'toxic'. In brief: 2018 was not for the faint-hearted.

For better or for worse, not much of this geopolitical madness was directly reflected in the productions of Shakespeare described in the following pages. There is no obvious generic or thematic way of structuring these reflections, so I begin with two of my favourite productions outside London in 2018, both (to my surprise) of *Henry V*, before heading North to 'Shakespeare's Rose Theatre', a temporary playing space that popped up in York for a summer season. After an account of the RSC's four main-house offerings in Stratford-upon-Avon, I finish with three intimate productions from Liverpool, Bristol and Newbury.

One thing has become clear on my first outing as a *Survey* reviewer: while we might have more words at our disposal than a newspaper critic (and a very different remit), we have less space per production than a reviewer might in, for example, *Shakespeare Bulletin*. This is no bad thing but it does necessitate a process of radical synecdoche – a mere handful of salient parts must stand in for the whole. Pages of notes shrink to a few paragraphs, and I am very conscious of having to overlook the contributions of many theatre workers to the creation and smooth-running of these productions. I am also full of renewed respect for the job done by previous *Survey* reviewers, not least for the quality of their writing and the density of their insights.

## A BRACE OF HENRIES

I saw Antic Disposition's touring production of *Henry V* in Holy Trinity Church, Stratford, on 15 November, four days after the centenary of the Armistice of the First World War. Outside the church, it had been an especially febrile day in the ongoing saga of Brexit. Inside, all was still and retrospective. A few yards from Shakespeare's grave, a temporary exhibition on Stratford during the Great War foregrounded morale-boosting professional and student productions of *Henry V*. Ben Horslen and John Risebero's production, set during the Great War and performed by an Anglo-French cast, originated in 2015 when it was devised to honour the anniversary of Agincourt; it was punctuated by plangent song settings of poems by A. E. Housman.

The action was framed by a halting procession of the wounded that consciously echoed John Singer Sargent's painting *Gassed*. Finding himself in a hospital near the village of Azincourt, an English private removed a copy of *Henry V* from his knapsack and presented it as a '*cadeau, pour remercier*' to a French soldier. A young French nurse – spying the potential for a spot of drama therapy – began to read the Chorus, casting the men and her fellow nurse as she did so. When she spoke of 'imaginary *puissance*', the second word was so clearly her language that it neatly reminded us of the hybridity of 'our' own tongue. (The effect was repeated at 4.0.43 when 'largess universal' became '*largesse universale*'.) With the French and British stationed at either end of a traverse playing area, there ensued a theatrical version of the Christmas Day Anglo-German football match in no-man's-land – a 'game' during a temporary truce – the main difference being that the two sides here were actually allies in the First World War (though not, of course, in Shakespeare).

After an intentionally ropey beginning in which the men fumbled their way through 1.1, and everyone seemed baffled by the Salic Law, the clunky acting quickly shaded into convincing performances and the framing device largely receded. This, for me, somewhat complicated the status of Henry's soliloquies. What is *actually* happening in 'Upon the King' when spoken by a private in the First World War pretending to be Henry V? Here it was given 'straight' by Nathan Hamilton's boyish and earnest King with no sense of an injured soldier trying out this argument or persona from below, as it were. There's clearly an art to the economy of frame-intrusion but on a number of occasions it would have been powerful to remind us of the 1915 context (when, for example, Westmoreland wished for more soldiers, or when Henry learned of the 10,000 French slain).

The first major reintroduction of the frame came just before the interval and was devastating. Henry, compelled to punish Bardolph for the theft of the plate, held a gun to his face. This can hardly be best practice in drama therapy and the soldier playing Bardolph had a massive episode of shell shock, a fit that was acted with complete and disturbing conviction by James Murfitt. The nurses swept to his aid and the men sang a calming, melancholy setting of Housman's 'The Long Road' ('Trudge on, trudge on, 'twill all be well, / The way will guide one back').

Another of the production's powerful coups was to interrupt the play-within-the-play with noises off from the Front. It did this twice: first, midway through Agincourt when the altar-end of the church reverberated to a sudden rumble of cannons and flashes of flare lights. It was almost enough to rattle the chancel's most famous bones. All the soldiers, French and English, turned to face the Front and sang 'The Agincourt Carol'. The second interruption felt like a variation on the closing moments of *Love's Labour's Lost*. After a straightforward wooing scene between Henry and Katherine (played by

the younger of the two nurses), Henry gave the epilogue, gesturing to Shakespeare's grave on 'our bending author', and all embraced. A dispatch arrived, Mercadé-like, with the command that the men should return to the Front. 'Henry' and 'Katherine' had an emotional farewell, and the English and French fell into line and exited in separate directions, the French into the maw of the darkened chancel, there to meet their makers, Shakespeare and God.

Elizabeth Freestone's touring version of the same play for Shakespeare at the Tobacco Factory (Bristol) conjured an altogether more secular and political world. Modern-dress but with some anachronistic throwbacks (thirties' microphone stand, anti-aircraft arc lights), this spry and inventive production played out on six movable metal platforms with gravel underfoot. It began with a boozy party to celebrate (I think) the wedding of Pistol and Quickly. A sozzled and semi-undressed Harry passed out, alone, then remained on stage during the Chorus, only to be discovered by Ely and Canterbury in 1.1. Their encomia about Hal's reformation felt premature; this hung-over body was far from a 'paradise' and the 'spirits' it contained were more vodka-based than 'celestial' (see 1.1.31–2). Nevertheless, Ely and Canterbury spoke the lines as they dressed and refreshed Hal; others then brought restorative coffee as a heavily cut 1.1 merged seamlessly into 1.2 and Harry all too suddenly found himself surrounded by hawkish suits and special advisors, subtly inching this fog-headed boy towards war.

This was not only a war with the French – more subtly, Ben Hall's Henry was at war with the words the script demanded he utter. He repeatedly made a frustrated growl to himself after the role forced him to perform a series of unpleasant tasks for the first time, whether being angry at the French ambassador, condemning Cambridge to death (three traitors became one here) or ordering the execution of Bardolph. As in the Antic Disposition production, the latter moment provided one of the highlights of the evening. In 3.6, Bardolph was brought captive into the camp headquarters; when he saw his King and old mate, he pleaded

'It's just a plate, Hal!' Hal coldly responded 'We would have all such offenders so cut off' (3.6.108), and this acted as a direct instruction to Fluellen to push Bardolph to his knees and garrotte him with a piece of cable. It was excruciatingly slow work and everyone struggled to watch, especially Harry. When it was finally over, Nym launched himself at the King but was knocked out cold by an attendant. Harry, clutching the plate that Bardolph had stolen to his chest, was a traumatized wreck. There ensued a queasy silence, broken by Montjoy's entry. (By the way: Pistol's later lines about Harry being 'a heart of gold, a lad of life', etc. (4.1.45ff.) didn't tally with his shocked reaction to Harry putting Bardolph to death.)

Freestone's adaptation of the text was fresh and inventive throughout, and her most interesting move was to absorb the role of the Dauphin into that of Katherine. Heledd Gwynn's crop-haired Katherine had the striking androgyny of the young Sinead O'Connor and a streetwise sense of fashion (tight lilac suit, big looped earrings, black fingernails). She it was who sent the tennis balls to Henry: three luminous pink ones set in black foam in a small steel firearms case, a gesture that was both playful and deeply sinister.

So formidable was this adversary that I spent a long time during the first half wondering what would happen when Harry met Kathy in Act 5, or indeed how or why such a badass (who clearly hated the English) would get through the giggly language lesson. As it happened, the latter was cut but resurfaced brilliantly in the endgame of the battle of Agincourt. Pistol's prisoner was Charles Duke of Orléans, previously established as Katherine's boyfriend. Pistol, just following orders, coupéd his gorge. Orléan's body then lay onstage throughout the inventory of the French and English dead. When Harry concluded 'Take it, God, / For it is none but Thine' (4.8.111–12), Katherine entered and rushed to the corpse of her lover (Figure 35). Lacking coherent words for her angry grief, she named his body parts in French and English, a dazzling and moving rebuke to the watching English victors. After performing this improvised rite, she rose to the microphone and delivered the verdict: '*votre langage est contemptible*'. She returned to cradle her lover; Harry redundantly ordered the 'Te Deum'.

When they met again in 5.2, it was predictably awkward. On 'I will not part with a village of it' (5.2.174), he knelt to her and she simply shoved him over. How could this possibly fadge? The resolution was something of a letdown. He forced a kiss on her, she repelled him, beat his chest, then broke down, sobbing. Eventually, she rose to her feet and offered him her hand; it would have been truer to the power and the logic of this performance if she had planted a boot in his groin and stalked off. But this was a rare misstep. What I admired throughout this performance and that of all the company was the way in which none of the characters was simplified, satirized or diminished – everyone had dignity and life and a story.

## SHAKESPEARE'S ROSE THEATRE, YORK

'Shakespeare's Rose Theatre' was the brainchild of a former private banker and current arts entrepreneur, James Cundall. It is perhaps no coincidence that Cundall is a direct descendant (via a couple of vowel shifts) of Henry Condell. We have recently seen a pop-up Globe in Melbourne and 'container' Globes in Buenos Aires and elsewhere, and the principle was the same here: a temporary structure, very broadly approximating an early modern theatre, plonked in an urban setting. As its name implies, 'Shakespeare's Rose Theatre' was not overfussy about historical veracity. (The idea of calling it 'Henslowe's Rose' presumably didn't detain anyone for too long.)

York has a long and proud tradition of civic theatre and, with the recent advent of the biennial York Shakespeare Festival, is fast becoming a Northern Powerhouse of Shakespearian performance. This temporary playing space, located in a car park beneath the picturesque Clifford's Tower, was a very welcome addition to the city's cultural landscape.

35 *Henry V*, 4.8, Bristol Tobacco Factory and touring, directed by Elizabeth Freestone for Shakespeare at the Tobacco Factory. Heledd Gwynn as Katherine and Zachary Powell as Orléans. Photograph by Craig Fuller.

The fourteen-sided polygonal auditorium was only one part of the package, for in order to enter it you had first to navigate a small Elizabethan-themed village of food vendors and outdoor exhibits. The former featured 'artisanal' modern comestibles, the latter tended to focus on the more grisly aspects of early modern life (bear-baiting, mannequins in stocks, that kind of thing). A small Romeo and Juliet-themed botanical area provided leafy relief.

The theatre space itself was a complex system of scaffolding and cladding that was never likely to give the illusion of time-travel, but was entirely fit for purpose as an outdoor venue for Shakespearian drama. The stage ran the entire width of the space (and was therefore not tapered like the various iterations of the Rose); a balcony protruded centre stage from which

actors could descend stairways on either side. I counted eight onstage entrances and a further three from the pit, meaning that directors had every opportunity to ricochet our attention around the space. A self-supporting roof covered the stage and obviated the need for columns; sightlines were excellent from every part of the house.

The groundlings' pit was both smaller and significantly more relaxed than at Shakespeare's Globe (more expensive, too: £15). At early performances, ushers had encouraged everyone to stand but abandoned this policy when the pit was less than full and as the mercury rose. As is now usual, this was one of the hottest UK summers since records began, and it was counterintuitive – if not positively hazardous – to stand in the sun when you could sit in the shade. At the performances I saw,

36 The interior of Shakespeare's Rose Theatre, York. Photograph by Paul Prescott.

while most groundlings chose to sit towards the back of the pit, a handful opted to stand right at the lip of the stage. One man stood alone for most of *Richard III*, just off-centre but in everyone's eye-line, reading a paperback copy of the play. Solo eccentrics aside, the net effect of a half-empty pit was to create patches of dead space. For the actors, it must sometimes have felt as if they were pouring energy into a non-conductor.

The stage was floor-boarded and clad in wood but the other hemisphere of the theatre, the audience's half, consisted of exposed metal scaffolding (Figure 36). Most creative labour had been expended on the fresco above the stage –

a beaming sun (of York?) face radiating into starry constellations of blue, yellow and white.

I saw all four productions in quick succession over two sweltering days. It may have been the theatrical equivalent of Stockholm Syndrome, but the quality of the shows really did seem to improve incrementally.

\*\*\*

Juliet Forster's production of *A Midsummer Night's Dream* was a solid, largely uncomplicated and low-risk affair. If you've seen ten productions of *Dream*, the chances are you've seen one like this at least twice. It was memorable mainly for Sara Perks's costume designs for the forest which drew on

English folk iconography and legend: bones, antlers, horns, twigs and a dark, late autumnal palette, like a charred silver birch. While striking in themselves, these designs did tend to blend in with the brown backdrop of the permanent set, meaning that this – the only non-tragedy of the season – lacked colour and warmth.

In an unorthodox move, not only were Hippolyta/Theseus doubled with Oberon/Titania, but the move into the woods effected a gender flip so that Hippolyta became Oberon, and Theseus, Titania. (This added a new, autoerotic dimension to the lines in which Titania and Oberon accuse each other of consorting with these mortals.) You could see why Hippolyta would willingly enter such a flipped dream state and want to wear the trousers. Amanda Ryan had played her as thoroughly pissed off in 1.1 and, in an interesting interpolation, she subsequently overheard all of Lysander and Hermia's plot to head off into the woods. There were some pay-offs. Theseus/Titania's line 'out of this wood do not desire to go' (3.1.144) and corresponding capture of Bottom echoed the backstory of Theseus's capture of Hippolyta, as if the character had learned nothing yet and still treated others as coercible objects. But when the time came for the pair to revert to their former identities, I couldn't detect a transformation. As they removed their foresty over-clothes, there was no obvious sense that they were turning back into their 'real' selves. Here, of course, the text doesn't help much. Rather than reflecting on the far-out experience of the night, it requires them mainly to talk, like the posh people they are, about dogs and hunting. It was therefore hard to see how the fierce vexation had performed the requisite couples' therapy.

Damien Crudden's production of *Macbeth* was in many respects a traditional affair of beards and furs and blood. We were broadly in the Middle Ages. In a self-effacing Director's Note, Crudden wrote that 'The play seems to block itself' (which sounds a bit spooky) and that he hoped the 'words, live music, great swordplay and performances [would] carry the weight of this production'. Indeed, of the four York productions, this was the least conceptual.

The major exception was the treatment of the witches. When they (two female, one male) first met, there was nothing remotely witchy or supernatural about them; they were simply poor folk, the medieval precariat. Sensing the arrival of Macbeth and Banquo, they donned animal-skull headpieces, contorted their bodies and adopted a weird vocal register that bordered on parody. It quickly emerged that in their day jobs these three were servants to the Macbeths. Very trusted ones at that: Lady Macbeth read most of her husband's letter to the two female witches/servants (dismissing them on 'King thou shalt be'). The full trio soon reappeared as the three murderers who disembowelled Banquo; later, they bore silent witness from the balcony to the Macbeths' post-banquet meltdown.

The Hecate scene was highly original. 'Hecate' was really Lady Macbeth's waiting-woman and the mastermind of this peasants' revolt; as such, she was also a budding playwright who had scripted the 'witches'' lines for their final encounter with Macbeth. 'Thrice the brinded cat hath mewed', etc., was a dress rehearsal, crisply concluded with 'O, well done, I commend your pains' (4.1.39), here offered as an approving director's note.

While enjoying the novelty of this concept, I couldn't quite see how it stacked up. The precariat was enacting revenge on the warrior class, specifically Macbeth, by (a) goading him on to commit regicide; then (b) executing his orders when he wanted, for example, Banquo or Lady Macduff and her kids murdered; while (c) messing with his head, even to madness. As a method of class warfare, it seemed peculiarly long-winded. At the conclusion, Hecate / Lady Macbeth's waiting-woman was handed Macbeth's head by a rather squeamish Malcolm. The soldiers exited and she and the head were left on the balcony for a *da capo* ending; below her the three witches/servants re-ran the opening lines of the play, pausing at 'There to meet with . . .', at which point they looked up to Hecate for guidance, only to be answered by an inscrutable smirk.

The festival's remaining shows – *Romeo and Juliet* and *Richard III*, both directed by Lindsay Posner – were colourful, intelligent and very well acted by a different company of actors than had featured in *Macbeth* and *Dream*. *Romeo and Juliet* was set in Verona in 1932, a decade or so into Mussolini's dictatorship. As with all Shakespeare productions set in fascist Italy, at least two scenes took place in an outdoor café. In one of these (2.3), Mussolini's voice barked out of a radio; the only other explicit manifestation of the fascist context was when Tybalt entered in 3.1 with a trio of Blackshirts. After the muted colours of both *Macbeth* and *Dream*, and despite the occasional Blackshirt, this production was refreshingly zesty on the eye. Sue Wilmington's bold costumes popped out beautifully against the brown background. Movable props – wooden crates of apples, flower stands, bicycles – nicely textured the space.

The titular roles were well cast, in the sense that they both looked like the kind of actors who are commonly cast as Romeo and Juliet. But Alexander Vlahos and Alexandra Dowling can't help that, and both had some good moments. At their meeting, the rest of the party climbed upstairs to the balcony to observe, with their backs to the audience, a firework display. On 'palm to palm is holy palmer's kiss', a firework exploded, giving Romeo a split second to work out how to move the conversation on to facial congress. They kissed. Another firework. At least on the afternoon I saw it, Dowling wasn't leaning on Juliet's usual gag lines and 'what satisfaction . . . ?', 'Where is your mother?!', 'How art thou out of breath . . . ' weren't quite landing. She delivered most of the 'faint cold fear' (4.3.15ff.) soliloquy quietly, sitting at the foot of her bed, and this stillness both helped the actor and foregrounded the fact that the space's sightlines and surprisingly good acoustics allowed for an almost conversational intimacy.

Elsewhere, there was strong and interesting work throughout the cast. Shanaya Rafaat's Mercutio (one of two female Mercutios this year) sported a Louise Brooks helmet and modern attitudes; she attended the Capulets' ball beneath a Napoleon hat topped by extravagant tricolore plumes. Her default daywear – gent's slacks, waistcoat, shades – was more progressive than the Veronese norm; during her ribald taunting of the Nurse, a 'respectable' couple left the café, appalled at her degenerate appearance and behaviour.

More at home in this macho world was Robert Gwilym's murderously bald Lord Capulet – a Cockney gang boss, the Mad Frankie Fraser of Verona. He attended his own ball dressed as Julius Caesar (with Lady C in an extravagant Cleopatra get-up) and seemed to enjoy a little too much putting Tybalt in a painful headlock on 'you are a saucy boy'. Throughout, Gwilym alternated between (and sometimes combined) bluster and menace. The lines sounded so natural in the East End persona that when, *à propos* of Paris and Juliet's projected wedding, he said 'We'll keep no great ado – a friend or two' (3.4.23), what I actually heard was 'Nothing fancy – a few mates round for a bit of a knees-up'. (And his actions later contradicted this: on 'so many guests invite as here are writ' (4.2.1), he passed a *stack* of invitations to the maid.) This was maybe not an original conception of the part, but it was very charismatically executed.

An hour before I saw Posner's *Richard III*, we had the first rainfall in what felt like living memory, the splotches and puddles in the pit an autumnal blast before the winter of discontent. The show opened in a fashion I primarily associate with Cheek by Jowl, i.e. the company paced out purposefully, hit their respective places, and regarded the audience with steadfast neutrality. Pause. Then cue the opening bass guitar (bomp ba bomp, bomp ba bomp) from 'Come on Eileen', to which the company swayed its hips before bursting into a full-on coronation party.

Dyfan Dwyfor's Richard entered on the balcony and hurtled into an equally upbeat rendition of the opening soliloquy in which there was nothing indulgent, lingering or psychologized, nor was there a recognition of the site-specific (this was, after all, the local lad coming to life again in a car park). Dwyfor was a lop-sided ball of energy and bustle, young, black-bearded, facially inseparable from the hipster baristas of the city. His left side was near-paralysed, his arm crooked into his abdomen and his hand often fanned over his crotch in a way

37 *Richard III*, 4.2, Shakespeare's Rose Theatre, directed by Lindsay Posner. Dyfan Dwyfor as Richard III. Photograph by Anthony Robling.

that felt almost oppressively symbolic (Figure 37). 'He cannot live, I hope' was delivered in a rush, without the obvious midline pause, and he continued to gallivant in this fashion through the encounters with Clarence, Hastings and Anne. When he offered the latter his dagger, there was no see-saw, no will-she, won't-she, about the exchange, no pause even between the two halves of 'take up the sword or take up me'. When he played 'I'll have her,

but I will not keep her long' (1.3.217) again without pause, one could only conclude that this was a Richard who did not want or need the audience to find him funny. This suspicion was confirmed later, in the scene with the Lord Mayor, when three very playable gag lines ('Oh do not swear, my Lord of Buckingham'; 'Will you enforce me to a world of cares?'; 'Call them back again') flew by in quick succession.

Dwyfor was very good in the hectic 'songs of death' sequence, scuttling and skittering between incoming messengers, adversity a welcome aphrodisiac. In Act IV, his mother describes how his bold, courageous manhood was replaced by the milder tone of his recent career. This, then, felt like a return to form, a restoration of manhood (the fragility of which was perhaps signified by the placing of that protective hand over his groin?).

A good production of *Richard III* needs to be more than a one-man band, and there was real quality across the board in this show. Edward (Dale Rapley), Clarence (Richard Teverson), Richmond (Edward Sayer) and Elizabeth (Emily Raymond) – all knew how to work their way in a pacey, structured and lucid fashion through rhetorical set-pieces.

The production was in modern dress but without too many obvious contemporary political parallels. The scene in which the court is reconciled ended (as in Richard Eyre's 1990 NT production) with a group photograph: in a year in which scores of journalists have been murdered across the globe, it was a sinister touch that only one photo journalist was allowed to cover the event and that his vulnerability was signalled by a bullet-proof PRESS vest.

It was recently announced that 'Shakespeare's Rose Theatre' will return to York with four new productions in the summer of 2019. This is good news. And it is a clear sign of the financial viability of the enterprise that a duplicate Rose will, as if by parthenogenesis, also pop up next summer in the grounds of Blenheim Palace, Oxfordshire, with revivals of the four shows discussed here. Some aspects of this venture were improvable (the tickets were a little pricey and both companies were very white) but, on the whole, the pop-up space proved a very hospitable environment for these accessible, well-made and sometimes inventive productions.

## THE ROYAL SHAKESPEARE COMPANY

Disembarking (or deplaning) visitors to Birmingham International Airport in 2018 might have noticed a large advertisement for the RSC sheathing the jet bridge at Gate 29. One section read 'JOURNEYS END IN LOVERS MEETING', while the next enjoined the weary traveller to 'EXPERIENCE A DIFFERENT KIND OF THEATRE'. For long-term fans of the RSC (among whom I count myself), the ad raised a question: what *is* different about the kind of theatre made by the RSC? The question felt doubly plangent in 2018, a year in which some great figures from the Company's history died. The passing of John Barton and Cicely Berry (following that of Peter Hall in 2017) made a great crack, and a series of commemorative events in Stratford and London movingly captured their formative contributions to the evolution of a company that was, in the 1960s and 1970s at least, distinctly 'different'.

One sign of the RSC's difference in 2018 might have been the fact that all three main-house shows in the summer season were directed by women. This was a welcome landmark; in recent years, it has felt as if female creatives have been shunted into the smaller spaces of the Swan and The Other Place to make what the RSC now routinely refers to as 'mischief'.

More than anyone else, Erica Whyman embodies (even drives) the progressive wing of the current RSC and, from a purely political perspective there was much to applaud in her approach to *Romeo and Juliet*. Her largely young cast was racially and socially inclusive, and each performance gave local high-schoolers the chance to participate in the Prologue, which was split between and repeated by multiple speakers. The casting of relatively inexperienced and unknown actors as Romeo, Juliet and Mercutio contrasted strongly with, for example, Kenneth Branagh's 2016 West End production (screen stars for the lovers, Derek Jacobi as Mercutio). The expectation, then, was for a fresh, contemporary, hormonal production that would capture something of the lived experience of young adults in the UK in 2018. The result – at least on the two nights I saw it – was a curiously abstract and under-powered production.

The tone was set by Tom Piper's minimalist, non-committal set, the main feature of which was a large revolving cube centre-stage, open on two sides. While the pre-publicity for the show had perhaps suggested a *verismo* approach, this set didn't really locate us anywhere. Structurally, the cube enabled a balcony scene, a cell, a tomb, but it did not provide a sense of place or suggest a communal landscape, let alone conjure the kind of urban spaces referred to in the programme. It was left, then, to the company to create a sense of community, but there was nothing to distinguish the two families or their followers, and we were meant to be blind and deaf to other conventional markers of identity such as accent, race and gender. I found myself wondering: Who *are* these kids? They didn't appear to have phones or jobs or schools or postcodes; they didn't drink, do drugs, practice veganism, flirt with socialism. The lack of specificity reduced them to free-floating signifiers of 'young adult' and, on a largely empty stage, left them exposed.

There was throughout this production a problem of hasty, unvaried and sometimes unmotivated delivery. Romeo's 'Ay me, what fray was here?' lacked any obvious stimulus (Piper's set was as clean as ever, with no visible symptoms of the fray) and the younger actors often struggled to make the ideas and images of the lines their own. It was not that they were embarrassed by lines such as 'I would I were thy bird' – more that they rattled through them, speaking 'by the book', as it were, rarely surprising themselves (and therefore us) with the words they found themselves saying. I began to sympathize with Friar Lawrence: 'slowly and surely! They stumble that [speak] fast.' (Andrew French's Friar and Beth Cordingly's Escalus were both role models of tempo, phrasing and authoritative stage presence.)

Whether or not I (well-wishing but unconvinced) enjoyed the show was perhaps beside the point. Many first-time visitors to the Royal Shakespeare Theatre (and to the UK theatres to which this show toured) will have come away having seen a cast that looked and sounded like modern Britain, and might just have concluded that Shakespeare is not the exclusive preserve of the middle-aged and the middle classes. If so, job done.

While Whyman's *Romeo* felt underconceptualized, the same could not be said for Polly Findlay's *Macbeth*. This show had two very Big Ideas: that *Macbeth* is like a horror movie and that *Macbeth* is about Time. (Well-written programme articles were helpfully dedicated to both propositions.)

The Time motif registered in a number of ways, some subtle, some not. The stage was pre-set with Duncan asleep in his bed, crown resting on the corner angle of the headboard. A teenage girl in pyjamas – Donalbain, his carer – sat against the bed, attempting a Rubik's cube while, downstage and in a large triangular formation, three younger girls (Witches) played sleepily with dolls. Upstage right: a wall-mounted bell, a large indoor fern and a row of plastic waiting-room chairs on which sat two adults (later revealed to be the Porter and Lady Macbeth). Upstage left: more chairs and the kind of corporate water dispenser found in gyms or hotel lobbies. Nothing of note happened in the fifteen minutes between the first audience admission and the advertised start, as if the purpose of this pre-set was to create a kind of pulse-relaxing dead time, a suspended lull from which the action could erupt. Once it had, the passing of time was foregrounded when, for example, Banquo impatiently checked his watch while Macbeth spoke his extended aside in 1.3, or when a full minute of near-silence elapsed as the Murderers waited for the arrival of Banquo and Fleance while the Porter ate a packet of crisps.

Findlay's most obvious and controversial choice occurred at the end of Macbeth's soliloquy in 2.1. The wall-mounted bell eerily rang of its own accord and invited Macbeth to murder Duncan. As Eccleston crept upstage, the Porter (who never left the stage in this production) stepped forward and clicked a button on his watch. This activated a red digital display above the stage which then proceeded to countdown from 2.00.00 (i.e. 2 hours) to 0.00.00. The use of a countdown is not unprecedented – in the *Roman Tragedies*, Ivo van Hove alerted his audience to the fact that there were, for example, twenty-five minutes until the death of Cleopatra. But in those productions, the information was flashed briefly and acted as a kind of historical irony alert and subliminal pacer. Findlay's clock was stubbornly supraliminal (above the threshold, or centre-stage door) and unavoidable.

The message: from the murder of Duncan, Macbeth is living on borrowed time, and the production was artfully designed so that the clock should finally count down to 0.00.00 at the exact second that Macbeth breathed his last. This necessitated a somewhat odd onstage demise. The first time I saw the show, the long fight was clearly choreographed so that Macbeth and Macduff could repeat certain actions in order to run the clock down. But at 0.00.17, and midway through these manoeuvres, the clock unexpectedly spasmed and went straight to 0.00.00, much to everyone's consternation. This was a wretched anti-climax. My notes at this point simply read 'FFS'.

The horror effects were uneven. Michael Hodgson's sinisterly omnipresent Porter did capture something of the banality of evil, chalking up Macbeth's victims in proliferating strokes on the brick façade of the proscenium. And, with eight minutes to go, there was a hallucinogenic strobe-lit sequence of unsettling images – the Porter creepily cradling a baby, a Witch on a swing – but this was too little, too late. I suspect the original intention of casting pre-teens as the Witches was to make them a triadic version of the terrifying Grady sisters in Kubrick's *The Shining*. But these slightly self-conscious little girls in their strawberry onesies and white booties were really rather endearing. And, whereas the power of Kubrick's girls depends on their showing up unexpectedly every now and then for a few seconds of sheer terror, Findlay's girls were over-exposed and even made to shift stage furniture, which acts of child labour did little to multiply their villainy.

Kubrick used inter-titles in *The Shining* to indicate the passing of time, and Findlay did something similar here by projecting short slogans ('WHEN THE BATTLE'S LOST AND WON', 'FEARS AND SCRUPLES SHAKE US') above the stage. The word 'LATER' was frequently projected, but, given that no scene was described as 'EARLIER',

it was somewhat superfluous to inform us that time was working in its regular linear fashion.

In the run-up to opening, Christopher Eccleston had spoken compellingly about class and regional biases in Shakespearian casting. As Macbeth, he spoke in his native Salford accent and seemed to be channelling what he perceived to be his outsider status. His was a bitter, angry Macbeth, shot through with stroppy irony. When naming '*The Prince of Cumberland*: that is a step . . .' and when talking to the Murderers of 'certain friends', he adopted a camp lisp to signal manly disdain; he accompanied his reference to the 'English epicures' with the hand gesture that, in the UK at least, denotes a 'wanker'. He was in a somewhat different play from Niamh Cusack's refined and fragile Lady Macbeth, and their scenes together were unusually testy. On their reunion in 1.5, they nicely avoided the cliché of the passionate clinch on his return from the battlefield; instead, he did something quite odd and interesting, slamming his heavy kit bag down repeatedly on the floor as if squashing large scorpions. Cusack, too, was more than capable of surprising choices. Hers was a notably athletic final scene in pyjamas and tiara, skittishly covering large areas of the playing space, even descending into the front row of the auditorium and soliciting an audience member to give her his hand (5.1.64).

I would have liked to see these performances later in the run. To Eccleston's credit, he admitted in a newspaper interview that he 'definitely wasn't ready when we opened' and that he had since stopped 'trying too hard'.[1] Both he and Cusack are seriously diligent as well as inventive actors, and I have no doubt that their performances had grown substantially by the time this production reached London.

I'm not sure what the idea was behind Ed Bennett's Macduff but he must surely be the first actor in that role to be required to wear a false

---

[1] See www.metro.news/weekend-christopher-eccleston-on-feeling-shut-out-from-shakespeare-and-finally-landing-his-dream-role-macbeth/1274511.

stomach. This prosthetic girth sat beneath an elegant cardigan and the overall look was cuddly architect. Had he grown his belly out of sympathy for his pregnant wife? Was this now ante-natal best practice, to 'feel it like a man'? Bennett's performance, though, was excellent. He took a full 4 seconds before 'My children, too?' (courtesy of the digital clock, one could easily measure such pauses), before repeating 'all, all, all, all, all, all, all' with increasing intensity, jabbing his finger into Ross's chest. A very human moment – brain and tongue stammering to come to terms with real horror.

Fiona Laird's boisterous and very busy *Merry Wives of Windsor* began with an unusual apology for the quality of Shakespeare's writing. As the lights faded, audio played of a young woman delivering a letter to Shakespeare's London lodgings ('Mr Shakespeare, Mr Shakespeare! A letter for you!' etc.). The animated head of the letter's author, Good Queen Bess 'erself, was then projected onstage as she rattled off the tenor of the missive: Shakespeare *must* write a play about Falstaff in love (see Nicholas Rowe) and do it in a week (see *No Bed for Bacon*). Shakespeare – the comic hack – groaned and set about the task.

Having implied that the play we were about to see was, frankly, not up to much, Laird then inserted a second prologue in which we were introduced to the residents of this modern-day Windsor in a series of flashy choreographic vignettes. Here's the Page family with Anne a sulky bimbo, all heels and lashes and extensions, swiping left on her Tinder app! Here's Fenton the goofy love interest striking romantic poses then pratfalling over his own feet!

While this did efficiently introduce us to the *dramatis personae*, it also felt like we had skipped the play and gone straight to the curtain call. Ten minutes had passed before Shallow *et al.* initiated something resembling a plot.

If Whyman's *Romeo* had struggled to create a sense of place and community, there was no such problem here. On Lez Brotherston's excellent maximalist set – two revolving, half-timbered houses; garish *nouveau riche* furniture – we were in contemporary Essex. Or rather in that vapid, fake-tanned version of it depicted in the long-running TV 'reality soap' *The Only Way Is Essex* (*TOWIE*) (2010 – the crack of doom), in which we follow the semi-scripted adventures of lads and ladettes in the nightclubs and tanning salons of Brentwood, Essex. *TOWIE* is one of the clearest symptoms of the fact that, as a society, we have agreed that it's OK to laugh at people who volunteer to go on television, especially if they are poorly educated narcissists. (Although, on the global stage, reality TV really has had the last laugh by getting another not-very-bright, orangey narcissist into the White House.)

In the USA, a current vogue is to give this play a local habitation and name (e.g. *The Merry Wives of Bloomington*). Such productions trade on the affection audiences have for their home towns, while also confirming their suspicion that in Bloomington (or San Jose or Milwaukee), all the women are strong and most of the men are harmless chumps. In staging a *Merry Wives of Essex*, Laird opted for something quite different: a cheerful embrace of a TV-generated stereotype that could unite audiences in the Midlands and London in their own sense of superiority to that benighted county north-east of the capital.

Parts of Essex voted heavily in favour of leaving the European Union, and Laird and her team integrated a slew of state-of-the-nation gags, many of which revolved around immigration and other preoccupations of Brexit Britain. Dr Caius entered, flustered and sweaty after a busy round of visits, muttering '*il fait chaud . . . les grandes affaires . . . Brexit . . . catastrophe!*' The Fat Woman of Brentford became a Romanian maid from Brentwood, Elena Popescu (Ford: 'I'll Popesc-you!'). The lads hired to assist in the gulling scenes were Jan and Radek from Poland. They discussed the pros and cons of taking the gig in (surtitled) Polish, with Radek complaining that 'My dissertation isn't going to write itself'; in the second gulling scene, they compared Ford's jealousy to a passage in Proust, even gesturing to an inflatable swan and making an erudite pun on *Swann's Way*. Ford's alter ego was Mr Jakoff, a UK-based Russian with suspiciously new money. There was internal immigration, too: we had a Welsh

38 *The Merry Wives of Windsor*, 4.2, Royal Shakespeare Theatre, directed by Fiona Laird. David Troughton as Falstaff and Beth Cordingly as Mistress Ford. Photograph by Manuel Harlan.

nationalist Sir Hugh who sang 'Bread of Heaven' to gee himself up for the duel, and then, when the audience were encouraged to join him for an encore, scolded us: 'Rubbish! Think Welsh welly not English porridge!' As such interpolations imply, this production wasn't slavishly committed to the text Shakespeare had apparently cobbled together in a tricky week in the mid-1590s.

Everything was thrown at each scene of this show to maintain the manic and cartoonish atmosphere, whether it was Anne Page's mechanical purse dog yapping at the hapless Slender, an anarchic remote-control golf caddy causing chaos during a chase scene, or the steam that rose from Dr Caius's pen as he frantically scribbled his letter of challenge. Amid this mayhem, the production was grounded by the performances of Rebecca Lacey (Page) and Beth Cordingly (Ford) as the wives. The letter scene was played, as the

production poster had promised, in a beauty spa (shades here of Bill Alexander's 1985 wives in curlers under hairdryers). Lacey and Cordingly avoided over-playing either the initial cattiness or the later conspiratorial glee; the only time they laughed was at Page's line about hatches and going to sea (2.1.88ff.). This was a down-to-earth friendship of two equally smart and resilient women. Elsewhere, Vince Leigh's unconventional Frank Ford had the air of a recently retired rock star – both the best-looking and most insecure man in town. I liked the way he underplayed the soliloquies, eschewing the easy laughs on trusting a Welshman with his butter, etc., and attempting to introduce a modicum of psychological reality amid all the cranked-up mayhem.

The major casualty of the contemporary Essex setting was David Troughton's Falstaff. Troughton brought his customary energy, intelligence and peerless diction to the role, but – surrounded by all-too-legible stereotypes – it wasn't clear who this man was supposed to be. In his early scenes, he squeezed into a vast Union Jack waistcoat, a bedraggled John Bull with ginger comb-over. But if this was meant to align him with a Brexity agenda, why were his followers (a 'tough girl' Bardolph, a finger-snapping gay Pistol) so youthful and 'cosmopolitan'? Perhaps this was Falstaff as anachronism. The first gulling scene was set on a blinged-up poolside – lime recliner on astroturf, de-luxe faux-gold barbecue – into which he waddled in absurd Edwardian tennis gear (with multiple knee braces): the wrong sport and the wrong century (Figure 38). (On 'have I caught thee?', he ran the tennis racket head over the length of Mistress Ford's reclined body like a metal detector – a 'seductive' move that nicely revealed his pecuniary motives.) Perhaps the ultimate humiliation for this out-of-time Falstaff was to exit the gulling scene not in a buck-basket but in a fetid wheelie-bin.

***

Expectation is a key theme of *Troilus and Cressida*, and the pre-publicity for Gregory Doran's production tickled skittish spirits with three promises: (a) that the company would be 50/50 men and women; (b) that the action would be set in a world inspired by the *Mad Max* movies; (c) that the whole thing would pulsate to a specially commissioned score by Dame Evelyn Glennie, doyenne of UK percussionists.

Nikki Turner's set was dominated by an enormous mobile consisting of the dangling detritus of the twentieth century (wheel hubs, car radiator grills, etc.), hanging 'like a rusty mail / In monumental mockery' (3.3.146–7). Upstage, five container crates. On a relatively bare stage, Turner's impressive costumes did much of the work. The National Theatre's 2018 *Macbeth* had been wrongly described by many critics as *Mad Max*-inspired, but in terms of imitative homage, here at the RSC was the real thing: goggled messengers on customized motor-bikes, massively muscled strongmen (Theo Ogundipe's Ajax) on superfluous stilts,

a dieselpunk depiction of a future age scattered with the fragments, scraps and relics of those that have come before it.

Other than inspiring some terrific costumes and keeping the props department in gainful employment constructing baroque multi-horned motorbikes, I wasn't convinced that the full implications of the post-disaster setting were really observed. There was no sense of a scarcity of resources, nor of the deprivations of a siege, nor of a toxic or unforgiving climate (Achilles' default setting was topless, most other characters went for layered grungy). Nor did the production draw an analogy between Helen's position as a captive and the fugitive women of *Mad Max: Fury Road*, trying to escape their fate as enslaved breeders. In short, nearly everyone moved and acted as they might in any other Shakespeare production. (Charlotte Arrowsmith's Cassandra was an exception: she had a distinct and engaged body language, percussively stomping out her prophecies with her feet.) I also wondered if *Mad Max* – which is, if memory serves, short on meaningful dialogue and long on insanely adrenal chase sequences – is the most obvious context for this wordy and largely uneventful play.

There are only false gods in *Mad Max*, but there were real ones in this world. When Ulysses invited us to 'hark what discord follows' when degree is not observed, she lifted her arms, discordant sounds emerged from the musicians' galleries, and the massive rusty mobile wobbled ominously. This struck me as odd: surely the point here is not that Ulysses actually believes what she is saying, let alone thinks that anything metaphysical is going to shift the stalemate. Similarly, when Calchas (here Cressida's mother) oversaw the rigged lottery, she invoked the heavens and the mobile shook its rusty locks. Again, at the moment that Cressida agreed to see Diomede the next day ('Ay, come, do. / I shall be plagued') – she looked up and the junkyard heaven gave a disapproving wobble.

As promised, Glennie's percussive score was integral to the experience. At least two of the instruments – the Glennie concert aluphone and the barimbulum – are of her own invention, and these and other metallic clamours frequently interrupted speech in the opening scenes. (After the curtain bow, the percussionists performed a well-earned *Stomp*-like encore on the stage, including a wall-mounted drum downstage left that had not, surprisingly, been used in the show itself. I was reminded of Joseph Roach's dictum that 'luxury is the performance of waste'.)

Unlike the previous three shows, which played in rep with many overlapping cast members, the company for this *Troilus* had been specially assembled, and boasted some very experienced performers in relatively minor parts (e.g. Amanda Harris as a cocky Aeneas, and Suzanne Bertish, a shock-haired, intentionally hammy Agamemnon). Doran also had at his disposal very distinguished actors such as Oliver Ford Davies (Pandarus) and Sheila Reid (Thersites), although I couldn't help thinking that it might have worked better if the cerebral Davies had played Thersites and the diminutive and larky Reid had given a cheeky Auntie Pandarus.

Adjoa Andoh's was a significantly more energetic Ulysses than is typical, full of sudden gestures and tonal shifts (Figure 39). Perhaps she was relishing driving the plot, perhaps she felt responsible for generating energy in some of the more sluggish passages. Flipping the gender of the character led to some interesting pay-offs: her 'sluttish spoils' jibe at Cressida became an acidic piece of horizontal misogyny; and, on her departure from Achilles' tent, Patroclus's reference to 'A woman impudent

39 *Troilus and Cressida*, 1.3, Royal Shakespeare Theatre, directed by Gregory Doran. Adjoa Andoh as Ulysses and Suzanne Bertish as Agamemnon. Photograph by Helen Maybanks.

and mannish grown' (3.3.210) was spat in the direction in which she'd exited. Her villainy was also clearly signalled by the fact that she shot Patroclus dead from a kind of book-depository position on top of one of the upstage container units.

Daniel Hawksford gave a solid, centred, unfussy performance as a Hector whose end was even more ignominious than usual. Someone here had the odd idea that Achilles is actually a useless fighter; when he and Hector met in single-combat in 5.6, Achilles cack-handedly dropped his spear, moved very clumsily and was easily bested. It was even more of a moral outrage when the Myrmidons massacred Hector, spectacularly backlit by dozens of orange lanterns, like so many setting suns (see 5.9.5).

At the other end of the tonal scale, there were some nice comedic touches. In the procession of returning warriors, Troilus's self-consciousness at being eyed by Cressida led to a series of goof-ups (dropped helmet, tripping upstairs) only partially redeemed by splashing his hair with sacred water then tossing his head back like a shampoo model. The characterization of Menelaus as a barely articulate, red-wigged bone-head, however, tipped over into caricature (something John Barton's notes on the play, reprinted in the programme, warned against).

If not strictly futuristic, Amber James's Cressida was certainly the most contemporary person onstage. After she was suspected of begging a kiss from Troilus, her 'I am ashamed. O heavens, what have I done?' (3.2.135) was comic mock regret; this assertive and knowing woman was not about to conform to a cliché of feminine reticence. In the morning-after scene with Troilus, her 'Are you aweary of me?' and 'Do you think I will?' were direct, authentic and displayed a rare ability in this verbose world to cut through the crap with simple questions. In her short coda to the overhearing scene, James gave an anguished scream before 'Ah, poor our sex!' (5.2.111), in an effort to make those words an epitaph on the victimization of women, rather than the colon before the sexist lines with which Shakespeare ends her part in the play. In this production (as in others before it), Cressida was brought back on in the final moments, in this case in the same suspended orb from which Helen spoke the Prologue. For a second, I wondered whether she would speak some part of the Epilogue. But no – her fate was silence, clamped, like Helen, in the cage of her notorious identity.

\*\*\*

To return to the question with which this section began: based on these four productions, does the RSC currently provide a theatrical experience that is 'different'? It's a broad question and not one that can be fully unpacked here. One could argue that certain aspects of these shows, rather than being distinctive, were actually squarely in line with broader trends. Whether it be cross-gendered casting, 50/50 male/female companies or an increasing number of actors speaking in their own accents rather than British Received Pronunciation (RP), the RSC is generally, as it were, getting with the wider programme. But what struck me most about this season was the fact that three out of the four shows' primary conceptual and design referents derived from TV and film (horror films such as *The Shining*, *The Only Way is Essex*, the *Mad Max* films). This might be pure coincidence – equally, it might be a symptom of the way in which we reach for the familiar in uncertain times. Either way, this 'different kind of theatre' looked oddly familiar. With the increasing importance of cinematic relays, is it possible – even on a subconscious level – that directors and designers are opting for something that they know already looks good on a rectangular screen: that the cinematic tail is wagging the theatrical dog? Just a hunch; let's see what happens in 2019.

## BRISTOL, LIVERPOOL, NEWBURY

These final three productions, although geographically dispersed, had important things in common: all were medium-budget productions with middle-sized casts of eight to ten actors taking place in well-established, intimate venues. All three were symptomatic of the strong standard of

Shakespearian production to be found outside of London.

Adele Thomas's production of *Macbeth* bene-fitted from the tight quarters of the Tobacco Factory's in-the-round playing space. The stage floor (which must be crossed to reach your seat) was covered with pungent shreds of black rubber, the opposite of a 'sure and firm-set earth' (2.1.56). The major design leitmotif was of white boxes, whether the glowing cubes held by the Witches or the thanks-for-having-me present that an unwitting Fleance gave to Lady Macbeth on arrival at Dunsinane. These white boxes thus seemed to symbolize both prophecy and the exchange objects of a gift culture. I saw an early preview and I suspect their significance might have been further clarified by press night (likewise that of the blindfolded, somewhat static, Gaelic-speaking weird sisters).

Katy Stephens's Lady Macbeth required no clar-ification. Preview be damned – this performance was fully formed, precisely delineated and clearly the fulfilment of a long-term ambition to play the role. She entered in dressing gown and socks, the depressed day-wear of the left-behind and bereaved woman. On the invocation, she bur-rowed into the rubbery earth to discover a black mirror. She set this against a pillar and from a diagonal distance asked to be unsexed in its reflection. She grasped herself between the legs on 'Unsex me *here*', and the 'compunctious visit-ings' could only be read as menstruation and, metonymically, childbirth. She had, in effect, cursed herself with sterility.

She would revisit this primal scene often, cli-mactically when sleep-walking. Here she scrambled again into the earth to reach the conclu-sion that 'hell is murky'; on 'this little hand', she again reached between her legs, then quickly pulled her hand back up for inspection. Whatever she saw then – whether blood (equalling menstrua-tion and therefore not a hoped-for pregnancy) or no blood (confirmation of her unsexed state?) – triggered her terminal despair. Her maternal instinct had earlier surfaced in the way she hugged Fleance to her while, tongue-tied and discombo-bulated, she attempted to welcome Duncan to her

house. Perhaps her child had died in hospital, like the apparition that appeared to Macbeth, a boy in white vest, long-johns and an oversized ruff attached to an intravenous drip, a tree sprig at the bottom of the bag. Certainly, the glass that Banquo bore in the show of kings was the same black mirror into which she had earlier unsexed herself.

Although this show played at the Tobacco Factory, it was not (like the *Henry V* described above) a production by the company 'Shakespeare at the Tobacco Factory'. It was – Stephens's perfor-mance aside – more conservative than the *Henry*, but will have served as a very solid introduction to the play to the many students taking notes around me.

The most striking feature of Gemma Bodinetz's *Othello* at the Liverpool Everyman was the gender-flipping of the titular character (Figure 40). The UK currently has a female Prime Minister, the most senior police officer is Cressida Dick, and the British Army appointed its first female General in 2015. Golda Rosheuvel's General Othello had no doubt overcome many of the obstacles faced by her real-life counterparts, but with the key difference that she was a black lesbian operating in a white man's world. Her first entrance in a simple sleeveless dress, sandals and a bold yellow and black headscarf signalled some-one who wasn't trying to pass as either masculine or white. For this 'old black dam' (*sic*) to be ordering white boys around while also being in a same-sex marriage was meant to feel doubly transgressive. The fact that Emily Hughes's Desdemona was a 'lipstick lesbian', a trophy younger wife in con-ventional and expensive outfits, must have both galled guys like Roderigo and, later, played on Othello's insecurities (maybe she's just dabbling with lesbianism and will actually abandon me for some bulky stud like Cassio?). When Othello rebuked Desdemona ('Proceed you in your tears, Oh well-painted passion'), Desdemona wasn't actually crying; the lines were thus a way of demeaning her to the effect of: 'you're just a little girl, not a grown-up like me – I always knew you were not strong enough to make this relationship work'.

40 *Othello*, 1.3, Everyman Theatre, Liverpool, directed by Gemma Bodinetz. Golda Rosheuvel as Othello and Emily Hughes as Desdemona. Photograph by Jonathan Keenan.

The production was set in a near future that looked very like now. The Duchess of Venice checked her iPad for military updates, and Patrick Brennan's Iago was a techno stalker who filmed Desdemona and Cassio on his phone ('Ay, smile upon her, do', 2.1.172ff.) and later showed the clip to Roderigo to illustrate the 'index and obscure prologue'. Brennan played Iago at a rattling pace – had he learned this from the 'busy insinuating rogue' who had previously turned his own wit the seamy side out with jealousy (cf. 4.2.135ff.)? He was at his best in 3.3 when he was forced to slow down, weigh his words (line 124) and focus on his quarry. The scene was nicely staged as the morning-after-the-night-before in a makeshift mess hall over breakfast (Desdemona munching on a piece of toast, Othello spooning down a bowl of what looked like *Cheerios*). For once,

the business of the scene was not war-related paperwork but the more mundane task of cleaning up breakfast plates. When Iago refused to reveal his thoughts, Othello shoved the hot tray trolley into his midriff – the first indication she might have a short and violent fuse.

This production had a slight issue with pronouns and other markers of gender. Despite changes like 'old black ram' to 'old black dam' in 1.1, when Brabantio arraigned Othello in front of the Duke, he spluttered 'here is the man!' but without any ironic inflection. Desdemona said 'but here's my husband' and alternated between calling Othello 'my lord' and 'my love'. Later, Iago implored 'Good ma'am, be a man', which doubly confused the matter. This happens quite a lot in gender-flipped productions and should be remediable.

The eight-strong cast worked hard all night and I especially enjoyed Marc Elliot's metrosexual Roderigo (older and handsomer than is usual in this role) who showed up in Cyprus with matching designer suitcases and in tight pedal-pusher chinos and pink shirt, ready for a Mediterranean holiday.

He would have been better off spending a balmy night at the Watermill Theatre, Newbury, where Paul Hart's charming, whacky *A Midsummer Night's Dream* played throughout the sweltering summer. The already small stage was cluttered with ropes, trunks and clothes rails, a haunted Edwardian theatre, more *Woman in Black* than ancient Athens. The transition to the woods was effected by the swift dropping and raising of a red curtain to reveal an arboreal mural on the upstage wall. Magical interventions were denoted simply: Puck played a single note on the piano prompting Helena's light-bulb resolution to tell Demetrius of the lovers' flight. Interpolated musical numbers included Victoria Blunt's Bottom crooning 'Blue Moon' to prove that she was not afraid, and Jamie Satterthwaite's Oberon singing 'I put a spell on you' to the sleeping Titania. (My only complaint about the music was that we didn't hear a lot more of Tyrone Huntley's Lysander, fresh as he was from his award-winning turn as Judas in Regent's Park's *Jesus Christ Superstar*.)

There was quite a deal of (rehearsed) ad-libbing and some fun ideas: when the 'Battle with the centaurs' was mooted, a topless 'Athenian eunuch' jumped excitedly onstage, ready to perform – 'Alright?' he asked the audience in a suspiciously deep voice before being dispatched by Theseus's 'We'll none of that' (5.1.46). Elsewhere, I enjoyed Emma McDonald's Hippolyta whose thick accent suggested she hailed from somewhere deep in the Amazon basin; so sternly and assertively did she accuse Quince of speaking the prologue 'like a child on the recorder' (5.1.123) that the analogy had the force of a Brazilian proverb.

After years of being home to the all-male Propeller company, it was refreshing to see a 50/50 gender split in this young cast. And it is a sign of how far and how quickly we've come in the last decade that it now feels unremarkable to see a woman playing Bottom or a partially deaf actress signing most of Hermia's lines in British Sign Language. The direction of travel is clear and offers some small grounds for optimism as we brace ourselves for 2019.

# PROFESSIONAL SHAKESPEARE PRODUCTIONS IN THE BRITISH ISLES, JANUARY–DECEMBER 2017

## JAMES SHAW

Most of the productions listed are by professional companies, but some amateur productions are included. The information is taken from *Touchstone* (www.touchstone.bham.ac.uk), a Shakespeare resource maintained by the Shakespeare Institute Library. *Touchstone* includes a monthly list of current and forthcoming UK Shakespeare productions from listings information. The websites provided for theatre companies were accurate at the time of going to press.

### ALL'S WELL THAT ENDS WELL

Cambridge Shakespeare Festival. Downing College Gardens, Cambridge, 10–29 July.
www.cambridgeshakespeare.com

### ANTONY AND CLEOPATRA

Royal Shakespeare Company. Royal Shakespeare Theatre, Stratford-upon-Avon, 11 March–7 September; Barbican Centre, London, 30 November–20 January 2018. Broadcast in cinemas worldwide 24 May.
www.rsc.org.uk
Director: Iqbal Khan
Cleopatra: Josette Simon
Mark Antony: Antony Byrne
Part of the Shakespeare's Rome season.

*Adaptation*

*Roman Tragedies*
Toneelgroep Amsterdam. Barbican Theatre, London, 17–19 March. First staged at the Barbican in 2009.

Director: Ivo van Hove
Six-hour conflation of *Coriolanus, Julius Caesar* and *Antony and Cleopatra*. The theatre doors remained open and an electronic display announced the minutes until significant dramatic moments. In Dutch with English subtitles.

### AS YOU LIKE IT

Civil Brawl Theatre Company. Number One Shakespeare Street, Stratford-upon-Avon, 3–5 April.
http://civilbrawltheatrecompany.co.uk
Modern-day setting with some gender-reversed roles.

LAMDA. POSK, London, 11–20 April; Theatre Royal, Bury St Edmunds, 26–27 April.
www.lamda.org.uk
Director: Bill Alexander

The HandleBards. St George's Theatre, Great Yarmouth, 5 June and tour to Chelsea Physic Garden, London, 14–15 September.
www.handlebards.com
Four-strong all-female troupe.

MadCap Theatre Productions. Ryde School with Upper Chine, Isle of Wight, 18 June and tour to Greyfriars House and Gardens, Worcester, 13 August.
www.madcaptheatreproductions.co.uk

Regents Park Open Air Theatre, London, 6–28 July.
http://openairtheatre.com
Director: Max Webster

Shared Experience. The Theatre by The Lake, Keswick, 7 July–4 November and tour to Broadway Theatre, Letchworth, 29 November–2 December.
www.sharedexperience.org.uk
Director: Kate Saxon

## Adaptation

*Rosalind*
James Cousins Company. Lakeside Arts, Nottingham, 3 March and tour to Jerwood DanceHouse, Ipswich, 5 May.
www.jamescousinscompany.com
Choreography: James Cousins

*7/7 The Dance of Life in Seven Steps*
Hungarian State Theatre. Studio, York Theatre Royal, 15–16 May.
www.yorktheatreroyal.co.uk
Choreographer: Baczó Tünde
Dance adaptation reimagining the seven ages from a female perspective. Part of the York International Shakespeare Festival.

## THE COMEDY OF ERRORS

Illyria Theatre Company. The Hawth Amphitheatre, Crawley, 17 June and tour to Manor Farm, Corsley, 10 September.
www.illyria.co.uk

Derby Shakespeare Theatre Company. Minack Theatre, Penzance, 14–18 August.

## CORIOLANUS

Titus Theatre Group (Iran). Temple Hall, York St John University, 20 May.
Directors: Hamed Asgharzadeh and Javad Ebrahimi Nezhad
Shown on screen due to actors having been declined visa entry to UK for York International Shakespeare Festival.

Royal Shakespeare Company. Royal Shakespeare Theatre, Stratford-upon-Avon, 15 September–14 October; Barbican Centre, London, 6–18 November.
www.rsc.org.uk
Director: Angus Jackson
Coriolanus: Sope Dirisu
Part of Shakespeare's Rome season.

## Adaptation

*Roman Tragedies*
Toneelgroep Amsterdam. Barbican Theatre, London, 17–19 March. First staged at the Barbican in 2009.
Director: Ivo van Hove

Six-hour conflation of *Coriolanus*, *Julius Caesar* and *Antony and Cleopatra*. The theatre doors remained open and an electronic display announced the minutes until significant dramatic moments. In Dutch with English subtitles.

## HAMLET

Icarus Theatre Collective. Lawrence Batley Theatre, Huddersfield, 17 January and tour to King's Theatre, Southsea, 3–4 April.
www.icarustheatre.co.uk
Director: Max Lewendel
Cast of nine.

Almeida Theatre, London, 17 February–8 April; Harold Pinter Theatre, London, 9 June–2 September.
www.almeida.co.uk
Director: Robert Icke
Hamlet: Andrew Scott
Gertrude: Juliet Stevenson

Leicester Drama Society. The Little Theatre, Leicester, 24–29 April.
www.thelittletheatre.net
Director: Pip Nixon

The Discarded Nut Theatre Company. The Lights, Andover, 10 May and tour to Theatre Royal, Winchester, 4 June.
www.discardednut.co.uk
Director: Noel Jones

Cambridge Shakespeare Festival. St John's College Gardens, Cambridge, 10–29 July.
www.cambridgeshakespeare.com

Kenneth Branagh Theatre Company and RADA. The Jerwood Vanbrugh Theatre, London, 1–23 September.
www.rada.ac.uk
Director: Kenneth Branagh
Hamlet: Tom Hiddleston
Fund-raising production for RADA.

Progress Theatre, Reading, 12–21 October.
http://progresstheatre.co.uk
Director: Aidan Moran
Female Hamlet.

## Adaptation

*Rosencrantz and Guildenstern are Dead*

The Old Vic Theatre, London, 25 February–29 April.
www.oldvictheatre.com
Playwright: Tom Stoppard
Director: David Leveaux
Rosencrantz: Daniel Radcliffe
Guildenstern: Joshua McGuire

*Re-member Me*
Almeida, London, 19 and 26 March, 2 April.
http://almeida.co.uk
Director: Jan-Willem Van Den Bosch
Playwright: Dickie Beau
A frustrated actor ruminates on the realization that he will not play Hamlet. Played on the same set as the Almeida's *Hamlet* directed by Robert Icke.

Approximately Right Productions (in association with Park Theatre). Park Theatre, London, 22 August–16 September.
Director: Simon Evans and David Aula
90-minute version played by three members of one family.

## Opera

Glyndebourne Theatre Company. Glyndebourne, Lewes, 11 June–6 July and tour to Theatre Royal, Plymouth, 1 December.
www.glyndebourne.com
Composer: Brett Dean
Libretto: Matthew Jocelyn
Director: Neil Armfield

## HENRY IV PARTS I–2

### Adaptation

*Henry IV – a Pub Wake*
Bronzehead Theatre. Eagle & Child, York, 14–18 May and tour to Wig & Mitre, Lincoln, 1 June.
www.bronzeheadtheatre.co.uk
Director: Tom Straszewski
Conflation of parts 1 and 2.

## HENRY V

Antic Disposition. Southwark Cathedral, London, 2–3 February and tour returning to Southwark Cathedral, London, 21–22 February.

www.anticdisposition.co.uk
Director: Ben Horslen and John Risebero
Set in World War I.

Tread the Boards Theatre Company. Attic Theatre, Stratford-upon-Avon, 30 March–23 April.
www.treadtheboardstheatre.co.uk
Director: John-Robert Partridge

### Adaptation

*Into the Breach*
The Old Red Lion, London, 3 April and occasional touring performances to October.
Playwright and performer: Mark Carey
A novice actor plays Henry for the village drama group.

*Henry V (Man and Monarch)*
Theatre Royal, York, 19–20 May.
Director: Brett Brown
One-man show exploring Henry with dialogue from *Henry IV* plays, *Henry V* and *Henry VI*.

## HENRY VIII

York Theatre Royal. King's Manor, York, 30 March–1 April.
www.yorktheatreroyal.co.uk
Director: Ben Prusiner
Promenade performance.

## JULIUS CAESAR

Guildford Shakespeare Company. Holy Trinity Church, Guildford, 4–25 February.
www.guildford-shakespeare-company.co.uk
Director: Gemma Fairlie

Royal Shakespeare Company. Royal Shakespeare Theatre, Stratford-upon-Avon, 3 March–9 September; Barbican Centre, London, 24 November–20 January 2018.
www.rsc.org.uk
Director: Angus Jackson
Part of Shakespeare's Rome season.

Crucible Theatre, Sheffield, 17 May–10 June.
www.sheffieldtheatres.co.uk
Director: Robert Hastie

Bristol Old Vic Theatre School. Bristol Old Vic, Bristol, 9 June–1 July.

www.bristololdvic.org.uk
Director: Simon Dormandy
Julius Caesar: Julian Glover
Cast predominantly comprising Bristol Old Vic Theatre School graduates.

Storyhouse Theatre, Chester, 23 June–30 July; Grosvenor Park Open Air Theatre, Chester, 3–27 August.
www.storyhouse.com
Director: Loveday Ingram
Included a local community chorus.

*Adaptation*

*Roman Tragedies*
Toneelgroep Amsterdam. Barbican Theatre, London, 17–19 March. First staged at the Barbican in 2009.
Director: Ivo van Hove
Six-hour conflation of *Coriolanus*, *Julius Caesar* and *Antony and Cleopatra*. The theatre doors remained open and an electronic display announced the minutes until significant dramatic moments. In Dutch with English subtitles.

### KING LEAR

Little Goblin Productions and Art Vic Theatre Company. Theatro Technis, London, 30 May–10 June.
www.theatrotechnis.com
Director: Victor Sobchak

Cambridge Shakespeare Festival. St John's College Gardens, Cambridge, 31 July–19 August.
www.cambridgeshakespeare.com

Shakespeare's Globe Theatre, London, 10 August–14 October.
www.shakespearesglobe.com
Director: Nancy Meckler
Lear: Kevin McNally

Minerva Theatre, Chichester, 22 September–28 October.
www.cft.org.uk
Director: Jonathan Munby
Lear: Ian McKellen
McKellen first played Lear in 2007 for the RSC.

*Adaptation*

Orange Tree Theatre, London, 13 May–10 June.

www.orangetreetheatre.co.uk
For school audiences. Abridged version with a cast of four.

*Queen Lear*
Bard in the Botanics. Botanic Gardens, Kibble Palace, Glasgow, 12–29 July.
www.bardinthebotanics.co.uk
Director: Jennifer Dick

*King Lear Retold*
The Civic Theatre, Barnsley, 19 October.
www.barnsleycivic.co.uk
Performer: Debs Newbold
Solo storytelling with modernized language.

### LOVE'S LABOUR'S LOST

Royal Shakespeare Company in collaboration with Chichester Festival Theatre. Theatre Royal Haymarket, London, 9 December 2016–18 March.
www.rsc.org.uk
Director: Christopher Luscombe

*Adaptation*

Royal Academy of Music's Musical Theatre Company. Hackney Empire, London, 29 June–2 July.
Director: Bruce Guthrie
Composer: Michael Friedman
Musical adaptation. UK premiere first staged at Shakespeare in the Park in New York in 2013.

### MACBETH

Theatr Genedlaethol Cymru. Caerphilly Castle, 7–15 February.
www.chapter.org
Director: Arwel Gruffydd
Welsh-language production.

The Dukes Young Actors. The Dukes Theatre, Lancaster, 22–25 March.
http://dukes-lancaster.org
Director: Liz Stevenson

The AC Group. Jack Studio Theatre (previously Brockley Studio Theatre), London, 4–22 April.
www.brockleyjack.co.uk
Director: Thomas Attwood

Sutton Coldfield Town Hall Theatre Company. Town Hall, Sutton Coldfield, 23–27 May.
www.townhallsuttoncoldfield.co.uk
Director: Benjamin Field

Iris Theatre Company. St Paul's Church (The Actors' Church), London, 21 June–29 July.
http://iristheatre.com
Director: Daniel Winder

Barbican Theatre, London, 5–8 October.
Director: Yukio Ninagawa
In Japanese with English surtitles.

Devil You Know Theatre Company. CLF Theatre, the Bussey Building Peckham, 31 October–18 November.

*Adaptation*

*Macbeth – Shakespeare for Younger Audiences*
Dorfman Theatre. National Theatre, London, 6–20 February.
www.nationaltheatre.org.uk
Director: Justin Audibert

Splendid Productions. Blake Theatre, Monmouth, 8 February; Quarry Theatre, Bedford, 7 March; Waterside Arts Centre, Sale, 17 March.
www.splendidproductions.co.uk
Directors: Kerry Frampton and Matt Wilde
60-minute version including comedy, physical theatre and song.

*Macbeth & Twelfth Night*
Purple Cast Productions. The Bread and Roses Theatre, London, 21 March–1 April.
Directors: Wendy A. Jeffries and George C. Francis
Abridged 60-minute versions separated by an interval.

*The Devil Speaks True*
Goat and Monkey Theatre Company. Lighthouse (previously known as Poole Arts Centre), Poole, 27 April.
Adaptation from Banquo's perspective.

*MacBlair*
Falling Sparrow Productions. The Warren (Studio 3), Brighton, 5–7 May and 3–4 June.
Playwright: Charlie Dupre
Macblair and Macbrown meet three weird journalists in the House of Commons.

*Wyrd Sisters*
New Wimbledon Theatre, London, 9–13 May.
Author: Terry Pratchett

Adaptor: Stephen Briggs

Oddsocks Theatre Company. Pavilion at the Park, Bedford, 10 June and tour to Workington Hall, Cumbria, 1 September.
www.oddsocks.co.uk
Comic version.

*The Macbeths*
Citizens Theatre, Glasgow, 27 September–14 October.
Director: Dominic Hill
70-minute version concentrating only on the titular characters.

*Lady M.*
1623 Theatre Company. Derby Theatre, St Peter's Quarter, Derby, 5 November.
www.1623theatre.co.uk
A performer develops a tightrope-walking drag queen called Lady M.

*Macbeeth*
Red Squash Theatre Company. Hen and Chickens Theatre, London, 12–16 December.
60-minute comic version.

*Opera*

Teatro Regio Torino. Festival Theatre, Edinburgh, 18–20 August.
Director: Emma Dante
Composer: Giuseppe Verdi

## MEASURE FOR MEASURE

Cygnet Theatre Company. New Theatre (also Cygnet Theatre), Exeter, 22 March–1 April.
https://cygnettheatre.co.uk

Bard in the Botanics. Botanic Gardens, Kibble Palace, Glasgow, 14–29 July.
www.bardinthebotanics.co.uk
Director: Gordon Barr
Cast of four.

## THE MERCHANT OF VENICE

Shake-Scene Shakespeare Theatre Company. The Cockpit Theatre, London, 3–7 October.
http://shake-sceneshakespeare.co.uk
Cue-script performance.

*Adaptation*

*Gratiano: Grist to the Mill*
Studio, York Theatre Royal, 18 May; Assembly Hall, Edinburgh, 3–28 August.
Playwright and performer: Ross Ericson
A sequel from Gratiano's perspective.

*Opera*

Royal Opera House, London, 19–20 July.
www.wno.org.uk
Composer: André Tchaikowsky

## THE MERRY WIVES OF WINDSOR

Festival Players. Kington and Dormston Village Hall, Dormston, 13 May and tour to Winterbourne Medieval Barn, Winterbourne, 29 August.
http://thefestivalplayers.co.uk
Director: Michael Dyer
All-male production.

Cambridge Shakespeare Festival. Robinson College Gardens, Cambridge, 31 July–26 August.
www.cambridgeshakespeare.com

The Lantern Theatre, Sheffield, 15–25 November.
http://lanterntheatre.org.uk

## A MIDSUMMER NIGHT'S DREAM

The Young Vic, London, 16 February–1 April.
www.youngvic.org
Director: Joe Hill-Gibbins

Further Stages Theatre Company. New Wimbledon Studio Theatre, London, 8–9 April.

Daniel Taylor Productions. Epstein Theatre (formerly Neptune Theatre), Liverpool, 25–29 April.
www.epsteinliverpool.co.uk

Grosvenor Park Open Air Theatre, Chester, 9 June–27 August.

Merely Theatre. The Dell (RSC), Stratford-upon-Avon, 10–11 June; N16 Globe, Bedford Hill, 15 September; Trinity Theatre, Tunbridge Wells, 28 September.
http://merelytheatre.co.uk
Cast of five.

Chapterhouse Theatre Company. Hampton Court Castle Gardens, 15 June and tour to The Oates Collections, Selbourne, Hampshire, 27 August.
www.chapterhouse.org

Guildford Shakespeare Company. Racks Close, Quarry Street, Guildford, 15 June–1 July.
www.guildford-shakespeare-company.co.uk
Director: Lotte Wakeham

The Pantaloons Theatre Company. Denmead Junior School, Waterlooville, 21 June and tour to Diss Corn Hall Open-Air, 3 September.
http://thepantaloons.co.uk

Civil Brawl Theatre Company. Number One Shakespeare Street, Stratford-upon-Avon, 16–19 and 23–26 July.
http://civilbrawltheatrecompany.co.uk
Director: Richard Nunn

Cambridge Shakespeare Festival. Trinity College Gardens, Cambridge, 31 July–19 August.
www.cambridgeshakespeare.com

Unfolds Theatre Company. The Rose Playhouse, London, 1–26 August.
www.rosetheatre.org.uk
Director: Alex Pearson

Northern Spark Theatre and Bite My Thumb. Carriageworks Theatre, Leeds, 8–9 September; Guiseley Theatre, Leeds, 16 September; Halifax Playhouse, Halifax, 29–30 September.
www.northernsparktheatre.co.uk

*Adaptation*

*Thisbe*
Door Ajar Theatre Company. Theatre Royal, Stratford East, 21–25 February; Aberdeen Exhibition and Conference Centre, 10 March; Theatre Royal, York, 21–22 March.
www.doorajartheatre.com
Playwright: Samantha Sutherland
Sequel from the perspective of the daughter of Helena and Demetrius.

The HandleBards. Norden Farm, Maidenhead, 13 June and tour to Phoenix Theatre & Arts Centre, Bordom, 16 September.
www.handlebards.com
All-male cast of four.

Creation Theatre Company. Clapham Omnibus, Clapham, 16–30 June; 5 July–5 August.
www.creationtheatre.co.uk
Director: Zoe Seaton
Promenade treasure hunt.

Flute Theatre, Orange Tree Theatre and English Touring Theatre. Orange Tree Theatre, Richmond, 16–28 October.
www.orangetreetheatre.co.uk
Participatory performance for children on the autism spectrum aged 10+.

*Drugged Love: A Night in Midsummer*
Civil Brawl Theatre Company. Number One Shakespeare Street, Stratford-upon-Avon, 13–15 and 19–22 November.
Playwright and Director: Kathryn Harper
LGBT-themed play based on *A Midsummer Night's Dream.*

## *Ballet*

Ballet Cymru and Riverfront Theatre. Blackwood Miner's Institute, Blackwood, 24 May and tour to Salisbury Arts Centre, Salisbury, 8 December.
http://welshballet.co.uk
Composer: Felix Mendelssohn
Choreography: Darius James

*The Dream*
Royal Opera House, London, 2–10 June.
www.roh.org.uk
Part of a triple bill in tribute to Frederick Ashton.

Ballet Theatre UK. Theatre Royal, Bury St Edmunds, 1–2 March; Epsom Playhouse, Epsom, 9 March.
www.ballettheatreuk.com
Composer: Felix Mendelssohn

## *Opera*

Durham Opera Ensemble. Gala Theatre, Durham, 17–18 February.
Composer: Benjamin Britten

Aldeburgh Festival Orchestra. Snape Maltings Concert Hall, Aldeburgh, 9–14 June.
Composer: Benjamin Britten

## MUCH ADO ABOUT NOTHING

*Love's Labour's Won or Much Ado About Nothing*

Royal Shakespeare Company in collaboration with Chichester Festival Theatre. Theatre Royal Haymarket, London, 9 December 2016–18 March.
www.rsc.org.uk
Director: Christopher Luscombe

Bowler Crab Productions. Half House Farm, Three Oaks, Sussex, 16–25 June and tour to St John's Centre, Bexhill-on-Sea, 8 July.
www.bowler-crab.com

Cambridge Shakespeare Festival. King's College Gardens, Cambridge, 10–29 July.
www.cambridgeshakespeare.com

Shakespeare's Globe Theatre, London, 14 July–15 October.
www.shakespearesglobe.com
Director: Matthew Dunster
Benedick: Matthew Needham
Beatrice: Beatriz Romily

Rondo Theatre Company. The Rondo Theatre, Bath, 22–25 November.
http://rondotheatre.co.uk

## *Adaptation*

Shit-Faced Shakespeare. Leicester Square Theatre, London, 11 April–16 September.

*I Know You of Old*
Golem Theatre Company. The Hope Theatre, London, 13 June–1 July.
www.golemtheatre.co.uk
Playwright: David Fairs
An alternative play created from rearranging Shakespeare's text.

*Much Ado about Hero*
Theatre N16, London, 17–21 October.
www.theatren16.co.uk
Playwright: Lexi Clare
Musical version.

## OTHELLO

Shakespeare at the Tobacco Factory. The Tobacco Factory Theatres, Bristol, 16 February–1 April and tour to Wilton's Music Hall, London, 16–20 May.
www.tobaccofactorytheatres.com
Director: Richard Twyman

Shakespeare's Globe. Sam Wanamaker Playhouse, London, 23 February–16 April.
www.shakespearesglobe.com
Director: Ellen McDougall
Othello: Kurt Egyiawan
Iago: Sam Sprueilleach
Cassio played as Michelle Cassio.

SISATA. Lighthouse (previously known as Poole Arts Centre), Poole, 12–13 May and tour to Edmondsham House and Gardens, Edmondsham, 23 July.
www.sisata.co.uk

National Youth Theatre and Frantic Assembly. The Ambassadors Theatre, London, 26 September–8 December.
Director: Simon Pittman

Bowler Crab Productions. St Mildred's Church, Tenterden, 28 October and tour to St John's Centre, Bexhill, 2 December.
www.bowler-crab.com

### Adaptation

*Waiting for Othello*
Studio, York Theatre Royal, 17–18 May.
Director: Jan Naturski
Two immigrants audition for the role of Othello.

*Otelo*
CASA Festival. Southwark Playhouse, London, 26–30 September.
http://southwarkplayhouse.co.uk
Playwright: Viajeinmovil
Puppetry version focusing on Desdemona's murder.

### Ballet

Birmingham Royal Ballet Triple Bill: *Arcadia/Wink/The Moor's Pavane*. Everyman Theatre, Cheltenham, 5–6 May.

### Opera

*Otello/Othello*
Kent Opera. The Old Market, Brighton 23 May.
Composer: Giuseppe Verdi

*Otello*
Royal Opera House, London, 21 June–15 July.

www.roh.org.uk
Director: Keith Warner

## PERICLES

### Adaptation

*Pericles – All at Sea*
Multi Story Theatre Company. Everyman Theatre, Cheltenham, 8–9 March.
www.multistorytheatre.co.uk

## RICHARD II

Clatterhouse Theatre Company. Drayton Arms Theatre, London, 15 March–1 April.

## RICHARD III

Schaubühne Berlin. Barbican Theatre, London, 16–19 February.
Director: Thomas Ostermeier
In German with English surtitles.

Northern Broadsides Theatre Company. Hull Truck Theatre, Hull, 4–27 May; The Viaduct, Halifax, 30 May–3 June.
www.northern-broadsides.co.uk
Director: Barrie Rutter

Arcola Theatre, London, 11 May–10 June.
www.arcolatheatre.com
Director: Mehmet Ergen
Richard III: Greg Hicks

The Malachites. The Rose Playhouse, Bankside, London, 11–23 July and on tour.
www.themalachites.co.uk
Director: Benjamin Blyth

Antic Disposition Theatre Company. Peterborough Cathedral, Cambridgeshire, 14–15 July and on tour to Centre du Village, Beauville, France, 3 August. First staged in 2015.
www.anticdisposition.co.uk
Directors: Ben Horslen and John Risebero

Front Foot Theatre Company. The Cockpit Theatre, London, 12 October–4 November.
http://frontfoottheatre.com

Barons Court Theatre, London, 30 October–19 November.
Set in the 1960s East London with Richard played by two actors as the Kray twins.

## ROMEO AND JULIET

Merely Theatre Company (in association with The Production Exchange). Theatre Royal, Lincoln, 2 March–3 March and tour to Kings Theatre, Edinburgh, 20–22 September.

West Yorkshire Playhouse. Quarry Theatre, WYP, Leeds, 3–25 March.
www.wyp.org.uk
Director: Amy Leach
Included a local community chorus.

Shakespeare's Globe Theatre, London, 22 April–9 July.
www.shakespearesglobe.com
Director: Daniel Kramer
Gender-reversed casting for Mercutio.

Victor Harvey Productions. Union Theatre, London, 29 April–20 May.
www.uniontheatre.biz
Director: Andy Bewley
Romeo and Juliet played as two gay footballers playing for rival teams.

Watermill Theatre, Newbury, 10–13 May and tour returning to Watermill 18–22 July.
www.watermill.org.uk
Director: Paul Hart

Everyman Company. Everyman & Playhouse, Liverpool, 27 May–7 June.
www.everymanplayhouse.com
Director: Nick Bagnall
Gender-reversed casting of Juliet as Julius.

Shakespeare in the Square. St James's Square, London, 4 July and tour around London garden squares.
www.shakespeareinthesquare.co.uk
Director: Tatty Hennessy

Butterfly Theatre Company. Glastonbury Abbey, 14–16 July.
www.glastonburyabbeyshop.com
Promenade performance.

Mayhem Theatre Company. Cannizaro Park, London, 26–29 July.
www.mayhemtheatre.co.uk

Cambridge Shakespeare Festival. King's College Gardens, Cambridge, 31 July–26 August.
www.cambridgeshakespeare.com

### Adaptation

*Romeo and Juliet – Shakespeare for Younger Audiences*
Stratford Circus, London, 18 January–1 February; National Theatre, London, 11–24 February.
www.nationaltheatre.org.uk

*Romeo and Juliet – The Timeless Tale Reimagined by a Cast of Five*
Actors from the London Stage. Cockpit Theatre, London, 2–3 April.
http://thecockpit.org.uk

Theatr Iolo. Studio 2, Theatr Clwyd, Mold, 5–8 April.
www.theatrclwyd.com
Combining circus skills and theatre.

*Oddsocks Romeo and Juliet – Mods v. Rockers*
Oddsocks Theatre Company. Lichfield Garrick, Lichfield, 17–18 May and tour to St James Garden, Liverpool, 31 August.
www.oddsocks.co.uk/theatre

*West Side Story*
Dolman Theatre, Newport, 23–25 June.
www.dolmantheatre.co.uk
Composer: Leonard Bernstein

The Three Inch Fools. Eastbury Manor House (National Trust), Barking, 9 June and tour to The Globe at Hay, Hay-on-Wye, 16 August.
www.threeinchfools.com
60-minute version with a cast of five.

Flute Theatre. Orange Tree Theatre, London, 16–28 October.
www.orangetreetheatre.co.uk
Performance for young people with autism, and their families. Children and actors play sensory games to unravel Shakespeare's story.

*West Side Story*
Orbit Theatre Company. New Theatre, Cardiff, 7–11 November.
www.newtheatrecardiff.co.uk

## Ballet

Moscow City Ballet. Chichester Festival Theatre, Chichester, 3–4 January; Richmond Theatre, London, 18–22 January.
Composer: Prokofiev

Ballet Theatre UK. Pomegranate Theatre, Chesterfield, 12 January.
www.ballettheatreuk.com
Composer: Prokofiev

English National Ballet. Southbank Centre, London, 1–5 August; Hippodrome, Bristol, 21–25 November.
www.ballet.org.uk
Choreographer: Rudolf Nureyev
Composer: Prokofiev

Russian State Ballet and Opera House. Theatre Severn, Shrewsbury, 15 October and tour to Theatre Royal, Norwich, 4 April 2018.
Composer: Prokofiev

## Opera

*I Capuleti e i Montecchi*
Popup Opera. Off Quay, London, 7 March and tour to West Wight Association 70th Anniversary, Freshwater, Isle of Wight, 8 April.
http://popupopera.co.uk
Composer: Vincenzo Bellini

*A Village Romeo and Juliet*
New Sussex Opera. Lewes Town Hall, 22 March and tour to Devonshire Park Theatre, Eastbourne, 2 April.
www.newsussexopera.org
Composer: Frederick Delius

## THE TAMING OF THE SHREW

Get Over It Productions. The Cockpit Theatre London, 23–27 January; Bread and Roses Theatre, London, 21–25 February.
http://getoveritproductions
Director: Paula Benson
All-female cast.

Lazarus Theatre Company. Jack Studio Theatre, Brockley Road, London, 18 July–5 August.
www.lazarustheatrecompany.com
Director: Sara Reimers

LAMDA, London, 29 November–7 December.

www.lamda.org.uk
Director: Rebecca Frecknell
Reverse-gender production.

## Adaptation

*Kiss Me Kate*
Kilworth House Theatre, Leicestershire, 31 May– 6 July.
www.kilworthhousetheatre.co.uk
Director: Matthew White

*Kiss Me Kate*
Ilkley Playhouse, 5–17 June; Minack Theatre, Penzance, 24–28 July.
www.draminack.com
Director: David Kirk

*The Taming of the Shrew?*
Bard in the Botanics. Botanic Gardens, Glasgow, 23 June–8 July.
www.bardinthebotanics.co.uk
Director: Gordon Barr
With additional material from *The Tamer Tamed, or The Woman's Prize* by John Fletcher.

## THE TEMPEST

Royal Shakespeare Company. Royal Shakespeare Theatre, Stratford-upon-Avon, 8 November 2016– 21 January; Gala Theatre, Durham, 3 February; Barbican Centre, London, 30 June–18 August.
www.rsc.org.uk
Director: Gregory Doran
Prospero: Simon Russell Beale

Southwark Playhouse. Southwark Playhouse, London, 6–28 January.
http://southwarkplayhouse.co.uk
Director: Amy Draper
For school audiences.

Sea-change Theatre. The Rose Playhouse, London, 22 June–2 July.
www.sea-changetheatre.com
Director: Ray Malone
90-minute version from all-female company.

## Adaptation

The Salon Collective. The Cockpit Theatre, London, 11 December 2016–15 January.

# PROFESSIONAL SHAKESPEARE PRODUCTIONS

www.thesaloncollective.org
Cue-script production.

Royal Shakespeare Company. Swan Theatre, Stratford-upon-Avon, 3–4 February and tour to The Other Place, Stratford-upon-Avon, 23–25 March.
www.rsc.org.uk
Director: Aileen Gonsalve
For younger audiences.

*The Buried Moon*
Petersfield Shakespeare Festival at Bedales. The Rose Playhouse, Bankside, London, 3–13 May.
www.petersfieldshakespearefestival.co.uk
Director: Jake Smith
Playwright: Laura Turner
Prequel exploring the relationship between Miranda and Caliban.

Bilimankhwe Arts. EM Forster Theatre, Tonbridge, 2 October and tour to Lakeside Arts Centre, Nottingham, 27 October.
www.bilimankhwe-arts.org
Director: Kate Stafford
Abridged version omitting King of Naples and all courtiers except Ferdinand.

## TIMON OF ATHENS

Bard in the Botanic Gardens, Kibble Palace, Glasgow, 23 June–8 July.
www.bardinthebotanics.co.uk
Director: Jennifer Dick
Gender-reversal casting for Timon.

## TITUS ANDRONICUS

Royal Shakespeare Company. Royal Shakespeare Theatre, Stratford-upon-Avon, 23 June–2 September; Barbican Centre, London, 7 December–19 January 2018.
www.rsc.org.uk
Director: Blanche McIntyre
Titus: David Troughton

## TWELFTH NIGHT

Chipstead Players. The Courtyard Theatre, London, 6–14 January.
www.chipsteadplayers.org

Director: Sarah Branston

Civil Brawl Theatre Company. The View, Stratford-upon-Avon, 12–15 and 17–21 January.
Director: Ashleigh Aston

National Theatre. Olivier Theatre, London, 15 February–13 May.
www.nationaltheatre.org.uk
Director: Simon Godwin
Malvolia: Tamsin Greig
Gender-reversal casting of Feste and Malvolio, with Malvolio rechristened Malvolia.

Clatterhouse Theatre Company. Drayton Arms Theatre, London, 17–31 March.
www.thedraytonarmstheatre.co.uk

Merely Theatre. Theatre Royal, Lincoln, 2 March–3 March and tour to Kings Theatre, Edinburgh, 20–21 September.
http://merelytheatre.co.uk
Cast of five.

Shakespeare Up Close. Orange Tree Theatre, London, 18–26 March.
www.orangetreetheatre.co.uk
Director: Alex Thorpe
Abridged version with cast of six.

Watermill Theatre, Newbury, 6 April–6 May and tour returning to the Watermill 18–22 July.
www.watermill.org.uk
Director: Paul Hart
Gender-reversal casting of Antonio and gender-blind casting of Sir Toby.

Royal Exchange Theatre, Manchester, 13 April–20 May.
www.royalexchange.co.uk
Director: Jo Davies
Transgender casting of Feste.

Shakespeare's Globe Theatre, London, 18 May–5 August.
www.shakespearesglobe.com
Director: Emma Rice
Gender-reversal casting of Malvolio. Emma Rice's final production as Artistic Director of the Globe.

Rain or Shine Theatre Company. Sandhurst Village Green, 2 June and tour to Butleigh Cricket Club, Butleigh, 28 August.
www.rainorshine.co.uk

The Three Inch Fools. Ightham Mote (National Trust), Kent, 3 June and tour to Mapperton Gardens, Beaminster, Dorset, 20 August.
www.threeinchfools.com
Cast of five.

Sun & Moon Theatre. The Dell, Stratford-upon-Avon, 18 June and tour to Palace Theatre, Paignton, 12 August.

RoughCast Theatre Company UK summer tour, July.
www.roughcast.co.uk
Director: Mark Burridge

Folksy Theatre Company. Cottiers Theatre, Glasgow, 11 July and tour to Hare Hill Garden, Macclesfield, 26 August.
www.folksytheatre.co.uk

Shooting Stars Theatre Company. Tea Lawn, Lauderdale House, 10–20 August and tour.
www.shootingstarstheatre.co.uk

Royal Shakespeare Company. Royal Shakespeare Theatre, Stratford-upon-Avon, 2 November–24 February 2018.
www.rsc.org.uk
Director: Christopher Luscombe
Malvolio: Adrian Edmondson
Viola: Dinita Gohil

*Adaptation*

*Macbeth & Twelfth Night*
Purple Cast Productions. The Bread and Roses Theatre, London, 21 March–1 April.
Directors: Wendy A. Jeffries and George C. Francis
Abridged 60-minute versions separated by an interval.

## THE TWO GENTLEMEN OF VERONA

Guildford Shakespeare Company. University of Law, Guildford, 14–29 July.
www.guildford-shakespeare-company.co.uk

## THE TWO NOBLE KINSMEN

Royal Shakespeare Company. Swan Theatre, Stratford-upon-Avon, 17 August–7 February.
www.rsc.org.uk
Director: Blanche McIntyre

## THE WINTER'S TALE

Cheek by Jowl Theatre Company. Citizens Theatre, Glasgow, 24–28 January and tour to Bristol Old Vic, Bristol, 25–29 April. First staged in 2016.
www.cheekbyjowl.com
Director: Declan Donnellan

Royal Lyceum Theatre, Edinburgh, 10 February–4 March.
http://lyceum.org.uk
Director: Max Webster

*Opera*

English National Opera. London Coliseum, London, 27 February–14 March.
www.eno.org
Director: Rory Kinnear
Composer: Ryan Wigglesworth

## POEMS AND APOCRYPHA

*The History of Cardenio* by William Shakespeare, John Fletcher and Gary Taylor
Richmond Shakespeare Society and Cutpurse. Mary Wallace Theatre, Twickenham, 18–25 March.
www.richmondshakespeare.org.uk
Director: Gerald Baker

*Venus and Adonis*

Royal Shakespeare Company with Little Angel Theatre. Swan Theatre, Stratford-upon-Avon, 26 July–4 August.
www.rsc.org.uk
Director: Gregory Doran
Puppet version.

*Venus and Adonis*

Noontide Sun and Close Quarter Productions. Edinburgh Festival Fringe, Lodge No. 1, Edinburgh, 2–28 August; and at the Rose Playhouse, London, 10–15 October.
www.thenoontidesun.com
Director: David Salter
Solo performance.

# PROFESSIONAL SHAKESPEARE PRODUCTIONS

### Analyse Thou

Ruff Trade Theatre Company. OFS Studio, Oxford, 21 April.
Playwright: Jodana Janse van Vuuren and Lee Woodward
Comedy featuring counselling sessions for a selection of Shakespeare characters.

### Bard Heads; Third Witch from the Left and Call Me Oz

Finding the Will Theatre Company in association with The Everyman Theatre.
The Old Red Lion, London, 2 April; Penlee Park Open Air Theatre, Penzance, 23 July; Cygnet Theatre, Exeter, 21 October.
Playwright and Performer: Jules Heads and Richard Curnow
Two 'talking heads' performances featuring Osric and one of the witches in Macbeth.

### The Complete Deaths

Spymonkey. Minerva Theatre, Chichester, 14–18 February.
www.spymonkey.co.uk
Director: Tim Crouch
Seeventy-four onstage deaths delivered by a cast of four.

### The Complete Works of William Shakespeare (Abridged)

Attic Theatre, Stratford-Upon-Avon, 18 May–11 June.
www.theattictheatre.co.uk

### Othellomacbeth

Home Theatre (formerly Cornerhouse), Manchester, 14–29 September; Lyric Theatre Hammersmith, London, 5 October–3 November.
Director: Jude Christian
Abridged versions, separated by an interval, with the Othello women reanimating to become the witches in the second half.

### The Second Best Bed

Worcester Repertory Company. Yvonne Arnaud Theatre, Guildford, 21 January; Timsbury, Bath, 26 January.
www.worcester-rep.co.uk
Playwright: Avril Rowland
Solo piece from the perspective of Anne Hathaway.

### Shakespeare, Tolkein, Others and You

Park 200, London, 4–9 July.
Director: Jez Bond
Performer: Ian McKellen
One-man show of theatrical anecdotes.

### Shakespeare and his Black Mates

Presented by Museumand. The National Caribbean Heritage Museum. Playhouse, Nottingham, 2 November.
Playwright: Lynda Burrell and Fran Hajat
A young William Shakespeare observes a tavern scene which inspires creative ideas.

### Shakespeare and the Character of Kingship

Society of Antiquaries of London. Burlington House, London, 29 January.
Performer: Simon Russell Beale
Dramatic readings from Shakespeare's history plays. Released on DVD by Society of Antiquaries of London.

### The Shakespeare Revue

Clwyd Theatr Cymru, Mold, 19–23 September.
www.theatrclwyd.com
Adaptors: Christopher Luscombe and Malcolm McKee

### Shakespeare's Lost Women

Petersfield Shakespeare Festival at Bedales. The Rose Playhouse, Bankside, London, 3–13 May.
www.petersfieldshakespearefestival.co.uk
Director: Jake Smith

*Shakespeare's Will*

Through the Square Theatre Company. Alma Tavern Theatre, Bristol, 16–17 June.
Playwright: Vern Thiessen
The fallout from the reading of Shakespeare's will in 1616.

*William Shakespeare's Long Lost First Play (Abridged)*

Reduced Shakespeare Company. Pleasance, Playhouse Theatre, Norwich, 4 February and tour to Gilded Balloon, Edinburgh, 3–28 August.

Abridged version of a 'new' play discovered in a Leicester car park.

*Your Bard*

Royal Oak and Castle, Pevensey, 3 March; and tour to Kemnay Village Hall, Aberdeenshire, 14 May.
www.nicholascollett.com
Playwright and Performer: Nicholas Collett.
William Shakespeare defends his authorship claims against an anti-Stratfordian professor.

# THE YEAR'S CONTRIBUTIONS TO
# SHAKESPEARE STUDIES

## 1. CRITICAL STUDIES
*reviewed by* CHARLOTTE SCOTT

In homage to Patricia Parker's brilliant and baroque book, *Shakespearean Intersections: Language, Contexts, Critical Keywords*, I start where I should end with the 'arsy-versy' or the preposterous, as a new collective noun for a group of books on Shakespeare. In this amblongus pie of textual delicacies, Parker addresses 'key' terms through which other words or phrases may be unlocked or interconnected. Returning to many of the avenues and intersections that Parker explored in her – now classic – *Shakespeare from the Margins*, the book devotes itself to the ebullient performances of meaning that take place across the drama and invites us to the often indigestible feast of language as both a guest and an onlooker. Following the surprising verbal behaviours, reversals and different senses of before and after, Parker begins with *Love's Labour's Lost* and 'the obscene and most preposterous event' with which the play starts. Focusing on the ways in which Armado introduces the audience to the disruptive world of the before (pre) that now comes after (posterior), we follow the fissures and breeches, ends and beginnings, body parts and processes through which the play frustrates its discoveries and defers its endings. The extraordinarily detailed and accomplished way in which Parker observes behaviours and behavioural patterns of words through this most starchy of plays points to

an unending delight in the tractability of language and the capacity of the imagination to trace such pyrotechnical displays across the page. Tracing the patterns that words may make across the play and through the mouths of its characters, Parker shows the contextual ways in which words are harnessed and redeployed through the cornucopian vessel of the play world. Demonstrating that exploring the 'preposterous' is 'to engage in a reconsideration of word play and structural play not simply for formal reasons', but to situate that wordplay within the broader contextual histories of order, hierarchy, bodily function and normative categories of gendered and social expectation, Parker sets out the terms of the book's enquiry and the importance of the 'arsy-versy' (John Baret's phrase) in Shakespeare's conception of progress. Following the categories of 'proper order', Parker moves to *The Taming of the Shrew*, where she discusses arts and arses in the context of 'the "sodomitical", suppositional, and substitutive resonances of "supposes"'. In *A Midsummer Night's Dream*, she addresses the quince in Athenian weddings and the 'medlar' or 'open arse' of the play's emphasis on 'love-potions, sexuality, unruly women, and female speech, as well as on the question of fruitfulness and fruitful issue'. The following chapter attends to preposterous recall in *Henry V*, including a brilliant reading of the multiple performances of Burgundy and the recursive 'bending' of the play's Epilogue, where we are encouraged to go backwards in order to go forwards. On *Othello*, Parker returns to her interest in the geopolitical contexts of Brabant, Spain and Ottoman power. The final chapter on *Cymbeline* draws together the many preposterous strands of Shakespeare's imagination through a focus on the 'back-door' and the 'women's part' in the importance of transvestite theatre as a place of recognition as well as supposition. Parker has always been one of the most trenchant and dazzling observers of word behaviour and her command of the almost incorrigible and mischievous elements of Shakespeare's language is an art in itself. The vibrant way in which she conjures contexts and allusions, recalls, suppositions, bends, behinds and breaches draws out the spectacular ways in which meanings are networked across the plays, but also the audiences and how the word becomes a powerful token or gift through which we can explore the rich complexities of belonging to Shakespeare's play worlds. Where, perhaps, the book loses focus is in performance and how much of this sparkling display remains evident for the audience member where 'quick bright things' can, like Lysander's love stories, 'come to confusion'.

Speaking of things with a parted eye, Brett Gamboa's *Shakespeare's Double Plays: Dramatic Economy on the Early Modern Stage* explores the nature of double-meaning in Shakespeare's plays. Here the idea of doubleness extends from the pun, through the actor's body, to doubling up roles so that dramatic meaning becomes networked to a range of instances that are simultaneously embodied, theatrical, symbolic and linguistic. 'How Shakespeare puns with actors' is the central concern of Gamboa's book, and within that enquiry he engages with a fundamental concern of representation: being and seeming. The paradox of acting, as Gamboa sees it, when the actor is required to be both character and professional impersonator, is further extended in Shakespeare by the multiple uses of the same actor for different roles. Doubling roles is more than just expedient in a smaller acting

company; it is strategically vital in 'orchestrating possibilities for the thematic patterning and resonance between or among characters through the unifying agent of a single actor who doubles in these roles'. Referring to the 'actor-character's core duality', Gamboa develops a compelling thesis for the interactions between character and actor that are, in Parker's terms, 'preposterous', because they bring, through recall and pun, the back to the front, and what has gone forward to the backs of our minds. This visual punning produces similar effects to Parker's linguistic fireworks because the audience has a half-memory of an alternative conversation – say in the doubling of Polonius and the grave digger – that is both far away and near at hand. Central to Gamboa's thesis are the multiple opportunities that doubleness provides: from a theatrical or performative perspective, there are endless possibilities in the admission of artifice; and from a conceptual angle, we can appreciate the anamorphic potential of complex questions of morality or gender, sexuality or faith away from the conventional positions of antithesis. Understanding character in this way – as a series of positions, densely occupying various dimensions within the fiction – allows the spectator to participate in the challenge of reconciling or 'harmoninz[ing] multiple and contradictory personas at a single point of perception'. Exploring the idea of representation through the multidimensional interactions between spectator and character, Gamboa sets out the importance of doubleness in the history of artifice, as well as belief. Beginning with *Hamlet*, Gamboa attends to Polonius and his precarious position between the fictional worlds of the play and the audience: analysing the moments he becomes the actor who almost forgets his lines, or waffles on about genre, Gamboa establishes the enhanced presence of disruption which allows Shakespeare to 'blend the real and the imaginary': '[s]ince theatre is an art energized by constantly staving off its own disintegration, doubling roles provides an unparalleled means of enhancing its fundamental attractions'. Focusing on the ways in which doubling 'admits the fiction of the fiction', Gamboa produces a very fluent, well-argued and compelling account of the theatre's self-referential abilities to animate, as well as unsettle, the unity of character. There is something especially invigorating about Gamboa's focus on the positive processes of disruption which do not strive for unity or naturalism, but rather gather in celebration around the fractious and fractured nature of representation: 'the haunted illusions that result gain a greater pretension to something like truth because of the hierarchies established within them'. Exploring the diversity and range required of actors in order to double roles, the book goes on to investigate the theatrical expectations afforded by the body's ability to inhabit multiple roles. Considering Shakespeare's passionate commitment to exploiting the opportunities of doubling, Gamboa persuasively argues that we need to grasp the implications of doubling in order fully to appreciate Shakespeare's play-making. Within this context, he provides some fresh and attractive arguments for the reconsideration of certain roles, as well as bodies: most significantly, Gamboa suggests that adult men played women (an argument that is especially convincing in *Macbeth*) and that lead actors often played multiple roles. Thinking about the logistics of costume changes, the shorthand of certain staging conventions, and the theatrical necessity of particular deaths to keep the cast to size opens up a wealth of opportunities to appreciate the inter-illusions of the play worlds, as well as the strategies that support them. Repositioning Shakespeare's play worlds as written for small casts focuses our attention on some of the incongruities that the text may produce (unexplained deaths, departures, behaviours, etc.) but also leaves open the problem of crowd scenes, battles or, indeed, the opening to *Titus Andronicus*. Here Gamboa examines our limiting historical allegiance to verisimilitude and offers different possibilities about the maximum number of speaking bodies needed (consider *Henry V*'s Chorus's invitation to think a 'thousand parts divide one man'). Similarly, the bias towards naturalism has skewed our understanding of the representation of children as well as women, and Gamboa presents 'a more persuasive casting theory'

for the multiple use of adult males in these roles. Thinking through both structure and substitution, the book then analyses the prevailing ways in which the potential for doubling enhances the play world's larger commitments to the physical body as a site of meaning that can be replaced as well as reinvented. *Shakespeare's Double Plays* follows a narrative arc in which Shakespeare appears to become more adept at and indebted to the art of doubling: Lear's poor fool, *Measure*'s '[a]n Angelo for a Claudio', Hermione's dead son reborn as a daughter, as well as Hamlet's uncle-father produce a myriad of theatrical puns which support the ingenuity of Shakespeare's dramaturgy. Working on the basis that Shakespeare wrote for a cast size of between nine and twelve actors, Gamboa produces a fascinating and brilliant account of the significance of doubling – not only as the province of the mercurial and efficient playwright, but as the source from which Shakespeare's theatrical energy flows.

Continuing the focus on theatrical ingenuity, we turn to Tom Rutter's *Shakespeare and the Admiral's Men: Reading Across Repertories on the London Stage, 1594–1600*, which examines the 'reciprocal influence' between Shakespeare's work and the playing company. Moving beyond the more generally accepted inspirations of Marlowe and Kyd, Rutter identifies the significance of plays by George Chapman, William Haughton and Anthony Munday, as well as those anonymous works performed by the Admiral's Men which contributed to the wider authority of the repertory. Understanding the dynamic and referential relationships that existed between the playing companies and the ways in which these generated new plays allows us further to understand the formative networks of repertory theatre. Central to this focus is a critical emphasis on 'the artistic choices they made and the aesthetic effects generated by their adherence to and rejection of earlier practice'. The range of theatrical material offered by the Admiral's Men supports Rutter's inquiry into the intertextual relationship between the company and the playwright. One of the most compelling elements of this account is its expansion of the terms of influence through which plays and playing companies developed. Rutter is aware that his focus is somewhat skewed in its emphasis on a single author and repertory, but the work he produces here has wider impacts for the ways in which we consider the intertextual and developmental opportunities that playwrights and companies exploited in each other. Despite the canonical emphasis on Shakespeare, one of the great pleasures here is the focus on obscure and unfamiliar plays. In the first chapter, Rutter considers the anonymous Admiral's 1594 play *A Knack to Know a Knave* and Richard Edward's *Damon and Pythias* in relation to *The Merchant of Venice* as well as *The Jew of Malta*: here he explores the precedents through which Shakespeare was able to exploit the commercial and theatrical impacts of plays bringing together 'faithful friends' and 'a usurer's daughter'. More revealing, I think, are the networks of influence that Shakespeare chose to exclude and the development in dramatic genre afforded by these plays. Keeping a keen eye on Marlowe, Rutter examines how other writers of the 1590s were also reworking Marlovian material, and how playwrights including Munday and Peele, as well as the authors of anonymous plays such as *Captain Thomas Stukely*, exploit the opportunities that Marlowe's work had produced for both imitation and satire. Within these contexts, Rutter focuses on place, social status, genre, narrative and allusion to determine the extents to which playwrights 'treated comparable materials', and whether this can produce something equating to a 'company style' or 'corporate identity'. Extending this inquiry to whether the company held any comprehensive or consistent positions, Rutter interrogates the question of religion and affiliation through the figures of John Oldcastle and Robin Hood. The chapter on *As You Like It* is especially compelling in this regard since it positions the play's forest exile within the community of beliefs about Robin Hood and the social, religious and political contexts reconfigured by Munday in *The Downfall*. Exploring such affiliations and expositions, Rutter concludes that 'Admiral's Men dramatists expressed attitudes and deployed motifs open to interpretation from other religious perspectives, from Catholic nostalgia to radical puritanism', and that there was 'significant overlap between their audience and that of the Lord Chamberlain's Men'. Rutter's emphasis on the 1590s is largely keyed into the period before the Admiral's Men moved to the Fortune in 1600, and what he produces is a very informative and well-argued book that seeks to open up the sympathetic and intertextual dynamics between plays and repertory. I learned a lot from this book, and Rutter convincingly develops the field to show how playgoers of the 1590s moved between their playhouses within an allusive atmosphere through which plays were consciously networked into, or referenced by, each other. The plays are thus pollenated by audiences to develop a powerful and rich ecology of Elizabethan theatre.

Onto a different ecology and into the woods we find Anne Barton's posthumous book, *The Shakespearean Forest,* the main text annotated, edited and compiled through the dedication of Hester Lees-Jeffries, and flanked by contributions by two of Barton's ex-students, Adrian Poole and Peter Holland. Adrian Poole sets out the genesis of the book in the Northcliffe and Clark Lectures that Barton gave at University College London and Cambridge, respectively, over the 1990s and early noughties. Establishing the context for Barton's brilliant career, her powerful contribution to Shakespeare studies, as well as the extraordinary fact that she was the first female fellow of New College, Oxford, and a 'senior figure from outside Cambridge', Poole outlines the formative role that Barton played in the 'significant increase in the number of women fellows in the 1990s and beyond'. Peter Holland provides a compassionate, charming, respectful and funny eulogy to Barton's career, which began with an undergraduate essay submission to *Shakespeare Quarterly* and ends with her as the doyenne of Cambridge, the summer before she died, reciting snatches of Richmond Lattimore's poetry in the dwindling light of her rooms over a glass of wine, with friends. Holland's admiration for Barton extends beyond the impact of her scholarship to the ways in which she demonstrates, at that moment and always, 'her lifetime of learning' and why it mattered. The book begins with a journey into the woods where Barton sets out the contexts for understanding forests, their opacity, tracks, mythologies and deep literary heritage that establishes the formidable images of cultural association. Tracing the interrelationships between sixteenth- and seventeenth-century forest ecologies and timber use, the first chapter identifies the many faces of Shakespeare's forests (Arden never gets dark, for example) and the increasingly populous areas they provide for his characters to be 'cut historically and socially adrift'. It is perhaps a legacy of the book's genesis in lectures that readers may struggle at times to find a linear argument or thread that brings the different sections together. It is episodic in nature and provides a series of detailed, clever and informative insights that cut across moments and plays as well as literary cultures and heritages. Sometimes, I felt as though I was in the presence of a conversation, transfixed by the paths trodden and the references and allusions, insights and connections made and where the speaker would go next. Moving from vibrant textual detail to broader concerns about deforestation, Barton sets out to explore the forest as an embodied space and theatrical entity, full of life and symbolism, history and imagination. Considering the artificial forest of royal pageants, Barton explores what staging a forest might look like and how the theatre responded to the many visual cues needed to define its forest spaces. From the 'sylvan spectacle' of the 'Forrest Salvigne' to the 'complex woodland set' of Inigo Jones's design, Barton investigates over the scenic potential of forests and trees, including Herne's Oak, structural posts, Tantalus, Lorel's chestnut, golden apples and the 'property tree [which] is both too real and not real enough'. Within this rich and layered tradition, the forest is so suggestive, so powerful in its ability to conjure emotions and images beyond the control of specific set designs or backdrops that we need only hear the word 'desert' to imagine the perilous space of dramatic destiny. Exploring the wood as *neminis* (the place of no one), as chaos, as lively imagining, and as ritual or cultural experience, Barton introduces us to a vibrant range of images, interlocutors and intertexts through which

the forest can take shape. In *Macbeth*, for example, Barton examines the phenomenon of the green man and leaf masks in which 'Shakespeare's audience may well have understood the walking wood in *Macbeth*, each of Malcom's soldiers obscured behind a "leafy screen" hewed from Birnam Wood, as we do not: the ritual bringing in of spring to a Scotland unnaturally arrested in winter by the usurper'. Thinking beyond the space of the forest to its inhabitants, Barton attends to the figure of the wild man, as both spectre of social disintegration and strategic political disguise. Where, for Shakespeare, the wild man remains a central figure of concern across his drama, for other writers of the period the character seems to have hit his vogue in the 1590s. Moving from the wild man to Robin Hood, Barton examines the relationship between the forest as organic space and the outlaw as embodied figure of concealment. Looking at historical impersonations of Robin Hood, Barton engages with the drama 'where characters with distinct identities of their own elect to put on Robin's hood'. Compelled by the ambivalent figure of the outlaw-hero, Barton examines the mercurial nature of the figure that could produce 'an honourable kind of thievery'. There's a huge amount of detail in the book – from specific English woods to forest mythologies; pageants, masques, paintings, engravings, emblem books, maps and frontispieces; plays, tales, modern and early modern fictions, as well as anecdotes and imaginings that range from the fourteenth to the twenty-first centuries – and Barton alludes to an extraordinary variety of authors, some only in passing and others in more detail. She generally stays clear of going into detail about the more thematically complex subjects – women, fairies and dryads, for example – but she does acknowledge the points at which the history of 'nature' and of the 'forest' collide. In the last chapter, we return to the four plays in which the forest occupies a powerful position: *As You Like It, A Midsummer Night's Dream, The Two Gentlemen of Verona* and *Titus Andronicus*. Considering the multiple nonverbal roles that the forest plays, as well as its performative fabric – trees as testimony and woods as witnesses – Barton studies 'the gift of the forest' and what it gives to the characters who pass through, converge or take refuge in it. Ending on the movement of Birnam Wood, she writes that Shakespeare

invested that disturbing image with meanings far more complex than those in his source: the forest invading the city, the urban attacked (as so often) by the alien wild, but also and conversely, as in the traditional rites of May morning, when tree branches were customarily carried into houses and towns, the forest not as an enemy but as a symbol of renewal.

This powerfully and productively ambivalent forest remains at the heart of Barton's lovely book as a testimony to the power of the human imagination and the truth of nature.

## LOVE'S NOT LOVE

The King of France's prescient observation that '[l]ove's not love / When it is mingled with regards that stand / Aloof from the entire point', begs the interminable question as to what exactly the point is from which love must not be aloof? In *Shakespeare, Love and Language,* David Schalkwyk attempts to answer that question, although he stays clear of *King Lear*, by asserting that 'love is not an emotion' but 'a form of action and disposition'. Setting out to explore how love manifests linguistically and conceptually in a selection of Shakespeare's plays, Schalkwyk powerfully attests from the outset that love is a doing more than a feeling word and one in which a staggering range of intentions and expressions can inhere. From the assertion of love in rape, violence, loathing and dishonour, Schalkwyk sets out the contentious and often disgraceful ways in which love can be averred in defence of both violation and vilification. There is, of course, another more conventional side to love in which both the doing and the expressing of it belong to something more like care, devotion, protection, desire and affection. Part of the project here is to unpick not only the contingent and conflicted behaviour of the affect but the linguistic complexities through which Shakespeare weaves his narratives of love so that it can be both 'horrible' and heart-warming. Although

the idea of desire is central to the book's focus on love, Schalkwyk takes time to establish that, for Shakespeare, often 'desire is transformed into love' and therefore should be recognized as a process through which 'language and action' are negotiated. The distinction between desire and love is important to the book's focus on love as a 'performative concept', as Schalkwyk states 'love acts rather than simply is or feels', and here we see the emphasis fall on the speech act as well as the verbal need to establish the position of the thing that is being desired as want, both as a lack and a need. The significance of being without is central to the history of both desire and love and propagates the effective processes by which love can be mobilized across the centuries as something transhistorically powerful. Yet, where desire can more specifically be associated with lacking – assuming that desire does not hold its form when the conditions are fulfilled – love asserts itself as bound by the unique conditions of the individual and therefore irreducible to a single concept or expression. The dynamic, dialogic nature of love can be found at the 'edges', between people, words, imagination and ideal; love is at its most legible in human subjectivity. Organized largely according to genre, *Shakespeare, Love and Language* analyses the pursuit and expression of desire in relation to the values and expectations of the play worlds through which it is expressed. Drawing on contemporary texts as well as critical theories, both early and modern, each chapter analyses the effects and expressions of desire as something fulfilling (both erotically and emotionally) as well as destructive (socially and bodily). One of the most compelling avenues that the book explores is the idea of 'provisional' love: in other words, love which stands on the threshold of being expressed but is contingent until embodied in 'passionate utterance'. The emphasis then on language is what brings love and desire into focus as affective sites of human relationships wherein fantasy, fiction, oaths, obligations, gifts, proximity and status offer ways of being in love as well as recognizing it as such. In *As You Like It*, for example, Schalkwyk observes the fantasy of social transformation, embodied by Rosalind and Adam, which 'is the forging of a performative capacity or agency to pledge oneself to another freely within a set of social laws, rather than merely occupying a slot in a preconditioned space'. Pledging oneself is usually at its most powerful for Schalkwyk within the terms of service that he explored in *Shakespeare, Love and Service* (Cambridge, 2008), and many of the arguments about friendship, subordination, fungibility and bonds are reinvigorated through a focus on the characters' capacity to love and 'the singularity of imaginative bestowal' that unites the disparate elements of 'passionate utterance'. The book asserts its complex relationship to love as something that unsettles but perhaps should not surprise us: Katherina's lament that Petrucchio's cruelty is carried out 'under the name of perfect love' is no surprise to the toxic world of the domestic abuser, and yet the idea that love could manifest as a justification of violence is presented as something of a surprise to Schalkwyk: as Armardo says, '[a]nd how can that be true love which is falsely attempted? Love is a familiar. Love is a devil.' There is perhaps a paradox here in which 'love' has been mobilized over the centuries by men to support a range of endeavours from the adorable to the abhorrent, and, despite Schalkwyk's perspicuity, he rallies the ranks of Plato, Lacan, Wittgenstein, Derrida and Cavell to discuss once again the male terms through which (mostly) women's erotic value has been defined. 'Love is not love', it seems, but a 'range of often-contradictory emotions or feelings over time', and would presumably, like Juliet's rose, by any other name smell as sweet. There are some wonderful insights in this book – powerful and evocative explorations of want and desire – but Shakespeare and love is more than the history of the men who have described it, and there needs to be some acknowledgement of the ways in which women have been shaped by, as well as excluded from, that discourse.

The focus on language remains prominent in *The Bible on the Shakespearean Stage: Cultures of Interpretation in Reformation England* (ed. Thomas Fulton and Kristen Poole), which provides a fortuitous return to the art of interpretation, and this collection offers an utterly absorbing account of what biblical knowledge meant to the period. Bringing together an emphasis on Reformation and Counter-reformation debates, as well as practices of reading and exegesis, the essays in this collection begin by exploring the networks through which the Bible is being read and disseminated in early modern Europe, its identity as a text within a confluence of changing cultural and religious expectations, and the apparatus – textual, visual, audible – through which scripture could be understood. As the introduction explains, how you read your Bible in the early modern period was not only revealing in terms of spiritual identities but also in terms of hermeneutic practices and the powerful ways in which those practices and principles were being shaped by a culture which had radically reappraised the *sola scriptura*. Moving beyond Naseeb Shaheen's study of biblical references, this collection shows the diverse ways in which references to the Bible can be traced beyond allusion and through the fascinating networks of religious and social interaction in the period. As a structural, generic, linguistic, allusive, visual or dialogic experience, the Bible is everywhere in Shakespeare's plays. As the editors quickly establish, '[t]he Bible, then, was not just the most read, but also the most methodologically scrutinized text in the early modern period'. 'Lived experience' travels alongside such reflective practices so that reading becomes an intermediary process of translation. Beginning with Reformation hermeneutics, the first section, which comprises two chapters, historically situates the Bible within a European context. Bruce Gordon offers a fascinating array of key figures and texts in the delivering of Reformation Bibles, and Aaron Pratt brings the focus more specifically to England and the material and media networks – including printers and bishops, almanacs and calendars – that support the creation of a New Testament. Here Pratt makes the fundamental point about how we calculate success on the basis 'that translation is what drove reception', but in fact shows a more whimsical and historically contingent text. The second section, which focuses on reading practices, provides some detailed explorations of how the 'word' is interpreted and used in various plays, including *Measure for Measure*, *Richard II* and the Henriad. Here, hermeneutics takes centre-stage as the essays examine the dramatic power of interpretation. Beginning with Angelo's mastication of God's name, the second section's three essays bring together the literal and the figurative, 'the discursive modes that privilege puns in a religious context' (Poole) and 'Shakespeare's creative engagement with Protestantism's aspirational longing' (Groves). Adrian Streete provides an excellent essay on *Titus Andronicus* and 'the generative interplay between the Roman rhetoric of oratory and the biblical rhetoric of lament' through which the play attempts to come to terms with the language of grief as it is felt 'as both stasis and excess'. Turning towards biblical allusion and the experiences of wonder that intertextuality unlocks, the following two essays in this section examine *Pericles* and *The Winter's Tale*, where, for Richard Strier, 'Shakespeare seems to have seen how fully a humanist awareness of the limits of art runs parallel to the biblical (and Reformation) critique of idolatry'. The final sections focus more specifically on the social implications of certain figures or paradigms, and Shaina Trapedo's essay on *The Merchant of Venice* is nothing short of brilliant as it explores the 'Daniel paradigm' not as one of 'cultural assimilation, but its opposite: the ability to remain distinct from the larger (corrupt) social world'. The analysis is further complicated by the 'fact that Portia takes the name "Balthasar" – a name that had been given to Daniel upon arrival at the court of Nebuchadnezzar in Babylon as a way of erasing his Jewish identity'. Trapedo's point that *Merchant* 'opens itself to questions concerning the constitutive, epistemic, and critical affordances and risks attached to all forms of human interpretation' resonates at different levels throughout the collection. Thomas Fulton's concluding essay on the 'theology of politics' brings the many layers into the later end of the early modern period where the problem of interpretation itself allows the secular to be admitted into the politics of theology. This wonderful collection of essays shows the richly layered experiences of scripture available to sixteenth- and seventeenth-century playgoers, and the formative structures through which interpretation and information are made possible. The book is a rich resource not only for scholars of the Bible, but for anyone with an interest in cultural processes of reading and interpretation as well as the status of the text.

## LOOK, WHERE SADLY THE POOR WRETCH COMES READING

Happily keeping the text in view, Julie Maxwell and Kate Rumbold's *Shakespeare and Quotation* supports a two-part approach to how Shakespeare quotes and is quoted. The collection of essays, which attempts to span the 'history of four centuries of quoting Shakespeare', begins by trying to tease out the differences between quotation, allusion, 'borrowing' and intertextuality. This is not as rewarding a task as one might hope, and the introduction is somewhat muddled in its pursuit of a clarification of these terms. Quotation and recitation, borrowing and adapting, using and repeating become a little lost in the need to pinpoint the movements of words from one place, text or mouth to another. The most engaging essays here deal with the social history of appropriation and the wonderful but no less opaque instances in which Shakespeare's words reinvent themselves in a multitude of surprising situations and instances. The essays forage among the woodlands of sententiae, sources, resources, citation and pre-history to explore quotation as a form of detachment and bricolage, with many questions as to why certain words and phrases make it to the status of quotation and what the 'longer-term fortunes of these circulating words and phrases' might be. As the thrust of these questions suggests, there is much that is speculative here, and this speculation, alongside a critical need to find some kind of 'practice' in quotation, leads to an emphasis on 'circulation', but without the drive of Greenblatt's 'social energy' (note: I quote here in order to draw the Shakespearian to *Shakespearean Negotiations* in an attempt to raise an awareness of the predominantly anecdotal thrust of the argument, or perhaps as a shorthand for flagging up the relevance of new historicism). The first section of the book attends to early modern 'bursts of words' as indications of authority, affiliation and authorship. Looking at translation and 'learned' plagiarism, these essays situate Shakespeare within an emerging but energetic tradition of reiteration and one-upmanship. There is a particularly good essay on *Lucrece* by Kevin Peterson, which illuminates the powerful use of adage and allusion in the fabric of the poem's emotional range, as well as in its self-conscious analysis of posterity. The largest sections of the book deal with the eighteenth century onwards, and are especially interested in the ways in which cultural appropriation takes effect through quotation, as both literary practice and intellectual affiliation. Moving through fiction, poetry, film and social media, the essays attempt to engage the multiple forms and iterations of Shakespeare, both as and in quotation. The least compelling element of this collection is the attempt to wrest a quotation methodology which will then produce a comprehensive attitude to the study. Part of the magic and mystery of quotation is precisely its dependence on ellipsis – both in how the words of others stand in for something that we attempt to say but ultimately cannot say, and how such acts are a process of disassociation (not my words, as it were) and attachment (words I've chosen but not originated). It's these Nietzschean effects that get lost here when the essays lean towards understanding quotation as 'a practice in its own right' rather than as meta-metaphor or, to quote Craig Raine, as 'a parable of transmission'.

One of the best books I've read this year is *Believing in Shakespeare: Studies in Longing*, by Claire McEachern, which brings together many of the strands present in other work and produces an immensely intelligent, rewarding and nuanced account of how feeling functions as a central guide to the experience of knowing as well as believing. Building on and extending the more recent turn towards re-examining the impact of the Reformation on experiences and models of belief, and exploring the effects of a Protestant emphasis on interpretation and doubt, McEachern puts the focus on how empathy can emerge through knowledge as a shared process of discovery rather than an individual position of faith. Beginning with a wonderfully clear statement of intent, McEachern establishes that the book will focus on 'two experiences of believing': '[b]elieving in a play and believing in salvation'. At first, the implicit corollary between salvation and playgoing seems sensationalist, but the book goes on to define its philosophical focus as attuned to the experiences of revelation as supported by anagnorisis and enlightenment. Turning to 'pity' and 'charity' rather than the more conventional terms of Coleridge's 'suspension of disbelief', McEachern produces a brilliant and ambitious re-examination of precisely what is at stake for the terms and conditions of theatrical experience. Beginning with an assessment of the vocabularies of belief as they have been conditioned by soteriology, Chapter 1 asserts the importance of distinguishing what early modern Protestants did believe in, as opposed to what they rejected. Tracing the routes from believing to knowing, Chapter 2 attests to the formation of belief as an 'unabashedly interested conjecture from affective experience to celestial futures, an evidence-based practice distinct from faith, on the one hand, and confirmed knowledge, on the other'. The second section develops the theme through narrative techniques, including irony and suspense, and the structures in which genre establishes and exploits 'mistaken belief'. Weaved throughout is an attention to compassion, character and techniques of recognition through which probability and knowledge are rehearsed. Over the course of the book, McEachern provides some in-depth readings of *Much Ado*, *Othello*, *Richard II*, *The Tempest* and *King Lear*. Drawing on a wonderful range of texts from Greek tragedy to the 'self help industry of practical piety', cosmology and climate, place and time, the book develops its own compassionate register of belief which is neither relativist nor irresponsible, but shaped by an awareness of denouement and death and the theatrical necessity of both.

In *Shakespeare's Reading Audiences: Early Modern Books and Audience Interpretation*, Cyndia Susan Clegg also focuses on the structures and practices of reading through which different communities learnt to interpret. Largely focusing on elite groups of learned humanists, Clegg begins by establishing that Hamlet's response to the travelling players 'suggests that Shakespeare understood that what audience members read may have affected their reception of his plays'. To this end, she focuses on how we might trace the networks of texts available to courtly culture, as well as the more quotidian practices of textual engagement in the wider public. Beginning with a focus on the 'noble mind', and how the plays conceptualize their audiences, Clegg examines the 'cluster reading experience' and the self-reflective ways in which such practices inform Shakespeare's drama. Teasing out the potential impact that reading may have had on audience experience, as well as how reading networks and groups can be identified and imagined, Clegg attempts to reconstruct the 'audience'. Holding tight to the idea of different reading communities, each chapter positions a particular text or texts at the centre of its enquiry, in most cases the play world to which it belongs or which is referenced, and then extrapolates 'how a cluster of readers who knew that text might respond to Shakespeare's work'. What's not entirely clear are the methods or data through which popularity and dissemination are being addressed. How do we know, for example, that 'books on English legal theory' were 'clearly popular'? Clegg largely bases her assumptions on number of editions as well as translations and references, all of which has been the mainstay of supporting scholarly enquiry into the subject of early modern literacy, but, as Aaron Pratt's essay in *The Bible on the Shakespearean Stage* shows, this is not always a reliable indication. The chapters on law, its interpretation and application, are largely focused on Christopher St Germain and the emphasis on justice as well as conscience. The readings of various plays, including *Merry Wives, Othello* and *Henry V*, illuminate the relationships

between act and implication, as well as, in the case of *Othello*, 'the play's forensic structure'. Focusing on 'proof' and 'doubt', alongside women and foreign law, Clegg explores the fascinating Homily '[a]gainst whoredom and adultery'. Here Clegg finds Othello, conditioned by the 'moral dichotomy that the play sets up between Venetians and the outsider', not a rationalized murderer, but an agent of justice 'whose marital love is framed by his understanding of an explicit legal code that punishes female infidelity with death'. Attending to Calvinist introspection and the 'problem of evil in *Macbeth*', Clegg establishes that the fault, dear readers, lies not with the witches or Macbeth but in the failure to 'understand the power and nature of evil'. The final chapter, which is a standout favourite for me, examines different interpretations of *Richard II*, both before and after Essex's 'aristocratic intervention'. How Elizabethans understood their history is heightened here by Clegg's excellent analysis of 'how rebellion became an interpretative trope' for the 'dramatic representation of politics'. Pursuing a much more nuanced line in relation to contemporary historical writings, Clegg supports the view that 'readers accustomed to entertaining seemingly incompatible perspectives would be prepared both to weep for Richard and to blame him'. The emphasis that the chapter brings to 'alternative and sometimes contradictory perspectives' supports a much more complex and rewarding experience of a play which has traditionally been read as politically divisive. Revisiting the commonplace assumption that Act 4, Scene 1 is excised for its representation of a deposed monarch, Clegg persuasively argues that it was more likely to be as a result of its proximity to Robert Persons's *A Conference About the Next Succession to the Crowne of Ingland*, which 'not only flouted England's statutory prohibitions against writing on the succession; it violated every statutory definition of treasonous and seditious writing' in its support of the Spanish claim to the English throne. It was not Shakespeare's play *per se* that made deposing a king on stage so dangerous but the propaganda that followed, which allowed rebellion to take such a terrifying hold of the public imagination. Exploring the relationships between John Haywood's *Henrie IIII*, Persons's *Conference*, and *Richard II*, Clegg explains that 'Coke's inferences about Haywood's book and present times might have remained simply an obscure part of the historical record if the government had not decided to use them as evidence of Essex's treasonous intentions in the 1601 rising.' *Shakespeare's Reading Audiences* is much more than its title suggests: it's a wholly compelling and fascinatingly argued revision of the cultural and literary networks that contribute to the interpretative communities that make up the public sphere.

In B. J. Sokol's *Shakespeare's Artists: The Painters, Sculptors, Poets and Musicians in his Plays and Poems*, however, the focus is on the makers and viewers of art, rather than books. Concentrating not just on the artworks themselves but on the figures and characters responsible for them, Sokol begins to untangle the knotted and compelling attitudes to the production of aesthetics and the pleasures and problems they produce. More controversially, perhaps, the book attempts to consider what Shakespeare's artists might 'think and feel', and in the process to lay claim to a 'contextual framework' through which their presence can be either explained or understood. Crucial to Sokol's thesis is art, less as a thing, image or object, but as a 'transaction', so that the 'beholder's share' is a central element of the process, which is not driven by imagination, *per se*, but by the aesthetic effects manifest in that experience. Historically nuanced to the terms of renaissance art, the book explores the production of artifice as both inspiration and labour. Tracing changing perceptions of artifice and inspiration, creation and imagination, Sokol identifies the developing attitudes through which the artificial begins to assert its affective authority. Beginning with Shakespeare's narrative poems, the book establishes the figure of the visual artist and the many ways in which Shakespeare exploits the motif of the painter, the painted image and the sympathetic or frustrated viewer. Here we encounter the familiar rhetoric of reading art, and Sokol unpacks some of the poems' explorations of ekphrasis, paragoni and blazon, for example. Continuing its focus on the visual arts, the book extends its analysis through the mobility of the terms of 'painting' to denote both a thing and an action. Sokol includes *Arden of Faversham* in his line-up as 'possibly' a Shakespearian text, and provides an engaging account of poison, passion and painting. Giulio Romano features significantly in the book, and there are some wonderfully detailed explorations of the status of Hermione as statue. Considering the figure of the 'poet' in Shakespeare's plays, from Venus to Orlando by way of the Sonnets, Sokol analyses the self-critical nature of the figure though which the 'contrary impulses' of love must be redeemed. The second half of the book turns to music and musicians, and Sokol provides a historically attentive analysis of the representation of musicians, including mythological musicians and the 'kinds of music indicated by Shakespearean play texts'. Sokol discusses *Twelfth Night* and medieval minstrels, social status, comedy and lyricism, 'where Shakespeare's complex depiction of Feste demonstrates both despised and admired aspects of being an artist', as well as a concern with performance and pedagogy and the 'thuggish vituperation' of *Romeo and Juliet*. Especially occupied by how musicians were regarded socially and culturally, and the absence of madrigals on Shakespeare's stage, Sokol develops his argument through 'vacuous noise' and 'insubordination'. Drawing on a number of mythological musicians, including Orpheus and Apollo, Sokol focuses in on the satyr Marsyas and his relationship to *The Merchant of Venice*, and Babys, whom he perceives as helping us 'untangle certain textual and structural conundrums in *Othello*'. Paying special attention to the scene in *Othello* in which the recently disgraced Cassio hires some 'wake-up musicians' to play underneath the bedroom window of Othello and Desdemona, Sokol provides an evaluation of the links between Cassio's new role in the play as one who, 'in forsaking his former conscience and delicacy becomes the blustering Captain figure of the commedia, a character easily associated with Babys-like, inappropriately blaring, wind instruments'. In an afterword, considering the 'joyousness of art', Sokol ends with a contemplation of the art maker as creator and cornucopian vessel in which the effects of poetry linger as both joy and sadness.

## SEX, SOLILOQUIES AND THE CITY

In *Shakespeare and London*, Duncan Salkeld provides a comprehensive and useful book for students to familiarize themselves with the contexts in which the early modern theatre was developing and the city that supported it. Drawing together allusions through the plays of Shakespeare's contemporaries, including Marlowe, Jonson, Marston and Chapman, Salkeld attempts to bring the London of Shakespeare's theatre into the distant worlds of his plays and to render it, even briefly, 'ridiculously familiar'. According to Salkeld, '[w]hile Shakespeare owed his success to London, it seems he was always attempting to transport his audience out of it'. Understanding the city in which Shakespeare's art thrived, Salkeld puts together some of the vistas and views of the teeming life of the capital. Driven largely by the seedier sides of London, Salkeld reimagines the contexts in which the lawless and destitute, itinerant and irreverent drove the energies of the rapidly expanding city. Salkeld has a novelistic eye on the archives in which he reconstructs possible local allusions or triggers for Shakespeare's place names, characters or events, in which speculative details provide marvellous fodder for the re-imagination of Elizabethan London. Beginning with the links between Stratford-on-Avon and London, the book asserts that Shakespeare was foremost a 'countryman' and this sense of 'exclusion' permeates his work. The binary distinction between the town and the city, as well as the country and the city, is important to Salkeld's trajectory, and he makes a virtue of Shakespeare's emotionally peripheral relationship to the city which launched his career. The second chapter, which focuses more specifically on London locations and makes a case for the relevance of topography, explores areas, including Clerkenwell, Shoreditch, Bishopsgate and Bankside, as they may have been referred to, however fleetingly, in the plays. Often these

moments take Salkeld into the archives, where he retrieves compelling and often curious details about specific persons or events, including Shakespeare's tax dodges and itinerant London lodgings. The history plays provide the most fodder here for local reference, as well as Edmund Shakespeare's proximity to the Globe. The following chapters deal with London-based theatre people, including the Burbage family and the less well-known 'unsavoury characters' of Luce Bayman and Gilbert East, as well as the 'scandalous' figures of Christopher Beeston and George Wilkins. The emphasis here, as elsewhere, is on the seamier side of London and the inherent drama in Shakespeare's associations with a morally dubious social world. The final chapters explore authority in the shape of both institutions and individuals, and Shakespeare's reaction to bureaucratic power through its resistance on stage. Linking the stage to the city through playwrights, shareholders, carpenters, actors, allusions and aggravators, Salkeld produces a narrative history of London in fragments through the various associations and allusions made visible by what remains of Shakespeare's traces there, not only in the archives but also in the plays.

Another very useful book for teaching is Neil Corcoran's *Reading Shakespeare's Soliloquies: Text, Theatre, Film*. Tackling the form and function of the soliloquy, Corcoran sets out to establish the various ways in which isolated speeches function both within and without the play worlds, and their incumbent relationship to both poetry and thought. Beginning with Macbeth's 'Is this a dagger', Corcoran explores the 'extreme state of mind' present in this speech, and locates the psychological efficiency with which Shakespeare prepares both Macbeth and the audience for this moment. Remaining alert to the aside as a prefiguration of the space that the soliloquy will inhabit, Corcoran draws on the internal dynamics of the play world as well as the potential physical responses that have been amplified in film or stage versions of this speech. Exploring the fluctuating spaces that the soliloquy can support, whether of self-communion, reflection, performativity, irony or delusion, Corcoran sets out to open up the various interpretative opportunities they afford. Investigating the authority of the soliloquy, Corcoran draws on its formal properties, image clusters and networks, as well as verbal triggers and echoes. Moving between the 'hazardous' and 'magnificent' opportunities that Shakespearian soliloquies offer, the book produces highlighted text boxes to guide the reader towards a concrete sense of the speech's significance, as well as its key attributes. Focusing on the representation of emotion as well as the practical functions of analogy helps Corcoran situate the soliloquy within the developmental arc of Shakespeare's art. The hermeneutic opportunities afforded by the soliloquy are developed through a focus on the analogous function of allusion and the surrogate ways in which the mind is shown to search out precedents in moments of extreme or heightened emotion. Some of the less obvious effects emerge in discussion of Falstaff and the prose soliloquy that 'become[s a] site of adverse judgement'. Exploring the semantically dense texture of these prose soliloquies, Corcoran demonstrates the 'riot of discrete contemporary particulars' that evince Falstaff's selfhood. The second part of the book attends to the broader philosophical and psychological issues that the idea of speaking to oneself precipitates, and its necessarily complex ties to questions of faith, ontology, mental health and epistemology. Addressing the idea of the self, Corcoran provides a more sophisticated exploration of what such terms mean and how we might identify the 'self' as character or interiority rather than distinct bodily part. The concept of 'thinking aloud' becomes central to this rendition of the self, and Corcoran surveys the divergent dynamics created by those who speak the lines to the audience or to, as it were, a mirror. The latter section of the book uses specific performances and actors to anchor a close reading of the delivery of soliloquies and the affects produced and techniques employed. Here various actors explore and explain how they inhabited their role and the particular ways they needed to prepare for the soliloquies, and how they belonged to their character. Revealing how actors work with direction as well as the challenges

of language and rhythm, these essays situate the soliloquy at the heart of character performance and narrative engagement.

In *Queer Shakespeare: Desire and Sexuality*, Goran Stanivukovic, begins by asserting that, in 'Shakespeare's world of desire the choice of an object of desire and of language through which desire is verbalised are separate'. Reinvigorating the focus on queer studies, with a powerful nod to the controversial ex-Artistic Director of Shakespeare's Globe, Emma Rice, Stanivukovic extends queer discourses to consider almost anything that expresses itself as non-normative or non-binary: there are essays on the witches and weather in *Macbeth*; worthy love, as '(not) love' in *The Two Gentlemen of Verona*; identity, marriage and clothing in *Cymbeline*; orthography in *Much Ado About Nothing*; insertions, meandering, letters and semen in *The Merchant of Venice*; 'glass' in the sonnets; and a 'grim view of life' in *Measure for Measure*. The focus on materiality evinced by the last two essays I mention here is particularly interesting. John S. Garrison's chapter on the sonnets examines glass not as transparent, but as an object of mediation which 'mitigates relations between people, as well as between people and their desired objects and experiences'. Developing this through an analysis of orientation and objectification, Garrison understands glass as 'enabling multiplicity' which then 'grants access to queer erotic arrangements'. Uncoupling the mirror from its traditional relationship to self-knowledge, this essay supports the glass as an object of estrangement through which we can experience desires and things other than ourselves. Melissa Sanchez's essay on *Measure* retains the material focus but is keenly invested in the body and the intersections between human and non-human life which provide the play with its critical structures of social taxonomy. Addressing the play's anxious commitment to procreation, as well as its desacralization of human life, 'depicting the human creature as little better than the inanimate matter – the dust – from which she or he came and to which he or she will return'. Considering the role of the prostitute within the structures through which women's bodies are socialized, Sanchez makes a compelling argument for Kate Keepdown's status as a prostitute and the 'circumstances of procreative sex that appear to have doomed her to the slow death of those outside the protective category of *bios*'. Troubling the identities of 'virtuous sex', Sanchez's essay provides a stimulating addition to scholarship on the play, in which we can move beyond the binaries of life or death characterized by humanist scholarship, towards an appraisal of the 'material, inhuman dimension of reproduction ... [through which we can] appreciate the difficulty of drawing a line between virtuous and shameful sex'.

Continuing to consider the difficult lines of distinction between virtue and shame, Patricia Akhimie's *Shakespeare and the Cultivation of Difference: Race and Conduct in the Early Modern World* addresses the 'imbrication of race, class and conduct' in the early modern period, with a particular focus on the language of conduct. Central to this focus is the representation of blackness as fixed and immutable, incapable of development or progression and therefore denied potential social or cultural opportunities for betterment. Within these terms, Akhimie seeks 'out such forms of oppression and prejudice ... [to] demonstrate that they are by-products of a conduct system in which social identity is understood as both fixed and fluid'. Understanding the rigidity of social groupings as extending beyond race to class, Akhimie observes a 'spectrum of mutability to immutability': where 'immutability, a pitiable condition, was then associated with visible, bodily marks that were themselves immutable and understood as inherited and thus natural'. Supporting the focus on environmental and social factors that produce and inhibit change, the book explores an ideology of cultivation in which opportunity serves the interests of the dominant group. Understanding race as a 'structural relationship' between human difference and power relations, Akhimie unpacks 'processes of inclusion and exclusion', the 'peculiar logic whereby different bodies are assigned different values', and the 'pain' that this causes and the indelible marks it leaves behind. Beginning with the 'cultivating process' and the social groups included and excluded from

that process, Akhimie analyses the potential for transformation as it becomes available through the terms of conduct. Bringing together a range of early modern discourses on identity, behaviour, mobility, education, bodily markers and imagined potential, Akhimie exposes 'the epistemic violence toward stigmatized others that lies at the heart of self cultivation', as well as the 'somatic markers' that support social oppression. Akhimie's wider focus on class-based social oppression is especially engaging for the ways in which it allows her to bring characters like Caliban and Othello, for example, into conversation with figures like Malvolio or the Dromios of *The Comedy of Errors*. Her approach seems especially productive for the formative ways in which the body becomes a marker of difference, a 'liability', as well as abuse, so that images of disfigurement become assertive social motifs in the quest for change. The implications that this has for concepts of the natural are particularly key in terms of the limits of mutability and the plays' many compelling intersections between those characters who want to absolve themselves of their nature as well as deny its existence. Recognizing the 'outspoken' figures of resistance that the drama presents, Akhimie explains, 'Shakespeare's outspoken characters offer critiques of a system of class or rank that is ostensibly held to be both just and permanent ... These characters present accounts of how inferior status is not inherited but assigned, stamped on, inflicted, and enforced, and then later presented as the dictate of nature.' Predominantly focusing on conduct literature, *Shakespeare and the Cultivation of Difference* analyses how an ideology of cultivation – at once mutable for some social groups and fixed for others – suppresses a profound critique of prejudice. The first chapter deals with *Othello* and the terms of 'marking' through which the martial, bodily and ocular processes of the play produce a 'pernicious stigma' through which Othello may be examined and abbreviated. Here the focus on travel literature opens up a dialogue within 'alternate systems of value and codes of conduct' whereby 'Othello plans to accept the culpability that blackness signifies, giving his life to protect a fiction'. In Chapter 2, Akhimie turns to *The Comedy of*

*Errors* and the bruised body of the servant. Understanding the repeated beatings that the twin servants experience not as temporary signs of comic bodily function but as an 'indelible somatic marker', Akhimie positions the bruise 'not as the stable sign of a flawed individual whose faults have garnered punishment, but [it] instead serves to brand groups of people who suffer continual, arbitrary, and violent suppression at the hands of social betters'. Exploring domestic and household manuals, Akhimie argues that the subservient body becomes forcefully stigmatized to wear its subordination. Akhimie brings some clever and fresh perspectives and approaches to a familiar subject, but in doing so she paves the way for a fundamental shift in how we can understand the pernicious machinations of social oppression. In her third chapter, observing the socially preserved entertainments of the ruling elite, Akhimie examines *A Midsummer Night's Dream* and the relationships between leisure and labour through which power, both imagined and experienced, can be asserted. In this way, the aristocratic leisure the play promotes is produced by the animals, mechanicals and lovers who have been the subjects and objects of 'sport'. The final chapter on *The Tempest* brings together colonial discourses on improvement and social mobility. Attending to the pervasive language of cultivation and nurture, Akhimie explores the principles of disfigurement through which Caliban's body is identified as a 'weed to be plucked rather than cultivated'. The implications for his resistant 'nature' and Prospero's fruitless 'humane' 'pains' can be re-read within the contexts of Akhimie's arguments for mutability and the marked body of racial prejudice as one that can never change. There are many wonderful elements to this book, not least its powerful scrutiny of social differentiation, but it also gives rise to new conversations, I think, about the relationships between not only race and class but gender, too, and the formative and biological ways in which the drama asserts claims to

naturalness as a critique of the oppressive principles of reproduction.

\*\*\*

To conclude this year's round-up, we turn to time and Lauren Shohet's edited collection, *Temporality, Genre, and Experience in the Age of Shakespeare: Forms of Time*. In this collection, which grew out of a Shakespeare Association of America conference, the contributors present philosophically nuanced accounts of how we can approach time as an experience, a principle, a structure or a form in some of Shakespeare's works. The essays range from the diachronic to the synchronic, historical time, inhabited and embodied time, to the experiences of shared time that support genre, across a variety of plays. Perhaps unsurprisingly, history and tragedy feature most prominently, with essays by Andrew Griffin on *Henry V* and Philip Lorenz on *Henry VIII*; and Rebecca Bushnell on *Antony and Cleopatra*, William Carroll on *Hamlet, Macbeth* and *King Lear*, and Meredith Beales on *King Lear*. There are two especially engaging contributions on non-Shakespearian drama: essays from Lucy Munro on the publication and performance of *The Knight of the Burning Pestle*, and Lara Dodds on a 'narrative counterfactual' of *The Tragedy of Mariam* and the competing experiences of time that support the 'ambiguity of tragedy'. Focusing on 'some of the affordances of theatre for thinking about time', the collection examines the ways in which the drama imposes on and engages with our sense of the uncanny, and how multiple forms, and platforms, intersect with time to produce a broader vocabulary for understanding the 'temporal roots of our experience' and the profoundly unstable architectures of genre. There is a wide range of approaches here – from the typographical, performative, semantic, recursive, imagined, inherited, abbreviated and embodied – and a desire to understand the multifaceted nature of time to produce different and often competing experiences for the audience, as well as the reader. Valerie Wayne's essay on *Cymbeline* concludes the collection with an analysis of the 'two halves' of the play and the 'temporalities that occur generally in phenomenological experience, as well as staging the densities particular to its own early modern time'. Pursuing these experiences through the dissonance of collapsed time, Wayne observes the 'foldable density' of a time that is both then and the should-have-been hereafter.

## WORKS REVIEWED

Akhimie, Patricia, *Shakespeare and the Cultivation of Difference: Race and Conduct in the Early Modern World* (London, 2018)

Barton, Anne, *The Shakespearean Forest* (Cambridge, 2018)

Clegg, Cyndia Susan, *Shakespeare's Reading Audiences: Early Modern Books and Audience Interpretation* (Cambridge, 2018)

Corcoran, Neil, *Reading Shakespeare's Soliloquies: Text, Theatre, Film* (London, 2018)

Fulton, Thomas, and Kristen Poole, *The Bible on the Shakespearean Stage: Cultures of Interpretation in Reformation England* (Cambridge, 2018)

Gamboa, Brett, *Shakespeare's Double Plays: Dramatic Economy on the Early Modern Stage* (Cambridge, 2018)

Maxwell, Julie, and Kate Rumbold, *Shakespeare and Quotation* (Cambridge, 2018)

McEachern, Claire, *Believing in Shakespeare: Studies in Longing* (Cambridge, 2018)

Parker, Patricia, *Shakespearean Intersections: Language, Contexts, Critical Keywords* (Philadelphia, PA, 2018)

Rutter, Tom, *Shakespeare and the Admiral's Men: Reading Across Repertories on the London Stage, 1594–1600* (Cambridge, 2018)

Salkeld, Duncan, *Shakespeare and London* (Oxford, 2018)

Schalkwyk, David, *Shakespeare, Love and Language* (Cambridge, 2018)

Shohet, Lauren, ed., *Temporality, Genre, and Experience in the Age of Shakespeare: Forms of Time* (London, 2018)

Sokol, B. J., *Shakespeare's Artists: The Painters, Sculptors, Poets and Musicians in his Plays and Poems* (London, 2018)

Stanivukovic, Goran, ed., *Queer Shakespeare: Desire and Sexuality* (London, 2018)

# 2. SHAKESPEARE IN PERFORMANCE
### *reviewed by* RUSSELL JACKSON

However sophisticated or assertive a director or designer may be, it is the actor and his or her body that carry the ultimate authority in most kinds of theatre, especially in 'live' performance. 'Liveness' is a category debated in a number of the works reviewed this year, and evidence from the archive is always both invaluable and to be questioned. Nevertheless, the power of the actor to 'fix' posthumously an image of a character, assisted in this case by the photographer's camera, is asserted in Angus McBean's photograph of Richard Burton as Prince Henry in the Shakespeare Memorial Theatre's 1951 production of *Henry IV, Part Two*, which forms the front cover of *Shakespeare by McBean*, edited by Adrian Woodhouse. The upward gaze is intense, the pupils raised towards the crown that the young man's hands hold a half-inch or so above his brows. He seems at once determined and tentative, caught a moment before he submits to its actual and symbolic weight. This powerful image of one of the play's crucial moments is also an icon of the actor-as-king, and of the actor's profession, comparable to Hogarth's painting of Garrick as Richard III, Lawrence's portraits of John Philip Kemble as Hamlet and Sarah Siddons as Lady Macbeth, or Sargent's majestic image of Ellen Terry as Lady Macbeth holding a crown above her head. McBean's sombre black-and-white photograph of Burton is balanced on the back cover, in vivid but subtle colour, by Keith Michell as Orsino and Vivien Leigh as the disguised Viola in Act 2, Scene 4 of *Twelfth Night*. Leigh's gaze is firmly fixed on Michell, whose open shirt reveals a pendant against his bare chest – probably the jewel he will send to Olivia – while the flowing sleeves of his richly decorated dark-green gown suggest the passionate aesthete whose eyes meet the intensity of Cesario's. Unlike Burton, Michell and Leigh are photographed on what is recognizably a stage set, that for the 1953 Stratford production. Both photographs exemplify McBean's gift as a dramatic photographer whose

pictures always tell a story, whether of some element of a play's narrative or of the inner life of the actor-as-character. In many cases, that of Leigh being the most significant, they also tell the story of the photographer's relationship with his subject. This handsome collection of McBean's theatre photographs, predominantly but not exclusively drawn from his work at Stratford-upon-Avon, reflects an approach to the theatre that prizes glamour, with actors posed with appropriate forcefulness and thoughtful focus, and actresses (the gendered term is appropriate) depicted with glamour and grace. Many of the portraits, especially those of women, have been enhanced by skilful retouching, although this has its own value, as it renders the impression that lighting and make-up would produce onstage. Sometimes McBean, like Cecil Beaton, was capable of making actresses look like debutantes, and vice versa. Occasionally he smoothed even male visages – including that of Burton as Prince Henry – to an extent that would seem old-fashioned by the middle of the 1960s. Sometimes his dramatic effects might be vetoed by an actor: Ian Bannen 'killed' images of his 1961 Hamlet. (Woodhouse reproduces one of these, 'not passed for publication', on page 36 of his comprehensively informative introduction.)

As well as taking individual portraits, McBean attended a dress rehearsal, making a list of scenes and situations, then held his own photo-call onstage with costumes, props and appropriate scenery. The resulting images were used in the theatre's publicity and in the souvenir programmes of individual seasons, and collected volumes covering a span of years from 1952 to 1958. For the 1958 season brochure, he produced 'an extraordinary montage of 39 cut-outs of his photographs of Stratford performers, which could wind in a giant "S" down the front cover, as well as a "straight" photograph for the back cover of a table laden with lobster, fruits and wines to advertise the theatre's riverside restaurant' (29–30). Catering is rendered as a fine art, in keeping with the brochures' presentation of the Stratford theatre as a glamorous and fashionable venue. For that year's brochure, McBean was 'credited with all photographs, unless otherwise acknowledged'. In 1959, six photographers are credited. Although Tony Armstrong Jones's pages for *Othello* are superficially in the familiar chiaroscuro style, some deliver a stronger sense of the spontaneity of performance, while the director, designer and 'lighting expert' (Tony Richardson, Loudon Sainthill and Michael Northen) are casually dressed and strike nonchalant poses in their full-length portraits. Perhaps, they seem to suggest, this is no longer a theatre in which men must wear a jacket and tie for rehearsals. (Nevertheless, for the time being, the dress code remained 'smart casual.')

McBean could be larksome, as when he blacked out some of Angela Baddeley's teeth in a portrait of her as Juliet's Nurse – an effect that, as Woodhouse points out, was not achieved onstage. He experimented with multiple exposures and montages and, beyond the range of his documenting of performances, using quasi-surrealistic effects and painted backdrops, as in a striking photograph of Peggy Ashcroft as Portia in *The Merchant of Venice*. With its large format and generously sized high-quality reproductions, *Shakespeare by McBean* reflects a theatre whose values have been superseded in the course of five decades, but at their best the illustrations convey the spirit of the productions and, above all, the quality of the actors' work.

The actor's work on his role forms the centre of both Antony Sher's *Year of the Mad King: The Lear Diaries* and Paterson Joseph's *Julius Caesar and Me: Exploring Shakespeare's African Play*. Sher played King Lear in an RSC production directed by Greg Doran in 2017–18. Joseph describes his work on Brutus for the 2012 RSC production of *Julius Caesar*, also directed by Doran. Preparation through research leads into the creative act itself, which has an element of letting go, which Paterson conveys vividly:

Trying to work out what a character means, why he does what he does; what he might walk like, talk like,

look like; what burns inside him, how does he see the world about him … what are his longings and motivations. And then, forgetting all that and walking like a blank sheet of paper on to the stage – daring yourself to be painted with all the research and sculpting you have been doing through the rehearsal period, trying, bravely, to simply *be*. (14)

Antony Sher, whose research on his characters includes painting and sketching, describes what Greg Doran calls 'the big sketch', when the play is 'put on its feet' for the first time in the rehearsal room. This complements Joseph's account from the dual perspective of actor and director: 'This is the moment when [Greg] discovers if his instincts about the production, forged over months of thought, discussion and meetings, are proving sound and true. In a way, rehearsals are simply the test drives of a vehicle that has been built beforehand. You can make adjustments or even major changes, but the basic structure already exists' (193).

John Caird, quoted in Jonathan Croall's *Performing Hamlet: Actors in the Modern Age* suggests a corresponding degree of tentativeness in his approach as director:

If you have an open relationship with the actors you'll get plenty of surprises … You can analyse a character as much as you like beforehand, but you won't get much out of it until an actor plays it. Then the magical chemistry happens, the combination of the actor's personality and the written role gives it the absolute reality that Shakespeare intended, but could never exactly prophesy because he didn't know the actors. (144)

Caird leaves out an important factor: Shakespeare *did* know the actors for whom he was writing, so that, although he could not anticipate what Simon Russell Beale would make of Hamlet, he would have had a pretty good idea of what he would get from Burbage. Even then, of course, he might hope that his actor would surprise him once the play was 'on its feet'. (And we can only speculate as to what Hamlet would tell Burbage about himself.) Did Burbage perhaps write 'Hamlet's advice to the players' – or at least suggest its salient points? ('Don't you think we need a bit here where he gives them some sort of briefing?' – 'Perhaps, but not about *The Murder of Gonzago*, that would give the game away too soon' – 'What about something on acting in general?' – 'Such as?' – 'Well . . . ')

The personal reflections of Sher and Joseph and the reportage of Croall – whose book includes his observation of Caird's 2000 *Hamlet* production as well as interviews with five other actors – are within a theatrical tradition that values the actor's and director's exploration of the text in terms of the psychology of the individual in relation to carefully constructed 'given circumstances'. Joseph gives an invaluable account of the production's creation of 'our Africa . . . a place of huge monuments and negligible pastoral care', where 'the dictator, the great conqueror, had surrounded himself with greedy sycophants, who had syphoned off the resources of a prosperous country for their own venal ends'. Rather than anchoring the play in a specific country, this would enable actors and director to 'deal with the essence of the play' rather than 'being bogged down in a lot of irrelevant history' (95–6). With another element of the 'given circumstances', it was decided to base the accents on a fusion of RP and Kenyan English, which in any case was found to vary from speaker to speaker in such matters as the sound of '-ion' word endings. Joseph points out that it was only after making these 'foundational choices' with the accent and dialect coach Penny Dyer that he could 'begin to slowly learn the lines for Brutus, making an educated guess as to what the final accent might sound like' (61–2). *Julius Caesar and Me* outlines the long and sometimes challenging process by which a group of actors and a director worked together. Tensions between colleagues are acknowledged and dealt with; difficult transitions, in this case between rehearsal room and theatre (with a detour into the film studio), are negotiated; and performances adjust to the less 'given' circumstances of audience responses.

*Year of the Mad King*, like Sher's previous production diaries, explores the intertwining of personal life with creativity, focusing more closely than Joseph on the individual's quest for a character, but similarly attentive to the collaborative nature of the task. Sher's writing exemplifies the degree to which reports of the demise of 'character criticism', like those of the death of the author, have been greatly exaggerated, especially in the theatre. In an actor's career, one role can inform another, if only by contrast. Sher was struck by the perception that Lear and Falstaff were 'both portraits of old age, deeply perceptive, though deeply contrasting':

Given that the two of them are in my system at the moment, I can't help noticing how different their speeches look in my scripts. Falstaff's speeches are in prose, fat and wide on the page, big blocks of verbiage: wild, wise, funny, stupid, spiteful, scared. Lear's speeches are in verse, and on the page they're like tall edifices of iambic pentameter, drumming with power, burning with fury and curses. And then later on they're like Falstaff again, just wise and scared. Just two old men . . . (58)

Like his response to a particular view of Table Mountain, which seemed to Sher, with the mad king in his mind, to have 'a King Lear look to it' (47), this is a personal epiphany that would later feed into his performance. Sometimes a breakthrough comes to an actor in rehearsal as a shared exprience. Joseph as Brutus and Cyril Nri as Cassius found a key to their relationship in betrayal – not just of their political cause, 'but the betrayal of one sibling by another'. In a 'momentous, game-changing leap into the heart of the play', on a 'tired, grey afternoon' they 'launched into the scene for the final time that day' and 'something extraordinary happened': 'We both reverted to children. Not just men who were arguing in a childish way. Actual children who felt passionately about their own righteous wounds in that profound way that only children can. We roared, yes, but we also wept, pouted and despaired of ever being understood by the one person who had always understood us' (77).

Directors working in this tradition, fusing psychological realism with formal and intellectual perceptions, deal like actors in creating and developing a production's emotional context. In his *Hamlet* production, John Caird was anxious to eliminate the political background, 'much of which he felt

Shakespeare may have added at a later stage' (132), and chose to emphasize the play's religious aspect. In the course of two months of weekly discussions with Simon Russell Beale, they agreed that the play was essentially about a group of people 'who all loved or wanted to love each other, but whose love was destroyed by circumstances' (135). It is clear that this, rather than Danish political matters, would appeal as a source of creativity in the rehearsal room, but the removal of a significant element arguably distorted the play. In this respect, and in the daily interactions with his cast chronicled by Croall, Caird was establishing an 'actor's theatre' approach. Nevertheless, he edged closer towards a relatively low-tech version of 'high-concept' directors' theatre. The 'concept' lay in the presentation of the play's events as though reenacted by the 'ghosts' of the characters, and the cathedral-like set where trunks and suitcases were manoeuvred to establish location. Croall summarizes the critical response to this aspect of the production, and to the religious dimension emphasized by the set and the music: 'There is also some uncertainty about [Caird's] concept of the actors as ghosts, and a general dislike of the luggage-based scene-shifting' (171). (My own response was that this suggested not so much Sartre's *Huis clos* as the lost-property room at a railway station, though Russell Beale was, as might be expected, a moving, intellectually articulate and emotionally honest Prince.) Other Hamlets in Croall's gallery include Jude Law, a far more energetic, and, as the director Michael Grandage puts it, 'very physical' actor who 'use[d] his body to tell the story, so he inhabited the soliloquies physically as well as verbally, finding Hamlet's inner life through his exterior life' (104). Law tells Croall about the inspiration he drew from other performances he had seen, but this was an influence that was inevitably discounted by the need to 'bring yourself' into the part, 'to be honest and rooted in your own emotional network' (105). There is nothing especially surprising about this approach, but it is yet another reminder of the extent to which a director sets up the context – in this case described by Grandage as 'a dynamic and modern production' – in which a performance can be created.

Croall surveys a range of performances from the 1950s to the present decade, drawing on a variety of published sources as well as the five interviews he himself conducted. Many of the actors testify to the role's effect in bringing out aspects of their creativity, or even their personality, which they either were unfamiliar with or had in some cases suppressed. Maxine Peake's account of her Hamlet at Manchester's Royal Exchange Theatre is especially interesting. The starting point was 'an old Danish legend, where Prince Hamlet was actually the tale of a girl princess disguised as a boy' – in other words, the theory elaborated by Edward P. Vining in *The Mystery of Hamlet* (Philadelphia, 1881) and given its fullest artistic expression in Asta Neilsen's 1920 film. The director Sarah Franckom describes how one day at rehearsal Peake said: 'I don't think I am a woman. I might have a female body, but I don't want to be a woman. I might want to be male, but I'm confused' (117). Peake's description of the feeling reflects the ways in which this discovery informed her performance. After some research into transsexual people ('both of us have got quite a few trans friends'), they arrived at the decision to play Hamlet as 'a man trapped in a female body', effectively the mirror image of Neilsen's Prince/ess: 'I felt it was a way of accessing bits of me as an actress that I've not been able to access before. I don't always feel female. At RADA I was a bit of a tomboy, and they said I needed to be more feminine. That's so wrong: being boisterous doesn't mean you're not feminine' (118).

In 1979 at the Half Moon Theatre in London, Frances De La Tour played an androgynous Hamlet: 'I didn't approach the part as a woman, I just studied the role as any actor would. I was dressed in trousers and jacket, so I could be seen as androgynous. My hair was long and curly and I wore no make up, so I was just a young person.' Croall cites a review by Michael Billington – favourable where several others were dismissive – that reflects the gender confusion attached not so much to the actress as to the role itself: 'She is tough, virile and impassioned' in a 'good performance, compact with every male virtue except femininity' (44).

Male and female identities figure inevitably in Robert Shaughnessy's study of *As You Like It* in Manchester University Press's 'Shakespeare in Performance' series. The productions range from Nigel Playfair's Shakespeare Memorial Theatre staging of 1919 – notorious for its stylized costumes and settings and for having discarded the stuffed Charlecote stag carried on by Duke Senior's co-mates and brothers in exile in 4.2 – to Peter Stein's *Wie es euch gefällt* (Schaubühne, Berlin, 1977). Stein's audiences were made to stand for about forty minutes in 'a vast, high-ceilinged chamber with ice-blue featureless walls, representing the court … a realm from which all traces of the natural world had been eradicated', before being led into a 'stunning, meticulously detailed forest'. This 'combination of the hyperreal with the non-real', freighted with emblematic as well as naturalistic scenic elements, writes Shaughnessy, 'was of inexhaustible (and for some reviewers, exhausting) visual richness, and of a vision of a green utopia that, Stein knew, was an impossible dream' (121). The fact that the production was staged in a disused film studio suggests comparison with the lavish 'studio realism' of Paul Czinner's 1936 film, featuring his wife Elisabeth Bergner and the young Laurence Olivier, and contrasts with the out-and-out anti-realism of many other productions and the use of 'real nature' in the largely location-bound BBC TV version directed by Basil Coleman (1978) and the 'Japanese' landscape of the film by Kenneth Branagh (2006). Any production of the play, with or without a fully realized, or even appropriated, natural environment, necessarily touches on the hyperreal in the figure of Rosalind. Shaughnessy successfully frames his discussion of performances within the gender politics, as well as attending to the broader cultural politics (or, simply, politics), of their time. The all-male productions of Clifford Williams (National Theatre, 1967–9) and Declan Donellan (Cheek by Jowl, 1994–5) make for intriguing comparisons with Buzz Goodbody's 1973 RSC production, with Eileen Atkins's Ganymede in a denim pantsuit among a forest of plastic poles, and Christine Edzard's 1992 film, in which Emma Croft disguises herself in the non-gender-specific

clothes of a street dweller in an industrial wasteland. In such productions, as in a number of others, Rosalind's exclamation (or question) 'Well, this is the Forest of Arden' (2.4.14) takes on a new meaning: 'Is this what we came all this way for?' At the National Theatre, Williams, who took over as director when John Dexter withdrew, 'inherited a production concept whose scope for queer reading was, as far as mainstream traditions of Shakespearean performance were concerned, unprecedented', but 'went out of his way to minimize its more radical implications' (133). Shaughnessy underlines the extent to which this production was of its time with reference to the outdated effect of its later revivals: like Atkins's denims in 1973, the contemporary fashions on display would soon lose a sense of immediacy. Although most of the male actors playing women eschewed exaggerated 'feminine' mannerisms, the overall effect of unreality in Arden recorded by reviewers was of general camp. In Declan Donellan's production, featuring Adrian Lester's commanding, tender and funny Rosalind, the 'prevailing theme' was that of 'the fundamentally performative nature of identity – and in particular of sexual and gender identities' (145). The fact that this Rosalind, one of the defining performances of the role in the late twentieth century, was also male and black added to a sense of 'relevance' to contemporary issues that went beyond the fashionable playfulness of Williams's production.

The 1967 National Theatre *As You Like It* also features in Shaughnessy's volume in the Arden Shakespeare 'Shakespeare in the Theatre' series: *The National Theatre, 1963–1975: Olivier and Hall*. There it takes its place in a broader discussion of the social and theatrical contexts of the newly created company. In his examination of Laurence Olivier's *Othello* (1965) and *Shylock* (1970), Shaughnessy addresses the complexities of the racial politics of both performances, and takes account of their partial preservation in the form of film and television productions. Stuart Burge's film of John Dexter's *Othello* production suffers from having a studio set that is effectively a larger version of that used on stage at the Old Vic, whereas John Sichel directed a 'richly textured' quasi-naturalistic television version of Jonathan Miller's *Merchant of Venice* that was 'not just a decorative backdrop to its central performance . . . But a context and rationale for it.'

The difference in approach to *Othello*, on the part of Olivier as actor and Miller as director, was marked: Dexter's production, rooting Olivier's Moor in racial fantasies that produced a white man's imagining of how a black man should move and speak, pitched his performance into a void space that could exist nowhere but in a theatre; Miller, by placing Shylock with some historical and cultural precision, anchored the play's world in history. (44–5)

Like many of his insights, this is grounded in Shaughnessy's grasp of the multiple contexts of performance and impressive command of the archival evidence, as well as the reactions of critics. As he observes, by the time of Hall's 1975 *Hamlet*, 'reviewers of almost every NT production were used to treating them as tests of institutional policy and achievement', with reference to 'the demand that the work should self-evidently justify the organisation's financial advantages and institutional privileges' (179). As well as productions directed by the 'home team', Shaughnessy discusses the unhappy marriage between the National and two directors from the Berliner Ensemble in the 1971 *Coriolanus*; Franco Zeffirelli's Italian-language *Amleto*, imported for a visit in 1964; and the same director's festively 'Sicilian' *Much Ado About Nothing*, directed for the National's company in 1965. Appropriately enough, Tom Stoppard's *Rosencrantz and Guildenstern are Dead* (1965) takes its place alongside such notable productions of Shakespeare's plays as the company's opening production of *Hamlet,* directed by Olivier himself; the aforementioned *As You Like It, Othello* and *Merchant of Venice*; and Hall's *Hamlet* and *Tempest*.

Shaughnessy draws on the theatre's archives to unravel – so far as can be achieved – the *Rashomon*-like tale of the 1971 *Coriolanus* and the artistic differences between the Berliner Ensemble directors and the cast and production team. For Peter Hall's productions at the Old Vic, there is the important testimony of the director's

autobiography and his published diaries. In using these, Shaughnessy is telling 'less the story of those events than a story about the stories that have been spun around them' (180). The diaries have to be read alongside the kind of evidence from the NT archives drawn on extensively by Daniel Rosenthal in *The National Theatre Story* (2013), and now collected by him in the selected missives of *Dramatic Exchanges: The Lives and Letters of the National Theatre* (2018). Complementing one another, Shaughnessy's and Rosenthal's books provide a detailed and engrossing picture of a major cultural institution whose managers and staff have sometimes had to engage with conflicting personalities and artistic imperatives in its directors, while responding to crises in funding and social pressures. Most of the letters in *Dramatic Exchanges* concern the work of contemporary playwrights, but light is shed on some important Shakespearian productions, including correspondence between Hall and Ian McKellen on the use of onstage audience members as non-speaking extras in the 1984 *Coriolanus* (194–6). Postcards, letters and internal memos reflect the unfolding crises that attended Richard Eyre's 1989 *Hamlet*, including the withdrawal of Daniel Day-Lewis and the death of his successor in the title role, Ian Charleson. (216–20). There are also a number of intriguing 'might-have-been' performances. These include Orson Welles as director of the 1970 *Merchant of Venice*; Emma Thompson (presumably as Rosalind) in *As You Like It*; Ralph Richardson as Julius Caesar; Ronnie Barker as Falstaff; Eileen Atkins as Ophelia; and Geraldine McEwan as Desdemona. In themselves, all these would have been audience-pleasing choices.

A radically different approach, not merely to Shakespeare but to performance in general, is described in Ayanna Thompson's account of the theories and practice of Peter Sellars, whose attitude to pleasing the audience is positively defiant. At an early stage in his career, in 1975–6, during a gap year between Phillips Andover College and Harvard, and in the light of a number of 'long form' productions in Paris, as well as seeing, on 'six different occasions', a Bread and Puppet

Theatre show that 'ran over four hours long', Sellars 'began to develop his sense that audiences do not need to enjoy a performance for it to make and have a profound impact on them' (xxi). At first enraged by Patrice Chéreau's Paris Opera production of *The Tales of Hoffmann*, he told Thompson in a phone interview, he could remember 'everything about the production' forty years later, supporting his belief that that 'The destination is not opening night; the destination is the rest of life' (xxi). On the other hand, his *Macbeth/Play*, a mash-up of texts by Shakespeare and Beckett, ran for a mere eighty minutes, and impressed reviewers despite the fact that, without prior knowledge of the two plays, it would be incomprehensible. Citing the example of Noh theatre in his programme notes, Sellars made it clear that (in Thompson's words) 'immediate comprehension is not a goal for which he strives' (xxxiv).

Thompson's description of Sellars as 'a thinking person's director' seems to imply that other kinds of director do not encourage reflection. Perhaps it is more a matter of radical energy, of the kind that has kept avant-garde artists marching forward at least since Wagner. Sellars 'challenges audiences to grapple, struggle and wrestle with Shakespeare collectively in the moment of production and individually as the production both deepens and recedes in one's memory'. Because his work 'does not invite linearity or even full intellectual comprehension', Thompson has her work cut out in attempting 'to engage with Sellars's Shakespeare productions in the complex ways they invite and desire' (liii). It is a sign of the formidable nature of the task that she takes fifty-three pages (in small Roman numerals) of 'Introduction' before embarking on it. But, despite this caveat, the book achieves an informative and well-argued evaluation of the productions and the career: linearity and intellectual comprehension prevail. Even so, it takes the thirty-one pages of Chapter 1 to adumbrate the 'context' of Sellars, a voraciously eclectic wunderkind, before, in a chapter on 'Purpose, process, technique', Thompson is in a position to analyse and evaluate the productions themselves. In this, her attention to the variety and arresting vitality of some of the work is exemplary, including detailed 'case studies' of Sellars's best-known Shakespearian productions, *The Merchant of Venice* (1994), *Othello* (2009), *A Midsummer Night's Dream* 2014), and *Desdemona*, written by Toni Morrison and Rokia Traoré (2011–12). Sellars's aversion to audiences making sense of his productions does not preclude their effectiveness as provocations, but in the case of Thompson's book he took this to an unusual length, objecting to her choice of a cover photograph, which showed 'a stunning image' of Philip Seymour Hoffman as Othello and John Ortiz as Iago 'locked in a moment of homosocial tension' on a bed formed of video screens showing bloody hands.. This was 'entirely too legible', for Sellars: 'a book cover that a reader would look at once, understand, and therefore not feel the need to re-examine in the future'. Thompson concluded that he was 'absolutely right', because the production 'upended everything [she thought she] knew about *Othello*'. She had 'struggled with so much in that production, hating it the first night [she] saw it, loving it the second night, and feeling haunted by it and conflicted about it eight years later' (129). The photograph appears in the body of the book, and that on the cover, presumably in response to Sellars's objection, has the same actors in what may be a moment from the same sequence, but with Hoffman leaning close to Ortiz, who sits with his hands clasped in front of him as if he were a penitent seeking absolution. It is, indeed, a mysterious image, and the note on the back cover merely identifies it as from a production of *Othello*, so perhaps the decision was a good one. But it is also consonant with the director's desire to remain enigmatic, taking a stand against interpretation.

By way of contrast, in Dominique Goy-Blanquet's 'Shakespeare in the Theatre' volume, Patrice Chéreau emerges as devoted to clarity and intelligibility. He was commended, even by 'his harshest critics', for 'his unique talent for conveying the story through an image'. In the book's cover photograph, Gérard Desarthe as Hamlet sits near the edge of what must be the grave trap, meditatively poking a stick at Yorick's skull. This cannot tell the whole story of the production first seen at Avignon in 1988, and does not reveal the effect of the set, 'a seventeenth-century palatial façade laid down before the high walls of the medieval Palais des Papes "like a fallen giant"' (98). Nevertheless, as a representation of one aspect of the production – Hamlet's relentlessly intellectual engagement with emotions – it is as eloquent as McBean's photograph of Burton as Prince Henry. Chéreau's preparation for the play was what might be expected from a person who, from an early age, had been an *habitué* of seminars and libraries as much as of theatres, and of what he called 'this trade that does not have a respectable name but that I endure and practice nonetheless with tenderness and violence' (xii). Goy-Blanquet makes extensive use of the archive documenting the director's notes and annotated scripts, and creates a portrait of the theatre artist as an intellectual – sometimes one experienced as arrogant by his actors, but always impassioned in the search for physical embodiments of the script's emotional as well as intellectual life. His customary method in approaching a play 'is to read all he can find about its past history, context, parallels, echoes, then discard everything. Start from the raw text, the bare set, the nude flesh, bodies level with the ground among raised pillars of aggressive machinery.' As for violence, he 'admits to a fascination' with it, comparing human relations to a rugby scrum 'all linked in embrace, throwing kicks at each other' (104). For *Hamlet*, his comprehensive preparatory reading included a specially commissioned translation of John Dover Wilson's *What Happens in Hamlet?* (1935), and he worked closely with the poet Yves Bonnefoy, whose translation formed the basis of the script. Although *Hamlet* was by no means Chéreau's only theatrical engagement with Shakespeare, Goy-Blanquet's account of this engrossing and at times startling production forms the centrepiece of her study of a director whose sensibility combined a formidable array of intellectual and artistic influences with a flair for visceral effects. When the ghost of Hamlet's father entered on horseback, his mount rearing up in the face of the terrified sentries, or when Hamlet and Laertes confronted each other in a startlingly dangerous sword fight at the end of the performance's four hours, one experienced the danger of Hamlet's predicament with a directness rarely matched in the theatre. *Shakespeare in the Theatre: Patrice Chéreau* conveys the complexity and sophistication of a major director's engagement with Shakespeare, and his success, despite an at times rarefied and cerebral approach, in sharing that enthusiasm with audiences.

Ivo van Hove's Shakespeare productions, including his six-hour compendium of *Roman Tragedies*, characterized by Kate Bassett as a 'multimedia epic', are prepared meticulously over a long period by him and his associates at the Toneelgroep Amsterdam, but are typically rehearsed with the actors over a matter of a few weeks. As Bassett observes, in *Ivo van Hove: From Shakespeare to David Bowie*, edited by Susan Bennett and Sonia Massai, one of his principal aims is to 'find expressionistic and symbolic correlatives for the emotional states and the ethos in which a play's characters are caught'. In *Othello*, a punchbag hanging from a chain downstage, 'not actually pummelled but coupled with the amplified sound of boxing at curtain-up', established 'a barracks gym setting and denote[d] a whole ill-boding culture of macho competitiveness and violence'. This was 'a fine example of van Hove's mature work fusing the realistic and significantly stylized with assurance' (43). It suggests the concreteness of van Hove's stage images, and the ways in which, often enhanced by the use of video and the manipulation of the performance space, he seeks a directness of communication. In his director's notes for the Los Angeles performance of *Roman Tragedies* in 2007, van Hove wrote that in the heavily edited versions of *Julius Caesar* and *Antony and Cleopatra* (the performance also included *Coriolanus*) the audience would be presented with 'case studies' in 'a big conference about politics' (59). Events would be staged with the use of the familiar channels of communication, available to the audience through live action or, when they chose, video feeds, breaking down conventional boundaries between performance and auditorium spaces. Joseph V. Melillo describes the practice, especially notable in the *Roman Tragedies* as performed at Brooklyn Academy of Music (BAM), as one of 'offering the audience multiple prisms through which to view the story and its characters'. Melillo cites the *New York Times* critic Ben Brantley's observation that '[c]utting-edge technology is only deployed in the service of that most ancient *raison d'être* of the theatre, catharsis' (51).

Compared with the accounts of Sellars and Chéreau, this collection of essays and texts reflects the distance between their agendas and that of van Hove, although he describes Chéreau as his 'idol', with particular reference to his use of sound in an 'emotional and atmospheric way' (7). Van Hove and his team aim for a freer, more 'open' experience, in which (Sonia Massai suggests) the effect is to 'pry classical plays open for their audiences to experience them as raw and relevant from within, as if they were unfolding, quite literally, all around them' (21). Massai identifies van Hove's 'life goal' as 'to make great theatre for a mass audience and not for the initiated few' (28). The accusations of solipsism sometimes levelled at Sellars, with his lack of interest in the audience's understanding of a play, is altogether foreign to van Hove's theatre, even though they have employed much of the same technology. Taken together, the 'Shakespeare in the Theatre' studies of Sellars and Chéreau and *Ivo van Hove: From Shakespeare to David Bowie* reflect the diversity of postmodern Shakespeare productions by directors whose work has not invariably been enjoyed or admired, but has never failed to stimulate.

Politically charged theatre work under very different circumstances is the subject of Emily Oliver's *Shakespeare and German Reunification*, which examines (as her subtitle indicates) 'the interface of politics and performance' in the two Germanies that existed before the *Wende* of 1989, and the subsequent reinstated nation. Before the *Wende*, unavoidable political engagement, or at least professions of it, prompted British and American scholars to hold up German theatre – particularly in the German Democratic Republic (GDR) – 'as a supposed paragon of what theatre can actually achieve, if it does not pander to consumer tastes' (43). Whilst, in the East, theatre practitioners were obliged to adhere to the notion of productions that were 'faithful to the work' (*werktreu*), in the West, 'The theatrical avant-garde of the 1960s and 1970s saw it as their task to redefine the theatre's function and transform it into "an instrument of 'Aufklärung' or anti-bourgeois agitation"' (62; quoting Wilhelm Hortmann). This caused 'a rift between West German theatre and its traditional core audience' that can be measured in terms of attendance figures: despite a simultaneous increase in population figures, audience numbers decreased by 24 per cent between 1970 and 1990, and the average subsidy per spectator rose from €11.50 in 1970 to €96 in 2002 (62). In other words, as in the old Hollywood saying, the customers stayed away in droves.

The *Wende* put the system of subsidy across Germany under additional strain. In the last decade of the century, in theatres across the newly unified country, there was a consensus that it was necessary to maintain the 'unique features of the German public theatre', which Oliver identifies as 'regional diversity, multi-genre theatres, rotating repertoire, and permanent ensemble' (191). This was a situation that some artistic directors reacted to with pragmatism – Oliver cites the efforts of the Maxim-Gorki-Theater in East Berlin to cope with the ageing ensemble resulting from the inherited system of tenure – while others responded with defiance. Hans Neuenfels at the Volksbühne in West Berlin turned 'a financially sound long-run theatre with no fixed ensemble into an institution with a rotating repertoire and permanent ensemble' (211). By one estimate, at the Freie Volksbühne, the cost per ticket in subsidy had risen by 1990 to DM505. After leaving his successor with just enough to pay off the remaining actors and administer the closure of the theatre in 1992, in June 1993 Neuenfels directed a production of *A Midsummer Night's Dream* at the Schiller Theater: 'Dressing his cast in black, Neuenfels directed a nightmare scenario, including snowstorms, and a rain of blood after Oberon's final blessing. A despotic, middle-aged Theseus/Oberon was locked in a bitter marriage dispute with Hippolyta/Titania ... At the end of the

"Pyramus and Thisbe" interlude, the mechanicals were gunned down by Theseus' bodyguards.' Interpreted by some as 'a bitter indictment of the city's treatment of its artists', rather than a 'directorial quirk', and characterized by Oliver as a 'protest through highly aestheticized means', the 'expensive effects and absence of comedy in his production may well have helped to justify the theatre's closure' (211).

Neuenfels's Coriolanus-like gesture, amounting to 'I banish you', has its roots not only in his temperament (and flair for mismanagement) but also in the theatrical culture that nurtured him. But such extreme and often grotesque 'quirks' could be a valuable element of the radicalism with which directors in East and West Germany had sought to confront conventional expectations. In the East, the task was more formidable. In one of his most uncompromising interventions, Heiner Müller's *Macbeth nach Shakespeare* (*Macbeth 'after'* [or *'based on'*] *Shakespeare*: 1982) 'no longer depicted the sacrilege of murdering a rightful king, but instead showed a relentless power game among thanes', downplaying the supernatural element and showing that 'the feudal power struggle takes place against the background of an oppressed peasantry'. In an inserted scene, a peasant was flayed in the background while Macduff read a passage from Ovid's *Metamorphoses*. (Presumably this was the flaying of Marsyas in Book Six.) Like Müller's other dealings with 'Shakespeare' the iconic cultural brand, as well as the plays written by the author, *Macbeth nach Shakespeare* had an uncompromising grimness comparable to Edward Bond's *Lear* and even Howard Barker's *Gertrude: the Cry*. Its political implications were emphasized by the repeated use of the word 'work' (*Arbeit*) by Lady Macbeth to refer to the killing of Duncan, and by Macbeth to refer to the murder of Banquo. As well as being criticized for its brutality and 'lack of hope for humanity', the production was accused of 'misrepresenting peasants': in other words, failing to support the ideals of the GDR's 'workers' and peasants' state' (*Arbeiter- und Bauernstaat*) (99–100).

Two new books deal with the less hazardous adventures to be had in working with reconstructions of early modern performance spaces, although one of the theatres in question is the subject of some contention regarding its pedigree. In *Playing Indoors: Staging Early Modern Drama in the Sam Wanamaker Playhouse*, Will Tosh, a lecturer and research fellow at Shakespeare's Globe, describes the thinking behind this new addition to the range of theatre spaces geared to the exploration of late sixteenth- and early seventeenth-century performance techniques. The detailed case studies of productions, interviews with actors and other practitioners, and striking illustrations provide a comprehensive picture of the advantages of the Sam Wanamaker Playhouse (SWP), and the ways in which productions of the indoor theatre repertoire have benefitted from them. Nevertheless, there are also disadvantages. This is not a 'reconstruction' of a theatre that once existed, nor does it follow the plan for any such, although a fair case is made for its illustrating the kind of theatricality represented by the Blackfriars (xvii). It is 'inspired by a set of plans for a small indoor theatre drawn up by an ageing Royalist architect in the 1660s' and is 'based upon our collective knowledge about seventeenth-century indoor theatres, with [Tosh admits] all the scope for disagreement and compromise that such collective knowledge entails'. It is 'a more contested, complicated structure than the outside Globe', and 'in some ways ... raises more questions than it answers – but it poses questions we had not previously thought to ponder'(xix).[1] Tosh does his best to make a virtue of the fact. He contends that the playhouse 'offers an astonishingly broad range of spectatorial vantage points which differ markedly from the experience of watching a play in a more familiar theatre'. Not everyone will welcome the prospect of the 'ideal spectator' being a figure who, in Tosh's phrase, is 'disarmingly exploded' (xxii) by what in other terms amounts to a theatre with awful

---

[1] On the SWP's credentials, see Holger Scott Syme, 'Pastiche or archetype? The Sam Wanamaker Playhouse and the project of theatrical reconstruction', *Shakespeare Survey 71* (2018), 135–46

sightlines and, just to make matters worse, very uncomfortable seating. (For my part, I should admit that I have always thought moving indoors was an excellent development in the history of the theatre, but not on these terms.)

Tosh gives a convincing account of the interpretive impact of experience of candlelit performances in an exquisite but confined space. He observes that 'While the Globe's pillared stage lends itself to figure-of-eight travel, the SWP's movement dynamic is side-to-side, a subtle seesawing of stage-left and stage-right to ensure the upper-gallery patrons get a fair share of the action' (82). Nevertheless, it is not clear how the techniques called for when performing 'in the round' in the SWP differ markedly from those required in more modern (and less cramped) spaces with a similar configuration. As for the effect on the actors of the 'non-unitary spectator', Tosh claims that it encouraged performers to consider their characters' moral reputations 'more critically and more flexibly than in a "conventional" theatre' (46). Which set of conventions is being evoked? Those of end-on theatres with or without a forestage, thrust stages, or even the equally conventional 'black box'? Are the 'moral reputations' of characters any less available for scrutiny in these, or indeed in a rehearsal room? The actor Peter Hamilton Dyer observes of the vertical dimension of the space that 'it's an act of will to pick yourself up, and throw [the performance] up ... It's a greater challenge for an actor to stand up and look up, particularly when you've got the lure [of an appreciative audience in the lower gallery and pit] right in front of you' (79). There is no gainsaying this as a professional's personal experience, but similar comments have been made about working in other theatres, including the Swan in Stratford-upon-Avon, and, for that matter, in many proscenium-arch houses where an actor has to 'reach the back of the gallery' as well as the stalls and dress circle. The author is frank about the problems presented by the 'unforgiving viewing angles', and the case for the virtues of this

particular 'non-unitary' theatre has to be regarded as 'not proven'.

Work with an 'early modern' stage of a very different kind is described by the contributors to *The New Fortune Theatre: That Vast open Stage*, edited by Ciara Rawnsley and Robert White. The New Fortune at the University of Western Australia is, so far as the evidence allows, a reconstruction of the theatre built in London in 1600. The New Fortune's architect, Marshall Clifton, notes that the known dimensions of the original have been adhered to: '55 feet square between balconies and 27½ feet by 43 feet wide of the stage' (52). The project dates back to 1964, taking advantage of 'a building containing academic offices in a three-storey structure around a rectangular open quadrangle' (79) to realize the vision of Professor Allan Edwards (1909–95), chair of the University's English department for thirty-four years from 1941. The theatre historian Philip Parsons describes how 'the vast stage seems to fill the theatre. It invites freedom of movement fit for creatures larger than life, who will dominate the crowded world of ordinary men pressing in close, around, above, below' (61: is this an intentional echo of John Donne?). Robert White reviews the theatre's first fifty years, celebrating the generosity of the space, and the ways in which the stage fosters a rhythm of acting 'passing in circles and figure-of-eights rather than "backwards" and "forwards" or sideways, and facing up and down to the different levels rather than "forwards," in order to involve all the audience simultaneously'. This makes for an interesting comparison with Will Tosh's account of the SWP, conjuring up the sense of an audience that is not so much 'unitary' as unified, with 'no spectator ... more than a cricket pitch's length away from the actors' (18). Other essays by scholars, actors and directors describe the experience of directing and acting at the New Fortune, including productions of work by the poet, novelist and playwright Dorothy Hewett. Her account of the theatre's first production, *Hamlet* in 1964, evokes the excitement of discovery: 'without a backward glance, without hesitation, I threw the proscenium arch over my shoulder and embraced this tremendous world of giants who are still, miraculously, men' (67). The overall impression created by the collection is of a theatre as open to experiment and innovation as its stage is large and accommodating. The collective experience seems to be one of the vitality and versatility of its particular kind of 'liveness'.

'Liveness' of another kind, less easily assessed although now a major aspect of spectatorship, is the subject of *Shakespeare and the 'Live' Theatre Broadcast*, edited by Pascale Aebischer, Susanne Greenhalgh and Laurie E. Osborne. The history of the video and film recording and live broadcasting of theatre performances is traced by Greenhalgh in the first chapter of Part One ('Wide Angle'), which is followed by chapters discussing the place of such broadcasts in the marketplace, the cinema audience's experience of them and the 'emerging audience behaviours'. Interviews with performers and audience members inform the chapters in Part Two ('In the Theatre'), and Part Three ('Close-ups') examines case studies of specific theatres and events. The final section ('Reaction Shots') moves across the globe to consider the view (literally) from Japan, Hong Kong, Bologna and North-east Ohio, with an essay by Aebischer on a broadcast of *Roméo et Juliette* from the Comédie Française. Taken together, the contributions present an informative and comprehensive overview of a cross-media phenomenon that is developing as rapidly as the technical means available. Accounts of the effect of the paraphernalia of broadcasting on the experience of the 'live' audience and the actors, and on the specific choices made by directors (notably in Peter Kirwan's essay on the web-stream of Cheek by Jowl's *Measure for Measure*) suggest the many factors that qualify the authenticity of the mediated experience. In terms of the visual effect of a play, opera or ballet, film or video necessarily privileges some moments at the expense of others, although with the passage of time directors have become more adept at balancing a view of the whole scenic picture – especially important in ballet – with the privileged focus on details. There is also attention to the paratextual elements of the transmissions, such as

introductions, interval talks and behind-the-scenes interviews, and the impact of 'live' transmission on the theatres themselves. This is a timely and thought-provoking collection, with implications for the study of earlier film and television as well as for its immediate subject.

Two recent books on the relationship between Shakespeare and the cinema offer differing but complementary approaches. In *Shakespeare's Cinema of Love, a Study in Genre and Influence*, R. S. White argues for the influence of Shakespeare's plays on film genres. White differs from Stanley Cavell, whose influential *Pursuits of Happiness* (1981) proposed Shakespearian origins for the Hollywood 'comedy of remarriage', for example in suggesting *The Taming of the Shrew* as the model for films that deal with 'power relations in the journey towards marriage, and underlying marriage itself' (51). With respect to conventions themselves, White suggests, Shakespeare 'rarely if ever uses a convention simply as an unchallenged datum, but rather … seeks to suggest some plausible motivation or human significance behind the convention, which can make it come alive in quite different historical times and contexts'. An important aspect of this proposition is that films using the generic structures but without reference to his works or name may be 'more "faithful" to the generic sources than antiquarian productions that do use Shakespeare's name yet make little attempt to provide a contemporary significance to his stories' (69). White's approach supports discussion of an impressive range of films, so that the reader finds enlightening and sometimes provocative commentary on (for example) George Cukor's *Holiday*, Billy Wilder's *Double Indemnity* and even the television series *The Flintstones* (as a point of reference for the systematically anachronistic fun of *The Boys from Syracuse*), as well as the 'usual suspects' of Shakespeare/Film Studies. (Yes, *Casablanca* is there too.) The effect is sometimes dizzying, but invariably acute and diverting, as is appropriate for the topic. White positively revels in the pleasures of comparison and analysis.

Jeffrey Knapp, in *Pleasing Everyone: Mass Entertainment in Renaissance London and Golden-*

*Age Hollywood* may at first seem to be indicating an uncomplicated comparison between two performing arts industries, both geared to attracting a mass audience – in Hollywood's case, globally – and both relentless in the pursuit of material for adaptation and offering an enticing prospect for would-be scriptwriters. But Knapp's project goes much further, proposing a sophisticated analysis of the inclusiveness of the plays themselves, as well as their more obvious strategies as accessible entertainment. Thus, in the final scene of *The Winter's Tale*, the silent presence of the newly elevated Shepherd and his son means that 'It's not one class or another that partakes of the revelation', but 'optimally, for Shakespeare as for Paulina, it's everyone' (164). In another telling example, Knapp points out that allusions to the audience in *Hamlet* 'befit the plot of fallen sovereignty that the play inherits from *1 Henry IV*: they register the gravitational force that the multitude exert over any figure who hopes to prove "most royal" when he is "put on" the "stage"' (112). It is characteristic of Knapp's dexterity that, from the tragedy of *Hamlet*, he can turn (as it were, 'on a sixpence') to the backstage movies of Busby Berkeley, in a chapter, 'One step ahead of my shadow', whose epigraph is from James Cagney: 'Never relax. If you relax, the audience relaxes.' Jonson jostles with Shakespeare (and many others), and seemingly disparate films are juxtaposed, so that *Citizen Kane* is placed alongside the shopgirl-marries-boss's-disguised-son comedy *My Best Girl* (1927) to illustrate the mode Knapp identifies as 'scatter-form'. In the case of these two films, the result is not so much a formalistic exercise in comparison as a proposition regarding the standing of cinema as art, as an analysis of the kind of tension between containment and dispersion represented in Welles's film by the apparent fragmentation of narrative and, in a striking objective correlative, the jigsaw frustrating Kane's wife Susan Alexander. (Like Mary Pickford's character in *My Best Girl*, Susan is a former shopgirl.)

One difficulty of giving an account of the year's contributions to Shakespeare studies is that publishers seem to waver in their decisions as to which year a book will be delivered in, or even what date they will put on the verso of the title page. Given that the essays in any volume of dispatches from the front line will probably have been written two years before its arrival, a work that aims to represent the state of the discipline is not likely to catch the very latest news. Discussions of performances are especially subject to this inhibition when they have to capture the insistent forward movement of the avant-garde. Nevertheless, the *Oxford Handbook of Shakespeare and Performance*, edited by James Bulman, contains, within its xxviii and 669 pages, contributions by 'leading figures in the discipline' that reflect both the current situation and likely forward direction of 'Shakespeare and Performance' scholarship. The back flap of the dust-jacket promises 'critical examinations of the direction and progress of debates, as well as a foundation for future research'. The claim is amply justified. As the editor announces, the essays 'represent the current attempts of critics to come to term with that slippery entity called performance, wherein a Shakespearean text is made flesh by theatrical representation' (1). The title's choice of 'and' rather than 'in' accommodates the wide range of definitions available for 'performance'. A comprehensive account of the individual essays would occupy a separate review article, and to single out some for commendation might suggest implicit preference for a few among the many. But several of the essays, all of which contribute to the overall strategy, propose a direct challenge to assumptions. In one section of 'Shakespeare's property ladder: women directors and the politics of ownership', Kim Solga addresses the critical response to Phyllida Lloyd's all-female *Julius Caesar* and *Henry IV*, noting that 'a number of reviewers ... argued that Lloyd's all-female casts created fresh insights *about* the implications of Shakespeare's plays as opposed to insights *into* them', demanding 'a dialogue with them and their conditions of performance and their original conditions of production in order to be of significance to a twenty-first century audience' (115). Solga's feminist interrogation of the institutions within which directors such as Lloyd and Katie Mitchell have to operate, and the ways in which their work is commonly assessed, has implications beyond her immediate purpose. Important in itself, it also offers a matrix for the study of other aspects of Shakespearian performance. Similarly, Stephen Purcell's '"It's all a bit of a risk": reformulating "liveness" in twenty-first century performance of Shakespeare', raises questions of 'authenticity' in the experience of performance beyond the essay's immediate topic. Purcell's contribution can be read alongside Anthony B. Guneratne's 'Shakespeare's rebirth: performance in the age of electro-digital reproduction', and, moving over into more familiar territory of Shakespeare/Film Studies, Scott Newstok's 'Making "Music at the Editing Table": echoing Verdi in Welles's Othello'.

'Handbook' may be something of a misnomer, as the volume can hardly be held in one hand and probably calls for a library-style book rest, but publishers have a limited choice. 'Companion', 'Guide' and other titles have already been claimed. Perhaps 'vademecum' will come back into vogue? That would be appropriate, if less commercially viable, for a work that will accompany study and debate and repay repeated visits as well as judicious sampling on the part of its target clientèle (the 'blurb' again) of 'scholars and graduate students'. Like the variety and quality of the other works reviewed here, in a world hard pressed to find cause for optimism, it suggests that Shakespeare 'in' or 'and' Performance is an exciting and promisingly open field.

## WORKS REVIEWED

Aebischer, Pascale, Susanne Greenhalgh and Laurie E. Osborne, eds., *Shakespeare and the 'Live' Theatre Broadcast* (London, 2018)

Bennett, Susan, and Sonia Massai, eds., *Ivo Van Hove: From Shakespeare to David Bowie* (London, 2018)

Bulman, James C., ed., *The Oxford Handbook of Shakespeare and Performance* (Oxford, 2018)

Croall, Jonathan, *Performing Hamlet: Actors in the Modern Age* (London, 2018)

Goy-Blanquet, Dominique, *Shakespeare in the Theatre: Patrice Chéreau* (London, 2018)

Joseph, Paterson, *Julius Caesar and Me: Exploring Shakespeare's African Play* (London, 2018)

Knapp, Jeffrey, *Pleasing Everyone: Mass Entertainment in Renaissance London and Golden-Age Hollywood* (New York, 2017)

Oliver, Emily, *Shakespeare and German Reunification: The Interface of Politics and Performance* (Oxford, 2017)

Rawnsley, Ciara, and Robert White, eds., *The New Fortune Theatre: That Vast Open Stage* (Crawley, Western Australia, 2018)

Rosenthal, Daniel, ed., *Dramatic Exchanges: The Lives and Letters of the National Theatre* (London, 2018)

Shaughnessy, Robert, *Shakespeare in the Theatre: The National Theatre, 1963–1975: Olivier and Hall* (London, 2018)

Shaughnessy, Robert, *Shakespeare in Performance: As You Like It* (Manchester, 2018)

Sher, Antony, *Year of the Mad King: The Lear Diaries* (London, 2018)

Thompson, Ayanna, 'Rawnsley' *Shakespeare in the Theatre: Peter Sellars* (London, 2018)

Tosh, Will, *Playing Indoors: Staging Early Modern Drama in the Sam Wanamaker Playhouse* (London, 2018)

White, R. S., *Shakespeare's Cinema of Love: A Study in Genre and Influence* (Manchester, 2016)

Woodhouse, Adrian, *Shakespeare by McBean* (Manchester, 2018)

# 3. EDITIONS AND TEXTUAL STUDIES
*Reviewed by* PETER KIRWAN

Following two years that have featured major new Complete Works projects, 2017–18 has been something of a year of consolidation and diversification in the world of Shakespeare editing. The projects surveyed in this essay comprise primarily new introductions, revised editions and a new series reorienting the Arden Shakespeare at practitioners. The reframing of existing edited texts at new audiences has been accompanied by some thoughtful work reflecting on both the history and future of Shakespeare in print, making this a good year to reflect on how today's texts are shaping future histories.

## NEW EDITIONS

Jesse M. Lander and J. J. M. Tobin's Arden 3 edition of *King John* replaces E. A. J. Honigmann's 1954 edition, last updated in 1962. Surprisingly little has apparently changed in the last fifty-five years, according to an edition that is outstanding in its defence of and appreciation for the play, and in its coverage of the play's fortunes pre-1900, but less informative regarding the last century. The introduction touches briefly on only four productions post-Beerbohm Tree (1899), with most attention given to the Globe's 2015 production, largely because that production's return to antiquarian ideas in its dumb shows, medievalism and church settings precisely evokes the tradition that peaked with Tree (110). The verdict is that none of the productions of the early twentieth century 'appears to have made much of an impact' (103), an oddly passive locution that sidesteps the critical edition's role in *making* that impact. The omission of productions that take a more explicitly oppositional stance, both in politics and in aesthetic (most notably Maria Aberg's much-discussed 2012 production), leaves this edition of *King John* somewhat mired in the histories it so eloquently critiques.

The advantage of the play's thinner reception history and relatively uncomplicated textual state is the freedom for Lander and Tobin's introduction to focus on detailed interpretive issues, with an eye on further-reaching debates around history plays and historiography. The play itself 'sounds a sceptical note regarding traditional historiography and its attempt to establish the truth of the past' (32) and is 'preoccupied with the question of historical representation . . . constantly aware of its complicated relationship to the received historiography of the reign that it depicts' (2). To this end, the edition is invested in challenging assumptions about the play that have been reinforced by the tendency to judge it in terms of 'real' history.

Lander and Tobin dispute that the play tones down the anti-Popery of Peele's *The Troublesome Reign of King John* (which this edition treats as Shakespeare's primary source) as much as is often suggested (16), and argue that almost nothing in it would qualify as an endorsement of Protestantism (20). The play's fundamental preoccupation is rather 'the slipperiness with which arguments are attached to various political projects' (21). The most important figure who emerges is Pandulph, the play's true Machiavel, a savvy operator who manipulates and deceives but is not a superhuman force (26–7). The play is 'corrosive of all value systems' (25), refusing to draw clear lines between right and wrong, and in a particularly insightful passage the editors suggest that the real question is not who should succeed to the throne, but who has the authority to adjudicate (29); Philip of France's claim to police the world is as woolly as John's claim to the crown.

Lander and Tobin touch on much of what makes this play unusual – the relative absence of English common people or specific English locations (with exceptions including the Lincoln Washes) – as well as the ongoing debates about heredity and England's place in the world that are common to several history plays. 'The play presents a version of little England opposed to foreign entanglements and adventures' (15), especially in the way the play retreats in on itself towards the end, withdrawing from the international locations of earlier acts. The political consequences, the editors argue, are far more important than the religious ones; their distinguishing of Pandulph's political aims from his theological position makes clear that the emphasis is on the political consequences of papal intervention rather than an exploration of Reformation religious thought (51). Indeed, the conflicting loyalties of the post-Reformation world are precisely what lead to the play's most gripping drama, particularly in the pivotal scenes of the taking and breaking of oaths.

Perhaps the edition's most important insight, though, is that this play is an example of 'passionate history' (56), which the edition identifies as the play's most 'important innovation, an attempt to represent the way in which passions shape history' (65). The editors argue that characters are emblematic of passions, which has always been central to criticism of Constance (grief), but applies also to John (rage), Hubert (guilt) and others. A pleasure of this section of the introduction is the editors' detailed application of the play's rhetorical strategies of repetition to questions of characterization and clues for performance, which feeds in to the extended section on the play's afterlives.

More so than is usual for an Arden edition, the editors recount moments in Shakespeare's performance and textual history that are general to the plays rather than specific to *John*, such as the role of the 1734–5 Tonson–Walker price wars in making Shakespeare cheaply available (68–9). The discussion is largely focused around a handful of key moments in the play's afterlife, each given several pages of treatment, including Cibber's anti-Catholic *Papal Tyranny* (finally staged in 1745); Kemble's 1823 historical extravaganza, whose playbill listed its historical sources (83); and Macready's 1842 version, lauded for its 'celebration of English History and English Poetry' (92). By the mid nineteenth century, both the performance and critical discussion of the play were inextricable

from historicist impulses, with the rise of Magna Carta as an important moment in Whig historiography and the 1797 exhumation of John's body both influencing representation. The antiquarian trend culminated in Tree's 1899 production, including a large-scale tableau of the sealing of Magna Carta, allowing him 'to display a historical fact as punctual, vivid, existing beyond the rhetoric of praise and blame' (102) and promising a bright future for England. Tree's version was also the first Shakespeare production to make its way to film, a fact which launches the introduction (though disappointingly not drawing on Judith Buchanan's work on that film, including its now-lost scenes).

There is very little by way of new textual insight; the main original contribution is to draw attention to a woodcut in Foxe's *Acts and Monuments* whose depiction of the death of John's murderer accords with that in the play, reinforcing the importance of Foxe as a source. The textual discussion makes rather absolute distinctions between what it calls the 'dialogue text' and 'directions text', and between 'foul papers' and other forms of document, that are somewhat out of keeping with more recent critiques of these categories; certainly, the editors are rather too sure that the inconsistencies in speech prefixes and stage directions rule out prompt copy (118). The edition sets out the difficulties with the Folio's act and scene division, which it suggests emerge from the compositors differently interpreting the number '2' in the transcript they worked from (133). This edition follows Theobald in removing the scene break after Constance sits on the ground – 'Here is my throne, bid kings come bow to it' (3.1.74) – making the action continuous with the arrival of Kings John and Philip, on the assumption that this best represents stage practice when the play was first performed. Other issues are dealt with less clearly; the editors note that the question of whether the Citizen of Angiers and Hubert are a single character is one of the most debated difficulties (114), but never explain that this is because of the speech prefix '*Hubert*' appearing intermittently throughout 2.1, an idiosyncrasy not recorded in the collation. Better are the notes on the play's odd dramaturgy, including a large number of minor characters appearing onstage for very brief moments.

A unique feature of the edition, for an Arden text, is marginal indications throughout the text showing where each new column of Folio text begins, a useful addition. There are few major emendations of note, with most deviations from the Folio copy-text derived from eighteenth-century editors. There is more intervention in the stage directions; a note in the introduction points out that the moment where King Philip takes King John's hand is ambiguous (124) and suggests that the most obvious place is 3.1.135 when Pandulph enters; however, the editors include the direction both here *and* at 3.1.192, at which point a note suggests that editors argue also for it taking place as early as 3.1.161. While alerting readers to the ambiguity is helpful, including the SD twice in the text is more confusing. Of more value throughout is the detailed glossing and commentary, which demonstrate the editors' wealth of expertise. There are notes here drawn from productions that receive no mention in the introduction; detailed local comparisons with *Troublesome Reign*; detailed discussion of ambiguous meanings, such as Constance's 'calf's skin' insult to Austria at 3.1.129; and sensitive unpackings of the rhetorical flourishes and political implications of the play's speeches. The relatively full stage directions draw on a broad range of interventions from the editorial tradition, with this edition's original contributions mostly clarifying the stage picture, such as at 2.1.299 where Lander and Tobin specify (sensibly) that the two armies leave via opposite exits.

With the third edition of *The Norton Shakespeare* now out, it was inevitable that new single editions would follow, and the first are Gordon McMullan's *Romeo and Juliet* and Grace Ioppolo's *A Midsummer Night's Dream*. The relationship between *The Norton Shakespeare* and the Norton Critical Editions is different in each case: the stand-alone *Romeo and Juliet* shares the exact text and glossing of the Q2 edition in the *Complete Works*, with McMullan providing a new introduction and textual note, whereas Ioppolo's *Midsummer Night's Dream* is entirely independent of Lukas Erne's edition for the *Complete Works*, offering a relatively lightly annotated conflated edition of the play. Unlike the revised Norton Critical *Othello* (reviewed below), there is relatively little contribution from either editor: the bibliographies are unannotated, and the editors restrict themselves to a single introduction of around fifteen pages.

McMullan begins his introduction with the argument that this is not a 'simple play' (ix), and argues that the challenge is to come to the play afresh. The introduction demonstrates the play's complexity through sensitive analysis of a number of key sections, beginning with the conflict between assertion and restraint that characterizes the opening brawl, setting up a working-class masculinity that turns out to be a feint (xi). For McMullan, the play is far more interested in role-playing: '[m]asculinity is negotiated in the play not as something fixed and unchanging but as the product of stereotypes and subject-positions' (xi). The performativity of roles, as in Romeo's self-personation of a courtly lover, is formally mimicked in the use of sonnets that rhetorically circumscribe the 'spontaneous' dialogue of the titular lovers when they meet (xiii). McMullan is particularly influenced in his introduction by Dympna Callaghan's argument that the play helped shape the post-Reformation ideal of romantic, freely chosen love (xvi) that is challenged immediately in the play by Mercutio's homosocial principle, veering into misogyny (xvii). These insights stand for McMullan as examples of the play's complexity, inviting careful attention to the play's critical history.

The unique value of McMullan's edition is its creative and extensive appendix of sources, adaptation and criticism, unusually fulsome even for this series. Lengthy excerpts from five sources (da Porto, Bandello, Boaistuau, Brooke and Painter) are followed by extracts from Kareen Seidler's translation of a *c.* 1680 German adaptation that followed Q2 closely while also creating the new comic character 'Pickleherring', and from the conclusion of Thomas Otway's *The History and Fall of Caius Marius*. The rich selection of critical writings is introduced by Stanley Wells's magisterial 1996 essay on 'The challenges of *Romeo and Juliet*', privileged in its placement as a primer for deeper exploration of the play's complexities. The work that follows shows a fine eye for variety and representation: the pre-twentieth-century includes Helena Faucit, alongside the inevitable figures of Johnson, Hazlitt and Coleridge, while more recent inclusions privilege female scholars' responses to the play. Highlights include Wendy Wall's 2006 essay on the implications of textual variants for the play's kinship relations, Gayle Whittier's 1989 article on the embodiment of the sonnet (and the 'sonnetizing' of the body) and Sasha Roberts's treatment of the play's identity politics from 1998. Performance is also well represented, with Niamh Cusack and David Tennant reflecting on playing the title characters, Courtney Lehmann and Barbara Hodgdon writing on the Zeffirelli and Luhrmann films (an extract of Luhrmann and Craig Pearce's screenplay is also included) and Susan Bennett discussing the 2012 Iraqi Theatre Company's production. What emerges from this hefty anthology is a play that speaks to a wide range of pressing issues, and McMullan makes a fine case for the play's return to advanced-level syllabi.

Grace Ioppolo's *A Midsummer Night's Dream* is a thinner volume, just over half the size of *Romeo and Juliet*. Ioppolo begins her introduction with Peter Brook (ix), whose seminal production she sees as something of a blessing and a curse for the play, suggesting that the production has led to the play becoming 'limited and fixed' by its shadow (x). From this, Ioppolo offers an efficient summary of current scholarship on the play's original circumstances of production, rightly avoiding attempts to pin down the original performance to a specific wedding occasion and arguing that the delay in the play's publication may have suggested popularity onstage (xii). She notes that the Folio text seems to contain influence from both outdoor and indoor playhouse practice (xiii), and offers a succinct summary of other textual features, such as the signs of revision in Q1 (xv) and the variants of the Folio text (xvi). Brook dominates Ioppolo's summary of the play's fortunes in performance,

with later productions given a single paragraph (xxi). In introducing the play's critical history, Ioppolo particularly privileges the play's fortunes in the light of gender theory since the 1970s, emphasizing the misogyny and abuse directed towards the play's women (xxiv), and more recent attention to postcolonial aspects (xxvi).

Ioppolo's text is clean, and very lightly annotated throughout (certainly compared to the Norton 3 edition). The text is eclectic, based primarily on Q1 but with F variants 'that appear to result from revision or correction' interpolated (66). The Textual Variants list is particularly diligent in recording variants in stage directions or speech prefixes, though there are one or two errors in relation to the editorial tradition (e.g. Ioppolo's note on 1.1.10 'New-bent' says that 'Now bent' is a Folio reading, when it is also the reading of the copy-text and 'New' was an emendation original to Rowe). This edition has Philostrate act as master of the revels in 5.1, incorporates F's direction at the end of 3.2 that *'The lovers sleep all the Act'*; and prefers the common emendation 'Now is the mural down' at 5.1.202, for F's 'morall downe' or Q's 'Moon vsed'.

Ioppolo's selection of critical materials differs markedly from McMullan's in its bias towards older writing; the majority of McMullan's materials date from the last thirty years, whereas Ioppolo includes only one piece from the last twenty years, and that is Peter Brook's 2013 reflection on his 1970 production. While there is something of a vacuum in relation to recent work on the play, therefore, the edition offers several classic commentators on the play (Pepys, Rowe, Johnson, Hazlitt, Swinburne, Wilson Knight), with Lynda Boose (1982) and Margo Hendricks (1996) representing the post-1970 state of play concerning gender and race theory. However, the edition wonderfully concludes with an extended excerpt from Robert Cox's *Merry Conceited Humours of Bottom the Weaver* and the full libretto of Henry Purcell and Elkanah Settle's *The Fairy Queen* (1692), two extremely useful resources for students of early adaptations of the play.

372

## REVISED EDITIONS

The most substantially revised edition among this year's releases is Jonathan Bate's revisiting of his 1995 *Titus Andronicus*, with forty-two pages of new material in the introduction. Bate's edition has a better rationale than most for the 'Arden 3.5' treatment, given the original edition's claim (based on then-recent but quickly discredited attribution scholarship) that the play was by Shakespeare in its entirety. While Bate recanted in his 2011 edition of the play for the RSC Shakespeare, the Arden edition offers a welcome clarification.

Bate addresses the attribution issue with commendable honesty: A. Q. Morton's test 'was enough to convince the present editor of what he wanted to hear: that the play which he admired so much (while so many others did not) was entirely Shakespeare's' (125). The original 1995 argument is left to stand, while the 'Reconsiderations and Reinventions' set out the strong evidence for Peele's hand in the first act. An interesting indication of broader shifts in attitudes over the last twenty years is Bate's note that his 'defensive' treatment of the play equated quality with sole authorship; acknowledgement in 2018 of Peele's presence, of course, for Bate, does not diminish the play's achievement. The text of the play and commentary are not altered in light of the acceptance of Peele's authorship, even to note where words such as 'brethren' indicate Peele's presence, but this is consistent with the majority of the revised Ardens.

Perhaps conscious of not wanting to leave space for future recantation, Bate cautiously addresses a number of other recent textual theories. He inclines towards the argument that the three companies on the quarto's title page performed the play in succession rather than together (134), and thinks that Henslowe's 'ne' may refer to Shakespeare's contribution in 1594. He suggests that Shakespeare took over from an ill Peele, or rewrote an older version of the play, rather than collaborating directly. Finally, he remains ambivalent about whether the sacrifice of Alarbus and murder of Mutius were later additions, and whether Middleton wrote the fly-killing scene as suggested by the *New Oxford Shakespeare*; while Bate feels the case is less strong than for Peele, he defers to other scholars to test these arguments (146).

Bate is on more confident ground when he moves onto the play's reinventions on the world stage. Silvio Purcărete's 1992 Romanian National Theatre production and Gregory Doran's 1995 Market Theatre / National Theatre version dominate the discussion, setting up the play's 'profoundly contemporary' value in productions that 'used the combination of the Roman, the Elizabethan and the contemporary to explore questions of political violence' (149). After some briefer mentions of other recent productions, Bate concludes with more substantial discussion of Julie Taymor's film, which co-executive producer Steve Bannon (yes, that one) thankfully failed to turn into a sci-fi extravaganza (159). The attention to performance throughout this concluding section brings the edition up to date with the play's renewed fortunes on the contemporary stage and screen.

The year's two revised New Cambridge Shakespeare editions offer very different levels of intervention. Tom Lockwood contributes seventeen new pages to Molly Mahood's *The Merchant of Venice*, beginning with a tribute to his late predecessor and her edition, which emphasizes the play as one that asks its audience to be sceptically alert to how language is used (53). Lockwood covers a great deal of ground as he surveys recent productions, critical approaches and other transpositions of the play, from a New York auction in 2015 to Howard Jacobson's *Shylock is My Name* (2016). The emphasis here is on material that will be useful for the reader looking to get up to date on the play from a range of angles, including the growing interest in the play's homoeroticism, interrogations of the cultural construction of Jewishness, and the importance of material culture as an emerging context for the play.

Christina Luckyj, on the other hand, provides a completely new introduction to Norman Sanders's *Othello*, an invigorating and often surprising read that offers a consistently insightful synthesis of the play's major issues and contexts. For example, while discussing the obvious early responses to the play, she also points out that the presentation of the play as part of wedding celebrations in 1613 suggests that some early audiences responded to it as a moving love story (2); and while the sources section dutifully describes Cinthio's short story, Luckyj also draws attention to the lesser-known histories of Turks and bondslaves in circulation at the time.

The standout section, 'Strangers as allies', argues that Venice was known as home to a wide variety of 'strangers', and uses the play's setting to argue that all of the main characters are represented as 'strangers' to an English audience. The Spanish name 'Iago' may have immediately roused hostility in an audience for its association with a hostile European power that persecuted Moors in its own country, but Luckyj is more invested in demonstrating Iago's connections to older feudal and chivalric relationships, as opposed to the new capitalism embodied in the 'arithmetician' Cassio (9). Desdemona, meanwhile, is associated with Venice, speaking the language of contract and consent rather than authoritarianism, in line with the liberal professions of the city (12). It is precisely this liberality that Iago plays on, and in a brilliant passage Luckyj explores how Desdemona's heroism in the public sphere of Venice changes in Cyprus, where the herald of her beauty becomes a drunken brawler and Iago narrows the spheres in which she can move. All three main figures are initially defamiliarized 'only to be drawn into a close sympathetic alliance with the audience' (24), a view which informs Luckyj's sensitive exploration of Othello, covering the ways in which he might be racially defined while noting that it is Othello's 'strangeness' that wins Desdemona as he portrays himself as a romance hero and endurer of trials.

Another rich section recounts the intense critical battles surrounding the play, especially in reference to race and gender, and the intensity of these disputes supports Luckyj's sense that the play resists any singular reading, just as it complicates easy binaries within the text (50). The lingering influence of older racist and sexist readings is a clear issue for contemporary criticism, and Luckyj notes the extent to which Desdemona continues to be praised by reviewers for her 'attractive defencelessness' (56). She argues that blackness was largely incidental to performances of the title role until the nineteenth century, although actors of colour have had more or less exclusive rights to the role since the 1980s. Luckyj concludes her introduction with the perennial problem of *Othello*s, rarely stated as explicitly as here – that productions have to work hard to keep Othello and Desdemona at the heart of the play: '[i]n the best productions, *Othello* pulls us in opposite directions and, in doing so, wrenches us apart' (76). Luckyj's practical insight and deft handling of competing positions makes this a richly rewarding read.

The other recently revised *Othello* is Edward Pechter's second edition of his own 2004 Norton Critical Edition. This is a light but thorough revision, its minor alterations spread throughout the volume. To take a typical scene, 3.4 (197 lines) contains three new glosses, all aimed at the student reader, and a longer explanation of the distinction between venial and mortal sin (112). The minor changes are invariably justified, and the section on 'Text and editorial procedures' (125–32) is substantially unchanged.

The particular value of the Norton Critical Editions is the lengthy appendices containing excerpts of critical material. This edition removes more than it adds: pieces by Lynda Boose on the handkerchief, Mark Rose on chivalry, and Patricia Parker on the 'secret place' of women all disappear, and in their place appear a short 1979 piece by Stanley Cavell and a bizarrely edited compilation of passages from Lois Potter's (excellent) book on *Othello* in performance. This section of the new edition is, I feel, rather poorer for the omissions.

Pechter's new introduction notes that the emphasis on the play's contemporary relevance makes it even more important to acknowledge the traditions that may, even unconsciously, shape 'our desire and understanding' (xi). The main revisions are to his own essays, '*Othello* in its own time' and '*Othello* in theatrical and critical history'. The former is split into three sections focusing on 'Strangers', 'Women' and 'Theater'. 'Strangers' concentrates on romance and travel writing in the period, noting the early modern fascination with the other, before moving on to discussion of Turk plays. Drawing on a series of representations of 'Moors' in the early modern period, Pechter points to the 'lack [of] coherent stability required' to register racial attributes *as* racial (145), and argues that the religious turn – focusing on a Moorish and a Muslim Othello – has been of particular help. The section on 'Women' is only lightly rewritten, but the section on 'Theater' is mostly new, and ambitiously explores the hypothetical affective parameters of experience for early modern audiences. Pechter argues that the sophisticated genre understanding of early audiences would have enabled interpretation of the play as symbolic and intensified rather than reflective of reality (161). The play itself, however, shows the extent to which lived reality is overtaken by 'fantasy or fiction' (163).

Pechter's overview of the theatrical and critical history of the play is also lightly revised, but the most notable new material includes discussion of Lolita Chakrabarti's *Red Velvet* (2012); a more pointed critique of nineteenth-century silencings of Desdemona (207–8); and an extended overview of *Othello* in modern times. Pechter concentrates on the shifts in the social context of commentary across the twentieth century, moving from psychoanalytic approaches that led to the ascendancy of Iago to the sociopolitical concerns that have led to Othello's return to the centre of the play. Pechter concludes, however, that 'Iagocentrism' remains 'the dominant mode of engaging [with] *Othello*' (216). An extensive, useful and helpfully annotated bibliography concludes the edition; one wishes that the new Norton Critical Editions had kept this feature.

## EDITING FOR PERFORMANCE

Although published in 2016, the special issue of *Shakespeare Bulletin* curated by C. K. Ash, José A. Pérez Díez and Emma Smith is worth highlighting in the year that sees the launch of the new Arden Shakespeare Performance Editions. The issue's introduction argues that there has been a lack of 'focus on the real-time interaction of editing and performance' (2). The issue brings together a range of approaches that aim to 'reanimate playbooks'. Stephen Purcell offers a practice-based discussion of the clowning scenes of *Doctor Faustus*, arguing that both A and B texts allow space for improvisation (13), based on a fascinating live workshop during which actors and audience members were invited to memorially reconstruct an improvised scene. Nora Williams offers a detailed examination of editorial applications of [*Aside*], with the text and recent productions of *The Changeling* as her case study; her nuanced appreciation of the interpretive implications in practice will be a useful resource for all editors musing over adding asides to their text. Similarly practical in its implications is Ash's essay on proverbs, which models 'activated commentary' (89) in relation to *Macbeth*. Ash's call is for specialist editions that prioritize '"playable" information' (94), which manifests in her glossing of 'There's no art / To find the mind's construction in the face' to consider the proverb's dramaturgical function and suggested characterization as well as simple meaning. Such detailed work would necessitate an electronic rather than print edition, and Brett D. Hirsch and Janelle Jenstad conclude the special issue to advocate for digital editions as the future of performance-sensitive editing. As well as highlighting the potential of the digital edition to incorporate several different end-users and approaches to editing, the authors discuss a forthcoming *Digital Renaissance Editions* text of *Fair Em* that hopes to incorporate short workshopped sequences exploring textual cruces into the digital text (118–19). The potential for digital editions to include performance-based research that informs editorial choices (such as that explored by Díez in his contribution) is ripe for further exploration.

The remaining contribution is a series of interviews conducted by Abigail Rokison-Woodall with theatre practitioners, about their interaction with texts. What emerges are the contingency and practical application of the engagement, with Trevor Nunn in particular insisting on there being no rule of thumb, and the decisions of editors being acknowledged or rejected as the needs of rehearsal demand. Gregory Doran complains about the extent and literariness of notes in an Arden edition, and Lucy Bailey worries about over-punctuation in the service of readers. From the actor's perspective, Simon Russell Beale eschews performance history but appreciates source material. The insights are not individually surprising, but practitioners consistently ask for texts that give access to straightforward information and which admit of flexibility of performance, pronunciation and organization. Rokison-Woodall's contribution is a prolegomenon of sorts to the new Arden Performance Editions, for which she shares the general editorship with Michael Dobson and Russell Beale. The first five volumes in the series are available at the time of writing, covering some of the most regularly performed plays, and offer a major intervention in creating editions suitable for rehearsal room use.

The primary achievement is design. The text is in a large font, on verso only, with substantial white space and a pleasingly bendy spine; far more so than the main Arden Shakespeare editions, these editions are a pleasure to read aloud from while standing. The recto contains glosses, significant variants and notes on pronunciation and metre. The prefatory materials are deliberately brief and efficient – the General Editor's introduction is in bullet points – focusing on information that is directly utilizable by performers. The relatively bare-bones approach is refreshing, and while this inevitably leads to omissions in the supporting materials, it also allows often-overlooked points of interest to gain an unusual prominence.

The series introduction sets out its principles, and in doing so raises important questions about what kinds of information matter for practitioners. The editors wish to 'set our actor-readers' imaginations free' (vii; all references to these preliminaries are from Rokison-Woodall's *Hamlet*) by making alternative readings visible. A strength of the introduction is its avoidance of dogmatism,

emphasizing the ambiguity involved in many decisions; this also means that the persistent trend for treating Folio punctuation as representing Shakespeare's thoughts is given short shrift (ix). The editors follow the Arden 3 texts, with the primary difference being lineation in the case of multiple consecutive short lines, where the editors reorganize to admit of different possibilities; the Arden 3 *Hamlet*'s 1.1.17–18, for instance, becomes a single multiply staggered line in the Arden Performance Edition. Other important sections focus on metre (where the detailed explanation of scansion and an excellent separate 'Note on metre' will be indispensable for students as well as actors) and pronunciation, with each edition not only giving preferred pronunciations but also explaining the principles on which words (especially names) change their number of syllables to fit the verse line.

In the push for brevity and clarity, there are some small elisions of nuance, some of which are more significant than others. 'The Globe' is the assumed venue throughout the series introduction, and the absence of mention of the Blackfriars complicates the claims of the 'Scene divisions' section that '[a]ct and scene division originate with the First Folio' (xv); it seems misleading not to note that, for *some* plays at least, act divisions may have some root in early indoor performance. At other times, the editions retain old theories that have been substantially challenged in recent years, such as that of memorial reconstruction for Q1 *Hamlet*, and in instances such as these it is a shame that the Performance Editions rehearse the older positions.

But the emphasis here is on utility for performance, and the detail is in the individual annotations. Biblical references and proverbs are marked up in order to allow actors to be self-aware of their characters' utilization of common sayings; shifts between verse and prose, or 'you' and 'thou', are highlighted for their changes in tone of address; rhyme has a number of different effects. Where the Arden Performance Editions succeed is in creating an edition that gives actors practical tools for delivering the text and making informed choices about interpretation. A pleasure of the individual editions is their idiosyncratic choices of what to focus on, consistent only in the editors' sense of what will interest producers of the play.

Rokison-Woodall focuses much of her introduction to *Hamlet* on the key textual differences. In a deviation from the Arden Q2 *Hamlet*, the edition includes Folio-only passages and variants commonly used in performance. While Q1 is assumed to be a memorial reconstruction, the section on this text is one of the edition's most valuable, particularly in setting out how Q1's placement of 'To be, or not to be' changes the trajectory for the actor, and explaining how and why many modern productions have preferred this placement (xxxiv–xxxviii). Another insightful section covers the play's distinctive transitions between verse and prose, noting how Claudius, Laertes and Polonius all switch between verse and prose, often in sympathy with the person they are talking to (xli–xliv); this is accompanied by the play's nuanced utilization of 'you/thou' distinctions, which Rokison-Woodall considers as giving potential clues to the actor during the nunnery scene, among other examples.

Rokison-Woodall's *Midsummer Night's Dream* sums up the basic genealogy of the early witnesses, imagining F as a version of Q2 marked up from prompt copy, which is in line with Arden 3, even though the edition is based on Harold Jenkins's Arden 2 text. As with her introduction to *Hamlet*, the beauty of Rokison-Woodall's introduction is the nuanced attention to metre, rhyme and address in relation to characterization. She points out that traditional class-based distinctions between verse and prose are reversed in the final scene, where the onstage spectators heckle in prose (xxxiii); that 'thee/thou' are used in contexts of both love and superiority, often between the same characters; and that the word 'Athenian' oscillates between three and four syllables throughout. An especially useful feature is the clear, student-friendly introduction to the play's metrical variety, from alexandrines and heroic stanzas to ballad metre and trochaic tetrameter (xxxiii–xxxviii).

Paul Menzer's *Romeo and Juliet* follows Arden 3 in using Q2 as copy-text, while Q1 is described as probably a memorial reconstruction. Menzer's introduction to Q1 picks up on subtleties of that text's indications to actors, including the unique SD '*All at once cry out and wring their hands*' (4.5.48.1), which he suggests may be a rare indicator of overlapping dialogue (xxxii). The attention to verse and prose feeds into the observation that verse is regularly used to restore order throughout the play, and culminates in a beautiful close reading of Romeo and Juliet's sonnet (xxxix). Menzer also notes some key challenges for the theatre, including the early texts' lack of any reference to a 'balcony' (xliv); the difficulty of finding actors of an appropriate playing age for Juliet (xxxix); and, in a fascinating conclusion, the unique fact of Romeo dying in ignorance of his errors (xlv).

Anna Kamaralli makes a passionate case for the value of *Much Ado About Nothing* at a time when many are working to ensure women's voices are heard (xxxiii). The rich introduction focuses on the play's prosody and stagecraft. The 'highly distinctive choice to have upper-class characters speak in prose during scenes of romantic declaration' (xxxvi) gives fewer clues but more freedom to actors. Other insights include the falling away of Hero's feminine endings when defending herself against accusations; the use of 'thou' for intimate conversations; and the flirting quality of euphuistic dialogue (xliv). The remainder of the introduction takes a more proactive stance in relation to performance options, as in her argument that the 'unfortunate racist implications' (xlvii) of references to Jews and Ethiopians can easily be cut. She also reminds the reader that Margaret and Ursula are not servants, and that the distinction between public and private spaces shapes what is possible throughout the play.

Finally, Paul Prescott's *Othello* is based on E. A. J. Honigmann's Arden 3 text, but with some small changes (xxxiv), including – in line with Ayanna Thompson's remarks in her recent revised introduction to Honigmann's edition – reassigning 'This Lodovico is a proper man' (4.3.34) to Desdemona, for whom Honigmann felt it was 'out of character' (xxxiv). This edition also 'retains Q's saltiness' (xxxvii) in restoring the oaths removed in F, and also draws attention to the many other synonyms for 'fucked'. Prescott is attentive throughout to the stage history and playable options, noting for instance the stage tradition, inaugurated by Rowe, of Othello grabbing Iago during the 'collaring scene' (xxxv); the myriad possibilities for business during short lines (xliii); and the status games implicit in the choice of 'thou' and 'you' throughout. Another surprising (to me) observation is Desdemona's relative comfort in both verse and prose throughout.

The individual texts all follow house style in the organization of the glossing, and I conclude with some general notes about the texts. The recto page aligns glosses on the left, and textual variants and pronunciation/metrical guides on the right. As everything is in the same font, the page can sometimes become cluttered, particularly in *Hamlet* and *Othello*, though this is a small price to pay for the uncluttered presentation of the dialogue on the verso. Textual variants are simply set out in the form 'Q2 – a-praying F – praying' (*Hamlet* 3.3.73) or '*SD*/ Rowe; not in QF' (*Othello* 3.3.57.1), and performers will be able to compare quickly. I feel that the edition would benefit from some common-sense pruning to alleviate the pressure on page space – I am not sure, for example, that the line 'No' (*Hamlet* 3.3.87) needs the explanation 'line is short by 9 syl. in Q2'. Pleasingly, the metrical guides are demarcated by bold for stressed syllables, making it much easier to see and identify these instructions. The glossing throughout is efficient, offering simple modern synonyms in most cases; the glossing is not exhaustive, but all of the editors make appropriate judgement calls on words or phrases whose historical specificity or modern rarity may cause questions.

There are small variations in practice. Rokison-Woodall offers slightly fuller scansion and pronunciation advice (especially in *Hamlet*) than the other editions, while Kamaralli includes far more interpretive notes (e.g. '*Leonato begins, but suffers a failure of imagination*' at 2.3.111, or '*Claudio and Don Pedro may hear this as they exit*' at Beatrice's 'Dead, I think'

(4.1.110)). But the volumes are generally consistent with one another, and the attention to fine detail of performance will make these editions invaluable in the classroom as well as in the rehearsal room; students will particularly benefit from the detailed assistance with reading aloud. It will be interesting to see how many volumes the new series produces, especially as it may be the less-often-performed plays that benefit most from the close attention to performative options in these texts, but the series is off to a strong start.

## TEXTUAL LEGACIES

The first legacy of this review is a sad one, with the festschrift to Barbara Mowat that makes up *Shakespeare Quarterly* 68.1 followed shortly by her passing. Paul Werstine begins by offering a tribute to Mowat's textual scholarship, noting her particular influence in the paradigm shift away from editing according to the New Bibliography's hypothetical categories of manuscript and towards version-based editing. While the heyday of that paradigm may already be past, the essays in this collection take Mowat's work as their inspiration. David Bevington leads off with a beautifully expressed series of questions and difficulties facing the editor, concluding with his observation that '[a]ll paraphrase, all translation, is inadequate' (20). His litany of inadequacies includes: glosses that require more learning to understand than the text they attempt to elucidate; bracketed stage directions that limit the options for plausible stage action; and paradigms of spatialization and location that are inappropriately imposed on scenes whose logic depends on a fluid theatrical space. Throughout, Bevington calls for an annotating practice that acknowledges its own limitations and strives for better.

Alan Galey and Rebecca Niles adapt Mowat's interest in material texts to their argument that Shakespeare is 'mediated by complex technological systems' that include digital technologies (22). Defending the principle that 'wrestling with new media is what Shakespeareans do' (55), the authors offer a pre-digital history of modelling practices that grapple with presenting the data provided by Shakespearian text and performance, from model boxes and line numbers to LEGO Batman figures arranged atop a Folio facsimile. The article is an important reminder to would-be editors that their intellectual labour is inextricable from the affordances of the medium. Their essay is followed by Sonia Massai's exploratory paper, which notes that 'single-text editing has reinforced the notion that "the play" is still the main semantic unit through which we can access and understand early modern English drama' (57), and deconstructs the ontology of the whole to imagine what editing Shakespeare 'in part' might look like. Massai is interested in the wide variety of ways in which the elements contained within a traditional edition might be broken up, and calls for an approach that emphasizes intertextuality – for example, editions that create connections between the openings, or 'incipits' (69), of plays such as *King John* and *King Lear*, or which connect plays according to the practices of extracting and anthologizing undertaken by early readers. Following a fascinating short piece by Stephen Orgel on grimoires and the wide availability of books on natural magic in the early modern period, the special issue concludes with Eric Johnson's touching words on the aspirational standards that Mowat's work embodies.

After reading Emma Depledge's *Shakespeare's Rise to Cultural Prominence: Politics, Print and Alteration, 1640–1700*, it will be difficult for future historians of Shakespeare's afterlives not to privilege the Exclusion Crisis as a pivotal moment in the consolidation of Shakespeare's ubiquity. Depledge's book shares the argument of her 2017 collection *Canonising Shakespeare: Stationers and the Book Trade, 1640–1740* (co-edited with Peter Kirwan and hence, for obvious reasons, not reviewed here) for the impact of the late seventeenth- and early eighteenth-century book trade on Shakespeare's legacy, but in much finer detail.

Depledge's book is a magisterial synthesis of book history, theatre history and adaptation studies (with adaptations referred to here as 'alterations' in deference to the preferred terminology of Restoration authors). The primary focus is on

1678–82, the years of the Popish Plot and the repeated attempts to bar James, Duke of York, from the throne. Depledge sets up her case with a diligent set of correctives to received narratives of Shakespeare's presence in print and performance during 1642–77. Countering arguments that Shakespeare was unavailable during the closure of the theatres, she draws attention to the 'abbreviated or redacted' Shakespeare texts (14) that circulated during the Commonwealth years, many of which show indications of having been designed with surreptitious performance in mind. That many of these texts clearly give prominence to Shakespeare's name and/or characters indicates for Depledge that 'his works were more readily available to consumers' than has previously been acknowledged (39), leading her to conclude that it was the period 1660–77 that marked the low point in Shakespeare's popular profile. The publication pattern of 'unaltered' Shakespeare shows an early (or anticipated) enthusiasm for Shakespeare culminating in the Third Folio of 1663/4, but then a huge drop-off during which Shakespeare 'was not offered for sale for almost a decade', and only one of two new playbooks was attributed to Shakespeare (47). This finds its corollary in a stage presence which, while at first glance fulsome, rarely advertised Shakespeare's name, particularly in prologues. The celebrated alterations of this period by Davenant, Dryden and others were highly topical, but rarely advertised their connection to Shakespeare.

With Shakespeare's low visibility established, Depledge then devotes three chapters to the all-important Exclusion Crisis. Here the integrated methodologies of book history and theatre history expand to include Depledge's subtle literary critique of the Shakespearian alterations produced during this period, including Shadwell's *Timon of Athens* (1678), Crowne's *Misery of Civil War* (1679) and Tate's *Richard the Second* (1680) and *The Ingratitude of a Common-Wealth* (1681), which she argues resonated strikingly with the politics of their moment. The parallels allowed authors and companies to explore the issues of their day while using Shakespeare's name to 'divert attention away from the altered play's politics' for the purposes of avoiding censorship (83). The detailed work on the alterations will be of particular value to historians of the period, especially in the bravura argument for the recurring introduction of new rape subplots in the alterations, 'Tory in tone, and ... associated with both rebellion and an absence of strong paternal care' (112). These alterations emphasized 'the need for strong, legitimate male rule, while celebrating male virility, caring fathers and loving husbands' (128), and restored Shakespeare's place in the billing. Feminist Shakespeare scholarship will need to grapple with the implications here of the interweaving of Shakespearian authority and rape at the point of Shakespeare's ascension to a culturally privileged status.

The book concludes with a return to print culture, exploring the paratexts of printed Shakespearian alterations, which now both acknowledge and, in many cases, stage the presence of Shakespeare, in the form of a Ghost. A peculiar feature of the narrative is that playbills and printed playbooks advertised the alterations as new and radically altered, while prologues and epilogues delivered in the theatres presented them as old and politically neutral (148). The authority of Shakespeare and his adaptors was mutually reinforcing and brought Shakespeare back into the national conversation, in ways that Depledge shows in her final chapter were consolidated towards the turn of the century. Shakespeare's vendibility in the print marketplace (including in the 1685 Fourth Folio) increased, establishing the market value that was a core context for the eighteenth-century editorial tradition. Depledge's integrated study of page and stage establishes a nuanced revision of a story too often told in broad brush strokes, and will be essential reading for future historians of Shakespeare's afterlives.

Paul Salzman's *Editors Construct the Renaissance Canon, 1825–1915* is a short, efficient monograph that fills a temporal and intellectual lacuna between Jeremy Lopez's *Constructing the Canon of Early Modern Drama* (Cambridge, 2013), with its focus on histories of anthologizing, and Gabriel Egan's *The Struggle for Shakespeare's Text* (Cambridge, 2010), which picks up the editorial history of Shakespeare from 1902. While Salzman's book claims to trace 'a new history of the transmission of Renaissance writing through a rich and heterogeneous editorial tradition' (3), the emphasis here is on the work of a few key editors: Alexander Dyce, James Orchard Halliwell-Phillips, Alexander Grosart and R. B. McKerrow.

The pleasure of the book is in the thick contextual attention to the careers of prolific editors beyond Shakespeare; perhaps its most significant achievement is a sensitive exploration of Dyce as one of the most important anthologizers and editors of women's poetry. Dyce's approach to editing was one of comprehensiveness, moving through volume after volume of the complete works of Greene, Webster, Middleton and more, before culminating with Shakespeare. By contrast, 'where Dyce's editorial principle was one of completeness, dependent upon being comprehensive, Halliwell was driven by a focus on Shakespeare, so that many of his diverse projects had what we might call a Shakespearean end' (43). The two men's progression towards their Shakespeare editorial projects of 1853–65 (Halliwell) and 1857 and 1864–7 (Dyce) occurred in the light of Malone's Variorum and Collier's forgery scandal, which Salzman sees as an important moment in editing being reconceived as a historicist enterprise (57).

A feature of this book is the detailed examination of Halliwell's voluminous edition and attention to the accompanying scrapbooks that can still be found in various archives, and which serve as a kind of supplement to the edition. In the detailed discussion of Halliwell's integration of facsimiles, illustrations and sources, Salzman paints a portrait of an innovative technological endeavour that opens up intellectual questions explored recently in Alan Galey's *The Shakespearean Archive* (Cambridge, 2014). Frustratingly, though, despite references on pages 41, 52 and 59 to imminent discussion of Dyce's edition of Shakespeare, that edition receives only brief mention. The remainder of the book touches more briefly on Shakespeare, primarily in the work of Horace Howard Furness and the Globe Shakespeare (which Galey covers in much more detail), but offers useful insight into more neglected projects, including Grosart's prolific work on obscure authors (editions which remained current until the advent of EEBO), McKerrow's edition of Nashe, Furnivall's six-column *Canterbury Tales*, and Montague Summers's work on Aphra Behn. These projects, Salzman concludes, retain their influence in the recent resurgence of interest in authorially based complete works projects, and offer a useful final reminder to textual historians of the ongoing influence of even those editorial projects usually consigned to the footnotes of Shakespeare's publishing history.

### WORKS REVIEWED

Ash, C. K., José A. Pérez Díez and Emma Smith, eds., Reanimating Playbooks: Editing for Performance, Performance for Editing, special issue of *Shakespeare Bulletin* 34 (2016), 1–127

Bate, Jonathan, ed., *Titus Andronicus*, rev. edn (London, 2018)

Depledge, Emma, *Shakespeare's Rise to Cultural Prominence: Politics, Print and Alteration, 1640–1700* (Cambridge, 2018)

Ioppolo, Grace, ed., *A Midsummer Night's Dream* (New York, 2018)

Kamaralli, Anna, ed., *Much Ado About Nothing* (London, 2018)

Lander, Jesse M., and J. J. M. Tobin, eds., *King John* (London, 2018)

Mahood, M. M., ed., *The Merchant of Venice*, 3rd edn (Cambridge, 2018)

McMullan, Gordon, ed., *Romeo and Juliet* (New York, 2017)

Menzer, Paul, ed., *Romeo and Juliet* (London, 2017)

Pechter, Edward, ed., *Othello*, 2nd edn (New York, 2017)

Prescott, Paul, ed., *Othello* (London, 2018)

Rokison-Woodall, Abigail, ed., *Hamlet* (London, 2017)

Rokison-Woodall, Abigail, ed., *A Midsummer Night's Dream* (London, 2017)

Salzman, Paul, *Editors Construct the Renaissance Canon, 1825–1915* (Basingstoke, 2018)

Sanders, Norman, ed., *Othello*, 3rd edn (Cambridge, 2018)

Werstine, Paul, ed., special issue of *Shakespeare Quarterly* 68.1 (2017), 1–92

# ABSTRACTS OF ARTICLES
## IN *SHAKESPEARE SURVEY 72*

RAMONA WRAY

*Henry V* **after the War on Terror**
The period since 9/11 has seen unprecedented numbers of *Henry V* productions
and the first major film in almost thirty years. By prioritizing the fields of debate
that surround Thea Sharrock's *Henry V* (2012), the article argues that the 'War on
Terror' has transformed the meanings of Shakespeare's greatest history.

RANDALL MARTIN

**Economies of Gunpowder and Ecologies of Peace: Accounting for
Sustainability**
Shakespeare creates a vision of ecological accountability and sustainability from
bookkeeping quantification and appraisal, which critiques commonplace
assumptions about spoils recouping the costs of war, challenges the emergent ethos
of unlimited extraction and growth exemplified by the gunpowder revolution, and
points to a contemporary ethos of peace and post-growth prosperity within earth-
bound ecosystems.

ELISABETTA TARANTINO

**Shakespeare and Religious War: New Developments on the Italian
Sources of** *Twelfth Night*
This article shows how the cluster of sources of *Twelfth Night*, which now includes
Grazzini's *La Strega*, points to issues of religious strife and engagement with the
'mountainish inhumanity' concept in *Sir Thomas More*. At a general level, it
discusses Shakespeare's use of sources and his access to Italian material.

MICHAEL HATTAWAY

**'Thou Laidst No Sieges to the Music-Room': Anatomizing Wars, Staging
Battles**
Evidence in Shakespearian texts reveals that, although sieges and duels were shown,
larger battles were ritualized or diverted into a 'battle box' behind the stage, and
represented by music and sound effects. Agincourt in Olivier's screen version *Henry
V* is climactic, but the film ends with a Spenserian pageant of mutability.

ROS KING

**Shakespearian Narratives of War: Trauma, Repetition and Metaphor**
This article describes both the repetition of war motifs in Shakespeare's work
(within and across plays), and the use of Shakespeare with military veterans
suffering from PTSD. In acting out the stories Shakespeare is telling, the
veterans allow themselves to confront traumatic war experiences. The process, in reflecting the structures of repetition and metaphor in Shakespeare's
plays, also offers new insight for criticism, education and performance.

EOIN PRICE

**War Without Shakespeare: Reading Shakespearian Absence, 1642–1649**
Scholars commonly stress Shakespeare's ubiquity, but in the English Civil War Shakespeare's plays seem to have formed a smaller part of the literary landscape. This article considers why that might be the case, what took Shakespeare's place, and how this relative obscurity may have helped his later canonization.

IRENA R. MAKARYK

**Antic Dispositions: Shakespeare, War and Cabaret**
Focusing in particular on twentieth-century Ukraine, this article explores the Hamletesque 'antic disposition' of cabaret – its grotesque, satirical, adversarial, yet playful and intelligent nature – as a way to respond critically and with authenticity to war, fake news and the madness of their strongman adherents.

REIKO OYA

**The Comedy of *Hamlet* in Nazi-Occupied Warsaw: An Exploration of Lubitsch's *To Be or Not to Be* (1942)**
Arguing for the deep anger that underlies the comedy of Lubitsch's *Hamlet*-inspired film, this article discusses its role and its reception in wartime culture and politics. There is a particular focus on the play's most famous soliloquy and its cinematic treatment, and a comparison with its immediate source and issues of censorship.

ZOLTÁN MÁRKUS

**The Lion and the Lamb: *Hamlet* in London during World War II**
By discussing the paradoxical history of Shakespeare productions in wartime London (including Donald Wolfit's 'Lunchtime Shakespeare' series), the article argues that *Hamlet* productions in 1944 in general, and the Haymarket Theatre's staging (Hamlet: John Gielgud; director: George Rylands) in particular, succeeded in re-establishing Shakespeare as a cultural icon of a national(istic) tradition and unity.

DIANA E. HENDERSON

**Dividing to Conquer or Joining the ReSisters: Shakespeare's Lady Anne (and Woolf's *Three Guineas*) in the Wake of #MeToo**
Triangulating Shakespeare's playtext, performance practices and fifteenth-century history, post-#MeToo analysis of *Richard III* 1.2 makes visible both the gaslighting of Lady Anne and how unexceptional women are routinely sidelined, diminishing attention to violence beyond battlefields. A coda reveals comparable divide-and-conquer use of weaponized rhetoric to dismiss Virginia Woolf's feminist pacifism.

CHRISTINA WALD

**The *Homeland* of *Coriolanus*: War Homecomings between Shakespeare's Stage and Current Complex TV**
Addressing the methodological question of how we can argue for an oblique cultural impact of Shakespeare's plays on contemporary culture, this article explores the controversial television series *Homeland* as part of the afterlife of *Coriolanus*. *Homeland*'s focus on the conceptual spectrum between 'turning' and 'returning' provides a productive lens for the political concerns and aesthetic choices of *Coriolanus*, itself marked by a careful dramaturgy of serialization.

GABRIEL EGAN

**Scholarly Method, Truth and Evidence in Shakespearian Textual Studies**
The new computational methods of Shakespearian study use evidence that is primarily numerical (the counts of occurrences of phenomena) and statistical (asking whether chance might produce the numbers found). This article offers Shakespearians unfamiliar with numerical approaches some guidance on evaluating them and reasons for bothering to do so.

LISA HOPKINS

**Beautiful Polecats: The Living and the Dead in *Julius Caesar***
This article argues that puns in *Julius Caesar* are not just wordplay but help to explain why the main character dies halfway through. It argues that the sense of doubleness which accrues to Caesar is articulated through wordplay, and explores what happens if some characters' names are heard as puns.

MELISSA CROTEAU

**Ancient Aesthetics and Current Conflicts: Indian *Rasa* Theory and Vishal Bhardwaj's *Haider* (2014)**
In 2014, director Vishal Bhardwaj adapted *Hamlet* into the Bollywood film *Haider*, transforming the 'rotten' state of Denmark into the divided region of Kashmir. Ancient Indian *rasa* theory posits that all elements in a performed narrative must focus on eliciting powerful emotion from the audience. In *Haider*, the *karuna* (sorrow, pathos) *rasa* is evoked vividly, through acting and other aspects of *mise-en-scène*, to condemn the appalling corruption and violence perpetrated by official authorities in India, as well as by Indian and Pakistani militants.

ELIZABETH MAZZOLA

**Failure to Thrive**
By representing mothers next to children they love or cast aside, Shakespeare suggests that – just as there are good breasts and bad breasts, caring mothers and cold ones – there are children who learn to belong and others who don't, who refuse the process or are repudiated by it.

MICHAEL GRAHAM

**Tippett's *Tempest*: Shakespeare in *The Knot Garden***
An analysis of Michael Tippett's psychoanalytic *Tempest* opera, *The Knot Garden* (1970), which elucidates how the composer uses Shakespeare's play as a vehicle to explore crucial contemporary themes of 'forgiveness and reconciliation, amongst [modern] individuals at war with each other'.

SAMUEL FALLON

**Tautological Character: *Troilus and Cressida* and the Problems of Personation**
*Troilus and Cressida* stages a conflict between two modes of 'personation': one expressed in practices of distinction, and the other rooted in imitative performance. The tension between these two modes reflects changing early modern conceptions of personhood and explains the troubling irresolution of the play's characters.

PETER J. SMITH

**'Rude Wind': *King Lear* – Canonicity versus Physicality**
This article proposes that we should confront the canonical centrality of Shakespeare's putatively greatest play with an awareness of its physicality – a human body, tortured and even decaying. Such an approach exposes the play's insistent materiality and, in so doing, demonstrates the fallacy of readings which champion its metaphysical, philosophical or even theological status.

ELENA PELLONE
AND DAVID SCHALKWYK

**Content but Also Unwell: Distributed Character and Language in *The Merchant of Venice***

This article seeks to reinvigorate scholarly enquiry into the nature of Shakespearian character as experienced in performance. We use a historic performance of *The Merchant in Venice* (an adaptation of Shakespeare's play) in the Venetian Ghetto in 2016 to reveal something crucial and often unnoticed about Shakespeare's multi-faceted conceptualization of character.

SONYA FREEMAN LOFTIS

**This Autistic Island's Mine: Neurodiversity, Autistic Culture and the Hunter Heartbeat Method**

While the Hunter Heartbeat Method has helped some autistic children develop skills, the programme's rhetoric casts the autistic subject as an incomplete human being. The programme builds on cultural assumptions that Shakespeare can 'cure', thus translating Shakespeare's cultural capital into a symbol of the medical model of disability.

JUDITH ROSENHEIM†

**The Senecan Tragedy of Feste in *Twelfth Night***

This article discusses the character of Feste in *Twelfth Night*. Feste's words and deeds exhibit an array of Stoic meanings so pervasive, wide-ranging and evidently intended as to make this philosophy the defining element of his character, and thereby of the play's tragic undertones.

# INDEX

# INDEX

# INDEX